REFORMING THE ADMINISTRATION OF JUSTICE IN MEXICO

Contributors

Mario Arroyo Juárez

Sigrid Arzt

Elena Azaola

John J. Bailey

Marcelo Bergman

Robert Buffington

Hugo Concha

Wayne A. Cornelius

Irasema Coronado

Héctor Fix-Fierro

Rosa Aída Hernández

Robert M. Kossick, Jr.

Ana Laura Magaloni Kerpel

Rubén Minutti Z.

Marcos Pablo Moloeznik

Héctor Ortiz Elizondo

Pablo Parás

Pablo Piccato

Benjamin Nelson Reames

Alejandra Ríos Cázares

Allison Rowland

Sara Schatz

David A. Shirk

Carlos Silva

Elisa Speckman Guerra

Jeffrey K. Staton

Kathleen Staudt

Robert O. Varenik

Guillermo Zepeda Lecuona

Reforming the

Administration of Justice

in Mexico

edited by

Wayne A. Cornelius and David A. Shirk

UNIVERSITY OF NOTRE DAME PRESS AND
CENTER FOR U.S.-MEXICAN STUDIES, UNIVERSITY OF CALIFORNIA, SAN DIEGO
NOTRE DAME, INDIANA, AND LA JOLLA, CALIFORNIA

Published by the University of Notre Dame Press
Notre Dame, Indiana 46556
www.undpress.nd.edu
All Rights Reserved

Manufactured in the United States of America

Library of Congress Cataloging-in-Publication Data

Reforming the administration of justice in Mexico / edited
by Wayne A. Cornelius and David A. Shirk.
p. cm.
Includes bibliographical references.
ISBN 13:   978-0-268-02292-1 (pbk. : alk. paper)
ISBN 10:   0-268-02292-5 (pbk. : alk. paper)
1. Criminal justice, Administration of — Mexico.   2. Crime — Mexico.
3. Police — Mexico.   I. Cornelius, Wayne A.   II. Shirk, David A., 1971–
HV9960.M6 R44   2006
364.972 — dc22
2006028977

∞ *The paper in this book meets the guidelines for permanence and durability of
the Committee on Production Guidelines for Book Longevity of the
Council on Library Resources.*

CONTENTS

Part V. Best Practices and Policy Recommendations

Preface

The research project whose results are summarized in this volume began to take shape in 1997, at a time when Mexico's democratic transition was gaining momentum (the ruling Institutional Revolutionary Party lost control of the Chamber of Deputies in that year's midterm elections) and concern was rising among scholars as well as public officials about the country's dysfunctional justice system as a potential obstacle to democratic consolidation. Urban crime and violence had increased sharply in the post-1994 period, and "personal insecurity" had become one of the foremost preoccupations of Mexicans in all social classes. On the U.S. side of the border, law enforcement authorities and politicians viewed with alarm the growing backwash of organized crime in Mexico into the United States, particularly in the form of drug-related violence. Moreover, it was widely believed, among both U.S. and Mexican elites, that the crux of Mexico's economic development problem was the lack of enforceable contracts and other aspects of commercial and constitutional law.

Clearly, this was a public policy domain that merited much greater engagement by scholars of Mexico. In no other area of the U.S.-Mexico relationship was there such a large gap between the quantity and quality of extant scholarly research and the degree of interest and urgency among U.S. and Mexican policymakers. The research gap was notable even in general surveys of judicial system problems in Latin America, which gave only passing mention to the Mexican case or treated it superficially. The paucity of reliable data was limiting the ability of scholars to provide useful policy prescriptions.

In planning our project, we sought to provide a comprehensive, up-to-date, multidisciplinary assessment of Mexico's justice system. We invited more than forty leading practitioners of anthropology, history, law, sociology, and political science from the United States, Mexico, and Britain to participate in the conceptualization and execution of the project. While new empirical research and database creation were urgent priorities, we were very much aware of the need for theory-building to guide the empirical work and historical analysis to chart the evolution of contemporary justice system problems. We adopted a multi-level analytic perspective, designed to illuminate not only the functioning of key national institutions in the justice system but also important developments at the state and local levels. While issues of institutional design and capacity were central to the project, participating researchers also delved deeply into patterns of citizen participation in the justice system and how the system impacts different segments of Mexican society. Finally, we looked abroad, to identify relevant lessons from other Latin American countries that have attempted to reform their justice systems, and suggest new opportunities for U.S.-Mexican collaboration in addressing law enforcement problems.

This project was made possible by generous grants from the William and Flora Hewlett Foundation, the Tinker Foundation, and the University of California's Consortium on Mexico and the United States (UC MEXUS). Additional support was provided by the American Bar Association-LALIC, the United States Agency for International Development, Bajaintermex, L.L.C., and Marathon Oil. In-kind contributions were made by Yolanda S. Walther-Meade, L.A. Cetto, and Cervecería Tecate.

We are indebted to the numerous institutions that have hosted and provided staff support for the project's planning meetings, workshops, and conferences: the Center for U.S.-Mexican Studies at the University of California, San Diego (especially staff members Graciela Platero and Diana Platero); the Trans-Border Institute at the University of San Diego; the Center for Strategic and International Studies (CSIS); the Centro de Estudios Sociológicos at El Colegio de México; the Centro de Investigación y Docencia Económicas (CIDE); the Centro de Investigación y Estudios Superiores en Antropología Social (CIESAS); the Centro Internacional de Estudios Sobre la Seguridad (CIESS); Democracia, Derechos Humanos y Seguridad (DDHS); the Instituto Ciudadano de Estudios Superiores Sobre la Inseguridad (ICESI); the Instituto de Investigaciones Jurídicas (IIJ) at the Universidad Nacional Autónoma de México (UNAM); the Instituto Nacional de Ciencias Penales (INACIPE); the Instituto para la Seguridad y la Democracia (ISD); and La Ronda Ciudadana.

Throughout the project, David Shirk served ably and with tremendous dedication as its principal coordinator, joined by John Bailey, Arturo Alvarado, and myself as co-coordinators. Alejandra Ríos Cázares provided essential research, administrative, and editorial assistance, as well as support for Web site development. Additional research assistance was provided by Robert Donnelly, Veronica López Arrellano, and Jhanelle Johnson. Undergraduate interns who assisted with different aspects of the project include Matt Fisher, Vicki Kraus, Monica Ohtsuka, Kimberly Mitchell, Yuko Matsumoto, Takayuki Okada, Fabiana Sánchez, Sara Sawairi, Giuliana Schroeder, Juliana Sugano, Jackie Shiroma, and Ana Takayama. Sandra del Castillo, our editor, once again demonstrated her matchless skills in bringing this volume to publication. Patricia Rosas translated all of the chapters originally written in Spanish.

Finally, this project would not have been possible without the contributions of dozens of leading experts and practitioners—some who contributed chapters for this volume, others who enriched our discussions and critiqued our work—who came together frequently during the past five years in a spirit of collegiality and concern for promoting the rule of law in Mexico. Marcelo Bergman, Hugo Concha, Réne Jiménez, Miguel Sarre, and Alexander Ruiz Euler served effectively as working group coordinators and advisers to us during the project. Pablo Piccato, Elisa Speckman, Pablo Parás, Arturo Arango, and Cristina Lara provided essential databases. Among practitioners, special thanks are due to Secretary of Public Security Alejandro Gertz Manero, Assistant Attorney General Alejandro Ramos, Border Commissioner Ernesto Ruffo Appel, Mexico City Police Chief Marcelo Ebrard Casaubón, and Baja California Governor Eugenio Elorduy.

The numerous deficiencies in the administration of justice in Mexico that we have identified in this volume are highly complex, closely interrelated, and deeply embedded in Mexico's society and political system. Solving these problems will require a Herculean effort, sustained over several decades. We hope that this volume will help to launch a new generation of policy-oriented research on Mexico's justice system that will be instrumental in making the system more effective and democratically accountable.

Wayne A. Cornelius
La Jolla, California, July 21, 2006

CHAPTER 1

Introduction: Reforming the Administration of Justice in Mexico

DAVID A. SHIRK AND ALEJANDRA RÍOS CÁZARES

One of the greatest challenges facing Mexico today and for the foreseeable future is that of ensuring the rule of law through the effective administration of justice. For the past decade, Mexicans have consistently ranked crime, corruption, and injustice among their top concerns. Their preoccupations about public security and access to justice have been partly a response to real increases in crime, especially violent crime. However, they also reflect the public's enormous frustration with the inability of Mexican government and law enforcement officials to effectively guarantee public security, accountability, and access to justice. Even after the 2000 elections—the watershed event that ostensibly confirmed Mexico's transition to democracy—the public's general perception is that lawlessness prevails because government and law enforcement officials remain indifferent, inept, or corrupt.

Unfortunately, all evidence suggests that these negative public perceptions of Mexican authorities are well founded. Poor training, inadequate resources, inefficient procedures, and case backlogs are pervasive throughout the criminal justice system. In addition, official corruption, abuse of authority, limited transparency, a general lack of accountability, and even the direct involvement of public officials and law enforcement agents in criminal activity are sufficiently common to justifiably undermine the pub-

The authors wish to acknowledge the contributions and improvements made by Arturo Alvarado, John Bailey, Wayne Cornelius, David Eisenberg, Barak Hoffman, Pablo Piccato, Benjamin Reames, Allison Rowland, Kathleen Staudt, Brittany Thatcher, Robert Varenik, and other collaborators over the course of several drafts of this chapter.

lic's trust. One concrete result of these severe problems is that the vast majority of total crimes in Mexico go unreported, and only a tiny fraction of reported crimes are actually punished.[1] The state's failure to adequately prevent, prosecute, and punish crime results, in turn, in greater criminal impunity and significant frustration for victims of crime. Meanwhile, too many individuals who are ultimately charged with crimes are themselves deprived of due process, go long periods in jail without formal sentencing, obtain inadequate legal defense, and suffer significant human rights abuses by law enforcement authorities (see Azaola and Bergman, this volume).

Over the last decade, a steadily growing public outcry demanding that authorities address these problems has provoked a nationwide debate on the need to reform the administration of justice in Mexico. Despite the movement toward a more competitive political system and some significant advances in Mexico's justice system during the last decade—including the restructuring of the judiciary and key agencies, major blows against organized crime, and a number of state-level reform initiatives—there has not been a significant improvement in the overall effectiveness, transparency, and accountability of the system. The slow change from a regime of single-party hegemony to a regime of multiparty competition and political alternation has not been accompanied by an improvement in the real and perceived effectiveness of the state to guarantee order, justice, and government accountability. To continue its democratic consolidation, Mexico needs to secure the protection of citizens' basic legal rights and personal security, equal access to justice, and an accountable state. Reforming the administration of justice has therefore become an essential task for Mexico's continued democratization.

DEMOCRATIC GOVERNANCE AND THE RULE OF LAW IN MEXICO

During the 1980s and 1990s, the literature on democratic transitions in Latin America and Eastern Europe placed much emphasis on the necessary incentives and conditions for transforming existing authoritarian regimes into democratic systems.[2] However, as Pilar Domingo points out, in the

---

[1] "[F]ewer than one in five inquires concludes satisfactorily" (Zepeda Lecuona, this volume).

[2] That is, much of this literature initially focused on identifying the pathways to democracy or the circumstances required for dictators to surrender authority to democratic actors (O'Donnell and Schmitter 1986; Di Palma 1990; Huntington 1991; Mainwaring et al. 1992; Przeworski 1991; Rueschemeyer, Stepehens,

urgency to identify and establish "the minimal democratic rules of the game," much of the initial literature on democratization overlooked a crucial element of democracy: the rule of law (Domingo 1996: 2). Many newly emerging democracies experienced a rising tide of crime, violence, and corruption that ultimately detracted from the performance of democratic institutions on multiple levels. This was especially true in Latin America, where a history of weakness and corruption in judicial institutions has combined with several new trends that are complicating the provision of order, accountability, and access to justice, including severe economic crises, rapid social and demographic change (urbanization), and powerful domestic and transnational crime syndicates. In response, scholars from multiple disciplinary approaches to social scientific inquiry in Latin America have sought to analyze and find solutions to a wide range of interrelated rule of law challenges, including crime and public insecurity, corruption, unprofessional and ineffective policing, human rights abuses, violence against women and minorities, vigilantism, ineffective and squalid prisons, and criminal recidivism.[3]

In spite of the agreement on the relevance of the rule of law and the need to address its challenges, there is no consensus about the definition of the concept. In this introduction we consider the rule of law to consist of at least three broad components: the regulation of individual behavior within

---

and Stephens 1992), and later on the design of electoral institutions capable of promoting representative and sustainable democratic systems of government (Grofman and Lijphart 1986; Lijphart and Aitkin 1994; Lijphart and Grofman 1984; Lijphart and Waisman 1996; Taagepera and Shugart 1989). As the process of democratic consolidation progressed, scholars began to analyze other issues of institutional design that would yield greater stability and effectiveness in democratic governance, including the nature of executive-legislative relations (Lijphart and Waisman 1996; Linz and Valenzuela 1994; Mainwaring and Shugart 1997; Shugart 1995), the strength of party organizations (Camp 1996; Di Tella 1998; Mainwaring 1999; Mainwaring and Scully 1995), and the distribution of national-local power within political systems (Carmagnani and Bidart Campos 1993; Gibson 2004; Montero and Samuels 2004; Samuels 2003; Tulchin, Selee, and Clemente 2004). In short, much of the literature on democratization and democratic consolidation focused on pressing problems of institutional design that concerned would-be political reformers and newly established democratic governments.

3 Domingo 2004; Domingo and Sieder 2001; Gloppen, Gargarella, and Skaar 2004; Jarquín and Carrillo Florez 1998; McAdams 1997; Salvatore, Aguirre, and Joseph 2001; Ungar 2001; O'Donnell, Vargas Cullell, and Iazzetta 2004; Bailey and Dammert. 2006.

society under the law (order), the accountability of the state and its representatives under the law (accountability), and access to justice through the law (access).[4]

The first component of our definition of the rule of law is the maintenance of "order" in terms of the provision of security, the regulation of social conduct, and the resolution of grievances according to a previously devised legal code. Order maintenance implies the existence of effective mechanisms for addressing deviant behavior from established law. "Accountability," the second component, refers to a State that is itself committed to be responsive to its citizens, to protect their individual rights, and to abide by the established legal order. Accountability is crucial to contemporary notions of the rule of law, in which groups and individuals in society must be protected from arbitrary or improper conduct by the State and its representatives. Finally, the notion of "access" requires that the enforcement of the law be efficient and predictable and that people have equal access to justice and equal treatment before the law itself. This component of the rule of law is based on the relatively modern and inherently normative understanding that the law must be effective, swift, and just.[5]

With regard to this definition of the rule of law, we must make two important observations. On the one hand, as our definition suggests, the manner in which "order," "accountability," and "access" are achieved is highly dependent on the nature and conduct of the State. Our definition is intrinsically linked to contemporary notions of democracy, especially liberal democracy. Unlike autocratic political systems, where society is essentially subject to the will of those in power, democratic systems place State power in the service of society through popular sovereignty. Certainly, autocratic political systems often boast a significant degree of "order" and may even achieve a semblance of State obedience to the law.[6] However,

---

[4] For a good discussion of these three elements as components of the rule of law, see Kleinfeld Belton 2005.

[5] When enforcement of the law is slow, irregular, inefficient, or inherently inimical to basic individual rights, the law is inadequate or even pernicious. Further, when individuals do not have access to justice, they may be inclined to subvert the law by taking matters into their own hands; under the above definition, vengeance and vigilantism are inconsistent with the rule of law.

[6] For example, Robert Barros (2003) argues that the collective nature of decision making in the Chilean military dictatorship from 1973 to 1990 was what contributed to a meticulous and rigorously respected institutional order that provided restraints equivalent to the rule of law.

with regard to constraints on State behavior and the provision of access to justice, authoritarian actors are ultimately only as subject to the law as they choose to be. Any restraint they may exercise is ultimately not externally binding or is at best extremely difficult to enforce from outside the State.[7] Hence, according to our definition, the rule of law is not compatible with authoritarian rule.

On the other hand, we argue that society at large plays a key and complementary role to that of the State in the provision of the rule of law. Societal traditions and norms both guide individual conduct and provide the fundamental basis of the law (Black and Mileski 1973). Likewise, groups and actors in organized civil society—professional associations, civic activist groups, and other self-organizing communities—play a key role in holding the State accountable for its actions and in advocating for access to justice.

To establish the rule of law—through an effective justice system that emphasizes strong preventive institutions, equitable access, effective resolution of grievances, civilian oversight, basic personal security, and the protection of individual rights—is an essential part of democratic consolidation (Ungar 2001). However, to consolidate the rule of law is necessarily an ongoing process and not an end goal, and is therefore one of the most elusive virtues to which any democracy can aspire. Indeed, even advanced, industrial democracies face continual challenges in protecting their citizens from crime, injustice, and inappropriate behavior from agents of the State. For instance, at different times and degrees over more than two centuries of representative government, the United States has experienced significant levels of crime, official corruption, and abuses of state power at virtually all levels of government. Moreover, it was not until the 1960s that the United States established universal access to key protections for the accused (such as the Miranda rights), free access to legal defense counsel, and standards and practices to promote "professional" policing. The rule of law must therefore be understood as a slowly attained and constantly evolving quality.

---

[7] Indeed, even in the case of Chile—where some scholars suggest that the Pinochet dictatorship was a regime "bound by law"—recent revelations suggest that illegal and corrupt government behavior occurred even at the highest levels. In March 2005, a U.S. Senate report produced by a subcommittee of the Committee on Governmental Affairs alleged that General Augusto Pinochet embezzled more than US$13 million, which was deposited to 125 offshore bank accounts, many of them in the United States (U.S. Senate Press Release 2005). Consider also the limits of the rule of law in China as discussed by Turner-Gottschang, Feinerman, and Guy 2000.

Table 1.1. Transparency International Corruption Perception Index Ratings of Selected Latin American Countries, 1995–2005

	1995	1996	1997	1998	1999	2000	2001	2002	2003	2004	2005	Average
Argentina	5.2	3.4	2.8	3.0	3.0	3.5	3.5	2.8	2.5	2.5	2.8	3.2
Belize	n.a	n.a	n.a	n.a	n.a	n.a	n.a	n.a	4.5	3.8	3.7	4.0
Bolivia	--	3.4	2.1	2.8	2.5	2.7	2	2.2	2.3	2.2	2.5	2.5
Brazil	2.7	3.0	3.6	4.0	4.1	3.9	4	4	3.9	3.9	3.7	3.7
Chile	7.9	6.1	6.1	6.8	6.9	7.4	7.5	7.5	7.4	7.4	7.3	7.2
Colombia	3.4	2.7	2.2	2.2	2.9	3.2	3.8	3.6	3.7	3.8	4.0	3.2
Costa Rica	n.a	n.a	6.4	5.6	5.1	5.4	4.5	4.5	4.3	4.9	4.2	5.0
Cuba	n.a	n.a	n.a	n.a	n.a	n.a	n.a	n.a	4.6	3.7	3.8	4.0
Ecuador	n.a	n.a	n.a	2.3	2.4	2.6	2.3	2.2	2.2	2.4	2.5	2.4
El Salvador	n.a	n.a	n.a	3.6	3.9	4.1	3.6	3.4	3.7	4.2	4.2	3.8
Guatemala	n.a	n.a	n.a	3.1	3.2	n.a	2.9	2.5	2.4	2.2	2.4	2.7
Honduras	n.a	n.a	n.a	1.7	1.8	n.a	2.7	2.7	2.3	2.3	2.6	2.3
Mexico	**3.2**	**3.3**	**2.7**	**3.3**	**3.4**	**3.3**	**3.7**	**3.6**	**3.6**	**3.6**	**3.5**	**3.4**
Nicaragua	n.a	n.a	n.a	3.0	3.1	n.a	2.4	2.5	2.6	2.7	2.6	2.7
Panama	n.a	n.a	n.a	n.a	n.a	n.a	3.7	3	3.4	3.7	3.5	3.5
Paraguay	n.a	n.a	n.a	1.5	2.0	n.a	n.a	1.7	1.6	1.9	2.1	1.8
Peru	n.a	n.a	n.a	4.5	4.5	4.4	4.1	4	3.7	3.5	3.5	4.0
Uruguay	n.a	n.a	4.1	n.a	4.4	n.a	5.1	5.1	5.5	6.2	5.9	5.2
Venezuela	2.7	2.5	2.8	2.3	2.6	2.7	2.8	2.5	2.4	2.3	2.3	2.5
Average	4.2	3.6	3.6	3.3	3.5	3.9	3.7	3.4	3.5	3.5	3.5	3.6

Achieving the rule of law is an especially difficult challenge for new democratic governments, given that the process of regime change (the process by which the apparatus of the State itself is reformed or replaced) is often inherently destabilizing, particularly in developing countries. Whether brought about by political negotiation, revolution, or external imposition, regime change eliminates, disrupts, or significantly modifies political institutions and norms. In particular, regime change often involves a transformation of the structure and function of the coercive organizations of the State: the police, the penal system, and the military. The effects of this transformation may be inherently destabilizing for the organizations themselves, may occur too slowly for the needs and preferences of citizens, or may otherwise strain relations between the State and society.

Democratic transitions also lead to increases in both the demand for justice and the public's intolerance for violations to the law. This is due to: (1) the inauguration of an electoral democracy that increases the expectations of government performance and its ability to provide collective goods, such as access to justice (especially among traditionally neglected groups), and (2) a greater degree of transparency in government performance that affects the information citizens obtain and use to evaluate the government. When new democratic governments are unable to cope effectively with increasing expectations and demands—and when the expansion of basic freedoms (such as freedom of expression) places bureaucratic ineptitude at the center of public opinion—public frustrations are likely to increase. The outcome is a cycle of high expectations, governmental ineffectiveness, media exposure, public frustration, and greater demands. This cycle is of key concern because it threatens to erode support for democracy and increase the appeal of populist or authoritarian formulas that may ultimately work to undermine the rule of law.

These challenges appear to be broadly applicable to countries of the so-called Third Wave of democratization during the last quarter of the twentieth century. In all the regions where the Third Wave had its greatest impact—Africa, Eastern Europe, and Latin America—the new freedoms of democracy were accompanied by significant problems of crime, violence, and disorder, along with poor improvements in combating corruption. Table 1.1 presents some statistics on the perception of corruption for some Latin American countries in the last ten years.[8]

---

[8] See Finn 1991; Godson 2003; Kaufmann 2001; McAdams 1997. On rule of law challenges in post-Soviet Russia and Eastern Europe, especially organized

In Mexico, while official rates of reported crime declined significantly from the 1940s to the 1970s—a period of strong economic growth—a series of economic crises in the 1980s and 1990s was accompanied by sharp increases in certain forms of crime, especially robbery and theft (see figure 1.1).[9] Nationally, Mexicans reported 63 crimes per 100,000 inhabitants each month between 1997 and May 2005.[10] This statistic obscures subnational dynamics, however, because average reported crime rates varied significantly across states during the same period (see figure 1.2). For example, during this period Tlaxcala residents reported 29 crimes per month per 100,000 residents, while Baja California residents reported 218.

Over the last two decades, Mexico's levels of crime and violence have been accompanied by serious problems of corruption, organized crime (especially narco-trafficking), widespread impunity, and abuse of public authority. As a result and despite Mexico's democratic transition, there is a lack of public confidence in the Mexican government's ability to guarantee basic security and the rule of law (table 1.2). In particular, citizens continue to express very low confidence in Mexican police as law enforcement agents (table 1.3).

Furthermore, despite an apparent leveling off—and possibly a slight decline—in Mexico's crime rate since 2000, citizens' perceptions of "public security" as a primary national problem have generally increased over the course of recent years (figure 1.3).[11]

---

crime, see Bonnell and Breslauer 2001; Howard 1991; Jakobsen 2003; Kelley 2003; Marshall 2003; Sachs and Pistor 1997; Smith and Danilenko 1993; Varese 2001; Volkov 2002; Webster 1997; Webster, De Borchgrave, and Cilluffo 2000; Williams 1997. Regarding rule of law challenges in newly emerging Latin American democracies, see Buscaglia 1998; Chávez 2004; Domingo and Sieder 2001; Jarquín and Carrillo Florez 1998; Johnson 1990; Ungar 2001. Regarding other developing democracies, see Ellmann 1992; Hassall 1997; Jackson 2005; Lobban 1996; Zeleza and McConnaughay 2004.

[9] Alvarado and Arzt 2001; Fix-Fierro and Jiménez Gómez 1997; González Ruiz, López Portillo V., and Yáñez R. 1994; Magaloni et al. 1994; M. Taylor 1995.

[10] Sistema Nacional de Seguridad Pública. The data up to 2001 were compiled by Arturo Arango and Cristina Lara; these data are available at www .seguridadpublicaenmexico.org.mx/crisada/estadistica/estadistica.htm. Data for 2002–May 2005 were compiled by the authors from INEGI statistics (www.inegi.org.mx).

[11] There is a lack of public data on how people perceived public insecurity before 1997, and data for the 1997–2000 period are not public.

Figure 1.1. Criminal Charges Filed in Mexico at State-level Jurisdiction, per 100,000 Inhabitants, 1926–2001

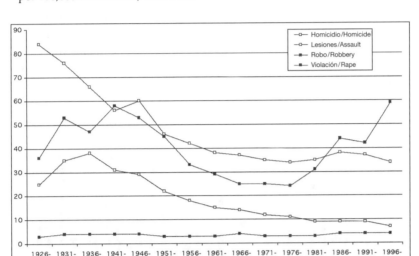

Source: Database compiled by Pablo Piccato on accused criminals (*presuntos delincuentes*) by criminal charge, crimes of state-level jurisdiction, 1926–2001.

These data show that Mexico's new democratic leaders must respond to public demand by addressing the deterioration of domestic security, by creating better mechanisms to keep public officials under control, and by securing equal access to justice. Otherwise, public officials risk a severe political crisis since Mexico's real and perceived failing rule of law may undermine support for democratic governance. As then–Mexico City Police Chief Marcelo Ebrard observed in May 2003: "Our justice system does not work. It is clear that if we do not resolve this problem, not only will we have an increasingly difficult situation, we may also provoke political problems of a magnitude that we cannot imagine, because the impression that exists—the public's perception—is that the legal system does not work."[12] This volume scrutinizes the key challenges that Mexico faces in reforming its justice system and identifies possible strategies for improving the rule of law.

---

[12] Comments by Marcelo Ebrard, in *Conference Report: Reforming the Administration of Justice in Mexico*, from a conference hosted at the Center for U.S.-Mexican Studies, University of California, San Diego, May 15–17, 2003.

Figure 1.2. Monthly Average Crime Reporting Rates in Mexico per 100,000
Inhabitants, 1997–May 2005

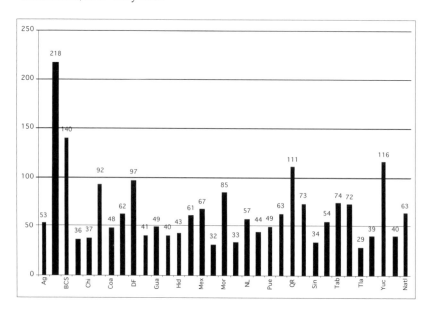

Sources: 1997–2001: Seguridad Pública en México (www.seguridadpublicaenmexico.org.mx).
These data are based on INEGI's *Anuarios Estadísticos Estatales* for 1997–2001. Data
for 2002–May 2005 come from the electronic version of *Anuarios Estadísticos Estatales*, available at www.inegi.gob.mx.

Table 1.2. Perceptions of Federal, State, and Local Efforts to Fight Crime

In the fight against crime: *Do you think the federal (state, local) government is
effective?*

	Good Performance	Bad Performance	No Opinion	Total
Federal government	31%	45%	24%	100%
State government (includes Federal District)	36%	42%	22%	100%
Local government (municipalities)	43%	37%	20%	100%

Source: *Reforma* newspaper, Mexico City, July 30–31, 2005, national phone survey.

Table 1.3. Rating of Trust in Mexican Institutions on a 10-Point Scale

	April, 04	July, 05
Universities	n.a	8.1
Church	7.7	7.7
Army	7.5	7.7
National Human Rights Commission	n.a	7.4
Federal Electoral Institute	6.7	7.1
Mass media	7.0	6.9
President	6.1	6.2
Supreme Court	5.7	6.1
Businessmen	5.3	5.3
Political parties	4.7	5.1
Senators	4.7	5.0
Police	**5**	**4.9**
Labor unions	4.8	4.7
Legislative deputies	4.2	4.5

Source: Consulta Mitofsky, "Confianza en Instituciones," National Home Survey, July 2005, p. 3 The question asked was: In a scale like the one used in the school, where 0 is nothing and 10 is a lot, please tell me how much you trust … .

Figure 1.3. Percentage of Citizens for Whom Insecurity Is Most Important Problem

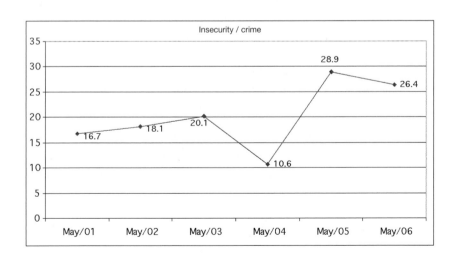

Source: *Reforma* newspaper, Mexico City, July 30-31, 2005, national phone survey.

ORDER: REDUCING CRIME AND CRIMINALITY IN MEXICO

Any discussion of crime and criminality must begin with a major caveat: obtaining accurate, reliable, and comprehensive statistical indicators about crime and law enforcement is extremely difficult, particularly in Mexico. In general, there are essentially three kinds of crime: (1) crimes that are unobserved by the victim or authorities, (2) crimes that are known but not reported, and (3) crimes that are known and reported.[13] Many crimes in Mexico fall into the first two categories and—because hard data on such crimes are essentially impossible to obtain—are commonly referred to by Mexican criminologists as "black data" (the *cifra negra*). Underreporting results from many factors. Although victims or witnesses may feel disinclined to report crimes due to humiliation (a common reaction in rape cases) or indifference (for example, among witnesses to minor traffic violations), underreporting in Mexico is too often related to inconvenience or a lack of confidence in the justice system.

That is, many victims perceive that the process of reporting crimes is highly bureaucratic and time consuming, and may even lead to further victimization by authorities. Furthermore, given high rates of criminal impunity (that is, the improbability of apprehension and punishment) in Mexico—because police and the judicial system are often ineffective or corrupt—victims also perceive that reporting a crime is a futile exercise. A recent survey on crime and victimization in Mexico shows that only 25 percent of those who were victims of crime between 1999 and 2005 reported the crime to the public prosecutor (*ministerio público*); and of those who reported a crime, 63 percent were disappointed with the performance of the public prosecutor.[14]

When crime data *are* collected in Mexico, the methods for collection are often significantly flawed in ways that prevent effective investigation or analysis. Thus, not only is there a lack of information about crime in Mexico, there is also a lack of credible information and clear priorities for the data needed to confront the problem of insecurity. For example, Mexican authorities often fail to collect data about the victim (such as age, sex, employment, relation to the offender, and so on) or the circumstances of the

---

[13] Comments by Arturo Arango in *Conference Report: Reforming the Administration of Justice in Mexico.*

[14] See "Encuesta Internacional sobre Criminalidad y Victimización, ENICRIV–2004," http://www.consulta.com.mx/interiores/99_pdfs/15_otros_pdf/oe_2004_ENICRIV_ICESI.pdf.

crime (specific location, time of day, damage or loss suffered by the victim, and so on). Moreover, most police units—such as "preventive" and "auxiliary" police (which provide support to banks and private businesses)—do not even collect and report crime statistics.

Additionally, because prosecutors are generally able to obtain convictions with a single charge, crime data are often collected in ways that obscure the multiple infractions that might be involved in a given incident. For example, a homicide suspect carrying an illegal weapon and drugs may only be charged with the most serious offense in order to streamline the process of prosecution. Furthermore, individual police and different agencies have enormous discretion in categorizing a crime; as a result, there is no uniform analytical framework to permit systematic comparison. Likewise, generalization across other sources (such as opinion polls) is complicated by variations in definitions, sample populations, and methodology.

All of these points suggest that crime statistics in Mexico have major flaws. Nonetheless, at a minimum, the imperfect crime data available provide a point of departure for analysis and improvement in data collection. Experts estimate the incidence of crime in Mexico by tabulating: (1) the rate of "known crimes" as indicated in victimization surveys;[15] (2) the "apparent crime" reported and crimes under investigation or "preliminary inquiry" (*averiguación previa*); (3) "investigated crimes"; and (4) crimes resulting in arrest and sentencing. Agencies of the executive branch (including the police and attorneys general) collect and manage data in the first three categories, while the judiciary (including the courts, magistrates, judicial police, and so on) operate and manage data in the third and fourth categories. Statistics on public security are eventually compiled from state-level attorneys general and published by the National Institute of Statistics, Geography, and Informatics (INEGI) and the Ministry of Public Security (SSP). Data on suspects (*probables delincuentes*) and convicted criminals (*delincuentes sentenciados*) are published in judicial statistics bulletins. Reports

---

[15] The Citizens' Institute for Security Studies (ICESI) recently published two major surveys on crime and victimization: The International Survey on Crime and Victimization (Encuesta Internacional sobre Criminalidad y Victimización), 1999–2004, and the Third National Survey on Public Safety (Tercera Encuesta Nacional sobre Inseguridad), 2005. ICESI is a civic organization sponsored by academic institutions (Universidad Nacional Autónoma de México, Instituto Tecnológico Autónomo de Monterrey, and the Este País Foundation) and the private sector.

of selected crime indicators can also be obtained from the president's annual report and those of state and local executives.

The first section of this volume examines notions of crime, historical crime trends, and contemporary patterns of criminality in Mexico. Experts generally assert that our understanding of crime is socially constructed and that the reactions crime provokes from the State and from the general public are shaped by that construction (Buffington 1994; Speckman Guerra 2002). Robert Buffington begins therefore with a detailed discussion of the construction of crime and criminality in modern Mexico, providing a cautionary tale for would-be modern-day reformers. Buffington points out that public and governmental reactions have historically failed to properly diagnose and prescribe solutions to Mexico's crime problems. Across multiple phases in Mexico's history, different criminal justice paradigms portrayed endemic social crises as "crime waves"; villainized society's "undesirables" (from the traditional petty thief or *ratero* to the modern *norteño* narco-trafficker); produced concerted efforts to measure public opinion about crime through new methods and technologies; and led to the patchwork construction of new laws and structural reforms. The result of these often misguided criminological frameworks has been the development of suboptimal policy responses, self-perpetuating dilemmas, and the accumulation of anomalies, contradictions, and failures in the judicial system. Thus, from Buffington's perspective, the problem with criminological paradigms and reform efforts in Mexico is that they have ultimately proved cyclical and self-defeating.

Pablo Piccato's study of crime trends in Mexico City likewise illustrates the persistence of Mexico's criminal justice challenges over the better part of the twentieth century. Piccato's presentation of long-term historical data in Mexico City reveals an apparent contradiction between popular perception and quantitative statistical evidence. On the one hand, multiple testimonies collected throughout the century show that crime (particularly violence, theft, and corruption) was a permanent concern for the inhabitants of the city. On the other hand, despite the noticeable increases in the last two decades, official indicators suggest that (with important exceptions, such as Baja California, Baja California Sur, Quintana Roo, and Yucatán) crime has generally tended to level off or decline over the course of the twentieth century and into the twenty-first century (see figure 1.4).

Piccato blames underreporting for the apparent contradiction between the popular perception of a constant "crime wave" and the declining statistical incidence of crime. Given the corruption and resource limitations of law enforcement authorities, today's victims choose not to bring the vast majority of all crimes to the attention of the police.[16]

Figure 1.4. Crime Rates in Mexico City, Baja California, and Nationwide during the Fox Administration

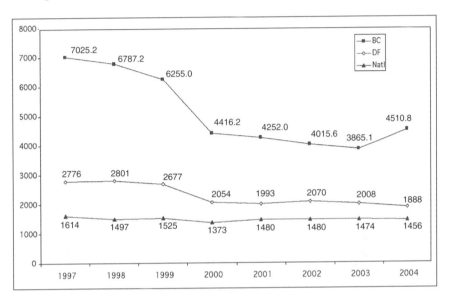

Source: Seguridad Pública en México. These data are a systematization of data from the Secretaría de Seguridad Pública and INEGI's *Anuarios Estadísticos Estatales*, www.seguridadpublicaenmexico.org.mx/crisada/estadistica/estadistica.htm.

A major contribution of Piccato's chapter is his discussion of how certain Mexico City communities have been forced to develop their own internal norms for adjusting to crime and other social problems in order to avoid falling into a state of anomie or unfocused collective violence. Indeed, Piccato underscores the way that society adapts in the absence of effective state responses to crime and insecurity, and illustrates that these adaptations can play an important role in promoting the rule of law.

Meanwhile, little is generally known about criminals in Mexico. While the criminal himself is a central focus of criminological studies elsewhere, he is practically nonexistent in studies on crime in Mexico. However, some

---

[16] Zepeda discusses rates of reporting in his chapter in this volume.

important exceptions have helped illuminate the social construction, organization, and individual calculus of crime and criminality.[17] The objective of such analyses must necessarily be to evaluate the extent to which societal transformation and institutional reform can affect the conditions that lead to criminality and the ultimate calculus of choosing to commit a crime.

Accordingly, in their coauthored chapter, Elena Azaola and Marcelo Bergman present the results of the first major study of prisoners in Mexico, conducted by a team of researchers at the law school of the Centro de Investigación y Docencia Económicas (CIDE). Official data on prisoners and incarceration in Mexico are still very rare and contain little detailed information. Hence the authors provide unique insights into the kinds of crimes committed by inmates, personal background and socioeconomic status of prisoners, treatment and access to justice in the course of arrest and prosecution, and prison living conditions.

According to Azaola and Bergman, Mexico's imprisoned population nearly doubled—from 87,700 to 177,500 inmates—between 1992 and 2003. The authors explain that this increase was partly due to real increases in crimes committed, but was also due to increasing the number and duration of drug-related sentences (as has also occurred in the United States; see Blumstein and Beck 1999). In other cases, where officials have discretion to alter sentences, prison personnel are often too overloaded to allow for review or early release. Some other problematic characteristics of Mexico's prisons that Azaola and Bergman reveal—such as the large numbers of convicts awaiting court verdicts, due to an unreliable parole system— illustrate unresolved challenges elsewhere in the Mexican justice system. Other patterns—such as inhumanely overcrowded facilities, insufficient basic services such as food, medicine, and clothing, and the overrepresentation of individuals who could not afford adequate legal defense—invoke Dostoevsky's observation that a society is best judged by the treatment of its prisoners (figure 1.5).

Yet, as Azaola and Bergman point out, these findings do not suggest that Mexico is unique or different from other Latin American countries. Rather, they illustrate the low priority that public officials throughout the hemisphere have placed on using their prison systems to promote rehabilitation and reduce recidivism. Meanwhile, knee-jerk reactions to perceived

---

[17] Azaola 1990; Bailey and Godson 2000; Buffington 2000, 1994; Piccato 2001; Piccato, Pérez Montfort, and del Castillo Yurrita 1997.

increases in crime have produced inadequate, counterproductive policies (raising penalties and so on) that will not adequately address the problem.

Figure 1.5. Official Estimates of Prison Overcrowding in Mexico, 1998–2004

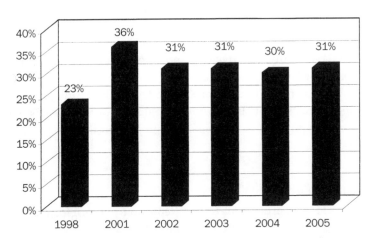

Sources: For 1998: Secretaría de Gobernación, Dirección General de Prevención y Readaptación Social. For 2001–2004: Secretaría de Seguridad Pública, "Organo Administrativo Desconcentrado. Prevención y Readaptación Social."

ACCOUNTABILITY: LAW ENFORCEMENT AND JUDICIAL REFORM

Recent research published by the Center for U.S.-Mexican Studies at the University of California, San Diego suggests that problems of insecurity in Mexico tend to be more tied to citizens' "perception of the government's ineffectiveness in enforcing the law than to perceptions of crime itself" (Bailey and Chabat 2001). Indeed, many analysts contend that Mexico's public safety "crisis" lies less in the increases in crime and violence of the mid-1990s than in the inability of the criminal justice system to adequately and responsibly address them.

In part, this failure is the result of problems of institutional design and dysfunction, some of which date from the days of Spanish colonial rule and others from more than a century of authoritarian rule under the Porfiriato and Institutional Revolutionary Party (PRI) hegemony. These problems are frequently reflected in the lack of professionalism and improper behavior of actors within the legal system. Indeed, the entire justice system in Mexico suffers from a poorly trained and weakly professionalized police force and legal profession. While Mexican policing has been one of the few areas of government growth in an era of massive downsizing, these efforts have not been accompanied by significantly greater effectiveness and accountability in the system.

That these are ultimately issues of institutional design means that throwing additional resources at the problem will not provide adequate solutions. Real progress requires comprehensive institutional reforms that increase the integrity, effectiveness, and accountability of the state apparatus itself in order to ensure greater access to justice for Mexico's citizens. This volume therefore directs particular attention to the organizations and institutional roles of public security and judicial personnel--the military, police, public prosecutors, lawyers, and judges—in the functioning of the justice system.

Policing and Prosecution in Mexico

A recent U.S. Department of Justice Report on police reform asserts that "security is important to the development of democracy and police are important to the character of that security." According to this report, "democratic" police organizations must adopt norms in which police: (1) hold as their primary mission protection and service to individual citizens; (2) are constrained by law, not "by directions [from] particular regimes and their members"; (3) protect human rights, particularly those freedoms essential to democracy; and (4) are transparent in their operations and subject to external review (Bayley 2001: 13–15). According to the author of this report, "promoting police reform is widely regarded as a key element of democratic governance. Assisting in the democratic reform of foreign police systems has become a front-burner issue in American foreign policy" (Bayley 2001: 5).

Major innovations in policing and legal reform began to gain ground in North America and Europe in the 1960s and 1970s and have done so more recently in Latin America with the course of democratization. However, Mexico falls short and has been slow to adopt such standards. In part, the behavior of police organizations in Mexico is the product of decades of rule by a corrupt political system and the selective application of justice dating back to Spanish colonialism and its nineteenth-century legacies.[18] During

---

[18] Barrón Cruz, Silva, and Yáñez R. 2004; Rohlfes 1983; Vanderwood 1981; Yáñez R. 1999.

the twentieth century, Mexican police and criminal investigators operated in a context where machine-style monopoly politics encouraged impunity, incompetence, and antagonism, much as they did under entrenched political machines in the United States.[19] The result has been a significant deviation from the norms of modern democratic policing.

A growing number of scholars have turned their attention to problems of policing and public security in Mexico.[20] However, until recently, studies of Mexico's criminal justice system remained relatively isolated and awaiting an integrative theory, comparative insights, and a more comprehensive analysis of the problems at hand. This volume provides a number of studies and recommendations that help to fill this void. In his chapter, Benjamin Reames presents a useful overview of police organizations in Mexico. As Reames discusses, Mexico fits the general pattern in Latin America of having an organizational separation between order maintenance and investigative functions, in the form of the preventive police (*policía preventiva*) and judicial police (*policía judicial*).

Moreover, despite having very large numbers, Mexico's civilian police organizations are generally afflicted by practical human and material resource limitations that reduce their effectiveness, professionalism, and levels of public confidence. Indeed, police salaries are low even by Mexican standards (see table 1.4), and other types of benefits (such as life insurance) and basic equipment (bullets, bulletproof vests, and uniforms) must often be purchased by the officers themselves. Reames argues that, above and beyond these problems, the Mexican system suffers from particularly "confusing organization and inefficient use of personnel," "frequent internal reorganizations," and important problems of coordination. Reames explains that the Fox administration sought to overcome these challenges by unifying some of the nation's police organizations and increasing the investigative capacity of police.

In his chapter, Guillermo Zepeda Lecuona looks explicitly at the problem of criminal investigations and argues that police functions are too limited to properly assist prosecutors, undermining the effective administration of justice in Mexico. Zepeda looks specifically at the role of the public prosecutor's office in the investigative phase of a crime known as

---

[19] Regarding twentieth-century policing in Mexico, see González G. 1983; López 1988; Martínez de Murguía 1999; Martínez Garnelo 1999. Regarding policing in the United States, see Walker 1977; Wilson and Boland 1979.

[20] Alvarado and Arzt 2001; Davis and Alvarado 1999; del Villar 2001; González Ruiz, López Portillo V., and Yáñez R. 1994.

the "preliminary inquiry." Since most Mexican police have no legal authority to investigate crimes, the public prosecutor's office plays a critical role. However, because this office is responsible for both conducting investigations *and* prosecuting crimes, the public prosecutor is considered a "privileged party," with major advantages vis-à-vis the legal defense of the individual accused of a crime. Moreover, given that police do not have investigative capacity, public prosecutors' offices in Mexico are significantly overburdened because they handle investigations of *all* reported crimes, rather than dealing only with the subset of crimes that result in prosecutions.

Table 1.4. Daily Average Income by Sector, February 2005
(average daily minimum wage is US$4.05)

Police[a]	Manufacturing	Maquiladoras	Construction	Services
$13.45	$35.77	$23.33	$15.27	$22.09

Source: Salario Mínimo General y Remuneraciones Nominales Promedio de los Asalariados en Grupos de Actividad Seleccionados. Mexico: Secretaría del Trabajo y Previsión Social.
Note: Exchange rate in February 2005: US$1 = MX$11.16.
[a] Average wage of a policeman in the Preventive Police in Mexico City in February 2005 (Policía Bancaria e Industrial).

Hence Mexico's prosecutors spend most of their time fulfilling basic investigative functions that might be better done by police organizations, as they are in other countries. The prosecutors' excessive workload necessitates a high degree of discretion in the selection and investigation of cases, though this discretion is generally unregulated and unsupervised. The result, according to Zepeda, is that a relatively small number of reported crimes for which a suspect is identified (less than one in four) and an even smaller number of suspected criminals (less than half) are brought to trial. But what is especially needed to improve the institutional capacity of prosecutors in criminal investigations, Zepeda argues, is greater independence for units charged with investigating crimes, the creation of a career civil service at the state level to increase professionalism, and the injection of greater accountability through "a clear system of regular and autonomous external supervision" linked to the established system of judicial oversight.

On the other hand, as Robert Kossick and Rubén Minutti argue in this volume, part of the problem is the lack of the competition and balancing power provided by capable defense councilors who are decently equipped to challenge prosecutors.[21] Indeed, for many Mexicans the idea of providing law enforcement with more resources and authority is difficult to accept because of the accurate perception that police themselves are so often corrupt and abusive. In his chapter, Carlos Silva develops a classification of the cases of police abuse in Mexico City, focusing particularly on the motivations found in the daily practices of police units. Drawing on findings and recommendations of the Human Rights Commission of the Federal District from its founding in 1994 to 2003, Silva developed a classification that takes into account the legal and organizational factors that contribute to corrupt practices and behaviors among police. He finds three main modalities of corruption and abuse: (1) as a substitute for proper investigation and prevention, (2) as a means of unlawful economic gain, and (3) as punishment for challenging the "power" of the police. Silva then identifies five major contributors to corruption and abuse in Mexico: (1) the characteristics of individual police personnel; (2) the organizational procedures for recruitment, training, and internal management; (3) the particular context of interaction; (4) macro-level socioeconomic factors; and (5) the existing legal framework for regulating police functions. Overall, Silva paints an extremely critical picture of the current state of police behavior in Mexico and illustrates the urgent need for reform in the new democratic context.

All of the above challenges that undermine the overall effectiveness of police have contributed in turn to a troubling trend: the "militarization" of policing. The militarization of Mexican policing manifests itself in at least two ways: a high involvement of former military personnel in Mexican police organizations, and significant involvement of the armed forces themselves in domestic law enforcement activities, particularly with regard to the war on drugs. The prevailing wisdom in Mexico appears to be that involving the highly respected armed forces in the fight against narcotrafficking is a necessary evil.[22] This involvement began well ahead of the Fox administration. If it has not existed throughout the entire history of policing in Mexico (Barrón Cruz, Silva, and Yáñez R. 2004), it certainly was in place by the time President Miguel de la Madrid declared in 1986 that

---

[21] See also Gilman 2001; Human Rights First 2001; Reding 1995.

[22] According to General Alvaro Vallarta Cecena (Ret.), "The army has to take the risks [of corruption], like when a doctor ... attends a sick person. He runs the risk of contracting the contagious disease" (Kraul 2002).

narco-trafficking represented a national security crisis. Later, President
Ernesto Zedillo substituted career military officers and soldiers for civilian
law enforcement personnel in the criminal justice systems of several states,
most notably in Chihuahua and the Federal District (Mexico City).

Yet, according to Sigrid Arzt's chapter in this volume, during the Fox
administration the armed forces in Mexico significantly expanded their
role and presence in the distinct areas of security, intelligence, and justice.
Indeed, the appointments of General Rafael Macedo and other high-
ranking military officers to civilian law enforcement positions at the outset
of the Fox administration were evidently intended as part of a serious
campaign to enhance the integrity of the Mexican justice system.[23] The
incorporation of military personnel was accompanied by increased U.S.-
Mexico collaboration and resulted in major blows against drug-trafficking
cartels. Notably, in early 2002 Mexican and U.S. officials accomplished a
long-standing goal—the disruption of the Tijuana cartel—when local officials in Mazatlán, Sinaloa, killed Ramón Arrellano-Félix and elite counter-
narcotics units in Puebla arrested Benjamín Arrellano-Félix. One year later,
the Fox administration captured Osiel Cárdenas, head of the Gulf cartel,
who was later incarcerated in La Palma, the same maximum security penitentiary holding Benjamín Arrellano-Félix. Unfortunately, despite these
accomplishments, Mexico experienced continued violence as remnants of
the Tijuana and Gulf cartels—still coordinated by their imprisoned leaders—battled rivals seeking control of lucrative northern drug corridors into
the United States.[24]

In the end, the militarization of domestic security and policing raises
serious concerns about the potential for increased corruption within the
armed forces and about their overall effectiveness in contributing to public
safety. Yet present civilian alternatives do not appear well suited for the
challenges at hand. Indeed, the resignation of Attorney General Rafael
Macedo—partly in response to public criticism over the attempt to prose-

---

[23] It is worth noting that, prior to taking office, Fox pledged to abolish the Office of the Attorney General (PGR) but instead relied heavily on the agency
during his term. See Smith and Ellingwood 2000.

[24] The resulting violence included the retaliatory murder of half a dozen Mata-
moros prison guards, the brazen assassination of Nuevo Laredo's police chief
only hours after being sworn in, and dozens of killings (several of which
were perpetrated by masked commando units, or "Zetas," allegedly coordinated by Osiel Cárdenas and apparently comprising former military personnel).

cute Mexico City mayor and presidential hopeful Andrés Manuel López Obrador for failing to comply with a court order—provoked criticisms that his successor, Daniel Cabeza de Vaca, lacked the experience and credibility to effectively manage the office (Barclay 2005). For Arzt, then, the most urgent priority is to establish institutionalized civilian counterbalances within the executive branch, in other branches of the federal government, and in society as a whole.

Key Actors in the Mexican Legal System

In addition to a focus on police, this volume also places substantial emphasis on the professional role of key actors—including lawyers and judges—in the Mexican legal system. After years of neglect in Latin America, judicial reform and the professionalization of legal actors have become major priorities for strengthening democracy and the rule of law.[25] In Mexico, as Schatz, Concha, and Magaloni discuss in their chapter, the last set of major judicial reforms came at the outset of the administration of Ernesto Zedillo (1994–2000). These reforms consisted primarily of top-down initiatives to modestly restructure and increase professionalization at the highest levels of the judiciary, rather than at the level where most criminal justice takes place. Thus the Zedillo-era reforms fell far short of resolving Mexico's systemic justice-sector problems.

The urgency of deeper and more substantial reforms was made clear by a scathing 2002 United Nations report critiquing persistent problems in the Mexican justice system: the disorganization of the legal profession, problems of lawyer-prisoner accessibility, harassment and intimidation of lawyers and human rights defenders, trial procedure violations (including the use of forced confessions), the inefficiency of injunction procedures (*amparo*), inadequate access to justice for indigenous persons, the lack of special legal procedures for children and adolescents, the utter failure to resolve the brutal serial murders of hundreds of women in Ciudad Juárez since 1994, a lack of equality and access for women, and a general lack of transparency and accountability throughout the justice system (Cumaraswamy 2002).

Nonetheless, it seems that reform of the justice system will depend on the prevailing theories and arguments of politicians and actors in the legal

---

[25] Begné Guerra 1995; Buscaglia 1998; Chávez 2004; Domingo 2004; Domingo and Sieder 2001; Jarquín and Carrillo Florez 1998; Reyes 2001; M. Taylor 1995.

system and their ability to convince a skeptical public that they have succeeded in developing viable solutions after many failures. Drawing lessons from a historical perspective, Elisa Speckman Guerra looks at how the connection between statute and the administration of justice is impacted by social change. In particular, Speckman argues that judges, lawyers, and policymakers have been the crucial agents of change in past reforms to the administration of justice in Mexico. The social and political context in which these actors operate is therefore key to understanding the prospects and direction for legal change. Using interviews and public pronouncements of lawyers and judges, Speckman studies the legal codes of 1871–1931 to explain the emergence of the 1931 legal system, which brought about major changes in Mexico's criminal codes in response to a significant rise in violence and drug-related crime during the 1920s.

According to Speckman, as occurred in other countries, these reforms reflected socially constructed notions of crime and legal theories that predominated at the time. For Speckman, changing legal discourse brought a critical shift that ultimately tended to constrain judicial prerogatives, make punishments harsher, emphasize incarceration, and generally abandon the belief that law enforcement could reform individual criminal behavior. This was the beginning of a new era in Mexican criminal justice that coincided with the consolidation of the state apparatus and the new political context that developed after the Mexican Revolution. Similarly, reforms at the current transitional stage of Mexico's political development will similarly hinge on the discourse of scholars and legal experts, the theories and priorities that they identify as most germane to Mexico's contemporary circumstances, and their efforts to integrate these to the juridical status quo.

What is troubling about this prospect is the significant lack of professional standards among Mexico's 40,000 practicing lawyers, which Héctor Fix-Fierro discusses in his chapter. Fix-Fierro focuses especially on undergraduate legal education, since Mexican lawyers need not obtain a graduate degree in order to practice law. As Fix-Fierro points out, the current state of legal education has been undermined by a veritable explosion in the number of law programs in Mexico and a lack of oversight of them. The diversity and proliferation of such programs have resulted in enormous variation in the quality of legal training. Moreover, would-be lawyers are not required to take a standardized bar examination or any assessment of their qualifications with regard to professional responsibility and ethical conduct in the practice of law. There is also no requirement for lawyers to belong to a bar association in order to practice law, nor are there any professional requirements for continuing legal education for lawyers and judges.

The lack of regulation by the government or professional associations gives lawyers enormous leeway and little accountability to the public. The deficient oversight of the legal profession leaves practically no defense against a disloyal, negligent, or dishonest lawyer, as such individuals are very rarely prosecuted or convicted for crimes related to their professional practice. As a result, in the above-mentioned 2002 United Nations report, the president of Mexico's largest bar association (the 2,000-member Mexico City–based Colegio de Abogados) admitted that "the legal profession in Mexico might be one of the worst in the world insofar as disciplinary procedures were concerned" (Cumaraswamy 2002). According to Fix-Fierro, a decisive factor for reform will therefore be an open and public debate on how to regulate legal education, access to the profession, and the overall role of lawyers in the administration of justice in Mexico.

Complementing Fix-Fierro's evaluation of lawyers, Jeffrey Staton's chapter focuses on the role of judges in the reform of Mexico's justice system. According to Staton, it is obvious that judges intimately affect the success of reform efforts since reform packages are designed to influence judicial performance. However, the exact role judges play in reshaping judicial institutions is less clear. Although judges and the judiciary are traditionally viewed as apolitical, Staton argues that judges can play an active role as "agenda setters" in shaping public debate and initiatives for reform.[26] Judges may consult directly with legislative reformers or even influence public opinion by "going public." Staton argues that this creates a fundamental dilemma for judges as they try to manage the judiciary's public relations at the same time that they are expected to remain "apolitical."

Staton focuses on the role of ministers of the current Supreme Court (all appointed with the restructuring of the federal judiciary in late 1994), who engaged in lobbying efforts directed toward national policymakers and

---

[26] There are historical reasons for the traditionally apolitical role of the Supreme Court. In 1882, in the wake of the so-called Iglesias-Vallarta dispute, a constitutional reform was passed to prevent members of the Supreme Court from serving provisionally as chief executive. However, the larger implication of the Iglesias-Vallarta dispute was that it institutionalized the notion that the Supreme Court should remain outside of the "political realm." See Barragán 1994.

mounted an aggressive public relations campaign designed to connect the Court directly to the Mexican public. Their efforts produced mixed results. On the one hand, the Court successfully supported reforms for judicial efficiency and administrative control over the functioning of the court system. On the other hand, the Mexican Congress rejected key proposals to increase the Court's powers of constitutional interpretation (such as strengthening *amparo* rulings) and judicial independence. Hence, in contrast to Speckman's findings, Staton concludes that successful lobbying by the judiciary may convince executives or congressional delegates to consider reform proposals, but this does not ensure that those proposals will be enacted.

ACCESS TO JUSTICE: CIVIC PARTICIPATION AND OVERSIGHT

In recent years a number of desperate and even extreme reactions from the public have illustrated the severity of Mexico's rule of law challenges and the need to integrate civil society in the process of justice reform. On June 27, 2004, a quarter of a million Mexicans dressed in white marched in the streets of Mexico City to protest the government's failure to address problems of crime and violence (Alcaraz and Cortés 2004; Thompson 2004). Four days later, in response to their demands, Fox unveiled a ten-point plan that included an increase in spending on security from US$250 million to $350 million for 2004 and to half a billion dollars for 2005.[27]

In the weeks that followed, however, capital-city residents took out their frustrations on suspected criminals and even police in a series of vigilante acts and mob lynchings, one of which resulted in the televised beatings and murders of two federal police officers in November 2004.[28] While this was the most widely reported incident in recent years, vigilantism and public lynching have been common in Mexico, though predominantly in

---

[27] The ten points were: (1) a meeting of the National Security Council (CNSP) to address the issue; (2) the incorporation of state prosecutors in the CNSP; (3) coordination with state governors; (4) more effective coordination of police; (5) greater transparency in the area of security; (6) increased budget for security; (7) a media campaign to promote a culture of legality; (8) total quality and service in attention to reported crime; (9) a new system of attention to victims of crime; and (10) the constant purification of PGR and SSP police forces (Kraul 2004; Ruiz and Arvizu 2004).

[28] McKinley and Thompson 2004. In reaction to public outrage over the incident, Fox fired Mexico City Police Chief Marcelo Ebrard.

rural, poor, and indigenous communities, where the absence of effective law enforcement leads to a reliance on informal means of justice.[29] Though such responses may reflect community norms and even long-standing local traditions, the punishments imposed can vary widely from (and even violate) established Mexican law (CNDH 2003).

Such extreme and desperate reactions from society point to the severity of Mexico's rule of law challenges and the enormous frustration of a population in search of justice. Citizens have an overwhelming lack of confidence in the justice system, which suggests an exceedingly low level of "customer satisfaction" and a significant legitimacy problem for the Mexican government. Reforms and new policy measures are needed to provide greater civic access and oversight, which can be channeled toward the overall improvement of the justice system. Above all, civil society and individual communities must be made integral parts of justice reform in Mexico, rather than the casualties of injustice. This volume pays special attention, therefore, to the relationship of civil society and individual citizens to Mexico's criminal justice system—the degree of access to justice— from various perspectives.

In their chapter, Robert Kossick and Rubén Minutti provide an overview of the problems of citizen access to justice from a legal and judicial perspective. These authors argue that insufficient access is particularly exacerbated by the lack of professionalism and accountability in the legal community. These problems are especially acute, they suggest, with regard to public defenders, who are ultimately responsible for holding the government accountable to the law. According to Kossick and Minutti, Mexican public defenders are too often burdened by excessive caseloads, offered inadequate compensation, and poorly regulated. These problems in turn explain the high level of incompetence and even corruption among public defenders in Mexico. Not surprisingly, the lack of adequate legal counsel disproportionately affects poor and indigenous persons; indeed, the latter often lack adequate translation at different stages in criminal proceedings and tend to be overrepresented among prisoners being held in pretrial detention.

Over the last decade, efforts to improve public legal defense have included the creation of the Federal Institute of the Public Defender (IFDP),

---

[29] One *Washington Post* report described a rural Mixtec community that had buried one murderer alive with his dead victim (a life-long friend killed in a drunken fight) and reprimanded rapists with minor restitution to the family or only a few hours of jail time (Sullivan 2002; see also Kraul 2004).

significant increases in the number of public defenders and civil counselors, and the development of new training resources. The authors recommend that these important advances should be complemented by further measures to strengthen licensing requirements and regulation of the legal profession, and to increase the opportunities and incentives for the provision of legal assistance through pro bono and supervised student involvement in IFDP cases. With regard to the improvement of legal practice and professional responsibility in general, Kossick and Minutti also note the increased requirements for federal judicial candidates, greater efforts to monitor judicial assets, partial provisions to prevent the commingling of attorney-client funds, and the development of a new federal transparency law. Ultimately, however, what is critically lacking is the development of better oversight mechanisms to ensure greater accountability. Kossick and Minutti suggest that such mechanisms would include the development of a U.S.-style network of mandatory state and national bar associations, obligatory standards for professional responsibility, and increased access to information about the professional conduct of legal actors.

Meanwhile, the real and perceived barriers between citizens and the justice system are an impediment to the latter's proper functioning and must be addressed. To examine societal reactions to Mexico's security crisis, Pablo Parás provides an innovative assessment of public opinion surveys to determine how crime affects levels of trust, or "social capital," between individuals in society. The concept of social capital has been widely employed as an explanatory variable that impacts other phenomena, such as democratic system performance. However, drawing on survey data from Mexico City, Parás constructs a causal model that demonstrates that social capital can itself be affected by levels of crime and violence in a society. That is, when citizens feel unsafe or have been victimized by crime, their levels of trust in other citizens and institutions decline significantly. Parás's findings suggest that continued high levels of crime and violence may have significant negative implications for democratic consolidation in Mexico, in the sense that public insecurity contributes to lessen support for democracy, democratic institutions, and norms that promote active citizenship.

Rosalva Aída Hernández and Héctor Ortiz address issues of accessibility to justice for Mexico's indigenous population. These authors argue that Mexico must undergo reforms to ensure that its judicial system recognizes and incorporates the cultural diversity of the nation. Their central argument is that "the refusal of the legislature and judiciary to recognize cultural diversity" is a determining factor in the slow pace of incorporation of cultural diversity into the concepts and practice of Mexican law. According to Hernández and Ortiz, the origin of the problem is historical and resides in the coexistence of two separate systems—European and indigenous—based on distinct concepts of justice.

Hernández and Ortiz argue that the influence of French liberalism and other liberal doctrines was centered on a "politics of acculturation and integration of indigenous peoples into a homogeneous and blended national culture." However, despite such efforts at homogenization, "parallel spaces for the delivery of justice" have been tolerated throughout Mexico's history. Those spaces correspond to a plurality of normative practices that indigenous people have maintained and adapted to resolve community problems. The result is the coexistence of two systems with distinct concepts of responsibility (collective versus individual) and of justice (reconciliation versus punishment). According to the authors, "Juridical pluralism has therefore been a consistent reality in Mexico since its independence, partly the result of indigenous tradition, and partly the legacy of colonial law that created a parallel legal system for the native population through the Indigenous Republics." These authors' work illustrates that Mexico's particular circumstances as a highly diverse nation will involve special challenges in establishing the rule of law, but they will also create opportunities to draw on established practices that long predate the present order.

Also contributing to the discussion of innovative society-driven solutions to rule of law problems, Kathleen Staudt and Irasema Coronado examine the role of civic activism for access to justice in hundreds of unresolved "femicides" in the Ciudad Juárez–El Paso region. Drawing on extensive research on antiviolence organizing in this border region, Staudt and Coronado examine civic organizing efforts to address the brutal murders of over 380 girls and women over the last decade (a third of which involve gruesome forms of mutilation).

Providing vivid illustrations of the incompetence and unresponsiveness of public authorities, Staudt and Coronado point out that when the Ciudad Juárez murders first attracted public attention, elected officials dismissed them by blaming the victims. Publicly, officials questioned why victims went out late at night or dressed in "provocative" ways, which communicated to the bureaucracy and the public that the victims were responsible for their own fates. Underscoring the lack of professionalism in Mexican policing discussed throughout the volume, police investigations were compromised and shoddy: police files were often incomplete, and investigators were careless about evidence collection and the treatment of victims' remains. Indeed, evidence was often fabricated, and remains were misidentified, causing victims' families—often treated with disrespect—to relive the murders over and over. Further, official explanations given to victims' families and the public were often inconsistent, undermining whatever trust that remained in a population already skeptical of their police.

Hence, in the face of official incompetence and apathy, the families of victims and other concerned citizens began to organize to pressure for justice. The authors assert that, despite Mexico's transition to democracy, civic activists still have great difficulty obtaining political accountability, professional responses from the criminal justice system, or even acknowledgment of public problems, particularly those affecting women and families from poverty backgrounds. In fact, some activists face threats, harassment, and intimidation for their efforts to make public problems and government unresponsiveness visible. Still, Staudt and Coronado stress that the civic work of nongovernmental organizations has been vital in pressing governments to be accountable, and they discuss the conditions for successful cross-border organization. Staudt and Coronado insist that the problems found in Ciudad Juárez are ultimately binational and therefore require government and activist strategies tailored to the unique context of the border region, where shared problems often fall through the cracks of international jurisdiction.

SOLUTIONS: PROMOTING REFORM AND BEST PRACTICES

Mexico's democratization was accompanied, even propelled, by a significant decentralization of government authority and capability.[30] Hence the process of justice reform may hinge critically on the development of best practices and innovative strategies for improving the administration of justice at the state and local levels. The final section of this volume includes a series of case studies and recommendations on how to improve key areas of the justice system at the subnational level.

Robert Varenik begins this assessment with a focus on Mexico's painful dilemma in the area of public security and policing. While Mexican police forces utterly lack public trust, Varenik observes, the nation also finds itself

---

[30] Arnaut Salgado 1998; Cabrero Mendoza 1998; Cornelius, Eisenstadt, and Hindley 1999; Fox and Aranda 1996; García Bátiz and Centro Universitario 1998; Giugale and Webb 2000; Lybecker 2003; Ortega Lomelín 1994; Oxhorn, Tulchin, and Selee 2004; Rodríguez 1997; Shirk 1999; Torres Ramírez 1986.

in the midst of the most troubling period of criminality in its modern history. This fact only exacerbates the enormity of the multiple challenges involved in vetting, retraining, and upgrading police forces at every level and across the nation. Faced with dual emergencies and urgently seeking to placate a public clamoring for action, politicians run a great risk of seizing upon an approach that is too facile and insufficiently considered. Varenik stresses the importance of institutionalizing accountability and offers concrete recommendations on how to achieve it.

According to Varenik, the central fact of policing everywhere is that police exercise broad discretion in a low-visibility, low-scrutiny environment. Although this is not necessarily a bad thing (since effective police work requires good police "judgment"), it also means that monitoring and regulating discretion is a first priority. Accountability is the operative principle behind a series of mechanisms for regulating the exercise of broad discretion and limiting bad, illegal, or nonperformance by police. For Varenik, demonstrated accountability is also a key to credibility. As a practical matter, Varenik admits that, even assuming that a consensus develops to focus on accountability, many difficult choices—what sort of mechanisms are needed (and wanted), what level of public transparency, what mix of internal and external controls—will confront would-be reformers. Varenik recommends drawing lessons from other countries that have successfully addressed the difficult challenge of police reform: South Africa, Peru, Australia, Brazil, Colombia, the United States, and Spain's autonomous Catalán region.

In his case study analysis, Mario Arroyo provides a thorough analysis of Mexico City's efforts to implement reforms modeled on the "zero tolerance" initiative utilized by New York Mayor Rudolph Giuliani. Zero tolerance drew on the "broken windows" theory of criminal justice, which identifies a link between low-level infractions (such as vandalism) and more serious crimes (such as theft and violence).[31] By targeting minor crime with increased police presence and a more sophisticated technological approach to monitoring minor infractions (such as the use of GIS technologies to identify trouble spots), advocates of the "broken windows" theory suggest that levels of overall crime will be seriously diminished because likely or "would-be" criminals will be caught before their activities escalate from minor to major forms of crime. In addition to offering significant criticisms

---

[31] Dunham and Alpert 2001; Harcourt 2001; Kelling 1999; Kelling and Coles 1996; McArdle and Erzen 2001; R. B. Taylor 2001.

of the "broken windows" theory—most notably, that crime rates started declining in New York prior to Giuliani's term in office (primarily due to an improved economy and an increased absolute number of police)—Arroyo notes that there would be serious challenges in implementing the "Giuliani model" in Mexico. In particular, Arroyo reiterates Zepeda's view that police in Mexico lack the necessary authority and capacity—including forensic training—to properly investigate crimes. In this author's view, when combined with the abuse of authority on the part of corrupt police that Silva noted, this creates an infertile context for implementing zero tolerance programs.

Bringing further attention to the importance of the subnational arena, Allison Rowland considers the role of municipal governments in reforming Mexico's justice system, taking as a starting point the consistent failure of municipal public security policies in Mexico. She argues that, although reliable statistics on crime at the local level are neither available nor particularly relevant, it is possible to establish a systematic framework for understanding governance in Mexican municipalities to help explain the common problems encountered in local public security. Thus her research incorporates a consideration of the broader institutional limitations of municipal government in Mexico, as identified in recent literature on this topic. Applying this framework to research in six municipalities, Rowland concludes that Mexican local governments suffer from built-in weaknesses that impede effective policymaking and implementation in multiple public policy areas, including law enforcement and security. Generally speaking, municipal governments confront administrative and technical limitations, difficulties in management of relationships with local communities, and insufficient attention and assistance from state and federal authorities.

In crime prevention and control, local governments also deal with a unique set of issues and challenges. Their scope of action is limited in comparison to the state and federal levels, given that local police only have jurisdiction to "prevent" crimes and maintain order. Therefore, municipalities must depend on other levels of government for investigative policing and prosecution. This can result in frustration for police officers when municipal capacity to arrest suspects surpasses state ability (or interest) to investigate or prosecute a crime. In addition, local governments are forbidden from trying to fight certain types of crime, including organized crime, in spite of the profound impacts that such activities may have on crime within their jurisdictions. Thus, especially in areas where drug trafficking has become a problem, local police are allowed to do very little.

Rowland's findings hold several policy implications. First, she calls into question the effectiveness of increasingly common proposals for the centralization of crime-fighting functions at the national level, as well as current national policies that implicitly define the local crime problem as merely one of insufficient financial resources. The fact that municipalities suffer common, systemic difficulties in developing effective anticrime policies suggests that there may be better ways to help local governments improve their responses to crime and fear of crime. These solutions will likely be closely linked to efforts that continue the strengthening of democratic institutions and processes. This is the case because electoral competition has come to act as an incentive for better local government performance by better reflecting the preferences and the rights of local residents nearly everywhere in the country. In the future, national and local civic organizations—such as the Centro de Investigación para el Desarrollo, A.C. (CIDAC); Democracia, Derechos Humanos y Seguridad, A.C. (DDHS); Instituto Nacional de Ciencias Penales (INACIPE); Instituto para la Seguridad y la Democracia, A.C. (INSYDE); Instituto Ciudadano de Estudios sobre la Inseguridad (ICESI)—may take on greater importance in providing expertise to help improve law enforcement professionalization.

Finally, to examine the connection between Mexican democratization and justice-sector reform at the subnational level, Marcos Pablo Moloeznik examines the impact of partisan changes in the state of Jalisco. Specifically, Moloeznik analyzes the legal, human rights, and security policies instituted by Governors Alberto Cárdenas Jiménez (1995–2000) and Francisco Javier Ramírez Acuña (2000–2006), both from the National Action Party (PAN). Moloeznik argues that political alternation at the state level has not improved the situation in public security. According to this author, seven major factors limit the administration of justice at the state level: (1) excessive centralism intensified by the creation of the National Public Security System in 1995; (2) the militarization of public security; (3) the privatization of security; (4) the strengthening and consolidation of organized crime; (5) the internationalization of policing or intensification of global cooperation in the fight against organized crime; (6) unresolved tensions between law enforcement and the protection of human rights; and (7) excessive emphasis of authorities on quantitative rather than qualitative results. These trends all contribute to reduced state autonomy in the provision of public security, Moloeznik argues, and, therefore, to less effectiveness. To address these negative trends, Moloeznik offers several proposals, including clarification of the concept of (and responsibilities for) domestic security, re-evaluation of the notion of systemic public security, cleansing of public security agencies, and greater linkages between law enforcement, higher education, and civil society.

CONCLUDING OBSERVATIONS:
PROSPECTS FOR JUSTICE-SECTOR REFORM IN MEXICO

Though Mexico experienced some significant improvements in certain aspects of its justice system in the 1990s—notably, reforms in 1996 under President Ernesto Zedillo which promoted greater professionalism at higher levels of the judiciary—many serious deficiencies, noted above, persisted. Later, the defeat of the PRI in the July 2000 presidential election was perceived as a watershed that would lead to sweeping changes on a number of fronts. Early on, the PAN's Vicente Fox delivered change in areas within his purview as president. In his first months in office, Fox made initial gains in rooting out corruption by purging Mexico's federal customs operations, firing 48 regional directors and over 1,000 customs officials (roughly 20 percent of all customs employees) (Kraul 2001). As noted earlier, Fox also stepped up the involvement of military officials in the provision of domestic security and achieved significant successes in the disruption of key narco-trafficking organizations. Another significant early Fox initiative was the passage of a new transparency and freedom of information law (Ley de Transparencia y Acceso a la Información Pública). One of the most important results of this law was to disclose information from the national intelligence archives, resulting in efforts to prosecute crimes committed during Mexico's "Dirty War" of the 1970s.

Among the most important reforms introduced early in the Fox administration were the creation of new federal law enforcement agencies and a national structure for coordinating them. Notably, with the establishment of a new cabinet-level department, the Ministry of Public Security (SSP) brought about the (re)creation of the Federal Preventive Police (PFP) as well as the restructuring of the National Public Security System (SNSP) initiated under President Zedillo.[32] Later, in 2001, Fox issued a presidential decree creating the Federal Investigative Police (AFI)—a cognate to the U.S. Federal Bureau of Investigation—to replace and augment the functions of the former Federal Judicial Police (PJF).

---

[32] In the 2003 conference that generated many of the chapters in this volume, then-Secretary Gertz asserted that "the problem is not management" but rather the low caliber of Mexican police units.

Still, even after these changes, Mexico faced continued rule of law challenges and experienced significant setbacks over the course of the Fox administration. The escape of convicted narco-trafficker Joaquín "El Chapo" Guzmán in early 2001 underscored both the impunity with which Mexico's most powerful drug lords operate and the limits of Mexico's justice system. The SSP was weakened by administrative turnover, with three different secretaries—Alejandro Gertz Manero, Ramón Martín Huerta (who died in a helicopter crash in September 2005), and Eduardo Medina Mora—serving in the post during Fox's term. The Fox administration also suffered criticism for its failure to address human rights and to protect advocates.[33] Furthermore, the aforementioned demonstrations and acts of vigilantism during the Fox administration, especially in 2004, underscored the public's frustration with official corruption and incompetence. In 2005 a series of scandals and prison riots (one instigated by major narco-traffickers incarcerated by the Fox administration) brought public attention to many of the severe problems in the Mexican penal system (Aponte 2005). Also in 2005, the international ramifications of Mexico's rule of law challenges became clear when U.S. Ambassador Tony Garza issued two State Department warnings for visitors traveling to Mexico and closed consular facilities in Nuevo Laredo in an effort to "punish" Mexico for failing to control crime and violence on the border (Althaus et al. 2005; Reuters News Service 2005).

Facing these challenges, the Fox administration's most significant initiative with regard to the justice sector was a major package of constitutional reforms and new legislation presented to the Mexican Congress in March 2004 and still under consideration by the legislature at the time this volume went to press (table 1.5).[34] The initiative was developed through consulta-

---

[33] Particularly controversial was the death of Digna Ochoa, a prominent human rights lawyer in Mexico City, in October 2001; authorities hold that Ochoa committed suicide, but her supporters insist she was brutally murdered for her fight against injustice.

[34] In July 2004, in collaboration with the Mexico Project at the Center for Strategic and International Studies, the Center for U.S.-Mexican Studies hosted a roundtable on the new reform package with high-ranking U.S. and Mexican officials, scholars, and experts on the rule of law. In April 2005, in collaboration with the Mexican Senate, the Center for U.S.-Mexican Studies' Project on Reforming the Administration of Justice in Mexico produced an exhaustive technical analysis of the Fox justice reform package and several alternative proposals, which has helped to move forward the debate. See González Placencia, Negrete Sansores, and Zepeda Lecuona 2005.

tion with law enforcement authorities, legal experts, academics, and non-governmental organizations, as well as comparative analyses of legal systems in the United States, Europe, and Latin America.[35]

Fox's justice reform package comprised six new laws, reforms to eight existing laws, and several constitutional amendments to achieve three types of changes: structural, procedural, and professional.[36] The most significant structural changes sought by the administration included the unification of federal police forces, the autonomy of prosecutors from the executive power, and the creation of a separate criminal justice system for minors. The reform package also attempted to introduce major procedural changes, including police investigation of crimes, the presumption of innocence until proof of guilt, the use of oral argument in trial proceedings (and thus presumably greater transparency, efficiency, and swiftness), and the possibility of plea bargaining. Finally, Fox's proposals sought to require increased professional qualifications for key legal actors in Mexico, particularly defense attorneys.

All of these proposed changes were intended to generate greater transparency, stronger protections for both victims and defendants, and more efficient and swift administration of justice. Yet critics of the Fox reform package have pointed to the impracticability of the massive changes proposed as well as the hazards of importing foreign legal concepts into the Mexican criminal justice system.[37] Changing the structure and function of Mexican police and legal institutions would incur enormous financial costs, including converting existing courtrooms to accommodate public access and adopting new technologies (such as stenographic equipment). New courtroom procedures would require significant retraining and certification for thousands of legal practitioners. In the meantime, the transition to a new system would bring the potential for major procedural errors and other miscarriages of justice. Furthermore, as in any major systemic reform, the prospect of change would potentially disadvantage established benefi-

---

[35] The reform package gave particular consideration to the recommendations of the above-mentioned 2002 report from the United Nations Commission on Human Rights.

[36] Mexican Embassy in the United States, http://portal.sre.gob.mx/usa, last accessed October 27, 2005. See also the Office of the President's Web site, www.seguridadyjusticia.gob.mx.

[37] For a critical appraisal of President Fox's initiative, see "Análisis Técnico de la Propuesta de Reforma al Sistema de Justicia Mexicano," especially the appendix, at www.usmex.ucsd.edu.

ciaries of the status quo without measurable compensation: those trained under the old system would lose their "investment" in prior training and experience.

Table 1.5. Key Fox Administration Proposals for Reforming the Administration of Justice in Mexico

Structural	Unification of federal police forces (AFI and PFP) and systems of criminal intelligence. Creation of Federal Public Prosecutor General (Fiscalía General de la Federación) with prosecutorial autonomy from the executive power. Creation of new judges for supervision of pretrial processes, sentencing, and resolution of jurisdictional conflicts. Creation of a separate juvenile justice system.
Procedural	Federal, state, and local police investigation of crimes. Constitutional adoption of a presumption of innocence in trial proceedings. Oral and adversarial argument in trial proceedings. Requirement that a judge be present for all indictments. Creation of abbreviated processes (such as plea bargaining) and alternative dispute resolution mechanisms.
Professional	Standardization of criteria for police training. Requirement that criminal defendants be represented by a licensed attorney.

Source: Mexican Embassy in the United States, http://portal.sre.gob.mx/usa, last accessed October 27, 2005.

Finally, some critics of the Fox reform package voiced nationalistic concerns, noting that its provisions clearly responded to external criticisms and sought to introduce legal practices common in other countries. The active role of foreign agencies and nonprofit foundations in promoting reform of Mexico's justice system fueled long-standing suspicions that outside forces—particularly from the United States—were conspiring to manipulate Mexico's domestic politics. In fact, several U.S.-based agencies and foundations—the United States Agency for International Development (USAID), the William and Flora Hewlett Foundation, the Tinker Foundation, and the MacArthur Foundation—have funded major projects to promote justice reform in Mexico in recent years.[38] Indeed, generous support from the Hewlett Foundation and the Tinker Foundation made possible the project that produced the studies contained in this volume, as well as a comprehensive policy analysis to assist the Mexican Senate in its consideration of the Fox reform package.[39] Thus, given past violations of Mexican sovereignty, such prominent involvement of U.S. organizations in Mexico's domestic affairs aggravated nationalistic sensibilities and raised suspicions about the origin and intent of the Fox reform initiative.

Whatever the source of objections, at the time that this volume went to press none of the elements of Fox's justice reform package had been signed into law. Unlike the virtually omnipotent PRI presidents of the past, Fox's ability to pass legislation to promote reform in multiple policy areas was severely limited due to resistance from an opposition-dominated legislature. Hence the ability of the Fox administration to promote substantial changes in the Mexican justice system—or virtually any major reform agenda, including fiscal reform and energy-sector reform—was severely limited. Certainly, the justice reform initiative might have been more effective had Fox presented his plan much earlier (rather than into the last third of his term) and worked to build consensus across party lines from the beginning of his time in office.

Still, even if the federal legislature had fully supported his policies, it is quite doubtful that Fox would have been able to transform Mexico's justice system in a single six-year term. Certainly, during the Fox administration official crime rates generally appeared to stabilize from their mid-1990s swell. However, this may have had as much to do with economic trends—and Mexico's recovery from the 1994 peso devaluation—as any policy instituted by the administration. Moreover, promoting the rule of law—especially governmental accountability and responsiveness—is not merely about reducing crime. The rule of law is not a policy output but rather a process that must be continually refined in a democratic system. In the United States and elsewhere, political competition and the alternation of political parties in elected office have proved essential to reform over the last century. It is reasonable, therefore, to expect that democratic competition will be a driving force for justice-sector reform in Mexico, even though

---

[38] For analyses of other international programs for promoting the rule of law, see Domingo and Sieder 2001.

[39] "Análisis Técnico de la Propuesta de Reforma al Sistema de Justicia Mexicano," www.justiceinmexico.org.

the absence of reelection is a serious impediment to both accountability and responsiveness. Yet, so long as the serious rule of law challenges discussed in this volume persist, justice-sector reform will undoubtedly remain among voters' top priorities. Thus politicians will have an incentive to demonstrate a credible commitment to resolve the problems that voters care about the most.[40]

In Mexico's increasingly decentralized political context, public choices and actors at the subnational level will have an important role in the process. As this volume and an ample body of research suggest, during the course of Mexico's democratization, state and local governments began to play an increasing role in proposing solutions to key policy challenges. Thus, like other progress in Mexico's democratic consolidation, true, long-term reform of the justice system will likely need to occur at the state and local levels. Some recent developments at the subnational level—oral trials, alternative dispute resolution mechanisms, and mediation of legal disputes—are very promising in this regard. An impressive wave of reforms in these areas has already begun in states like Coahuila, México State, and Nuevo León. Interesting proposals of reform are currently under consideration in Aguascalientes, Chiapas, Chihuahua, Oaxaca, Querétaro, and Zacatecas. In a new collaborative research initiative spearheaded by CIDAC and the Trans-Border Institute at the University of San Diego,[41] these state and local initiatives will be the focus of the next phase of research for the project that inspired this volume.

In the meantime, this volume provides scholars, policymakers, and the public with an overview of the severe challenges facing Mexico in the reform of its justice system. Confronted with such overwhelming and immediate challenges, it is easy to fall prey to self-fulfilling pessimism. A longer-term view, however, offers the advantage of an obtainable horizon and reachable goals. We, and other authors in this volume, take the more optimistic view that the problems confronting Mexico can be resolved over the longer term in the course of its democratic consolidation.

---

[40] Indeed, all three major parties adopted justice-sector reforms as part of their platform for the 2006 federal election.

[41] www.cidac.org.mx and www.justiceinmexico.org.

References

Alcaraz, Yetlaneci, and Nayeli Cortés. 2004. "Sacuden al país," *El Universal*, July 28.

Althaus, Dudley, Ioan Grillo, James Pinkerton, and Patty Reinert. 2005. "Border Travelers Warned of Violence," *Houston Chronicle*, January 27.

Alvarado, Arturo, and Sigrid Arzt, eds. 2001. *El desafío democrático de México: seguridad y estado de derecho*. Mexico City: El Colegio de México.

Aponte, David. 2005. "Vulnera narco penales de máxima seguridad," *El Universal*, January 4.

Arnaut Salgado, Alberto. 1998. *La federalización educativa en México: historia del debate sobre la centralización y la descentralización educativa (1889–1994)*. Mexico City: Centro de Estudios Sociológicos, El Colegio de México and Centro de Investigación y Docencia Económicas.

Azaola, Elena. 1990. *La institución correccional en México: una mirada extraviada*. Mexico City: Siglo Veintiuno.

Bailey, John J., and Jorge Chabat, eds. 2001. *Transnational Crime and Public Security: Challenges to Mexico and the United States*. La Jolla: Center for U.S.-Mexican Studies, University of California, San Diego.

Bailey, John, and Lucía Dammert, eds. 2006. *Public Security and Police Reform in the Americas*. Pittsburgh, Penn.: University of Pittsburgh Press.

Bailey, John J., and Roy Godson. 2000. *Organized Crime and Democratic Governability: Mexico and the U.S.-Mexican Borderlands*. Pittsburgh, Penn.: University of Pittsburgh Press.

Barclay, Eliza. 2005. "Prospects Grim for Mexican Justice Clean Up," *Washington Times*, May 28.

Barragán, José Moctezuma. 1994. *José María Iglesias y la justicia electoral*. Mexico: Instituto de Investigaciones Jurídicas.

Barrón Cruz, Martín Gabriel, Carlos Silva, and José Arturo Yáñez R. 2004. *Guardia Nacional y Policía Preventiva: dos problemas de seguridad en México*. Mexico City: Instituto Nacional de Ciencias Penales.

Barros, Robert. 2003. "Dictatorship and the Rule of Law: Rules and Military Power in Chile." In *Democracy and the Rule of Law*, ed. J. M. Maravall and A. Przeworski. Cambridge: Cambridge University Press.

Bayley, David H. 2001. *Democratizing the Police Abroad: What to Do and How to Do It*. Washington, D.C.: U.S. Department of Justice, Office of Justice Programs, National Institute of Justice.

Begné Guerra, Alberto. 1995. "La reforma del poder judicial federal," *Nexos* 18, no. 205: 16–18.

Black, Donald J., and Maureen Mileski. 1973. *The Social Organization of Law*. New York: Seminar Press.

Blumstein, Alfred, and Alan Beck. 1999. "Factors Contributing to the Growth in U.S. Prison Populations." In *Crime and Justice: A Review of Research*, ed. M. H. Tonry. Chicago: University of Chicago Press.

Bonnell, Victoria E., and George W. Breslauer, eds. 2001. *Russia in the New Century: Stability or Disorder?* Boulder, Colo.: Westview.

Buffington, Robert Marshall. 1994. "Forging the Fatherland: Criminality and Citizenship in Modern Mexico." PhD dissertation, University of Arizona.

———. 2000. *Criminal and Citizen in Modern Mexico.* Lincoln: University of Nebraska Press.

Buscaglia, Edgardo. 1998. "Obstacles to Judicial Reform in Latin America." In *Justice Delayed: Judicial Reform in Latin America*, ed. E. Jarquín and F. Carrillo Florez. Washington, D.C.: Inter-American Development Bank.

Cabrero Mendoza, Enrique. 1998. *Las políticas descentralizadoras en México, 1983–1993: logros y desencantos.* Mexico: CIDE and Porrúa.

Camp, Roderic Ai. 1996. *Democracy in Latin America: Patterns and Cycles.* Wilmington, Del.: SR Books.

Carmagnani, Marcello, and Germán José Bidart Campos. 1993. *Federalismos latinoamericanos: México, Brasil, Argentina.* Mexico: El Colegio de México, Fideicomiso Historia de las Américas, and Fondo de Cultura Económica.

Chávez, Rebecca Bill. 2004. *The Rule of Law in Nascent Democracies: Judicial Politics in Argentina.* Stanford, Calif.: Stanford University Press.

CNDH (Comisión Nacional de Derechos Humanos). 2003. "Primer certamen nacional de ensayo: linchamiento: justicia por propia mano." México, D.F.: CNDH.

Cornelius, Wayne A., Todd A. Eisenstadt, and Jane Hindley, eds. 1999. *Subnational Politics and Democratization in Mexico.* La Jolla: Center for U.S.-Mexican Studies, University of California, San Diego.

Cumaraswamy, Dato' Param. 2002. *Independence of the Judiciary, Administration of Justice, Impunity: Report on the Mission to Mexico. Report of the Special Rapporteur on the Independence of Judges and Lawyers.* Economic and Social Council of the United Nations. Submitted in accordance with Commission on Human Rights resolution 2001/39.

Davis, Diane, and Arturo Alvarado, eds. 1999. "Liberalization, Public Insecurity, and Deteriorating Rule of Law in Mexico City," *Working Papers in Local Governance and Democracy.*

del Villar, Samuel. 2001. "El desafío de la seguridad pública en el Distrito Federal." In *El desafío democrático de México: seguridad y estado de derecho*, ed. Arturo Alvarado and Sigrid Arzt. Mexico City: El Colegio de México.

Di Palma, Giuseppe. 1990. *To Craft Democracies: An Essay on Democratic Transitions.* Berkeley: University of California Press.

Di Tella, Torcuato S. 1998. *Los partidos políticos: teoría y análisis comparativo.* Buenos Aires: A-Z.

Domingo, Pilar. 1996. *Rule of Law, Citizenship and Access to Justice in Mexico.* Mexico City: División de Estudios Políticos, Centro de Investigación y Docencia Económicas.

———. 2004. "Judicialization of Politics or Politicization of the Judiciary? Recent Trends in Latin America," *Democratization* 11, no. 1 (February): 104–27.

Domingo, Pilar, and Rachel Sieder. 2001. *The Rule of Law in Latin America: The International Promotion of Judicial Reform.* London: Institute of Latin American Studies, University of London.

Dunham, Roger G., and Geoffrey P. Alpert. 2001. *Critical Issues in Policing: Contemporary Readings.* Prospect Heights, Ill.: Waveland.

Ellmann, Stephen. 1992. *In a Time of Trouble: Law and Liberty in South Africa's State of Emergency.* Oxford and New York: Clarendon and Oxford University Press.

Finn, John E. 1991. *Constitutions in Crisis: Political Violence and the Rule of Law.* New York: Oxford University Press.

Fix-Fierro, Héctor, and Juan Ricardo Jiménez Gómez, eds. 1997. "La administración de la justicia en México," *Revista AMEINAPE* (Querétaro: Asociación Mexicana de Egresados del INAP de España, A.C.).

Fox, Jonathan, and Josefina Aranda. 1996. *Decentralization and Rural Development in Mexico: Community Participation in Oaxaca's Municipal Funds Program.* La Jolla: Center for U.S.-Mexican Studies, University of California, San Diego.

García Bátiz, María Luisa, and Centro Universitario de Ciencias Económico Administrativas. 1998. *Descentralización e iniciativas locales de desarrollo.* Jalisco, Los Angeles, and Mexico City: Universidad de Guadalajara; Program on Mexico, University of California, Los Angeles; and Juan Pablos Editor.

Gibson, Edward L. 2004. *Federalism and Democracy in Latin America.* Baltimore, Md.: Johns Hopkins University Press.

Gilman, Denise. 2001. *Legalized Injustice: Mexican Criminal Procedure and Human Rights.* New York: Lawyers Committee for Human Rights.

Giugale, Marcelo, and Steven Benjamin Webb. 2000. *Achievements and Challenges of Fiscal Decentralization: Lessons from Mexico.* Washington, D.C.: World Bank.

Gloppen, Siri, Roberto Gargarella, and Elin Skaar. 2004. *Democratization and the Judiciary: The Accountability Function of Courts in New Democracies.* London: Frank Cass.

Godson, Roy. 2003. *Menace to Society: Political-Criminal Collaboration around the World.* New Brunswick, N.J.: Transaction.

González G., José. 1983. *Lo negro del Negro Durazo.* México, D.F.: Editorial Posada.

González Placencia, Luis, Layda Negrete Sansores, and Guillermo Zepeda Lecuona. 2005. *Análisis técnico de la propuesta de reforma al sistema de justicia mexicano.* Coordinated and with an introduction by Cuitláhuac Bardán,

David A. Shirk, and Alejandra Ríos. México, D.F.: Instituto de Investigaciones Legislativas del Senado de la República and the Center for U.S.-Mexican Studies, University of California, San Diego.

González Ruiz, Samuel, Ernesto López Portillo V., and José Arturo Yáñez R. 1994. *Seguridad pública en México: problemas, perspectivas y propuestas*. Mexico: Coordinación de Humanidades, Universidad Nacional Autónoma de México.

Grofman, Bernard, and Arend Lijphart. 1986. *Electoral Laws and Their Political Consequences*. New York: Agathon.

Harcourt, Bernard E. 2001. *Illusion of Order: The False Promise of Broken Windows Policing*. Cambridge, Mass.: Harvard University Press.

Hassall, Graham. 1997. "Democracy in Asia Revisited," *Asian Studies Review* 21, no. 2: 2–17.

Howard, A. E. Dick. 1991. *Democracy's Dawn: A Directory of American Initiatives on Constitutionalism, Democracy, and the Rule of Law in Central and Eastern Europe*. Charlottesville: University Press of Virginia, for the United States Institute of Peace.

Human Rights First. 2001. *Legalized Injustice: Mexican Criminal Procedure and Human Rights*. New York: Human Rights First.

Huntington, Samuel P. 1991. *The Third Wave: Democratization in the Late Twentieth Century*. Norman: University of Oklahoma Press.

Jackson, Nicole. 2005. "The Trafficking of Narcotics, Arms and Humans in Post-Soviet Central Asia: (Mis)Perceptions, Policies and Realities," *Central Asian Survey* 24, no. 1: 39–52.

Jakobsen, P. V. 2003. "Reviving the Judicial and Penal System in Kosovo." In *The United Nations and Regional Security: Europe and Beyond*, ed. M. C. Pugh and W. P. S. Sidhu. Boulder, Colo.: Lynne Rienner.

Jarquín, Edmundo, and Fernando Carrillo Florez. 1998. *Justice Delayed: Judicial Reform in Latin America*. Washington, D.C.: Inter-American Development Bank.

Johnson, Lyman L. 1990. *The Problem of Order in Changing Societies: Essays on Crime and Policing in Argentina and Uruguay*. Albuquerque: University of New Mexico Press.

Kaufmann, Daniel. 2001. "Misrule of Law: Does the Evidence Challenge Conventions in Judiciary and Legal Reforms?" Washington, D.C.: World Bank.

Kelley, Donald R. 2003. *After Communism: Perspectives on Democracy*. Fayetteville: University of Arkansas Press.

Kelling, George L. 1999. *Broken Windows and Police Discretion*. Washington, D.C.: U.S. Dept. of Justice, Office of Justice Programs, National Institute of Justice.

Kelling, George L., and Catherine M. Coles. 1996. *Fixing Broken Windows: Restoring Order and Reducing Crime in Our Communities*. New York: Martin Kessler.

Kleinfeld Belton, Rachel. 2005. *Competing Definitions of the Rule of Law: Implications for Practitioners.* Carnegie Papers Rule of Law Series, no. 55. Washington, D.C.: Carnegie Endowment for International Peace.

Kraul, Chris. 2001. "Mexico Corruption Fight Nets Cache of Contraband," *Los Angeles Times*, September 23.

———. 2002. "Mexican Army Unit to Be Disbanded amid Drug Probe," *Los Angeles Times*, October 17.

———. 2004. "In Mexico, Vigilantism Rises on Surge of Crime, Public Disgust," *Los Angeles Times*, August 22.

Lijphart, Arend, and Don Aitkin. 1994. *Electoral Systems and Party Systems: A Study of Twenty-Seven Democracies, 1945–1990.* Oxford: Oxford University Press.

Lijphart, Arend, and Bernard Grofman. 1984. *Choosing an Electoral System: Issues and Alternatives.* New York: Praeger.

Lijphart, Arend, and Carlos H. Waisman. 1996. *Institutional Design in New Democracies: Eastern Europe and Latin America.* Boulder, Colo.: Westview.

Linz, Juan J., and Arturo Valenzuela, eds. 1994. *The Failure of Presidential Democracy.* Baltimore, Md.: Johns Hopkins University Press.

Lobban, Michael. 1996. *White Man's Justice: South African Political Trials in the Black Consciousness Era.* Oxford and New York: Clarendon and Oxford University Press.

López, Jesús Antonio Sam. 1988. *La policía judicial en México.* Mexico: n.p.

Lybecker, Donna L. 2003. "Decentralization of Mexican Environmental and Water Policy: Baja California and Sonora." PhD dissertation, Colorado State University.

Magaloni, Beatriz, Edna Jaime, Luis Rubio F., and Héctor Fix-Fierro. 1994. *A la puerta de la ley: el estado de derecho en México.* México, D.F.: Cal y Arena.

Mainwaring, Scott. 1999. *Rethinking Party Systems in the Third Wave of Democratization: The Case of Brazil.* Stanford, Calif.: Stanford University Press.

Mainwaring, Scott, Guillermo A. O'Donnell, and J. Samuel Valenzuela. 1992. *Issues in Democratic Consolidation: The New South American Democracies in Comparative Perspective.* Notre Dame, Ind.: University of Notre Dame Press, for the Helen Kellogg Institute for International Studies.

Mainwaring, Scott, and Timothy Scully. 1995. *Building Democratic Institutions: Party Systems in Latin America.* Stanford, Calif.: Stanford University Press.

Mainwaring, Scott, and Matthew Soberg Shugart. 1997. *Presidentialism and Democracy in Latin America.* Cambridge: Cambridge University Press.

Marshall, D. 2003. "Strengthening Indigenous Police Capacity and the Rule of Law in the Balkans." In *The United Nations and Regional Security: Europe and Beyond*, ed. M. C. Pugh and W. P. S. Sidhu. Boulder, Colo.: Lynne Rienner.

Martínez de Murguía, Beatriz. 1999. *La policía en México: ¿orden social o criminalidad?* México, D.F.: Planeta.

Martínez Garnelo, Jesús. 1999. *Policía nacional investigadora del delito: antología del origen, evolución y modernización de la policía en México*. Mexico: Porrúa.

McAdams, A. James. 1997. *Transitional Justice and the Rule of Law in New Democracies*. Notre Dame, Ind.: University of Notre Dame Press.

McArdle, Andrea, and Tanya Erzen. 2001. *Zero Tolerance: Quality of Life and the New Police Brutality in New York City*. New York: New York University Press.

McKinley, James C., and Ginger Thompson. 2004. "Lynchings of Policemen Ignite Outrage at Violence in Mexico," *New York Times*, November 25.

Montero, Alfred P., and David Samuels, eds. 2004. *Decentralization and Democracy in Latin America*. Notre Dame, Ind.: University of Notre Dame Press.

O'Donnell, Guillermo, and Philippe Schmitter. 1986. *Transitions from Authoritarian Rule: Tentative Conclusions about Uncertain Democracies*. Baltimore, Md.: Johns Hopkins University Press.

O'Donnell, Guillermo, Jorge Vargas Cullell, and Osvaldo M. Iazzetta, eds. 2004. *The Quality of Democracy: Theory and Applications*. Notre Dame, Ind.: University of Notre Dame Press.

Ortega Lomelín, Roberto. 1994. *Federalismo y municipio*. Mexico: Fondo de Cultura Económica.

Oxhorn, Philip, Joseph S. Tulchin, and Andrew D. Selee. 2004. *Decentralization, Democratic Governance, and Civil Society in Comparative Perspective: Africa, Asia, and Latin America*. Washington, D.C., and Baltimore, Md.: Woodrow Wilson Center Press and Johns Hopkins University Press.

Piccato, Pablo. 2001. *City of Suspects: Crime in Mexico City, 1900–1931*. Durham, N.C.: Duke University Press.

Piccato, Pablo, Ricardo Pérez Montfort, and Alberto del Castillo Yurrita. 1997. *Hábitos, normas y escándalo: prensa, criminalidad y drogas durante el porfiriato tardío*. México, D.F.: CIESAS and Plaza y Valdés.

Przeworski, Adam. 1991. *Democracy and the Market: Political and Economic Reforms in Eastern Europe and Latin America*. Cambridge: Cambridge University Press.

Reding, Andrew. 1995. *Democracy and Human Rights in Mexico*. New York: World Policy Institute.

Reuters News Service. 2005. "Mexico Scolds U.S. Ambassador for 'Punish' Boast," *Houston Chronicle*, August 18.

Reyes, Corinna A. 2001. "Unlikely Alliances: The Politics of Judicial Reform in Mexico." Paper prepared for the 2001 congress of the Latin American Studies Association.

Rodríguez, Victoria Elizabeth. 1997. *Decentralization in Mexico: From Reforma Municipal to Solidaridad to Nuevo Federalismo*. Boulder, Colo.: Westview.

Rohlfes, Laurence J. 1983. "Police and Penal Correction in Mexico City, 1876–1911: A Study of Order and Progress in Porfirian Mexico." PhD thesis, Tulane University.

Rueschemeyer, Dietrich, Evelyne Huber Stephens, and John D. Stephens. 1992. *Capitalist Development and Democracy*. Chicago: University of Chicago Press.

Ruiz, José Luis, and Juan Arvizu. 2004. "Fox presenta plan contra delincuencia," *El Universal*, July 2.

Sachs, Jeffrey, and Katharina Pistor. 1997. *The Rule of Law and Economic Reform in Russia*. Boulder, Colo.: Westview.

Salvatore, Ricardo Donato, Carlos Aguirre, and G. M. Joseph. 2001. *Crime and Punishment in Latin America: Law and Society since Late Colonial Times*. Durham, N.C.: Duke University Press.

Samuels, David. 2003. *Ambition, Federalism, and Legislative Politics in Brazil*. Cambridge: Cambridge University Press.

Shirk, David A. 1999. *New Federalism in Mexico: Implications for Baja California and the Cross-Border Region*. [San Diego, Calif.]: San Diego Dialogue.

Shugart, Matthew Soberg. 1995. "The Electoral Cycle and Institutional Sources of Divided Presidential Government," *American Political Science Review* 89, no. 2: 1–17.

Smith, Bruce L. R., and G. M. Danilenko. 1993. *Law and Democracy in the New Russia*. Washington, D.C.: Brookings Institution.

Smith, James F., and Ken Ellingwood. 2000. "Fox Lays Out Plan to Overhaul Justice System in Mexico," *Los Angeles Times*, July 5.

Speckman Guerra, Elisa. 2002. *Crimen y castigo: legislación penal, interpretaciones de la criminalidad y administración de justicia, Ciudad de México, 1872–1910*. Mexico: Centro de Estudios Históricos, El Colegio de México and Instituto de Investigaciones Históricas, Universidad Nacional Autónoma de México.

Sullivan, Kevin. 2002. "In Mexico Hinterland, Life Beyond the Law," *Washington Post*, March 15.

Taagepera, Rein, and Matthew Soberg Shugart. 1989. *Seats and Votes: The Effects and Determinants of Electoral Systems*. New Haven, Conn.: Yale University Press.

Taylor, Michael. 1995. "Why No Rule of Law in Mexico: Explaining the Weakness of Mexico's Judicial Branch," *New Mexico Law Review* 27: 141–66.

Taylor, Ralph B. 2001. *Breaking Away from Broken Windows: Baltimore Neighborhoods and the Nationwide Fight against Crime, Grime, Fear, and Decline*. Boulder, Colo.: Westview.

Thompson, Ginger. 2004. "Hundreds of Thousands in Mexico March against Crime," *New York Times*, June 28.

Torres Ramírez, Blanca. 1986. *Descentralización y democracia en México*. Mexico City: El Colegio de México.

Tulchin, Joseph S., Andrew D. Selee, and Adriana Clemente. 2004. *Decentralization and Democratic Governance in Latin America*. Washington, D.C.: Woodrow Wilson International Center for Scholars, Latin American Program.

Turner-Gottschang, Karen, James Vincent Feinerman, and R. Kent Guy. 2000. *The Limits of the Rule of Law in China*. Seattle: University of Washington Press.

Ungar, Mark. 2001. *Elusive Reform: Democracy and the Rule of Law in Latin America*. Boulder, Colo.: Lynne Rienner.

U.S. Senate Press Release. 2005. "Levin-Coleman Staff Report Discloses Web of Secret Accounts Used by Pinochet." Washington, D.C.: Senate Committee on Homeland Security and Governmental Affairs.

Vanderwood, Paul J. 1981. *Disorder and Progress: Bandits, Police, and Mexican Development*. Lincoln: University of Nebraska Press.

Varese, Federico. 2001. *The Russian Mafia: Private Protection in a New Market Economy*. Oxford: Oxford University Press.

Volkov, Vadim. 2002. *Violent Entrepreneurs: The Use of Force in the Making of Russian Capitalism*. Ithaca, N.Y.: Cornell University Press.

Walker, Samuel. 1977. *A Critical History of Police Reform: The Emergence of Professionalism*. Lexington, Mass.: Lexington Books.

Webster, William H. 1997. *Russian Organized Crime*. CSIS Global Organized Crime Project. Washington, D.C.: Center for Strategic and International Studies.

Webster, William H., Arnaud De Borchgrave, and Frank J. Cilluffo. 2000. *Russian Organized Crime and Corruption: Putin's Challenge*. CSIS Global Organized Crime Project. Washington, D.C.: Center for Strategic and International Studies.

Williams, Phil. 1997. *Russian Organized Crime: The New Threat?* London: Frank Cass.

Wilson, James Q., and Barbara Boland. 1979. *The Effect of the Police on Crime*. Washington, D.C.: Department of Justice, Law Enforcement Assistance Administration, National Institute of Law Enforcement and Criminal Justice.

Yáñez R., José Arturo. 1999. *Policía mexicana: cultura política, (in)seguridad y órden público en el gobierno del Distrito Federal, 1821–1876*. México, D.F.: Universidad Autónoma Metropolitana and Plaza y Valdés.

Zeleza, Tiyambe, and Philip J. McConnaughay. 2004. *Human Rights, the Rule of Law, and Development in Africa*. Philadelphia: University of Pennsylvania Press.

PART I

Crime and Criminality in Mexico

CHAPTER 2

The Social Construction of Crime in Mexico

ROBERT BUFFINGTON

Confronted with the undeniable "realities" of crime—its victims, its economic costs, its pernicious effects on social relations, its corrupting impacts on politics and the administration of justice—an academic essay that stresses its social constructed-ness cannot help but seem a bit specious. What, in the face of these realities, does it matter that preceding generations have looked at crime and criminality somewhat differently than has our own? There may not be a satisfactory answer to this question. Very possibly, faced with the exigencies of the present, historical context is important only to historians. So if this chapter appears tentative, if the broadly sketched periods and patterns it identifies lack sufficient specificity, if the tensions it analyzes seem mostly outdated, if it has little apparent relevance to pressing administrative and institutional needs, my hope is that there is at least some comfort in knowing that we have been here before, that our predecessors have confronted and weathered similar crises.

This chapter has two parts. The first gives a broad overview of four major phases in the social construction of crime and criminality in Mexico since the Independence era, and analyzes the "logic" or pattern underlying each of them. The second explores some of the dialectical tensions that render problematic any attempt at periodization. Both parts are speculative rather than definitive. In both, I attempt to tease out any possible "lessons" the past might hold for analysts and policymakers in the present, especially for those committed to "reforming the administration of justice in Mexico."

The theoretical insight that informs the chapter as a whole is borrowed from Émile Durkheim's classic *The Rules of Sociological Method*. "Crime is … necessary," Durkheim argues; "it is bound up with the fundamental conditions of all social life, and by that very fact it is useful, because these conditions of which it is a part are themselves indispensable to the normal evolution of morality and law ... [because] where crime exists, collective sentiments are sufficiently flexible to take on a new form, and crime sometimes helps to determine the form they will take." Thus, while Durkheim acknowledges that "although crime is a fact of normal sociology, it does not follow that we must not abhor it," he reminds us that any society's engagement with crime and criminality is normal, productive, and even indispensable to social "evolution" (Durkheim 1979: 65). In another classic text, *Discipline and Punish*, Michel Foucault (1979) also elaborates on the indispensable, productive aspects of crime and criminality. His concerns about the social ramifications of criminological discourses and technologies of power inform this essay as well. Foucault's pessimistic vision, however, emphasizes the coercive, disciplinary character of criminal justice systems. For that reason—and in the spirit of this volume—I have preferred Durkheim's more optimistic (and positivistic) approach to "productive" crime. A willing suspension of disbelief, perhaps, but defensible in these trying times.

PHASES AND PATTERNS IN THE SOCIAL CONSTRUCTION OF CRIME AND CRIMINALITY

Theorists like Durkheim and Foucault remind us that crime is normal and productive, as much as we might wish it were otherwise. To further complicate matters, crime is an inherently unstable phenomenon that can only be understood in historical context. Article 4 of the 1871 Mexican Penal Code offers a straightforward definition of the term: "Crime is: the voluntary infraction of a penal law, doing that which it prohibits or neglecting to do that which it demands" (Código Penal 1890: 7). The definition is both elegantly precise and deceptively simple. Elegant because it eschews moral-ethical judgments that might encourage extra-legal sanctions; deceptive because it ignores moral-ethical judgments implicit in penal law. In fact, a clear example of moral-ethical judgment is embedded in the definition itself: the prominent use of the heavily freighted "voluntary" reflects classic nineteenth-century liberal notions of "free will." Moreover, as Elisa Speckman Guerra's chapter in this volume demonstrates, this moral-ethical position was already under attack from positivist criminologists in Mexico and elsewhere by the end of the century (although it still persists in modified form in Mexican penal law). Less obvious are the ideological biases of the penal law's elite drafters and interpreters, biases grounded in a profound suspicion of the lower classes and ethnic minorities.[1] Pablo Piccato's chapter informs us that lower-class urban communities had their biases as well—accepting male violence in defense of honor while ignoring crimes of violence against women and children—even though those biases only rarely made it into law. The point here is not that a crime is hard to define in and of itself—the Article 4 definition is both sufficient and practical—but that its characteristics necessarily reflect the attitudes toward crime and criminality of a particular society at a given historical moment. In other words, while crime as an abstract concept can be considered as any act that does what the law prohibits or neglects what it demands, crime as an actual phenomenon must be acknowledged—whether by historians or policymakers—as socially constructed and historically contingent. "Something that is easily forgotten in official, journalistic, and scientific views of the problem of crime," Piccato points out, "[is that] defining an act as a crime was always the product of public discussions and, often, of informal arrangements."

Attitudes toward crime and criminality in Mexico can be divided into four phases. Using foundational political events as convenient if somewhat arbitrary signposts, these four phases can be sketched as follows: 1810–1855 (Independence to Ayutla); 1855–1910 (Ayutla to Revolution); 1910–1982 (Revolution to Economic Crisis); 1982–present (Economic Crisis to Democratic Transition). As might be expected with something as inevitable and endemic as crime, there are obvious continuities that run through these different phases. And since crime is nothing if not messy and transgressive, there are also frequent overlaps between them.

Perhaps because of these many continuities and overlaps, each of the four phases appears to follow a similar pattern, a pattern that bears a passing and not entirely coincidental resemblance to the shifting scientific paradigms analyzed by Thomas Kuhn in *The Structure of Scientific Revolutions* (1970). This resemblance is likely due to the prominence of the social sciences (and their adaptation of scientific methods) in shaping and defining (but not determining) each of these phases. Although Kuhn restricts his analysis to the "hard" sciences, his paradigm model brings a certain conceptual clarity to an extraordinarily complex historical problem, and I borrow it here for that reason. The pattern has five overlapping stages that develop something like this:

---

[1] On elite biases in Mexican criminology and penology, see Buffington 2000; Piccato 2001; Speckman Guerra 2002.

- A sustained period of social upheaval produced by and contributing to a major shift in the nation's political economy.

- The generalized perception of endemic crises, represented in public opinion as a crime wave and taking the form of a series of moral panics about the state of the nation.

- A concerted response (especially but not exclusively on the part of state policymakers), represented in public opinion as a war on crime and taking the form of "new" discourses, practices, institutions, and technologies of social control.

- The consolidation of a new criminal justice paradigm, often in the form of new laws and institutions, along with its inevitable contestation and negotiation by vested elite interest groups and the often-targeted popular classes.

- The accumulation of "anomalies"—inconsistencies, contradictions, failures—in the dominant criminal justice paradigm that render it unstable and thus vulnerable to the next sustained period of social upheaval (which restarts the cycle).

The Independence to Ayutla phase (1810–1855) begins with the early-nineteenth-century wars for Independence and the transition from colony to nation-state. A rehearsal of the unique combination of political and economic factors that precipitated this sustained period of social upheaval is impractical here. No respectable historian, however, would deny the pervasive sense of moral panic, beginning with the Hidalgo revolt and persisting through the Santa Anna era, that runs through most contemporary accounts of the period. Prominent in these accounts is the familiar presence of criminalized *villains du jour*, whether collective actors like Hidalgo's mestizo peasant hordes and Mexico City's notoriously unruly crowds or sinister individuals like the ruthless rural bandit and the treacherous urban *lépero*. Given the chaotic conditions of early nationhood, it is hardly surprising that the concerted response to these crises was more discursive than institutional, with frequent social commentaries and occasional studies by prominent public intellectuals like José Joaquín Fernández de Lizardi, Vicente Rocafuerte, Mariano Otero, and José María Luis Mora.

Most commentaries reflected "enlightened" notions of crime and punishment, with obligatory references to the classic criminology of Cesare Beccaria, the utilitarianism of Jeremy Bentham, and penitentiary experiments in the United States and Britain. Most deployed these notions in the eclectic, non-doctrinaire fashion that would come to characterize Mexican criminology.[2] In this first phase, the consolidation of a criminal justice paradigm was above all a constitutional affair as ruling elites struggled to develop the appropriate legal infrastructure for the new nation. Even among elites, contestation rather than negotiation was the order of the day as enlightened commitments to equality before the law ran up against centuries of *fueros* (corporate privileges especially for the Church and military) and other forms of legalized social inequality. Anomalies multiplied with each succeeding constitution. Liberal revolution in 1855 and the appearance of a definitive new constitution in 1857 failed to resolve these anomalies, and another sustained period of social upheaval, more destructive than the first, quickly ensued.

The Ayutla to Revolution phase (1855–1910) follows a similar trajectory as civil wars and foreign interventions contributed to yet another round of moral panics. Most were directed at the same villains as before. But as civil strife intensified into civil war, all sides sought to demonize their political opponents, and the traitor—the betrayer of *la patria*—became a much reviled, often tortured, and sometimes executed criminal. In the initial stages, the response to this crisis was primarily discursive as well, culminating in a new "modern" penal code in 1871 that its author, Antonio Martínez del Castro, hoped would end "the state of anarchy we have endured for so long [which] has sown distrust among the citizenry, engendered hatreds, and … resulted in mutual isolation, in the selfish pursuit of private interests, and in disregard for the public good" (Martínez de Castro 1968: 133). As in the first phase, however, discursive consolidation failed to produce social stability, and concerned policymakers took advantage of the *pax porfiriana* to begin the institutionalization and professionalization of Mexico's criminal justice system with model prisons, police reforms, statistical studies, and penal code revisions. Piccato's chapter documents the failure of these reforms to address the crime problem in any substantial way. Nevertheless, they did "produce" important discursive and ideological effects by representing the regime's commitment to "Order and Progress" and, in that sense, helping to legitimate its rule.

As "anomalies" began to accumulate in Martínez de Castro's classic liberal paradigm, the positivist criminology of Cesare Lombroso and Gabriel Tarde found a responsive audience among the growing ranks of aspiring

---

[2] See Buffington 2000 and Speckman's discussion of late-nineteenth- and early-twentieth-century Mexican criminology in her chapter in this volume.

(but not yet professional) Mexican criminologists. As Speckman explains, classic liberal criminology assumed that criminal behavior was a rational choice and punished the crime in order to discourage the criminal. Positivist criminology, however, insisted that most criminal behavior was irrational, even abnormal, and sought to defend "decent" society from sociopathic criminals with punishments directed at criminal "types" rather than their crimes per se. Effectively resisted or co-opted by legal professionals still committed to a liberal criminal justice system (although, as Speckman notes, they frequently endorsed the positivist principles "in theory"), positivist criminology remained a paradigm in waiting. The sustained period of social upheaval that began in 1910 marked the beginning of its ascendancy.

The third phase in the social construction of crime and criminality is the longest and most clearly paradigmatic. Closely linked to the rise and decline of the political party that would become the Institutional Revolutionary Party (PRI), it begins with the 1910 Revolution and ends with the 1980s political and economic crises. That the Revolution qualifies as a sustained period of social upheaval is hardly controversial, nor is the notion that it generated moral panics of all sorts. In addition to the usual suspects, Piccato (2001) has identified some "new" villains: the ubiquitous petty thief or *ratero* (a descendent of the traditional *lépero*) and the unabashedly modern Grey Automobile Gang (a forerunner of the *norteño* narco-trafficker in his flashy SUV). Moreover, as Piccato explains, policymakers increasingly expanded criminal categories like *raterismo* or *nacrotraficantes* to include a broad spectrum of the lower classes often identified with specific neighborhoods like Tepito in Mexico City or specific regions like the northern border cities or Sinaloa.

After the Revolution, positivist criminology supplanted liberal criminology as the dominant criminal justice paradigm, and postrevolutionary policymakers turned to a new generation of professional criminologists to lend their expertise in "social defense" to the state's project of national redemption. As Speckman's chapter details, the appearance of a positivist penal code in 1929 met with some resistance, especially from within the legal establishment; and a more "pragmatic" penal code—one that incorporated the doctrine of social defense only "up to the point permitted by our constitutional framework, our judicial traditions, and our social and economic conditions"[3]—was adapted in 1931. The inauguration of a pro-

---

[3] From Alfonso Teja Zabre, "Exposición de motivos presentada al Congreso Jurídico Nacional," in Buffington 2000: 125. Both codes were intended for the Federal District and territories but set the standard for the states.

fessional journal for criminologists, *Criminalia*, two years later further anchored these gains.

Sociologist/historian David Garland uses the term "penal welfarism" to characterize mid-twentieth-century attitudes toward crime and punishment in England and the United States (Garland 2001). Encouraged by the state's reformist ambitions, Mexico's expanding ranks of criminal justice professionals took a similar tack, although institutional constraints and lack of resources made serious efforts at penal welfare something of a sham (as they often were elsewhere). Nonetheless, ideological commitments to social reform and individual rehabilitation gave a sense of paradigmatic stability to the criminal justice project—something it had lacked up until that time—and thus complemented the relative political stability of the PRI years. Moreover, while penal welfarism was fatally undermined by conservative regimes in the United States and England during the 1980s, criminal justice professionals in Mexico continued to espouse penal reform and reintegrationist principles for at least another decade. At the same time, the gradual decline of PRI hegemony took its toll on the criminal justice system as critics relentlessly exposed its many failings, from inadequate institutions to inefficient practices to widespread corruption.

A series of catastrophic political and economic crises beginning in the 1980s—devaluations, earthquakes, assassinations, armed revolt—characterizes the fourth phase in the social construction of crime and criminality in Mexico. It is too early to tell if the pattern will hold for this cycle, but preliminary indications are that it will. Certainly, moral panics over political corruption (including political murders), organized crime (especially narcotrafficking), serial murders, and kidnappings (traditional and express) appear with depressing regularity, as do laments over the Colombianization of Mexico.

The sense of moral panic is especially strong in Mexico City. This is due in no small part to the long history of the capital's crime problem, a historical legacy that exacerbates current fears. Piccato (this volume) contends that, for Mexico City residents, "the police and judiciary have been perceived ... as sources of insecurity and unmerited harassment rather than protection" since the beginning of the twentieth century (if not before). In his chapter, Mario Arroyo Juárez reaches a similar conclusion, arguing that "for more than seven decades of authoritarian rule the principal objective [of the police] was to provide security not to citizens but to the regime." In recent years, however, things have gone from bad to worse. Arroyo reports that nearly 80 percent of Mexico City crimes go unreported because most victims consider the police to be ineffectual, corrupt, and probably criminal themselves. A successful prosecution rate of only 7 percent for reported crimes suggests that those concerns are well founded. The introduction to Robert Varenik's chapter captures the desperate mood. He insists that "the nation finds itself in the midst of the most troubling period of criminality in its modern history ... [and] the perception [is] that crime is more common, better organized, more dangerous, and generally more out of control than before." The crime statistics provided by Piccato and others support this perception, and their wide dissemination likely contributes to the pervasive sense of desperation throughout Mexico.

In the introduction to *Organized Crime and Democratic Governability*, John Bailey and Roy Godson break down "images of the political-criminal nexus" into four categories: contained corruption, centralized-systemic (formal), centralized-systemic (formal and shadow), and fragmented-contested. While they acknowledge that all four images coexist in Mexico, Bailey and Godson argue that only the fragmented-contested image "fits with our understanding of the disruptions and dislocations brought on by the dual transition ... from macroeconomic adjustment policies ... [and] the beginning stages of liberalization and democratization ... [to] microeconomic measures designed to strengthen market forces ... [and] social welfare policies ... redesigned to target resources more effectively" (Bailey and Godson 2000: 20). Read against the historical patterns sketched out above, I would argue that these four images of the political-criminal nexus reflect the late-twentieth-century crisis in the penal welfarist paradigm: the first image (contained corruption) is typical of a stable paradigm able to respond effectively to challenges, the second and third demonstrate the destabilizing power of the paradigm's anomalies, and the fourth shatters the paradigm altogether—an accurate reflection, as Bailey and Godson imply, of the current state of affairs.

The concerted response to paradigmatic instability has already begun, running the gamut from academic gatherings like the one that gave rise to this volume, to publicity stunts like the controversial hiring of former New York City Mayor Rudolph Giuliani as a Mexico City crime consultant. Consolidation of a new criminal justice paradigm, however, is still a ways off (and not just in Mexico). At the moment, Mexican policymakers (like their colleagues elsewhere) are experimenting with a range of options, from conservative approaches (broken windows, zero tolerance) to neoliberal "rational choice" models to a modified penal welfarism. If past responses have any predictive value, their approaches will be as eclectic and pragmatic as those of their predecessors.

Whether eclecticism translates into a stable paradigm any time soon is another matter. According to Arroyo, most recent attempts at criminal justice reform have been primarily theatrical (aimed at placating a distraught citizenry) and/or half-hearted (grossly underfunded, poorly supervised, and so on). For example, Arroyo argues that public officials embraced "zero tolerance" (and paid US$4.3 million to Giuliani) without taking into account important differences between Mexico City and New York, money and attention that might have been better spent on police salaries and training. Other imported ideas like designated "high-crime areas" (*zonas de alta incidencia delictiva*), "broken windows" policing of minor property crimes (like graffiti and vandalism), and special police squads (the Mexican equivalent of SWAT teams) fail to address the structural problems that produce crime zones in the first place, and tend to encourage police abuses, especially in targeted areas, without significantly reducing criminal activity. In these instances, eclecticism looks more like a problem than a solution. Certainly, Arroyo's and Varenik's insistence on the need for police accountability, transparency, better pay and training, and serious structural reorganization seems obvious enough, and the managerial approach may well represent the paradigm of the future, although *"menos política, más administración"* has never played particularly well outside of technocratic circles.

This overview clearly suffers from both overcompression and oversimplification. Nevertheless, I would argue that it has a certain heuristic and even practical value. For example, as the term itself implies, moral panics have a desperate and intemperate quality that often distorts the situation they purport to explain. Periods of political and economic "structural adjustment" are indeed traumatic and require widely publicized drastic measures (jailing prominent political figures, firing thousands of Mexico City policemen, hiring celebrity consultants). And as Arroyo and Varenik remind us, they also require considerable patience and sustained reflexivity. These qualities—often forgotten by policymakers and public opinion in the midst of a moral panic—are restored by historical perspective. "Crime," Durkheim reminds us, "is bound up with the fundamental conditions of all social life," and public concerns about crime, including periods of intense moral panic, are nothing new.

Durkheim's insistence that public concerns about crime and criminality are essential to the formation of the "collective sentiments" that bind societies together suggests further possibilities. If we must "abhor" the very real damage crime does, we should also be attentive to *and take advantage of* its positive effects. Since before Independence, Mexican national identity has been closely tied to the crime and criminality that mark its boundaries. Octavio Paz's appropriation (via Samuel Ramos) of Porfirian criminologist Julio Guerrero's stereotypical mestizo criminal—masked, macho, violent, insecure—as the Mexican national type in *Labyrinth of Solitude* is probably the best-known example. But the widespread (and transnational) popularity of *narcocorridos* and rock groups with names like Maldita Vencidad y los Hijos del Quinto Patio suggest that criminality and national identity remain inextricably linked in the public imagination. For all its destructive qualities, then, crime also performs a creative function: the discourses and debates it generates help the public to make sense of sustained periods of social upheaval; and in so doing, they shape the collective sentiments essential to sustaining national identity—a crucial step in the restoration of social order. Intervention in public discourse, however, is a tricky matter, especially when informed by overcompressed and oversimplified historical narratives.

PERIODIZATION AND ITS DISCONTENTS

If historical overview has its virtues, it also has several major drawbacks, drawbacks that must be taken into account by any conscientious analyst. There are too many to deal with here, but three drawbacks (posed as questions) are especially germane to the issues at hand:

- Does paradigm-driven periodization distort complex historical processes?
- How (and by whom) is a criminal justice paradigm constructed?
- What constitutes public opinion?

The answer to the first question (Does paradigm-driven periodization distort complex historical processes?) is "yes" on at least two counts. First, any attempt to impose a causal chain (crisis→perception→response→ consolidation→anomalies→crisis) on a complex historical process like the social construction of crime and criminality obscures the fact that the "stages" and "phases" that it produces are just as likely to be synchronous (and mutually constitutive) as they are diachronic (or in a cause-effect relation). This is obvious for the current situation in Mexico and was probably just as obvious in past situations. Even where a causal chain is defensible, as in the succession of disciplinary paradigms within criminology and penology (classic→positivist→penal welfarist→neoliberal), the overlapping of "stages" and "phases," as well as the constant rearticulation of existing discursive elements within them, expose the arbitrary nature of any periodization scheme. Second, the question of timing must be confronted head on. The overview given above is structured around historical events in Mexico. Thus, although it notes foreign influences on Mexican developments, from Beccaria to Lombroso to Giuliani, it situates the paradigm shifts themselves firmly in Mexican national time. However, many legal historians take a more internationalist approach that focuses on the dissemination and assimilation of "imported" ideas. On both counts, more attention to the dialectical tensions between synchronous and diachronic causation and between endogenous and exogenous developments would help "correct" the inherent flaws in the paradigm model. This would not only give us a better sense of past paradigm shifts but would also shed much-needed light on the process of paradigm development currently under way.

The second question (Whose paradigm are we talking about?) also highlights the need for a dialectical approach. In this case, however, the dialectical tensions occur between and among interest groups and social classes within Mexico. By definition, a criminal justice paradigm is a hegemonic construct in the fullest sense of the word—a bundle of working concepts that sets the parameters of public discourse and institutional practice. At the same time, hegemony is not monolithic. Like the discourses and practices that structure it, hegemony is constantly being negotiated and contested by elite interest groups operating from within the power structure and by marginalized groups resisting or seeking accommodation with the powerful. Piccato's chapter, for example, highlights the role of urban communities in controlling violence in response to the manifest failures of the state to ensure their safety. This scenario, all too familiar in the present crisis, indicates paradigmatic fragility at the social margins. Under most circumstances, however, the process of negotiation and contestation functions to keep hegemonic paradigms flexible, responsive, and therefore acceptable (if far from ideal) even to the "opposition." To call this "the consent of the governed" is perhaps going too far. Nevertheless, to ignore the internal dynamics of paradigmatic hegemony would be a huge mistake, whether for historians looking at the past or for policymakers seeking solutions in the present. Consensus is both impossible and undesirable; paradigmatic hegemony (and the sense of a functional, if much contested, social order that it confers) is both possible and very much to be desired.

Another drawback to historical overviews (What constitutes public opinion?) is closely related to the problem of paradigmatic hegemony. Like hegemony, the notion of public opinion pretends to a coherence that it promises but can never deliver. Even a cursory glance at media reporting, opinion polls, and electoral processes reveals complex discursive fields constructed around differences of opinion rather than consensus. If there is any consensus in public opinion, then, it is hidden in the unstated premises of hegemonic paradigms, not in the ebbs and flows of an easily identifiable "collective sentiment." And the best way to get at those unstated premises—the discursive heart of public opinion—would be to follow Foucault's advice in *The Archeology of Knowledge*. "One must characterize and individualize," he suggests, "... these dispersed and heterogeneous statements; the systems that govern their division, the degree to which they depend upon one another, the way in which they interlock or exclude one another, the transformation that they undergo, and the play of their location, arrangement, and replacement" (Foucault 1972: 34). A tall order to be sure but essential to any real understanding of public attitudes toward crime and criminality—an understanding vital to any serious attempt at "reforming the administration of justice in Mexico." Thus an archeological exploration of historical and contemporary discourses on crime and criminality, as evidenced in the chapters by Speckman and Piccato, should be one of the principal goals of this project.

FINAL THOUGHTS

To begin with gross generalizations and conclude with self-critique might seem counterproductive. I would argue instead that both strategies are essential. In *The Consequences of Modernity*, sociologist Anthony Giddens points out that modernity, especially in its later stages, is characterized by an intense reflexivity that constantly revises our understanding of the world in order to ensure ongoing "progress" across the spectrum of human knowledge about the natural and social worlds (Giddens 1990). Intended to increase our control of both worlds, reflexivity also works to heighten our sense of insecurity. The fevered pitch of contemporary moral panics might be a negative by-product of modern reflexivity. Certainly, the chapters by Arroyo and Varenik report on *and* reflect a sense of desperation that shows little sign of abating, at least not in the foreseeable future. Despite some negative consequences, however, what is needed is not less reflexivity but approaches and projects grounded in sustained self-critique (including at the institutional level, as Arroyo and Varenik suggest). Only in that way can we begin to talk about meaningful reform.

A hopeful postscript

Driving through the southwestern U.S. borderlands (from Las Cruces to San Diego) on my way to the conference that gave rise to this collection, I spent several hours listening to Mexican border radio, a deliberate cultural re-immersion of sorts by a native borderlander after nine long years in the upper Midwest. The talk-show commentators and callers were obsessing about two things: sex and crime. The first obsession was no surprise since sex provides an irresistible hook for wide-ranging discussions of interpersonal relations. The second obsession—or, more precisely, the tone of the second—was somewhat unexpected. Sensational crime has always attracted a lot of attention (José Guadalupe Posada's lurid broadsides spring to mind), and indeed these discussions often centered on shocking, if anecdotal, accounts of assaults, kidnappings, and murders. What seemed unusual to me was the willingness, even eagerness, of all concerned to turn these discussions into sustained and penetrating critiques of contemporary social relations, in particular, the responsibilities of the state vis-à-vis its citizens and the responsibilities of citizens vis-à-vis the state *and* each other. This spontaneous use of mass media as a public sphere in which citizens engage in "rational-critical" debate over the nature of society and government—all too rare in discussions about crime (or terrorism) in the United States—can only further the development of participatory democracy in Mexico. Arroyo and Varenik persuasively argue that informed and patient public support is essential to the success of any reform project. This admittedly anecdotal evidence suggests that the general public may be ready and even eager to back reform efforts, even as they remain deeply suspicious of the criminal justice system. The devastation wrought by rampant crime is a high price to pay, and panicked responses always run the risk of undermining the democratic processes that concerns about crime help stimulate. High price or not, an engaged and demanding citizenry cannot help but be a tremendous boon to Mexico's future.

References

Bailey, John, and Roy Godson. 2000. "Introduction." In *Organized Crime and Democratic Governability: Mexico and the U.S.-Mexican Borderlands*. Pittsburg, Penn.: University of Pittsburg Press.

Buffington, Robert. 2000. *Criminal and Citizen in Modern Mexico*. Lincoln: University of Nebraska Press.

Código Penal para el Distrito Federal y Territorio de la Baja-California sobre delitos del fuero común y para toda la República sobre delitos contra la Federación. 1890. Madrid: Establecimiento Tipográfico de Pedro Núñez.

Durkheim, Émile. 1979. "The Normal and the Pathological." In *Classics of Criminology*, ed. Joseph E. Jacoby. Prospect Heights, Ill.: Waveland.

Foucault, Michel. 1972. *The Archeology of Knowledge and the Discourse on Language*, trans. A.M. Sheridan Smith. New York: Harper Colophon.

———. 1979. *Discipline and Punish: The Birth of the Prison,* trans. Alan Sheridan. New York: Vintage.

Garland David. 2001. *The Culture of Control: Crime and Social Order in Contemporary Society.* Chicago: University of Chicago Press.

Giddens, Anthony. 1990. *The Consequences of Modernity*. Cambridge: Polity.

Kuhn, Thomas S. 1970. *The Structure of Scientific Revolutions*. Chicago: University of Chicago Press.

Martínez de Castro, Antonio. 1968. "Exposición de motivos del Código Penal," *Criminalia* 34, no. 3 (March 30).

Piccato, Pablo. 2001. *City of Suspects: Crime in Mexico City, 1900–1931*. Durham, N.C.: Duke University Press.

Speckman Guerra, Elisa. 2002. *Crimen y castigo: legislación penal, interpretaciones de la criminalidad y administración de justicia (Ciudad de México, 1872–1910)*. Mexico City: El Colegio de México/Instituto de Investigaciones Históricas, Universidad Nacional Autónoma de México.

CHAPTER 3

A Historical Perspective on Crime in Twentieth-Century Mexico City

PABLO PICCATO

A historical perspective of crime in twentieth-century Mexico City must start by addressing an apparent contradiction between the qualitative and quantitative evidence. Multiple testimonies collected throughout the last century show that crime (particularly violence, theft, and extortion) was a permanent concern for the inhabitants of the city, and was always thought to be too common. Yet statistical evidence shows decreasing criminal rates after the Mexican Revolution and continuing until the 1980s. Are these rates the product of the state's preferences and limitations, rather than objective facts? Or are there other factors, invisible to quantitative sources, that explain the contradiction? After a brief examination of the statistical data, this chapter focuses on other kinds of evidence to attempt a satisfactory explanation and present an overview of criminal practices in Mexico during the twentieth century.

Rather than singling out one factor, I will advance two arguments. First, historically, crime in Mexico City was indeed frequent and disruptive but, because of police and judicial corruption, it was not always registered by statistics; furthermore, corruption encouraged crime by lowering the chances of punishment. Second, the inhabitants of the city and its surrounding urban communities maintained a degree of control over crime by channeling conflict through informal negotiations. Those negotiations involved policemen and judicial representatives, but they became less effective in the last decades of the century because of the increasing importance of corruption, organized violence, and drug trafficking as factors in crime. Urban communities also chose to ignore certain kinds of crimes, such as violence against women and children. Thus, rather than privileging a given political explanation, this chapter will explore the combination of circumstances, attitudes, institutions, and practices that converge in the problem of crime.

Two photographs taken at police stations (*delegaciones*) define the ambiguity of the relationship between the inhabitants of Mexico City and the representatives of the state. In figure 3.1, taken in the mid-1950s, photojournalist Nacho López shows a suspect making a point with his eloquent hand and eyes to the broad-shouldered prosecutor facing away from the camera. Next to the suspect, a policeman raises his finger, probably to correct the suspect's story. In figure 3.2, probably from Ciudad Netzahualcóyotl in the early 1970s, two men are also seen across the police station desk. The one on the right is arguing, while the other is handing some crumpled bills to an official outside the frame. These two images portray something that is easily forgotten in official, journalistic, and scientific views of the problem of crime and justice in Mexico City: defining an act as a crime was always the product of public discussions and, often, informal arrangements. This chapter will shift the point of view from the official side of the desk (where the two photographers placed themselves) to the other side, where crime was a problematic category.

TRENDS

The statistical evidence shows clear general trends in crime rates in the Federal District during the twentieth century: an increase, reaching the highest levels, during the last decade of the Porfiriato (1876–1911, the period of Porfirio Díaz's domination of national politics); a decrease beginning in the 1920s, when compilation of data resumed after the Revolution, up to the 1980s; and then a new and steep increase continuing to the present day. Breaking down these trends by type of crime, we can identify some nuances: sexual violence increased steadily throughout the century; theft had clear peaks after 1929, World War II, and in the last couple of decades; homicide decreased steadily, as did the ratio of violent crimes to crimes against property.[1]

These statistics have serious biases. One is that they reflect the attitudes of police and judicial authorities regarding crimes they believed deserved

---

[1] See Beltrán and Piccato 2001 and Piccato 2003; see also Ruiz Harrell 1998. I am grateful to Ira Beltrán, John Mraz, and the participants of the "Reforming the Administration of Justice in Mexico" conference, particularly David Shirk and Wayne Cornelius, for their comments on this essay.

Figure 3.1. Man and Police in Mexico City.

Source: Photo by Nacho López, 1954, in Mraz 2003: 134.

Figure 3.2. Paying Off the Police.

Source: Vélez-Ibáñez 1983: 83.

to be prosecuted (for example, theft before the Revolution, drug consumption since the 1940s), as well as their lack of interest in prosecuting others (arguably rape, which had a low ratio of guilty sentences). While police chiefs could demand that officers increase arrests, thus bringing numbers up (Sodi 1951: 215), courts suffered a chronic scarcity of resources that limited their ability to deal with new cases. Finally, not all crimes resulted in arrests: in most cases, and for reasons we will examine presently, victims decided not to bring crimes to the attention of the police.[2]

This said, however, statistical information can be considered reliable in demonstrating long-term trends. The Federal District trends are similar to those in the rest of the country, and the administrative biases that affect the accuracy of the numbers seem to be constant throughout the period. A preliminary analysis of the factors that may be related to changes in crime rates suggested that multiple variables are important: literacy, income, and government expenditure. Improvement in social indicators like literacy (which itself reflects state welfare strategies) partly explains decreasing rates. The strongest correlation, however, was with the ratio of persons charged (*consignados*) to the number sentenced—in other words, the gap between indictments and guilty convictions (a measure of the effectiveness of prosecutions and *consignado* rates).

This suggests that, apart from socioeconomic variables, trends are also the result of victims' and offenders' perceptions of the efficacy of the police and judicial system: if crime was less likely to be punished, offenders had greater incentives to commit crimes and victims had fewer reasons to press charges. The state, in other words, can have an impact on crime rates but not always in the intended direction. Crime rates will go up, as they did during the Porfiriato and the last decades of the twentieth century, when socioeconomic pressures coincide with a state that emphasizes repressive police strategies yet does not pay much attention to the inefficacy of the judicial system. Falling between "judicial" and "social" hypotheses about criminality, this interpretation of historical trends combines multiple socioeconomic factors with an effort to understand popular and institutional definitions of crime and reconstruct patterns of criminal practices that probably respond to those perceptions but also to other factors that are specific to each kind of practice.

---

2 Hayner 1946: 436; Borras 1987: 12; Aguirre, de la Torre, and Ramírez Heredia 1999: 90; *El Universal*, October 14, 1920, p. 9.

PERCEPTIONS OF CRIME

The clearest challenge to statistical evidence of decreasing crime rates comes from police news, particularly the *nota roja*—gruesome, sometimes voyeuristic descriptions that have reached thousands of readers through newspapers, magazines, comics, books, and, more recently, television. Since the late nineteenth century, murderers and professional criminals have been objects of widespread attention, to the extent that specialists blamed the *nota roja* for immorality and rising crime and officials considered censoring it. Shocking photographs, such as those in the weekly *Alarma!*, lured many readers, but it was the genre's effort to make narrative sense of crime and its perceived constant rise that made it a staple of newsstands, as well as a valuable historical source.

The *nota roja* reporter was always close to police sources, so close, in fact, that witnesses and suspects could confuse him with a police officer. At the same time, the skillful and scientific police detective (notably exemplified by Alfonso Quiroz Cuarón) was often at the center of the press reports because he knew the world of criminals so well. Taking cues from Mexican criminology (about which Quiroz Cuarón was a well-known author), the *nota roja* chronicled criminal practices to uncover the habits of a well-defined sector of society, the "criminal population." Emphasizing the police perspective, the *nota roja* often did little more than describe the horrors and tragedies of the police station or crime scene and reproduce the officials' speculations as to the causes of crime (usually passion, greed, or drugs).[3]

The *nota roja* reporter's proximity to the police contrasts with this medium's relative detachment from the judicial process. Trials lasted months, and they were dull affairs conducted by judges and clerks in unattractive spaces. Until 1929, after which jury trials were no longer used, juries heard highly publicized cases that combined famous suspects, eloquent lawyers, and avid audiences. The print media and radio relayed debates and interrogations that took place over the span of a few hours or days (even months after the events), conveying all the drama lacking in the official written record (Macías González 1999; Ortega Ramírez 1990: 27–64). Yet in most cases, these media showed little interest in following proceedings after the police made an arrest or the public prosecutor (*agente del ministerio*

---

3 Monsiváis 1980: 199, 336, 362; González Rodríguez 1990: 11; Téllez Vargas and Garmabella 1982: 9, 38; Rubenstein 1998: 152; del Castillo 1997; Roumagnac 1923: 148–49; Aguilar 1941: 99–102. See as an antecedent the *Gaceta de Policía*, published in the 1900s with the support of the Department of Police.

público) presented a suspect to the judge. For reporters, guilt was the product of the detective's skill and the suspect's obvious psychological and moral features. In the readers' perspective, this detachment also expressed a tacit assumption: preventive detention of a suspect during the investigation and trial of a crime was usually long and painful, and in and of itself constituted punishment. Formalizing guilt with a criminal sentence was of little consequence since justice had already been served with the suspect's indictment (Roumagnac 1933; Azaola Garrido 1996: 76, 91).

Starting in the 1970s, however, news coverage of police and police matters became more ambivalent. Although established reporters like Eduardo Téllez considered the Mexican police corps one of the best in the world and praised Federal District police chief Arturo Durazo Moreno (1976–1982), others like Ramón Márquez criticized police corruption and ineptitude. The popular interest in the *nota roja* was by no means a vindication of the police institutions portrayed in Nacho López's photo essays (figure 3.1). Rather, the figure of Durazo Moreno crystallized the public's perception of the police as corrupt and involved in political repression (Márquez 1980: 345; Téllez Vargas and Garmabella 1982: 235, 257, but also see 258, 261; Mraz 2003: 129). *Lo negro del Negro Durazo*, a book written by Jorge González González, Durazo's bodyguard, was an editorial success in the 1980s. It described the corruption and violence of a police chief who had been directly appointed by President José López Portillo. The book underscored the connections between Durazo and nightclubs, prostitution, and criminal activities like kidnapping and drug trafficking, as well as his illegal use of public resources (González González 1983). In the words of Sergio González Rodríguez (1990: 10), the book continued the *nota roja* tradition but also described "nepotism, the symbiotic nexus between underground and formal businesses, official criminality, and vulgar picaresque." That nexus was also the key to understanding the popular perception of the Mexico City police and judicial system, not as part of a state apparatus designed to fight crime, but as a "mafia" tied together by a code of silence, corruption, and violence.[4]

Not surprisingly, many of González González's claims about Durazo are difficult to substantiate. Yet they point to certain continuities in police

---

[4] In breaking with that silence, González González confessed fifty murders that he had committed on the order of President Gustavo Díaz Ordaz and other officials. The confession was followed by a disarming expression of patriotism: "Even we hit men love Mexico in our own way" (González González 1983: 17).

practices. Assertions of corruption, abuses, and political involvement by the higher ranks of the police, which date back to the Porfiriato, became very visible in the early 1920s. Later, during the years of political stability under the Institutional Revolutionary Party (PRI) in the mid-twentieth century, police chiefs apparently became adept at cultivating a favorable press. Yet, by contrast, Durazo's tenure marked a historic shift because, critics asserted years later, it internalized and systematized long-standing connections between the Federal District's police and various illegal businesses. The criminal organization that allegedly developed inside the ranks of law enforcement—"the brotherhood" ("*la hermandad*")—resisted attempts by higher political officials and even army officers to control it.[5]

Yet, rather than demonstrating the existence of a criminal organization within the city's police, the following pages will explore how the belief in such an organization shaped public perceptions of criminal practices, impunity, and official involvement in twentieth-century Mexico City. As one reconstructs public evidence of these practices, it becomes clear that Durazo's work was exceptional for its scale and notoriety, but not because of its content and structure.

Graft quite visibly occupied the lowest level of the connection between crime and the police; the "bite" (*la mordida*) was in widespread use throughout the twentieth century. Police officers and other government representatives on the street (such as health inspectors) extracted money from drivers, established merchants, street vendors, and persons suspected of crimes and misdemeanors. Since the first years of the twentieth century, if not before, policemen took bribes for granted, as a way to complement their low salaries and to support a pyramidal structure that—through quotas and the leasing of uniforms, street corners, guns, identification cards,

---

5 Aguirre, de la Torre, and Ramírez Heredia 1999: 60–61; *La Jornada* 2000; Téllez Vargas and Garmabella 1982: 286. For purges, reforms, and militarization of police hierarchies, see Obregón to Governor of the Federal District, 21 Nov. 1921, Archivo General de la Nación, Fondo Presidentes Obregón-Calles (hereinafter AGN, POC), 122-D2-P-4; Obregón decree, 2 Jan. 1922, AGN, POC, 731-P-14; Inspector General de Policía to President, 9 Aug. 1924, AGN, POC, 104-P-106; *El Universal*, September 16, 1929, sec. 5, p. 1; Leobardo Cruz to Presidente Municipal, 27 Dec. 1917, Archivo Histórico de la Ciudad de México (hereinafter AHCM), Policía Presos Penitenciaría, 3664, 2; *El Universal*, January 12, 1918, p. 1; *Excélsior*, October 2, 1929, sec. 2, p. 1; González González 1983: 63; Aguirre, de la Torre, and Ramírez Heredia 1999: 61, 66–67, 68. For attitudes toward the police, see Ramírez Plancarte 1941: 53, 560–61; Barrera Bassols 1997; Mraz 2001.

and tow trucks—funneled income up to the upper ranks. Many suspects and victims saw the inherent unfairness of having to protect themselves against corrupt police and public prosecutors. Like the men in the photos presented above, they often had to beg or buy their way out of police stations. Beatings and torture by the police only raised the cost of failing to pay a bribe after arrest.[6] Although graft was probably not restricted to police stations and criminal courts, its impact on public perceptions of crime was greater when it involved police, judicial, and prison officials who victimized the poor and let wealthy or influential suspects go free.[7]

Illegal but nonviolent practices (punishable under the law but often not perceived as criminal by the majority of the population) were also a source of profit for the police. This was true for abortion, with doctors and midwives funneling a steady flow of protection money to the police (Ortega Ramírez 1990; González González 1983: 191). Gambling was a more prominent activity; it blossomed in the 1920s, both in Mexico City and in Mexico's border with the United States, as U.S. tourists flocked to Mexico to escape Prohibition. Although gambling was subject to government regulation during the administration of President Álvaro Obregón, the police were involved nevertheless, a fact denounced by the press.[8]

Smuggling was another activity that thrived during the twentieth century. In the early 1940s, smugglers brought products that were small in volume but high in value, such as jewels or drugs, which were often sold in respectable stores. However, contraband goods soon became associated

---

[6] *Excélsior*, November 24, 1921, sec. 2, p. 1; Hayner 1946: 429; Aguilar 1941: 143; Toribio Esquivel Obregón to Manuel Macías, 16 May 1907, Archivo Toribio Esquivel Obregón, Universidad Iberoamericana, Caja 21, exp. 1, f. 320; Luis Cabrera to Rafael Nieto, 13 June 1922, Archivo Calles Torreblanca, Fondo Fernando Torreblanca, ser. 010203, exp. 1/2: Cabrera, Luis, inv. 142; *El Universal*, June 7, 1930, p. 1; Muñoz Martínez 1995: 123, 127; Mraz 2003: 129, 139; Sodi 1951: 118; Nelligan 1988: 111; Azaola Garrido 1996: 77, 83; Borras 1987: 69; Vélez-Ibáñez 1983: 83; CNDH 1997: 21; *El Demócrata*, September 25, 1914, sec. 1, pp. 3–5.

[7] See *El Universal*, January 19, 1918, p. 1; María Luisa Mena to President Calles, 17 May 1926, AGN, POC, 811-G-186; Nelligan 1988: 30; Abogado Visitador to Comisaría de la Cuarta Demarcación, 23 July 1919, AHCM, Justicia Comisarías, 2717, expedientes 11, 13, 15.

[8] Inspector General de Policía to Presidente Municipal, 13 Aug. 1917, AHCM, Policía Presos Penitenciaría, 3664, 2; Álvaro Obregón to Governor of the Federal District, 11 Apr. 1921, AGN, POC, 425-R-1; *El Universal*, October 7, 1920, p. 12; Meyer 1977: 304; Sodi 1951: 216.

with street peddling, particularly in the Tepito neighborhood, where the sale of stolen goods was common (Aguilar 1941: 127–28; Smith 1903: 72–73). Peddlers had been subject to police harassment and extortion since the Porfiriato. When they began trading in smuggled goods, they also attracted government inspectors from the Treasury Department (Secretaría de Hacienda).[9] In Tepito, the open sale of contraband became an important source of employment during the second half of the century, following an expansion of street commerce in general. Its stability was made possible by the clientelistic relations that existed between the neighborhood merchant associations and the PRI. The importance of these relations was directly linked to the street merchants' vulnerability to inspectors and policemen: in the absence of specific regulations, all street sales were, in one way or another, illegal. Organizations worked as "mafias" that sold protection. In exchange, authorities benefited from, among other things, the mobilization of *tepiteños* in PRI demonstrations (Reyes Domínguez and Rosas Mantecón 1993; Eckstein 1972: 60; Lewis 1961: 349; Borras 1987: 32).

Although most people did not regard it as a crime, prostitution emerged as a legal gray area in the twentieth century, encouraging extortion and even violence against sex workers on the part of the police. Prostitution had been regulated as a public health issue since the 1860s, and sex workers had to register and undergo periodic examinations, which exposed them to police extortion. This risk led many of them to work from the streets, where the threat of random violence was always present, or in brothels, where madams mediated the relationship with health inspectors and police. Prostitution was deregulated in the 1930s, and legal punishments were directed against pimping, viewed as male exploitation of working-class women. Yet, with its links to cabarets, dance halls, and hotels, the prostitution business remained a feature of Mexico City nightlife. Brothel owners recruited young women through deception or force. The sex workers' life stories often began with domestic violence, followed by rape, forced labor, and ultimately prostitution. Young female migrants to Mexico City, in particular, found themselves alone and helpless in a city that seemed indifferent to their plight. Even among women who found some financial autonomy through prostitution, the stigma was costly in terms of

---

[9] Isabel Reza and 12 signatures to Presidente del Ayuntamiento, 25 Jan. 1901, AHCM, Policía en general, 3642, 1342; Tomasa Pérez and 7 signatures to Presidente del Ayuntamiento, 3 July 1915, AHCM, Policía en general, 3645, 1768; *El Universal*, January 10, 1917, p. 1; Aguilar 1941: 30; Piccato 2001a: chaps. 1–2; González González 1983: 166.

social capital and was a powerful factor keeping them in the business. Meanwhile, although neighbors denounced cabarets and cantinas as centers of vice and crime, prostitution in Mexico did not prompt the kinds of police campaigns or public scandals seen in other countries.[10]

Police protection also extended to criminal activities like car theft, kidnapping, and robbery. Auto theft became commonplace during the Revolution and was soon linked to other organized criminal practices that required protection. The famous case of the Grey Automobile Gang (*Banda del Automóvil Gris*) exemplified this new criminal trend: this sophisticated group of educated Mexicans and foreigners, who robbed wealthy homes and stole government funds, operated with the complicity of revolutionary generals. Even street vendors who trafficked in stolen goods paid bribes to the police.[11]

Drug trafficking, which swelled during the twentieth century, involved the complicity of officials on a much broader scale—at many levels of government and in a range of institutions. Marijuana, cocaine, opium, heroin, and morphine, which had been in use since at least the late nineteenth century, were criminalized in the early decades of the twentieth, largely due to pressure from the United States (Astorga 1996, 2000: 172; Roumagnac 1904: 107, 109, 113; Pérez Montfort 1997). Drugs were linked to varied social and cultural groups; long before it became associated with the 1960s counterculture, marijuana was used by soldiers, prisoners, and young men of the social elite.[12] Cocaine evolved from miracle drug to upper-class vice. A prohibition on the use of opium was initially enforced among Chinese immigrants, but morphine and heroin soon attracted upper-class consumers. These culturally and socially diverse practices were identified as a "social problem" and criminalized. The result was the development of an

---

[10] Nelligan 1988; Roumagnac 1904: 181, 196; Hayner 1946: 429; Bliss 2001; Monsiváis 1980: 198–99, 327; *El Universal*, June 7, 1930, p. 1; *El Universal*, June 18, 1930, p. 5; AHCM, Gobernación, 1110, 43; *Excélsior*, October 10, 1929, sec. 2, p. 1; Subinspector 4th District to Ayuntamiento, 24 Jan. 1920, AHCM, Presos penitenciaría, 3665, 12; Guy 1991.

[11] Piccato 2001a; Mérigo 1959; *Excélsior*, October 25, 1921, p. 1; Aguilar 1941: 123–24; *La Nación*, July 30, 1912, p. 6; *Excélsior*, October 1, 1929, p. 1; Archivo Judicial, Distrito Federal, Reclusorio Sur (hereinafter AJ-RS), 23196, 1; Lewis 1961: 230–31, 350–52, 356.

[12] *El Universal*, October 9, 1916, p. 4; Gamboa 1922: 211; Roumagnac 1904: 210; Peón del Valle 1935.

underground distribution network that enjoyed official protection.[13] Drug sales expanded early in the century through a decentralized system of market stalls and drugstores, and by the 1930s national and international gangs were vying for control of this market. In addition to simultaneously harassing and protecting drug dealers, police at all levels were directly involved in the sale of seized drugs.[14] According to Luis Astorga, the public record since the 1940s shows fewer politicians and more police involved in drug-trafficking scandals. In Astorga's view, this is a consequence of the centralization of drug-case prosecutions in the Office of the Attorney General (PGR) and the interest of the political class in this highly profitable business. The last three decades of the twentieth century witnessed several highly publicized cases of complicity between drug traffickers and federal, state, and local officers. Meanwhile, the increased availability of illegal drugs in Mexico, along with the addition of cheaper alternatives (particularly solvents), has added another facet to the violent and legally ambiguous interactions between the police and Mexico City residents, down to the level of schoolchildren.[15]

Astorga and others describe the links between police and criminals in drug trafficking as analogous to those of "the brotherhood." This interpretation implies that the police do not simply facilitate crime; they are a direct cause of crime and are positioned at the very center of a broad, secretive network involved in illegal activities, a network often referred to as "the mob" (el hampa). Police and judicial corruption and the impunity of powerful criminals are core factors in social perceptions of crime in Mexico City.[16]

Yet a strictly moral or legalistic interpretation leads to an erroneous view of police corruption as the only cause of serious crime and low criminal prosecution rates. We must remember that, for centuries, Mexico City has been characterized by an informal sector of the economy operating at

---

13 Pérez Montfort 2000: 114; AHCM, 18 Mar. 1916, Policía en general, 3645, 1777; AHCM, 23 Jan. 1919, Presos penitenciaría, 3665, 13; AHCM, 23 Aug. 1918, 3664, 5; ACHM, 11 Jan. 1918, 3665, 10.

14 Astorga 2000: 174; Pérez Montfort 2000: 115, 124, 130; Argüelles 1935: 322, 326; Aguirre, de la Torre, and Ramírez Heredia 1999: 61; Hayner 1946: 429; Aguilar 1941: 128; Peón del Valle 1935: 140; Eckstein 1972: 56; El Universal, September 16, 1929, p. 1.

15 CNDH 1997: 255; Astorga 2000: 167, 169, 173, 187; New York Times 2003.

16 El Universal, June 30, 1930, p. 3; Aguilar 1941: 145; Hayner 1946: 429; Cohen 1996: 11.

the margins of the law but tolerated by the authorities (Francois 1998). Although the private use of public resources for personal gain was nothing new in independent Mexico, the twentieth century became the century of corruption as the Porfiriato (which, in collective memory of the postrevolutionary era, was marked by order and propriety) gave way to a "new bourgeoisie" enriched by the Revolution (Katz 2000: 94, 96; Taracena 1960: 5, 98–99; Meyer 1977: 304–305).

Corruption has been studied as a manageable aspect of the relationship between the postrevolutionary state and civil society. In his work on Guadalajara, de la Peña found that bribes in exchange for official protection allowed the survival of a large informal sector, a part of the economy that gained importance as industrialization gave way to a decentralization of economic activity. Bribes and protection were part of a "network of exchanges of favors" that involved various sectors of the official party machinery and, in the protection of business groups, relied on traditional patronage and reciprocity networks (de la Peña 2000: 118, 122, 123). Similar conditions were found in Tepito (Reyes Domínguez and Rosas Mantecón 1993). But it is during the later decades of the twentieth century (hence Durazo's paradigmatic importance) that public perceptions reflect corruption on a new scale: penetrating all levels of government, fostering violence, and evading the citizenry's ability to turn it to their own advantage.

If illegality is not the same as crime and if corruption cannot be treated as a predatory crime, a more productive question for understanding recent changes in crime rates in Mexico might address the impact of police and judicial misconduct on the more common patterns of crime. It is hard to evaluate that impact through crime rates; by definition, offenses committed by those in charge of prosecuting them are rarely punished (but see Aguilar 1941; Lovera 1990: 13). However, if we focus on people's experiences of police and judicial action against the most common predatory offenses, we can venture a different hypothesis: prosecution and punishment were so uncertain that, for the majority of Mexico City's lower-class population, the state was not a reliable partner in dealing with crime, and justice was biased in favor of the rich. In the case of theft, for example, during the first three decades of the century, the goal was to restore property rather than to punish the thief; this objective was pursued via negotiations, which ran parallel to the prosecution process, between victims and suspected perpetrators.[17] Judicial outcomes were highly uncertain unless one of the actors

---

[17] Piccato 2001a: chap. 6; AJ-RS, 1074694, 8; AJ-RS, 1067902, 8.

had the financial wherewithal to influence the result. In light of this uncertainty regarding the judicial process, some suspects and their families looked for help from religious or magical interventions, while victims sought out seers to help them recover stolen property (Azaola Garrido 1993: 40, 37; Lewis 1961: 308).

Since punishment was unlikely and most victims belonged to the lower classes, the cost of committing a crime appeared to would-be committers of crime to be relatively low.[18] Corruption in the courts and among the police created many ways for criminals to escape punishment (flight, bribes, and so on) in what criminologists have aptly called a "lottery of impunity" (Ceniceros and Garrido 1936: 93). This is supported by the strong inverse relationship between the number of indictments and the number of criminals actually sentenced. Going beyond this evidence of corruption, the remainder of the chapter examines two criminal practices that seem to have distinguished twentieth-century Mexico City: domestic abuse and juvenile delinquency.

GENDER, AGE, AND VIOLENCE

Domestic abuse—or, more accurately, gender violence, because it is structured by gender inequality and is not necessarily restricted to the intimate space of the household—is one of the most damaging and least investigated aspects of crime in twentieth-century Mexico City. The public health costs of drug addiction, the wages of corruption, and the loss of property and labor involved in crime and its punishment have been the subject of multiple studies (Quiroz Cuarón 1958; Quiroz Cuarón and Quiroz Cuarón 1970; Azaola Garrido 1996). However, we have yet to evaluate the impact on society at large of the violence of men against women, adults against children, and offenders against victims who, by virtue of the attack, are perceived as "feminized" (weak and passive).

There is convincing evidence of certain patterns of such violence, some of them centuries old. They include coercion linked to domestic labor and prostitution; violence by husbands, lovers, and fathers; rape committed by relatives or friends, which sometimes pushed women into prostitution or other activities where their sexual integrity was no longer a valuable asset; and harassment, robbery, and sexual violence on nighttime streets, under-

---

[18] Borras 1987: 48; Azaola Garrido 1996: 121; Quiroz Cuarón, Gómez Robleda, and Argüelles 1939: 104; *El Diablito Bromista*, October 13, 1907, p. 3.

mining women's freedom to use public spaces.[19] Women's violence against children or other family members is often the direct result of a husband's abuse.[20] The gendered structure of aggression is clear: the control of women's labor and sexuality through the exercise of masculine attributes (physical strength, aggressiveness, domination of public spaces) extends through the spheres of public life, work, and the household (Selby, Murphy, and Lorenzen 1990: 175–76; see also Bourdieu 2000; Brownmiller 1976).

It is not appropriate, then, to understand male violence as an unintended consequence of modernization and the disruption of traditional values. Violence of man against man in twentieth-century Mexico City strongly suggests that one's honor remained a paramount concern, including among the lower classes. The clearest evidence of this lies in the rules that were applied to fights between men, rules similar to those followed in dueling to ensure fairness and to avoid involving the authorities. Guns, which had become more common since the Revolution, increased the likelihood of a lethal outcome—which probably kept many such encounters from taking place—yet honor and reputation remained as factors in violent encounters.[21]

However, the practices associated with gendered violence suggest a caveat to the classic model of honor as an active male concern and a passive female virtue. Personal stories collected by anthropologist Oscar Lewis reveal a nuance that explains the prevalence of abuse against wives, daughters, and lovers: while men were willing to fight over the smallest insult to their reputation, they were not necessarily willing to fight for the love of a woman. The prize might not be worth the risks, especially if the lady proved fickle, according to Roberto, one of Lewis's informants. Despite his skill with the knife, Roberto preferred to forget a former lover

---

[19] See Piccato 2001b; Nelligan 1988; Lewis 1961; Lovera 1990; Stern 1995; Tutino 1998; Penyak 1993.

[20] Gutmann 1996: 200, 208, 209. In a sample of women convicted of homicide, 70 percent had suffered mistreatment, neglect, abuse, or abandonment by their families, 66 percent from their husbands, and 60 percent from the police (Azaola Garrido 1996: 129, 72, 99, 102). Although closer to a *nota roja* treatment, also see Nelligan 1988: 52.

[21] See AJ-RS, 781394, Battery 1901; Aguilar 1941: 22–23; Piccato 2001a: chap. 5. Mexican criminologists have explained "proletarian delinquency" as a cultural trait of the lower classes; see Quiroz Cuarón, Gómez Robleda, and Argüelles 1939: 135; Wolfgang and Ferracuti 1967: 280. But also see Gutmann 1996: 200. On modernization and anomie, see *Excélsior*, October 11, 1929, p. 5; Roumagnac 1904: 282; Guerrero 1901: 111, 157–58.

rather than fight her husband (Lewis 1961: 205, 293, 400–401). The reluctance to fight over a woman is not surprising if we view it in the socioeconomic context of domestic abuse, which Lewis also documented. The respect afforded a woman and the value of her work diminish with each instance of abuse or "dishonor," thus also decreasing the social cost of committing gender violence.

The rate of sexual offenses (rape, abduction, statutory rape) increased slowly but steadily in twentieth-century Mexico City, unlike the trend that prevailed for most other crimes. The same disclaimers about official statistics apply here: social and institutional reluctance to deal with it means that gender violence was more common than official evidence would suggest. Women who were victimized faced numerous obstacles if they decided to press charges: skepticism on the part of the police and judges, humiliating medical examinations at police stations, and their parents' negotiations with suspects for a promise of marriage.[22] In addition, the law lessened the punishment for husbands and parents who used violence, including deadly force, against adulterous wives or disobedient children (Martínez de Castro 1891; Código Penal [1929] 1929; Código Penal [1931] 1938: 294). More importantly, social attitudes (which were also embraced by women) discouraged the state's intervention in the intimacy of the home, placing an additional burden on victims who dared bring such private affairs into the open. The gradual increase in rates of sexual offenses may therefore express women's greater willingness to challenge those attitudes, to talk openly about rape, and to use penal institutions and community networks to negotiate conflict with men.[23]

Juvenile delinquency was first identified as a social problem in Mexico City early in the twentieth century, and its importance has increased in recent years.[24] Like violence against women, it seemed to be a symptom of urban growth and modernization. The postrevolutionary period saw a proliferation of studies and regulations dedicated to treating and rehabili-

---

[22] Piccato 2001a; Mraz 2003: 137; Roumagnac 1910: 81–96; AJ-RS, 1067905, 2v–3.

[23] Sentence against Antonio Castellanos Navarrete, Jan. 1914, AGN, Fondo Secretaría de Justicia (hereinafter SJ), vol. 892, exp. 3961; Azaola Garrido 1996: 95, 101; Piccato 2001a: chap. 5. A specialized branch of the public prosecutor's office devoted to sex crimes was established in 1990; Lovera 1990: 16, 17. See also Selby, Murphy, and Lorenzen 1990: 176; Lewis 1961: 299. For the intervention of state agencies, see Lewis 1961: 432–33.

[24] La Voz de México, January 18, 1890, p. 2; Macedo 1897: 14–15, 29–30; El Universal, October 15, 1923, p. 7.

tating young offenders (Ceniceros and Garrido 1936; Azaola Garrido 1990; Roumagnac 1912: 41–46; Borras 1987: 13). Research focused on the kinds of crime committed by children and adolescents (vandalism and theft more often than violence against persons) and explained these as overdetermined urban phenomena, the product of poverty, disrupted families, promiscuity, lack of schools and parks, movies and "unhealthy" literature, drugs and alcohol, and "urbanism" in general (Hayner 1946: 436; Buñuel 1950; Ceniceros and Garrido 1936: 62, 63, 65, 75).

Youth gangs have been a defining feature of criminality in twentieth-century Mexico City. Particularly since the 1970s, young gangsters (*chavos banda*) in poor colonias, such as the western hills of Santa Fé, represented a threat of violence and property crime linked to drugs and rock and roll, against which the state seemed helpless. Youth sections in city jails and correctional institutions, like the adult prisons, were characterized by violence, coercive sexual practices, and drug consumption (Roumagnac 1912; Mellado 1959; Azaola Garrido 1990, 1993). Reform efforts brought professionals other than lawyers into the young offenders' institutional setting, but the changes only created additional uncertainty about outcomes.

Because of the position functions these youth gangs held for their members, it is not correct to define them as mere criminal organizations. For Lewis's informants, membership in the Tepito neighborhood gang was a matter of community pride. Members' rankings were based on their fighting skills. Girls could be protected, but they also had their own gangs, which, like the boy gangs, combined intimidation and solidarity.[25] Many practices associated with juvenile delinquency are convincingly explained as the result of survival strategies in which the streets are an extension of socializing and economic activities ideally set in the home or workplace. Marginal economic activities—working as informal porters, selling newspapers and lottery tickets on the street, trading in stolen goods, and even selling drugs—gave minors access to short-term income.[26] Children's presence in the urban labor market often reflected family demands: for boys, bringing in money from work on the streets was crucial for the household's economic survival; for girls, domestic labor, especially child care, imposed harsh conditions and often generated conflicts over the legitimacy of step-parents' demands (Azaola Garrido 1990: 34 and 1996: 136; Hayner 1946:

---

[25] Lewis 1961; *El Imparcial*, July 1, 1908, p. 7; Borras 1987: 126–27, 163; Aguilar 1941: 15.

[26] Reyes Domínguez and Rosas Mantecón 1993: 46, 56; *El Imparcial*, January 8, 1900, p. 3; Ceniceros and Garrido 1936: 113–18; Azaola Garrido 1993: 35.

436–37, 433n). Furthermore, testimonies show that minors' criminal behavior often had its roots in abuse and neglect at home—as attention was directed to younger siblings, as fathers abandoned one household to move to another, and as adolescents were subjected to violence, including sexual abuse (Ceniceros and Garrido 1936: 98–100, 109, 121; Azaola Garrido 1993: 40–41; Lewis 1961).

The social impact of juvenile delinquency and its connections with gender violence can best be examined in specific urban communities. Although other areas of Mexico City have been known for their gangs, Tepito stands out as the one where popular lore, literature, and ethnographic testimony permit a closer look. By documenting the urban poor's efforts to maintain strong social networks despite adverse circumstances, such sources provide a useful counterbalance to the temptation to equate poverty with anomie and crime.[27]

Tepito, which grew out of irregular settlements on what was, at the time, the northern outskirts of Mexico City, held a reputation as "the cradle of crime" throughout the twentieth century. It shared several features with other lower-class areas of the city—notably a shortage of housing, urban infrastructure, and security.[28] Two interconnected strands of evidence debunk any stereotypes. First, Tepito's inhabitants have waged a constant struggle for basic services that other areas of the capital enjoy, all the while maintaining a special, informal relationship with authorities who alternatively harassed them and turned a blind eye to their street commerce and ancillary economic activities. As mentioned previously, illegality and corruption have shaped the interactions between the *barrio* and the state, generating a perception of the police and judiciary as brutal, dishonest, and

---

[27] Hayner 1946; Lomnitz 1977; González de la Rocha 1994; Lewis 1969, 1961. Yet Lewis himself defined his object of study as "the culture of poverty ... a subculture of its own," resembling in the mechanisms of its perpetuation the criminal subcultures studied by criminologists (Lewis 1961: xxiv). See also Wolfgang and Ferracuti 1967. For critiques of Lewis, see Reyes Domínguez and Rosas Mantecón 1993: 49; Gutmann 1994. A valuable literary testimony is found in Ramírez Rodríguez 1972. On the empirical weaknesses of subcultural explanations in criminology, see Braithwaite 1989: 21–27; Bottomley 1986: 138; Taylor 1994: 479–80.

[28] *El Imparcial*, July 6, 1908, p. 4 and July 3, 1908, p. 1; *El Universal*, October 28, 1920, p. 4; Cossío 1937: 31; appeal by Antonio Rodríguez, 11 Apr. 1914, AGN, SJ, vol. 893, exp. 4337; AHCM, Policía en general, 3643, 1600; clipping from *El Imparcial*, August, 11, 1902, p. 1.

ineffective.[29] Second, Tepiteños have expended considerable effort to dispel their neighborhood's reputation as a place of crime, and they have taken it upon themselves to deal with the disruptive consequences of theft and violence. Their statements tend to portray violence and criminality as something in the past, even as they acknowledge that residents of certain streets or buildings in the *barrio* "were all crooks, the flower of the underworld" (Lewis 1961: 145, 397; Reyes Domínguez and Rosas Mantecón 1993: 34; Borras 1987: 33).

Two patterns stand out in these responses to the crime problem. On the one hand, neighbors in Tepito and other communities have organized. In addition to issues related to street commerce, public health, and housing that have prompted past mobilizations (particularly after the 1985 earthquakes), street security is a key concern for neighborhood organizations. Their approach, in contrast with the police's blanket treatment of the *barrio* as a den of criminals, emphasizes the need to offer treatment and alternatives to young people who commit crimes because of drug addiction.[30] On the other hand, residents of Tepito (and other areas of Mexico City) have developed approaches to violence that, at the cost of feeding their areas' bad reputations, have helped them structure conflict and contain crime through the use of shame. As noted above, concern with honor seems to better explain male-to-male violence than do theories about the poor as innately violent. While Tepiteños, particularly young men, frequently fought one another, they did so to consolidate loyalties and hierarchies that strengthened, rather than undermined, the social networks embodied in gangs. These concerns crystallized in the flourishing of boxing in the *barrio*, at the same time that men and women criticized *machismo* and gratuitous violence (Lewis 1961; Novo 1996: 1, 33). Fighting codes expressed local pride but also the power of shaming. For example, neighbors condemned petty theft, which meant that a transgressor lost social capital. Shaming was probably more effective than law enforcement at restoring the property and personal safety that crime put at risk (Lewis 1961; Braithwaite 1989, 1993; Piccato 2001a: chap. 5).

---

[29] Borras 1987: 160; Gutmann 1996: 215; Lewis 1961: 216, 350; AGN, SJ, vol. 891, exp. 3691 [1914]. And from the AJ-RS: 781323, 434207, 1074715: 1–2, 518295, 430159.

[30] Reyes Domínguez and Rosas Mantecón 1993: 118–19, 127; Vélez-Ibáñez 1983: 88; Borras 1987: 18, 40–41, 160, 165; Safa Barraza 1998: 233, 237; Gutmann 1996: 215–16; AJ-RS, 281, 596570. From the AHCM, letter to Consejo Superior de Salubridad, 13 Apr. 1901, Policía en general, 3642, 1420; and 3644, 1686.

CONCLUSIONS

This chapter has emphasized continuities in criminal practices and social perceptions of crime in Mexico City. Juvenile delinquency and gender violence have persisted at about the same levels despite considerable public attention to the former. Politically charged issues, such as drugs and police corruption, have also carried over since at least the early postrevolutionary period, thus challenging the apparent exceptionality that recent crime statistics suggest.

I have attempted to be quite explicit about the sources that combine to portray "crime" in contemporary eyes: official statistics, the *nota roja*, word of mouth, and testimonies of Mexico City inhabitants. In spite of their biases, it has been my premise that, if examined critically, these sources consistently reveal several features of crime in twentieth-century Mexico City:

- The police and judiciary have been perceived by the population as sources of insecurity and unmerited harassment rather than protection.

- Corruption among the various representatives of the state involved with crime prevention and punishment has become a factor in crime by reducing the perceived cost of transgression, offering ways to escape prosecution, and discouraging victims and their communities from denouncing crimes.

- Gendered violence against women and children remains a widespread pattern, one that has not been fully addressed in terms of its impact on other, more visible criminal practices such as juvenile delinquency.

- Urban communities have dealt with crime through informal mechanisms, such as shaming, that avoid or make a selective use of penal institutions.

These assertions can be further explored through an analysis centered on social capital, such as that presented by Pablo Parás in this volume. Concern with honor and its link to violence, for example, can be framed in terms of protecting social networks that hold great importance for survival. At the cost of being labeled an optimist (a grave accusation against a historian), I contend that such an analysis will show that civil society in Mexico City has multiple and increasingly effective ways to deal with the problem of crime, including but not limited to electoral politics. Victims, particularly women, seem increasingly willing to face prejudice and institutional inertia to fight against abuse. Urban communities have dealt with crime and other social problems through more than a century without falling into a state of anomie, and rarely have they succumbed to the temptation of rioting and other forms of unfocused collective violence.[31] Despite all of their problems, Tepiteños seem to remain strongly identified with their *barrio*. Urban communities, of course, are not impervious to change, but the evidence thus far suggests that they can adapt their organizations and relations with the state to changing criminal practices.

The recent increase in crime rates had the positive effect of placing the problem of crime at the center of public debate, thus attracting multiple actors to talk about the state's obvious failure in this area. This could lead to electoral success for supporters of "strong-handed" or "zero-tolerance" approaches against criminals. Paradoxically, these state-centered recipes often coexist with strategies that encourage managerial approaches to crime through privatization of security services and outsourcing of the design of security strategies.[32] Because the majority of Mexico City residents view the state through critical eyes and recognize the inequalities of privatized security, we can expect a skeptical attitude from civil society toward purely repressive strategies—one that is portrayed indirectly in the police station photographs. Encompassing both a state that is less powerful than it is willing to recognize and criminal practices that are inevitable parts of everyday life, a historical perspective can help civil society find more inclusive responses to crime.

References

Aguilar, José Raúl. 1941. *Los métodos criminales en Mexico, cómo defendernos.* Mexico City: Lux.

Aguirre, Eugenio, Gerardo de la Torre, and Rafael Ramírez Heredia. 1999. *Crónicas de una ciudad ganada.* Mexico: Diana.

Argüelles, Benjamín. 1935. "La delincuencia de los toxicomanos y su tratamiento en las prisiones." Paper read at the Memoria del Primer Congreso Nacional Penitenciario, Mexico City, November 24–December 3, 1932, convened by the Dirección Antialcohólica, Mexico City.

---

[31] Report to Inspección General de Policía, 18 July 1915, AHCM, Policía en general, 3645, 176; Ramírez Plancarte 1941: 427, 525; Lear 2001; Rodríguez Kuri 2000.

[32] See the chapter by Mario Arroyo in this volume. Also see Cohen 1996; *El Universal* 1923; Garland 1996.

Astorga, Luis. 1996. *El siglo de las drogas. Espasa hoy*. Mexico City: Espasa-Calpe Mexicana.

———. 2000. "Traficantes de drogas, políticos y policías en el siglo XX mexicano." In *Vicios públicos, virtudes privadas: la corrupción en México*, ed. Claudio Lomnitz. Mexico City: CIESAS.

Azaola Garrido, Elena. 1990. *La institución correccional en México: una mirada extraviada*. Mexico City: Siglo Veintiuno.

———. 1993. *Los niños de la correccional: fragmentos de vida*. Mexico City: CIESAS.

———. 1996. *El delito de ser mujer. Hombres y mujeres homicidas en la ciudad de México: historias de vida*. Mexico City: CIESAS/Plaza y Valdés.

Barrera Bassols, Jacinto. 1997. *El caso Villavicencio: violencia y poder en el porfiriato*. Mexico City: Alfaguara.

Beltrán, Ira, and Pablo Piccato. 2003. *Crimen en el siglo XX: fragmentos de análisis sobre la evidencia cuantitativa*. At http://www.columbia.edu/~pp143/fragme~1.

Bliss, Katherine Elaine. 2001. *Compromised Positions: Prostitution, Public Health, and Gender Politics in Revolutionary Mexico City*. University Park: Pennsylvania State University Press.

Borras, Leopoldo. 1987. *A mano armada: la delincuencia en la ciudad de México*. Mexico City: Universidad Nacional Autónoma de México.

Bottomley, Keith A. 1986. *Crime and Punishment: Interpreting the Data*. Philadelphia, Penn.: Open University Press.

Bourdieu, Pierre. 2000. *La dominación masculina*. Trans. J. Jordá. Barcelona: Anagrama.

Braithwaite, John. 1989. *Crime, Shame and Reintegration*. New York: Cambridge University Press.

———. 1993. "Shame and Modernity," *British Journal of Criminology* 33, no. 1: 1–18.

Brownmiller, Susan. 1976. *Against Our Will: Men, Women and Rape*. New York: Bantam.

Buñuel, Luis. 1950. *Los olvidados*, ed. Luis Alcoriza. Mexico City.

Ceniceros, José Ángel, and Luis Garrido. 1936. *La delincuencia infantil en México*. Mexico City: Botas.

CNDH (Comisión Nacional de Derechos Humanos). 1997. *Procuración de justicia y derechos humanos: Análisis de recomendaciones de la Comisión Nacional de Derechos Humanos*. Mexico City: CNDH.

Código Penal para el Distrito y Territorios Federales. 1929. Mexico City: Talleres Gráficos de la Nación.

Código Penal para el Distrito y Territorios Federales y para toda la República en Materia de Fuero Federal [1931]. 1938. Mexico City: Botas.

Cohen, Stanley. 1996. "Crime and Politics: Spot the Difference," *British Journal of Sociology* 47, no. 1: 1–21.

Cossío, José Lorenzo. 1937. "Algunas noticias sobre las colonias de esta capital," *Boletín de la Sociedad Mexicana de Geografía y Estadística* 47, no. 1: 5–41.

de la Peña, Guillermo. 2000. "Corrupción e informalidad." In *Vicios públicos, virtudes privadas: la corrupción en México,* ed. Claudio Lomnitz. Mexico City: CIESAS.

del Castillo, Alberto. 1997. "Prensa, poder y criminalidad a finales del siglo XIX en la ciudad de México." In *Hábitos, normas y escándalo: prensa, criminalidad y drogas durante el porfiriato tardío,* ed. R. Pérez Montfort. Mexico City: CIESAS/Plaza y Valdés.

Eckstein, Susan. 1972. "The Poverty of Revolution: A Study of Social, Economic and Political Inequality in a Center City Area, a Squatter Settlement and a Low-Cost Housing Project in Mexico City." PhD dissertation, Columbia University.

El Universal. 1923. "Primer Congreso Criminológico y Penitenciaro Mexicano," October 12.

Francois, Marie Eileen. 1998. "When Pawnshops Talk: Popular Credit and Material Culture in Mexico City, 1775–1916." PhD dissertation, University of Arizona.

Gamboa, Federico. 1922. *La llaga.* Mexico City: Eusebio Gómez de la Puente.

Garland, David. 1996. "The Limits of the Sovereign State: Strategies of Crime Control in Contemporary Society," *British Journal of Criminology* 36, no. 4: 445–71.

González de la Rocha, Mercedes. 1994. *The Resources of Poverty: Women and Survival in a Mexican City.* Cambridge: Blackwell.

González González, Jorge. 1983. *Lo negro del Negro Durazo.* Mexico City: Posada.

González Rodríguez, Sergio. 1990. "Prólogo." In *Crimen, terror y páginas: antología,* ed. P. Ortega Ramírez. Mexico: El Nacional.

Guerrero, Julio. 1901. *La génesis del crimen en México; estudio de psiquiatría social.* Paris: Vda. de Ch. Bouret.

Gutmann, Matthew C. 1994. "Los hijos de Lewis: la sensibilidad antropológica y el caso de los pobres machos," *Alteridades* 4, no. 7: 9–19.

———. 1996. *The Meanings of Macho: Being a Man in Mexico City.* Berkeley: University of California Press.

Guy, Donna. 1991. *Sex and Danger in Buenos Aires: Prostitution, Family, and Nation in Argentina.* Lincoln: University of Nebraska Press.

Hayner, Norman S. 1946. "Criminogenic Zones in Mexico City," *American Sociological Review* 11, no. 4: 428–38.

Katz, Friedrich. 2000. "La corrupción y la Revolución Mexicana." In *Vicios públicos, virtudes privadas: la corrupción en México,* ed. Claudio Lomnitz. Mexico City: CIESAS.

La Jornada. 2000. "Durazo, de cruel jefe policiaco a benefactor de alcohólicos," August 6. At http://www.jornada.unam.mx/2000/ago00/000806/010n1gen.html.

Lear, John. 2001. *Workers, Neighbors, and Citizens: The Revolution in Mexico City.* Lincoln: University of Nebraska Press.

Lewis, Oscar. 1961. *The Children of Sánchez: Autobiography of a Mexican Family.* New York: Random House.

———. 1969. *Antropología de la pobreza: cinco familias.* Mexico City: Fondo de Cultura Económica.

Lomnitz, Larissa. 1977. *Networks and Marginality: Life in a Mexican Shantytown.* New York: Academic Press.

Lovera, Sara. 1990. *Policías violadores, violadores policías.* Mexico City: Majo.

Macedo, Miguel. 1897. *La criminalidad en México: medios de combatirla.* Mexico City: Secretaría de Fomento.

Macías González, Víctor Manuel. 1999. "El caso de una beldad asesina: la construcción narrativa, los concursos de belleza y el mito nacional posrevolucionario (1921–1931)," *Historia y Grafía* 13: 113–54.

Márquez, Ramón. 1980. "Yoko: historia de un impune crimen policial." In *A ustedes les consta: antología de la crónica en México,* ed. Carlos Monsiváis. Mexico City: ERA.

Martínez de Castro, Antonio. 1891. *Código penal para el Distrito Federal y Territorio de la Baja-California sobre delitos del fuero común y para toda la República Mexicana sobre delitos contra la Federación [1871].* Veracruz and Puebla: La Ilustración.

Mellado, Guillermo. 1959. *Belén por dentro y por fuera.* Mexico City: Cuadernos Criminalia.

Mérigo, Juan. 1959. *La banda del automóvil gris y yo!* Mexico City: n.p.

Meyer, Jean. 1977. *Historia de la Revolución Mexicana. Período 1924–1928.* Vol. 11, *Estado y sociedad con Calles.* Mexico City: El Colegio de México.

Monsiváis, Carlos. 1980. *A ustedes les consta: antología de la crónica en México.* Mexico City: ERA.

Mraz, John. 2001. "Today, Tomorrow and Always: The Golden Age of Illustrated Magazines in Mexico, 1937–1960." In *Fragments of a Golden Age: The Politics of Culture in Mexico since 1940,* ed. G.M. Joseph, A. Rubenstein, and E. Zolov. Durham, N.C.: Duke University Press.

———. 2003. *Nacho López, Mexican Photographer. Visible Evidence,* vol. 14. Minneapolis: University of Minnesota Press.

Muñoz Martínez, Aurora. 1995. "Seguridad pública y derechos humanos de los capitalinos." In *Los derechos humanos en México durante la transición sexenal,* ed. D. Fernández. Mexico City: Universidad Iberoamericana/Centro de Derechos Humanos "Miguel Agustín Pro Juárez."

Nelligan, Mauricio. 1988. *Mujeres que matan: prostitución y homicidio femenil en México.* Mexico City: Edamex.

New York Times. 2003. "Mexico: Officers Held In School Drug Sales," April 12.

Novo, Salvador. 1996. *Viajes y ensayos: letras mexicanas.* Mexico City: Fondo de Cultura Económica.

Ortega Ramírez, Patricia. 1990. *Crimen, terror y páginas: antología.* Mexico City: El Nacional.

Penyak, Lee Michael. 1993. "Criminal Sexuality in Central Mexico, 1750–1850." PhD dissertation, University of Connecticut.

Peón del Valle, J. 1935. "La lucha contra la toxicomanía en México." Paper read at the Memoria del Primer Congreso Nacional Penitenciario, Mexico City, November 24–December 3, 1932, convened by the Dirección Antialcohólica, Mexico City.

Pérez Montfort, Ricardo. 1997. "El veneno 'faradisíaco' o el olor a tortilla tostada: fragmentos de historia de las 'drogas' en México, 1870–1920." In *Habitos, normas y escándalo: prensa, criminalidad y drogas durante el porfiriato tardío*, ed. R. Pérez Montfort. Mexico City: CIESAS/Plaza y Valdés.

———. 2000. "De vicios populares, corruptelas, y toxicomanías." In *Juntos y medio revueltos*, ed. Ricardo Pérez Montfort. Mexico City: Sones-Unios.

Piccato, Pablo. 2001a. *City of Suspects: Crime in Mexico City, 1900–1931*. Durham, N.C.: Duke University Press.

———. 2001b. "El Chalequero, or 'the Mexican Jack the Ripper': The Meanings of Sexual Violence in Turn-of-the-Century Mexico City," *Hispanic American Historical Review* 81, nos. 3-4: 623–51.

Quiroz Cuarón, Alfonso. 1958. *La criminalidad en la República Mexicana y el costo social del homicidio, derecho penal contemporáneo*. Mexico City: Universidad Nacional Autónoma de México.

Quiroz Cuarón, Alfonso, José Gómez Robleda, and Benjamín Argüelles. 1939. *Tendencia y ritmo de la criminalidad en México, D.F.* Mexico City: Instituto de Investigaciones Estadísticas.

Quiroz Cuarón, Alfonso, and Raúl Quiroz Cuarón. 1970. *El costo social del delito en México: symposium sobre el costo social del crimen y la defensa social contra el mismo*. Mexico City: Botas.

Ramírez Plancarte, Francisco. 1941. *La ciudad de México durante la revolución constitucionalista*. Mexico City: Botas.

Ramírez Rodríguez, Armando. 1972. *Chin-chin el teporocho*. 8th ed. Mexico: Novaro.

Reyes Domínguez, Guadalupe, and Ana Rosas Mantecón. 1993. *Los usos de la identidad barrial: una mirada antropológica a la lucha por la vivienda. Tepito 1970–1984*. Mexico City: Universidad Autónoma Metropolitana.

Rodríguez Kuri, Ariel. 2000. "Desabasto, hambre y respuesta política, 1915." In *Instituciones y ciudad: ocho estudios históricos sobre la ciudad de México*, ed. C. Illades and Ariel Rodríguez K. Mexico City: FP-Sones-Unios.

Roumagnac, Carlos. 1904. *Los criminales en México. Ensayo de psicología criminal. Seguido de dos casos de hermafrodismo observado por los señores doctores Ricardo Egea... Ignacio Ocampo*. Mexico City: n.p.

———. 1910. *Matadores de mujeres*. Part 2 of *Crímenes sexuales y pasionales*. Mexico City: Ch. Bouret.

———. 1912. *Los criminales en México. Ensayo de psicología criminal. Seguido de dos casos de hermafrodismo observado por los señores doctores Ricardo Egea … Ignacio Ocampo.* 2d ed. Mexico City: El Fénix.

———. 1923. *Elementos de policía científica: obra de texto para la Escuela Científica de Policía de México.* Mexico City: Botas.

———. 1933. "Mis recuerdos de Belém," *El Nacional,* September 24.

Rubenstein, Anne. 1998. *Bad Language, Naked Ladies, and Other Threats to the Nation: A Political History of Comic Books in Mexico.* Durham, N.C.: Duke University Press.

Ruiz Harrell, Rafael. 1998. *Criminalidad y mal gobierno.* Mexico City: Sansores y Aljure.

Safa Barraza, Patricia. 1998. *Vecinos y vecindarios en la ciudad de México: un estudio sobre la construcción de las identidades vecinales en Coyoacán, D.F.* Mexico City: CIESAS.

Selby, Henry A., Arthur D. Murphy, and Stephen A. Lorenzen. 1990. *The Mexican Urban Household: Organizing for Self-Defense.* Austin: University of Texas Press.

Smith, Eaton. 1903. *Flying Visits to the City of Mexico and the Pacific Coast.* Liverpool: Henry Young and Sons.

Sodi, Carlos Franco. 1951. *Don Juan Delincuente y otros ensayos.* Mexico City: Botas.

Stern, Steve. 1995. *The Secret History of Gender: Women, Men, and Power in Late Colonial Mexico.* Chapel Hill: University of North Carolina Press.

Taracena, Alfonso. 1960. *La verdadera revolución mexicana.* Mexico City: Jus.

Taylor, Ian. 1994. "The Political Economy of Crime." In *The Oxford Handbook of Criminology,* ed. M. Maguire, R. Morgan, and R. Reiner. New York: Clarendon.

Téllez Vargas, Eduardo, and José Ramón Garmabella. 1982. *¡Reportero de policía! El Güero Téllez.* Mexico City: Océano.

Tutino, John. 1998. "El desarrollo liberal, el patriarcado y la involución de la violencia social en el México Porfirista: el crimen y la muerte infantil en el altiplano central." In *Don Porfirio presidente … nunca omnipotente: hallazgos, reflexiones y debates, 1876–1911,* ed. R. Falcón and R. Buve. Mexico City: Universidad Iberoamericana.

Vélez-Ibáñez, Carlos G. 1983. *Rituals of Marginality: Politics, Process, and Culture Change in Urban Central Mexico, 1969–1974.* Berkeley: University of California Press.

Wolfgang, Marvin E., and Franco Ferracuti. 1967. *The Subculture of Violence.* London: Tavistock.

CHAPTER 4

The Mexican Prison System

ELENA AZAOLA AND MARCELO BERGMAN

This chapter describes the most important characteristics of the Mexican prison system, and it analyzes the role played by that system within the set of institutions dealing with crime control in Mexico. We particularly want to understand which of the various functions assigned to the prison system are performed satisfactorily and which are brushed aside or not addressed at all. The chapter also touches on the most relevant changes in criminal activity that have occurred in Mexico in the past decade and the actions that the security and justice institutions are carrying out to contain it, as well as the principal problems that Mexico's prison institutions face. For this task, we have compiled a series of both primary and secondary data from a variety of sources. We make use of statistical information from official sources,[1] and we also present some of the results and the main conclusions from a survey we took of 1,615 inmates in prisons in three Mexican states.[2] One of the purposes of that survey was to glean what the prison population thinks about the dissuasive abilities of the security forces as well as about the performance of Mexico's law enforcement and prosecutorial agencies.

Translation by Patricia Rosas.

[1] Throughout this chapter, when no other source is cited, the information comes from Mexico's Public Security Ministry (Secretaría de Seguridad Pública, or SSP).

[2] The survey was conducted during the first half of 2002 using random sampling procedures. It included 1,615 inmates in 15 prisons: 1,010 in the Federal District, 512 in México State, and 93 in Morelos State. Taken together, the prison population in these states is, in round numbers, 35,000 inmates, or one-fifth of Mexico's entire inmate population of 177,000. For the complete survey results, see Bergman et al. 2003.

THE PRISONS

Mexico has 447 prisons: 5 under federal jurisdiction, 330 run by the states, 103 run by municipalities, and 9 under the jurisdiction of the Federal District. The prison populations vary significantly from place to place. Prisons in the Federal District are the most populous, with two of its facilities holding a little more than 8,000 prisoners. Next are the state facilities, which, in most cases, have a population of between 500 and 5,000, with the average being about 1,000 inmates. The federal facilities have approximately 500 inmates each, and the municipal ones have even lower populations. At the federal level, there are three maximum security prisons (in México State, Jalisco, and Tamaulipas), one minimum security prison, and a prison for the mentally infirm.

The prison population is 96 percent men and 4 percent women, a ratio that has held constant in recent decades and is similar to those found in countries at a level of development similar to Mexico (Azaola 1998). Of the total prison population, 57 percent have been sentenced and 43 percent are awaiting sentencing, a ratio that has been more or less constant since 1994.

In terms of jurisdiction, 26 percent of inmates nationwide are accused of federal jurisdiction (*fuero federal*) crimes and 74 percent are accused of local jurisdiction (*fuero común*) offenses, another ratio that has not changed appreciably in the past decade. It is worth noting, however, that because of drug trafficking, the states along Mexico's northern border (Baja California, Sonora, Chihuahua, and Tamaulipas) have a significantly higher proportion of people imprisoned for federal jurisdiction crimes in comparison to the rest of the nation (table 4.1). The data we gathered in our survey in three states reveal a composition in terms of types of crime that is similar to that in other states, with the exception of those in northern Mexico, where a higher percentage of crime is drug-related (table 4.2).

Increase in the Prison Population

Since the mid-1990s, Mexico's prison population has increased at an unprecedented rate, doubling in a little over ten years (see table 4.3). In fact, Mexico now has 175 prisoners for every 100,000 inhabitants, compared to only 104 per 100,000 just ten years ago (see figure 4.1). The prison population increased at an average annual rate of 9 percent in the 1990s, with the most pronounced growth visible after 1996 (see figure 4.2). Only in 2002 did the growth rate appear to be declining, possibly because of prison overpopulation.

Table 4.1. Prison Population by Jurisdiction, 2001

State	Prison Population	Local Jurisdiction	Federal Jurisdiction (%)
Federal District	22,371	18,878	3,493 (16%)
Baja California	11,855	7,235	4,620 (39%)
Sonora	11,409	6,536	4,873 (43%)
México State	10,807	9,705	1,102 (10%)
Veracruz	9,050	7,929	1,121 (12%)
Tamaulipas	8,741	4,797	3,944 (45%)
Michoacán	8,083	6,176	1,907 (24%)
Jalisco	7,153	5,778	1,375 (19%)
Chihuahua	6,714	3,747	2,967 (44%)
Sinaloa	6,373	3,946	2,427 (38%)
Tlaxcala	603	n.d.	n.d.
Campeche	1,063	n.d.	n.d.
Aguascalientes	1,068	n.d.	n.d.
Baja California Sur	1,069	n.d.	n.d.

Source: Órgano Administrativo Descentralizado Prevención y Readaptación Social, Secretaría de Seguridad Pública, November 2001.
n.d. = no data.

Mexican prisons today are overflowing, with an average excess population of 35 percent. However, in certain states the prison population exceeds available capacity by more than 100 percent. According to the National Human Rights Commission (CNDH), the prisons in Baja California, Nayarit, Chiapas, Sonora, Tamaulipas, Oaxaca, Puebla, and the Federal District are in particularly difficult situations because of overpopulation.

Factors behind the Increased Prison Population

Notably, the factors underlying the 100 percent increase in the prison population that occurred between 1992 and 2003 include increased crime rates, changes to the criminal code that resulted in tougher sentences, and administrative measures that prolong prison stays.[3] We will analyze each briefly.

---

[3] In some places the increase has been even greater. In the Federal District, for example, the prison population tripled between 1993 and 2002, from 7,800 inmates to 23,000 (Tenorio 2002a).

Table 4.2. Inmate Population by Crime Type (percentages)

State	Property Crimes	Violent Crimes	Drug Trafficking	Other[a]	Total
Federal District	33%	50%	6%	11%	100%
México State	21%	64%	5%	10%	100%
Morelos	16%	46%	22%	16%	100%
Percent of total	26%	54%	8%	12%	100%

Source: Prison Survey, CIDE, 2002.
[a] Includes sex crimes, white-collar crime, and others.

Table 4.3. Prison Population in Mexico, 1992–2003

	Population (1000s)
1992	87.7
1993	91.6
1994	92.7
1995	93.5
1996	101.2
1997	109.9
1998	124.7
1999	135.3
2000	155.1
2001	165.6
2002	176.4
2003[a]	177.5

Sources: Secretaría de Gobernación 1992–2000; Secretaría de Seguridad Pública 2001–2003.
[a] Until April 2003.

Figure 4.1. Inmate Population in Mexico

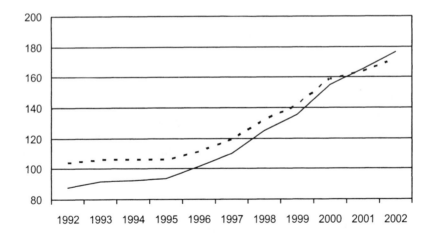

Source: SSP 2003.

Figure 4.2. Annual Rate of Increase in Mexico's Prison Population

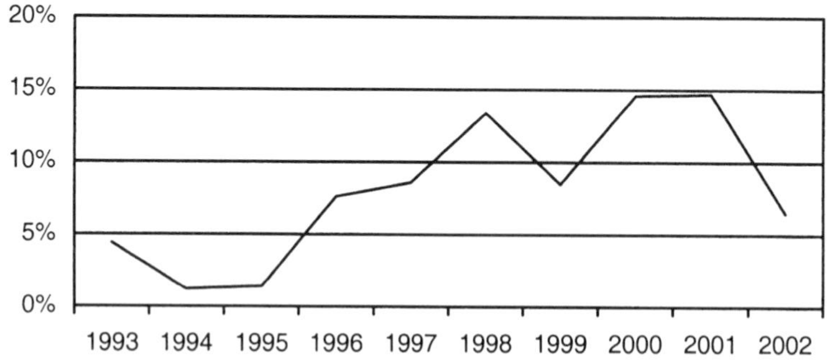

Source: SSP 2003.

Rising Crime Rates

The number of reported crimes in Mexico increased from 809,000 in 1991 to 1,517,000 in 2001, an increase of 88 percent in only ten years. The maximum was reached in 1997, with 16.18 crimes reported per 100,000 inhabitants. That figure declined to 14.26 in 2000 but grew again, to 15.1, in 2002. The states with the highest crime rates are Baja California, the Federal District, and Quintana Roo. It is worth noting that this increase in the number of reported crimes has taken place despite victimization surveys that all show that the percentage of unreported crimes has also increased year after year since 1995. Indeed, according to these surveys, between 70 and 80 percent of the crimes during that time went unreported.[4] It is also worth considering that only 7 percent of reported crimes go to trial, meaning that 93 percent go unpunished (SSP 2003; Zepeda 2002).

Tougher Sentences

Another factor contributing to the increase in the prison population is the 1994 Criminal Code reform, which reclassified a number of crimes as seri-

---

[4] We refer to surveys by the newspaper *Reforma*, the magazine *Este País*, the Instituto Ciudadano de Estudios sobre la Inseguridad research center, and the ACNielsen polling company.

ous, with the result that increased sentences were assigned to them. For a variety of crimes, the possibility of parole was removed, so that certain offenders now serve longer sentences. This is the case with the so-called crimes against health (*delitos contra la salud*) or drug-trafficking crimes, for which the law no longer grants any reduction in the sentence decreed by the judge.

Administrative Measures

One should also consider that the length of time an inmate stays in prison is ultimately decided not by the judge but by the technical personnel in the prison facilities, who have broad power to grant or deny early release or parole. This results in actual sentences that are not necessarily proportional to the seriousness of the crime, as well as the granting of paroles in an arbitrary or untimely manner, especially because prison personnel must review far more case files than they can conceivably handle. For example, in the Federal District, each official empowered to grant parole is responsible for processing between 400 and 2,000 case files, which explains why paroles are not granted in a timely manner.

There are no studies showing which of these (or other) factors have had the greatest impact on the growth of the prison population. Nevertheless, some data suggest that what we are seeing may be not so much an increase in the flow of prisoners into the institutions as an increase in the "stockpile" of prisoners. That is, initial evidence points to an increase in the population due to the extension of sentences rather than to the number of people entering prison. Regarding this, an examination of court sentencing statistics for 1998, 1990, and 2000 by type of crime shows that the prison population grew by more than 20 percent even though the total number of sentences handed down increased by only 1.8 percent (see table 4.4).[5] Although the sentences for violent and drug-related crimes showed a significant increase (9 percent), the data also show that for most crimes, the number of sentences did not increase in step with the increase in reported crimes and the increase in the prison population. The court statistics also show that between 1998 and 2000 the number of sentences for which an imprisonment of three or more years was decreed increased, whereas those sentences for fewer than three years declined (INEGI 2003). Even though a

---

[5] Shortly after 1998, judicial data became available at this minimal level of disaggregation.

more analytical study remains to be done, the preceding information shows that the increase in criminal activity is not reflected in the number of arrests nor in the number of sentences handed down. However, the harsher penalties in the justice system could indirectly be the result of an increase in criminality.

Table 4.4. Number of Sentences Passed by Type of Crime, 1998–2000

Type of Crime	1998	1999	2000	Total
Drug-related crime	7,684	7,487	8,719	23,890
Use of firearms	n.a.	1,687	1,879	3,566
Homicide	5,006	4,988	4,938	14,932
Bodily harm	20,918	22,316	22,809	66,043
Rape	2,513	2,596	2,589	7,698
Sexual abuse	438	564	762	1,764
Robbery	41,991	43,463	41,133	126,587
Fraud	1,791	1,618	1,592	5,001
Property damage	6,074	5,979	5,859	11,838
Usurpation and ouster	2,027	1,509	1,628	5,164
Burglary	1,823	1,775	1,837	5,435
Threats	910	951	937	2,798
Use of illegal weapons	11,267	10,538	8,404	30,209
Other	18,278	19,233	19,496	57,007
Total	120,720	124,704	122,582	368,006

Source: Arango 2004.
n.a. = not available.

A COMPARATIVE PERSPECTIVE

Criminal activity in general, and the prison population in particular, have been rising throughout Latin America in recent years. The increase in crime is particularly notorious in large urban centers (Wacquant 2000). For example, between 1992 and 1999 the Latin American prison population grew 56.4 percent (see table 4.5), with the only exception being Venezuela, which had massive parole and reprieve programs during that time (Ungar 2003). Although the growth in Mexico's prison population for that period was close to the average, Mexico still has one of the highest rates of incarceration (per 100,000 inhabitants) of any Latin American country. Among the countries at a similar development level, only Chile and Colombia surpass Mexico's rate.

Viewed from another angle, Mexico also does not surpass the Latin American average for prison overpopulation or the deplorable level of institutional services (see table 4.6). Below, we will analyze in detail these topics for the case of Mexico, but here we will only note that services such as the minimum rights guaranteed to inmates are systematically violated, and that there is no social or institutional incentive to remedy that state of affairs. In summary, although the situation in the prisons and the increase in criminal activity have become serious problems, Mexico still falls within the average range for the Latin American region, where institutional ineffectiveness and rising crime clearly worsened throughout the 1990s.

SOME FEATURES OF THE CRIME RATE

As we discuss below, the distribution of inmates based on crime committed relates to the law enforcement system's capacity to capture suspects and the judicial system's capacity to punish offenders. That is, the composition of the prison population is not simply a function of the distribution of crimes actually committed multiplied by the duration of the sentences handed down. Rather, it depends on the ability of justice system institutions to capture and sentence offenders. Inmates serving time for violent crimes constitute the largest group. This is not only because their sentences are longer; it also reflects the increase in that type of crime during recent years.

Violent robbery (a category in which the victim is intimidated or assaulted, similar to armed robbery in the United States) is the crime that has increased most during the past decade or so. For example, whereas in 1990 one violent robbery occurred for every two that were not violent, by 1997, 55 percent of the robberies were violent. In 1994 only 28 percent of the assaults in Mexico City were perpetrated with weapons, and only one in ten robbery victims was injured. By 1999 those figures had risen to 70 percent and one in three (Ruiz Harrell 1998 and various articles in *Reforma* in 2000). In our 2002 survey, 57 percent of those charged with violent robbery admitted having used a weapon, as did 56 percent of those charged with crimes against people. In summary, the increase in the number of inmates is a reflection of the imposition of harsher sentences and higher violent-crime rates.

Table 4.5. Latin American Prison Populations, 1992, 1996, 1999

Country	Total Prison Population			Percent Increase, 1992–1999	Inmates (per 100,000 inhabitants)
	1992	1996	1999		
Argentina	21,016	34,228	38,604	84	107
Bolivia	n.a.	6,235 (1997)	8,315	33	102
Brazil	114,377	148,760	194,074	70	113
Chile	20,989	23,567	30,852	47	205
Colombia	33,491	46,747	57,068	70	153
Costa Rica	3,346	4,722	8,526	155	229
Dominican Republic	10,800	10,387	14,188	31	170
Ecuador	7,998	10,957	8,520	7	69
El Salvador	5,348	7,996	6,868	28	109
Guatemala	n.a	6,387	8,169	28	69
Honduras	5,717	9,480	10,869	90	172
Mexico	87,723	101,200	139,707	59	143
Panama	4,428	7,322	8,517	92	303
Paraguay	n.a.	3,427	4,088	19	75
Peru	17,350	23,174	27,452	58	107
Uruguay	3,037	3,268	4,012	32	123
Venezuela	n.a.	22,791	14,196	-38	60

Source: Prepared by the authors, based on Ungar 2003.

n.a. = not available.

Table 4.6. Latin American Prisons: Overpopulation, Inmates Awaiting Sentencing, and Cost per Inmate[a]

Country	Overpopulation (%)	Percent Awaiting Sentencing	Cost per Inmate (US$)
Argentina[b]	140 (average)	70 (average)	Varies by province
Bolivia	162	70	$26/inmate/month
Brazil	181 (average)	45	Varies by state
Chile	150	51	n.a.
Colombia	137	43	$1.44 (food only)
Costa Rica	167	moderate numbers	n.a.
Cuba	175 (approx.)	moderate numbers	n.a.
Dominican Republic	215	74	n.a.
Ecuador	143	severe backlog	n.a.
El Salvador	135	75+	n.a.
Guatemala	101	62	n.a.
Honduras	109	90	$0.40 (food & health)
Mexico	133 (average)	43	Varies by state
Nicaragua	113	moderate numbers	$0.58 (food only)
Panama	126	severe backlog	n.a.
Paraguay	212	80–90	n.a.
Peru	141	65+	$0.75 (food only)
Uruguay	125	70+	n.a.
Venezuela	160	70+	$1.86 (total cost)[c]

Sources: Prepared by the authors based on Ungar 2003, Observatoire international des prisons, 1995, Ministerio de Justicia y Derechos Humanos de Bolivia, Instituto Nacional Penitenciario de Colombia, and Reuters, "Peru Admits Jails Packed with Unsentenced Inmates," April 24, 1996. (The Vice Minister for Justice in Peru noted that the proportion of inmates awaiting sentencing was almost 90 percent.)

[a] Although Guatemala's overall prison population is approximately the same as its installed capacity, some prisons are overpopulated by up to 170 percent. In Brazil, almost 200,000 inmates are housed in a system designed for only 145,000 (*Economist*, February 24, 2001, p. 37).

[b] In federated countries like Argentina, with separate prison systems for each province, there can be marked differences between provinces.

[c] *El Universal*, March 21, 1995.

Reported crimes. In a situation of optimal equilibrium when controlling for the severity of the sentence, prisons should house a proportion of inmates whose crimes reflect the distribution of crimes actually committed in society. One could measure criminal activity by reported crimes or by the results of victimization surveys. Because there are no standardized victimization surveys in Mexico, crime reports have to be used to measure criminal activity; however, the public's confidence in the justice institutions and their perceived effectiveness influence this variable. That is, when the public perceives the institutions to be effective and trusts them, crime reports will tend to increase; when the reverse is true, those reports will decline, without that decline implying a reduction in criminal activity. The latter appears to have been the situation in Mexico during the last decade (Azaola 2002).

According to official sources, crime peaked in 1997, after which it began to decline somewhat. The decline has been more noticeable in some crime categories than in others. The number of reported robberies, for example, declined by 10 percent between 1997 and 2001, while reports of car theft rose 2 percent. Something similar can be seen regarding violent crimes: homicide declined 11 percent, but bodily harm and rape both increased 12 percent. Moreover, whereas other crime categories declined, criminal damage, threats, fraud, and embezzlement have increased. Compared to overall cases reported in 1997, cases in 2001 declined by only 4 percent. In 1998, of all crimes reported, robberies accounted for 43 percent; bodily harm, 18 percent; criminal damage, 10 percent; drug-related crimes, 5 percent; threats and fraud, each 4 percent; and homicide, 3 percent. Regarding robberies, the average was 583 per 100,000 inhabitants. According to another classification, the breakdown in 2001 was as follows: 37.2 percent robbery, 17.9 percent bodily harm, 9.8 percent criminal damage, and 35.1 percent for all other crimes (SSP 2003). As can be seen, crimes reported to the authorities evince a strong bias in that the most prevalent are those that are minor and receive short sentences. Thus, at least at first glance, the prison population does not closely reflect the distribution of criminal activity that actually occurs.

Cities. The cities with the highest crime rates in Mexico in 1998 were Tijuana, with 3,429 crimes per 100,000 inhabitants; metropolitan Mexico City with 2,851; Ciudad Juárez with 2,803; and Guadalajara with 2,779. In these cities, robbery represents between 45 and 61 percent of all crimes committed.

Drug-related crimes. Our survey indicated that 8 percent of inmates were serving a sentence for a drug-related crime, primarily for selling drugs. In

56 percent of the cases, the inmate was charged with selling marijuana, and in 34 percent, cocaine. It is important to note that 10 percent of those charged with selling prohibited substances indicated that they had acted in complicity with the authorities, principally the police. According to information that the inmates provided, the average value of the drugs sold was 1,168 pesos (approximately US$100). Thus, for the vast majority, the gain realized from the illegal transaction was very low. Indeed, only in 10 percent of the cases did it exceed 3,900 pesos (approximately US$400). This means that most of these inmates are serving a sentence for having sold a very small quantity of illegal drugs. What we find in abundance in the prisons, then, are not major drug traffickers but small-time pushers or, possibly, consumers who were arrested with small quantities that barely exceeded the amount tolerated for personal consumption.

Robbery. According to our survey data, in the prisons studied, almost 25 percent of those serving a sentence for robbery had stolen less than 1,000 pesos, and almost half had stolen less than 6,000 pesos. Notably, more than 70 percent of the inmates serving time for this type of crime claimed that they could have avoided going to prison had they had the financial resources to bribe the authorities at the time of arrest. We can infer that those who commit robberies on a grander scale, and thus have more money, effectively manage to avoid punishment. Thus the justice system concentrates primarily on punishing property crimes perpetrated by small-time criminals. Indeed, according to the survey, only 5 percent of those serving time for property crimes had stolen amounts over 75,000 pesos. This reinforces the perception that the institutions charged with investigating, prosecuting, and punishing crime clearly fail to punish that segment of criminals who perpetrate major crimes.

The foregoing allows us to conclude that the prisons in our study do not house the most dangerous criminals, but rather those whose arrest posed less difficulty for the authorities. The differential access to resources, such as defense attorneys, and the possibility of using bribery to avoid being brought to justice give rise to a great many poor people being incarcerated while a large number of professional criminals remains outside prison walls.

Violent death. Homicide has always been among the top ten causes of death in Mexico. Notably, although the national homicide rate fell from 78 per 100,000 inhabitants in 1930 to 15 per 100,000 inhabitants in 2002, the most pronounced drop occurred between 1930 and 1970. From 1970 to 2000, the rate remained more or less stable. Mexico ranks among the top ten countries worldwide in violent death rates. Among the others are Colombia, with a rate of 54 per 100,000 inhabitants, El Salvador with 60, and Brazil with 20. In contrast, the rate is only 1.7 per 100,000 inhabitants in Chile, 1.5 in Japan, and 0.7 in Spain. The United States, after reaching a rate of 9.5 in 1990, has managed to reduce its rate to 5.8 per 100,000. The average death-by-homicide rate worldwide is 8.8 per 100,000, but Mexico, with 15.2 murders per 100,000 inhabitants, has nearly double that rate (WHO 2002). In the three Mexican states surveyed, 10 percent of the inmates were serving time for voluntary manslaughter (*homicidio doloso*) and 5 percent for involuntary manslaughter (*homicidio culposo*). However, we must remember that those serving time for these crimes are overrepresented in the sample because, due to the gravity of the offense, their sentences are longer than those of inmates serving time for other crimes.

Kidnapping. In 2001 the public prosecutors' offices reported 345 kidnapping cases nationwide, or an average of almost one per day. However, Coparmex, a business association, notes that an additional 297 cases were not reported to the authorities. Thus there were actually 642 cases of kidnapping that year, without counting the so-called express kidnappings, which last only a few hours. In the surveyed states, 4 percent of the inmates are serving sentences for kidnapping.

MAIN PROBLEMS WITH THE PRISONS

Mexico's prisons exhibit marked organizational shortcomings and serious functional deficiencies. In 2001 Alejandro Gertz Manero, head of Mexico's Public Security Ministry (SSP), recounted some of the main problems that the Mexican prison system faces. He acknowledged the existence of criminal networks and kinship networks among administrative personnel, guards, and inmates, which has led to high levels of corruption in the prisons. He also mentioned the sale of favors to inmates or their families by prison staff, and he added, "the structures for social rehabilitation are perhaps one of the gravest focal points for corruption that exist in the country." The prison system has the infrastructure to build a data network, but it uses less than 10 percent of the existing capacity, resulting in a serious absence of suitable and current technical information. For example, there is no databank containing the fingerprints of those serving time for local jurisdiction crimes, nor is there verifiable information available on prisoners, either those who are undergoing trial or those who have already been sentenced (Gertz Manero 2001).

According to the SSP, between 1998 and 2002 more than US$5 million were invested in the construction of sixty-two new prisons. However, thirty-two of them were never finished because of a shortfall of an additional $1.5 million. The SSP also indicated that, during this same period, more than US$40 million was invested in training, arms, equipment, transportation, and infrastructure in the security and justice sectors, yet crime rates keep rising. The 2001–2006 National Public Security Program (PNSP) also acknowledges that "the country's jails are full of petty criminals and people who could not pay for an effective defense." Of the more than 165,000 people who were incarcerated in 2001, it is estimated that 7,000, or only 4 percent, were highly dangerous.

According to the PNSP,

> The absence of financial resources and qualified personnel results in a shortage of reliable security systems and in inefficiency in the performance of custodial duties, since these are not performed according to the law and regulations currently in force. This fosters high levels of corruption in all its forms and modalities: trafficking in influence; backlogs in processing files; the introduction, sale, and consumption of drugs; extortion; prostitution; impunity; violence; and overcrowding (SSP 2003).

For its part, and only as an example, during 2002 the Human Rights Commission of the Federal District (CDHDF) reported that inmates in the city's prisons filed 1,600 complaints concerning the violation of various rights (see also United Nations 2003).

Our survey made it possible to document some of the problems mentioned above, and to do a more precise and detailed analysis about inmates' living conditions in Mexico's prisons. Some of the results are very telling. In terms of overcrowding, in some of the prisons in the study we found as many as ten inmates sleeping in cells designed to house only three, and as many as twenty sleeping in cells designed for five. In relation to the provision of basic necessities, 53 percent of the inmates interviewed believed that the food they were given was "insufficient," and 41 percent believed it was of poor or very poor quality. Similarly, 29 percent noted that they did not have a sufficient supply of drinking water.

With respect to charges for goods and services, 35 percent of the inmates said that family members had to pay to have the prisoner "sent for" when they came to visit; 29 percent paid to have food taken to them; 33

percent paid for the delivery of clothes or other basic items; 14 percent paid to have a conjugal visit; and 22 percent said they knew of inmates who had been granted parole in exchange for payment. The inmates also reported that their families had helped them during the six months prior to the survey by bringing them food (90 percent), medicines (49 percent), money (64 percent), or clothing or shoes (85 percent). Families also helped out by selling objects the prisoner had made (62 percent). However, 30 percent indicated that the treatment their family members receive when visiting the prison is poor or very poor. In regard to the issue of safety and order in the institution, 57 percent of the inmates said that they did not know about the prison system's internal regulations (*reglamento interno*). Similarly, 76 percent said that they felt less safe in prison than in the place they lived prior to being incarcerated, and 20 percent said that they did not feel safe in their cell. Fifty-six percent said they had been robbed inside the prison, some as many as ten times; and 10 percent reported having been beaten by guards or by other inmates within the previous six months.

Concerning inmates' participation in work and educational activities, only 37 percent of those interviewed reported that they participated in work programs and 55 percent in educational ones, despite regulations stipulating that these activities form the foundation for rehabilitation and are a requirement for granting an inmate parole. Regarding other types of payments for goods and services, 12 percent of the inmates said they paid to avoid doing janitorial work; 13 percent paid for food; and 27 percent paid to have their clothes laundered.

The foregoing data and other information obtained from our survey lead us to the following conclusions regarding the principal problems affecting Mexico's prison system:

- Almost all of the prisons in the study were in a sorry state, with deteriorating installations and furnishings and limited prisoner access to basic goods and services. These shortcomings undoubtedly have a negative impact on the prisoners' quality of life and, consequently, on relations and exchanges that occur among them and between prisoners and prison staff. One conclusion to be drawn from the generalized inadequacy of prison infrastructure is that prisons are low on Mexico's political agenda and hence unimportant in the nation's resource-allocation policy. In other words, prisons are not seen as deserving of investment; rather, they represent an area where officials always try to cut costs. The costs and benefits of such a policy have not been seriously considered in the debates surrounding the penal system, nor have the risks it entails been rigorously analyzed. The results of our survey indicate that continuing to view prisons as irrelevant or marginal is not a trivial issue, nor is it one without serious consequences.

- Given that family members supply prisoners with basic goods and services that the prison fails to provide or provides in inadequate amounts, the prisoners' families are in fact assuming a major share of the maintenance costs for the incarcerated population. This is a de facto admission that the punishments meted out by the justice system go beyond the inmate to include his or her family as well. Apart from being unlawful, the prevailing system disadvantages inmates who have no family or whose family cannot or will not assume these costs. Unfortunately, we find that this topic also has been ignored in ongoing debates, even though a discussion of the scope of prison functions is more urgently needed than ever before.

- Regarding the maintenance of order, legality, and security within penal institutions, our survey data support the hypothesis that a prison creates its own universe of relationships in a kind of paralegal regime. Thus, as several studies have documented, jails foster the existence of an informal organization that exists in parallel to the formal institutional order (Pérez 2000), with inmates living together under a regime that displays specific characteristics. This is yet another argument for an in-depth review of the role that the contemporary prison system performs in Mexico (Ciprés 2003).

- Another indicator of the need to revise the current model is the fact that prisons are in no condition to meet the legal precepts on which they are based—the doctrine of social rehabilitation through work, education, and occupational training. For many years, discussions in the field of penology have centered on rehabilitation, yet no satisfactory solution has been identified (CNDH 1995; Tenorio 2002b).

THE SECURITY AND JUSTICE SYSTEM'S OTHER INSTITUTIONS

In this section, we touch briefly on the other institutions active in the public security and justice system and involved, directly or indirectly, in the prison system. Some of our survey data illustrate features that are omitted in official statistics.

Police. Mexico has approximately 360,000 police officers, who perform both investigative and preventive functions. For most, their level of training and specialization is low and their capacity to investigate crime is poor. Corruption, abuse of power, and inappropriate use of force are widespread among the police, and efforts to stop these behaviors have not met with success. Systems of internal control are practically nonexistent, and both police and former police are frequently involved in organized crime, particularly drug trafficking and kidnapping. As a result, public mistrust of the police is high. For example, authorities in México State reported recently that nearly 90 percent of kidnapping rings that had been rounded up included one or more police officers or former officers.

The survey revealed that 13 percent of inmates had served in the armed forces or in the police force: 33 percent of those had been arrested for homicide, 27 percent for kidnapping, 25 percent for fraud or embezzlement, 19 percent for causing bodily harm, 14 percent for armed robbery, 11 percent for sex crimes, and 8 percent for drug-related crimes. The Public Security Ministry reported in 2003 that the National Public Security System had fingerprints for only 10 percent of the police in Mexico, and it was not even certain that those prints corresponded to the identified individuals.

Prosecutors. Mexico has a federal-level Office of the Attorney General (PGR), which prosecutes federal jurisdiction crimes, and thirty-two local-level offices, which handle local jurisdiction crimes. The performance of these offices is widely criticized.

Courts. The federal justice system includes 183 district courts, 74 appeals courts, and a Supreme Court. There are 830 criminal courts at the local level. Dissatisfaction with the performance of these public bodies is also widespread.

Our survey data on the performance of these agencies are illustrative, as discussed in the following paragraphs. Of the prisoners interviewed, 65 percent said they had confessed to agents from the public prosecutor's office (which is subordinate to the Office of the Attorney General). Of these, 50 percent confessed because they knew they were guilty, 23 percent because they were tortured, 12 percent because they were threatened, 3 percent on their lawyer's advice, and 2 percent on the advice of an agent of the public prosecutor's office. (The remaining 10 percent gave various other reasons.)

Inmates apparently received more information about their rights from the courts than from prosecutors. The proportion of convicted inmates who said they learned in court that they had a right not to testify was greater than the roughly 20 percent who were so informed by agents of the public prosecutor's office. Nevertheless, two-thirds of the inmates (66 percent) were not even told of this right in court, and a little more than a fourth (27 percent) did not have a lawyer when making their preliminary statement. Moreover, 71 percent of the prisoners reported that the judge was not present when they gave their preliminary statement, and 80 percent reported that they never had an opportunity to speak directly to a judge.

A portion of those interviewed understood that they might have avoided a prison sentence had they bribed the authorities. However, this perception of corruptibility was not distributed uniformly across the various agencies involved from the time of arrest through sentencing. Whereas 52 percent of those sentenced believed that they might have remained free had they bribed the police, the percentage drops to 37 percent at the stage involving the public prosecutors' offices, and to 27 percent at the stage involving court clerks and judges.

When the inmates were asked explicitly if any official had asked them for money or property in exchange for their liberty, the interviewees responded that the authorities who are most susceptible to bribery are, first, the judicial police and, in close second place, the preventive police (see table 4.7). This perception of corruptibility accords with that of the preceding paragraph: as the process moves forward, opportunities for corruption decrease.

Table 4.7. Inmates' Reports of Corruption in Prisons in Three Mexican States, by Agency, 2002

Agency	Percent of Inmates Asked for Money or Possessions
Preventive police	19%
Judicial police (justice administration)	**22%**
Public prosecutor's office (justice administration)	7%
Guards (prison system)	6%
Court clerks (courts)	4%
Judges (courts)	3%

Source: Prison survey, CIDE, 2002.

Specific questions also addressed the type of mistreatment or abuse that inmates might have suffered throughout the criminal proceeding. The answers, once again, vary depending on the agency (see table 4.8).

Table 4.8. Mistreatment and Abuse of Inmates in Prisons in Three Mexican States, by Agency, 2002

Agency	Percent of Inmates Threatened or Humiliated	Percent of Inmates Beaten or Tortured
Preventive police	16%	24%
Judicial police (justice administration)	**32%**	**41%**
Public prosecutor's office (justice administration)	6%	3%
Guards (prison system)	4%	4%
Court clerks (courts)	1%	1%
Judges (courts)	1%	1%

Source: Prison survey, CIDE, 2002.

Sixty percent of our interviewees noted that they had been arrested while committing a crime or shortly thereafter—that is, in flagrante delicto. The data also reveal that the likelihood of finding and arresting someone presumed to have committed a crime drops rapidly as time passes. The high proportion of inmates arrested in flagrante delicto allows us to infer that most arrests are made by the preventive police, and suggests that criminal investigations by the judicial police are largely unsuccessful and possibly seriously flawed. This being the case, it is possible to hypothesize that most successful prosecutions are for crimes of little complexity or importance. Similarly, it is likely that for most cases that go to trial, the public prosecutors' offices have not done in-depth investigations because in flagrante delicto cases do not require an actual crime investigation.

The data on both reported and perceived corruption indicate that the greatest possibility of avoiding prosecution comes at the moment of arrest. In this situation, the serious flaws in investigations conducted by the judicial police are even more troubling because they decrease the likelihood that criminals will be prosecuted. Our survey results enable us to suggest the following conclusions about the performance of Mexico's law enforcement and justice administration institutions:

- The highest levels of perceived and reported corruption occur at the point when the police arrest the criminal. This is the most important informal "exit door" that allows the criminal to avoid prosecution.

- Crime investigations by agents in the public prosecutor's office succeed in identifying only a small fraction of offenders. Most prisoners are arrested in flagrante delicto.

- Most prosecuted crimes are of little complexity or importance.

- The defense presented for those who reach trial is, in most cases, extremely inadequate and in some cases nonexistent. This deficit is even more pronounced while detainees are in the custody of the public prosecutor's office.

- There is a systematic violation of the minimum standards of due process from the moment of arrest through sentencing. This violation is most severe in the offices of the public prosecutor.

- The violations of civil liberties that were most frequently reported for the offices of the public prosecutor were failures to inform detainees of their right to remain in communication, their right to a defense attorney and to receive advice from that attorney before making a statement, and their right against self-incrimination.

- Half of the prisoners report having confessed to a crime because they were subjected to intimidation or torture.

- Given that the judge does not conduct the criminal trial nor participate in the hearings, the judge is not in a position to guarantee that the process is conducted according to legal standards of fairness and protection.

- During trial, a serious imbalance exists between the accuser and the accused, to the latter's detriment. This is due to the lack of an adequate defense and to the absence of a judge who, if present, could guide the proceedings.

- As a result of all of the above, the accused believe that the punishments they receive are unjust. This perception may be associated, at least in part, with a failure to observe the minimum standards that would make trials appear to be fair. These minimum standards include the presence of a judge, an adequate defense, and a satisfactory understanding on the part of the accused of what occurs during criminal proceedings.

CONCLUSIONS

The prison system in Mexico does not occupy a position of importance in the social project to fight crime. It does not correspond to an articulated and consistent anticrime policy, developed within a framework of respect for legality and constitutional guarantees. It seems to respond instead to a differential strategy that penalizes those who cannot avoid prosecution and sentencing.

The most relevant conclusions we can offer from our analysis of official data and our own survey results relate to the growth of Mexico's prison population, characteristics of the prisoners, the conviction process, and the performance of penal institutions.

First, Mexico's prison population has more than doubled in the last twelve years, from 87,000 inmates in 1992 to over 200,000 in 2004. Initial findings suggest that this increase responds more to harsher penalties and unwillingness to grant paroles than to the arrest of more criminals. The growth trend in the prison population and inmates' deteriorating living conditions are consistent with what is seen throughout Latin America.

Second, inmates are generally not the most dangerous criminals, but they are the poorest. The vast majority of the prison population is composed of inmates who committed relatively minor crimes. This stands in stark contrast to the high rates of very serious crimes found in the three states included in our study. The proportion of inmates incarcerated for serious crimes is very low, and evidence shows that criminals who commit major crimes frequently manage to avoid prosecution.

Third, there is a failure to comply with basic standards at all levels of law enforcement and justice administration. We can corroborate that at each step, from arrest to the suspect's confinement in prison, there is an alarming lack of adherence to minimum standards of due process. Basic principles are systematically violated in the offices of the public prosecutors. Serious procedural shortcomings exist in the hearings and sentencing which irretrievably undermine the credibility of the criminal justice system as a whole.

Fourth, in general, the institutions responsible for criminal justice administration are perceived as highly ineffective. The police arrest mostly petty criminals; the public prosecutors conduct inefficient criminal investigations, often failing to file charges; the judicial police undertake few investigations and those they complete are unsatisfactory; and the courts focus on validating the opinions of the prosecutors. The prisons, for their part, also fail to fulfill their purpose or respect their own regulations. All of this undoubtedly contributes to increased crime and also reduces the likelihood that inmates will reincorporate as law-abiding members of society.

These institutions' precarious performance undermines public confidence and erodes the very basis for the rule of law. Moreover, the cost of an inefficient criminal justice system is not paid by the guilty alone but also by society as a whole. A poorly functioning police force obliges those who want safety to hire their own security guards. The crime victim avoids reporting the crime to the public prosecutor's office—both out of fear of reprisal but also because of a suspicion that justice will not be done. The outcome is a failure to enforce a genuine rule of law, harming all of society by leaving it unprotected against crime. This further diminishes the public's trust in institutions, to the detriment of all.

References

Arango, Arturo. 2004. *Sistema de información delictiva: la estadística de seguridad pública en México*. Mexico: INACIPE/Center for U.S.-Mexican Studies.

Azaola, Elena. 1998. "Nuevas tendencias en la criminalidad femenina." In *Criminalidad y criminalización de la mujer en la región andina*, ed. Rosa del Olmo. Caracas: United Nations Development Programme.

———. 2002. "Mexico." In *Encyclopedia of Crime and Punishment*, vol. 3, ed. David Levinson. Thousand Oaks, Calif.: Sage.

Bergman, Marcelo, Elena Azaola, Ana Laura Magaloni, and Layda Negrete. 2003. "Mapa longitudinal de patrones e historias delictivas. Resultados de la encuesta a población en reclusión en tres entidades de la República Mexicana: Distrito Federal, Estado de México y de Morelos." Mexico City: Centro de Investigación y Docencia Económicas.

Ciprés, Pedro. 2003. "El sistema penal mexicano hacia el tercer milenio," *Revista de Ciencias Penales Inter Criminis* (Instituto Nacional de Ciencias Penales) 6 (April–June): 69–96.

CNDH (Comisión Nacional de Derechos Humanos). 1995. *La experiencia del penitenciarismo contemporáneo: aportes y perspectivas*. Mexico City: CNDH.

Gertz Manero, Alejandro. 2001. "Minuta de la comparecencia del Secretario de Seguridad Pública ante el Poder Legislativo" (Record of the appearance of the public security minister before the Legislature), October.

INEGI (Instituto Nacional de Estadística, Geografía e Informática). 2003. *Cuadernos de estadísticas judiciales*. Mexico City: INEGI.

Pérez, José Luis. 2000. *La construcción social de la realidad carcelaria: los alcances de la organización informal en cinco cárceles latinoamericanas (Perú, Chile, Argentina, Brasil y Bolivia)*. Lima: Pontificia Universidad Católica del Perú.

Ruiz Harrell, Rafael. 1998. *Criminalidad y mal gobierno*. Mexico City: Sansores y Aljure.

Secretaría de Gobernación. 1992–2000. *Estadísticas Penitenciarias, 1992–2000*. Mexico City: Government of Mexico.

SSP (Secretaría de Seguridad Pública). 2003. "Programa Nacional de Seguridad Pública 2001–2006," *Diario Oficial de la Federación,* January 14.

Tenorio, Fernando. 2002a. *El sistema de justicia penal en la Ciudad de México: ciudades seguras III.* Mexico City: Universidad Autónoma Metropolitana/Fondo de Cultura Económica/CONACYT.

———. 2002b. *Cultura, sistema penal y criminalidad: ciudades seguras I.* Mexico City: Universidad Autónoma Metropolitana/Fondo de Cultura Económica/CONACYT.

Ungar, Mark. 2003. "Prisons and Politics in Contemporary Latin America," *Human Rights Quarterly,* August.

United Nations. 2003. "Los derechos civiles y políticos, en particular las cuestiones de la tortura y la detención. Informe del grupo de trabajo sobre la detención arbitraria acerca de su visita a México (October 27, 2002 to November 10, 2002)." E/CN.4/2003/8/Add.3. United Nations.

Wacquant, Loïc. 2000. *Las cárceles de la miseria.* Buenos Aires: Manantial.

WHO (World Health Organization). 2002. *World Report on Violence and Health.* Geneva: WHO.

Zepeda, Guillermo. 2002. "Entre la delincuencia y la impunidad: el desempeño de las instituciones de procuración de justicia penal de México frente a los desafíos de la seguridad ciudadana." Manuscript.

PART II

Police and Policing in Mexico

CHAPTER 5

A Profile of Police Forces in Mexico

BENJAMIN NELSON REAMES

Public insecurity in Mexico—which, in addition to crime, involves the often corrupt and poorly functioning police forces—has been a primary public concern for many years. With the election of Vicente Fox to the presidency in 2000, expectations were high for the reform of public institutions. Though fragmented reform efforts had been under way in a number of policing institutions, Fox presented his first cohesive police reform proposal, the Iniciativa de Reforma en Seguridad Pública y Justicia Penal, on March 29, 2004. The major goal of the proposal was to unify some of the nation's police organizations and to give a greater number of police officers the power to conduct investigations. However, in early 2005 Fox reorganized and revamped the federal public security apparatus on his own in the wake of three incidents: the lynching of several police officers, a massacre in Cancún (related to police corruption), and narco-related murders of prison officials. To understand these proposed changes, and their counterproposals, it is important to develop an understanding of Mexico's policing institutions.

Mexico's police forces are similar in many ways to those of other Latin American countries, and function and jurisdiction emerge as two useful ways to understand the police. First, the legal structure is like that of other large federal democracies in the region (such as Brazil and Argentina) in that there are both federal police and relatively autonomous state police. Second, these forces are bifurcated into investigative (or judicial) police and patrol (or order maintenance) police departments. Further, the problems they face are common in Latin America: low pay, poor training, a lack of resources, disorganization, corruption, ineffectiveness, lack of public confidence, corruption, ill-defined or unachievable mandates, and increasingly severe crime problems.

The Mexican police are also unique in some respects. The Mexican policing system stands out for its confusing organization and inefficient use of personnel. Mexico's long border with the United States makes cooperation with U.S. law enforcement agencies an important task while concomitantly making drug trafficking and other organized crime a major challenge. Also unique is the fact that frequent internal reorganizations and the mix of centralized and decentralized policing mean that the policing organizations do not bear the traits of former militarization, as is the case in many Latin American countries, yet the ability to coordinate crime control activities is limited. The upshot is that the police forces of Mexico are rife with both problems and potential. As the front end of any judicial system, police forces must function effectively and fairly for the legal system to do the same.

A crucial first step is to make more sense of the various police forces themselves, their mandates and their powers, through an institutional lens, rather than solely through the important sociological and historical critiques that dominate the analysis of the police. This chapter describes the police forces of Mexico and identifies some of their major challenges. It is widely understood—and argued throughout this volume—that accountable and rights-respecting public security institutions are the backbone of democracy. Thus, if Mexican police can earn the confidence of the public, they would serve as a positive force in improving and consolidating confidence in the justice system and in legitimizing the democratic exercise of state power.

GENERAL BACKGROUND

As a large federation of thirty-one states and a federal district, Mexico maintains a complex variety of police forces with different functions and jurisdictions. Though estimates vary due to inadequate centralized data collection and changing conditions, it is safe to say there are about 400,000 police officers in the country (certainly more than 350,000) and about 3,000 different forces at municipal, state, and federal levels.[1] Besides the multi-

---

[1] These estimates amount to a ratio of about 1 police officer for every 260 citizens, assuming a population of 104,000,000 and a police population of 400,000. Estimates of the actual number of police come from Jane's 2004; Reuter's news reports following Fox's announcement of the proposal to re-

plicity of police forces in Mexico, the other outstanding features of the country's law enforcement organizations are their corruption, growing militarization, poor preparation, and ineffectiveness in the face of increasingly severe crime. Some causes and attempted redresses for these problems are explored, following the functional and jurisdictional descriptions of the police below.

There is no single police force that represents Mexico policing in a definitive way. However, reforms in three significant police institutions demonstrate the kaleidoscopic picture of Mexican policing. First, the federal Office of the Attorney General (PGR) recently established a new police force, the Federal Investigative Police (AFI), which replaced the notoriously corrupt Federal Judicial Police (PJF) by the presidential decree of Vicente Fox (2000–2006) on November 1, 2001. Efforts to develop the AFI into a professional, corruption-free force for the investigation of federal crimes are ongoing.

Second, the Federal Preventive Police (PFP) was created in 1999 by the initiative of President Ernesto Zedillo (1994–2000) to prevent and combat crime throughout the country.[2] The PFP came under the direction of the federal Ministry of Public Security (SSP) and has been assuming greater authority in stages over time, as its budget has grown and as it has incorporated and reorganized police departments from other major agencies such as those for migration, treasury, and highways.

Third, the Public Security Secretariat of the Federal District (SSP-DF), unlike the PFP and SSP, does not have national reach, but it does manage a combined force of over 90,000 officers in the Federal District (DF). The SSP-DF is charged with maintaining public order and safety in the center of Mexico City, where public insecurity and crime rates are the highest in the nation. As a result, there have been concurrent efforts to increase accountability and improve police effectiveness. Beginning in 1996, authorities began a dramatic restructuring of the SSP, which included replacing major officials with army officers. The most high-profile effort was Mexico City Mayor Andrés López Obrador's decision in 2002 to contract former New York City Mayor Rudolph Giuliani as a consultant to the SSP-DF.

The police in Mexico, properly understood, are the public security forces charged with the prevention and investigation of crimes; these

---

form the justice system (March 29, 2004); personal interviews; and data gathered from Mexican government Web sites.

[2] The PFP was created on December 13, 1998, so for all intents and purposes it did not come into existence until 1999.

forces are therefore meant to support the Office of the Public Prosecutor (Ministerio Público) and the judiciary. Given the changing, complex nature of these police institutions, two defining dimensions—function and jurisdiction—enable the clearest description.[3]

FUNCTIONAL DESCRIPTION OF THE POLICE

Mexico's police are divided into a dual set of preventive police (the order-controlling *policía preventiva*) and judicial police (the typically plainclothes, investigative *policía judicial*). The preventive police do what is often called "ostensive policing," maintaining order and public security in cities and towns; they do not investigate crimes and only assist the Office of the Public Prosecutor at its request. They are empowered to act according to police and governmental regulations (Article 21 of the Constitution).

The judicial police are an auxiliary to the Office of the Public Prosecutor and act under its authority and command. The judicial police belong to institutions known as *procuradurías generales*, which are important justice institutions usually translated as attorneys general offices. There are three key types of police actors in judicial law enforcement: police officers (*policías judiciales*); investigating agents of the public prosecutor (called *ministerios públicos*); and technical experts (*peritos*). Depending on their jurisdiction, judicial police enforce federal law (*fuero federal*) or local law (*fuero común*).

According to the National Public Security System (SNSP), municipal and state-level police forces employed some 280,000 officers in 1999. The nearly 34,000 preventive police of the Federal District and the federal preventive police raised the number to 319,600 preventive police in 1999. Today there are probably over 330,000 preventive police. Judicial police officers, which numbered 24,069 at the last official count in 1999, now almost certainly number over 25,000.

JURISDICTIONAL DESCRIPTION OF THE POLICE

There are four types of jurisdictions that affect the nature, activity, and organization of police institutions. They are the three levels of government—federal, state, and municipal—and the Federal District.

---

[3] This observation, like many others that appear without citation throughout this chapter, is owed to López Portillo Vargas 2002.

The Municipal Level of Government

The *municipio* (municipal government) represents the smallest autonomous unit of local government in Mexico. *Municipios* vary widely in size and may contain many smaller cities and towns. In this sense, municipal governments are often compared to county governments in the United States. Like U.S. counties that have sheriffs, Mexican municipalities can maintain a police force, though not all do. Unlike many sheriffs in U.S. counties, all municipal police chiefs are appointed rather than elected; also, Mexican municipal governments are only permitted to have preventive (not investigative) police functions.

Given the wide variation in the size and capability of Mexico's roughly 2,400 municipal governments, there are significant differences among local police forces. Roughly 12 percent, or 335 municipalities, have no police forces at all and are dependent on the state government to provide order. The vast majority of municipal governments—roughly 2,000 of them— have fewer than 100 officers, which implies that those police departments are not very developed and probably not very modernized. However, in large cities there is a tendency for municipal-level police to be much larger and more organizationally complex. Indeed, 87 of the largest *municipios* account for 68.7 percent of preventive police at all levels of government.

The Federal District

The Federal District covers a territory of 1,500 km and contains the heart of Mexico City and the seat of federal government. There are 8.7 million residents in the DF, according to 2002 estimates, and 18 million people in the metropolitan region. Mexico City is governed by a directly elected mayor, who appoints the heads of the Federal District's law enforcement forces: the public security secretary of the Federal District and the attorney general of the Federal District.

Preventive Police, Federal District

The Federal District stands out for having the highest crime rates in Mexico, as well as a very large preventive police force of approximately 34,000 officers (not to mention 40,000 auxiliary police and 15,000 bank police, to be discussed below). These nearly 90,000 officers work for the Public Security Secretariat of the Federal District. In 2000, the SSP-DF had six major divisions and a budget of about 10 billion pesos. The starting salary for a patrol officer of the SSP-DF was recently raised to 5,000 pesos per month (about US$500).

Like most police departments of major cities, the Federal District's preventive police are divided into regional subgroups (geographically defined police with specific jurisdictions) and into functional divisions with special responsibilities and resources. Slightly fewer than half of all preventive police are grouped into the geographical distributions of the so-called sectoral police (*policía sectoral*). The sectoral police of the Federal District are divided into six main regions, with usually three precincts in each (a total of sixteen precincts) and a number of sectors within each precinct (a total of seventy sectors).

The sectoral police compose the first of the five divisions; the remaining four divisions of the preventive police (over 17,000 of the 34,000) are organized into special functions rather than geography. The second division, the metropolitan police (*policía metropolitana*), consists of six special units: the public transit police, tourist police, grenadiers (*granaderos* protect the historic district), mounted police, the feminine police (the *policía femenil* work in schools, with juveniles, at public events, and in public parks and gardens), and the emergency rescue squad (ERUM).

The third division is a set of special squadrons (*fuerzas especiales*) consisting of four main groups: the helicopter squadron; the special unit, which specializes in motorcycles; the "task force" (*fuerza de tareas*) which deals with terrorist and bomb threats; and the Alfa group, which is a secretive, ad hoc force that works with the special unit and fights drug trafficking. The fourth division is roadway security (*seguridad vial*), which maintains a force of brown-uniformed police who patrol the roads and highways. An understaffed Internal Affairs is the final division.

Though the chain of authority is a source of common confusion, the SSP is not synonymous with the preventive police. There are two other separate forces, under the charge of the SSP but not part of the preventive police, that compose the "complementary police": the auxiliary police (approximately 40,000 strong), which guards official buildings and other specific locations like the airport; and the bank police (about 15,000 officers), which guards businesses, financial institutions, and banks. The forces function in a more ostensive capacity and in theory should allow for significant decentralization, the concentration of special resources within the preventive police, and the formation of reserve forces for order maintenance when necessary.

Judicial Police of the Federal District

The Federal District is also unique for maintaining its own force of judicial police: the Judicial Police of the Federal District (PJDF), organized under the Office of the Attorney General of the Federal District (PGJDF). The PGJDF receives complaints and reports of possible crimes and investigates them. They maintain 16 precincts (*delegaciones*) with an estimated 3,500 judicial police, 1,100 investigating agents for prosecuting attorneys, and 941 experts or specialists. The PGJDF annual budget exceeds 3 billion pesos.

States

The thirty-one states, like the Federal District, maintain both preventive and judicial police. The state-level preventive police are perhaps 90,000 strong. The judicial police, by definition, must enforce a set of laws or codes; in the states and the Federal District, the relevant jurisdiction is the local state law (*fuero común*). By the best but infrequent estimates, in 1995 there were 21,000 state-level judicial police officers (by now there are probably 25,000) in the State Judicial Police (PJE) organized under the Offices of the Attorneys General (Procuradurías Generales de Justicia).

Federal

The federal government has several major law enforcement organizations with national-level jurisdiction (*fuero federal*) for serious offenses such as drug trafficking and other forms of organized crime. Until recent reform proposals by the Fox administration, control of these organizations had been essentially split between two cabinet-level departments: the federal Office of the Attorney General and the Ministry of Public Security. These departments, as well as the intelligence organization of Mexico's Interior Ministry (Secretaría de Gobernación), are discussed below.

Federal Attorney General's Office

Mexico's federal attorney general (*procurador general de la república*) is appointed by the president and is presently the only cabinet official who must be approved by the Mexican Congress. President Fox appointed General Rafael Marcial Macedo de la Concha to this position, raising concerns that the PGR would become more militarized, as discussed more fully in Sigrid Arzt's chapter in this volume. The attorney general directs an office (the PGR) that functions as the equivalent of the U.S. Department of Justice. The PGR's mandate is to investigate and prosecute federal crimes such as drug trafficking, arms trafficking, kidnapping, and environmental and public health crimes. Under the Fox administration, the PGR has seen its budget grow from 5.6 billion pesos in 2001 to 7.2 billion in 2004, when it employed a staff of 21,838 persons.

The PGR reconfigured and renamed the Federal Judicial Police, which was much maligned for corruption and ineffectiveness. The Federal Investigative Police replaced the Federal Judicial Police and, at least nominally, invited comparisons to the U.S. Federal Bureau of Investigation (FBI). In 2004, AFI had a budget of 2.62 billion pesos, thus accounting for about a third of PGR spending. That same year the AFI's forces consisted of more than 5,000 judicial police officers, 1,600 investigators, and 450 specialists.

The PGR also oversees the Office of the Public Prosecutor, which has a separate judicial police force that operates nationwide. The rest of the PGR law enforcement apparatus (besides the delegations for each state) is divided into planning departments, internal controls, and, more notably, Deputy Attorney General Offices (*subprocuradurías*), which contain special units. Since the federal police are charged with some of Mexico's most vexing crime problems—staunching the flow of illegal drugs, solving kidnappings, and fighting other types of organized crime—it is worth mentioning some of the special offices for deputy prosecutors that have evolved over time.

First, the PGR's Special Anti–Organized Crime Unit (UEDO) appeared as a response to the phenomenon of organized crime. Organized crime was defined as a legal concept in Mexico's criminal code in February 1994 as "three or more persons organized under rules of discipline and hierarchy in order to commit, in a violent and repeated way or with the purpose of profit, any of the crimes legally defined." The Federal Law against Organized Crime (LFCDO) was passed in November 1996 to deal with the problem of drug trafficking, though other crimes (such as migrant smuggling, trafficking in arms or infants, and terrorism) were covered in the LFCDO as well.

Second, another unit within the PGR that has been important in the effort to combat drug trafficking and organized crime is the Office of the Special Prosecutor for Crimes against Health (FEADS). The FEADS appeared in 1997 after General Gutiérrez Rebollo, head of the National Institute to Combat Drugs (INCD), was arrested on charges stemming from association with leaders of the Juárez drug cartel. As a result of this high-level corruption, INCD was dismantled and FEADS was put under the direction of a civilian, Mariano Herrán. Under the same reorganization, the UEDO was assigned to operate out of FEADS headquarters in Mexico City. Two other key units within the FEADS were the Border Rapid Response Groups (Grupos de Respuesta Rápida Fronteriza) and the Special Anti–Money Laundering Unit (UECLD). UECLD was created in January 1998 to implement anti–money laundering legislation which dates from 1990. The problem of corruption in FEADS was not entirely solved, with agents in Tijuana and Monterrey being arrested for extortion and kidnapping. Both FEADS and UEDO have since been reorganized.

A third special office of the PGR is the Office of the Deputy Attorney for Special Investigation of Organized Crime (SIEDO), which received 357 million pesos of the 2004 budget. As currently organized, SIEDO contains six special units (with smaller, separate budgets) for investigating specific types of crimes: crimes against public health; terrorism and arms trafficking; money laundering and counterfeiting; human trafficking in minors, organs, and undocumented people; kidnappings; and robbery and auto theft. SIEDO is not to be confused with the Office of the Deputy Attorney for Special Investigation of Federal Crimes (SIEDF), which in 2004 received 15.9 million pesos. The four separate units under its direction cover cases related to intellectual property crimes, financial crimes, environmental damage, and public servants who obstruct justice.

The special offices of the PGR demonstrate the general rule that Mexican policing institutions try to reorganize themselves in a rational way to respond effectively to specific crime problems. However, for this functionality to be achieved, legislation must first address specific crime problems, as police institutions can generally only respond to established law. In other words, without specific laws that enable them to act, public institutions in Mexico—police departments included—find it difficult to pursue particular goals no matter how pressing. Another result is that official reorganizations and departmental shuffles tend to be quite frequent since ad hoc and internal changes in Mexico's type of bureaucracy are uncommon.

Federal Ministry of Public Safety

Sweeping reforms altered the public security landscape in January 2005, as this chapter was going to press. Widely seen as responding to the lynchings of federal police officers in the outskirts of Mexico City, President Fox revamped the federal public security apparatus. Fox created a federal security cabinet with himself presiding, though the chief of the SSP, Huerta (see below), will coordinate activities.

Moving toward greater integration, the cabinet will also include the attorney general (chief of the PGR) as a permanent member, among many other military officials. An Undersecretariat for Prevention and Citizen Participation has been transformed to work with a newly created Council of Citizen Participation (CPC) that will analyze government policies, monitor performance, and suggest courses of action. Miguel Ángel Yunes was appointed to the undersecretary post, and Tomás Valencia replaced retired Admiral José Luis Figueroa as commissioner of the SSP's preventive police.

The federal Ministry of Public Security is the second cabinet-level department that manages law enforcement organizations in Mexico. President Fox first appointed Alejandro Gertz Manero as his minister of public security; when Gertz stepped down in 2004 he was replaced by then-Deputy Interior Minister Ramón Martín Huerta. The SSP had a budget of 6.46 billion pesos for 2004 and a total staff of 22,900, including members of its police forces. Given Gertz's replacement and the reform package under consideration since early 2004, the future organization of SSP is not entirely certain. However, as currently constituted, the SSP oversees two important public security institutions: the Federal Preventive Police (PFP) and the National Public Security System (SNSP).

The PFP was created in 1999 at the behest of the Zedillo administration and with prompting from the SNSP to control crime throughout the country. The formation of the PFP was also catalyzed by legislation passed by the Mexican Senate in December 1998, calling for the creation of a national law enforcement body that would combine the Federal Highway Police (Policía Federal de Caminos), Federal Fiscal Police (Policía Fiscal Federal), and Federal Immigration Police (Policía Migratoria Federal). Initially, concerns focused on the fact that the new police force could be politically repressive toward opposition parties, and then critical attention turned to the military training, service background, and ethic of the new recruits.

The PFP has technical and operative autonomy and is headed by a commissioner named by the president. At the last major count in 2000, the PFP had 10,699 officers; 4,899 of these were from the military (3rd brigade of the military police), about 4,000 came from the Federal Highway Police, 1,500 from the Fiscal Police, and 600 from the Interior Ministry's intelligence agency (the National Information and Security Center, CISEN). These new members were then trained by the military. In short, rather than creating a new police force from scratch, the PFP has cobbled together a force with a decidedly militarized character.

The most recent restructuring of the PFP has left it with some notable attributes. Besides the typical training, development, and planning departments, there are unique coordinating departments (*coordinaciones*). Reflecting both the military and police background of the incorporated personnel, the Department for Regional Security is organized into four types of deployment: ports and borders, federal highways, other federal zones, and thirty-four regional commands. There is also a Department of Intelligence for Crime Prevention, which is organized internally to mimic closely the PGR units for analysis, information, and statistics, and for federal crimes such as trafficking, terrorism, and kidnapping. Finally, there are Federal Support Forces intended for disasters, special operations, and strategic deployments. The budget of the PFP in 2004 was nearly 3.6 billion pesos, which is more than half of the overall SSP budget.

Another important and relatively recent addition to the public security apparatus is the renamed Executive Secretariat of the National Public Security System (SE-SNSP), which began in 1994 with constitutional changes (Articles 21 and 73) that raised public security to the status of a state policy. The expressed idea was to coordinate public security efforts, plans, and data collection, as well as to systematically fight crime and address demands for public security.

The Zedillo administration followed the next year (1995) with legislation formally creating the SNSP. A key decision was to locate the SNSP within the Interior Ministry rather than in the Attorney General's Office and the Office of the Public Prosecutor. The law also created the National Public Security Council (CNSP) as a coordinating body for the SNSP. The council includes the minister of public security, who presides, as well as the thirty-one state governors, the attorney general, the mayor of the Federal District, and the military chiefs. Also created was a series of coordinating councils at the state and local levels, emphasizing the central government's role in data collection, coordination, and planning, rather than control. The SNSP has grown in budgetary terms from 226.6 million pesos in 1996 to 366 million pesos in 2004. By 1999, the resources that the federal and state governments together allocated to national security reached about 9 billion pesos.

Federal Ministry of the Interior

Mexico's cabinet-level Interior Ministry also oversees some domestic law enforcement functions, primarily in intelligence. In one of the few partisan appointments of his administration, President Fox named Santiago Creel as interior secretary. The appointment of a party ally as interior secretary may have reflected long-standing concerns about the department's traditional role in managing domestic intelligence and the often political nature of such intelligence (Aguayo Quezada 2001). The principal civilian intelligence agency in Mexico, overseen by the interior minister, is the National Information and Security Center, created in 1989. CISEN's primary function is to collect and process intelligence and security-related information. Its director initially served as "technical secretary" for the National Security Cabinet (Gabinete de Seguridad Nacional) created by President Carlos Salinas in 1988, at the beginning of his term. Salinas also created within the presidency the Coordinator for National Public Security (Coordinación de Seguridad Pública de la Nación) in 1994. The difference between these two offices was that the former was a standing staff office within the presidency, while the latter was a special response to the upsurge in public security problems in 1994.

It is worth noting that since drug-trafficking organizations proved successful in penetrating Mexico's security institutions, the anti–drug trafficking component of CISEN's intelligence and operations was transferred in 1992 to the newly created INCD and to its intelligence arm, the National Drug Control Center (CENDRO) and remained there during subsequent reorganizations under the FEADS.

MAJOR CHALLENGES IN MEXICAN POLICE ORGANIZATIONS AND POLICING

Corruption and inefficiency plague the Mexican police. In addition, low pay and lack of resources have hindered efforts at improving police performance, battling corruption, and professionalizing the forces. Moreover, even in consideration of the remarkably low number of crimes reported, Mexican police are often stretched beyond capacity. As noted throughout this volume, the lack of public confidence in the police has further eroded their ability to respond to crime: a survey in 1999 found that 90 percent of respondents in Mexico City had little or no trust in the police. Such a lack of public confidence translates into a lack of support—that is, an unwillingness to report crimes or assist in investigations, elements that are crucial to solving crimes. In more recent nationwide polls, only 12 percent of the population has expressed confidence in the police (Grupo Reforma 2004a, 2004b). In response to this crisis of public confidence, President Fox made reducing public corruption a key goal of his administration, and he gained international recognition for his efforts.

In 2001 Mexico moved up from 55th to 51st place on the global corruption index published by Transparency International, an advocacy nongovernmental organization (NGO). However, this improvement was short-lived. Mexico dropped to 57th position on the index in 2002, one notch better than China (at 58th) but well below Brazil and Peru (tied at 45th). In 2003, Mexico dropped to 64th position, again ahead of China, but one place below Peru.[4] Given concerns with corruption and crime, the management consulting firm A.T. Kearney reported in 2002 that Mexico's attractiveness to foreign investors dropped from fifth to ninth place worldwide.

Official corruption is prevalent within police organizations and is common to the very practice of policing in Mexico. Transparency International estimated in 2002 that the median Mexican household spends 8 percent of its income on bribes (*mordidas* or "bites").[5] As noted by Azaola and Bergman in this volume, police officers are among the officials most frequently extracting these *mordidas*. Corruption among the Mexican police force often takes on a pyramidal structure, with those at the bottom receiving low wages and the corrupt officials on the top sometimes taking in huge sums. The average police patrol officer in Mexico City earns a salary that is insufficient to support a family. It is frequently argued that *mordidas* allow police officials to augment their paltry salaries and avoid processing citizens for minor infractions.[6] However, a large percentage of these bribes flow upward, producing wealthy officers at the top and a wide base of still-impoverished patrol personnel at the bottom of the pyramid.[7]

---

[4] Mexico ranked 47th in 1997 and 55th in 1998. Information can be found at www.transparency.org.

[5] Police departments are not the only area of the criminal justice system where corruption is found. A recent United Nations Human Rights Commission special report on the independence of judges and lawyers warned that Mexico's justice system suffered widespread corruption. Based on testimonies, it estimated that 50 to 70 percent of federal judges were involved in acts of corruption, and stated that in some states, civil matters were not processed without the payment of a bribe.

[6] A fascinating response to this reality was the mayor of Ecatepec's decision to abolish all parking and traffic violations so that police officers would have to stop shaking down citizens for bribes (Sullivan 2003).

[7] Since much of this corruption occurs in Mexico City, this practice raises the question of if and how the "zero tolerance" recommendations of the Giuliani Group consulting firm will be implemented. If *mordidas* function to exchange

Training, preparation, and institutional support for the police are generally poor. For the preventive police, academic and professional training are recent additions to policy. Of the 58 police academies, 25 began training operations within in the last 23 years; most do not enforce a minimum educational requirement. Basic training lasts an average of 4.5 months; in the Federal District the period is 6 months. The majority of Mexican police officers have, at most, completed only elementary school. This situation has accelerated the erosion of institutional standards and postponed the modernization of the police. Police departments often lack tools to evaluate job performance, guidelines for performance, methods to ferret out corruption, technical support, and an understanding of human rights and community relations.

Meanwhile, overload is a significant problem in the Mexican criminal justice system, especially for police. When a complaint is received and a preliminary inquiry (*averiguación previa*) begun, a criminal case is opened. Alternatively, cases can be initiated when a law officer detains a person caught in the act of committing a crime. The person can be detained for up to 48 hours before being brought before a judge for a preliminary hearing. The judge has up to 72 hours to decide on three options: to jail the person subject to trial, to free the person on bail, or to free the person due to lack of evidence. If the person is not freed due to lack of evidence, the judge may ask the police to gather more evidence. When the investigation is complete, the judge concludes the trial portion of the process and issues a sentence (Lawyers Committee 2001). Part of the overload problem arises because investigating officers receive, on average, a new complaint each day of the year. Reported crimes practically doubled from 1991 to 1997, and reported crimes are only a small fraction of actual crimes. As Arroyo notes in this volume, this administrative backlog could worsen with more aggressive policing strategies, such as the "zero tolerance" strategy considered in Mexico City.

A final complicating factor or result of police corruption and ineffectiveness in Mexico is the proliferation of private policing, partially in response to the state's failure to provide security. According to a study by the Mexico City legislative assembly, in 1998 there were more private secu-

---

small bribes for not processing civilians through the criminal justice system, and if "broken windows" approaches to policing call for prosecuting minor crimes to prevent more serious ones, there is a necessary conflict. Also, many commentators have made the argument that *mordidas* are pyramidal, but special credit is due here to Fryer 1993.

rity guards than police. The number of Mexican private security companies has grown significantly in recent years, increasing roughly 40 percent from 1998 to 1999 alone (Jane's 2004a, 2004b). According to official figures, in December 2000 there were 2,984 private security companies registered, with 153,885 employees.[8]

The Mexican government has had serious problems regulating these companies, most of which are illegitimate since they lack the required legal permits. The inability to regulate or control these forces creates potential security problems. Since many of these companies are unregulated, some actually engage in criminality against their own clients, thus exacerbating the problem of insecurity. A substantial number of private security guards are former police officers or current officers who work as security guards while off duty; these dynamics increase the likelihood of police corruption.

CONCLUSIONS

Accountable and rights-respecting public security forces support democratic states. Where such police forces are incompetent or corrupt, citizens lose faith in public institutions and invest in private security. The police institutions of Mexico have the potential to improve the substantive quality of democracy for Mexican citizens if they embrace principles of transparency, efficiency, and democratic policing. The first step in tapping that potential is to clearly understand the police forces themselves, their mandate, their powers, and their problems. This chapter has attempted to advance this understanding.

Despite the relative comprehensiveness of jurisdictional coverage and the rational specialization of functions of Mexican police organizations, there are still numerous obstacles to effective policing in Mexico. Pervasive corruption and inefficiency detract from police performance and from the public's trust of police. These problems are compounded by poor police training, inadequate resources, and insufficient compensation. Furthermore, in the face of increasing levels of crime, even Mexico's most honest

---

[8] In 2000 *The Guardian* estimated that 200,000 Mexicans were employed as private guards by some 5,000 companies. In Mexico City, 510 companies are properly registered, with about 90,000 private guards working in the capital (Nelson 2000). *El Universal* reported on October 16, 2004, that the federal SSP had only counted 322 registered security companies and another 1,400 for state agencies, for a total of 1,722 businesses, which together employed 23,302 legitimate guards.

and best-trained police (as well as other actors in the justice system) find themselves overloaded and backlogged beyond capacity. Thus police reform in Mexico, considered in greater detail by other authors in this volume, must seek comprehensive solutions that address the multiple and systemic problems that compromise effective policing.

References

Aguayo Quezada, Sergio. 2001. *La charola: una historia de los servicios de inteligencia en México.* Mexico City: Grijalbo.

Fryer, Wesley A. 1993. "Mexican Security." At http://www.fas.org/irp/world/mexico/.

Grupo Reforma. 2004a. "Fox envía histórica reforma judicial a Congreso de México," March 29.

———. 2004b. "Gobierno de Fox presenta ley de reforma del sistema policial y judicial," March 30.

Jane's Sentinel Security Assessment. 2004a. "Internal and Security Forces: Mexico," September 9.

———. 2004b. "Executive Summary," September 9.

Lawyers Committee for Human Rights/Centro de Derechos Humanos "Miguel Agustín Pro Juárez." 2001. *Injusticia legalizada.* New York: Lawyers Committee for Human Rights.

López Portillo Vargas, E. 2002. "The Police in Mexico: Political Functions and Needed Reforms." In *Transnational Crime and Public Security,* ed. John Bailey and Jorge Chabat. La Jolla: Center for U.S.-Mexican Studies, University of California, San Diego.

Nelson, Zed. 2000. "Guns for Hire," *The Guardian,* December 9.

Sullivan, Kevin. 2003. "Mexican Town Forgoes Law for Order," *Washington Post,* September 8.

CHAPTER 6

Criminal Investigation and the Subversion of the Principles of the Justice System in Mexico

GUILLERMO ZEPEDA LECUONA

> *Present in all parts of a complex legal system is a conflict of author-*
> *ity between supra-level normative principles and lower-level norms*
> *and practices. A certain degree of ineffectiveness characterizes the*
> *first, whereas a degree of invalidity or illegitimacy characterizes the*
> *second. Conflict of authority is particularly serious in criminal law.*
> *Not only does it have direct effects on the liberty of citizens, but the*
> *distance between constitutional principles and law, and between*
> *law and jurisdiction, has also reached alarming proportions, result-*
> *ing in a de facto bleeding away of rights and an uncontrolled*
> *growth in arbitrariness*—Luigi Ferrajoli (1995: 27).

An initial review of Mexico's public security and criminal justice system
and an analysis of available empirical evidence reveal the legal weight and
practical preeminence of the federal Public Prosecutor's Office (Ministerio
Público), particularly in the investigative, preliminary-inquiry phase of a
crime (*averiguación previa*).[1] At both federal and state-level jurisdictions, the

---

The author gratefully acknowledges the Hewlett Foundation's generous support for this study. Translation by Patricia Rosas.

[1] Within criminal matters, the investigation of crimes is only one of the jurisdictions of the Office of the Public Prosecutor. It assumes the role of accuser during the criminal trial. In other matters, such as civil and family cases (and in
matters of *amparo* [injunction or appeal] in the federal jurisdiction), the prosecutor is the representative of society responsible for monitoring legality and
public interest. In some states, the attorney general continues acting as the
counselor-at-law and government attorney. At the federal level, although the
attorney general is no longer the president's legal adviser, the office retains

public prosecutor is the authority responsible for initiating and conducting the investigation of crimes. In fact, the public prosecutor has a monopoly in the area of criminal action (with slight and ineffective exceptions introduced in a 1994 constitutional reform) since most Mexican police have no practical or legal investigative capacity. At the same time, the prosecutor is also the accuser in criminal trial proceedings. Hence in legal parlance the prosecutor is referred to as the "privileged party" because of the legal characteristics and relative advantages he or she has compared to the defense attorney.

The few analyses conducted of the prosecutorial institution—at either a national level or comparatively—emphasize the broad powers of this office and the legal and investigative importance of its conduct. Thus it seems appropriate to devote a chapter in this volume to illuminating the role of the public prosecutor during the procedural phase and to the way in which that work affects the normative principles guiding the Mexican criminal system.

THE STARTING POINT: PUBLIC INSECURITY

Opinion polls and surveys show that Mexicans do not feel safe. They believe that criminals are continuously threatening their physical well-being, their lives, and their property. For example, in March 2002, the Citizens' Institute for Security Studies (ICESI) conducted the First National Survey on Public Insecurity (Primera Encuesta Nacional sobre Inseguridad Pública en las Entidades Federativas), in which 47 percent of respondents reported feeling somewhat or very unsafe; 34 percent, somewhat safe; and only 19 percent, very safe. Moreover, 75 percent of those interviewed believed that crime had increased in 2001 compared to 2000 (ICESI 2002: 30, 32).

Crime had begun to increase in Mexico beginning in the mid-1980s, but the growth in crime after 1994 was tremendous. The number of crime reports filed nationwide increased from 809,000 in 1991 to 1,111,000 in 1994, and to almost 1,500,000 in 1997 (figure 6.1). People often point out that the behavior of crime variables is linked to socioeconomic and political variables.[2] For example, unemployment and low-income indicators are associ-

---

the functions of government attorney. For example, it is the attorney general who, in the name of the executive, forwards cases of unconstitutionality to the Supreme Court. For more on this matter, see Fix Zamudio 2002.

[2] The causal mechanisms that attempt to explain correlations between these variables are a matter of great debate among criminologists, whose hypothe-

ated with the commission of property crimes such as robbery, whereas social equality variables predict violent crimes such as bodily harm and homicide (Fajnzylber Lederman, and Loayza 1998). This supposition largely holds true for Mexico. Crime reports began to increase notably during the economic and financial crisis of 1994–1995, when interest rates shot up and the economy suffered serious setbacks—factors that were reflected in high unemployment and declining household incomes for millions of families. However, it is worth noting that although Mexico's current economic indicators are less discouraging than those registered from 1994 to 1997, the crime rate remains high (1,398,000 crime reports were filed in local jurisdictions in 2001). Is crime here to stay? How can we reverse this trend in insecurity and violence?

Figure 6.1. Reported Local-jurisdiction Crimes for Mexico, 1991-2001 (per 100,000 inhabitants)

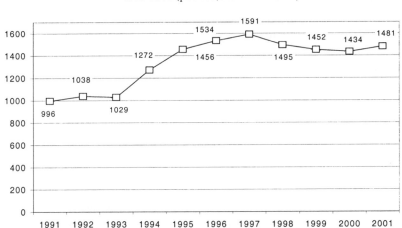

Source: Prepared by the author with data from INEGI 1991–2002.

ses and interpretations are highly varied and nuanced. Moreover, in empirical studies, the magnitude of the association and even the direction of some correlations vary enormously. (For the outline of this debate, see Fajnzylber, Lederman, and Loayza 1998; Kangaspunta, Joutsen, and Ollus 1998; Van Dijk 1996; Kahan 1997.) In Mexico, empirical research in the field of criminal sociology is just beginning.

The experiences of other societies that have suffered increased crime because of political instability or economic crises reveal the existence of a "crime inertia," which continues even after socioeconomic conditions improve. In Fajnzylber and colleagues' comparative analysis of crime and violence in Latin America, the effectiveness and soundness of the institutions responsible for combating crime largely determined whether a given society fell into a spiral of impunity and violence or, to the contrary, contained or even reversed the crime inertia. In other words, without ignoring the larger causal factors, it is clear that institutional structures have a significant effect in reducing crime and violence (Fajnzylber, Lederman, and Loayza 2001).

Obviously, it is fundamentally important that societies address the socioeconomic and political causes of citizen insecurity. An attempt to concentrate solely on institutional variables would be the equivalent of privileging punishment over both crime prevention and efforts to combat social problems. However, it is necessary—both during a crisis and after crime's social detonators have begun to diminish—to make crime syndicates and potential criminals painfully aware that they are confronting strong law enforcement and criminal justice institutions. Consequently, it is crucial that we diagnose and analyze the institutions in Mexico that are responsible for providing citizens with security services and criminal justice.

PROCESS AND PRINCIPLE: MEXICO'S INSTITUTIONAL RESPONSE TO CRIME

The Mexican Constitution stipulates that the procedural system or institutional design of the Mexican criminal proceeding belongs to a mixed law model. Article 21 establishes that the functions of indictment and trial are separate, a principle that is characteristic of the adversarial system. Yet the preliminary inquiry, under the direction of the public prosecutor, follows the outlines of the inquisitorial system. The Mexican criminal justice system can be explained more simply by separating it into four stages, during which various actors involved in public security policies and the criminal proceeding interact and interrelate (figure 6.2). The first stage, *preventive or citizen security measures*, encompasses crime prevention policies and police vigilance. The second stage is the *preliminary inquiry*, which occurs once a presumed crime has been committed; the public prosecutor directs specialists and the judicial police as they undertake the investigation. The third is the *criminal proceeding or the administration of justice*, during which the judge considers the prosecutor's arguments and, if the evidence supports it, issues arrest warrants. After the presentation of evidence and pleadings, the prisoner is sentenced or the case dismissed. The fourth stage, the *corrections system and social rehabilitation*, encompasses the set of institutions charged with administering punishment and monitoring the rehabilitation of offenders. Except for the third stage, which is the competence of the judicial branch, all steps fall under the purview of executive branch institutions.

Figure 6.2. Public Security and Criminal Justice Subsystems and the Social System

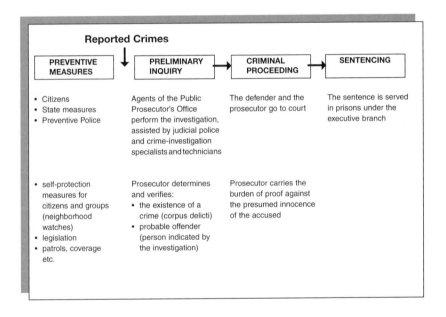

Source: Zepeda Lecuona 2004: 96.

The various stages are closely interconnected, and the performance of each has repercussions for the others. For example, the judicial branch has the constitutional role of reviewing the conditions under which a citizen is detained, in order to ensure that the constitutional requirements that would justify depriving a person of liberty are met. This stage is vitally important for controlling, checking, and, if necessary, punishing any abuse of force or power by other actors in the system, whether it be the preventive police, the judicial police, or the public prosecutor. Similarly, if the corrections system does not fulfill its mission of social rehabilitation, that precedent would result in high levels of recidivism, with serious repercussions for the public security system's preventive measures.

The normative and institutional framework also establishes a series of values or social agreements that determine the orientation of the criminal system by informing, shaping, and validating the structure and procedures. These values or agreements are the principles that govern the system; to avoid authoritarianism and arbitrariness, they inform and shape the set of rights and duties of private parties as well as those of the structure and procedures of the organizations responsible for investigation and criminal proceeding.

These principles are set forth (albeit not very systematically) in the Mexican Constitution, and they also appear in multilateral conventions and instruments to which Mexico is a signatory. The jurisprudence of the federal judicial branch, legislation, and legal doctrine all serve to interpret and articulate them. Authors differ over the number and content of the principles that govern criminal law. For simplicity's sake, these are the general categories around which the greatest doctrinal agreement exists: justice; the principle of legality; the principle of public or official prosecution; principles relating to the structure of the criminal proceeding and the conduct of the parties; and the principle of historical truth and the principles of evidence.

Justice is the ultimate goal of law and the inspiration that must guide all juridical institutions. It is the most abstract of the principles, and the other principles that govern the investigation and criminal proceeding are subordinate to it. One way to achieve an overview of the concept of justice is to note that it has both formal and substantive elements. To illustrate the first, one can point to the following definition from John Rawls, one of the seminal authors of the contemporary debate: "The correct rule as defined by institutions is regularly adhered to and properly interpreted by the authorities. This impartial and consistent administration of laws and institutions, whatever their substantive principles, we may call formal justice" (Rawls 1993: 76).

The effectiveness of this formal concept allows us to avoid a significant number of unjust acts, but the formal aspect is insufficient because it should also address the content of the provision being applied. The substantive notion, according to Rawls, must appeal to fairness, in the sense that all have the right to an extensive offering of equal basic liberties and an institutional design that considers the social and economic inequalities present among the members of society. Justice, like liberty and fairness, requires that, "Social and economic inequalities are to be arranged so that they are both (a) to the greatest expected benefit of the least advantaged and (b) attached to offices and positions open to all under conditions of fair equality of opportunity" (Rawls 1993: 105). An empirical analysis of the field of criminal justice in Mexico requires a fundamental consideration of both the formal and substantive aspects of justice because injustices can arise from the investigation and prosecution, both because of a divorce between the norm and what happens in reality and because substantively unjust provisions are impartially and consistently applied.

The *principle of legality* means that officials must adhere to legal mandates and that in criminal matters there is no room for arbitrariness or bending of the law for considerations of a political, economic, or even social nature. That is, the law must be applied exhaustively and without exception, as the legislation itself specifies. As Julio Maier has noted, this principle implies that "given a potentially prosecutable act, which can be pursued, there is an obligation to advance a criminal prosecution and, following the pertinent procedural formalities, arrive at a judicial decision that resolves the case according to the norms of criminal law, and bring the process to a conclusion" (Maier 2002: 830). The principle of legality seeks to offer juridical security and to minimize the opportunities the authorities might have to deviate from their legal mandates. The opposite of legality is the principle of opportunity, characterized by the introduction of opportunities for official arbitrariness and exceptions to the strict application of the legal mandate.[3] Because the law obliges the public prosecutor to investigate and determine whether there is a crime to prosecute, the principle of legality seeks to ensure that crimes do not go unpunished.

The *principle of public or official prosecution* shares traits with the principle of legality. Some authors even consider that the latter is included in the former. I treat them separately because of their great importance in the Mexican criminal justice system, particularly in regard to the public prosecutor's "monopoly of the criminal action" and the rights of victims and complainants.

---

3 Mexico's institutional framework has recently incorporated provisions that represent exceptions to the principle of strict legality. For example, so-called organized crime cases are governed by legislation that allows suspects to receive benefits and less harsh sentences if they cooperate with the authorities by giving information about their accomplices.

In Mexico, only the state can prosecute crimes. That attribute has been delegated exclusively (as a monopoly) to the public prosecutor, the sole party with authority to investigate crimes, examine the evidence, decide autonomously if a criminal action should be pursued, and carry out the criminal proceeding. Recently, following a reform to constitutional Article 21, this "monopoly of the criminal action" was breached when a provision was put in place making it possible to challenge the failure to pursue a criminal action.

The institutional environment within which the actors in the preliminary inquiry and the criminal proceeding interact is shaped by the *principles relating to the structure of the process and the conduct of the parties*. Among these principles, the two most notable are: (1) the separation of the institution that indicts (the public prosecutor) and the institution that prosecutes (the judge and criminal magistrates); and (2) the equality of the parties to a criminal procedure. However, in regard to the latter, laws and legal doctrine in Mexico make the public prosecutor a "privileged" party. The right to a hearing and adequate defense and the principle of cross-examination also fall within this category.

The *principle of historical truth and the principles of evidence* are also related to the aspect of legality. They seek to arrive at the truth of events and to act based on legal suppositions and the mandates that arise from them for determining, according to the facts of the case, whether a criminal action should be pursued and if the accused party should be acquitted or sentenced. Historical truth implies a genuine knowledge of the events that will be legally evaluated by the judge. It seeks to bridge the gap between legal or formal truth and the reality of events since, to the degree that both coincide, the law will be fulfilling its social goal of achieving justice based on the truth.

Figure 6.3 shows the dynamic interaction among participants in the criminal trial. The public prosecutor is the key actor, the only one who can initiate a criminal proceeding, under the restrictions to the "monopoly of the criminal action" already mentioned. In practice, those restrictions have been statistically insignificant (see Zepeda Lecuona 2004: 433ff), and for that reason the prosecutor appears as the obligatory mediator between the judge and the victims, offended parties, and society in general. There is no direct relationship between the victim and likely perpetrator. Consequently, rather than private vengeance, we have public prosecution, which is the responsibility of the public prosecutor who is both an impartial legal professional and a government official.

Figure 6.3. Constitutionally Established Principles and Guidelines
Articulated by the Law and Other System Norms

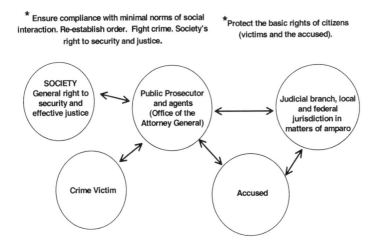

CRIMINAL LAW ENFORCEMENT AND THE PRELIMINARY INQUIRY: CASE OVERLOAD AND IMPUNITY

An initial review of available empirical evidence reveals the importance and practical preeminence of criminal law enforcement agencies and their protagonist, the public prosecutor. As Reames notes in his chapter in this volume, the preliminary inquiry is carried out by the Office of the Public Prosecutor, which is subordinate to the federal or state Office of the Attorney General. This procedure is a crucial and fundamental part of the institutional process for public security and criminal justice (see figure 6.4). It is at the heart of the problem of impunity. Empirical evidence indicates an inability on the part of prosecutors to duly respond to the public's demand for service. The principle of legality assumes that in every matter brought to their attention, the prosecutors must determine whether a crime has occurred. However, in Mexico, fewer than one in five inquiries concludes satisfactorily (18.25 percent) (see figure 6.5). The remaining 81.75 percent are not concluded, and consequently cheat those who file crime reports of their expectations for justice. The public prosecutor declines to investigate a significant 38.6 percent of reported crimes (*pendientes*), and 25.4 percent of reported crimes are closed for lack of evidence (*archivadas con las reservas de ley*). Some are closed either because the likely perpetrator is never captured (*consignados sin detenido*, 5 percent) or because the statute of limitations runs out (*por prescripción*, 12.8 percent).

Figure 6.4. The Crime Phenomenon and the Mexican Justice System, 2001

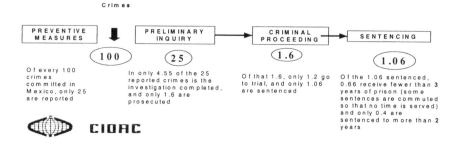

Sources: Author's estimates based on the proportion of reported crimes, from ICESI 2002: 32; completion of investigations from INEGI 2002, with information from the local public prosecutors' offices; court cases discharged and number of sentences based on *Cuaderno de Estadísticas Judiciales en Materia Penal* 10 (INEGI), with information from local courts.

Preliminary inquiries that are considered to have been concluded satisfactorily (the shaded parts of figure 6.5) fall into three categories. First, successful conclusion of a preliminary inquiry may occur when there is a crime to prosecute, a case is filed in the courts, and the accused is either captured or detained with an arrest warrant (*con detenido*) or appears voluntarily, having been out on bond or free under an injunction or appeal (*presentados*). Warrant detentions and voluntary detentions represent 3.3 and 3.1 percent, respectively, of all cases of reported crime. Second, 4.4 percent of preliminary inquiries are considered concluded if the matter falls outside of the public prosecutor's jurisdiction, as in cases that come under federal jurisdiction and must be turned over to the attorney general or that involve a minor and must be turned over to the child-protection agency (*no hubo competencia*). Finally, a case is closed definitively when it is determined that there is no crime to prosecute or that, despite the probability of a crime, the law allows it be closed, as, for example, when a victim drops the charges; this occurs in 7.4 percent of cases. These three categories of preliminary inquiries that are received and concluded satisfactorily sum to only 18.25 percent of all reported crime.

Figure 6.5. Preliminary Inquiries in Mexico, 2000

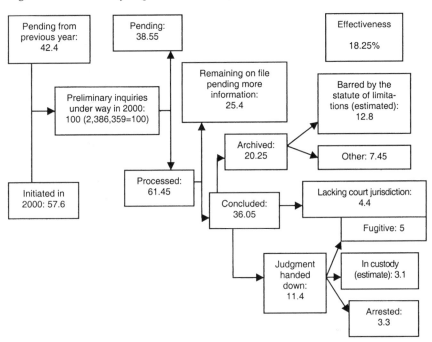

Source: INEGI 1998–2001. Durango is not included (Zepeda Lecuona 2004: 177).
Note: Only includes backlog from 1999.

These matters are considered "effectively concluded" because the prosecutors have fulfilled their obligation to clarify whether or not a case exists. Clarification occurs when it is determined that a crime has been committed (and the suspect has been arrested or the accused appears voluntarily), there is no crime to prosecute, or the nature of the matter (falling under federal jurisdiction or involving a suspect who is a minor) requires

Figure 6.6. Average Number of Crime Reports, by State-level Public Prosecutors' Offices, 2000

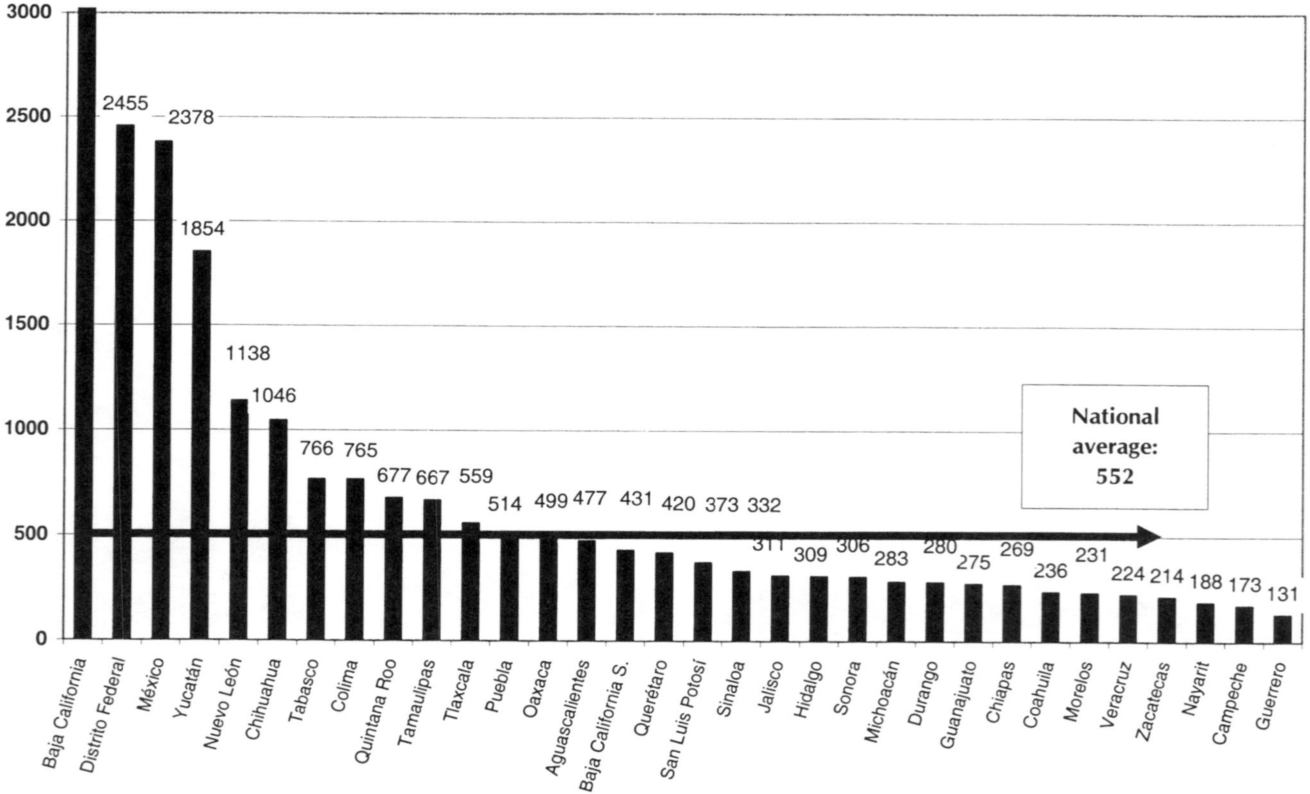

National average: 552

Source: Prepared by the author with data from INEGI 2000.

that the case be processed in another venue. The matters in which it is deemed that the prosecutors have not acted effectively are those in which the case is never investigated, it is closed for lack of evidence, the statute of limitations runs out, or there is a crime to prosecute and a case is filed in court but the presumed offender is never captured.

One of the main causes of this low level of effectiveness in the conclusion of criminal investigations is the prosecutors' heavy workload. There is no "filter" prior to the preliminary inquiry (see figures 6.2 and 6.4). In other countries, police headquarters or an office within the public prosecutor's office classifies and evaluates evidence, channeling minor infractions to other offices or dismissing clearly inadmissible cases. In Mexico, in contrast, all demands for a response concerning allegedly criminal acts are directed to the public prosecutor's office. Almost 10 percent of the caseload for that office consists of complaints on matters that are not properly considered crimes but that might become crimes (*consignaciones de hechos*). These reports are filed by individuals who want to show good faith and free themselves from any potential future responsibility in the matter.

Case overload has saturated the public prosecutors' offices. In 2000 each prosecutorial agency in Mexico's local jurisdictions had to process an average of 552 cases (see figure 6.6) in addition to the backlog from prior years. In the states for which disaggregated data are available, we can see that the workload is almost double the average because some agencies are assigned to the civil courts, where they perform the role of social representatives, overseeing the legality of trials. Thus the agencies are not only "investigative" or, as they are sometimes called, "interrogative," but they are also required to prosecute the case in court. With such workloads, it is obvious that they cannot provide quality service. Since these agencies must differentiate between cases as they administer scarce resources, they de facto empower themselves with discretionary attributes. These de facto discretionary powers (not only unregulated but also illegal) and the difficulties in oversight (supervisors cannot readily determine if a case is closed because an investigation cannot be effectively processed or because it has been marginalized intentionally or due to negligence) create room for impunity and opportunities for corruption.

The ineffectiveness of the public prosecutors' offices during the investigative stage and in presenting presumed offenders before the courts is very apparent, and it reflects a disquieting impunity. Only twenty-five of every hundred crimes are reported; of the total of reported crimes, in only 23.25 percent is a suspect identified, and in only 56.1 percent of the 23.25 percent does the suspect appear before a judge (when the culprit is caught in the act, arrested under a warrant, or turns him or herself in).[4] This means that only 3.3 percent of people who commit a crime will be brought to trial (see column 4 in table 6.1).

Table 6.1. Estimates of Criminal Impunity in Mexico during Preliminary Inquiry and the Fulfillment of Arrest Warrants (local jurisdictions, 2000)

Reported Crimes	Investigations Concluded	Appearance or Capture of Accused	Likelihood Accused Will Be Prosecuted
25%	23.25%	56.14%	3.3% (0.03263)

Source: CIDAC, based on data from INEGI 2000.

Even if we exclude the *cifra negra* (the "dark figure," or the proportion of crimes never reported to the authorities) and draw a conclusion based only on crime reports that are filed, we still find high levels of impunity (table 6.2); the likelihood that the suspect in a reported crime will be brought to court is only 13 percent (column 3 of the table).[5]

Table 6.2. The Contribution of Preliminary Investigations to Criminal Impunity in Mexico (local jurisdictions, 2000)

Investigations Concluded	Appearance or Capture of Accused	Likelihood Accused Will Be Prosecuted
23.25%	56.14%	13% (0.1305255)

Sources: Column 1, CIDAC, based on data from INEGI 2000; column 2, CIDAC, based on judicial statistics.

---

[4] Appearance before a judge occurs when the person appears voluntarily or is presented by the judicial or ministerial police without being under arrest, in virtue of having the right to release on bail. Similarly, this occurs when the accused appears before the judge under *amparo* (injunction or appeal).

[5] When impunity is presented in terms of table 6.1, the authorities argue that they cannot be held accountable for crimes that are never reported. However, it must be stressed that, in an indirect fashion, institutional conduct is basic to the proportion of crime reports filed by citizens. A victimization survey in Mexico found that 50 percent of victims who did not file crime reports stated that they opted not to do so because they considered it a "waste of time" and/or the process was "long and difficult," and 19 percent stated that they distrust the authorities (ICESI 2003: 18).

IMPACTS OF CASE OVERLOAD AND INEFFECTIVE INVESTIGATIONS ON THE EFFICACY OF JUSTICE SYSTEM PRINCIPLES

Inefficiencies, insufficiencies, and uncontrolled discretionary powers in the prosecutors' routine performance are all apparent during preliminary inquiries. These elements not only cause noncompliance with the principles of the criminal justice system, but they actually subvert them, creating situations that are utterly contrary to the intent of the system's institutional design. I comment briefly below on these subversions (also see figure 6.7).

Figure 6.7. The Subversion of the Principles of the Criminal Justice System

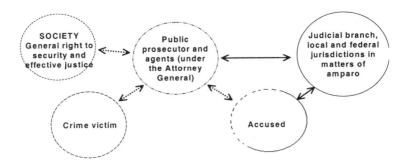

The Principle of Legality and the Public Prosecutor

Institutional, material, and labor conditions in the offices where public prosecutors work do not allow them to fulfill their important constitutional and legal mission. These conditions also impede prosecutors from meeting the public's expectations (the prosecutor is, after all, society's representative) and, especially, the expectations of complainants and crime victims.

The principle of legality dictates that all cases be investigated and that every matter (whether a serious crime or not, and whether a private party or the state initiates the complaint) be analyzed and investigated so that the material truth can be put at the service of criminal justice. This principle is not being met. Instead, in practice, the principle of opportunity comes into play. Cases are prioritized, with serious crimes processed more quickly while minor and potential crimes are marginalized. The Research Center for Development (CIDAC) has identified strategies used in offices of the attorneys general to cope with case overload. For example, certain matters (such as theft of cellular telephones or document robberies) are closed in order to avoid the bother of opening a criminal investigation. The victims receive "vouchers" so they can file claims with their insurance companies, arrange to replace stolen goods, or free themselves from liability related to the goods taken from them. Some discretionary budget allocations and the "filtering" and classification of case files are legitimate and necessary (though these are clearly distinct from refusing to investigate or marginalizing cases). Such administrative procedures occur in justice systems of countries throughout the world. However, in Mexico, in addition to the illegality of some of these modalities, most mechanisms are discretionary and are not duly regulated or subject to an adequate system of control.

Notable among the common anomalies in prosecutorial activity is the prosecutor's inability to directly supervise the investigation because of case overload. Many of the office's powers are informally delegated to the judicial police. Indeed, Juventino V. Castro has called the public prosecutor the "clerk of the judicial police."

Society, Victims, and Complainants without Effective Representation

The offices of the public prosecutors cannot fulfill the role of official investigator for the criminal matters presented to them. Criminal law, as "transpersonal" law (that is, added to the victim's individual grievance is the social injustice that the transgression of basic social norms signifies), has created the office of the public prosecutor, a legal expert who is responsible for the criminal investigation, who gathers evidence, and who represents society and the victim or complainant in their legitimate expectations of justice. However, facing the impossibility of investigating all cases, in practice the prosecutors lay much of the cost burden of the investigation on the victim. (For example, a victim must bring the facts and evidence directly to the official's desk if the case is to move forward.) In fact, unfair and unconstitutional barriers impede the filing of crime reports and the participation of the victim. In addition to the wait times, there are such practices as "ratification" of the crime report and validation of its provenance, as well as the high costs of participating in the preliminary inquiry and the criminal trial. Thus both the victim (whose rights have had constitutional status since 2000) and society seem to disappear from the process (figure 6.7); their rights are not duly protected, nor do they receive sufficient support from the authorities.

The Human Rights of the Presumed Offender

The rights of the presumed offender are very weak vis-à-vis the powers of the public prosecutor. In addition to being the investigating official, the prosecutor also has custody of the prisoner, so that only internal administrative controls exist, controls that have proven to be very lax. Moreover, legislation and jurisprudence have accorded great evidentiary weight to the preliminary inquiry. Thus this markedly interrogatory stage (investigating and evaluating the legal status of the accused, who is in the custody of the same authority that is investigating the case) is carried out by administrative officials and, basically, under internal administrative controls. Yet it is here that actions and inquiries take place that will have tremendous importance if the case comes to trial. Discretionary powers without effective controls are linked to uncertainty and human rights violations (many documented by the states' human rights commissions). Of the human rights commissions' recommendations, 70 percent are aimed at the criminal justice system (50 percent name public prosecutors' offices, and 15 percent name the corrections system).

POSSIBLE LINES OF ACTION

The offices of the state attorneys general can no longer tolerate merely superficial or cosmetic reforms. The Mexican criminal justice system requires profound transformation. We must recognize that the institution of public prosecutor and the way in which its offices operate no longer meet the needs of society.

The public prosecutor's office was created by, and has remained within the administrative sphere of, the executive branch in a country where, for decades, the powers of the presidency had no checks and balances. Today Mexicans suffer from a criminal justice system that incubated during decades of presidentialism. The public prosecutor, through legislative or judicial means, has received exaggerated faculties for which there is no accountability. The phrase "arbitrariness without effective controls" sums up the reach of prosecutorial powers. We have been very successful in our ongoing task of taking the bell off the cat.

These unchecked powers have not come about by chance. They are part of a vision of public power that made the executive desirous of conserving the scope of its dominion, with full discretion and without external controls. That dominion extends to the investigation and prosecution of crimes, including an uncontested faculty to assert its determinations before the court in order to convict prisoners. These powers have converted the public prosecutor's office into one more piece in an extensive network of control at the disposal of hegemonic political interests. In the selective application of criminal law, the goal of ensuring the punishment of the dissident and guaranteeing the impunity of the ally is largely the raison d'être of the current design of Mexico's criminal law enforcement institution.

A profound transformation is needed to guarantee the technical autonomy of the office responsible for investigating crime and prosecuting presumed offenders, to isolate that office from political ambitions and vicissitudes, to endow it with autonomy and a career civil-service structure, and to establish a clear-cut system of regular supervision by independent organizations. Once a new institutional design is in place that contains these elements of the rule of law (transparency and control in the exercise of powers), we will be able to address the infrastructural and organizational requirements for improving criminal investigation and for extending basic rights to both crime victims and those accused of crimes.

The basic challenge of a criminal investigation and the processing of crime reports is the organization of work and the system of case management. Better administration of those aspects would enable us to give full attention to the public's expectation for justice. In regard to case management, we must take measures in at least three areas: the authorities' capacity for immediate response; the classification (rather than prioritization) of cases (to give them specialized attention and to better channel scarce resources); and the organization of the investigative process to ensure that investigating officers have sufficient and highly trained personnel who can meet the demand for service.

Because criminal investigations and trials would be transparent and the powers of the authorities would be subject to a system of effective control, the proposed institutional design would also support the demand for respect for victims' and prisoners' basic rights. Additionally, victims and prisoners must be able to count on safeguards and have access to institutional instruments to contribute to—or even dispute—the work of the investigators. We must also have organizations and professionals who are responsible for effecting two constitutional principles that the current prosecutors have systematically forgotten (even though the label "prosecutor" arises from those very principles). The first is the public and official prosecution of crimes, a principle established to relieve victims of the high costs of investigating the facts and sponsoring the trial. The second is legality and good faith on the part of the investigating authorities, who must adhere to the mandates of the regulations that support the basic rights and dignity of the parties involved in a criminal investigation.

This is certainly only an initial list of areas in which an integral law enforcement reform should occur. That reform must take place in a way that articulates with reforms occurring within the police, the judiciary, and the corrections system. Each line of action merits a profound national debate and the elaboration of concrete diagnostics and specific programs for implementation.

Change will not be effortless given the institutional inertia that has had eighty years of encouragement. Uncontrolled discretion has resulted in a lucrative arbitrariness that will not be easily overturned. However, Mexican society must confront this challenge. Otherwise, given the current state of the nation's institutions, the scourge of crime inertia could continue, enveloping the country in a spiral of violence and impunity.

References

Fajnzylber, Pablo, Daniel Lederman, and Norman Loayza. 1998. *What Causes Violent Crime?* Washington, D.C.: Office of the Chief Economist for Latin America and the Caribbean Region, World Bank.

———. 2001. "Crimen y victimización, una perspectiva económica." In *Crimen y violencia en América Latina*, ed. Pablo Fajnzylber, Daniel Lederman, and Norman Loayza. Bogotá: World Bank/Alfaomega.

Ferrajoli, Luigi. 1995. *Derecho y razón: teoría del garantismo penal*. Madrid: Trotta.

Fix Zamudio, Héctor. 2002. *Función constitucional del Ministerio Público*. Mexico City: Instituto de Investigaciones Jurídicas, Universidad Nacional Autónoma de México.

ICESI (Instituto Ciudadano de Estudios sobre la Inseguridad A.C.). 2002. *Primera Encuesta Nacional sobre Inseguridad Pública en las Entidades Federativas: resultados finales*. Mexico City: ICESI. At http://www.icesi.org.mx.

———. 2003. *Segunda Encuesta Nacional sobre Inseguridad en las Entidades Federativas: resultados finales*. Mexico City: ICESI. At http://www.icesi.org.mx.

INEGI (Instituto Nacional de Estadística, Geografía e Informática). 2000. *Cuaderno de estadísticas judiciales*. Mexico City: INEGI.

———. 2002. *Cuaderno de Estadísticas Judiciales en Materia Penal*. Mexico City: INEGI.

———. Various years. *Anuarios estadísticos estatales*. Mexico City: INEGI.

Kahan, Dan M. 1997. "Between Economics and Sociology: The New Path of Deterrence," *Michigan Law Review* 95, no. 5: 2477–97.

Kangaspunta, Kristiina, Matti Joutsen, and Natalia Ollus, eds. 1998. *Crime and Criminal Justice in Europe and North America*. Helsinki: European Institute for Crime Prevention and Control (HEUNI).

Maier, Julio B. J. 2002. *Derecho procesal penal, Tomo I, Fundamentos*. 2d ed. Buenos Aires: Editores del Puerto.

Rawls, John. 1993. *Teoría de la justicia*. Madrid: Fondo de Cultura Económica.

Van Dijk, Jan J.M. 1996. "Cómo interpretar las estadísticas delictivas," *Revista Mexicana de Procuración de Justicia* (Procuraduría General de Justicia del Distrito Federal) 1, no. 1 (February): 77–98. Originally published as "Understanding Crime Rates: On the Interactions between the Rational Choices of Victims and Offenders," *British Journal of Criminology* 34 (1994).

Zepeda Lecuona, Guillermo. 2004. *Crimen sin castigo: procuración de justicia penal y ministerio público en México*. Mexico City: Fondo de Cultura Económica/ Centro de Investigación para el Desarrollo.

CHAPTER 7

The Militarization of the Procuraduría General de la República: Risks for Mexican Democracy

SIGRID ARZT

This chapter examines the political risks of the militarization of Mexico's Procuraduría General de la República (PGR, roughly equivalent to the U.S. Attorney General's Office) in the fight against organized crime during the first half of the administration of President Vicente Fox Quesada (2000–2006). It analyzes one of the most significant challenges for Mexico's new democracy: the expansion of the traditional functions of military personnel, manifested in their involvement in the fight against organized crime. This incremental role for the Mexican military appears in the context of a severe crisis of public insecurity, and it constitutes one of the least analyzed phenomena in studies on the consequences of Mexico's democratic transition.

This analysis has two fundamental premises. First, civilian institutions, particularly those dedicated to questions of public security, have been overtaxed by the fight against organized crime in, for example, matters such as drug trafficking. Second, although the military's collaboration in combating organized crime has had major successes, these must be viewed critically, taking into account possible political risks of that involvement for the military as an institution. These risks exist because of a lack of genuine civilian checks and balances to the work performed within the PGR by the armed forces, especially by the army and, to a lesser degree, the navy. The first part of this chapter clarifies how militarization is understood and how the involvement of the military in public security work developed during the first years of the Fox administration. The second part presents an accounting of the risks and achievements resulting from this militarization.

Translation by Patricia Rosas.

Finally, looking to the future, three scenarios are proposed concerning the militarization of the Mexican security apparatus.

THE PROCESS OF MILITARIZATION: THE CASE OF THE PGR

The process of militarization should not be understood as the mere presence of military personnel in civilian departments of the government—the Attorney General's Office or other posts related to public security and civilian intelligence—and their consequent participation in strategic decision making. Additionally, we must take into account three other considerations in addition to militarization:

- the lack of checks and balances to militarization, which clearly indicates institutional immaturity and, consequently, the fragility of democracy in Mexico;

- the lack of investment in training adequate numbers of civilian police to meet the challenge of combating crime; and

- an increasing concentration of human and economic resources in military police work—particularly those assigned to the Departments of Defense and the Navy (see table 7.1)—with less invested in the civilian police.[1]

Historically, little has been known about the Mexican military, given that the armed forces have lacked any culture of transparency whatsoever. The military's "political isolation" was part of the old arrangement in force throughout the rule of the Institutional Revolutionary Party (PRI) regime, when the military was subjected (only slightly, or not at all, to accountability and) to a civilian control strictly linked to the president and the PRI (Arzt 2002; Camp 1992). However, the difficulty in getting information about the operations of the armed forces in public security matters should not be attributed solely to shortcomings in the old regime. The facile response from President Fox when confronting public insecurity—increasing the military's involvement in combating organized crime—exacerbated this. At first glance, this decision sent a message that the new administra-

---

[1] For example, there has been a 20 percent cut in the budget of the National Information and Security Center (CISEN), along with a paring down of its personnel. Approximately 200 positions have been cut from CISEN's operations arm. Meanwhile, the PGR has been reorganized and the funding allocation for the armed forces has increased (table 7.1).

tion would use an iron fist in security matters. However, the involvement of the military does not necessarily translate into an easing of Mexico's insecurity crisis.

Table 7.1. Federal Budget Allocations during the Zedillo Administration (1994–2000) and First Half of the Fox Administration (2001–2003) (in pesos)

| | Office of the Attorney General | Armed Forces Budget | |
		Defense Ministry (SEDENA)	Navy (SM)
1996	1,727,633,200	9,903,535,800	3,430,803,900
1997	2,538,910,000	12,110,610,000	4,419,400,000
1998	3,485,930,600	14,220,780,100	5,883,545,400
1999	3,970,865,600	16,593,440,000	6,606,990,000
2000	4,875,030,000	20,400,873,690	7,971,606,100
2001	5,594,400,000	22,424,626,000	8,873,400,000
2002	6,932,500,000	22,705,420,000	8,518,470,000
2003	7,154,300,00	22,831,496,500	8,899,171,701

Sources: *Diario Oficial de la Federación*, December 31, 2000, January 1, 2002, and December 30, 2002.

The History of the Militarization of Public Security

Martín Barrón Cruz (2003) maintains that the involvement of the Mexican Armed Forces in police matters relating to public security is not a new phenomenon, asserting that it goes back to the birth of Mexico as an independent nation. This claim is, simultaneously, both true and untrue, and we must examine it with care. To compare the "militarization of public security" during Mexico's first century of independence with the current involvement of military personnel in the fight against crime is a complicated task.

First, the Mexican political situation between Independence and the establishment of the postrevolutionary civilian regime had a key characteristic: apparent or latent instability provoked by the conduct of actors in the system. Between 1821 and 1929, Mexico suffered two invasions, one by the United States (1846–1848) and another by France (1861–1867), two major civilian wars (the Reform and the Revolution of 1910), and innumerable armed domestic conflicts, insurrections, and short-lived governments. The only prolonged period of relative peace was the dictatorship of General Porfirio Díaz, which was certainly characterized by the presence of military power throughout the entire country. During that entire stage of Mexico's history, military forces had no other function than to involve themselves with the internal security of the government in power, that is, to impede a possible rebellion or coup d'état. The definition of public security in the nineteenth and at the beginning of the twentieth centuries is not comparable to the current definition. This is the case simply because the political and social dynamics of a stable civilian regime, which did not appear until after the Revolution, are very different from those of the governments and dictatorships headed by the military or the feeble civilian administrations that were continuously threatened by dissident military forces.

Second, although caudillos and generals were responsible for initiating the consolidation of the modern Mexican state at the end of the Revolution, the political system was gradually transformed into a civilian regime. In the process, the involvement of military authorities in government affairs was steadily restricted to limit their responsibilities solely to matters of national security. As the military presence in government offices was reduced, the modern concept of public security as a function that would be assigned to civilian authorities also emerged. The relative political stability of postrevolutionary Mexico propitiated—from at least 1940 until the present—the most prolonged period of civilian control of the security apparatus (rather than vice versa) in the history of the country. Therefore, contrary to Barrón's argument, the involvement of the armed forces in combating organized crime within a stable civilian regime in Mexico is a new phenomenon.

Militarization in Mexico has occurred concurrently with the evolving definition of national security following the sociopolitical events of the 1970s and 1980s. It is also essential to consider the political pressures exercised by the U.S. government during that time. Yet it was actually after the mid-1980s and around the beginning of the 1990s that a sector of the federal government began to take an interest in addressing the precariousness of the country's security and justice institutions, although those actions continued to be influenced by the connections and control of the ruling PRI regime.

The strengthening presence of the military apparatus in various government arenas—particularly those of security, intelligence, and justice—is a process that has been prescribed for the political apparatus, particularly since the administration of President Carlos Salinas de Gortari (1988–1994).

Salinas institutionalized the use of the armed forces in anti–organized-crime operations—at that time, primarily operations against drug traffick-ing—by including it in the National Development Program (Programa Nacional de Desarrollo, 1988–1994). This official document, which served as the centerpiece for public policy on security matters, recognized drug trafficking as a problem of national security, and as such legitimated the open participation of the military in fighting it (Toro 1995).

During the administration of President Ernesto Zedillo Ponce de León (1994–2000), the tendency to use the armed forces in public security work was furthered by the public security crisis, coupled with the disintegration of the institutions for security and justice administration. At the time, op-ponents to this strategy cited the risks inherent in the armed forces' par-ticipation in these activities: exposing the military to increased corruption, exposing the citizenry to possible human rights violations by the military, and invading the jurisdictions of civilian forces charged with combating crime. Ignoring these criticisms, Zedillo noted in his governing document on the war against drugs, "The Ministry of Defense contributed to the reduction in generalized violence arising from organized crime relating to drugs, chemical precursors, and firearms, as well as to the intensification in searching for, finding, and eradicating crops" (PGR 1995).

After December 1995, with the promulgation of the Law Establishing the General Bases for the National Public Security Council (Ley que Esta-blece las Bases Generales del Consejo Nacional de Seguridad Pública), the military's involvement in public security work became even more visible. The National Public Security Council (CNSP) integrated both the army and navy—and consequently the entire administrative structures of those agencies—in tasks related not only to the control of drug trafficking but also to security matters more generally. During the Zedillo administration, the defense minister, General Enrique Cervantes Aguirre, created and promoted the National Defense Program IV, which involved the geo-graphic restructuring of the armed forces in the fight against drug traffick-ers (La Jornada 2000a).

Because of the military's ever-increasing presence in domestic security and in the federal police apparatus, in March 1996 the Party of the Democ-ratic Revolution (PRD) and the National Action Party (PAN) challenged the participation of the armed forces in public security matters, based on Article 129 of the Mexican Constitution. In response, the Supreme Court noted that, "As long as the authorities need the support of the army, and considering that the armed forces are under the orders of the president, its participation in public security tasks does not violate constitutional precepts" (Cossío 2002). Moreover, the court validated the use of confessions extracted by the military, arguing that these arrests and interrogations were performed in the context of anti-drug activities and while assisting the Office of the Public Prosecutor and the Judicial Police (*Semanario* 1989: 148).[2] From then on, the military authorities were legally empowered to take statements. However, because they lacked adequate training for this task, they utilized torture in the interrogations. This has been widely denounced by human rights organizations, and it obviously impedes the development of the rule of law in Mexico.

By this time, the PAN had joined those who were calling for the establishment of stronger control mechanisms to monitor the military's involvement in public security tasks. During his presidential campaign, Vicente Fox promised to withdraw the armed forces from the fight against drugs, saying that soldiers who were working in areas that were the purview of the civilian police forces would be sent back to their barracks (*El Financiero* 2000). Later, a member of the Coordinating Body for Security and Justice in the transitional cabinet stated, "In the PGR's new structure, the military will not be given commands, such as those that they exercised illegally in the Federal Judicial Police and Federal Preventive Police forces." Another member, Francisco Molina, declared, "the army functions well doing the ancillary tasks of eradicating crops and aerial interception, because that does not require a capacity for criminology. The soldier is trained only to obey" (*Proceso* 2000).

The Militarization of the PGR during the Fox Administration

Upon assuming the presidency, Fox sought to demonstrate his resolve to take effective steps to halt the explosion in crime and to reduce impunity. Thus, contrary to his campaign promises to withdraw members of the military from the police and intelligence arenas, in forming his cabinet Fox named an active-duty general as attorney general. General Rafael Macedo de la Concha had been the attorney general for military justice during the

---

[2] A confession to the military authorities has evidentiary weight. The text states, "Although the army is not responsible for the prosecution of crimes, since that is the responsibility of the public prosecutor and the judicial police, according to Article 21 of the Constitution, a confession made to military authorities is valid if it is made in the context of the war on drugs and with the approval of the public prosecutor."

Zedillo administration. When Macedo's name went to the Senate for his ratification as head of the PGR, only the PRD voted against his appointment.

The presidential decision to appoint a general to head the PGR initially let Fox capitalize on major achievements in combating drug trafficking, especially those based on collaboration and coordination among the armed forces. However, these achievements or successes must be examined in light of a basic variable I will call "temporality" or "the political cycle." This is critical because today, as in the past, the fight against organized crime has been subject to politicization and partisanship. Thus we should not be surprised that certain achievements or themes of the public security agenda are publicized at election time. This was especially true in the past when the U.S. Congress was reviewing Mexico's annual certification as a partner in the war on drugs.

With the current increase in certain prerogatives given to the armed forces, the institutional legacy of civil-military relations from the PRI regime continues in the new context of the Fox administration. According to Alfred Stepan (1998: 93), military prerogatives are found when the military institution assumes that its members have acquired a right or privilege, whether formal or informal, to exercise particular control in certain arenas—in this case, those of domestic security and justice. Certainly it is apparent that the Mexican military has lobbied to gain more control over the public security apparatus. It would be a mistake, therefore, to think of the increased role of the armed forces in civilian law enforcement as being a product of unilateral decisions by the executive. Indeed, it is quite probable that the armed forces are seeking to gain ground in this area as part of a redefinition of tasks and challenges involving national security and adjustments in security matters, undertaken with an eye to the modernization of other militaries worldwide (Moskos, Williams, and Segal 2000).

The military currently enjoys considerable public respect, although perhaps less so in rural areas where its presence is more tangible and military personnel commit the most human rights abuses. In fact, surveys indicate that the Mexican army and navy enjoy as positive a public image as universities and churches, in sharp contrast to the levels of prestige of the federal government and the police (Arzt 2004).

Currently, the Mexican military, like other institutions in Mexico, is immersed in a process of adapting to new rules while attempting to protect long-standing ways of doing things. According to Felipe Agüero (1998), as the military seeks to maintain its power and influence in the new democratic context, that power will also have to be adjusted to and supported by formal legal arrangements. This is one of the most important tasks still pending: the renovation of democratic civil-military relations in Mexico and the establishment of clear legal boundaries for the participation of the armed forces in public security tasks.

The militarization in the public security arena is an ad hoc policy response by the Mexican political elite as it faces increasing organized crime, particularly drug trafficking. However, no tools are being developed with which to collect in-depth information about the conduct of the armed forces and the military's true impact in mitigating crime. It is revealing that after almost a decade of using the armed forces in anti-drug operations, the production and transit of narcotics through Mexico continues with ease and drugs have actually become more available on the streets of the country's main cities. The fact that the executive is seeking ways to reform the legal framework to address street sales of drugs is in some ways an indication of this failure (*El Universal* 2003a).

Meanwhile, exposing the military institution to the fight against organized crime can have serious consequences. One example of this is the increase in the number of officers and other members of the armed forces who have been tried for drug-related crimes, which has generated ample interest in the media (*El Universal* 2003b). Corruption is just one of the many risks created by the militarization of public security; there are serious concerns about civil-military interactions as well as the role and identity of the military itself. Greater attention to these risks is needed to evaluate the "overall picture" of drug trafficking and the institutional fragility of Mexico's apparatus for combating organized crime.

THE RISKS AND ACHIEVEMENTS OF MILITARIZATION

Today it is clear that militarization has had successes in fighting organized crime. However, these achievements should be evaluated critically, taking into consideration the political risks both for the civilian security institutions and for the army, air force, and navy. This section singles out two instances of risk that increased militarization creates. The first refers to the impact of militarization in the context of the civilian public security apparatus, where I identify six issues:

- the absence of civilian checks and balances (a weak Congress);
- the lack of accountability and transparency, which impedes ending impunity in the institutions of the security apparatus;
- human rights violations;

- weak coordination with other civilian authorities;
- a greater concentration of power in the PGR; and
- the presence of corruption, impunity, and institutional weakness.

The second instance, which is more rarely examined, involves the armed forces as an active participant in the process of militarization. I identify four basic effects on the institutional ethos:

- internal tensions;
- negative effects on military professionalization;
- an impact on intelligence gathering; and
- exposure to corruption and impunity existing in the police forces.

Checks and Balances: The Militarization of Civilian Security and Justice

Due to the military's takeover of civil authority in the face of civilian incompetence and professional shortcomings, the first major risk appears in the arena of the civilian public security apparatus. This decision to militarize—rather than improve—the civilian security apparatus is most visible through changes in the PGR, the backbone of Mexico's criminal justice system. The military's presence is visible not only in high-level appointments to the Attorney General's Office but also in the organizations that train the PGR's civilian police recruits, which are also now headed by active or retired military officers. This reproduces patterns of military training in civilian police departments. As yet, there is absolutely no evidence that this practice has a positive impact in the fight against crime, or that it has prevented impunity and institutionalized corruption. There are several problems related to the military's takeover of civil security, including limited transparency and the lack of civilian oversight, human rights violations, weak coordination with civilian authorities, and corruption. An examination of the militarization of the Attorney General's Office provides useful illustrations of these problems.

Inadequate Civilian Oversight

The institutional weakness of Congress to monitor the conduct of members of the armed forces, above all in its public security function, is not unique to Mexico but is constant in all Latin American governments (Basombrío Iglesias 1999). During the Fox administration, the militarization of the Attorney General's Office took place with little response from civilian authorities, and it continues without serious examination. General Macedo's appointment on December 7, 2000, as head of the PGR (appointment to this position has required Senate approval since 1995) occurred with 93 votes cast in favor by the PRI, PAN, and the Green Party (PVEM), and 15 votes cast against by the PRD.[3] Macedo's near-unanimous approval reflected the broad consensus among Mexico's major political parties which—having favored the use of military personnel to combat insecurity in their respective jurisdictions—generally support and rely without question on the participation of the armed forces for public security. Likewise, once Macedo was appointed, his testimony before the Justice and Human Rights Commission (Comisión de Justicia y Derechos Humanos) in both the Senate and the Chamber of Deputies has generally gone without rigorous questioning; fearful that it will be interpreted as a general indictment of the military as an institution, lawmakers generally treat the attorney general with deference.

It is worth noting in this context that advances in promoting transparency and accountability in other arenas have not contributed to greater civilian oversight of the PGR or other domestic security forces. Police forces, and military personnel in particular, resist being subjected to external control, as they are wary of intervention by nonprofessionals in their field and indignant of any sign of public mistrust (Ungar 2002: 67). Hence, when the Federal Law on Transparency and Access to Public Government Information (LFTAIPG) was promulgated, stipulations were included to ensure that information relating to public or national security would be excluded (see Articles 13, 14, and 15 of the law, published June 11, 2002, in the *Diario Oficial*). The result is that ongoing investigations, legal proceedings, and other actions by the PGR and other police agencies are at present legally shrouded from public scrutiny.

In short, the militarization of the PGR suggests that the armed forces have been able to expand their influence without serious civilian scrutiny, and they have been able to convince political elites that the military is the only entity capable of preventing the disintegration of the civilian security apparatus. In a nascent democracy, where the military has a culture lacking transparency and a history of human rights abuses, this continued

---

[3] The PRD opposition believed that, "allowing a military officer to take charge of the PGR further encouraged the derailment of the true work that is the jurisdiction of the military" (stenographic record from the Senate of Mexico, December 7, 2000; *La Jornada* 2000b).

(even expanded) role for the military in public security presents serious concerns. Indeed, according to Felipe Agüero, the militarization of civilian security, and especially the failure to distinguish lines of authority between civilians and the armed forces, severely undermines the quality of democracy (Agüero 1998: 384). Moreover, surveillance and supervision of public authorities are essential to democratization, particularly when an institution has been involved in acts of repression in the past. Therefore, unless civilian authorities create adequate checks and balances and civilian oversight mechanisms to monitor and correct the military's conduct, using the militarization of law enforcement as a way out of Mexico's insecurity crisis is a short-term strategy at best.

Human Rights Violations

The risk of more human rights violations due to militarization of public security is illustrated by a record of the PGR in recent years. In February 2003, for the second year in a row, Mexico's National Human Rights Commission (CNDH) announced that the PGR led all other security agencies in the number of complaints filed with the commission (Soberanes 2003).[4] The militarization of other civilian law enforcement forces, notably those of the Ministry of Public Security, was cited as a major contributing factor to human rights violations. According to CNDH President José Luis Soberanes (2003), "the activities entrusted to the Federal Preventive Police could compromise the respect for human rights, and the same happens with the participation of the military in public security tasks, since that is not an area appropriate to the army."

Nongovernmental organizations and international sources have expressed similar concerns. For example, the "Miguel Agustín Pro Juárez" Center for Human Rights reported that, with regard to arbitrary detentions in Mexico,

> PGR personnel from the Special Anti–Organized Crime Unit [UEDO], the AFI, and the Federal Judicial Police, as well as members of the Mexican army, occupy top positions among actors who violate individual liberties. Those acts result in the appropriation of other rights, such as victims' physical

---

[4] The PGR had six CNDH sanctions. It was followed by the Mexican Social Security Institute (IMSS) with five, the Ministry of Public Security (SSP) with four, and the Education Ministry (SEP) with three (Fox 2002: 573).

and psychological integrity and, when military and police personnel conspire with judicial authorities, the guarantee of due process and legal security ("PRODH Informe" n.d.: 4).

In 2002, in the wake of major revelations of corruption in a Sinaloan unit of the Mexican army, the U.S.-based Latin American Working Group issued a report asserting that "basic rights of citizens are being pushed aside," with escalating military involvement in the war on drugs contributing to "torture, arrests without warrants and even 'extrajudicial executions of civilians'" (Kraul 2002). Likewise, the U.S. State Department criticized "the extensive impunity that the security forces in Mexico continue to have" (U.S. Department of State 2002).

Weak Coordination with Civilian Authorities

The militarization of the PGR has brought increased coordination with the National Defense Ministry (SEDENA) and the navy, and significantly less reliance on ties to civilian law enforcement. An indication of this can be found in operations to combat organized crime conducted jointly by the PGR, SEDENA, and the navy, as well as in the expanded use of the army's Special Forces in lieu of PGR operatives. Currently, the Mexican army's Mobil Air Special Forces Groups (GAFES) are dedicated to carrying out the main anti-drug operations.[5] The GAFES are at the heart of the UEDO, which coordinates activities with the 7th Section of SEDENA (Anti-Drug Operations) in major operations against drug cartels. Through these efforts, the PGR and SEDENA managed to arrest Benjamín Arellano Félix, Adán Amezcua, and Gilberto García Mena, among other major drug traffickers.

However, despite their successes, these operations raise serious unanswered questions. What civilian control exists over these operations? What knowledge do civilian government entities have about these operations regardless of their level of success? What is the chain-of-command relationship between SEDENA and the PGR, given that military rank places the attorney general below the minister of defense? What is the mechanism for sorting out conflicts between civilian and military authorities in the

---

[5] U.S. institutions provided the initial training for the elite GAFES corps. Since 1998 the GAFES have had their own Special Forces School, with standardized criteria and specializations. The Mobile Air Special Forces Groups are experienced in anti-drug, anti-terrorist, and kidnapping-rescue operations. Nevertheless, as the authorities acknowledge, these groups are not free from corruption (*El Universal* 2003c).

event of crossfire in a particular operation? Certainly, public opinion has identified the capture of big drug-trafficking bosses as important successes for the Fox administration, but that alone does not address the complex dynamic of the security issues confronting Mexico.

Corruption, Impunity, and Institutional Weakness

During the first years of the Fox administration, the Ministry of Government Operations (SFP)—formerly known as the Ministry of Comptrollership and Administrative Development (SECODAM)—listed the PGR as one of the five federal institutions registering the highest levels of illicit acts and corruption. The others were the Ministry of the Treasury (SHCP), the Social Security Institute, the Energy Ministry, and the Mexican Petroleum Company (PEMEX). According to the Government Operations Ministry, at least 1,529 PGR employees, almost 10 percent of its entire workforce, were sanctioned for various types of violations during the first three years of the administration.

The size of the PGR administrative staff presents the Office of the Attorney General with one of its deepest structural challenges. It is incongruous that this institution, charged with reducing and containing federal-level crimes, has relatively few operational or field personnel. Of the nearly 18,000 PGR employees, 61 percent are administrative personnel, 10 percent are police, and only 4 percent are federal public prosecutors (*Excélsior* 2000). Added to this structural reality are low salaries and a major institutional deficiency in personnel recruitment. PGR salaries are less than half of the average level found in state-level offices of attorneys general (see table 7.2) and are not competitive with positions in other sectors. For example, a lead federal public prosecutor's salary is less than that of the head of the guard detail for a public official. In other words, a bodyguard earns more than the person responsible for conducting an investigation (table 7.2). Attorney General Macedo has promoted "salary modernization" within the PGR, which has helped bring PGR incomes more in line with those in other areas of public administration, but they still fall somewhat short.

In sum, this section has illustrated how the problems visible in the military takeover of civil authority indicate a considerable institutional immaturity and weakness in Mexican democracy. Below I consider the negative implications that this process has had for the military itself.

Table 7.2. Federal Budget Allocations for the Attorney General's Office

Position	Gross Salary (pesos)
Top-Ranking Civil Servants	
Attorney general of the republic	$224,557.10
Senior officer	213,190.89
Assistant attorney general	213,190.89
Special prosecutor	213,190.89
Assistant attorney general of the republic	207,991.11
Inspector general	176,682.90
Internal comptroller	160,620.82
Director general	160,620.82
State field officer	117,554.48
Commissioner of FEADS	176,682.90
FEADS coordinator general	176,682.90
Main Personnel	
Field Representatives	
Regional field officer	63,731.50
First field officer or from FEADS	48,195.05
Support field officer	38,606.70
FEADS backup	35,314.85
Federal Judicial Police	
Commander in chief	37,504.70
First commander	33,340.70
Second commander	27,911.55
First assistant commander	20,455.51
Second assistant commander	19,080.84
Agent "A"	17,607.09
Agent "B"	14,857.09
Agent "C"	11,557.09
Investigator for federal crimes	14,857.09
Federal Public Prosecutor's Office	
Chief, Special Prosecutor's Unit	49,428.90
Head agent	37,756.40
Adjunct agent	27,280.40
Assistant agent	22,476.45
Security Detail for Public Officials	
Chief of security agents	43,252.54
Assistant chief of security agents	35,887.93
Security agent "A"	30,386.17
Security agent "B"	27,794.93
Security agent "C"	25,216.27

Sources: Dirección General de Recursos Humanos, Dirección de Presupuesto y Sistematización, Subdirección de Operación del Sistema, PGR. January 2002.

Institutional Impacts on the Armed Forces

The second major impact of the militarization of public security is the potentially negative effect this process has on the armed forces themselves, both army and navy. These risks affect the armed forces' sense of identity and capacity for action. The basic question is, what happens when members of the armed forces are reassigned to perform activities—such as policing and public security—that are not strictly appropriate to the military discipline? I identify four basic problems: creation of tensions within the institution, a weakening of military professionalization, an impact on intelligence gathering, and putting the military at risk of exposure to corruption and impunity.

Diverted Mission of the Armed Forces

Theoretically, Mexico's military is supposed to provide ancillary support to civilian authorities, but in reality the military is the primary institution responsible for leading the war against organized crime, and it controls these operations. The Fox administration has been characterized by increasing coordination between the armed forces and the PGR in these activities. SEDENA, for example, established the administration's Coordinated Strategy against Drugs (Estrategia para el Combate Integral para las Drogas) (*El Universal* 2002). This strategy has components dedicated exclusively to "combating organized crime" and, more recently, to anti-kidnapping operations. According to Defense Secretary Vega García, successes in these areas have resulted from the use of the army's intelligence systems and collaboration with the PGR. The presence of a military man as attorney general, military commands in the departments of the Office of the Deputy Attorney for Special Investigation of Organized Crime (SIEDO) responsible for land and sea interception and operations, and the cooperation of the National Drug Control Center (CENDRO, also led by a military man) have all been crucially important in combating organized crime. It is very revealing that in the fight against crime, the armed forces have dedicated a combined force of almost 21,000 troops, while the PGR has only deployed about 3,000.

Distortion of Military Professionalization

The military career can be distorted when the processes of professionalization in the armed forces are truncated or diverted by participation in activities not appropriate for military personnel. Assigning military officers to public security tasks undoubtedly means that they lose out on other types of training and experience that would have been useful in their profession-alization as military personnel.

The military is one of the few institutions—along with the Ministry of Foreign Affairs (SRE)—that are known for long having a regulatory career-service framework. The military's participation in efforts to combat organized crime is a sore point in the career trajectory of military officers who perform public security tasks. Reassignment to police work has generated concern within the ranks of the armed forces because the regulatory framework is unclear in regard to where the performance of these tasks fits in the scheme of promotions, nor is it clear if participation in police activities contributes in any way to an officer's military résumé.

It is also important to talk about potential conflicts between hierarchies that militarization has created. Except for division generals who are retired, members of the army who work in the Office of the Attorney General are "commissioned"—that is, they do not entirely lose their responsibilities to SEDENA, and SEDENA can call up these "commissioned officers" at any time to perform tasks distinct from fighting crime. Therefore, based on rank and hierarchy, "commissioned officers" should be subordinate, first, to the head of SEDENA and not to the attorney general. Indeed, this could be applied to General Macedo himself, who, as a member of the military, should also answer to the head of SEDENA.

No legal framework yet exists to specify and delimit the boundaries of action for members of the armed forces in civilian departments, and that holds repercussions for careers in the military arena. The absence of this framework has led several members of Mexico's armed forces to refuse commissions in civilian areas because such a transfer could mean losing access to higher salaries or, as military service personnel themselves recognize, put them at greater risk of exposure to corruption (*El Universal* 2001). As stated in Article 29 of the Promotion and Compensation Law (Ley de Ascensos y Recompensas): "Promotions to the rank of colonel, brigadier general or general of a brigade, and division general will be conferred by the President of the Republic, based on professional merit, aptitude, and competence, as judged by that high official." However, Article 30 stipulates that "promotions will not be conferred on military personnel who are in any of the following situations: (a) on indefinite or special leave; (b) dishonorably discharged; (c) under prosecution."

This means, first, that the attorney general and army, air force, or navy personnel currently working in the PGR do not receive additional pay for the work and the responsibilities they carry out. Second, they are not eligible for promotion until they return to SEDENA or to their corresponding branch of the armed forces. Thus, having completed their six-year tour in the PGR, the generals, colonels, and lieutenant colonels are not entitled to promotions for which they would have been eligible had they not gone to the PGR. Third, military personnel working in civilian areas would not enjoy the rights pertaining to their branch of the military service because they are on furlough. This puts at risk the health and retirement benefits to which their families had been entitled, such as access to the Social Security Institute for Armed Forces Personnel (Instituto del Seguro Social de las Fuerzas Armadas).

Reallocation of Intelligence Capability

Today's military's intelligence apparatus is increasingly focused on developing criminal-intelligence capability, at the expense of intelligence in matters of national security. What is the armed forces' real ability to alert political leaders to a guerrilla threat or terrorist attack? For now, boundaries have not been set to define a clear concept of national security, in which laws would regulate both the civilian authorities and the military in the exercise of these tasks. On the other hand, the armed forces' growing participation in combating organized crime fosters the need for the military to create frameworks for criminal policy, something that is not in its purview and thus distorts the boundaries of the appropriate arena for military discipline.

Exposure to Corruption and Impunity

To involve the military in combating organized crime can result in the disintegration of the military institution and, consequently, in the loss of its prestige. An example of this is the "Narcotropa" scandal, which saw the arrest of forty-eight soldiers from the army's 65th Infantry Battalion deployed in Sinaloa. Both President Fox and Attorney General Vega García have repeatedly stated that anyone who embarrasses the army will be immediately turned over to military authorities. However, once again it is possible to see ambiguities in the application of the law; those soldiers who buckled to corruption should be tried by civilian courts, and not by military tribunals. With the exception of the arrest of General Jesús Gutiérrez Rebollo, a high-ranking officer who was tried by the civilian courts, most soldiers and officers involved with drug trafficking, particularly high-profile ones, have been turned over to the military justice system rather than to the civilian one. This gives wide latitude to the armed forces and keeps civilians out of the process (Pereira 2001). From this, it is clear that the military elite is maintaining its prerogative to "wash its dirty laundry at home" and to apply a policy of damage control in terms of its image and message. Unfortunately, this discretionary power emphasizes the impunity and lack of transparency in dealing with cases of military personnel suspected of drug-related crimes and human rights abuses.

A Double-Edged Sword: Militarization and the U.S.-Mexico Relationship

Despite the difficulties outlined above, the militarization process has had some favorable outcomes, which have important implications for the U.S.-Mexico bilateral relationship. It is important to point this out because, at the beginning of the war on drugs in the late 1970s, the role that Mexico's security and justice institutions took was primarily in response to U.S. pressures. However, as these pressures continued, the precariousness and deep weaknesses in Mexican government institutions dedicated to combating organized crime became apparent, as did the penetration of dirty money from the cartels. Given this reality, the United States looked favorably on the armed forces' involvement in public security work, particularly in fighting organized crime and drug trafficking. In the bilateral U.S.-Mexico framework, an undoubtedly important part of the security relationship is based on victories in combating those types of crimes. U.S. officials' favorable comments regarding the results achieved by the PGR and SEDENA are evidence of that.

With the dissolution of the annual certification process in the U.S. Congress and a post–September 11, 2001, turnabout in the focus of the U.S. government's domestic and external security apparatus—as attention shifted from the war on drugs to the war against terrorism—Mexico had to adjust to a new scenario. These new circumstances brought three important changes:

- Collaboration with the United States has intensified in information and intelligence exchanges. This has been particularly evident in counterterrorism work, although that comes in detriment to the work of combating drug trafficking, which is now a second-tier priority.

- There has been an improved flow of contact and support from U.S. authorities, which has translated into training and technical assistance for the Mexican military from U.S. experts (see table 7.3).

- In combating organized crime, but above all in liaison work related to the war on terrorism, there has been greater collaboration between Mexican military personnel and their U.S. counterparts.

Table 7.3. Number of Mexican Military Personnel Trained in the United States, 1983–2001

1983–1985	1986–1994	1995–1997	1998	2000	2001
293	821	1,910	1,085	622	1,363

Source: *Reforma*, November 7, 1997, at www.us.net/cip/facts/country.htm.

Both General Vega García and Attorney General Macedo have met with their U.S. counterparts to iron out the terms of the bilateral relationship on security matters and on combating organized crime. Those meetings have been particularly fruitful. First, the government in Washington has repeatedly expressed its satisfaction with the role that Mexico's armed forces play in anti–drug-trafficking tasks. Second, contacts, training, and technical assistance between the respective counterparts in the two nations have continued on course. Indeed, during his stay in the United States, General Vega García toured the academies where Mexican personnel are being trained.

Successes in combating organized crime, including the capture of major drug lords, were key to the development of this cordial environment. However, the events of September 11, 2001, shifted the U.S. administration's priorities to anti-terrorism work, and thus decreased the weight given to the results of anti–drug-trafficking operations. The United States is now much more focused on actions the Mexican government is taking to ensure security within its territorial boundaries and prevent Mexico from becoming a platform for a terrorist attack.

However, favoring the use of the armed forces in security tasks is a double-edged sword. On one hand, Washington currently seems to accept as inevitable the fact that responsibility for meeting domestic security needs cannot fall to any institution other than the military. On the other hand, in so doing, the United States is extending a blank check for the continuing involvement of the military in combating organized crime, without consideration of the political costs and domestic consequences for Mexican democracy.

SCENARIOS FOR MILITARIZATION

Based on the preceding discussion, we can suggest three alternative scenarios for a continued policy of militarization in Mexico's security and justice apparatus:

- If militarization continues as no more than an ad hoc policy response to the phenomenon of public insecurity, major institutional changes will not occur. Moreover, in security matters, the shortfall in trained professional civilian personnel will worsen. In the absence of a corresponding civilian force and civilian agencies to monitor the successes and failures of the military's participation in these security tasks, the armed forces will be able to define the public security agenda. In short, there will be no true democratic scrutiny.

- An attempt will be made to construct true public policy alternatives, in which the process of militarization could not be halted and the costs of exposing the armed forces to corruption could increase. Failure to move in the direction of incrementally removing the military from public security would place Mexican democracy at risk. The immediate implications include the emergence of subtle tensions within the armed forces, which could have grave consequences for the military's esprit de corps, integrity, and public reputation. Nevertheless, in the long run it will be the military alone (without any protection from those very politicians who have led it to participate more actively in public security) that will have to defend itself from the effects of its extensive participation in the security field: human rights violations, corruption, impunity, and, most likely, a loss of public prestige.

- The implementation of long-term policy, transcending political cycles, would allow Mexico to begin "civilian-izing" its police forces, achieving true civilian control by means of various institutional actors. These civilian organs would take the role of counterweights to actions undertaken by the armed forces, which are not subject to surveillance and institutionalized accountability. Such civilian accounting and oversight would go far beyond the measures the executive could implement, because civil society has to participate if genuine monitoring is to be achieved.

In summary, militarization poses political risks but, as has been apparent throughout this chapter, it also has its advantages. The big question will continue to be how effective and efficient the armed forces has been in combating organized crime, when we balance that against the ground lost in its proper labors of defending the nation (as contrasted to policing). As long as no policy is in place to establish the temporary nature of the military's presence in the public security arena, there will be serious hazards for Mexico's democracy.

References

Agüero, Felipe. 1998. "Legacies of Transitions: Institutionalization, the Military and Democracy in South America," *Mershon International Studies Review* 42: 383–404.

Arzt, Sigrid. 2002. "New Democracy, Old Arrangement: The Civil-Military Relations under Fox." Presented at the Center for Hemispheric Defense Studies, Brasilia, August 7–8.

———. 2004. "NGOs and the Construction of Civil Society in Mexico." Presented at the conference "Colombia and the NGOs," Center for Latin American Studies, University of Miami, March 5.

Barrón Cruz, Martín Gabriel. 2003. "Militarización de la seguridad pública en México: ¿actualización o permanencia histórica?" Project on Reforming the Administration of Justice in Mexico Working Paper. La Jolla: Center for U.S.-Mexican Studies, University of California, San Diego. At: http://repositories.cdlib.org/usmex/prajm/. Accessed August 2004.

Basombrío Iglesias, Carlos. 1999. "Militares y democracia en la América Latina de los '90: una revisión de los condicionantes legales e institucionales para la subordinación." In *Control civil y fuerzas armadas en las nuevas democracias latinoamericanas*, ed. Rut Diamint. Buenos Aires: Nuevohacer, Grupo Editor Latinoamericano.

Camp, Roderic Ai. 1992. *Generals in the Palacio: The Military in Modern Mexico.* New York: Oxford University Press.

Cossío, José Ramón. 2002. "Delincuencia organizada, seguridad pública y fuerzas armadas," *Revista de Justicia Mexicana* 4.

El Financiero. 2000. "Sorprende en Washington la designación de un militar en la PGR," November 29.

El Universal. 2000. "Evalúa su trayectoria intachable como jurista y militar," December 7.

———. 2001."Marinos desinteresados por PFP y PJF," December 13.

———. 2002. "Ejército combate narcotráfico," March 11.

———. 2003a. "Buscará facultar a los estados para combatir el narcomenudeo," June 26.

———. 2003b. "El ejército se abre y revela información," June 24.

———. 2003c. "Usan fuerzas de élite en lucha anticrimen," February 24.

Excélsior. 2000. "Resultados sobre seguridad, en 100 días: Macedo," December 14.

Fox, Vicente. 2002. "Recomendaciones de la CNDH a las autoridades de la administración pública federal, 2001–2002." In *II Informe de Gobierno, C. Presidente Vicente Fox Quesada.* September 1.

Kraul, Chris. 2002. "Mexican Army Unit to Be Disbanded Amid Drug Probe," *Los Angeles Times,* October 17.

La Jornada. 2000a. "La Sedena reestructuró la división territorial militar para garantizar la seguridad interior, afirma Cervantes Aguirre," February 20.

———. 2000b. "Rafael Macedo de la Concha fue ratificado como titular de la PGR," December 8.

Moskos, Charles, John Allen Williams, and David Segal. 2000. *The Postmodern Military, Armed Forces after the Cold War.* New York: Oxford University Press.

Pereira, Anthony. 2001. "Virtual Legality: Authoritarian Legacies and the Reform of Military Justice in Brazil, the Southern Cone, and Mexico," *Comparative Political Studies* 34, no. 5 (June).

PGR (Procuraduría General de la República). 1995. *Programa Nacional contra las Drogas, 1995–2000.* Mexico City: PGR.

Proceso. 2000. "Caso Macedo de la Concha: complicada ratificación," No. 1247 (December 3).

"PRODH Informe." n.d. "Miguel Agustín Pro Juárez" Center for Human Rights. At http:///www.sjsocial.org/PRODH/Publicaciones. Accessed August 2004.

Semanario Judicial de la Federación. 1989. 8th Session, Volume 3, Part II (January–June). *Jurisprudencia y Tesis Aisladas.* Tercer Tribunal Colegiado del Sexto Distrito. Delitos Contra la Salud.

Soberanes, José Luis. 2003. *Informe de actividades 2002.* Mexico City: Comisión Nacional de Derechos Humanos, February 12.

Stepan, Alfred. 1998. *Rethinking Military Politics.* Princeton, N.J.: Princeton University Press.

Toro, María Celia. 1995. *Mexico's "War" on Drugs: Causes and Consequences.* Boulder, Colo.: Lynne Rienner.

Ungar, Mark. 2002. *Elusive Reform, Democracy and the Rule of Law in Latin America.* Boulder, Colo.: Lynne Rienner.

U.S. Department of State. 2002. *Country Reports on Human Rights Practices. Mexico.* Washington, D.C.: The Department, March 31.

CHAPTER 8

Police Abuse in Mexico City

CARLOS SILVA

In some countries, including the United States, police brutality is considered nearly synonymous with the unjustified use of force during an arrest (Bayley 1996). But in Mexico, as in Latin America generally, police abuse refers to a broader set of events. This chapter, which focuses on Mexico's Federal District, examines the most disturbing forms of police abuse—those affecting someone's physical well-being (ranging from minor physical maltreatment to evident torture) and right to liberty (that is, situations in which a person is illegally detained). These elements do not operate independently of each other, and arbitrary detention can encourage, or even result from, the commission of other abuses. The conditions leading to police abuse reflect patterns that will be seen in the examples presented in this chapter. In the first pattern, the prevailing types of abuse are related to the nature of the tasks performed by each police force, because the abusive practices are a "means" for fulfilling those organizational functions.[1] A

Translation by Patricia Rosas.

[1] The police in the Federal District are divided by function into one group that is preventive in nature, charged with maintaining security and public order, and another that is investigative or judicial. The first is under the direction of the Ministry of Public Security (SSP) for the Federal District. The main SSP force is the preventive police (*policía preventiva*), with approximately 34,000 officers divided into units for patrolling and prevention, traffic control, and other specialized tasks. Two other complementary forces are the auxiliary police (*policía auxiliar*), with approximately 40,000 officers who guard public buildings and other high-profile places; and the bank police (*policía bancaria e industrial*), with approximately 15,000 officers who guard companies, banks, and financial institutions. The judicial police (*policía judicial*, with approximately 3,500 members) is under the direction of the Office of the Attorney

second pattern is visible in the Federal District police forces, where corruption networks have established their own objectives, pursued alongside formal duties: that is, abusive practices facilitate the search for illicit financial gain. The third pattern of abuse involves overreactions to challenges made to the real or symbolic power of police officers. Thus three modalities or logics of abuse exist: as a substitute for professional forms of investigation and prevention, as a means for graft, and as punishment for challenging police "power."

I review these patterns of abuse as they exist in the judicial police (*policía judicial*) and the police forces under the supervision of the Ministry of Public Security (SSP) in the Federal District. As a source of information, I use the recommendations issued by the Human Rights Commission of the Federal District (CDHDF 1994–2002) concerning members of Federal District police forces involved in cases of police abuse as defined in this chapter.

The factors that have been proposed to explain abusive police behaviors are categorized in the first section below. This analytical description of causal elements allows me to illustrate, in the following section, the major theoretical importance that these variables have for the various modalities of abuse. Those modalities are illustrated in instances of police abuse, which I describe and classify. In the third section, I propose possible areas for future research, and I pose the need to have access to the kind of information required for comparing causal theories and advancing our understanding of the phenomenon of police abuse in the Federal District.

FACTORS EXPLAINING POLICE ABUSE

The factors that theoretically (re)produce abusive police practices can be considered from five perspectives. Traditionally, the factors leading to excessive use of force have been categorized by only three perspectives: the individual, the organizational, and the situational (Friedrich 1980; Worden 1996).[2] Following the first perspective and given similar settings, variations

---

General for the Federal District, and it assists in investigations of reported crimes.

[2] The studies I cite as background in this chapter present dissimilarities in regard to the phenomenon or "dependent variable" they seek to explain. Depending on theoretical interests or the availability of data sources, these studies test models that seek to understand the use of force, the excessive use of force, police brutality, and so forth. However, they use definitions that do not closely match this chapter's definition of police abuse. These dissimilarities are fundamental for precisely defining theoretical causal factors and for the

in police officers' individual characteristics (sex, age, education, racial identity, prejudices, and so on) explain the existence of abusive responses. In the organizational approach, formal and informal aspects of the police force itself influence the behavior of officers in the street. Organizational characteristics—such as the system of rewards and sanctions, and the subculture of police work—determine the potential for abuse. From the situational perspective, the key to explaining abusive behaviors lies in the dynamic of the situations in which police-citizen interaction occurs. Situational constraints, such as a suspect's physical appearance, gender, or comportment and reaction, determine whether abuse will occur. Other authors note that this situational-sociological perspective has generally omitted structural-level variables (Holmes 2000). Thus, in a fourth, socio-structural, perspective, indices of economic inequality and crime for the various districts where police units operate are triggers for abuse. For the case of Mexico City, we must also consider a fifth perspective: the legal environment in which police activities unfold. This institutional approach cites elements in the legal framework that favor abusive police practices, such as, for example, parts of the Code of Criminal Procedure for the Federal District (Comité de Abogados 2001).

In summary, the factors explaining police abuse can be categorized into five approaches or perspectives: institutional, organizational, socio-structural, situational, and individual. Let us look more carefully at the theoretical logic of each.

The Institutional Perspective

In the institutional perspective, legal norms define the functions and attributes of the police forces and their personnel. Although police conduct is often viewed in terms of the gap between "real" practice and what legally "should occur," it cannot be denied that the legal framework either permits or restricts the space for arbitrariness, and it can even encourage abuse at the operational level of police conduct. That is, shortcomings in the laws that regulate the protection of civil liberties encourage the existence of abusive practices. The concern in this case is that the legal framework itself generates police abuse as a normal outcome (not just as an aberration).

---

significance of the results. In this chapter, given the type of information available, I do not test explicative models (something that must be an essential objective for future research), and I postpone an exhaustive discussion of this important point.

The Organizational Perspective

In the organizational perspective, formal and informal factors can explain abusive behaviors. Among the formal aspects are the criteria for recruitment and for education and training, the official culture of the organization, and its disciplinary and accountability mechanisms (Adams 1996; Worden 1996). In considering personnel recruitment as a causal factor in abuse, the supposition is that the low requirements that are set for the competency, background, and social origin of candidates result in the inclusion on the force of members unqualified to perform the functions of a police officer. In this connection, low salaries are a disincentive to attracting prepared individuals from better backgrounds. Police education refers, among others things, to training in the proportional use of force, the handling of firearms, and modern procedures for prevention and investigation. The lack of professionalization in these areas encourages the solidification of practices that are arbitrary and ineffective and that ignore the law in both the use of force and the attainment of the mission that is the responsibility of each force.

"Organizational culture" refers to the work philosophy "officially" pursued by the heads of the institution. Abusive behaviors are more likely when the official culture emphasizes the "war against crime" and when the model of "good policing" puts greater emphasis on winning that war than on respecting constitutional guarantees.

Finally, the design and proper functioning of the agencies of internal control and discipline are centrally important to inhibiting abusive behavior. Crime prevention and investigation is often invisible to the public eye and may be geographically dispersed, so if we are to achieve a police force that is more respectful of the public's individual rights, we must ensure that mechanisms of control and accountability play a central role.[3]

In the shaping of the organization, arbitrariness and difficulties in controlling police activities favor the importance of informal police practices, which can exist in a variety of relationships vis-à-vis the organization's formal norms. Informal practices can range from commonsense adaptations in response to the operational reality to an almost total replacement of "legal" functions by a parallel "informal" structure that develops illegal

---

[3] In his chapter in this volume, Robert Varenik notes that arbitrariness in police work is its most distinctive feature and its central problem. The principal solution is the construction of mechanisms of "accountability." In a country without a tradition of accountability, such as Mexico, this must be a core focus of any reform project.

objectives and conduct. Arbitrariness and invisibility in police practices favor the coexistence of three sets of rules. Formal rules can exercise effective sanctions, even if these might not be considered legitimate. Informal rules or "work rules" result from the daily pressures inherent in crime prevention tasks and the arresting of lawbreakers. Finally, rules of presentation come into play when, post facto, the actions of the police are reconstructed in legally acceptable terms. In that reconstruction, the high level of invisibility in police work creates considerable room for maneuver (Bayley 1994).

In relation to abuse, the most widely discussed trait of informal police culture is the deeply held belief that effective fulfillment of a mission demands a deviation from formal legality, particularly regarding individual rights and civil liberties (Chevigny 2002; Bayley 2002). Informal police culture has been described as being marked by three features: suspicion, internal solidarity, and social isolation (Reiner 1998; Buckner, Christie, and Fattah 1983). The culture of suspicion is the tendency to make snap judgments about whether a person might be a lawbreaker or be "dangerous." This leads to a tendency to operate with prejudiced stereotypes about potential "villains." Police work is made easier if officers accept the prejudices and discrimination already existing in the social environment. Moreover, police work itself emphasizes and spreads the stereotypes even further within the society.[4] Internal solidarity and social isolation, important resources in internal cover-ups of wrongdoing, are mutually reinforcing. The so-called organizational codes of silence are the other side of the coin of a system of nonautonomous, ineffective controls (Skolnick and Fyfe 1993).

The Socio-Structural Perspective

The socio-structural perspective considers the general characteristics of distinct groups with which the police interact and the social spaces for police conduct. One hypothesis, which derives from political theories of social control, notes that in societies with the sharpest social stratification or economic inequality, the dominant groups—in order to guarantee their social position and supremacy—make greater demands for the strengthen-

---

[4] In this connection, since these police procedures already incorporate widely held class distinctions, many are accepted as legitimate in the eyes of important groups in the population and even by some members of the groups most affected by surveillance and coercion.

ing of police powers (Jacobs and O'Brien 1998). The most privileged segments of society have a stronger public "voice" and more political clout for making their demands heard. Symmetrically, the subordinate segments of society lack a public presence that would allow them to complain about the level of force that the public security institutions exercise over them. Moreover, the subordinate groups experience high levels of coercion by police as "normal," or they may even support such actions when criminals or "suspects" are involved. Another hypothesis from the socio-structural perspective claims that the level of force used depends on the degree of social violence that officers face in their daily work. The possibilities for abuse increase in social arenas characterized by heavy violence (Reiner 1998).

The Situational Perspective

The situational perspective, which can also be termed "micro-social," generates explanatory factors relating to the interactions between the police and the public. Many of these factors can be seen as "triggers" of the pragmatic culture of policing, which specifies situations conducive to abuse. The factors that stand out in this perspective are the social space in which the crime occurs, the type of police mobilization, the behavior or crime that leads to police intervention, resisting arrest, the presence of witnesses, and the characteristics of the people with whom the police interact. If an interaction develops in a social space of low public visibility—inside a building, at night—or in micro-spaces that are known for criminal activity or that are considered dangerous, this can trigger an abusive event. These situational conditions activate an implicit, informal norm that legitimates a more rigorous or arbitrary use of police force.

With regard to the characteristics of a police mobilization, it is important to determine the number of police present, as well as whether the support of other officers was requested (Garner, Maxwell, and Heraux 2002). However, the driving force behind the effect of these factors does not follow a clear hypothesis. For example, the presence of police called in as backup can diminish the level of use of force by providing a sense of support should the suspect resist arrest, but for the officers who respond to the call, it can also generate an expectation of danger that can lead to excessive or unnecessary coercion.

The behavior resulting in a police intervention may be considered grave, in legal terms, or it may be viewed as merely antisocial or morally punishable. In both cases, the person can be located in a "normative space" in which there appears to be justification for strict control or informal penalization of the behavior. Faced with a case of abuse, it is important to identify whether the interacting person or persons resisted verbally or physically, and to what degree (Adams 1996; Terrill and Mastrofski 2002).

In relation to the personal characteristics of the "suspects," we can anticipate that a greater level of force will be used on people from lower socio-economic strata, on men, and on groups that are considered subordinate (ethnic minorities, youths). In this case, the hypothesis is that the use of coercion on the part of the police is distributed according to criteria that conform to people's social status.

The Individual Perspective

Finally, we can adopt the individual perspective or approach. In this case, a police officer's age, sex, educational level, work experience, attitudes toward the population, and previous police force experience predispose that officer to act in a certain manner (Brandl, Stroshine, and Frank 2001; Terrill and Mastrofski 2002). The "years on the force" factor appears at both the individual and organizational levels. This dimension of individual learning can be taken as an indicator of various formations (that is, training and experience), depending on the point at which an officer entered the force or greater knowledge of a department's informal culture. Characteristics of violence would be associated with what has been called a "work personality" of officers (Skolnick and Fyfe 1993), an attribute of the pragmatic culture of police work. Studies that have focused on officers' beliefs and attitudes as determinants of violence have, in general, taken two forms: officers' beliefs about human nature and their attitudes toward coercion.

In summary, the five perspectives and the main factors are:

- the institutional perspective: (1) the reigning legal framework as it relates to the functions and powers of the various police forces;

- the organizational perspective: (2) recruitment methods, (3) technical police training, (4) organizational culture, (5) internal and judicial controls, and (6) informal practices and pragmatic culture;

- the socio-structural perspective: (7) social stratification and (8) social violence;

- the situational perspective: (9) social environment, (10) behavior that motivates the interaction, (11) police mobilization, (12) resistance and presence of witnesses, and (13) characteristics of citizens or suspects; and

• the individual perspective: (14) characteristics and attitudes of the police officers themselves.

In the case of Mexico City, and the Federal District more specifically, there are significant shortcomings in available sources of information and systematized data. This makes it difficult to try to explain police abuse by means of multivariate analysis of the factors from one or several of the perspectives listed above. However, it is possible to use the cases of police abuse described by the Human Rights Commission of the Federal District (CDHDF) to illustrate repeated patterns. These patterns point to the presence of many of the causal factors outlined in the theories discussed above. Thus I can reaffirm the plausibility of those hypotheses even though it is impossible to know the real significance of these variables for the Mexico City case. After describing the most prominent features of Mexico City's police forces, I will classify cases of police abuse selected from the CDHDF's recommendations.

THE POLICE IN MEXICO CITY AND PATTERNS OF ABUSE IN THE FEDERAL DISTRICT

Police Force Autonomy

During the 1990s, academics and civil organizations produced various studies that reflected their growing consternation over problems in Federal District police forces. In particular, these studies documented horrible, but routine, cases of torture and high levels of systemic corruption. One of the most common approaches was to analyze the Codes of Criminal Procedure, which falls under the institutional perspective. Those studies attempt to determine the presence or absence of norms that could trigger abuse by the judicial police (de la Barreda Solórzano 1995; Comité de Abogados 2001). For example, withdrawing the evidentiary weight of confessions made in the presence of the police has removed an incentive for torture. However, stretching the definition of crimes in progress—in flagrante delicto—might lead to an increase in arbitrary or illegal detentions.

One of the most widely noted features has been the near-total lack of professionalism in the police forces (Ruiz Harrell 1998; Martínez de Murguía 1998). Poor preparation and a lack of familiarity with regulations and modern work techniques may well have constructed "normal" work practices that ignore the law and frequently involve abuse. The historical concretion of these practices, the already mentioned incentives in the legal framework, and the inefficacy or lack of controls have all been factors in turning the police forces into organizations with high levels of autonomy. Another even more disturbing aspect of this characteristic is the system of impunity that has developed internally in the organizations.[5] A clear indicator of the high levels of police impunity is the fact that only rarely are control mechanisms activated or officers effectively disciplined for committing abuses such as torture (Comité de Abogados 2001). Additionally, in general it is only when nongovernmental organizations or human rights commissions have applied strong pressure that abuse investigations are concluded and the responsible officers punished (Human Rights Watch 1999).

Whether because of organizational design flaws or informal practices that distort performance, it appears that the internal controls in the police forces themselves do not fulfill the anticipated objectives. The possibility of falsification of reports by officers is a clear example of the poor functioning of the control mechanisms. Beatriz Martínez de Murguía (1998) recounts cases involving the judicial police where the serious problem is less the notorious bizarreness of the police reports than it is the acceptance of those reports by other institutions in the justice system. Lamentably, this "system of impunity" does more than just protect the illegal conduct that develops in the fulfillment of the anticipated formal objectives. The police forces in Mexico have developed structures of criminal corruption that encompass a large part of the hierarchy. This reinforces and gives stability to the mechanisms for protecting officers who do wrong (and for mutual control through the possibility of accusations). In other words, the possibility of police abuse arises not only in the routine fulfillment of tasks but also in the overlapping of those routines with the involvement in graft, which develops more or less in parallel.

In Mexico City, particularly in the SSP's preventive police, the most common system of corruption is the practice of the rank and file paying "quotas" to superior officers. Money to pay these "fees" can only be obtained by taking bribes (*mordidas*) from a sizable number of citizens (Martínez de Murguía 1998). Another disturbing feature is the connection that officers establish with countless numbers of "collaborators." These

---

[5] In his chapter in this volume, Mario Arroyo argues that the three factors explaining the dysfunctional state of the Mexico City police are poor recruitment selection and training, impunity, and corruption.

personalized networks blur the boundaries between the police force and society, between public and private, opening the door to manipulation of the police by private interests (Martínez de Murguía 1998).[6]

In this scenario of deficient training, routine work practices that include abuse, networks of graft, and ineffective control mechanisms, we should not be surprised to find a culture whose self-interest is the utilization of its powers. Mild penalties and widespread social rejection and distrust encourage the use of coercion as a tool for symbolic reaffirmation against anyone who opposes the legal—or illegal—demands of "authority." However, we must also take into account that many traits of the pragmatic police culture are not far removed from the surrounding social culture; and although the concern over abuse has grown, such practices are interconnected with, and often legitimated by, the behaviors of citizens.

Patterns of Police Abuse in Mexico City

From the CDHDF recommendations, I have selected cases of police violations of individuals' physical integrity and personal freedom that allow us to observe and classify behavior patterns. Abuse is a constant in all the cases. A more generalized source of information about police-citizen interactions is not available, although ideally we should use data that would allow us to differentiate between situations that culminate in police abuse and those that do not. Moreover, the CDHDF recommendations are few when compared to the numbers of complaints brought before the commission. I also observe behavior patterns that repeat, indicating the presence of factors that trigger abuse. These patterns indicate a need for researchers to have access to better information in order to test the explanatory hypotheses.

The cases chosen are based on a social situation that generates an interaction—initiated by either the police or citizens—that culminates in abusive police behavior. Because I focus on police conduct, the involvement of other law enforcement or judicial offices (whether it be effective or negligent) is not central to the discussion. However, I consider these other actors to the extent that they may be contributing to the opportunities for abuse.

---

[6] High turnover and employment instability in the police, as well as growth in the forces themselves, may be among the factors favoring the formation of these "networks," which extend beyond the police force. Miguel Sarre (2001) cites both elements as causal sources of the criminality within the institutions charged with fighting crime.

Because of their gravity, a number of the CDHDF recommendations refer to cases of torture. Torture implies the use of various forms of physical coercion that cause great pain and harm. Their objective is to extract a confession or self-incrimination, to elicit information about a crime or other people, or "simply" to punish the prisoner. The factors that can lead to these acts are undoubtedly varied, but they must include the officers' psychological traits, the organizational culture, and enormous deficiencies in the system of controls and sanctions. However, the role of a confession in the criminal trial is the preferential factor; it has been the most widely discussed factor and the one for which solutions have been sought (de la Barreda 1995; Martínez de Murguía 1998; Comité de Abogados 2001). Given that a confession made before the police has greater evidentiary weight than other statements made later in the criminal process, it is believed that most cases in Mexico were "resolved" through confessions resulting from torture.

The 1993 constitutional reforms opposing torture have rectified this problem and appreciably improved the situation in Mexico. However, according to some observers, the improvements have been minor and torture continues to be an ongoing problem—and the norms and/or practices in the justice system continue setting a stage for its occurrence (Comité de Abogados 2001). The immense power that the judicial police and the Office of the Public Prosecutor (Ministerio Público) wield over the indictment is particularly noted. At any rate, no one believes that the problem has gone away.

Based on the cases of torture described in the CDHDF's recommendations, it is possible to deduce three causal logics. Empirically, these modalities can overlap and even reinforce each other. In the first, which is perhaps the most widely documented modality, torture plays an unfortunately routine role in how cases are "investigated" or "resolved." Under these conditions, torture is an expedient that replaces professionalism when investigating a crime or arresting someone during the commission of a crime. In the performance of police "functions," torture occupies a place in the way of doing things that is encouraged by law and established practice. On occasion, torture is passively condoned by other actors in the justice system, such as agents of the public prosecutor or public defender.

Second is the objective of obtaining graft. Money is demanded in exchange for not incriminating someone who is being tortured, or the goal of the torture is a prisoner's self-incrimination so that the police can make a profit by disposing of supposedly stolen goods. In parallel with the performance of their duties, the judicial police take advantage of opportunities that an investigation or an arrest of someone committing a crime offers for illicit gain, and torture can be a "means" of achieving that end. Here, the objective of graft is superimposed on, or set apart from, the goal of capturing the presumed lawbreaker.

The third modality involves situations that have nothing to do with implicating a person or with illicit gain. In this case, torture appears to obey a logic of sheer punishment. That is, the previous (often merely ridiculous) conduct of the detainee "deserves punishment." I will briefly illustrate these three logics of abuse.

One recommendation made during the early years of the CDHDF, that of 10/95,[7] describes a case of torture that was substituted for an investigation, when a parking lot attendant was tortured throughout an entire night in an attempt to obtain information about a stolen vehicle and the identity of the responsible parties. In Recommendation 2/97, faced with a doubtful delicto flagrante arrest for counterfeiting, the judicial police tortured a woman inside the police station itself to obtain information about her accomplices. More recently, in December 1999, as noted in Recommendation 5/02, two men, one a minor, were illegally detained and, in an attempt to get them to implicate a relative in a robbery, they were tortured next door to the offices of the public prosecutor. In this last case, it seems that an attempt to extort money was also a factor in the abuse. According to the recommendation, the judicial police sought to keep part of the supposedly stolen goods, and in the initial hours of the illegal detention they also tried to take advantage of the situation by demanding a payment from the family in exchange for freeing the pair (in other words, they were committing a kidnapping).

In other instances, the logic of graft via brutality appears in a "purer" form. In one of the first complaints that led to a CDHDF recommendation, that of 3/94, two judicial police used a baseless crime report to illegally detain and abuse two men. The officers removed items from the detainees' residence and demanded money in exchange for not initiating a robbery investigation. Recommendation 1/99 describes a case of private use of public force; a person was arrested illegally, robbed, and subjected to extortion because he owed money to a relative of the deputy director of the Attorney General's Office.

---

[7] The CDHDF numbers its recommendations by the year in which they were issued. Thus this was the tenth recommendation of 1995.

In yet other cases, the desire to inflict "punishment" is clearly the trigger for the abuse. In June 2000, according to Recommendation 7/00, the judicial police repeatedly tortured two men arrested for their participation in a robbery, one of whom had shot and killed an officer during commission of the crime. However, "punishment" can also be meted out for less serious conduct. As noted in Recommendation 11/97, a man was beaten, tortured, and falsely accused of robbery, though his only offense was having kicked the door of a judicial police patrol car that was blocking the entrance to the business he managed. Other cases to be discussed later in the chapter demonstrate that minor transgressions or a challenge to the police's right to "be in charge" can generate abusive responses. The examples presented thus far have involved abuses by the judicial police. Those cases are illustrative of some of the causal factors described above within the five theoretical perspectives: laws that empower the police to indict suspects, the lack of professionalism in conducting investigations, laxity in the system of controls, and a culture of overreaction in the use of force.

I now turn to CDHDF recommendations that involve abuses by officers from the SSP's preventive police. The kinds of duties performed by each police force create certain opportunities, such that specific abuses predominate in each force. For the judicial police, the fact that a "suspect" is present, in the flesh, during the interrogation influences the use of torture as a "normal" investigative tool. In the preventive police, in contrast, a lack of professionalism in the performance of police duties translates into abuse taking the form of arbitrary detentions and physical mistreatment. In the CDHDF recommendations, the documented cases of torture by the preventive police seem to fall mostly under the logic of "punishment" for having resisted arrest.

Examples of the first modality of abuse—as a substitute for professional conduct—can be seen in cases involving the preventive police as they attempt to control public demonstrations or in operations to catch people in the commission of a crime or while taking part in "suspicious" activities in areas that are considered dangerous. According to Recommendation 12/97, in an operation in the Anáhuac neighborhood the police apprehended scores of people without any apparent reason. Relatives and neighbors who complained were added to the list of offenders, and many were sent before a civil judge for "disturbing the peace," making arbitrary use of the Governing Rules for Civil Justice. Recommendation 14/97 calls attention to arbitrary detentions and abuse that occurred during an operation to control a demonstration by the Citizens' Assembly of Bank Debtors (Asamblea Ciudadana de Deudores de la Banca).

Arbitrary detentions and mistreatment also seem to arise from the pursuit of graft. It is common for police forces charged with crime prevention in Mexico City to systematically demand bribes in exchange for overlooking certain activities in public spaces. Recommendation 8/94 notes that both preventive and judicial police officers extorted money from clients of prostitutes. Arrests, appearances in Civil Court, and even mistreatment are among the possible consequences of refusing to pay a bribe. The first recommendation for 1997 compiled a series of complaints about routine extortions by the preventive police among people who derive their livelihood by washing cars in the streets. Refusal to pay the bribes led to mistreatment or an unnecessary appearance in Civil Court. Civil Court judges often act in ways that encourage the continuation of this abusive conduct.

It is not always possible to clearly separate abuse that follows a logic of punishment from the largely unprofessional fulfillment of police duties. In Recommendation 4/95, two teenagers who had stolen a couple of cases of soda were pursued by the judicial police in a patrol car. The police cornered them outside a house inhabited by "dangerous" people, who hurled rocks and bottles at the police from their rooftop. In reaction, the judicial police and preventive police mounted a joint operation involving numerous patrol cars, dozens of motorcycles, and members of four specialized groups from the two forces. They machine-gunned the front of the building, arrested and brutalized four adults and four minors, and reportedly attempted to rape a detainee.

Punishment inflicted for having questioned police authority is even clearer in Recommendation 10/97. Preventive police officers in a patrol car got into an altercation with four or five teenagers who had been listening to music and drinking in the street. The police retreated but, after radioing for backup, returned with at least ten patrol cars. The officers proceeded to drag the retreating young people from their houses and beat them in the street and in the patrol cars, injuring them so badly that they had to be hospitalized.

There are more examples. Another recommendation dealt with two brothers who refused to let a tow truck take their illegally parked car. They refused to pay a bribe, and they may have insulted, or even rushed, the police officer. The result? After subduing the two men, the driver of the tow truck and three preventive police officers beat them from head to toe, causing numerous injuries. In Recommendation 7/99, a man broke a lock that had been put on his delivery truck because he had not put money in the parking meter. When the police tried to arrest him, he resisted. The result? Agents of the bank police pinned the man to the floor while another agent repeatedly jabbed his knee into the detainee's stomach, causing severe internal injuries. These two events occurred at 1 p.m. and 6 p.m., respectively, in centrally located and heavily traveled neighborhoods. It seems that the presence of witnesses does nothing to discourage such excessive demonstrations of force.

Other cases seem to be related to police officers' personal traits, but these may also support the conclusion that only a small number of officers are responsible for most of the complaints (Adams 1996). Recommendation 8/99 notes that one officer had complaints against him for both kicking a woman in the stomach when she complained because he urinated on a tree near her door and sexual abuse of a minor. That such a person could remain on the force—and worse, that the investigation and administrative hearing for his offenses were marked by a lack of due diligence, as frequently occurs in such cases—are distressing indicators of conditions within the police and the Office of the Public Prosecutor.

In summary, both the judicial police and preventive police in Mexico City exhibit the three modalities into which I have classified abuse. These modalities can be separated analytically and, to a degree, empirically. Taking into account each police force's distinctive tasks and institutional relations, we can observe how each logic is linked, to a greater or lesser extent, to certain perspectives and causal factors, as described above, that figure in abuse.

Abuse as a means for resolving investigations points to institutional and organizational factors within the judicial police. From the institutional perspective, there are the excessive powers of indictment that the police and public prosecutor continue to possess in practice; and from the organizational perspective, there are deficiencies in investigative training and in effective accountability mechanisms.

For the preventive police, abuse as a means for fulfilling objectives is related, in the organizational perspective, to a lack of training in non-coercive problem-solving techniques as well as in the proper use of force. It is also related to the choice of policing strategy. However, more than strategy, it is the lack of accountability for how chosen strategies are implemented that opens the door to the potential for abuse. The relevant factors are societal, situational, and structural, given that the pursuit of a given path of action depends on characteristics of the social spaces in which the officer works or of the population with which the officer interacts. Understanding the relevant social variables will give us very useful information about how to change training programs and how to design organizational controls.

The lack of internal and external accountability, and of corresponding sanctions, is a principal factor behind networks of corruption that encourage abuse. We must also consider the influence of personnel recruitment mechanisms that reinforce, rather than weaken, those networks. A more effective system of incentives and sanctions is needed to break down the widespread and routinized networks of extortion, in which society is an active participant.

For its part, the logic of "punishment" seems to depend largely on the informal police culture and on attitudes that develop among the members of a force. However, formal organizational circumstances, such as training and systems for control and punishment, can affect that culture. Again, in order to be able to get feedback about mechanisms that might modify informal police culture, it is necessary to recognize the prejudices that infiltrate it and the situations that activate the excessive use of force. It is necessary to understand whether the determinants of this modality of abuse lie in the characteristics of the population, in its resistance behaviors, in the social spaces in which the officer works, or in the particular characteristics of an officer.

The descriptions that I have presented, based on cases in the CDHDF recommendations, point to the complexity of the police abuse problem in Mexico's Federal District. However, it is essential that we begin to research the question of which factors are the prime causes of abusive practices. Without a central focus on the issue of abuse, police reform will be ineffective. The principal obstacles to studying the issue of abuse lie in the failure to produce systematic information on police activities and the slim possibilities that researchers have for accessing information from within the police organizations themselves.

CONCLUSION: IMPROVING RESEARCH ON POLICE ABUSE

The lack of information and research on the police in Mexico is very serious. The gaps are related not only to police practices and informal structures (which are invisible in any police force anywhere in the world) but also to institutional memory and information, past and present, for the organization itself, and to the inability of researchers and the interested public to access that information.[8] Along with advances in accessing information from public organizations charged with providing security and justice, systematic internal and external information must also be created about police practices. Surveys among populations at high risk for being victimized by arbitrariness and police violence would help to reveal the incidence of the problem in the population. Such data are also needed if we hope to measure the results of any reform effort aimed at decreasing police abuse as a systematic pattern of conduct.

Current attempts to describe and explain police abuse draw on various methodologies and approaches. One involves a description of police work that includes its organizational-administrative structure as well as the routine practices of officers and the culture that guides those practices. For that approach, the preferred tool for obtaining information has been direct observation of police officers' daily routines or interviews with current or retired members of the force (Skolnick and Fyfe 1993). The construction of explanatory models concerning the use of force has relied on three types of information sources: official records, surveys of police officers or the public, and field observations (Adams 1996). Official records have included such things as criminal cases for excessive use of force, citizen complaints to police departments or external agencies, and police department arrest reports or reports on the use of force. Many of these records provide information on a sufficient number of cases to carry out an explanatory multivariate analysis. However, when doing the analysis, one cannot neglect the possibility that, rather than being a true indicator of police behavior, this information may be an organizational indicator (about the capacity, willingness, or strategy for collecting complaints or preparing activity reports).

Researchers evaluating police abuse in other cases have also relied on direct observation of police practices to avoid possible bias in information from official records. Taking police-citizen encounters as their unit of analysis, researchers have also explored situational and psychological factors as determinants for the use of force, though efforts must be made to avoid biases created by the observer's presence (Worden 1996; Terrill and Mastrofski 2002). The use of public surveys to gather information about police violence is another option worth considering for countries like Mexico, where official information systems still show serious problems in terms of access and validity. Surveys of the public have shown that the incidence

---

[8] It has already been noted that this is a relevant problem for Mexico; see López Portillo Vargas 2002.

of police use of force in the universe of reported police-citizen encounters is very low.[9] To delve deeper into the issue of police use of force, sampling must overrepresent those populations with the greatest risks of being victimized, or work with a sample of at-risk groups.

In the case of the Mexican police, the most widely utilized sources of information for documenting and analyzing abuse cases include: the legal frameworks regulating police behavior; human rights commissions' recommendations resulting from complaints; monitoring of cases that are societal or media "scandals"; and information available on the pragmatic functioning of the police, gathered through interviews with qualified informants. Also relevant is information gathered by international and human rights organizations (Human Rights Watch 1999; UNHRC 1998, 2000; CIDH 1998, 1999). However, few studies focus on *explaining* cases of abuse (Martínez de Murguía 1998; Comité de Abogados 2001). In the end, police institutions must be required to compile and make available reliable information about relevant police activities. Such information is essential to allow for a better assessment of police abuse in Mexico and to ensure organizational accountability to policymakers, watchdog organizations, researchers, and the public.

References

Adams, Kenneth. 1996. "Measuring the Prevalence of Police Abuse of Force." In *Police Violence: Understanding and Controlling Police Abuse of Force*, ed. William A. Geller and Hans Toch. New Haven, Conn.: Yale University Press.

Bayley, David. 1994. *Police for the Future.* New York: Oxford University Press.

———. 1996. "Police Brutality Abroad." In *Police Violence*, ed. William A. Geller and Hans Toch. New Haven, Conn.: Yale University Press.

———. 2002. "Law Enforcement and the Rule of Law: Is There a Trade-off?" *Criminology and Public Policy* 2 (November): 133–54.

Brandl, Steven, Meghan Stroshine, and James Frank. 2001. "Who Are Complaint-Prone Officers? An Examination of the Relationship between Police Officers' Attributes, Arrest Activity, Assignment, and Citizens' Complaints about Excessive Force," *Journal of Criminal Justice* 29, no. 6 (November–December): 521–29.

---

[9] In the United States, for example, the police used force or threatened to use force in only 1 percent of reported contacts; and in most cases, those surveyed indicated that their own actions (such as resisting or threatening) provoked the officers (Greenfeld, Langan, and Smith 1999).

Buckner, Taylor, Nils Christie, and Ezzat Fattah. 1983. "Policía y cultura." In *Policía y sociedad democrática*, ed. José María Rico. Madrid: Alianza.

CDHDF (Comisión de Derechos Humanos del Distrito Federal). 1994–2002. Recomendaciones de la Comisión de Derechos Humanos del Distrito Federal: 3/94, 8/94, 4/95, 10/95, 1/97, 2/97, 10/97, 11/97, 12/97, 14/97, 1/99, 7/99, 8/99, 7/00, 5/02. At www.cdhdf.org.mx.

Chevigny, Paul. 2002. "Conflict of Rights and Keeping Order," *Criminology and Public Policy* 2 (November): 155–59.

CIDH (Comisión Interamericana de Derechos Humanos). 1998. *Informe sobre la situación de los derechos humanos en México*. Mexico City: CIDH.

———. 1999. *Informe de seguimiento*. Mexico City: CIDH.

Comité de Abogados para los Derechos Humanos, Centro de Derechos Humanos "Miguel Agustín Pro Juárez." 2001. *Injusticia legalizada: procedimiento penal mexicano y derechos humanos*. Mexico City: Comité de Abogados para los Derechos Humanos, PRODH.

de la Barreda Solórzano, Luis. 1995. *La lid contra la tortura*. Mexico City: Cal y Arena.

Friedrich, Robert J. 1980. "Police Use of Force: Individuals, Situations, and Organizations," *Annals of the American Academy of Political and Social Sciences* 452 (November): 82–97.

Garner, Joel, Christopher Maxwell, and Cedrick Heraux. 2002. "Characteristics Associated with the Prevalence and Severity of Force Used by the Police," *Justice Quarterly* 19 (December): 705–46.

Greenfeld, Lawrence A., Patrick A. Langan, and Steven K. Smith. 1999. "Revising and Fielding the Police-Public Contact Survey." In *Use of Force by Police: Overview of National and Local Data*. National Institute of Justice, Bureau of Justice Statistics. At http://www.ojp.usdoj.gov/bjs/abstract/ufbponld.htm.

Holmes, Malcom. 2000. "Minority Threat and Police Brutality: Determinants of Civil Complaints in U.S. Municipalities," *Criminology* 38, no. 2: 343–67.

Human Rights Watch. 1999. *Abuso y desamparo: tortura, desaparición forzada y ejecución extrajudicial en México*. Mexico City: Human Rights Watch.

Jacobs, David, and Robert O'Brien. 1998. "The Determinants of Deadly Force: A Structural Analysis of Police Violence," *American Journal of Sociology* 103, no. 4: 837–62.

López Portillo Vargas, Ernesto. 2002. "La asistencia internacional para la reforma policial en México: una alternativa," *Este País*, November.

Martínez de Murguía, Beatriz. 1998. *La policía en México*. Mexico City: Planeta.

Reiner, Robert. 1998. "Policing the Police." In *The Oxford Handbook of Criminology*. Oxford: Oxford University Press.

Ruiz Harrell, Rafael. 1998. *Criminalidad y mal gobierno*. Mexico City: Sansores y Aljure.

Sarre, Miguel. 2001. "Seguridad ciudadana y justicia penal: frente a la democracia, la división de poderes y el federalismo." In *El desafío democrático de*

México: seguridad y estado de derecho, ed. Arturo Alvarado and Sigrid Arzt. Mexico City: El Colegio de México.

Skolnick, Jerome, and James Fyfe. 1993. *Above the Law*. New York: Free Press.

Terrill, William, and Stephen Mastrofski. 2002. "Situational and Officer-Based Determinants of Police Coercion," *Justice Quarterly* 19 (June): 215–48.

UNHRC (United Nations Human Rights Commission). 1998. *Informe del Relator Especial, Sr. Nigel Rodley*. New York: United Nations.

———. 2000. *Informe de seguimiento del Relator*. New York: United Nations.

Worden, Robert E. 1996. "The Causes of Police Brutality: Theory and Evidence on Police Use of Force." In *Police Violence*, ed. William A. Geller and Hans Toch. New Haven, Conn.: Yale University Press.

PART III

Civil Society in Action in the Border Region

CHAPTER 9

The Mexican Judicial System: Continuity and Change in a Period of Democratic Consolidation

SARA SCHATZ, HUGO CONCHA, AND
ANA LAURA MAGALONI KERPEL

The Mexican justice system is in a state of change as authorities attempt to address rising rates of crime and violence, ineffective police investigations, official corruption at multiple levels, and a resulting sense of insecurity and fear felt by citizens. This chapter provides an overview of the Mexican judicial system through a description of its legal institutions and their structure and functioning. Our description of the fundamental parameters of Mexico's justice system includes the constitutional history of the legal system, the complex structure and hierarchy of the Mexican court system and its provisions for the protection of individual rights, and the changing standards for the legal profession in an era of democratic consolidation and legal reform. In addition to a description of the regular court system, we also discuss several special federal judicial bodies and areas of administrative law. Specifically, we document a trend toward increased pluralism in judicial education, particularly since the 1994 judicial reforms, and the efforts to incorporate indigenous norms in the Mexican legal system. Overall, we see Mexico's current climate for legal change as positive but tempered against long-standing challenges that will complicate and sometimes hinder the process of reform.

Some of the material used in this chapter was adapted from Schatz 2002 and is used with the kind permission of ABC-CLIO, Santa Barbara.

HISTORICAL OVERVIEW AND LEGAL CONCEPTS

Highly advanced cultures—including those of the Olmecs, Mayas, Toltecs, and Aztecs—ruled what is today Mexico and parts of Guatemala for more than a thousand years before the Spaniards arrived. During that time, a complex oral legal tradition emerged in which traditional authority resolved conflicts. After Spain's conquest of Mexico, Spanish law governed disputes related to private law, commerce, property, family inheritance, and obligations among those of European ancestry in colonial Mexico. Nevertheless, the Spanish Crown also allowed for customary indigenous law and legal institutions—incorporated under the concept of *usos y costumbres* (uses and customs, or customary law)—provided they did not contradict established Spanish customs or Church doctrine (Clagett and Valderrama 1973; Stavenhagen 1994).

After three hundred years of Spanish colonialism, Mexico achieved independence in 1821 and adopted its first constitution in 1824. The 1824 Constitution was based on the 1812 Spanish Constitution and therefore carried over much of its Spanish law tradition to Mexico. The Constitution provided for a federal political system consisting of nineteen states, four territories, a federal district, and an independent judiciary. Internal armed conflict ensued between the conservative and liberal elements of the newly independent Mexican state, and many provisions of the 1824 Constitution were not implemented. By 1855 the previously independent judiciary was subordinated to the executive branch, and a new constitution was adopted in 1857 by the liberal element that had ascended to power (Arnold 1989: 469). The 1857 Constitution included such democratic rights as the separation of powers, the equality of all citizens before the law, the principle of innocence until proof of guilt, freedom of expression and of the press, the protection of private property, the abolition of special privileges for the clergy and the military, and agrarian reform.

Individual Rights and Amparo

The 1857 Constitution also allowed for a limited form of judicial review through the use of the *juicio de amparo* (injunction suit), which provided a partial but nonetheless initially effective form of individual rights protection. The word *amparo* literally means favor, aid, protection, or shelter. While *amparo* constitutes an original Mexican institution without exact equivalent in most other systems, legally the concept incorporates elements of several legal actions found elsewhere, including writs of habeas corpus, injunction, error of mandamus, and certiorari. Basically, an *amparo* suit may be filed to obtain a court ruling to temporarily or even permanently enjoin government action in a particular case. There are five types of *amparo*: (1) suits defending individual rights such as life, liberty, and personal dignity; (2) suits defending the individual against unconstitutional laws; (3) suits examining the legality of judicial decisions; (4) suits providing protection against administrative actions affecting an individual; and (5) suits protecting the rights of *ejido* (communal farm) residents. An *amparo* suit may be either direct (initiated in the Supreme Court or collegiate circuit courts) or indirect (initiated in a district court and heard by the previously mentioned courts) (Ávalos 2000; Fix Zamudio and Cossío Díaz 1995).

Judicial Restraint and Executive Dominance

The principle of judicial abstention from electoral and political matters by the Mexican Supreme Court was consolidated in 1882 when Chief Justice Ignacio Vallarta declared the Court "incompetent in origin—that it shall not intervene to solve political questions that correspond, by constitutional disposition, to other branches of government" (Jurisprudencia 1985: 272). This self-restraint enabled the Court's other powers to remain functional during long periods of dictatorship or one-party rule, when it was widely feared that the institution would be dissolved altogether by the executive powers (Barragán 1994). The historical self-restraint of the Supreme Court from ruling on issues of elections, electoral legitimacy, and electoral fraud also explains why a separate set of federal and state administrative courts exists for deciding election matters today.

In the course of the 1910 Mexican Revolution, the 1857 Constitution was replaced by the 1917 Constitution, which incorporated many of the major themes and concerns expressed during the Revolution, including the principles of no reelection, municipal autonomy, universal education, and protection of the national patrimony (Hernández and Portes 1985). However, the judicial power remained subordinate to the executive branch as the postrevolutionary regime was transformed into a unique Mexican-style authoritarianism, in which particular practices and forms of organization—as opposed to written laws contained in the Constitution—endowed the executive branch of government with almost unlimited political power (Rabasa 1912; Carpizo 1978; Garrido 1989). This held true because, from 1929 to 1997, the ruling Institutional Revolutionary Party (PRI) had near absolute control over the legislature and total loyalty to the president.[1] The primacy of the president in this system, despite his inability to be reelected, was mainly due to the president's de facto ability to determine his own successor (Weldon 2003). Mexican presidents also had ultimate authority in electoral matters and therefore controlled candidate selection for virtually all political offices.

Importantly, Mexican presidents historically controlled key aspects of the administration of justice. More specifically, the 1917 Constitution formally recognizes a cabinet-level official—appointed by the president—who presides over the Office of the Attorney General (PGR) and supervises all criminal prosecution. Until the 2000 election of Vicente Fox as president, all of Mexico's federal attorneys general except one (Antonio Lozano from the National Action Party [PAN], 1994–1996) were members of the PRI. The 1917 Constitution also originally established that the executive controlled the appointment of all kinds of judges and justices, was the top official in safety matters, commanded the biggest corps of police in Mexico City, and dictated general policy to all the security bodies through the Commission on Public Safety. Importantly, the prison system was also controlled by the president, which gave him the power to pardon anyone sentenced—and thus to eliminate most judicial penalties.

With such strong powers, the president was the chief administrator of justice, so that all criticisms concerning the administration of justice were also leveled against his performance and his bureaucratic apparatus. Thus, weak internal oversight within the criminal justice system is a partial legacy of excessive concentration of executive power and the long absence of checks and balances. Meanwhile, the lack of judicial autonomy continues to present a significant obstacle to the impartial administration of justice in Mexico. However, judicial institutions and actors have begun to play a more significant role in the context of Mexico's democratic transition and consolidation. Hence it is increasingly important to understand the structure and function of Mexico's judicial institutions and processes.

---

[1] The 1988 elections presented a brief exception within this period, since the PRI temporarily lost its two-thirds majority control of the Chamber of Deputies and therefore could no longer make constitutional reforms without a coalition partner.

MEXICAN JUDICIAL INSTITUTIONS AND PROCESSES

Mexico's supreme law, as in most countries, is found in its Constitution. Theoretically that document provides for the separation of powers into executive, legislative, and judicial branches of government; basic and fundamental human rights, including free speech, presumption of innocence, the right to an attorney in criminal matters, and rights to health protection; and guarantees of private property, protections for labor, freedom of belief and religion, freedom of contract, and other basic legal rights. However, as noted above, actual practice has been complicated by Mexico's particular political reality.

According to its Constitution, Mexico has a civil law system—derived from Roman law—in which judicial decisions are made through strict interpretation of formally legislated statutes. Article 71 of the 1917 Constitution specifically states that legislation is the only source of law. As a result, judicial decision making in Mexico (as in other civil law systems such as Canada and much of continental Europe) consists almost exclusively of interpretation of the law, without reference to other sources such as custom or precedent. This distinguishes Mexico and many other Latin American countries from the United Kingdom and most of the United States (except for Louisiana), which have common law systems that allow greater judicial interpretation of the law and references to legal precedents established in similar cases.

As noted earlier, Mexico has a federal system with separate judicial systems functioning at the national and state levels, though federal law is paramount in the case of conflict. Nationally, there is a three-tiered federal judiciary consisting of an appointed Supreme Court, 29 circuits, over 200 circuit courts, and about 250 district courts (as well as the courts under the authority of the Federal District). In addition, there are special courts for labor and fiscal matters, although any structured and organized overall system of administrative courts is lacking. Each state has its own supreme court and, except in the area of labor disputes, Mexican state legislatures can organize their own state tribunals in the areas of civil law, penal law, and administrative law. Beyond those areas, the states' power to legislate is quite limited. Local judges must always adjust their rulings to adhere to the federal Constitution, even when state law runs contrary. This is called the principle of "diffuse control of the Constitution" (Ávalos 2000; Herget and Camil 1978).

The Mexican Supreme Court

The Supreme Court is the highest body within Mexico's federal judicial branch, serving not only as the forum of last resort but also as the administrative and budgetary oversight institution for all courts (see figure 9.1). The Supreme Court hears a relatively large number of cases—18,241 between 1997 and 1999, in contrast to the 261 cases heard by the U.S. Supreme Court in the same period. The Mexican Supreme Court meets in plenary session for cases involving jurisdictional, constitutional, and agrarian issues. It divides and meets in two panels for other matters: the first panel handles criminal and civil cases, and the second deals with administrative and labor cases. A special office—the Federal Council of the Judiciary, or CJF—investigates acts of corruption, incapacity, and negligence among judges and serves to ensure compliance with established norms (Melgar Adalid 1998).

The Supreme Court is composed of eleven justices and one chief justice. The president nominates the candidates for the Supreme Court, and the Senate can approve the nomination with a two-thirds majority. The president also has the power to remove a Supreme Court justice with the approval of the Senate and the Chamber of Deputies. Supreme Court judges were originally appointed with life tenure. However, judicial reforms in 1994 altered the Supreme Court nomination process to make the judiciary more politically independent of the PRI regime. Since 1994, candidates must be law school graduates with ten years of professional experience, preferably in the judicial system, and they cannot have held a political position for at least one year before their appointment. The 1994 reform changed life tenure to a staggered fifteen-year fixed term, on the argument that fifteen years is sufficient to protect judicial independence for incumbent presidents, and has the advantage of allowing for healthy renewal of the highest tribunal (*Diario Oficial,* December 31, 1994). The current court membership was established in 1994. Every four years the court names one of its members as its president.

Previously, the Supreme Court's review of legislation was sharply restricted; the Court could declare a law unconstitutional only in regard to the individual in question (Domingo 2000; Schatz 1998). However, the 1994 judicial reforms also strengthened the Supreme Court by extending the reach of its powers of constitutional review by increasing the scope of its decisions. As Staton observes in this volume, the Court's recent proposals to further increase its powers of constitutional interpretation and independence from the executive and legislative branches of government have

Figure 9.1. Mexico's Court Structure

<u>Federal Courts</u>
- Supreme Court
- Circuit courts
- District courts

<u>Federal Administrative Tribunals</u>
- Federal Electoral Court (an administrative court to adjudicate election disputes)
- Federal District Court (an administrative court to deal with controversies arising from the government of the Federal District)
- Federal Tax Court (an administrative court that reviews fiscal controversies between an individual and the government)
- Labor Board of Conciliation and Arbitration (an administrative court to resolve controversies arising from labor disputes)
- Superior Court for Land Reform (an administrative court to deal with land reform disputes)
- Military tribunals (limited to military crimes by military personnel)

<u>State Courts</u>
- State Supreme Courts (primarily for review from state tribunals)
- State District Courts (for civil law, penal law, and administrative law)

been declined by the Mexican Congress. Still, the Supreme Court remains a significant factor in Mexico's democratic transition, and it has responded actively to the new political context. For example, in compliance with the new Freedom of Information Act, the Court began in June 2003 to place selected information on its new Web site, including jurisdictional and administrative information, civil servant salaries, telephone numbers, and parts of its rulings. Personal information from penal and family law rulings remain excluded from public access.

Lower Courts and Administrative Tribunals

The Mexican Constitution gives federal courts jurisdiction over controversies that arise from laws or acts by state or federal authorities that may violate individual guarantees; controversies between states or between a state and federal authorities; all matters involving federal laws and treaties; all cases in which the federal government is a party; all cases involving maritime law; and all cases that involve members of the diplomatic and consular corps. As noted above, the federal court structure has three tiers: district courts, circuit courts, and the Supreme Court. District courts serve as the lowest level of original jurisdiction (*primera instancia*) for federal cases and are presided over by individual judges. Circuit courts serve as federal appellate courts and are presided over by either a single judge or a grand jury of three or more judges. Both circuit and district judges are appointed by the Supreme Court to four-year terms, and they may be reappointed or promoted to a new position at the end of their four-year term. Circuit and district judges may be dismissed only for bad conduct. Unlike practice in the United States, there are no elected judges in Mexico at any level.

The federal judiciary has relatively greater authority than state judiciaries, which are generally weak (Ramírez 1994). Given the civil-law nature of the Mexican system, state justices' decisions establish no precedent and are therefore not even published in most states. Also, regional politics have a high degree of influence on state courts, particularly since the incumbent governor has power of appointment for state justices. At the state level, tenure is almost nonexistent. In the Federal District's Superior Court, for example, only seven out of forty-nine superior judges have tenure.

There are several federal judicial bodies that are not part of the regular court structure. The most important are the tax court, labor court, land reform court, and military courts. The Federal Tax Court is an administrative court with jurisdiction over controversies arising in fiscal matters between an individual and the government. The Federal Tax Court's responsibilities and structure are outlined by the Fiscal Code and the Organic Law of the Tax Court. Labor courts are administrative courts with responsibilities and jurisdiction over claims under the Federal Labor Code, disputes over collective bargaining, and strike-related matters.[2] The Superior Court for Land Reform, another administrative court, was created to deal with the backlog of land reform cases compiled for more than fifty years, whose resolution was supposed to be in the hands of the Ministry of Land Reform before the court's creation. Finally, the Organic Law of the Military Courts establishes the responsibilities and structure of courts governing the internal regulation of Mexico's armed forces.

Human Rights and Electoral Oversight Mechanisms

Mexican constitutional law and judicial structures have been crucial arenas for the protection of human rights and the establishment of free and fair elections in the course of Mexico's democratic transition and consolidation. The Constitution was modified in 1992 to create an independent National Human Rights Commission (CNDH). State governments were also required to establish their own human rights commissions. The head of the CNDH is appointed by the president and ratified by the Senate. Early on, from May 1993 to May 1994, the CNDH received more than twenty-four complaints a day at its office in Mexico City alone. As the offices spread throughout the country, the number of complaints rose to seventy-two a day. Some 70 percent of the claims before the commission came from poor people who could not afford the services of lawyers to engage in a lawsuit (González Oropeza 1996). The most common complaints included violations of prisoners' rights, abuse of authority by government officials, illegal detention by the judicial police, delay by the agents of the general prosecutor in bringing the accused before the courts, refusal to render health services at public institutions, false accusations and indictments, medical malpractice, denial of the constitutional right of petition, and torture.

The report of the CNDH president for 1993–1994 observed that fifty-three recommendations were issued against government agents who practiced torture, typically in an attempt to extract confessions. However, only seven of such cases were brought to trial. The role of the CNDH has been

---

[2] In a 2003 decision, the Supreme Court confirmed the Labor Court's status as an administrative body not pertaining to the regular federal judicial structure (*La Jornada* 2003a).

weakened by two factors: first, the CNDH cannot address issues related to political rights or to electoral, labor, or federal judicial matters; and second, its recommendations are not mandatory. Thus the CNDH remains an administrative commission with juridical personality but without punitive legal powers.

In an effort to clarify past state crimes, the CNDH publicized a special report in 2001 confirming direct governmental responsibility for at least 275 cases of forced disappearances of political activists in the so-called dirty war of the 1970s and 1980s. Following the presentation of the report, President Fox appointed a special prosecutor to investigate the disappearances and to bring criminal charges against the perpetrators. Human Rights Watch (2003) reported that, one and a half years later, the military was not fully cooperative with the investigation and the federal government was not supportive enough to move the investigation beyond the calling of witnesses to testify. The report concluded that the special prosecutor lacked sufficient material and human resources to overcome such serious obstacles as the lack of access to declassified military documents, resistance of military judges to cede jurisdiction to civilian courts for the prosecution of military personnel, and the idea held by many in the military that past crimes such as kidnapping or forced disappearances occurring in the 1970 and 1980s are too old to prosecute. In late 2003, the Supreme Court, in a historic appellate decision, acted for the first time to consider the question of whether the crimes of kidnapping that occurred during the "dirty war" were beyond the statute of limitation for prosecution (*Proceso* 2003a). The Court ruled that kidnapping was a "continuing crime," which opened the door for the criminal prosecution of "dirty war" offenders (*La Jornada* 2003b).

Special court structures have also served to strengthen procedural democracy in Mexico by providing a forum for the resolution of electoral disputes. The permanent Electoral Tribunal of the Federal Judiciary (TEPJF), located in Mexico City, is the highest legal court for deciding matters of elections (Eisenstadt 2004). Five regional electoral tribunals process election disputes only during election years. Prior to the 1996 electoral reforms, electoral magistrates were appointed by the president and approved by the Chamber of Deputies. At the request of the opposition parties, the 1996 reforms required the Supreme Court to propose candidates for the permanent and regional electoral tribunals, to be approved for a single eight-year term by two-thirds of the Senate. The essential function of the electoral tribunals is to hear questions of potential fraud and other violations of political rights relating to elections. Although the TEPJF was fully independent as of 2000, in many states where the PRI's political influence remained strong, standoffs occurred over election results and lines of legal authority between the federal electoral court, state electoral courts, and the PRI.

In addition to the TEPJF, the Mexican Constitution recognizes the Federal Electoral Institute (IFE) as a public institution with administrative autonomy and its own budget. The IFE is in charge of regulating all aspects of elections, including civic training and education, drawing electoral boundaries, regulating the rights and prerogatives of interest groups and political parties, registering and maintaining voter lists, preparing for election day, regulating poll watching, computing election results, and so forth. The IFE council president and eight council members are selected at the same time to seven-year terms with approval by two-thirds of the Chamber of Deputies. Additional council members with voice but no vote are proposed by the legislative power, representatives of the political parties, and a member of the executive branch.

Previously, elections were dominated by the PRI-controlled executive branch under the aegis of the Ministry of the Interior (Secretaría de Gobernación). Because of the conflict of interest created by giving the executive branch control over elections, electoral reforms were passed to ensure the IFE's complete autonomy; these reforms are seen as the definitive legal watershed in Mexico's democratization and transition to free and fair elections. The IFE has had an enormous impact in steering Mexico in this direction. Yet, despite its high operating budget, the IFE's authority remains limited: the federal electoral code did not give the IFE the authority to regulate either the private media or government expenditures during campaigns. In the past, both have been used to the unfair advantage of particular candidates. Nor did the electoral code give the IFE sufficient tools or powers to easily carry out some responsibilities within its mandate, such as monitoring campaign spending. Still, the IFE does possess the legal powers to confer financial penalties on political parties who violate campaign spending limits (WOLA 2000; Prud'homme 1998).

During the Fox administration, the IFE has grown increasingly autonomous and has actively asserted its authority in monitoring campaign spending limits and the sources of political contributions. In 2003 the IFE found the PRI guilty of overspending US$44 million in the 2000 presidential elections from public funds it obtained illegally from the official oil union. The IFE then fined the PRI US$89 million, the largest fine a Mexican political party has ever paid for breaking campaign spending laws (*La Jornada* 2003c). The IFE also approved a US$48 million fine in October 2003 against the coalition partners that brought Fox to power (the PAN and Mexico's Green Party [PVEM]) on the grounds that they violated campaign finance regulations by accepting foreign donations, exceeding spending limits, and engaging in other prohibited activities (*Proceso* 2003b). A special prosecutor's investigation into the case concluded that foreign campaign contributions were not illegal under the Mexican penal code (*News* 2002).

The TEPJF has similarly become more assertive of its regulatory powers in the post-2000 era. Nevertheless, in some cases resistance to the enforcement of its decisions by state-level PRI institutions was overcome only after Supreme Court rulings in its favor. Regarding gubernatorial elections scheduled for May 2001 in the state of Yucatán, the TEPJF declared in October 2000 that the composition of the electoral council of the State Electoral Institute (IEE) was invalid because of the unlawful overrepresentation of PRI supporters. The Yucatán state government initially refused to recognize the new electoral councilors designated by the TEPJF and denied them access to their office building. Only after a Supreme Court ruling in April 2001, less than two months before the elections, did state officials comply with the TEPJF order, paving the way for the election of the state's first PAN governor, Patricio Patrón Laviada. The TEPJF also annulled the gubernatorial elections in Tabasco in December 2000 due to serious irregularities, including vote-buying and excess official media time granted to the PRI. The decision overturned the victory of PRI candidate Manuel Andrade. The TEPJF ruled that an interim governor be appointed and that new elections for governor be held within three to six months of its December 2000 ruling. The PRI-dominated Tabasco congress extended the interim governor's term to eighteen months, but the Supreme Court declared this decision unlawful on March 8, 2001. The state congress then decided to schedule new elections for August 5, 2001, past the deadline set by the TEPJF.

PROFESSIONAL STANDARDS AND LEGAL EDUCATION

As Fix-Fierro notes in his chapter in this volume, there is a great need for an examination of Mexican legal training and professional standards, in both the judiciary and private practice. Presently, the federal judicial branch comprises 11 Supreme Court ministers, 6 counselors to the Federal Council of the Judiciary, about 718 federal circuit and district judges, and support staff working on their behalf (*Excélsior* 2000). A 1995 constitutional amendment formalized the process of recruiting federal circuit and district judges. This law now allows the newly established CJF to appoint federal district and circuit judges after a competitive examination based on the principles of "excellence, objectivity, impartiality, professionalism and independence" (Melgar Adalid 1998). Circuit and district judges must have at least five years of professional practice. About two hundred circuit judges and three hundred district judges have been nominated in the last five years under the new law. An informal federal career existed until 1994 in which young recruits would ascend the internal hierarchy of judicial posts up to the position of Supreme Court clerk. From there, they could be appointed at the proposal of one of the justices. The CJF has the power to appoint, assign, remove, suspend, or transfer judges, and thus there is no legal concept of tenure for federal judges. The Supreme Court retains the right to limited review of the council's decisions (Fix-Fierro 1998). Informal judicial career or direct appointment by the state governor remains the norm for state judges. In 2003 the Supreme Court initiated internal reforms to lower the salaries of administrators in the CJF to the level currently paid to circuit and unitary judges, in order to reduce the incentives for judges to remain on the bench (rather than become administrators in the judicial system) (*La Jornada* 2003d).

The typical public law school faculty consists of three to six full-time academics and from twenty to fifty part-time teachers who are active practitioners. The largest law school is the national law school at the Universidad Nacional Autónoma de Mexico (UNAM), one of the oldest universities in the hemisphere. The majority of federal judges and prosecutors are graduates of the UNAM. Most Mexican states also offer law degrees, including at the Benemérita Universidad Autónoma de Puebla, Universidad Autónoma de Sonora, Universidad Autónoma de San Luis Potosí, and so forth. Mexican universities also offer master's and doctoral degrees in law, with an emphasis on upgrading and modernizing specialized areas of law for Mexican legal practitioners. Fix-Fierro documents in this volume the recent dramatic growth in private law schools as a trend in legal education in Mexico.

Mexican law students are able to practice law after obtaining a law school diploma and receiving a state licensing certificate recognizing the diploma. Legal training consists of a five-year degree relying on lectures, hornbooks, and oral exams. There is no national or state bar examination as a prerequisite to practice law. Rather, membership in the most important bar association, the Mexican Bar Association (Barra Mexicana, Colegio de

Abogados), is voluntary and includes only a small percentage of practicing lawyers (about 1,800 total); most members are older, well-established lawyers who also do part-time teaching and writing. Thus the major requirement for state certification to practice law is a period of six months to one year of community service, through either legal aid or government agencies. This apprenticeship requirement allows the prospective new attorney to gain practical experience and provides aid to entities in need of legal assistance.

Judicial and Legal Education in a Period of Reform

The education and training of Mexican judges has become a topic of increased interest in light of the 1994 judicial reforms, which emphasized greater professionalism within the judiciary. The development of modern judicial education can be organized under three stages. In the first, during the 1950s and 1960s, judicial training was considered to be a type of specialized knowledge geared toward professional practice. Judicial training was quite basic and included nonsystematized courses and lectures. Students were supposed to learn the legal technicalities and customs necessary to work as a judge through on-the-job training. Several problems resulted from this type of judicial education, including a general lack of coordination between those who planned and made decisions within judicial institutions and those who educated future judges. The lack of a professional cadre of legal experts also led to occasional problems of clientelism, nepotism, and corruption, as many members of the judicial branch regularly hired trusted friends, known colleagues, and even family members for administrative positions. Other problems included a general resistance to change and the limited use of theoretical or applied knowledge as guides to judicial organization and practice.

The second stage of judicial training occurred within the context of the accelerated political and economic liberalization of the 1990s. Within this context of social change, judicial training has become conceptualized as a central part of this transformation, as illustrated by the creation of the Federal Council of the Judiciary in 1994–1995, which revolutionized the concept of judicial education in Mexico. The CJF became responsible for overseeing exams and increasing the requirements for professionals to work within the federal judiciary. Subsequently, judicial training became more specialized at different levels, and course material became more intense.

Judicial education thus acquired new relevance as a fundamental activity necessary to accelerate change in the nation after the 1994–1995 reforms.

Still, judicial education often remains seen as just another organizational and administrative activity undertaken by judicial institutions. Moreover, there is little consensus about how legal education should be organized in Mexico. There is currently a wide variety of initiatives to promote legal education within judicial institutions, in university law programs, and in multiple lectures and workshops on judicial education. Other Latin American countries undergoing legal reform have similarly experienced periods in which legal training initiatives were highly pluralistic (often with different aims and objectives), but they later developed greater consistency in their approaches. Thus the current phase in Mexico may be a period of transition. This transition will likely depend on the course of legal reforms that set the standards and requirements for actual practice.

Hence a third stage of development of judicial education and training may be on the horizon. In particular, some legal experts are calling for judicial training programs that rely more heavily on applied knowledge. In this model, future judges would be trained by teachers and judges who are in close contact with the daily demands of administering and imparting justice. Scholars at UNAM's Institute for Juridical Studies (IIJ-UNAM) have recently designed a new judicial training program that balances traditional academic legal studies with input from practicing judges and specialists from other professional fields.

The legal education of lawyers has also taken on new significance in the context of Mexico's accelerated processes of new political pluralism and commercial opening beginning in the 1990s. Lawyers have become ever more important as both old and new social conflicts have become increasingly legalized, and more and more citizens have turned to lawyers to solve, pacify, and even prevent conflicts. Some private universities have sought to adapt to these new legal realities by giving students applied legal training within the university setting. Traditionally, legal education in Mexico has stressed memorization of the civil code during the university period, whereas applied skills were generally acquired on the job. One private university in Mexico City, the Center for Teaching and Research in Economics (CIDE), seeks to provide students with analytic training in the application of law to concrete cases, an understanding of the social context within which law operates, and courses in ethics—all imparted within the university training period. This new emphasis also represents an effort to add another applied dimension to the traditional conceptual study of legal norms in the abstract. So, for example, in the CIDE course on commercial law, students learn global economic theories. In the study of family law, students are asked to find a legal answer to the question of maternity in cases of surrogate motherhood. These various innovative university initiatives all seek to expand and adapt legal and judicial education to meet the new professional challenges confronting the legal profession under conditions of political and economic opening.

PROMOTING LEGAL AND JUDICIAL REFORM IN MEXICO

The impartial administration of justice in Mexico is hindered by multiple factors. Budgetary constraints have historically hampered the extension and development of courts. As Reames notes in his chapter in this volume, low salaries for investigative judicial police (estimated at US$300 per month) and preventive police (estimated at US$200 per month) open the door to corruption and inefficiency in policing. Also, as Zepeda Lecuona points out in his chapter, the links between investigative judicial police and the public prosecutor creates a conflict of interest in the gathering of evidence and presentation of the state's case against a defendant. Moreover, the competence and professionalism of Mexican prosecutors is highly questionable. In 2000, one report by an internal commission described only 6.6 percent of the PGR's labor force as "legal, honest, efficient, professional, loyal, and impartial" (*La Jornada* 2000). Economic circumstances and the lack of legal professionalism in Mexico make it so that few defendants can find, or afford to hire, a competent attorney. Meanwhile, the Mexican court system suffers from serious problems of administrative backlog (*La Jornada* 2003e).[3]

In addition, government agents frequently act with a degree of impunity that fundamentally undermines the rule of law: every year government agents are involved in violations of due process rights, intimidation, torture, and even murder of independent labor organizers, opposition political activists, indigenous leaders and farmers, independent lawyers, human rights activists, journalists, gays, whistle-blowers, and clergy and laity who defend indigenous populations or support liberation theology. Authors of a Pulitzer prize–winning *Washington Post* series asserted that the Mexican criminal justice system harshly punishes petty crimes commit-

---

[3] The coordinator of the Commission of Penal Law of the Mexican Bar complained of an insufficient number of criminal courts for the number of cases, and noted that there still exists an imbalance in the Federal District Court system, which has eight criminal courts but twelve district collegiate courts, twelve labor courts, and fourteen administrative courts (United Nations 2002).

ted by the poor, while failing to provide an adequate system of juvenile justice or punishments for major offenses, such as kidnapping, white-collar crime, and organized crime (*Washington Post* 2002a, 2002b, 2002c, 2002d). Meanwhile, drug trafficking remains a serious problem; several federal judges were killed in recent years by individuals with alleged ties to the drug trade. Moreover, drug trafficking is also detrimental to the impartial administration of justice because it introduces greater corruption into the Mexican legal system (Bailey and Godson 2000: 1–2).[4]

No firm estimates exist for measuring the extent of drug-related or other corruption within the Mexican justice system, in part due to the secrecy surrounding acts of corruption but also because of the wide variety of public officials and members of society who participate in illegal transactions. A recent survey of the cases of 18 Federal District judges conducted by the federal Attorney General's Office reveals the complexity of social actors involved in crimes against the financial system.[5] In 2002 these 18 judges heard 150 cases, ruled with the Attorney General 86.9 percent of the time, and resolved 85 percent of the disputes. The cases demonstrate a variety of different types of social actors involved in corruption, businessmen as well as civil servants.[6] However, most citizens surveyed in a Mexico City poll in 2001 (71 percent) believed that government employees, not

---

[4] For example, according to extradition documents submitted by the government of Mexico in San Diego, California, in 1997, the Tijuana-based Arrellano-Félix cartel dispensed an estimated US$1 million in weekly bribes to Mexican federal, state, and local officials, who ensured that the movement of drugs continued unimpeded to the gateway cities along the southwestern border of the United States (U.S. Department of State 1997).

[5] Federal District judges are those who hear the majority of crimes against the financial system because it is in Mexico City that large-scale fiscal fraud, money laundering, and general high-profile crimes take place. Most state criminal judges tend to hear crimes against public health, illegal possession of arms, and trafficking in migrants (*Reforma* 2003a).

[6] There are many prominent examples of private-sector corruption and impunity in the commission of white-collar crime in Mexico. For example, one case filed against one hundred accomplices of the Juárez drug cartel involved alleged illicit enrichment by an ex-civil servant of the Federal Electricity Commission. Another involved allegations of the theft of US$1,150,442 by Mexican and French businessmen from the Ministry of Tourism. A suit was filed against functionaries of the Mexican Oil Union for granting an illegal scholarship to the son of a prominent PRI politician, and another case involved absolving the ex-head of the Mexican lottery from charges of embezzlement of public monies.

businessmen, were more corrupt (*Reforma Poll* 2001). Indeed, the majority of those surveyed (57 percent) believed that "an honest person who was given a public post was more likely to become corrupt than to stay honest." Yet despite this skepticism about government, 72 percent of those polled also thought the Fox administration would be able to reduce corruption to some degree.[7] The post-2000 period is therefore a crucial test for democratic government in Mexico, and it has involved key initiatives to promote the justice-sector reform on a number of fronts.

Opposition Governance and Justice-Sector Reform

During the period of growing opposition-party strength, including Mexico's first opposition-dominated federal legislature (1997–2000), various reforms were aimed at reducing corruption and improving the administration of justice. The left-leaning Party of the Democratic Revolution (PRD) won the mayoral post in Mexico City in 1997 and increased the monthly pay for new judicial police in Mexico City to a middle-class salary (about US$1,000). New entrance requirements were implemented to break the link between the police and criminality, including two years of college, an extensive background check, and no previous police experience. At the national level, a National Penal Sciences Institute (INACIPE) was created that offers master's degrees in victimology and criminal law. A new National Program to Combat Corruption went into effect in April 2000, including the development of a new ethical code for civil servants and the certification by federal agencies that they are successfully trying to combat corruption.

However, as noted earlier, the most active initiatives to reform the judiciary and the administration of justice have come since the installation of PAN candidate Vicente Fox as president in December 2000. The Fox administration has focused many of its activities on improving government agencies' accountability to law (Unger 2002: 8). For example, the Fox administration has made efforts to combat corruption more effectively by raising the salaries of federal public administrators, increasing training courses, implementing programs to detect and sanction corruption, and encouraging citizens to make government accountable. Most promisingly, obligatory human rights training is now required for all personnel in the

---

[7] This concurs with the opinion of the director of the nongovernmental organization Transparency International (dedicated to the study of corruption), who argues that the incremental Fox anticorruption reforms will likely achieve results by 2008–2010 (*Proceso* 2003c).

federal Office of the Attorney General. Likewise, the Fox administration implemented a new program to recruit personnel by means of examinations in the Public Prosecutor's Office, thereby promoting the professionalization of personnel within the criminal justice system; personnel who did not comply with professional requirements and standards were dismissed (United Nations 2002: 23). Where possible, Fox has sought redress for grievances committed by public authorities. For example, on humanitarian grounds, Fox ordered the release of two environmental activists who had been jailed based on forced confessions that the military had obtained in November 2001 through the use of torture.

Also worth noting has been the Fox administration's elaboration of a new set of juridical norms to regulate, coordinate, and make more public the way Mexico's intelligence and security agencies handle the public surveillance of citizens. Moreover, the Fox administration has worked closely with civil society to improve public access to and monitoring of the justice system in order to ensure accountability to society. In February 2001, the federal government also signed a cooperative agreement with eighty-three social organizations, political parties, businesses, and academic institutions to work together to fight corruption (United Nations 2002: 30). Subsequently, the passage of Mexico's Transparency Law in 2001 ensured that such groups would have access to the information required to hold public authorities accountable.

In response to both domestic and international criticism, the Fox administration also tried to increase the budget allocation for the judiciary by 77 percent in 2001, a significant increase over the judiciary's traditional share of 0.67 percent of the total budget. By 2002, the judiciary's budget had risen, but only to 1 percent of the total budget (Aprobación 2002). This places Mexico's judiciary budget as a proportion of total budget below such nations as Costa Rica (5.16 percent), El Salvador (4.51 percent), and Argentina (3.15 percent), but above nations such as Chile (0.93 percent), Bahamas (0.99 percent), and Belize (0.73 percent).

The Fox administration's most ambitious reform effort was a package of legislative initiatives and constitutional amendments introduced in 2004 that would dramatically overhaul key aspects of the Mexican judiciary. This reform package proposed a wide range of sweeping changes, including the structural separation of the functions of police investigation from prosecution, the use of oral trials, and greater professional requirements for public defenders. At the time of publication, the political prospects of passing all elements of Fox's reform package were relatively limited, given significant opposition and the perceived practical infeasibility of key provisions. However, the Fox reform package has at least succeeded in promoting a nationwide debate on the structure and function of Mexico's justice system. As these debates play out in the remainder of Fox's term and beyond, the role of the judiciary itself will be crucial in adapting new procedures and norms to the Mexican legal reality.

Asserting the Role of the Judiciary

Since 2000 the judiciary has actively expanded its influence and increasingly asserted its authority in the political system. The Supreme Court has extended the reach of federal law to the states, challenging some of the prerogatives that state governors had customarily enjoyed, including the largely unchallenged capacity to designate their subordinates and to control the state judiciary. For example, in 2003 the Supreme Court ruled that the attempt by the PRI governor of Colima to designate the head of the Labor Board of Conciliation and Arbitration violated the state congress's authority to approve the nominee (*Proceso* 2003d). In October 2001, five of six magistrates in Yucatán presented a constitutional controversy before the Court, accusing PRI Governor Víctor Cervera Pacheco of violating their judicial autonomy when he labeled them a mere "state entity" (rather than an independent branch of government) in his budget proposal. The Yucatán magistrates also claimed the governor had mounted a campaign of aggression against them. The Court ordered the presence of the heads of the executive, legislative, and judicial powers in Mexico City to resolve their differences in April 2003 (*Reforma* 2003b).

Also, after the 2000 transition, the Supreme Court acted to strengthen the legal position of municipalities vis-à-vis state law. In a 2003 decision, the Court ordered the Oaxacan state congress to reinstate a local municipal council governed under customary law that had been dissolved under state law. The Court ruled that the state congress failed to notify the municipal council of its impending dissolution, and thereby illegally deprived the council of the possibility of self-defense (*La Jornada* 2003f). The Court also struck down a México State law granting the state inspector general the power to intervene in, and request the destitution of, municipal treasurers.

Protecting Indigenous Legal Rights

The Mexican legal system incorporates concepts from both European and indigenous legal systems. More specifically, Article 4 of the Constitution officially recognizes the rights of indigenous peoples to their own cultural identity in accordance with local languages, cultures, means, customs, resources, and specific forms of social organization (Ávalos 2000). In particular, the concept of *usos y costumbres*, or customary treatment of indigenous legal issues under administrative courts, applies where there is no applicable law (Gessell 1997). Hence, in judicial and agrarian proceedings, Article 4 states that indigenous practices and judicial customs shall be taken into account in the terms that the law establishes. Still, as noted by Hernández and Ortiz Elizondo in this volume, indigenous peoples have traditionally had difficulty accessing justice in Mexico due to outright discrimination and basic economic inequalities. A recent United Nations report noted that indigenous people in the mountainous regions of Oaxaca State have to walk for seventy hours to reach the nearest court.

The 1994 Chiapas rebellion ultimately led to significant initiatives to improve legal conditions for indigenous people. On the day that the North American Free Trade Agreement (NAFTA) went into effect (January 1, 1994), the Zapatista Army of National Liberation (EZLN) initiated an armed uprising in the poor southern Mexican state of Chiapas. Among other grievances, the EZLN identified NAFTA clauses that ended special provisions for indigenous communal farms (*ejidos*) and the general marginalization of indigenous peoples as motivation for their rebellion. A series of formal talks between the government and the EZLN led to the signing of an initial agreement, the Agreement on Indian Rights and Culture (known as the San Andrés Accords), which was later elaborated as a legal initiative by the Peace and Harmony Commission (COCOPA).

As Hernández and Elizondo argue in this volume, the proposed CO-COPA constitutional reforms of 1996 raised indigenous rights to the level of formal constitutional guarantees of legal pluralism, including the right to self-governing political communities, the right to traditional systems of production, and the right to manage and operate their own development projects (EZLN Reforma 1996). Then-incoming President Fox pledged his political support for constitutional reforms promoting greater indigenous rights and presented a bill to Congress that incorporated the 1996 CO-COPA constitutional reforms. The law that Congress passed in 2001, however, significantly modified the 1996 agreements by restricting rights of autonomy and territoriality, rights also guaranteed by Resolution 169 of the International Labor Organization and ratified by the Mexican Congress in 1988. These included a concept of territoriality that defines the characteristics of an indigenous group, establishes the legal and political autonomy of majority-indigenous municipalities, and provides for collective owner-ship of the land and natural resources. In September 2002 the Supreme Court ruled on more than three hundred suits brought by hundreds of municipalities from the state of Oaxaca and elsewhere that raised constitu-tional challenges against the legislation. The challengers contended that the new law was unconstitutional because indigenous groups were not con-sulted on the legislation, as is required by Resolution 169.[8] The Supreme Court rejected all the appeals on procedural grounds, ruling that it had no jurisdiction to evaluate the constitutionality of a constitutional reform. The failure of the San Andrés Accords and the 2001 indigenous reform law means that custom remains a secondary source for law in Mexico.[9]

Increasing International Scrutiny

International treaties negotiated by the executive and approved by the Senate become binding in domestic law after their official domestic publi-cation in the federal government's Official Register (*Diario Oficial*). Accord-ingly, Mexican courts consistently equate treaties with legislative acts, affirm their incorporation into national law, and hold that they are binding throughout the land. Nevertheless, while Mexican judges are bound to give primacy to constitutional treaties over state laws, they are also bound to give primacy to the Constitution over international treaties (Cicero 1997). Hence, in the case of normative conflict, the traditional Mexican system would grant an injunction against the unconstitutional norms, with-out annulling an international treaty beyond the concrete cases brought to the courts.[10] This primacy of the Mexican Constitution, including the pro-hibition against life imprisonment and the death penalty, explains why the Supreme Court struck down a Fox proposal in late 2001 to facilitate the

---

[8] They also contended that the new law was not ratified by the required two-thirds majority in the sixteen state legislatures that would be affected by it, thereby also making the law unconstitutional (Ross 2002).

[9] Recently in Chiapas and elsewhere, some indigenous communities have cre-ated autonomous municipalities, which can elect their own representatives and use their lands and other resources according to custom but which oper-ate outside the boundaries of formal law (Reuters 2003).

[10] The interactions between treaties and domestic laws are not limited, of course, to instances of normative conflict. Indeed, the presumption is not that na-tional and international norms in force in Mexico contradict each other but that one supplements the other. For a greater discussion of the complex na-ture of this interaction, see Cicero 1997: 1045–86.

extradition of criminals—especially drug traffickers—to the United States, which employs both penalties.[11]

Nevertheless, there has been significant international attention to Mexico's rule of law problems—and corresponding pressure to improve its justice system. A scathing report from the United Nations Commission on Human Rights noted widespread problems of inefficiency, inaccessibility, corruption, case overload, and budgetary constraints as consistent complaints by both legal actors and the public at large. The same report decried the continuation of human rights violations in Mexico even under the Fox administration. These included violations of the rights of women and children, the harassment of lawyers and human rights defenders, violation of fair trial procedures, slavery-like working conditions for indigenous immigrants, continued high rates of impunity for criminals, police use of torture, and the lack of a uniform, enforceable code of ethics for the legal profession. The UN special rapporteur also claimed that 50 to 70 percent of all federal judges were corrupt but none was sanctioned by the Federal Council of the Judiciary (United Nations 2002: 18). This figure was quickly challenged in a "Counter-Report," in which the president of the Mexican Supreme Court asserted tellingly that "if in reality that level of corruption in the federal judicial system were real, there would be no democratic governance or social peace in this country, let alone the legal certainty that guarantees investment" (Suprema Corte de Justicia 2002: 1).

CONCLUSION

As the Mexican judicial system undergoes reforms to strengthen the rule of law during the period of democratic consolidation, we observe both continuity and change. With respect to continuity, efforts to achieve formal constitutional guarantees for indigenous rights remain conflictive, as has historically been the case. This is important because the attempt to legally define indigenous municipalities as fully autonomous regions, with legal and political standing and collective ownership over the land and its natural resources, is perceived by some to threaten the goal of national unity. Similarly, efforts to improve human rights in the administration of justice have been slow to change, although the National Human Rights Commis-

---

11 More specifically, the Foreign Ministry and Office of the Attorney General had sought to eliminate the constitutional requirement (Article 18) that the federal government ensure beforehand that no prisoner will be submitted to a life sentence prior to granting extradition (*Reforma* 2001).

sion reports that the overall number of incidents of torture has declined since 2000 (United Nations 2002: 22). The theme of continuity also characterizes persisting challenges in addressing increased indices of crime and violence as well as ongoing mistrust in the credibility of the criminal justice system. The harassment of human rights defenders—including death threats, kidnapping, and intimidation—has also continued into the Fox *sexenio*, particularly in the states of Chiapas, Oaxaca, and Guerrero (Amnesty International 2001). These obstacles continue to impede the development of a stronger rule of law in Mexico.

With respect to change, the intensification of both domestic and international scrutiny over the justice system has accelerated efforts to promote reform along with the process of Mexico's democratization and democratic consolidation. Initial reforms in the 1990s strengthened Mexico's legal institutions by increasing the scope of judicial decisions. Specialized judicial bodies such as the IFE and the TEPJF intensified their investigatory functions regarding violations of electoral laws, particularly since 2000. After 2000, the Supreme Court further extended the reach of federal law to the states, challenging some of the prerogatives that state governors customarily employed and hence fortifying the legal position of municipalities vis-à-vis state law. These rulings provide hope for the incremental strengthening of Mexican democracy through federalism, both horizontally across branches and vertically between the federal, state, and local levels of government.

Just as important, the recent plurality of theories and initiatives to improve judicial and legal education promises to infuse new ideas into both the legal system and society. Such intellectual transformations are vital to building a strengthened judiciary in a period of democratic consolidation. There are also signs of institutional change under Fox that reflect a greater commitment to transparency, accountability, and respect for the civil rights of Mexican citizens. Hence recent trends, along with further reforms to the Mexican judiciary, promise to serve as central elements in the construction of a robust rule of law. Nevertheless, continued systematic legal reform and the successful reform of Mexico's justice sector will be a long-term process.

References

Amnesty International. 2001. "Mexico: Daring to Raise their Voices," December.

Aprobación del Presupuesto para 2002. [Approved Budget of 2002]. At www.shcp.gob.mx\ori\docs\bo020106.pdf., p. 8.

Arnold, Linda. 1989. "La política de la justicia: los Vencedores de Ayutla y la Suprema Corte Mexicana," *Historia Mexicana* 39, no. 2 (October–December): 355–92.

Ávalos, Francisco A. 2000. *The Mexican Legal System*. Littleton, Colo.: F.B. Rothman.

Bailey, John, and Roy Godson. 2000. "Introduction." In *Organized Crime and Democratic Governability: Mexico and the U.S.-Mexico Borderlands*, ed. John Bailey and Roy Godson. Pittsburgh, Penn.: University of Pittsburgh Press.

Barragán, J.M. 1994. *José María Iglesias y la justicia electoral*. Mexico City: Universidad Nacional Autónoma de México.

Carpizo, Jorge. 1978. *El presidencialismo en México*. Mexico City: Siglo Veintiuno.

Cicero, Jorge. 1997. "International Law in Mexican Courts," *Vanderbilt Journal of Transnational Law* 30 (November): 1035–82.

Clagett, Helen L., and David M. Valderrama. 1973. "A Revised Guide to the Law and Legal Literature of Mexico." In *Comparative Law: Western European and Latin American Legal Systems*, ed. David S. Clark and John Henry Merryman. New York: Bobbs-Merrill.

Domingo, Pilar. 2000. "Judicial Independence: The Politics of the Supreme Court in Mexico," *Journal of Latin American Studies* 32: 705–35.

Eisenstadt, Todd. 2004. *Courting Democracy in Mexico: Party Strategies and Electoral Institutions*. Cambridge: Cambridge University Press.

Excélsior. 2000. "Designados, 200 magistrados y 300 jueces de distrito en 5 años," July 8.

EZLN Reforma 1996. "Constitutional Reforms Regarding Indigenous Rights: Comparative Chart of the COCOPA and the EZLN–Federal Government Agreements Signed on February 16, 1996." Internet edition. At http://www.ezln.org/ (accessed January 21, 2001).

Fix-Fierro, Héctor. 1998. "Judicial Reforms and the Supreme Court of Mexico: The Trajectory of Three Years," *U.S.-Mexico Law Journal* 6 (Spring): 1–22.

Fix Zamudio, H., and J.R. Cossío Díaz. 1995. *El poder judicial en el ordamiento mexicano*. Mexico City: Fondo de Cultura Económica.

Garrido, Luis Javier. 1989. "The Crisis of Presidentialismo." In *Mexico's Alternative Political Futures*, ed. Wayne A. Cornelius, Judith Gentleman, and Peter H. Smith. La Jolla: Center for U.S.-Mexican Studies, University of California, San Diego.

Gessell, Jeffrey N. 1997. "Customary Indigenous Law in Mexico," *Georgia Journal of International and Comparative Law* 26, no. 3: 643-71.

González Oropeza, Manuel. 1996. "The Administration of Justice and the Rule of Law." In *Mexico after Salinas*, ed. Mónica Serrano and Víctor Bulmer-Thomas. London: Institute of Latin American Studies, University of London.

Herget, James E., and Jorge Camil. 1978. *An Introduction to the Mexican Legal System*. Buffalo, N.Y.: William S. Hein.

Hernández, Octavio A., and Miguel Ángel Portes. 1985. *Derecho del pueblo mexicano: México a través de sus constituciones*. 3d ed. Mexico City: Cámara de Diputados.

Human Rights Watch. 2003. *Justice in Jeopardy*. New York: Human Rights Watch.

Jurisprudencia. 1985. "Poder judicial de la federación. Tesis ejecutorias, 1917–1985." Apéndice al Semanario Judicial de la Federación. Octava Parte. Jurisprudencia Comunal Pleno y las Salas. Mexico City.

La Jornada. 2000. [Translated Version]. "Honest and Efficient, Only 6% of the Personnel of the PGR in Five Areas," September 4.

———. 2003a. "Los tribunales laborales no se equiparán con los del Poder Judicial, decide la SCJN," June 4.

———. 2003b. "La desaparición forzada es un delito continuado, afirma Castro y Castro," October 31.

———. 2003c. "Hoy ratifica el IFE sanción contra el PRI," March 14.

———. 2003d. "Busca la Corte eliminar privilegios en la Judicatura," March 24.

———. 2003e. "Deficiencias en impartición de justicia, por falta de tribunales," June 20.

———. 2003f. "Ordena la Corte restituir en el cargo a funcionarios de Santiago Amoltepec," June 9.

Melgar Adalid, Mario. 1998. "Mexican Justice toward the 21st Century: The Federal Council of the Judicature: Formation, Branches, and Operation," *U.S.-Mexico Law Journal* 6 (Spring): 23–34.

News. 2001. "Congress Passes Spending Plan, 2001 Budget Finalized," December 30.

———. 2002. "Mexican Prosecutor: Campaign Contributions from Foreigners Legal," August 10.

Proceso. 2003a. "Atrae la SCJN el primer caso sobre la Guerra Sucia," No. 1405 (October 9).

———. 2003b. "Sanciona el IFE al PAN y al PVEM," No. 1405 (October 10).

———. 2003c. "Escándalos en Los Pinos afectan lucha anticorrupción de Fox: TI." No. 1405 (October 9).

———. 2003d. "Propina la Corte Nueva derrota jurídica al gobierno de Colima," No. 1378 (April 6).

Prud'homme, Jean-François, 1998. "The Instituto Federal Electoral (IFE): Building an Impartial Electoral Authority." In *Governing Mexico: Political Parties and Elections*, ed. Mónica Serrano. London: Institute of Latin American Studies, University of London.

Rabasa, Emilio. 1912. *La constitución y la dictadura; estudio sobre la organización política de México*. Mexico: Tipografía de Revista de Revistas.

Ramírez, F.T. 1994. *Leyes fundamentales en Mexico, 1808–1991*. 11th ed. Mexico City: Siglo Veintiuno.

Reforma. 2001. "Ratifica SCJN rechazo a cadena perpetua," October 2.

———. 2003a. "Elabora la PGR ranking de jueces," March 9.

————. 2003b. "Yucatan state judges," April 4.

Reforma Poll. 2001. "Corrupción: delito compartido," September 29.

Reuters. 2003. "Mexico City's Urban Indians Call for Autonomy," September 23.

Ross, John. 2002. "Mexico's Supreme Court Upholds Flawed Rights Law." MexBarb #1177. At www/chiapas/0915_chiapas.cfm.

Schatz, Sara. 1998. "A Neo-Weberian Approach to Constitutional Courts in the Transition from Authoritarian Rule: The Mexican Case (1994-97)," *International Journal of the Sociology of Law* 26, no. 2 (June): 217-44.

————. 2002. "Mexico." In *Legal Systems of the World: A Political, Social, and Cultural Encyclopedia*, ed. Herbert M. Kritzer. Santa Barbara, Calif.: ABC-CLIO.

Stavenhagen, Rodolfo. 1994. "Indigenous Peoples as Emerging Actors in Mexico and Latin America." Paper Presented at Woodrow Wilson Center, Washington, D.C.

Suprema Corte de Justicia. 2002. "El Informe del Relator de la ONU Desacredita sin Sustento al PJF: Góngora Pimental," Comunicado Número 515, Dirección General de Comunicación Social Comunicados de Prensa, April 11.

Unger, Mark. 2002. *Elusive Reform: Democracy and the Rule of Law in Latin America*. Boulder, Colo.: Lynne Rienner.

United Nations. 2002. "Civil and Political Rights, Including Questions of: Independence of the Judiciary, Administration of Justice, Impunity." Report of the special rapporteur on the independence of judges and lawyers, Dato'Param Cumaraswamy, submitted in accordance with the Commission on Human Rights Resolution 2001/39.

U.S. Department of State. 1997. "International Narcotics Control Strategy Report 1996." Report to Congress, March.

Washington Post. 2002a. "Disparate Justice Imprisons Mexico's Poor," July 6.

————. 2002b. "Kidnapping is Growth Industry in Mexico; Businessmen Targeted in Climate of Routine Ransoms, Police Corruption," September 17.

————. 2002c. "Mexico's Children Suffer in 'Little Jails,'" November 4.

————. 2002d. "The Union Boss Is the Only Man to See," December 26.

Weldon, Jeffrey. 2003. "Changing Patterns of Executive-Legislative Relations in Mexico." In *Dilemmas of Political Change in Mexico*, ed. Kevin J. Middlebrook. London: Institute of Latin American Studies, University of London.

WOLA (Washington Office on Latin America). 2000. "The Federal Electoral Institute," February 2, pp. 1–5.

CHAPTER 10

Justice Reform and Legal Opinion: The Mexican Criminal Codes of 1871, 1929, and 1931

ELISA SPECKMAN GUERRA

Historically, Mexican criminal law and major justice reform initiatives have been rooted in particular legal and sociological theories about crime and criminal behavior. However, this is not to say that Mexico's criminal justice system reflects a systematically determined or unified perspective. To the contrary, legislative and criminal justice reform has historically proven to involve a complex process of integrating new ideas into preexisting models of criminal justice. In this chapter I explore the philosophical currents and political processes that laid the foundation for Mexico's criminal justice system in the nineteenth and twentieth centuries by examining three distinct but interrelated phases in the development of Mexican criminal law. In the process, I give particular attention to the divergent theoretical perspectives on criminal law that have shaped legal debates and reform into the present.

LEGAL THEORY AND PRACTICE IN MEXICO

Throughout Mexico's history, there has been a gap between legal precepts and actual practice. At the end of the nineteenth and beginning of the twentieth centuries, intellectuals and government officials close to President Porfirio Díaz thought that the law did not respond to "reality" or to the needs of Mexican society. At the time, such elites argued that the 1857 Constitution and the Criminal Code of 1871 were inspired by legal theories that were appropriate for other nations but unrealistic for conditions in

---

The author thanks Laura Rojas and Diego Pulido Esteva for helping to compile the laws and legal texts. Translation by Patricia Rosas.

Mexico. Hence, to apply these laws would require waiting for the Mexican people to progress.[1] In other words, the gulf between legal precept and practice was justified by Mexico's political underdevelopment.

Years later, Silvio Zavala continued attributing the distance between the law and "reality" to the fact that the "intellectual lawmakers," the individuals charged with writing the laws, were unfamiliar with the society in which they lived. More specifically, because of the immense heterogeneity within the population itself, they could not write laws for all Mexicans. Instead of basing legal precepts on the "backward state" in which the majority lived, these lawmakers preferred to evoke an ideal and, through it, to "artificially accelerate" the process of civilizing the nation (Zavala 1930).

Both examples present an image of lawmakers who wrote laws with an ideal model in mind, whether or not they were aware of the distance between those laws and conditions in society. Both also illustrate the frustrations of lawmakers, lawyers, and even officials and judges who—although they agreed with the spirit of the law—believed that actual conditions made it impossible to apply the laws as written. In other words, these examples suggest a tension between legal ideals and practices that is ultimately the result of societal conditions.

Yet it is also likely that some legal experts, and perhaps even some public officials and judges, adhered to legal ideals other than those historically adopted. Still others may have actually preferred that legal precepts should reflect societal conditions (rather than vice versa).[2] This second option also suggests that there might have been experts and sectors of the population for whom the law seemed foreign and unfamiliar; in disobeying the law, they instead favored their own customs and practices.[3] In either case, it is quite possible that, in the process of legal discourse and legislation, these alternative viewpoints became blended with or otherwise modified the original ideals of lawmakers. Therefore, we must attempt to measure the law not only by its distance from "reality" and practice, but

---

[1] That idea, belonging to the "liberal-conservatives" (see, for example, Lombardo 1877; Macedo 1888; Urueta 1898a) has been studied by Charles Hale (1991: 59).

[2] In the final decades of the nineteenth century and the beginning of the twentieth century, an example of this was the influence of the positivist school on criminal law (Buffington 2001: 21–60; Piccato 1997; Speckman 2002a: 71–114).

[3] In the same period, an example is the resistance of the indigenous communities to the application of modern law and also the defense of their own mechanisms for resolving conflicts and applying justice (Marino n.d.).

also from the ideas of other contemporary legal experts (lawyers or judges) and even from the rest of society.

In this chapter, I work from the premise that we cannot study criminal law and its evolution as if it existed in a sterile and autonomous environment, independent from those who create and write it or from those who are affected by it. To do so would amount to accepting the utopian idea, inherited from eighteenth-century liberalism, that the law represents universal ideas or concepts. Quite to the contrary, laws arise from a certain political context and set of experiences, and they are, above all, the result of the actions and interests of specific actors. Hence those laws reflect that group's interpretation of social problems, its ideas about punishment and crime, and even its values, sympathies, prejudices, and fears. In other words, laws do not necessarily coincide with the interpretation, needs, and interests of other sectors, including lawyers, judges, and civil society. These possible divergences can also explain the distance between legal precepts and practice and between legal reforms and the thinking of legal experts.

Below, I examine these competing influences by exploring three major periods of Mexican criminal law, defined by the legal codes established or revised during 1871–1929, 1929–1931, and from 1931 to the late twentieth century. In evaluating each of these legal periods, I consider the proximity or distance between criminal legislation and juridical culture or public opinion by drawing on rigorous analysis of legal and procedural codes and regulations, as well as numerous books, pamphlets, and articles revealing the opinions of legal theoreticians and jurists.[4]

From these sources there emerge two distinct generations of jurists. The first, from the era of the Porfirio Díaz administration (the Porfiriato, 1876–1910), included Julio Guerrero, Miguel Macedo, Francisco Martínez Baca, Emilio Rabasa, Antonio Ramos Pedrueza, Carlos Roumagnac, Demetrio Sodi, Jesús Urueta, and Rafael de Zayas Enríquez.[5] After the Mexican

---

[4] In addition, to evaluate the position of judges and other judicial system officials, I employed a very useful survey taken in 1904 and published in the journal *Diario de Jurisprudencia*. The survey also appeared in the *Excélsior* and *El Universal* newspapers, and those two dailies, along with *El Siglo XIX*, *El Monitor Republicano*, and *La Voz de México*, helped me understand the opinions of other sectors of society.

[5] In addition to publishing various individual works and pamphlets, these men collaborated on journals such as the *Anuario de Legislación y Jurisprudencia*, *La Ciencia Jurídica*, *Diario de Jurisprudencia*, *El Foro*, and the *Revista de Legislación y Jurisprudencia*.

Revolution of 1910–1917, this group reunited in the Free School of Law (Escuela Libre de Derecho) and in 1917 formed the Association of Mexican Attorneys (Orden Mexicana de Abogados). In 1922, Macedo, Rabasa, and Ramos Pedrueza founded the Mexican Bar Association (Barra de Abogados) (see Speckman 2002b).[6] Other eminent jurists of the Porfiriato, such as Julio Guerrero, worked in the School of Jurisprudence of the National University (Escuela de Jurisprudencia de la Universidad Nacional), which later became the College of Jurisprudence (Facultad de Jurisprudencia) and eventually the College of Law and Social Sciences (Facultad de Derecho y Ciencias Sociales) of the National Autonomous University of Mexico (UNAM).[7] Hence the jurists of the Porfiriato continued to be influential until the end of the 1920s. At that point, Porfirian jurists were replaced by a second generation, comprising jurists such as Raúl Carrancá y Trujillo, José Ángel Ceniceros, Carlos Franco Sodi, Luis Garrido, Francisco González de la Vega, and Antonio Teja Zabre.[8]

In examining these major figures and their legal perspectives, I evaluate the extent to which dissension by legal theoreticians, legislators, "administrators of the law," and other social actors influenced legal reforms and their subsequent functioning in actual practice. The major argument advanced herein is that the theoretical, political, and social construction of criminal law often helps to explain the gulf between ideal and practice, as well as the overall process of legal reform.

THE CODE OF 1871 AND LEGAL REFORMS BEFORE 1929

The first criminal code for Mexico's Federal District was enacted in 1871, having been promulgated a year earlier. It remained in force throughout the Porfiriato, the Mexican Revolution, and until the formation of the ruling party in 1929. The Code of 1871 and, in general, criminal legislation issued after that were based on the premises of political liberalism, economic liberalism, and the classical or liberal school (see Speckman 2002a:

---

[6] They, along with other professors from the Escuela Libre de Derecho, including José Ángel Ceniceros, began publishing in *El Foro* around 1918.

[7] After 1921 the National University's School of Jurisprudence published the *Revista de Ciencias Sociales*, with the participation of both senior and junior faculty (among the first were Macedo, Rabasa, and Ramos Pedrueza, and among the second, Ezequiel Chávez, Luis Chico Goerne, Mario de la Cueva, Alfonso Teja Zabre, and Silvio Zavala).

[8] This group collaborated on the journal *Criminalia*, launched in 1933.

23–59). Following the tenets of the liberal school, the drafters of the criminal code believed that, under normal conditions, all adults—being equal—should enjoy the same freedom to act and have the same opportunities to know the nature and consequences of their actions. Thus adults were considered to be responsible when they violated a criminal law (Criminal Code of 1871, Arts. 4, 9, 11, 32, 34).

In contrast, it was supposed that children did not have a capacity for such discernment, or at least that their ability was more limited. Thus children under nine years of age—and in some cases, as old as fourteen—were exempt from or had only attenuated responsibility for criminal actions. Consequently, they were subject to punishments that were less severe than those meted out to adults, and children between fourteen and eighteen years of age who were convicted of a crime were interned in special institutions (Criminal Code of 1871, Arts. 127, 224–225). Under that logic, a children's court was established in 1926 to hand down preventive and educational sentences (medical treatment, guardianships, correctional education, and criminal corrections), review petitions from convicted and acquitted parties, and manage the correctional institutions ("Reglamento para la calificación de los infractores menores de edad," August 19, 1926).

The lawmakers also understood crime as a violation of the "social contract," an abstract, ahistorical pact in which individuals abdicate their natural freedoms in exchange for protection of their basic political rights by the government. Hence they understood crime as an offense against society as a whole. However, the criminals did not lose their rights; to the contrary, the laws held provisions for the rights of suspects, the accused, and the convicted.[9]

With the goal of guaranteeing equality under the law and in its application—elements essential to nineteenth-century liberalism—lawmakers also worked to standardize the sources and subjects of legal interpretation, and they eliminated exclusive benefits and special tribunals often available

---

[9] The 1857 Constitution, Arts. 16 and 18; the 1880 Code of Criminal Procedure, Arts. 23, 245, 248, 252, and 255; and the 1894 Code of Criminal Procedure, Arts. 105, 222, 225–226, 230, and 233. After the Revolution, the insistence on respect for individual rights continued (at least in the letter of the law). In 1911, state governors were urged to reorganize their security forces in order to reestablish order and respect for individual guarantees (Circular August 30, 1911). In 1917, the constituents broadened the list of rights (1917 Constitution, Art. 16); and in 1922, to guarantee the right to a defense, a new law and regulations mandating court-appointed defense counsel were issued.

solely to the privileged. In the process, they standardized the law itself, giving validity only to legislation produced by the "sovereign people" or by their representatives.[10] As a result, the concept and source of law was reduced to the edicts of the state, contributing to a tendency toward "judicial absolutism" (del Arenal 1999; Grossi 1991).

Besides ending pluralism in the sources and subjects of the law, lawmakers also tried to achieve full equality by erasing any possible differences in the application of the law. Thus punishment was based on the crime committed, without regard for the traits of the criminal. Nor was the individual character of the judge considered, since the lawmakers envisioned his role as merely applying a uniform and all-encompassing law code, with little need for exercising discretion or powers of judgment.[11] The criminal code enumerated in detail the foundations for determining the guilt or innocence of the accused and clearly specified the sentence that must be applied to each case. For some crimes, it stipulated a "midpoint" sentence, which could be increased or decreased by as much as one-third. In other cases, only a minimum and maximum penalty were set. To increase or reduce this penalty, the judge had to enumerate clearly identifiable attenuating or aggravating circumstances also set forth by the code.[12] Thus, historically, lawmakers assumed that each justice would be able to consistently deliver the correct application of the laws of the state.

Furthermore, Porfirian lawmakers sought to make criminal sentences sufficiently harsh to set an example (capable of dissuading others from committing crimes) and to achieve rehabilitation (since they believed correction was indeed possible). Because a prison term was believed sufficient to accomplish both those ends, lawmakers established fixed sentences, but they allowed for the possibility that the prisoner could influence the duration and conditions of the incarceration.[13] With the Revolution, this perspec-

---

[10] Constitution of 1857, Arts. 13, 14; Constitution of 1917, Art. 14; Criminal Code of 1871, Arts. 182–183; Criminal Procedure Code of 1880, Arts. 69–93, 158–161, 377–389; Criminal Procedure Code of 1894; Arts. 30, 51–72, 105–116, 247–249.

[11] However, in practice many judges were actually able to exercise substantial discretion in their decision making (see Speckman 2002a: 251–314).

[12] The weight of those circumstances was stipulated by placing them into four groups, each with a numeric value. Thus the judge was limited to noting and computing attenuating or aggravating circumstances, and based on the result of that mathematical operation he could lean toward either the maximum or minimum sentence (Criminal Code of 1871, Arts. 35–47, 66–69, 229–236).

[13] This was accomplished by dividing the sentence into three stages and detention or *libertad preparatoria* (parole) (see the 1857 Constitution, Art. 22; 1871

tive regarding sentences and prisons did not change, as is evidenced in the debates during the Constitutional Congress of 1917 and subsequent prison reforms (Buffington 2001: 132–62).[14]

Finally, Porfirian lawmakers authorized capital punishment but only in rare cases, such as treason, piracy, parricide, or first-degree murder (Constitution of 1857, Art. 23; Criminal Code of 1871, Arts. 560–566). Later, during the Revolution, various factions legislated decrees permitting the execution of common criminals—bandits, hijackers, kidnappers (see, for example, "Manifiesto del ejército libertador del centro y sur de la República," November 25, 1914, or "Decreto de Venustiano Carranza," October 9, 1916). Subsequent justifications for a more expansive application of the death penalty were developed in the context of the drafting of the 1917 Constitution. At that time, one of the commissions opined: "The moral poverty of the majority of the masses living within the Republic, who lack a solid civic education, which translates into a disposition for criminality, sets us apart from those exceptional nations where the level of culture and moral superiority of most people makes it possible to eliminate the death penalty from the repressive and preventive measures on which those countries rely" (Ceniceros and Garrido 1926a: 131–32). Proceeding with the commission's recommendation, the members of the constituent congress included the death penalty.

What were the opinions of legal experts and judges regarding the 1871 code and the prevailing legal justifications of the period? Examining books, theses, and articles on criminal law or criminology published between 1871

Criminal Code, Arts. 71–76 and 98–179; Ley reglamentaria sobre libertad preparatoria, December 20, 1871; Reglamento de los artículos 71–73 del Código Penal, August 23, 1877; Decreto que reforma varios artículos del Código Penal, September 5, 1896; Ley reglamentaria de la libertad preparatoria y de la retención, December 8, 1897; Ley que modifica el artículo 130 del Código Penal, December 20, 1911; and Decreto que reformó varios artículos del Código Penal, June 1927).

[14] In 1920 the prison review board was reorganized (Regulations, April 20, 1920). In 1923 Mexico's first national conference on prisons and correctional institutions was held ("Acuerdo autorizando al Gobernador del D.F. para que convoque a un Congreso Nacional de Establecimientos Penales y Correccionales," June 25, 1923; and "Circular ampliando la relativa al Congreso Criminológico y Penitenciario," July 20, 1923). And in 1924 the Technical Office for Prisons and Correctional Institutions Workshops was created ("Decreto cancelando varias partidas del presupuesto de egresos del Gobierno del D.F.," August 29, 1924).

and 1929, I found three currents: the traditional or liberal, the positivist, and the "eclectic" (similar to the "third school," as it was called in Italy). Ironically, the first school is less well represented than the others. Although some authors agreed with the prevailing opinions of Mexican lawmakers, and although existing legislation clearly shaped certain texts (such as official writings or manuals for teaching law), the publications of legal theoreticians generally tended to promote either positivist or eclectic views.

Positivist criminal legal theorists believed that human actions are determined by factors beyond will. Some of its adherents, particularly positivist champions of criminal sociology, located these factors in society, culture, or even the environment of the individual. However, the predominant view held by positivist defenders of criminal anthropology was that the causes of criminality were internal to the individual, resulting from mental or physical characteristics. In either case, positivists believed that because criminals were driven by factors beyond their own free will, they could not be held responsible for their actions. Nevertheless, positivists also recognized that criminals were a danger to the community, which needed to defend itself. Thus the principle of moral responsibility was rejected as a rationale for punishment in favor of the principle of social responsibility. Positivists conceived of a system of justice that varied based on the degree to which determinant factors for criminal or dangerous behavior were present in an individual (that is, the degree to which the individual's behavior was caused by uncontrollable factors). At the same time, given their belief that criminal behavior was not the result of free will, positivists doubted that criminals could be rehabilitated.

The eclectic school was characterized by its foundation in "scientism," the belief that the scientific method could be used to help lawmakers govern society by identifying appropriate measures to resolve social issues and ensure progress. While the positivist school shared that "scientific" inclination, the eclectic school had a basic belief that human beings exercise free will over their actions. Still, though eclectics generally sought to explain the causes of crime without falling into determinism, several within this school attributed criminal behavior to certain sociocultural or ethnic groups, such as mestizos and indigenous peoples.

Individuals who adopted an eclectic position did not make a radical critique of traditional liberal criminal codes, but instead proposed making certain changes. For example, the members of the criminal code review commission—convoked by the Justice Ministry from 1903 to 1912 and presided over by Miguel Macedo—respected the spirit of the Code of 1871 and fought only for the correction of its "imperfections, incoherencies, and deficiencies." Among these corrections were preventive confinement for alcoholics (the perceived connection between alcoholism and criminality illustrative of the casuistic tendency of the eclectic position); application of conditional sentences (based not on prior classifications but on the criminal's personality, as the positivist school also proposed), and the creation of penal colonies (for recidivists, but not for born criminals and the irredeemable, as the followers of Cesare Lombroso had desired).[15]

In addition, those who sympathized with the "third school" insisted on the need to create institutions for juvenile delinquents. In 1908 Miguel Macedo and Victoriano Pimentel fought to raise the age of personal responsibility from twelve to fourteen years (and the age of attenuated responsibility from sixteen to eighteen). They also fought for the creation of special tribunals and institutions for minors and for alternative sentences, such as sending a minor to live with a family or in a public shelter (Ceniceros and Garrido 1926b: 182–89). Demetrio Sodi, who believed that only educational experts would be able to determine the capacity of discernment in minors, insisted on the creation of special tribunals for such cases (Sodi 1917: 97–98). Years later, the participants in Mexico's first criminology and penology conference encouraged the creation of a child protection guardian, who would be responsible for getting laws enacted, monitoring the juvenile courts, and lobbying for policy on minors (*El Universal*, October 14–15, 1923).[16]

In contrast, adherents of the positivist school struggled for more radical change. They believed in the adoption of preventive measures to eliminate or control the factors leading to criminality. Following that idea, Emilio Rovirosa Andrade (1904) proposed "taking control of all individuals who, because of poverty, are threatened by crime, and relocating them in wild, unpopulated areas, where obtaining a basic subsistence will be easy." Positivist adherents also believed that sentences should be individualized, based on the threat posed by the criminal. Accordingly, they believed that the law code must be based on the criminal, not on the crime committed.

---

15 *Trabajos de revisión del Código Penal*, 1912–14, vols. 1, 3. The group comprised Manuel Olivera Toro, Victoriano Pimentel, Jesús M. Aguilar, Julio García, Juan Pérez de León, and, after 1911, Manuel Castelazo Fuentes, Carlos Trejo, Sebastián Lerdo de Tejada, and Emilio Monroy, and it had sporadic help from former justice ministers Demetrio Sodi and Manuel Calero.

16 The pioneering work of José Ángel Ceniceros and Luis Garrido (1926b) also reflects the concern for juvenile delinquency and its treatment.

For example, drawing on Enrique Ferri's categorization of "born criminals," "perpetrators of crimes of passion," and "random criminals," Miguel Macedo recommended conditional sentences or punishment for the latter two groups only if the offense were repeated (Macedo 1901, 1891). For his part, Octavio Medellín Ostos defended the need to "investigate the personal history, even the biological one," of defendants in order to guide the judges charged with the sentencing. He also maintained that judges should limit themselves to "affirming or denying the responsibility of the accused, who shall remain subject to technical specialists, doctors, and psychologists, who diagnose and dictate the treatment to be carried out in the reformatory" (*El Universal*, October 12, 1923). Similarly, Jesús Urueta argued for differentiated punishments in his assertion that "social surgery"— referring to deportation or capital punishment—must be applied to born criminals (Urueta 1898a, 1898b).[17]

In summary, legal theory vacillated between the ideas of the positivist school and those of the eclectic school. To the extent that judicial system authorities deviated from the traditional liberal perspective, they inclined toward the latter. Their position is known thanks to a 1904 survey by the Mexican Justice Ministry, undertaken in the framework of the revision of the criminal code, the results of which were published by the *Diario de Jurisprudencia*. Of the fifty-three people surveyed, only four (Emilio Rovirosa Andrade, Alberto Lombardo, Carlos Pereyra, and, to a lesser degree, Ismael Elizondo) believed that the law should be oriented according to the propositions of the positivist school.[18] The remainder (90 percent) proposed only minor reforms, not broad legislative reform. Among this latter group were the judges of the Tribunal Superior de Justicia (Superior Court) for the Federal District, criminal and correctional court judges, and other agents of the Office of the Public Prosecutor and public defenders.

The opinion of the other sectors of society is harder to reconstruct. I limit myself to only a few examples, all of them from the Porfiriato. The journals of the police profession as well as the official press—particularly *El Imparcial*—included organicist interpretations that harked back to the

---

[17] Teófilo Olea y Leyva defended the need to have an indeterminate sentence to combat criminal recidivism, as well as to establish reformatories for criminals who could be rehabilitated and penal colonies to which irredeemable criminals could be relegated (*El Universal*, October 16, 1923).

[18] The exceptions were relatively minor players in the hierarchy: Alberto Lombardo and Emilio Rovirosa Andrade were agents of the Office of the Public Prosecutor (Ministerio Público), and Pereyra was a public defender.

interpretations of the school of criminal anthropology. For its part, the Catholic journals (specifically those published by the Society of Jesus) and popular literature or broadsheets (specifically that of Antonio Vanegas Arroyo) show a clear yearning for the traditional conception of crime and punishment that existed during the Porfiriato. In synthesis, a panorama of interpretations existed in society, and they were not necessarily close to the liberal proposals or to the premises of the classical school of criminal law. Therefore, we again see the distance that existed between the ideas that were floating about in the community and the nature of criminal legislation itself (Speckman 2002a: 115–36, 173–250).

In short, during the Porfiriato many legal specialists or theoreticians disagreed with the underlying philosophy and spirit of Mexico's existing legal codes. However, the government did not promote radical legal reform because its own legitimacy lay in the liberal tradition. Moreover, even though they believed that the premises of liberal law were out of touch with social conditions in Mexico, functionaries of the court system (as well as adherents of the "third school") seemingly agreed with the laws as written, were generally opposed to radical reform, and at most recommended only minor changes.

Yet reform was also impeded because the defenders of the positivist school (and of the premises of criminal anthropology) did not themselves lead a movement for legal change. Like legal experts who supported the status quo, this group was close to President Porfirio Díaz, who presented himself as the heir of the liberal and nationalist struggle. They honored the heroes of that struggle (including Porfirio himself) and its symbols. As a result, the law was practically converted into a mythology that was untouchable by lawmakers and difficult for the regime's adherents to criticize. Hence, despite the distance between the legal status quo and the theoretical trends that predominated among the jurists, no group was inclined to spearhead a movement to promote legal reform during the Porfiriato.

THE CODE OF 1929

The Revolution became the watershed for a new direction in politics and the law. The jurists of the Porfiriato, now unbound from their commitment to Porfirio Díaz, could begin to actively promote legislative change. Yet, from the first call for proposals by the Justice Ministry in 1915, the process of reform would take over a decade. The executive branch did not receive authorization to reform the codes until 1926 (*Diario Oficial*, January 30,

1926, January 6, 1927, and January 14, 1928). In 1927 the drafting commission sent a preliminary proposal to the members of the Supreme Court, the Superior Court, the Attorney General's Office, the Bar Association, the Department of Health, and the Mexican Medical Association. The final version was completed in 1929, and on September 30 of that year President Emilio Portes Gil promulgated the criminal legislation that came into force on December 15, 1929.

Understanding the nature of the 1929 criminal code reform requires a careful review of the issues and limitations faced by its drafters. The drafting commission for the reform was convoked in 1925. In its final form, the commission consisted of Enrique Gudiño, Ignacio Ramírez Arriaga, and Manuel Ramos Estrada, and was presided over by José Almaraz. This commission took into consideration several proposals from a reform project developed by Miguel Macedo and his associates from 1903 to 1912. However, the Almaraz commission disagreed with these proposals for two reasons. First, the commission argued that the classical or liberal school, which was reflected in these proposals, "was totally bankrupt and could not continue to be the foundation for the entire edifice of criminal legislation." Second, the commission believed that the legal code required more than just minor reforms, because it did not fit the norms and conditions found in society. Basing its views on the ideas of the positivist school, the commission concluded, "The criminal reality, collected and organized into crime and sentencing statistics, will be the only thing to guide the direction of social defense" (Almaraz 1931: 12–13).

Still, the commission was limited in the extent to which it could promote radical change. The president of Mexico asked that the commission's reforms be limited to making "constitutional prescriptions"—that is, prescriptions that would respect the letter and spirit of the 1917 Constitution, which itself harked back to the liberal tenets of the 1857 Constitution. According to Almaraz, in light of that restriction, the members of the commission had to limit themselves to designing a "transitional code" and give up on the idea of a "perfect work based on modern trends" (1931: 24, 48–49). Thus some elements of the positivist school were introduced without fully eradicating the spirit of liberalism within the law.

One area where this created significant tension was with regard to the 1917 Constitution's stipulations about equality under the law, which made it impossible to apply the positivist principle of variable sentences. The commissioners were convinced that crime did not arise from free will but from "organic" and "social" determinism. That is, they believed that crime was the result of the criminal's "physical personality" (temperament) but also his "psychological personality" (character), both of which were determined by psycho-physiological inheritance and modified by the environment. Hence their positivist prescription would have been to individualize penalties based on the level of threat that a given criminal presented.[19] However, such case-by-case treatment contradicted the principle of equality contemplated by the Constitution. Hence the code would have to be followed based on decisions about the crime committed, without giving judges or authorities the power to vary the sentence or substantially change its duration in consideration of the criminal's individual characteristics.

Still, the commission worked to establish special stipulations about the aggravating or attenuating circumstances arising from the personality of the lawbreaker. For example, in order to let a judge consider the specific traits of the lawbreaker and the likelihood of rehabilitation, they gave the court the power to contemplate circumstances not included in the code and also to adjust the calculated weight of those factors that were already included. That opened the way for greater judicial discretion. Furthermore, convinced that a criminal's recidivism indicated anti-sociability, and thus the level of threat, the Almaraz commission increased the penalties for recidivists and introduced the concept of "habitual offenders," who were defined as those who show a "tendency to continue to commit crimes" (Almaraz 1931: 101, and 1941: 96–97; Criminal Code of 1929, Arts. 47–50, 55, 64–65, 175–176, 194).[20]

The commissioners also believed, as with regard to sentencing, that treatment of the convicted party should vary based on the personality of the criminal. The drafters insisted on individualized treatment for the convicted, and they opposed predetermination of the sentence or its length (Criminal Code of 1929, Arts. 105–113). Thus, in their view, specialized technicians should "separate criminals according to various criminal tendencies" and apply "scientific treatments that would transform, correct, cure, and reeducate them" (Almaraz 1931: 157; Criminal Code of 1929, Arts. 204–205). While the commission members believed in the possibility of rehabilitation and saw this as the ultimate goal of imprisonment, they also

---

[19] The Almaraz commission members discarded the principle of moral responsibility and were more concerned with the threat that criminals represented to society (Almaraz 1931: 18–19, 46).

[20] The custody and treatment of sentenced prisoners was assigned to the Supreme Council for Social Defense and Prevention, within the executive branch.

believed that the correctional system failed in achieving that objective. More precisely, they asserted that Mexican prisons had become nothing more than "free universities for the study of crime" and were transforming occasional and less dangerous criminals into "true professionals" (Almaraz 1931: 138).

To establish clear guidelines for improving sentencing and rehabilitation, the commission proposed a division into three groups: minors; "the mentally weak, deviant, or ill"; and adults. In contrast to the Code of 1871, adulthood was defined as beginning at sixteen years of age. On the other hand, following the wishes of the adherents of the "third school," the commission broadened the spectrum of sanctions applied to minors to include, for example, supervised release and probationary school (Criminal Code of 1929, Arts. 71, 121–124, 181–188). Moreover, there were stipulations for the mentally ill and habitual alcoholics and drug addicts, who had been exempt from responsibility in the 1871 code (Criminal Code of 1871, Arts. 34, 165). Having substituted the concept of responsibility for that of threat or peril, the drafters of the Criminal Code of 1929 included provisions for internment in hospitals, agrarian colonies, and mental institutions (Criminal Code of 1929, Arts. 72, 125–128, 189–192). Finally, as had been proposed by the Macedo commission, the Almaraz commission adopted a conditional sentence for adults. Based on Enrico Ferri's classification, and as Macedo himself had envisioned years before, the drafters wanted to give the "occasional criminal, by means of irreproachable conduct, the possibility of avoiding having to serve the decreed sentence" (Almaraz 1931: 53, 178; Criminal Code of 1929, Arts. 241–248).

Still, with some significant reservations, the Almaraz commission also contemplated the possibility that certain individuals represented too great a menace to society, or were so unalterably criminal in their orientation, that they could not be reformed. As noted above, the ideas of the positivist school asserted that the most dangerous and incorrigible criminals must be removed from society, through either capital punishment or exile to penal colonies. The commission considered that relegation to a penal colony should not apply in sentences for minor crimes; instead, it should be used only for "born criminals and the irredeemable" or those who had committed the most serious crimes (Almaraz 1931: 121; Criminal Code of 1929, Arts. 114–119). The possibility of the death penalty was even more controversial. In the end, after heated arguments on the topic and with Almaraz dissenting, the commission chose to eliminate capital punishment, a decision that Mexican President Emilio Portes Gil validated, reasoning that:

All the criminalists who support the terrible sentence have argued for its necessity based on the same underlying characteristic of "setting an example." Well now, many have been killed in our country to repress the commission of new crimes, and the results have been counterproductive. It even seems as if, in each case where the death penalty has been applied, there arise new incentives that stimulate the commission of the same crimes that made it indispensable to apply the example in the first place. It even seems as if the example of the executed person serves to exalt that convict in the eyes of the rest, awakening in others the morbid desire to end up in the same situation (cited in Ceniceros 1943: 362).

Overall, the 1929 code attempted to express the prevailing opinion of the moment, which had its roots in the thought of the 1880s. Thus the Almaraz commission proposed a body of law based on the ideas of the positivist school. The code incorporated some of the most significant propositions of the school, such as taking into consideration the criminal's personality and level of risk, granting judges greater freedom to decide the appropriate sentence and its length, and giving the Supreme Council for Social Defense and Prevention the ability to carry it out. It also included specific requirements, such as special treatment for minors and conditional sentences.

However, the positivist ideas promoted by the Almaraz commission had numerous detractors. The criticisms fell into three camps. First, some believed that the positivist school was passé.[21] That was the case for Alfonso Teja Zabre, who was surprised that the members of the drafting commission declared that their adherence to positivism made them modern. He maintained that the positivism doctrine had disappeared in Mexico after 1907 or 1908, and he accused the drafters of lacking familiarity with

---

[21] Despite this opinion, we find some authors whose ideas were still close to the positivist school. See, for example, Julio Guerrero's comments on the draft of the Criminal Code, in which he rejects free will and maintains that criminals act in response to determining factors, which could be either organic or shaped by the environment (Guerrero 1929: 19–25). Another example is the writing of Teófilo Olea y Leyva, representing the Barra de Abogados. In those comments, he applauded the influence on the commission of the proposal by Enrico Ferri (whom he considered the greatest specialist in criminal law in the world), and he praised some of his solutions, all belonging to the positivist school (Olea y Leyva 1929: 7).

newer theories, such as historical materialism, which understood law to be
the result of economic conditions and justice to be a class justice. He concluded, "The code of 1929 is extraneous to the trend toward socialization
and populism. It has the very shape of a bourgeois legal code, which is
accommodating toward the crimes of the privileged classes [and] deserving of being called a 'law against the poor,' as were earlier codes" (Teja
Zabre 1930: 54–55). Mario de la Cueva also believed that the times called
for an acceptance of the premises of historical materialism (de la Cueva
1930: 50–51).

Second, some believed that, despite the intentions of its drafters, the
1929 code was insufficient to meet the postulates of positivism. For example, José Ángel Ceniceros, Luis Garrido, and Francisco González de la Vega
maintained that it was not a "criminal code." In this view, such a code
should have established a relationship between the sentence and the personality of the criminal, and would have provided for indeterminate sentences. Instead, it continued to be a "crime code," based on predetermined
sentences that were proportional to the crime committed (Ceniceros 1929:
13, 1940a: 203; Garrido 1940: 240; González 1940: 254–55). Manuel Rivera
Silva presented the problem in light of these points:

> The 1929 legislation proudly wore the brand-spanking-new
> shirt of positivism. But for all its newness, it could not hide
> the rotten flesh of the classical school that lay underneath.
> The lawmakers of this era believed that having disguised the
> cadaver in trendy attire, the celebration for the new legisla-
> tion could go on. In their crazy enthusiasm, they failed to
> perceive, first, that the shirt of positivism had already turned
> the color of a shroud, and second, as noted, that it was too
> thin for the members of the classical school to hide under-
> neath it (Rivera Silva 1938: 567).

Finally, some of the 1929 code's detractors, including Carrancá y
Trujillo, Garrido, and González de la Vega, believed that intermingling the
ideas of positivism with the classical liberal codes had generated a contradictory, illogical, and inapplicable system. They argued that the blended
code "suffered from grave deficiencies of wording and structure, of constant cross-references, of duplication of concepts, and even flagrant contradictions, all which made its practical application difficult" (Carrancá y
Trujillo 1950: 77, 1940: 301). Garrido's criticism was that the 1929 code
"contained technical errors, lacked doctrinal unity, and exhibited lacunae

and contradictions" (Garrido 1952: 29). González de la Vega likewise charged that its application would be difficult because it was full of "omissions, contradictions, juxtaposition, overtaxed with theoretical definitions" (González de la Vega 1935: 20, 1940: 254).

Meanwhile, praise for the 1929 code was scant and centered on the influence that its drafters had on the modernization of the laws, which a new commission would complete. For example, González de la Vega admitted that the drafters had managed to "bundle together scientific concerns that until then had been dispersed, awakening in Mexican jurists the clear desire for an integral reform of the judicial-penal institutions, which, under the law of inertia, has resisted being displaced" (González de la Vega 1935: 21). Carrancá y Trujillo acknowledged the merit of the Almaraz commission: "By abolishing the venerable text of Martínez de Castro and opening the legal channels to the currents of criminal law in Mexico, it laid the plans for an integrated Mexican criminal reform" (Carrancá y Trujillo 1950: 79, 1940: 304). Giulio Belloni concluded that, "It is necessary to recognize José Almaraz and the jurists around him ... and give them credit for introducing a general orientation toward modern legislation through these laws, and afterward, for having seen the need to strongly oppose, even in the face of public opinion, the old metaphysical criticisms that arose against that orientation" (Belloni 1934: 27).

In the end, however, criticism predominated. Ceniceros maintained,

> The environment for the legislation is unfavorable and even hostile, both among the judiciary charged with applying it and among the litigants and professional associations. The authors of the laws have not been able to defend themselves seriously from technical criticisms. Instead, their tepid, inaccurate responses have consisted of generalizations, which have not been sufficient to satisfy public opinion (Ceniceros 1931: 79).

According to Garrido, various sectors of society were in opposition: "The press, the specialists, and even members of Congress carried out a campaign to discredit the decree" (Garrido 1952: 29). The daily newspapers reported on protests by some groups. There were the judges who demonstrated in front of a government building (*Excélsior*, December 16, 1929). Even taxi drivers, protesting sanctions against drivers who hit pedestrians, assembled on Paseo de la Reforma in protest and then paraded downtown, snarling traffic everywhere (*Excélsior*, April 18, 1929). Thus, added to the criticisms of the law specialists and theoreticians was the opposition of other groups, such as judges and lawmakers, as well as segments of civil society that would be affected by the new laws. All demanded that the law be repealed, leading to the creation of a new drafting commission only a few months after the promulgation of the 1929 code.

THE CODE OF 1931

Some critics of the 1929 criminal code sat on the commission for the drafting of a new code.[22] After almost two years of work, the commission finalized a version that was enacted in August 1931 and came into force one month later. In contrast to their predecessors, the new commission's members chose an eclectic and pragmatic approach because they believed that "the remedy for the failure of the classical school cannot be found in the positivist school." Furthermore, they admitted that "no school, nor doctrine, nor criminal system of any type can serve entirely as the basis for the criminal code." Still, faced with the need to acknowledge some affiliation, the commission declared its adherence to the "third school" (Criminal Code of 1931, "Exposición de motivos"). In the words of Ceniceros, "based on current criminal science, [the commission tried to move past] the abstract principles of the classical school," and it accepted some positivist hypotheses, such as "social responsibility and overcoming the troubling concept of punishment" (Ceniceros 1940a: 204, 210, and 1940b: 256, 257). However, they also took into consideration the contributions of current trends, such as historical materialism and the "new concepts of biology and the revision of social and spiritual values after World War I." Finally, the 1931 commission heeded Mexican "constitutional forms" and "traditions of jurisprudence," and paid attention to "social and economic conditions" and the patterns of criminality and crimes (Criminal Code of 1931, "Exposición de motivos"; Teja Zabre 1940: 340–41).

Although the drafters did not talk of determinism and viewed the criminal as "a human being who is absolutely equal to someone who has not committed a crime," they believed that actions are conditioned by biological, psychological, and social factors that are beyond the control of

---

[22] The group, comprising José Ángel Ceniceros, Luis Garrido, Ernesto G. Garza, José López Lira, and Alfonso Teja Zabre, wrote a draft disseminated in 1930 and 1931. At that same time, the executive was empowered to issue a new code (Decreto que faculta al Ejecutivo Federal para expedir los códigos penal y de procedimientos penales, January 31, 1930).

human will (Ceniceros 1940b: 256, 257, and 1940a: 204). Thus, leaving out the concept of will, they defined crime as "the act or omission that criminal laws punish" (Criminal Code of 1931, Art. 7). They also rejected the theory of moral responsibility, and instead they found their inspiration in the theory of social defense, but without taking it to its final conclusions (Ceniceros and Garrido 1934: 38; Ceniceros 1940a: 204). On the other hand was the belief that modern justice must:

> demand that the judge have the broadest powers to make decisions and apply penalties, based on objective and subjective traits of each case that is tried, so that, to the degree possible, the punishment be made appropriate to the criminal in question. In other words, the penalty must be individualized, according to the nature of the man against whom it would be applied, and this would be impossible without judicial decision-making powers. The law can afford the judge a foundation for individualization, but it cannot carry out the individualization itself because the judge alone can know the criminal, whose peculiarities vary from subject to subject (Ceniceros 1931: 91).

They did not believe in absolute judicial decision-making power—which they thought would require judges and magistrates who were amply trained in psychology and who were not appointed for political reasons or because of cronyism—but rather in a rational broadening of power that would remedy "the excessive, blind, brutal, and absurd rigidity of criminal metrics" (Ceniceros 1931: 98). To accomplish that, they broadened the spread between the minimum and maximum sentences stipulated for each crime. They eliminated the system of attenuating and aggravating circumstances found in the two previous codes and the system for numeric computation found in the 1871 code. Thus the judge could choose a sentence from within the span between the minimum and maximum penalties without having to consider preestablished factors or values. Instead, the judge could take into consideration the "nature of the action or the omission, the means employed for its execution, and the extent of the damage done and the risks run" as well as the traits of the criminal (Criminal Code of 1931, "Exposición de motivos," Arts. 51, 52; Ceniceros 1931: 91–99; Ceniceros and Garrido 1926a: 151; Ceniceros 1940b: 257–58, and 1943: 278–79).

Finally, with educational and rehabilitation goals in mind, the drafters held for a sentence that would allow for the correction of the criminal.

They opposed individualization, but they stipulated different sentences. For criminals who committed misdemeanors, the code contemplated conditional sentences or fines, whereas the habitual criminal was to be relegated to penal colonies (but not to the ones where the most dangerous criminals were sent, as the Code of 1929 had stipulated). For those who had committed the most serious crimes, they stipulated a sentence of up to thirty years in prison (since "the commission, having declared itself abolitionist in regard to the death penalty, found that it had to search for an effectively intimidating punishment"). They also opted for fixed prison terms, but they defended the need to separate criminals based on "an evaluation of their criminal condition" (Criminal Code of 1931, Arts. 25, 27, 78; Ceniceros and Garrido 1926a: 99–101; Ceniceros 1943: 362). They also made progress toward judicial individualization in the case of minors (which, like the Code of 1871, included anyone who was not eighteen years of age or older) and the mentally ill. As had the drafters of the Code of 1929, they left them "outside of the repressive penal function" and "subject to a policy of guardianship and education," without fixing a length for the term of correction or treatment (Criminal Code of 1931, "Exposición de motivos"; Art. 68; Ceniceros and Garrido 1926a: 152; Ceniceros 1940a: 207).

The most systematic critique of the new code came from Almaraz, who, curiously, touched on points similar to those that had been criticized in the Code of 1929. He believed that, given the eclecticism adopted by the commission, the corpus revealed "a lack of harmony and logical consistency," and he judged it to be "a hybrid legislation, which was in no way modern." He maintained that underlying the punishability of the committed crimes, attention continued to be paid to "legal rather than to real entities, to concepts and not to people." He argued that it ought to be based on the physical, psychological, moral, and social study of the criminal, since it would be possible to determine the appropriate treatment and its due execution only based on the results of that investigation. He criticized the survival of the qualitative predetermination of the sentence, as well as the restrictions placed on the judge in choosing a penalty and an appropriate length based on the personality of the lawbreaker. Moreover, he concluded that the drafters had erred in their intent to broaden the powers of judicial decision making, and that the premise that "there are no criminals, only human beings" was a farce (Almaraz 1941).

However, in the months following the promulgation of the code, the critics gradually fell silent. It is possible that, at last, the law reflected fundamental ideas that were generally accepted by the legal specialists of the day. Or, at minimum, the pragmatic and theoretically eclectic approach of the 1931 commission left something for all sides to appreciate. Also, it is quite possible that the 1929 code laid the groundwork for accomplishing major changes in the criminal justice system by promoting ample dialogue, debate, and public scrutiny. In any event, the 1931 code accomplished a substantial reform of the Mexican criminal justice system that would last into the twenty-first century. Contemporary efforts to reform this system will likely draw important lessons from its creation and evolution across the three periods covered herein.

CONCLUSION

The Criminal Code of 1871 responded to the premises of the school of legal theory and, in general, to the political model espoused by the segment of the Mexican elite that adhered to nineteenth-century liberalism. Victory over "conservatives" and the imperialists in the latter half of the nineteenth century had enabled the liberals to rise to power and to impose their legal vision and ideals regarding criminality, the administration of justice, and corrections. However, the classical liberal view was not an overwhelming consensus. Many jurists sympathized with the ideas of the positivist school, both in its Italian tendency (criminal anthropology and, to some degree, the "third school") and in its French variant (criminal sociology). Nonetheless, until the Revolution, no one—not the theoreticians and specialists, nor the judges, nor civil society—demanded substantial reform of the criminal laws. Moreover, even though many public officials often deviated from the law in actual practice, they also did not want to modify it radically because of their dedication to liberal philosophies and institutions.

The situation shifted after the end of the Revolution, which brought with it the promise of change. In the process of consolidating a new regime, reformers drafted new laws that adopted many of the principles that legal theorists had idealized but failed to promote during the Porfiriato: the ideas of the positivist school and the application of specific reforms (such as the adoption of conditional sentences and special institutions for juvenile delinquents). Still, at the same time, the drafters of the 1929 code were forced to align their work with the 1917 Constitution, which itself integrated much of the spirit and principles of the liberal school: equality before the law, free will, predetermined sentences, and a belief in the capacity for correction.

However, the 1929 code faced multiple criticisms and cannot be judged to be anything other than a failure. Critics objected to its overwrought and forced concessions to the principles of the liberal school, which resulted in technical errors; to its proclaimed closeness to the positivist school, which some now saw as outdated; and to its failure to address social issues or offer effective social reforms. For those reasons, it was repudiated by a variety of social actors, who vociferously demanded legal reform: a new generation of jurists who were replacing the theoreticians of the Porfiriato, judges, some lawmakers, and, in a novel development, certain sectors of civil society. Subsequent reforms in 1931 adopted many of the same propositions as the Code of 1929, but did so in a more pragmatic fashion; moreover, they did so in a language that was appropriate to postrevolutionary Mexico.

Yet, ultimately, both of these codes attempted to introduce some aspects of the positivist school without eradicating the essence of the classical or liberal school from Mexican criminal law. Hence, in the periods analyzed, we find two contrasting tendencies. On the one hand, the classical liberal criminal code remained in force for almost sixty years, despite the fact that many jurists disagreed with its premises and implementation. Moreover, the foundations of that legal system endured throughout the process of reform and consolidation that accompanied the Mexican Revolution. On the other hand, the 1929 code was in force for only a few months because, despite drawing together the strands of many ideas that were floating about, it provoked broad opposition. The 1931 reforms therefore necessarily adopted a more pragmatic approach to reform and achieved a broader consensus.

In the end, these examples give us important insights into the conditions and process under which criminal justice reform takes place. First, the proximity or distance of laws with respect to the "Mexican reality" or to the opinion of legal experts does by itself determine the possibility for reform and may have a variety of other effects. More specifically, distance between the law and reality may lead judges and public officials to deviate from the legal principles in actual practice (as occurred between 1871 and 1910). Hence, even long-standing opposition by legal theoreticians will not necessarily spark corresponding changes in the juridical landscape, even in the context of a sudden change in the political regime. In short, it is less the perceived legitimacy and effectiveness of established law than the level of political will and the degree of mobilization of leading public officials, legal theorists, and even elements of society in support of alternatives that determine the prospects for criminal justice reform.

Second, and related, is the fact that, even when so inclined and mobilized, proponents of reform may be significantly divided on the direction of change. This lack of consensus may result in a patchwork process of legal reform that ultimately integrates new and competing alternatives into the existing fabric of the law. Without a highly mobilized movement for legal reform that is based on a widespread consensus, efforts to promote a far-reaching transformation of the legal system are unlikely to result in the wholesale substitution of one legal system for another. Thus, to the extent that would-be reformers are able to advance bold proposals espousing new and distinct theoretical principles, they may be forced to settle for a piecemeal and pragmatic introduction of their vision to the existing framework. Moreover, once significant reforms have been enacted and accepted as legitimate, further evolution of the legal system is likely to be much slower and more measured than the pace at which social conditions and new theoretical perspectives develop.

References

Almaraz, José. 1931. *Exposición de motivos del código penal promulgado en diciembre de 1929*. Mexico City.

———. 1941. *Algunos errores y absurdos de la legislación penal de 1931*. Mexico City.

Belloni, Giulio A. 1934. "La ley penal mexicana de 1931," *Criminalia* 2, no. 2: 23–29.

Buffington, Robert. 2001. *Criminales y ciudadanos en el México moderno*. Mexico City: Siglo Veintiuno.

Carrancá y Trujillo, Raúl. 1940. "La legislación penal mexicana." In *Homenaje a Eugenio Florián*. Mexico City: León Sánchez.

———. 1950. *Derecho penal mexicano*. 3d ed. Mexico City: Antigua Librería Robredo.

Ceniceros, José A. 1929. "El nuevo código penal," *El Foro* 10, no. 4: 12–15.

———. 1931. *El código penal de 1929 y datos preliminares del nuevo código penal de 1931*. Mexico City: Ediciones Botas.

———. 1940a. "La escuela positiva y su influencia en la legislación penal mexicana," *Criminalia* 4, no. 4: 200–13.

———. 1940b. "El código penal mexicano." In *Homenaje a Eugenio Florián*. Mexico City: León Sánchez.

———. 1943. "Derecho penal." In *Evolución del derecho mexicano (1912–1942)*. Mexico City: Jus.

Ceniceros, José A., and Luis Garrido. 1926a. *La ley penal mexicana*. Mexico City: Ediciones Botas.

———. 1926b. *La delincuencia infantil en México*. Mexico City: Ediciones Botas.

———. 1934. *La ley penal mexicana*. Mexico City: Ediciones Botas.

de la Cueva, Mario. 1930. "Razón e historia en la elaboración del derecho," *Revista de Ciencias Sociales* 1, no. 2: 37–51.

del Arenal, Jaime. 1999. "El discurso en torno a la ley: el agotamiento de lo privado como fuente del derecho en el México del siglo XIX." In *Construcción de la legitimidad política en México*, ed. Brian Connaughton, Carlos Illades, and Sonia Pérez Toledo. Mexico City: El Colegio de Michoacán/Universidad Autónoma Metropolitana/Universidad Nacional Autónoma de México/El Colegio de México.

Garrido Luis. 1940. "La doctrina mexicana de nuestro derecho penal," *Criminalia* 7, no. 4: 240–47.

———. 1952. *Ensayos penales*. Mexico City: Ediciones Botas.

González de la Vega, Francisco. 1935. *La reforma de las leyes penales en México*. Mexico City: Secretaría de Relaciones Exteriores.

———. 1940. *Derecho penal mexicano*. Mexico City.

Grossi, Paolo. 1991. "Absolutismo jurídico y derecho privado en el siglo XIX." Bellaterra, Spain: Universidad Autónoma de Barcelona.

Guerrero, Julio. 1929. *Un código estrafalario*. Mexico City: Imprenta Azteca.

Hale, Charles. 1991. *La transformación del liberalismo en México a fines del siglo XIX*. Mexico City: Vuelta.

Lombardo, Alberto. 1877. "La pena de muerte," *El Foro*, Año II, 5 (59): 232.

Macedo, Miguel. 1888. *Discurso pronunciado en la Escuela Nacional de Jurisprudencia*. Mexico City: Imprenta de Antonio Vanegas Arroyo.

———. 1891. "Las condenas o penas condicionales," *Anuario de Legislación y Jurisprudencia* 8: 394–410.

———. 1901. "La condena condicional: innovaciones y reformas necesarias para establecerla en México," *La Ciencia Jurídica* 5: 297–326.

———. 1926. "Ideas sobre la reforma de los códigos," *El Foro* 8: 1–2.

Marino, Daniela. n.d. "El juzgado conciliador en la transición jurídica: Huixquilucan (Estado de México), siglo XIX." In *De normas, prácticas y sanciones: ensayos de historia social (Argentina, Brasil y México, 1850–1950)*, ed. Claudia Agostoni and Elisa Speckman. Mexico City: Instituto de Investigaciones Históricas, Universidad Nacional Autónoma de México. In press.

Olea y Leyva, Teófilo. 1929. "Proyecto de código penal para los Estados Unidos Mexicanos. Memorando de observaciones formado, en su vista, por la comisión de reformas legislativas de La Barra Mexicana," *El Foro* 10, no. 3: 7–15.

Piccato, Pablo. 1997. "El discurso sobre la criminalidad y el alcoholismo hacia el fin del porfiriato." In *Hábitos, normas y escándalo: prensa, criminalidad y drogas en el porfiriato tardío*, ed. Ricardo Pérez. Mexico City: CIESAS/Plaza y Valdés.

Rivera Silva, Manuel. 1938. "El positivismo y el código de 1929," *Criminalia* 4, no. 9: 567–69.

Rovirosa Andrade, Emilio. 1904. "Proyectos de reformas al código penal," *Diario de Jurisprudencia* II, 16–36: 199.

Sodi, Demetrio. 1917. *Nuestra ley penal; estudios prácticos y comentarios sobre el código del D.F. del 1ero de abril de 1872.* 2d ed. Mexico City: Librería de la Viuda de Ch. Bouret.

Speckman, Elisa. 2002a. *Crimen y castigo: legislación penal, interpretaciones de la criminalidad y administración de justicia (Ciudad de México, 1872–1910).* Mexico City: El Colegio de México/Instituto de Investigaciones Históricas, Universidad Nacional Autónoma de México.

———. 2002b. *La Barra Mexicana Colegio de Abogados.* Mexico City: Barra Mexicana de Abogados.

Teja Zabre, Alfonso. 1930. "Las nuevas orientaciones del derecho penal," *Revista de Ciencias Sociales* 1, no. 3: 50–55.

———. 1940. "Doctrina de la legislación penal mexicana." In *Homenaje a Eugenio Florián.* Mexico City: León Sánchez.

Urueta, Jesús. 1898a. "Delito y delincuentes," *Revista de Legislación y Jurisprudencia* 15 (July–December): 271–74.

———. 1898b. "Cirugía social," *Revista de Legislación y Jurisprudencia* 15 (July–December): 279–81.

Zavala, Silvio. 1930. "Nuestros legisladores y nuestras leyes," *Revista de Ciencias Sociales* 3, no. 1: 113–19.

CHAPTER 11

The Role of Lawyers in the Mexican Justice System

HÉCTOR FIX-FIERRO

In discussions about the administration of justice and judicial reform in Mexico, most analyses have centered on institutional aspects, such as corruption, organizational constraints, judges' training and professional abilities, and the like. Few studies, if any, highlight the (positive or negative) role of lawyers in the day-to-day operation of the justice system (an exception is Gudiño Pelayo 2003). This is all the more remarkable if we consider, for example, that no judge could decide a dispute without input provided by the parties, duly represented by their lawyers. Bench and bar depend on each other; sometimes they cooperate closely; sometimes they are at odds with each other. Their relationship could be described as a "friendly rivalry." Indeed, a very general observation tells us that the court's operation is dependent on the behavior and practices of other actors and organizations, lawyers and the bar prominent among them.

Mexican judges complain that attorneys sometimes constitute a significant obstacle to the efficient operation of the courts. For example, about a fourth of the state trial and appeals judges interviewed by Hugo Alejandro Concha Cantú and José Antonio Caballero Juárez mentioned "external factors" as the main obstacle to their activities, indicating that lawyers were among those external factors. They referred to the attorneys' lack of professional knowledge and questionable practices, such as using the press to apply pressure on the courts. About 40 percent of the civil judges and 55 percent of the criminal judges interviewed considered that attorney performance was "poor"; 18 percent found it to be outright "bad." When asked about the role of bar associations in their home state, 22 percent of chief judges said it was "unexceptional," and another 22 percent considered it "nonexistent." Several observed that the objectives of state bar associations were largely political, "flourishing" around election time. Finally, when asked about the training lawyers receive in law school, a sizable number of judges said they consider it to be "poor" (40 percent of appeals judges and 49 percent of trial judges) or "bad" (18 percent of appeals judges and 19 percent of trial judges) (Concha Cantú and Caballero Juárez 2001: 188, 215 ff.).

It may be that such opinions are biased. Even so, they are suggestive of the problems associated with lawyers' performance in the judicial process in Mexico. Unfortunately, there are no systematic studies on the quality of legal training and lawyers' performance in Mexico that would allow for a critical examination of the related problems. Nevertheless, existing data on the accelerated growth of law school enrollments in recent decades and the explosion of new, small, private law schools give cause to suspect a general decrease in the quality of legal studies, a suspicion that is confirmed by observers of the legal system (López Ayllón and Fix-Fierro 2003). In short, we can safely assert that the training and performance levels of a majority of lawyers (excluding a small, elite group) tend to be rather poor.

Why have legal education and the legal profession been left out of the sweeping changes introduced in the Mexican legal and judicial systems over the past two decades? Why are reforms in these two areas absent from the public agenda? One possible answer lies in the autonomy accorded to public and private law schools. Both must satisfy certain requirements in order to receive government recognition and the right to award law degrees, but those requirements are not very demanding. Further, law schools enjoy substantial autonomy in determining the type and quality of education they provide. The legal profession (or at least the corps of practicing attorneys) is not highly regulated by the government or by professional associations. Moreover, lawyers seem able to deflect attention from their professional performance. Where a case is lost and the "criminal" set free, or when an "innocent" is sent to prison, the public usually blames the judge, not the attorney. Finally, the fragmentary and unsystematic character of many reforms has effectively placed legal education and the legal profession well beyond the reforms' immediate objectives.

This chapter aims to highlight the role of lawyers in the justice system by providing a basic framework for analyzing their behavior and practices as these relate to the administration of justice in Mexico, especially in criminal cases. The chapter is divided into four sections. The first two provide a general overview of Mexican legal education and the legal profession, outlining the circumstances and conditions that surround the practice of law in Mexico. The third section examines two key areas in which lawyers' behavior may affect the administration of justice. And the last section offers a brief discussion of ideas for further research and reform.

LEGAL EDUCATION: AN OVERVIEW

Law Students and Law Schools: The Invisible Explosion

Higher education has expanded at an accelerated pace in Mexico in recent decades. In 1970, the total number of university students was 210,111 (about 0.45 percent of the population); this number had increased to 1,771,969 (or about 1.7 percent of the population) by 2002 (ANUIES 2002a). Enrollment in law schools has also risen, especially in the 1990s. Table 11.1 shows the number of law students, graduates, degrees, and programs between 1979 and 2002. During this period, the number of law students increased by 239 percent. Relative to the population, the increase was 119 percent. In 1997 law was the second-most-popular field in higher education; by 1999 it had climbed to first place, well above accounting and business administration.

In terms of law school enrollments, the number of law students as a percentage of total enrollment in higher education increased from 8.3 percent in 1979 to almost 12 percent in 2000. This is somewhat surprising; one might expect that the proliferation of new university programs would produce a relative reduction in the number of students choosing law and other "traditional" disciplines. If such a shift is occurring, it is taking place at a very slow pace. In 1997, accounting, law, business administration, and medicine accounted for 38.4 percent of total enrollment in higher education; in 2002, their share had dropped only slightly—to 33.9 percent— despite a considerable growth in new career options, such as computers and industrial engineering (ANUIES 1997, 2000, 2002a).

The gender composition among law students has also changed significantly. In 1979 women composed less than a third (28.2 percent) of law students; by 2002 they composed almost half, and in some schools (notably the law school at Mexico's National Autonomous University, or UNAM, in Mexico City) the percentage of women is even higher.[1] This even gender balance contrasts sharply with disciplines that are still regarded as predominantly "male" (engineering) or "female" (psychology). In law school at least, women seem to have attained equality.

---

[1] In 2001, women accounted for 59 percent of enrollment in the UNAM law school (ANUIES 2001).

Table 11.1. Law Students, Graduates, Degrees, and Programs, 1979–2002

	Number of Law Students				Graduates (previous year)		Degrees (previous year)		Programs
	Total	/100 K	% Women	% Enrollment	Total	% Women	Total	% Women	
1979	57,973	89	28.2	8.3	6,011	n.a.	n.a.	n.a.	87
1991	111,025	132	41.0	10.0	12,781	n.a.	6,077	n.a.	118
1997	155,332	162	46.7	11.9	20,983	45.7	10,960	42.0	309
2002	196,531	195	49.0	11.1	30,099	48.9	17,124	48.4	526[a]

Sources: ANUIES 1979, 1991, 1997, 2002a.

[a] This figure refers to the number of programs reported on the ANUIES Web site (www.anuies.mx) as of January 2004.

Notes: "Programs" refers to the number of facilities (*planteles*) that have independent student enrollment. One school or university may have more than one facility or program in one or more states or the Federal District. n.a. = not available.

Table 11.2. Law Students and Programs, 1991 and 2001

		Law Students				Law Programs		
		Private Law Schools		Public Law Schools			Private	Public
	Total	Total	Women	Total	Women	Total	Programs	Programs
1991	110,944	17,282 (15.58%)	6,875 (39.78%)	93,662 (84.42%)	38,528 (41.13%)	118	72 (61.02%)	46 (38.98%)
2001	189,864	85,911 (45.25%)	40,213 (46.80%)	104,481 (54.75%)	51,943 (49.71%)	506	431 (85.18%)	75 (14.82%)

Sources: ANUIES 1991, 2001.

Table 11.1 also shows that the number of law school graduates (students completing all coursework) increased fivefold from 1979 to 2002, and the number of students who obtained their law degree more than quadrupled between 1991 and 2002.[2]

Roughly a fourth and a fifth of law school students should graduate and obtain their degree each year. For example, 34,470 students began law school in 1997. Five years later (2001), the number of graduates was 87 percent of that figure; however, this percentage includes students who entered law school before 1997, so the number of students of the 1997 class who completed their program of studies on schedule is actually much lower (and it was even lower in previous years). A rigorous study of the performance of three classes of law students at UNAM after 1980 found that the number of students finishing law school after ten semesters (the normal length of studies) did not even reach 30 percent (Blanco and Rangel 1996). Although this fraction increased over succeeding years, it did so at a very slow pace. And despite the growing share of graduates, the number of degrees granted changed little between students who had begun law school fifteen semesters previously and those who had begun twenty semesters before, strongly suggesting that students who do not obtain their degree within a certain period are unlikely to do so later. About 20 percent of students in entering classes left law school before five years had elapsed; after ten years, between 9 and 13 percent were still enrolled.[3]

Of course, law students who do not meet all requirements for their degree and law license are not necessarily prevented from practicing law.[4]

---

[2] Not all graduates obtain the degree (*título profesional*) and official certificate (*cédula profesional*) that legally entitle them to practice law. Two disincentives for finishing law school are (1) that a significant number of students start working before or shortly after enrolling in law school, and (2) the requirement that they must write a dissertation to obtain their degree. Many law schools now offer a comprehensive exam in lieu of the dissertation, an option that many students prefer.

[3] According to a more recent assessment, an average of 1,433 first-year students enrolled in law school at the UNAM each year from 1997 to 2000. However, the number of students (from various generations) who completed the program dropped from 1,555 in 1997 to 1,084 in 2001. The decrease in the number of graduates coincides with the exit year of the first class to have followed the program of studies implemented in 1993 (Facultad de Derecho 2002: 16–18).

[4] Several state laws allow *pasantes* (students who have obtained at least 80 percent of their law school credits) to practice their profession for a limited period (up to three years).

In Mexico, lawyers do not hold a monopoly on the provision of legal advice, as they do in other countries; and a law degree is not necessary for representing clients in court in criminal, employment, and agrarian cases. Constitutional Article 20, section IX, provides, for example, that defendants in criminal proceedings have the right to an adequate defense—which they can present themselves or through a lawyer or someone they trust. If they do not choose, the judge will appoint a public defender. Unfortunately, the majority of public defenders are poorly trained (most are law students or recent law school graduates). Their pay is low, and they are very overburdened, which virtually compels them to deal perfunctorily with their cases (Lawyers Committee for Human Rights 2001: 45–47). Nevertheless, as a rule—at least in the Federal District—only a legal professional whose degree is duly registered with the proper authorities can represent clients in judicial and administrative proceedings.

Table 11.1 reveals the impressive growth in the number of law schools and programs, especially during the 1990s. Most of the new programs pertain to small, private law schools. Until the 1980s, the great majority of law students studied law at public universities; the largest programs were at the UNAM and the University of Puebla, with 10,000 and 12,000 students, respectively, in 1991. At that time, only a small proportion of law students attended private schools (either independent law schools or law schools within private universities). Most of the prestigious or best-known private law schools were established no earlier than the 1960s. Table 11.2 shows the increase in the number of private law school programs between 1991 and 2001.

Table 11.2 also documents the spectacular growth in enrollments in private law schools, which rose from fewer than 18,000 in 1991 to almost 86,000 in 2001, nearly a fivefold increase. The proportion of law students in private law schools, which was 16 percent in 1991, reached above 45 percent in 2001, while public law school enrollments rose by only about 10 percent. Meanwhile, the number of law programs (both public and private) increased from 118 in 1991 to 506 in 2001.

Most of the new law programs are at small private schools, with relatively small student enrollments. Between 63 and 70 percent of them have fewer than 250 students (see table 11.3). In 2001, for example, about 20 percent of private law facilities had fewer than 50 students, and 40 percent had fewer than 100. By contrast, public law schools are relatively large. In 1991, about half of all public law schools had between 1,000 and 2,500 students. Ten years later, public universities had added twenty-nine new law programs (though no new universities had been built), which indicates a decentralization of law programs within existing public institutions. Thus, by 2001 more than 40 percent of law programs had fewer than 500 students, and only a third had enrollments of between 1,000 and 2,500 students.

Two issues are of particular importance as we consider the rising number of law students and law schools, especially private institutions. The first is whether this increase signals the growing relevance of law and lawyers in Mexican society, or whether it indicates that legal education can be good business. That is, is this growth driven by supply or by demand?

In general terms, there is still a large unsatisfied demand for higher education in Mexico. Public universities have generally capped enrollment even though demand is increasing. At the UNAM, for example, the number of people wanting to enroll in the law school grew 10 percent annually, on average, between 1985 and 1995, from 7,856 to 20,627. Yet the number of admissions did not increase. In fact, it was reduced by about 15 percent, from 4,143 to 3,533 (Blanco and Rangel 1996: 128, 135), creating incentives for existing private institutions to establish law programs to meet this unsatisfied demand.

Creating a new law program requires little more than a classroom and an instructor, which also helps explain the proliferation of such programs. There is no real need to invest in ambitious research and publications programs, and a very basic library will suffice. Private institutions also benefit from the fact that they are subject to relatively little government control and regulation.

The second issue concerns the import of the public/private divide in legal education. There are no substantial differences between public and private law schools when it comes to curriculum, teaching method, or teaching faculty. But differences do appear in factors outside of the educational program per se—such as the students' socioeconomic position, which affects the professional contacts and opportunities they may have during their professional career. Students from working-class backgrounds are disadvantaged vis-à-vis upper-class students, who can draw on the support networks of their immediate families and their social environment. Instead, students from disadvantaged socioeconomic backgrounds must limit their professional networks, by necessity, to contacts they are able to cultivate in law school (Lomnitz and Salazar 2002). This differentiation seems to hold regardless of whether a lower-socioeconomic-class student graduates from a private or a public law school.

Table 11.3. Law Programs by Student Enrollment, 1991 and 2001

Student Enrollment	Public Law programs				Private Law Programs			
	1991 (N=46)		2001 (N=75)		1991[a] (N=72)		2001[a] (N=431)	
	N	%	N	%	N	%	N	%
Less than 50	1	2.17	4	5.33	11	15.28	94	21.80
51 to 100	2	3.35	2	2.66	10	13.89	83	19.26
100 to 250	3	6.52	12	16.00	25	34.72	135	31.32
251 to 500	4	8.69	15	20.00	15	20.83	63	14.62
501 to 1000	5	10.87	7	9.33	8	11.11	35	8.12
1001 to 2500	21	45.65	24	32.00	1	1.39	6	1.39
2501 to 5000	7	15.22	7	9.33	0	0.00	1	0.23
More than 5000	3	6.52	4	5.33	0	0.00	0	0.00

Sources: ANUIES 1991, 2001.

[a] Two private schools did not report enrollment in 1991, and thirteen did not report enrollment in 2001.

Another important trend in legal education in Mexico involves the establishment of institutions for specialized legal training. Law degree programs in Mexico generally do not include specialized training for the various roles within the legal profession (judge, public prosecutor, attorney); this need has been met via professional practice and/or part-time graduate-level study.

The oldest and foremost graduate law program is at the law school of the UNAM (the program began in 1951). By 2003, this program offered sixteen areas of specialization, in addition to a master's and a doctoral program in law. Public universities outside Mexico City have also established graduate programs in law, with most classes held on the weekend to accommodate professional schedules; and private universities have initiated graduate programs in Mexico City and elsewhere, with considerable success. Since most of the students are practicing lawyers, private universities (and public universities, to some extent) can charge sizable fees, enabling them to hire prestigious scholars and practitioners, both local and nonlocal, usually for individual weekend sessions.

In 2002, there were 9,797 students enrolled in 185 graduate-level law programs, an increase of almost 100 percent over 1998 (ANUIES 1998, 2002b). Of these, 2,790 were studying a specialization, 6,559 were in master's degree programs, and 448 were pursuing LLD degrees. However, when compared to the huge enrollment in undergraduate law programs, these numbers are relatively low (about 5 percent), confirming that an undergraduate degree in law suffices for most legal practitioners.

Traditionally, a few Mexican law students have studied in Europe (mostly in France, Italy, and Spain, where legal traditions are roughly similar to Mexico's). Since the implementation of the North American Free Trade Agreement (NAFTA) in 1994, however, it is very likely that an increasing number of law students—especially those hoping to practice law in the areas of business, trade, and finance—are studying in the United States and Canada.

Quality of Legal Education

The UNAM law school has long played a leading role in legal education in Mexico. Not only was it the country's oldest and most prestigious law school, it was also the largest—and a key center for recruitment into government (Lomnitz and Salazar 2002). Private law schools adopted the UNAM curriculum and even sought UNAM recognition for their programs and degrees. The prominence of the UNAM program has diminished somewhat in recent years, especially after the school introduced a new curriculum in 1993.

According to many observers, legal education at public universities in Mexico (the UNAM as well as some well-respected state universities such as Guanajuato, Veracruz, and San Luis Potosí) was reasonably good in the 1950s and 1960s. Program quality began to decline with the "massification" of public universities in the 1970s, when enrollments escalated to unwieldy levels. This untoward growth was an important factor in the surge of private universities, which were also made more attractive because they offered professional specializations (for example, corporate law) and the opportunity to forge significant personal relationships. Others among the private schools gained prominence by offering three-year (as opposed to the customary five-year) degree programs (López Ayllón and Fix-Fierro 2003).

When asked about the content and quality of legal education, the same observers described it as too traditional, stagnant, and still reflecting the legal-theoretical models of the nineteenth century. In parallel with this pattern, law books also continue to reproduce traditional legal ideas and models. In fact, the "classic" Mexican law books of the 1950s and 1960s are still widely used by law students and teachers (López Ayllón and Fix-Fierro 2003).

The great majority of law school professors are part-timers, legal practitioners who teach only a few hours a week. According to recent data, fewer than 140 of approximately 1,000 instructors at the UNAM law school are "career" faculty (*El Mundo del Abogado* 2002: 23). This makes it less likely that they will have up-to-date knowledge or use modern teaching techniques. Teaching methods still rely heavily on theoretical presentations and are rarely problem-oriented. They tend to present a view of the law that is isolated from both social reality and the social sciences (López Ayllón and Fix-Fierro 2003).

It should be noted, however, that technical legal skills are generally not the key criterion on which a law school graduate is judged. The legal profession is permeated by personal and social relationships (Dezalay and Garth 1995; Lomnitz and Salazar 2002), and law schools play a key role as recruiting centers and employment agencies. Because employers seem to expect only the most basic skills from a law graduate, the quality of education prior to law school may be much more important for recruitment.[5]

---

[5] According to Loretta Ortiz Ahlf, dean of the law school of the Universidad Iberoamericana in Mexico City, students entering law school display signifi-

The overall impression is that the education law school graduates receive is barely adequate. Some of the deficiencies may be offset by the training graduates obtain through legal internships. Unfortunately, this kind of learning is also viewed as problematic. According to the dean of a prestigious Mexico City law school, training during student internships in law firms (*pasantías*) is long, costly, and hit-or-miss. Students spend thousand of hours on very basic tasks (such as copying judicial decrees in courthouses) that do not create real professional expertise (Aranda García 2003: 58).

On the whole, objective criteria for evaluating law schools and law graduates are scarce. In 2000, the National Center for the Evaluation of Higher Education (CENEVAL, jointly established by universities, other institutions of higher education, and the Mexican government) began evaluating law graduates through a standard, multiple-choice test covering twelve areas (the history and philosophy of law, constitutional law, civil and criminal law, procedures, international law, and so on). According to CENEVAL's 1994–2001 report,[6] 8,160 law graduates from 59 institutions took the exam in 2000 and 2001; of these, only 309 (3.79 percent) scored in the "high" range.

More recently, the daily *Reforma* ranked seventy-two universities in the Mexico City metropolitan area on the sixteen most-sought-after fields of study (*Reforma*, August 26, 2002). The ranking resulted from a survey among students, on-staff and outside faculty, and employers. In the field of law, the five top-ranked schools were all private. The UNAM law school placed sixth, though the distance between the first and sixth positions was not sizable.

If the quality of legal education is generally poor and if legal technical skills are not decisive for the practice of law, then how can a more technically demanding legal system be sustained? Some law schools are attempting to modernize and update their curriculum and teaching methods. They are becoming more open to other disciplines and to foreign or international legal systems. They have established consortiums for exchanging faculty and students, hosting summer courses, and offering joint doctoral programs with foreign universities. However, the impact of these initiatives

---

cant deficiencies: "they do not devote time to reading, they cannot write, they do not have command of the language" (in Aranda García 2003: 58).

6 At www.ceneval.edu.mx (visited June 9, 2003).

on the quality of legal education in Mexico overall is likely to be limited in the short term.

THE LEGAL PROFESSION: AN OVERVIEW

Too Many Lawyers?

Unfortunately, little information is available about lawyers in Mexico, including how many there are. However, population census data for 1990 indicate that 141,539 individuals reported completing at least four years of higher education in law (7.5 percent of all professionals) (INEGI 1993).[7] Eighty-four percent of legal professionals were employed, but only some two-thirds seemed to be working in occupations related to the law (professionals and government categories).

Some information is also available on the number of registered legal professionals. According to data from the Education Ministry, of some 222,000 law degrees registered between 1945 and June 2002 (two-thirds of them recorded after 1990), the overwhelming majority were granted by public universities. The UNAM alone has granted more than 50,000. Of course, not all law degree recipients are practicing lawyers; according to one estimate, there are about 40,000 practicing attorneys in Mexico.[8]

As noted above, the public/private divide in legal education has had an impact in the legal profession, with private law school graduates enjoying a disproportionate presence in the top positions of the legal system. They have begun to win positions in government and the judiciary that previously seemed reserved for graduates of public law schools, and they are also rapidly displacing the older generation of business lawyers who attended public universities in the 1950s and 1960s (Dezalay and Garth 1995; Lomnitz and Salazar 2002; López Ayllón and Fix-Fierro 2003; Fix-Fierro 2003).

---

[7] Figures from the 2000 population census had not yet been released at the time of writing. In 1970, 35,333 individuals stated that they had completed at least four years of law studies (10.9 percent of all professionals) (Secretaría de Industria y Comercio 1972). Although the figures for 1970 and 1990 are not fully comparable, this means that the number of legal professionals quadrupled in absolute terms and almost doubled in proportion to the total population over a twenty-year period.

[8] Personal communication with Claus von Wobeser, former president of the Barra Mexicana Colegio de Abogados.

The Role of the Bar

Mexican lawyers need not be affiliated with a bar association to practice law. Because affiliation is voluntary and its benefits rather vague, it is safe to assume that only a small percentage of practicing lawyers belong to a professional association of this kind.[9]

State laws define the requirements for creating a professional association, as well as its rights and duties, and state authorities register professional associations and monitor their behavior. Professional associations are expected, in turn, to monitor their members' behavior, promote continuing education, and generally contribute to improving the profession. In addition, they may act as arbiters in disputes between a professional and a client. However, neither state authorities nor bar associations seem to take their monitoring responsibilities very seriously. Many bar associations have a code of ethics, but they do not enforce it. Even if they tried to do so, the fact that affiliation is voluntary deprives them of any leverage in applying effective sanctions.

As to advancing the profession, some bar associations organize conferences and seminars on new legislation, sometimes in cooperation with law schools. They occasionally make public statements in the press and other media on current issues of legal policy. However, even their members sometimes feel that their bar is more a social club than an effective organization of practicing attorneys. And at their worst, they are political pressure groups, bringing into serious question their commitment to strengthening the rule of law.

Indeed, one might question the very existence of a legal profession in Mexico. As a group, lawyers are divided, segmented, and weak. They neither have nor seek market control, nor do they seem intent on obtaining social prestige and political influence. While lawyers may to some degree empathize and identify with their fellow lawyers, the interests and opportunities of different groups of legal professionals diverge in significant ways, with increasing polarization between the public and the private sectors within the profession, as well as between the legal elite and the bulk of lawyers.

Thus the Mexican legal profession, assuming there is one, does not play a significant role in the process of institutional legitimacy or in the overall

---

[9] The Barra Mexicana Colegio de Abogados, which is based in Mexico City and has branches in several states, has some 2,500 active members.

governance of society. The fact that, until fairly recently, top government positions were held by politicians with law degrees may have lulled lawyers into thinking that the rule of law(yers) was firmly established. To the contrary, the rule of the *legal form* they came to symbolize did not necessarily equate with—and in a way precluded—the rule of law.

A Preliminary Conclusion

From the preceding overview we learn that: (1) legal education in Mexico has exploded in terms of the number of schools and students, while its quality has declined and is now generally poor; (2) legal professionals divide into a small, specialized elite and a large remainder, with graduates of private law schools increasingly occupying the most important positions in the private and public sectors; and (3) lawyers as a group are weak and disorganized, which keeps them from performing an important role in social governance in general and in the legitimization and reform of legal institutions in particular.

It is easy to see why the perception of the role of lawyers in the legal system is so negative. When asked about attorneys in their role as professionals, many lawyers, judges, and scholars deem that the majority are poorly qualified. One lawyer regarded lawyers as a group as "ignorant, arrogant, and presumptuous." They claim "a leading voice, but have little to say." They are "politically conservative" and "lack self-criticism." They do not realize "how narrow their intellectual horizon is." And as individuals, most seem to excel in the use of a cryptic language that overcomplicates matters and excludes non-lawyers from problem resolution.

LAWYER PERFORMANCE IN THE ADMINISTRATION OF JUSTICE: ASSET OR NUISANCE?

Lawyers perform many important functions, both direct and indirect, in the justice system. One example of their indirect influence is their role in teaching or providing practical training to young graduates interning in law firms. Among the direct functions are the following:

- Gatekeeping and access to the justice system. Lawyers may influence the likelihood that a dispute will go to court.

- Defense and representation. Lawyers translate into legal terms, and help enforce, the interests of defendants and clients.

- Legal evolution. Lawyers may bring new social problems to the justice system, thus promoting changes in the laws. Lawyer organizations may also play a role in the evolution of the rule of law as a whole.

- Time and costs of legal proceedings. Lawyers undoubtedly influence the costs and duration of legal proceedings.

- Confidence in the legal system. Lawyers act as intermediaries between the legal system and society.

In the following pages I attempt to describe a few relevant aspects of the behavior and performance of lawyers as these relate to the administration of justice in Mexico. Specifically, I address two of the functions stated above, with special reference to criminal law: professional representation and legal defense, and confidence in the legal system.

Quality of Professional Representation and Legal Defense in the Criminal Process

There are many good lawyers in Mexico, but the chance of finding one depends on the kind of law they practice, where they live (the best lawyers are concentrated in Mexico City, Guadalajara, and Monterrey), and what they charge.

Gaining access to a good criminal lawyer is difficult; there are relatively few of them, and the costs they incur in the criminal process are extremely high. Some of these costs derive from the lawyers' need for some minimal infrastructure for dealing effectively with their clients' needs (including being present at court hearings, detention facilities, and so on). Other costs derive from the different scenarios under which criminal proceedings take place. If a lawyer cannot stop the public prosecutor from bringing criminal charges before a judge (*consignación*) following the criminal investigation (*averiguación previa*), costs will mount as the lawyer fights to block a conviction (conviction rates are about 80 percent). Moreover, periodic changes in the legal code that increase criminal sanctions do little to enhance the dismal performance of the police and the prosecutor's office in the prosecution of criminals, but they certainly ratchet up the costs of legal representation.

An additional consideration for criminal lawyers is the risk involved in representing certain clients, as, for example, in drug-trafficking cases. Many defendants who need and deserve a good defense are shunned by lawyers because they are considered to be high risk. It is not surprising, then, given the potential costs and risks involved in criminal defense law, that many good lawyers leave this field to practitioners with questionable credentials.

Several recent studies and surveys provide useful insights into the quality of the services that criminal lawyers, including public defenders, provide. In general, these studies concur that the role of legal counsel in the criminal process tends to be marginal and poor in quality (Lawyers Committee for Human Rights 2001: 45ff.; Bergman et al. 2003; Pásara 2003).

Public defenders tend to restrict the evidence they present to their client's testimony, though it should be noted in their defense that most public defenders (particularly at the state level) lack the time to prepare a good defense. Private criminal lawyers are not necessarily any better.[10] Many of them take little advantage of the legal opportunities available to the defense (Pásara 2003), and they are often unaware of a defendant's basic rights. For example, they may not know that their client may refuse to answer any question and has the right to be released on bail. It is not surprising, then, that acquittals, which are very rare, generally occur because of a lack of evidence, not because of good lawyering.

A survey of prison inmates confirms some of our observations about criminal defense lawyers (Bergman et al. 2003: 48–49, 92ff.). Basically, inmates feel that they did not receive a competent defense. Forty-six percent stated that they had no defense at all, and 22 percent felt that they had been defended at a minimal level. Only 13 percent seemed satisfied with their lawyers. About 45 percent of these prisoners had dismissed legal counsel because their lawyer had "done nothing" to defend them (56.1 percent) or because they were simply "bad lawyers" (10.1 percent).

Why are so many criminal lawyers in Mexico so ineffective? The rules of criminal procedure give defendants and their lawyers the advantage in that that they need only identify a weakness in the public prosecutor's case; in theory, the principle *in dubio pro reo* (when in doubt, believe in yourself) should take care of the rest. However, while the public prosecutor tries to obstruct the defense lawyer's efforts, the obstacles are often much more fundamental. Despite the legal system's supposed presumption of the defendant's innocence, Mexican criminal procedure is geared, from the criminal investigation onward, toward conviction, and this affects the legal opportunities that are available to defendants. This context makes

---

[10] According to a criminal attorney, about 15 percent of criminal lawyers are very good, 30 percent are very bad, and the rest are average.

the public prosecutor the dominant figure by far (Pásara 2003), so that everything he or she does, or omits, will have a decisive impact on the outcome of the case. This is not to say, however, that the defense lawyer's performance is irrelevant. The studies and surveys cited above assume that a competent defense may lead, if not to an acquittal, at least to a better observance of the defendant's rights and legal procedures more generally.

Confidence in the Legal System

Perhaps lawyers have their most significant impact in their role as intermediaries between society and the justice system. The relationship between lawyers and judges, on one hand, and lawyers and their clients, on the other, significantly affects the operation and public perception of the justice system.

Judges lament that some lawyers try to pressure the courts via the media or by filing complaints against judges. These tactics frequently yield results; judges who feel intimated may opt to grant these lawyers' petition. In other cases, however, such tactics may prove counterproductive. As one lawyer put it, the case may get "hot" (politicized), making the public prosecutor keener to get a conviction and creating further complications for a successful defense.

The type of written procedure that prevails in the Mexican legal system has fostered what lawyers know (and abhor) as ex parte communication—that is, communication between the judge and one party, without the presence of the other party and that party's lawyer. Lawyers do not rely solely on their written complaints and motions. They always seek, and usually get, a personal interview with the judge. From the lawyer's viewpoint, these interviews serve multiple purposes. First, they allow the lawyers to find out "who they are dealing with." Second, lawyers may also find out if the judge has in fact become familiar with the case. And third, lawyers may determine if the judge is inclined to decide in a particular way, giving them additional opportunity to adjust their strategy. Many judges view the interviews as convenient and even necessary; written motions are "cold" and formulaic and do not allow for direct, personal contact between the judge and the parties. Most judges see no problems with the practice, given that both parties are granted the same "right" and judges can be trusted to treat them both fairly and impartially. However, some judges shun such interviews, wishing to avoid personal confrontations with litigants.

The problem with ex parte communications is that they are not regulated by the law but depend on the discretion of the judge. Not only do they open up an opportunity for making nonlegal arrangements, but the judge may also become sympathetic (or antipathetic) toward one of the parties involved, which could negatively affect the proceedings.

Seemingly unproblematic at first glance is the practice of judges to sometimes complement the efforts of a deficient lawyer, to the benefit of the lawyer's client. This *suplencia de la deficiencia de la queja*, which often favors the weaker party in criminal and employment cases, is granted even if it is not sought by the litigants. An appeals court will thoroughly review a case (in criminal cases, first examining the merits of the case and then its formal aspects) even before going into the specific grievances raised by a party. Judges view *suplencia* as an opportunity to go beyond a narrow definition of their role and to "do justice." Unfortunately, this helping hand on the part of the judges may well foster mediocre performance among less-than-competent lawyers. According to one lawyer, judges are very willing to examine new legal issues and ideas, but attorneys seldom raise them.

The most significant problem in the relationship between lawyers and their clients is that the latter are almost completely at the mercy of the former. In the absence of any constraints on their professional behavior, lawyers can exert a high degree of control over all aspects of the case. Although procedural codes give judges some tools (such as fines or criminal charges) with which to regulate a lawyer's behavior, these are generally not used in practice.[11] Lawyers are rarely prosecuted or convicted of crimes related to their professional performance. They are largely not accountable, and there is little recourse against a disloyal, negligent, or dishonest lawyer.

No wonder, then, that citizens hold lawyers in low esteem. In a survey conducted in Mexico City in 1996, a majority of respondents viewed lawyers as dishonest or very dishonest (Covarrubias y Asociados 1996). Opinions were even worse among respondents who had had contact with the justice system as compared with those who had not (54 percent and 41 percent, respectively). Respondents also listed lawyers as one of the main problems a citizen faces when he or she is involved in a legal dispute.

Moreover, lawyers can reinforce perceptions of corruption in the justice system. They often ask clients for "bribe money" for the judge, public

---

[11] See, for example, the Ley de Amparo, Arts. 90, 103 (judges may fine lawyers and litigants who act in bad faith or who challenge a decision without motive or cause) or the Federal Code of Civil Procedure, Art. 391 (the court may impose a disciplinary measure or bring criminal charges against a lawyer who fails to discharge his or her professional duties).

prosecutor, or other official,[12] though this money usually goes directly into the lawyer's own pocket. Of course, we should keep in mind here that many clients deliberately seek unscrupulous lawyers, believing (falsely) that this improves their chances of a successful outcome.

Although many courts and jurisdictions, especially at the federal level, are virtually free of corruption, the degree of corruption increases the lower one goes in the criminal justice system. This means that the possibility of correcting abuses can only take place, if it happens at all, at the very end of the process. Nevertheless, even though corruption is not uncommon at some institutional levels, corrupt practices are much less effective than is generally assumed. As one lawyer put it: in many cases money will not buy justice. At most, it may purchase an opportunity to be heard. Hence lawyers cannot rely on bribery and other corrupt practices to win their cases, though this is precisely what many of them seem to be doing.

CONCLUSION: AN AGENDA FOR RESEARCH AND REFORM

Lawyers function as intermediaries between the justice system and society. Lawyers may facilitate or obstruct access to the justice system. Their efforts to translate social expectations into legal concepts and arguments for presentation to the courts have profound consequences, not only on a client's chances of recovering damages or his or her freedom but also on society's confidence in the justice institutions themselves.

In previous sections I presented a very fragmentary description of legal education, the practice of law, and some aspects of lawyers' performance as these relate to the administration of justice in Mexico. Much more research is needed to gain a more detailed picture and more precise evidence regarding various areas of the law, procedural stages, jurisdictions, and groups of lawyers. Only a well-designed survey, for example, could elicit reliable information on the prevalence of specific problems. Of course, such a survey would need to encompass not only judges and lawyers, but also lawyers' clients and members of the society at large.

Such research is indispensable if judicial reform proposals currently under consideration in Mexico—such as the introduction of oral trials, especially for criminal cases—are to have any chance of success. For example, the success of a shift to oral trials—in which "decision of a case should be based (solely) on the outcome of a (preferably) single oral hearing"

---

[12] About 20 percent of prison inmates said their lawyer had asked for money to give to the public prosecutor and judge (Bergman et al. 2003: 94).

(Bender 1979: 437)—in terms of transparency, speediness, and so on, would depend heavily on the cooperation of lawyers, as well as on a thorough and intensive preparation for the hearing on the part of all participants.

This chapter allows us to envision three key target areas for near-term reform efforts. They are access to the profession, access to legal services, and professional accountability.

The need to revise the requirements that give access to the legal profession seems indisputable. If judges, notaries, public prosecutors, and even legal scholars must comply with ever-higher requirements in order to perform their roles in the legal system, why not practicing attorneys? There are no convincing reasons why these changes could not take the form of regulated practical training and an examination administered jointly by the courts and the bar association.

However, such reforms could give lawyers a virtual monopoly over legal advice, something that would have to be offset by measures to make access to their services more equitable and more affordable. For example, fees could be strictly regulated through legislation, as is the case in some European countries—though this would automatically generate problems of enforcement. Finally, effective mechanisms must be implemented to ensure lawyers' ethical behavior and to protect their clients' interests.

Such initiatives have been the subject of recurring discussion. For example, mandatory bar affiliation has been proposed as a means for controlling lawyers' behavior. Indeed, the Barra Mexicana, Colegio de Abogados, the most prestigious Mexican bar association, has debated this issue on several occasions beginning in the 1930s, without coming to a conclusion. Even the many lawyers who favor mandatory affiliation concede that it is not a panacea for the profession's ills (Barra Mexicana, Colegio de Abogados 2002: 61–65, 78), though it would be a first step and would probably spark little opposition within the profession.

An essential ingredient in any mechanism designed to make lawyers more accountable—be it mandatory bar affiliation or any other means—must be respect for clients' and defendants' interests and rights, whether through a special disciplinary jurisdiction, arbitration, or other dispute-settlement instruments.

To date, there has been no broad discussion on how to regulate legal education and access to the legal profession. Perhaps such a discussion is awaiting a fuller diagnosis of the problems. However, it is precisely such an open and public debate on the role of lawyers in the administration of justice that has been sorely missing.

References

ANUIES (Asociación Nacional de Universidades e Instituciones de Educación Superior). 1979, 1991, 1997. *Anuario estadístico. Población escolar de licenciatura en universidades e institutos tecnológicos.* Mexico City: ANUIES.

————. 1998. *Anuario estadístico. Población de posgrado.* Mexico City: ANUIES.

————. 2000, 2001. *Anuario estadístico. Población escolar de licenciatura en universidades e institutos tecnológicos.* Mexico City: ANUIES.

————. 2002a. *Anuario estadístico. Población escolar de licenciatura en universidades e institutos tecnológicos.* Mexico City: ANUIES.

————.2002b. *Anuario estadístico. Población de posgrado.* Mexico City: ANUIES.

Aranda García, Erick. 2003. "Entrevista con Loretta Ortiz Ahlf, Directora del Departamento de Derecho, Universidad Iberoamericana," *Cauces* 2, nos. 5–7 (January–September): 55–59.

Barra Mexicana, Colegio de Abogados. 2002. *80 años en la defensa de los valores del derecho (1922–2002).* Mexico: Barra Mexicana, Colegio de Abogados.

Bender, Rolf. 1979. "The Stuttgart Model." In *Access to Justice,* ed. Mauro Cappelletti and Bryant Garth. Vol. 2, book 2. Aalphen aan den Rijn: Sijthoff, and Milan: Giuffrè.

Bergman, Marcelo, Elena Azaola, Ana Laura Magaloni, and Layda Negrete. 2003. *Delincuencia, marginalidad y desempeño institucional: resultados de la encuesta a población en reclusión en tres entidades de la República Mexicana: Distrito Federal, Morelos y Estado de México.* Mexico City: División de Estudios Jurídicos, Centro de Investigación y Docencia Económicas.

Blanco, José, and José Rangel. 1996. *Las generaciones cambian: un estudio sobre el desempeño académico de la UNAM.* Mexico City: Universidad Nacional Autónoma de México.

Concha Cantú, Hugo Alejandro, and José Antonio Caballero Juárez. 2001. *Diagnóstico sobre la administración de justicia en las entidades federativas: un estudio institucional sobre la justicia local en México.* Mexico City: Universidad Nacional Autónoma de México.

Covarrubias y Asociados. 1996. "Entre abogados te veas," *Voz y Voto* 41 (July): 23–27.

Dezalay, Yves, and Bryant Garth. 1995. "Building the Law and Putting the State into Play: International Strategies among Mexico's Divided Elite." ABF Working Paper No. 9509. Chicago, Ill.: American Bar Foundation.

El Mundo del Abogado. 2002. "La Facultad de Derecho de la UNAM en cifras," vol. 5, no. 40 (August), 22–25.

Facultad de Derecho. 2002. "Proyecto de reforma al plan de estudios de la licenciatura en derecho." Unpublished document compiled by a special commission. Mexico City: Universidad Nacional Autónoma de México.

Fix-Fierro, Héctor. 2003. "Judicial Reform in Mexico: What Next?" In *Beyond Common Knowledge: Empirical Approaches to the Rule of Law*, ed. Erik G. Jensen and Thomas C. Heller. Stanford, Calif. Stanford University Press.

Gudiño Pelayo, José de Jesús. 2003. "La calidad en la justicia: corresponsabilidad de jueces, litigantes y partes," *Revista del Instituto de la Judicatura Federal* 16: 183–99.

INEGI (Instituto Nacional de Estadística, Geografía e Informática). 1993. *Los profesionistas en México*. Aguascalientes, Mex.: INEGI.

Lawyers Committee for Human Rights. 2001. *Injusticia legalizada: procedimiento penal mexicano y derechos humanos*. (Translation of *Legalized Injustice: Mexican Criminal Procedure and Human Rights*.) Mexico: Lawyers Committee for Human Rights/Centro de Derechos Humanos "Miguel Agustín Pro Juárez."

Lomnitz, Larissa, and Rodrigo Salazar. 2002. "Cultural Elements in the Practice of Law in Mexico: Informal Networks in a Formal System." In *Global Prescriptions: The Production, Exportation and Importation of a New Legal Orthodoxy*, ed. Yves Dezalay and Bryant Garth. Ann Arbor: University of Michigan Press.

López Ayllón, Sergio, and Héctor Fix-Fierro. 2003. "'Faraway, So Close!' The Rule of Law and Legal Change in Mexico (1970–2000)." In *Legal Culture in the Age of Globalization: Latin America and Latin Europe*, ed. Lawrence M. Friedman and Rogelio Pérez Perdomo. Stanford, Calif.: Stanford University Press.

Pásara, Luis. 2003. "Cómo sentencian los jueces del D.F. en material penal." Unpublished research report. Mexico City: Centro de Investigación y Docencia Económicas, June.

Secretaría de Industria y Comercio. 1972. *Resultados del IX Censo General de Población 1970*. Mexico: Secretaría.

CHAPTER **12**

Lobbying for Judicial Reform: The Role of the Mexican Supreme Court in Institutional Selection

JEFFREY K. STATON

A healthy judiciary is vital to a country's prospects for democratic consolidation and economic growth. Scholars suggest that an independent, well-functioning judiciary can constrain the state from violating fundamental civil liberties, provide an arena for the peaceful resolution of political and social conflicts, and increase investor confidence by stabilizing the norms under which property rights are protected (see O'Donnell 1999; Stone Sweet 2000; North and Thomas 1973). If a healthy judiciary can accomplish at least one of these normatively appealing goals, attempts to construct effective judicial systems should continue to be worthy of serious scholarship. In this chapter I ask how the behavior of high court judges might complement models designed to explain political decisions to build effective judicial systems. It is obvious that judges intimately affect the success of reform efforts (see Buscaglia and Dakolias 1996). After all, reform packages are largely designed to influence judicial performance. It is less clear how judges might influence institutional selection itself.

I argue that judges can do so in at least two ways. First, judges can help structure the portfolio of measures considered by reformers through consultation and direct lobbying. As highlighted by Speckman's contribution to this volume, Mexican judges have historically added their technical insight to legislative projects on administration of justice reform. Although this kind of influence may not change the general decision to delegate greater authority to the judiciary, it may well affect the substance of the delegation. Second, while judges are unlikely to have a direct influence over the outcomes of legislative bargaining, they may be able to affect public opinion concerning reform, and in that sense indirectly affect the preferences of reformers. This is to suggest that judges might be able to successfully go public.[1]

These possibilities of influence raise a number of subsidiary questions about judicial lobbying, both positive and normative. Under what conditions might judges successfully promote their reform proposals? Are there certain kinds of reforms that should be easier to promote than others? Assuming that there are conditions under which judges can successfully promote reform, is this a normatively appealing possibility? Although I do not develop and test a complete model here, I argue that answers to these questions ought to address a set of key political trade-offs. In particular, judges considering a public strategy to influence judicial reform are likely faced with a trade-off between effective public relations and the maintenance of an essentially apolitical image. How judges evaluate this trade-off may explain both the intensity of judicial public relations and the ultimate success of lobbying efforts. Similarly, legislators considering reform proposals likely face policy trade-offs between judicial independence and judicial accountability and between legislative authority and judicial power. Clearly the way legislators evaluate these trade-offs will affect the ability of judges to successfully obtain institutional reform.

I evaluate these claims by discussing the role played by the Mexican Supreme Court in the ongoing process of federal judicial reform.[2] The ministers of the current Supreme Court, all appointed following a massive change in the structure of the federal judiciary in late 1994, have played an intimate role in the development of the judicial reform agenda.[3] They have done so largely through direct lobbying efforts aimed at critical national policymakers, efforts aided by a highly aggressive public relations strategy designed in part to create an accurate mechanism through which the Court could speak to the Mexican public.

---

[1] This concept is famously developed in Kernell 1993: 2–6.

[2] I limit my discussion to the Court's role in developing the federal judiciary. Although the state judiciaries are clearly vital substantive points of interest, an expanded analysis would go quite beyond the scope of this chapter. The chapter by Schatz, Concha, and Magaloni Kerpel addresses the state judiciaries. For a recent study of the state judiciaries, see Concha Cantú and Caballero Juárez 2001.

[3] The ministers continue to promote further judicial reform. Indeed, the Supreme Court is currently coordinating an international discussion on reforming the administration of justice. Proposals for reform may be downloaded at the Supreme Court's Web site, www.scjn.gob.mx.

Although the Court has significantly helped frame the reform agenda, its influence over policy outcomes has been mixed. The Court has successfully advocated policies designed to increase the efficiency of the judicial branch and consolidate the Court's internal control over the administration of the judiciary. On the other hand, legislators have declined to implement key proposals concerning judicial independence and the Court's constitutional jurisdiction.

In what follows I discuss how judicial lobbying complements two kinds of models designed to explain the decision to delegate political authority to an independent judiciary. I then describe the Mexican Supreme Court's efforts to influence its own reform process and highlight the constraints the Court has faced. I conclude by discussing how future theoretical and empirical work might proceed.

BUILDING HEALTHY JUDICIARIES

Why might politicians delegate significant power to judges and work to make their courts more independent, accessible, and efficient?[4] This is a relevant question in studies of democratizing states, where developing the rule of law is a dominant concern. There are two approaches to modeling this process. The first—what has come to be called the insurance hypothesis—is an electoral theory.[5] The notion on this account is that ruling political elites face significant risks in democratizing states that lack effective courts, especially when such elites perceive a nontrivial probability of losing power. Increasing judicial independence, for example, allows judges to serve as a sort of insurance policy against possible future electoral losses, where the former minority might either attempt to retaliate for previous violations of civil liberties or radically change the state's legal structure. Independent courts empowered to exercise constitutional review are supposed bulwarks against such possibilities. Finkel (1997) offers such an explanation for the 1994 Mexican judicial reform briefly reviewed below.

An alternative model suggests that the state might attempt to build healthy courts in order to resolve a credible commitment problem (North and Weingast 1989). If the state is incapable of committing itself to its own rules, then the expected return to citizen investment in the regime likely

---

4 Prillaman (2001: 15–29) identifies accessibility, independence, and efficiency as the three crucial characteristics of a healthy judiciary.

5 For a recent example in the U.S. legal literature, see Ginsberg 2002; see also Finkel 1997.

will be lowered, and so will the incentive to invest.[6] The state may have greater difficulty generating revenue, in inducing compliance with social norms, and perhaps even in reducing competing revolutionary claims on power. Magaloni's analysis of the 1994 Mexican federal reform suggests that it was not an Institutional Revolutionary Party (PRI) insurance policy against future electoral losses, but rather an effort to institutionalize inter-party conflicts in order to avoid potentially disastrous clashes in an increasingly pluralistic political landscape (Magaloni 2003). A related story, offered by Schatz (1998), suggests that elites in transitional democracies might delegate authority to courts in order to change perceptions of governmental illegitimacy. On such an account, it might be argued that the 1994 reform was a means of convincing an increasingly relevant electorate that the government was becoming more willing to respect the rule of law and thus worthy of electoral support.

Both of these approaches place some needed theoretical rigor on the analysis of judicial reform, and they clearly generate testable hypotheses about the relationship between legitimacy, electoral uncertainty, and the inclination to create healthier judiciaries. Still, neither approach can offer much insight into the substance of judicial reform. It is one thing to suggest that the state ought to be more likely to delegate authority as electoral uncertainty increases; it is quite another to generate predictions about the particular kinds of authority granted. It is here that judges can play an important role by promoting well-defined alternatives for judicial reform. Judges themselves are likely to be more familiar than politicians with plausible institutional solutions to problems of judicial independence, citizen access to the justice system, judicial efficiency, and effective constitutional control. Moreover, as members of the state, judges should be able to gain access to relevant policymakers, a crucial condition for effective lobbying (see Hansen 1991). In that sense, it should come as no surprise that judges around the world exercise some degree of influence over the reform process in this regard.[7]

This kind of influence over the reform project is important but limited. While access to political leaders is likely necessary in order to frame the agenda, it is unlikely that access will be sufficient. Just like any lobbying

---

[6] A similar model is considered in Landes and Posner 1975, where independent courts are considered means for locking in the gains from cooperation in legislative bargains.

[7] For examples in the United States, see Winkle 1990; in Russia, see Solomon 2002; in Zimbabwe and Tanzania, see Widner 2001.

group, judges require political leverage in order to be effective. Absent a natural constituency, such leverage may be hard to come by. Of course, like politicians and interest groups, judges can turn to the media in order to generate public support. They can do so by giving speeches, granting interviews, writing editorials, and publishing books on important subjects of judicial reform (Widner 2001: 36). Still, appealing to the public presents judges with a trade-off. One of the serious problems courts face in transitional democracies is a lingering sense that the judiciary is overly politicized (Prillaman 2001: 19–21). Direct appeals to the public over such issues as the appropriate distribution of government expenditures are a political enterprise. As such, they may risk a concurrent judicial attempt to appear detached from politics. If judges care about developing an apolitical image, they may face a trade-off between the possible gains to be captured through effective public appeals and the costs of appearing politicized. Accordingly, the degree to which judges engage in public strategies to affect reform and their ultimate success should be a function of the way they evaluate this trade-off.

Even if judges are able to frame the legislative agenda over judicial reform, policy success is not guaranteed. And perhaps this is a good thing. As Speckman reminds us in her chapter, there is no assurance that judge-led reform proposals will be in the general public interest. Instead, such proposals ought to reflect the preferences of the judiciary itself, and those preferences may or may not be in accord with some ideal separation of powers. Proposals to both increase judicial independence from the elected branches and expand judicial powers of constitutional review also present legislators with difficult choices, especially if they value judicial accountability and their own prerogative over public policy. Granting judges greater independence weakly decreases the ability of elected officials to hold judges accountable for their behavior.[8] Also, granting greater constitutional review authority to courts weakly decreases legislative control over public policy. In short, legislators—and, implicitly, the people they represent—face trade-offs between judicial independence and accountability and between legislative control over public policy and judicial power. The success of judicial attempts to influence reform, as well as a normative evaluation of the appeal of judicial lobbying, will surely be a function of how legislators and their constituents evaluate these trade-offs.

---

[8] By "weakly decrease" I mean that greater independence will either produce no change in judicial accountability or will reduce it.

On the other hand, there are classes of reform proposals, like those concerning judicial efficiency, that are unlikely to present legislators with difficult policy choices. For example, typical solutions to judicial inefficiency include designing better legal education and judicial training, updating antiquated mechanisms for communication within the judicial hierarchy, and eliminating overly restrictive procedural rules (Prillaman 2001: 17–18). There may not be consensus over particular approaches to reducing inefficiency, and politicians might bargain over the costs associated with making courts more efficient. However, it is unlikely that efficiency proposals will undercut either legislative policy authority or the ability to hold judges accountable. Accordingly, in the absence of a significant legislative trade-off, we might suspect that judges will more successfully promote reforms designed to combat inefficiency than reforms over independence or judicial power.

MEXICAN SUPREME COURT MINISTERS AND JUDICIAL REFORM

In this section I discuss how the ministers of the Mexican Supreme Court have advanced their interests in reform though direct lobbying and public relations. I then review specific efforts the Court has made to promote reform in the elected branches of government. While the Court has successfully shaped the reform agenda, its efforts have not fully determined the outcomes of the reform debate.

Beginnings

On December 31, 1994, newly elected President Ernesto Zedillo published a series of recently adopted constitutional amendments altering the structure of the Mexican federal judiciary.[9] The amendments created an entirely new Supreme Court and started the ministers down a road of real political

---

[9] In the senatorial debate on the reform, members of both the Institutional Revolutionary Party (PRI) and National Action Party (PAN) spoke vehemently in favor of the proposal. A few *perredistas* (members of the Party of the Democratic Revolution, or PRD), however, stood against the reform, arguing that it did not adequately address the widespread problem of corruption and that it provided inadequate mechanisms for access to justice. In the end, however, 108 senators out of 112 present voted to pass the reform, *en lo general* and *en lo particular* as amended. For a fine review of the parties' arguments, see Carranco Zúñiga 2000: 109–17.

relevance. The 1994 reform has been thoroughly analyzed by a number of distinguished scholars, and accordingly I only note its key elements here.[10]

The Zedillo amendments reduced the size of the Supreme Court from twenty-six to eleven ministers and the number of benches from four to two.[11] As part of its transitory provisions, all members of the Supreme Court were forced to resign, and only two members were reappointed to the new Court. Under a new appointment procedure, the Senate selects each minister from a list of three nominees.[12] Once appointed, the ministers select a president from among their own number, who serves a four-year term. In addition to organizing the Court's administrative affairs, the president leads the seven-member Federal Council of the Judiciary (CJF), also created in 1994 in order to relieve the Supreme Court of much of its administrative responsibilities.[13]

The 1994 reform dramatically altered the Supreme Court's constitutional jurisdiction. The amendments created a new institution of abstract constitutional review, the action of unconstitutionality. This action complements Mexico's traditional means of constitutional review, the *amparo* suit. Designed in the nineteenth century, *amparo* grants jurisdiction to federal courts in order to address alleged governmental violations of individual rights. Legal effects in *amparo* are limited to the parties immediately involved in the case, and thus *amparo* restricts the degree to which Mexican

---

[10] For analyses in Spanish, see Fix Zamudio and Cossío Díaz 1995; Carranco Zúñiga 2000. For English-language reviews, see Fix-Fierro 2001; Domingo 2000.

[11] The benches previous to the reform separately specialized in civil, penal, administrative, and labor matters. Under the new configuration, the first bench hears penal and civil cases; the second hears labor and administrative cases.

[12] After the president submits the list, the Senate has thirty days to make an appointment, which it does via a two-thirds super-majority voting rule. In the event that the Senate fails to choose a minister within thirty days, the minister designated by the president is appointed. However, if the Senate rejects the entire list, the president must submit another. If the Senate rejects the second list, the president's designee is appointed (Constitución Política de los Estados Unidos Mexicanos [CPM], Art. 96). This procedure was tested in the winter of 2003, when Ministers Aguinaco Alemán and Castro y Castro retired. As of March 2004, the Congress had only appointed one new member to the bench: distinguished law professor José Ramón Cossío. The other seat remained vacant following a congressional deadlock over Vicente Fox's second *terna*.

[13] CPM, Art. 100. For a review of judicial councils in Latin America, see Fix Zamudio and Fix-Fierro 1996.

courts can significantly affect public policy.[14] In contrast, the action of un-constitutionality grants the Supreme Court the power to set general effects in a certain class of cases, as long as eight of the eleven ministers adopt the majority proposal. The reform also enhanced the Court's power in *constitutional controversies*, an action under which the Supreme Court rules on conflicts arising between two branches of the same level of government and disputes between governments of distinct levels in Mexico's federal system. Finally, in creating the action of unconstitutionality, reformers implemented a forgiving standing requirement that offers the power to challenge the constitutionality of laws to minorities of the state legislatures, minorities of either house of the national Congress, and federally registered political parties, among other agents of the state.[15] In short, the Zedillo reform drastically changed the institutional structure of the federal judiciary. Perhaps most important, by requiring the resignation of all then-current members, the reform paved the way for a new set of judges to revitalize the third branch of government.

A New Supreme Court

The eleven ministers who took the bench in early 1995 hoped to develop a trusted federal judiciary and turn the Court itself into an effective constitutional tribunal, one capable of systematically controlling constitutional meaning and ultimately creating conditions under which the rule of law might be fully realized.[16] The ministers would not easily attain this appropriate yet lofty goal. Both systematic and anecdotal evidence suggested

---

[14] The authoritative work on *amparo* is Burgoa O 1998. A terrific if somewhat dated work in English is Baker 1971.

[15] CPM, Art. 105 (II)A-F.

[16] In his first annual report on the state of the federal judiciary, President Aguinaco Alemán spoke to the goal of developing public trust. See Aguinaco Alemán 1998: 22–23. Further, many of the Court's administrative accords on the judiciary's internal design are justified as means of perfecting the Court's role as a constitutional court. See, for example, Acuerdo 6/1999 Considerando 4, whose exposition of motives states, "It is essential to permit the Supreme Court, as happens in other nations, to concentrate all of its efforts on the recognition and resolution of new issues or on those issues of such high importance that their resolution will influence the interpretation and application of the national judicial order." Also see Acuerdos 6/2000 Considerando 1, 9/1999 Considerando 7, all of which advocate the Supreme Court's position as a constitutional court.

that even after the 1994 reform, the Mexican public continued to consider the federal judiciary largely inaccessible to most people, unworthy of public trust, and subservient to the executive branch.[17] As noted by Fix-Fierro in his contribution to this volume, while members of the federal judiciary might have liked to blame attorneys and police for the failures of justice in Mexico, the ministers recognized that public opinion placed the blame on the judges.[18]

In order to help change the judiciary's public profile, the ministers began to develop further institutional reforms. Among a long list of interests, the Supreme Court desired changes in rules concerning the CJF, the judicial budget, the nature of the *amparo* suit, the power to initiate laws in Congress, and the ability to directly regulate the distribution of cases between the Court's benches and the collegial circuit courts of appeals.

Some elements of the Court's reform package could be carried out independently, but others required action from the elected branches of government. This situation presented two problems. Although the ministers could directly contact party leaders, cabinet officials, and the president, as unelected judges they lacked a natural constituency that they might leverage in conversations with public officials. More seriously, they had no effective way of explaining their proposals to the Mexican public and, as a result, no clear way of influencing legislative or executive policy interests through their own supporters. The reason? Neither print nor television media, which had historically ignored the Supreme Court, appeared prepared to accurately cover the judiciary. Jesús Aranda, one of the first reporters to provide daily coverage of the Court, described the situation as follows:

> Before [the reform], the Court was very closed off. There was a public relations office that would suddenly issue a press release, but reporters did not go to the Court. In the end, nothing was known or understood about the Court. This reflected the judiciary's situation in the country. Why? Because one always spoke of an executive or the legislature. The judiciary

---

[17] The results from a 1996 *Voz y Voto* poll suggest that nearly 50 percent of Mexico City residents who had no experience with the legal system believed the Supreme Court ministers themselves to be dishonest or very dishonest.

[18] See interviews with Ministers Palacios, Aguirre Anguiano, and Ortiz Mayagotia in Camacho Guzmán 1999.

was always seen as an appendage of the executive. The judiciary did whatever the president wanted.[19]

The result of this negative image and general lack of interest was that reporters were unfamiliar with the judiciary and thus unprepared to provide the kind of coverage that might allow the ministers to develop a consistent message.

In order to change this situation, the Supreme Court pursued a multidimensional media relations strategy. This work was originally organized by its own Office of Public Relations (DCS).[20] The DCS took out advertisements announcing the Court's autonomy. It published books, pamphlets, comics, and videos summarizing the Court's most salient decisions, describing its internal structure, and highlighting its new role in Mexican politics. The ministers themselves granted interviews with the media on a wide variety of topics (Staton 2002: 152–53). Further, the DCS was charged with developing accurate media coverage.[21] The judicial writing style is not reader-friendly; as a result, resolutions are unusually difficult to interpret without a reasonable familiarity with the law. To address this issue, the Supreme Court offered legal seminars for reporters so that they might better cover the intricacies of judicial resolutions.

Substantively, the DCS attempted to craft an image of an independent, apolitical Supreme Court, one responsible for an increasingly accessible and efficient judiciary. In order to help promote a consistent message, the DCS issued press releases announcing information on pending and resolved cases and on key administrative decisions taken by the Supreme Court and the CJF.

---

[19] Jesús Aranda, personal communication, June 6, 2001, Mexico City. Despite this perception, the Supreme Court has taken up the issue of legal education in its most recent effort to generate national debate on justice reform. As of March 2004 it had collected thirty proposals for institutionalizing the education of attorneys.

[20] I discuss the Court's public relations work in Staton 2002: 152–89.

[21] In particular, the DCS was required to help better inform the Mexican public about the actual structure and role of the federal courts through the media. The DCS was also asked to publicly yet professionally defend the judiciary's independence. The Court's public relations policy is published in *Compromiso, órgano informativo del Poder Judicial de la Federación*, no. 1 (July–August 1999): 21–22. Arturo Vizcaino Zamora, personal communication, June 10, 2000, Supreme Court of Justice of the Nation, Mexico City.

Figure 12.1 shows the number of press releases announcing case results and administrative decisions issued each quarter from January 1997 through June 2003.[22] With the exception of the first quarter of 1997, the Court consistently issued more press releases announcing administrative decisions than results of cases. However, while the number of releases on cases remained relatively stable until 2003, the number of administrative press releases skyrocketed beginning in 2001.[23] In fact, in the fourth quarter of 2002, the overwhelming majority of press releases (97 percent) announced administrative decisions or proposals, many of which directly concerned issues of judicial reform. For example, between 2001 and 2003, 14 percent of the Court's administrative press releases announced the opening of a new federal district court or circuit tribunal, an important element of its reform package to enhance judicial efficiency and increase access.[24] These administrative announcements frequently contained reviews of substantive messages the Court wished to promote. Indeed, 23 percent of the Court's press releases announcing the opening of a new court quoted a speech by a member of the Supreme Court or the CJF making an appeal for a constitutional reform of the judiciary's budgetary authority. Sixty-three percent of those same press releases contained a message reaffirming the Court's interest in promoting justice for all Mexicans.

Perhaps of greater interest, the number of press releases issued by the Supreme Court plummeted in 2003. While the Court averaged twenty-four releases per quarter between 1997 and 2002, it issued only five during the first two quarters of 2003. This reduced activity corresponds with the election of the Court's new president, Minister Mariano Azuela, and suggests that the ministers may have begun to seriously consider the risks of cultivating such a high public profile. I return to this issue below.

Although coverage of the Supreme Court has certainly grown since 1995, we should be careful about drawing causal inferences about the

---

[22] The codebook for these data is available upon request from the author. For the purposes of this figure, the coding is rather straightforward.

[23] The likely explanation for this pattern is that in 2001 the press offices of the Supreme Court and the Federal Judicial Council were consolidated. Insofar as the CJF does not resolve legal cases, the increase in total press releases resulting from combining the two press offices had to affect the number of administrative announcements only. On the reason for this consolidation, see Staton 2002: 183–86.

[24] Data and codebook available from the author upon request.

Figure 12.1. Supreme Court Press Releases by Quarter (1997-2003)

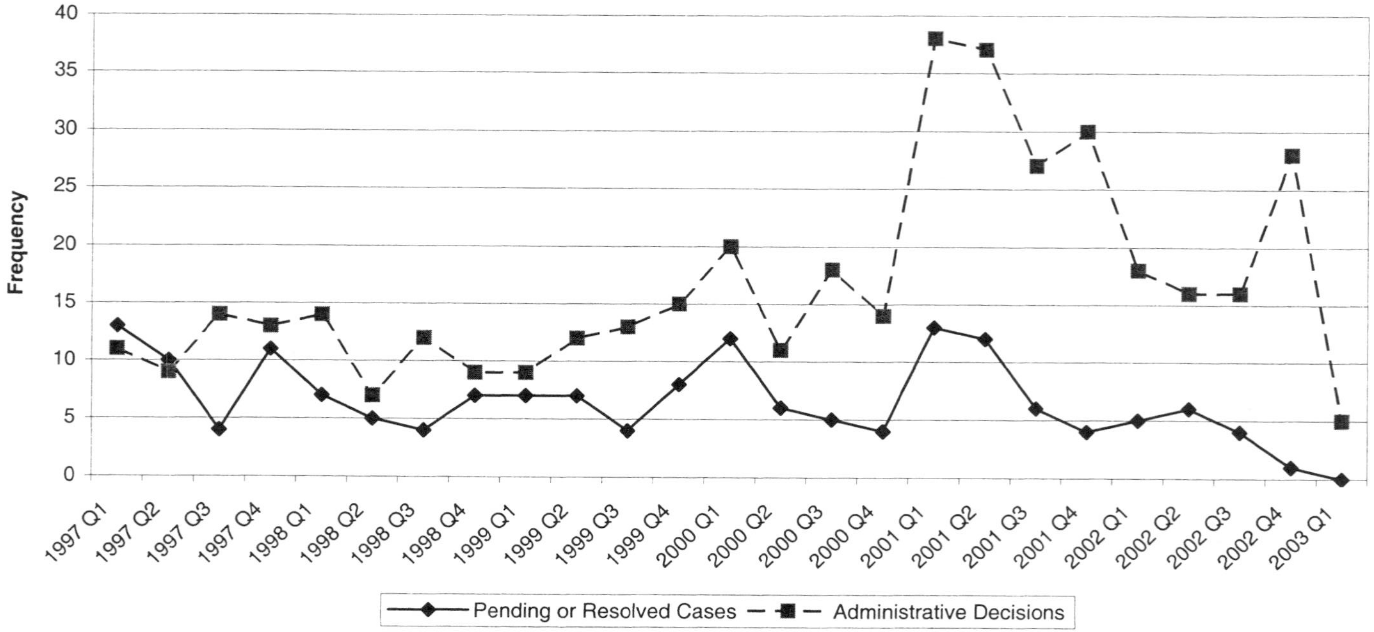

Court's effect on its own coverage.[25] Given the Court's new powers of constitutional review, it has increasingly resolved politically relevant cases, and those cases generate considerable interest in the press, independent of the Court's activities. It is also debatable whether the Court effectively crafted a new image or substantially increased public support for particular reform proposals.[26] Still, it is clear that by the end of 2002 the DCS and an increasingly cognoscente press corps offered the Court an effective mechanism for communicating its reform interests to the public. I now discuss examples of the Court's attempts to influence judicial reform.

Judicial Independence

Unsurprisingly, the Supreme Court has promoted institutional changes designed to increase the independence of the federal judiciary. The key proposal has been a constitutional amendment guaranteeing the judiciary a fixed yearly percentage of the federal budget. Constitutionally, the Supreme Court is empowered to submit a budget directly to Congress for its consideration, while the CJF submits a budget for the remainder of the judiciary. In practice, this requirement has meant that the Court negotiates directly with the president of Mexico (Fix-Fierro 2001: 33). The concern among the ministers is that this budgetary structure grants the legislature an unnecessary degree of control over the judiciary's activities (Aguirre Anguiano 2001). Despite the lack of a fixed budgetary provision, the judiciary's budget has grown tremendously over the past six years. Fix-Fierro (2001: 33) suggests that the current allocation is over four times as great as

---

25 A search at *La Jornada*'s Web site for news articles on the Supreme Court reveals the significant change in coverage. For example, a search for "Suprema Corte" in 1996 generates 460 hits. In contrast, an identical search in 2001 and 2002 generates 1,312 and 1,964 hits, respectively.

26 Data obtained by the newspaper *Reforma* on the Supreme Court's national approval suggest that in the days immediately following the Fox transition, 50 percent of Mexicans surveyed held a favorable opinion of the Court. Only 7 percent expressed a negative opinion; see Staton 2004. This result suggests a different understanding of the Court's image than that contained in Domingo 2000. By February 2002, however, only 39 percent of respondents issued a favorable opinion, while the percentage of respondents issuing a negative opinion had risen to 17 percent. Moreover, these latter results are confirmed by Fix-Fierro (2001: 39), who discusses a poll reported in *Este País* wherein only 36 percent of respondents suggested that they had between some and much confidence in the Supreme Court.

it was in 1995. However, for the ministers the issue is not how much the Court's budget has grown but whether the Court has to consistently seek legislative approval for increases.

The Court has promoted its budgetary reform initiative via direct lobbying and through more subtle forms of public relations. Roughly six weeks after Vicente Fox won the Mexican presidency, his transition team on justice and public security matters took part in a breakfast meeting with the eleven ministers of the Supreme Court. The subject of the meeting, which was widely covered by the national media, concerned a number of the president-elect's reform proposals for the justice system, none of which addressed the Court's budget reform.[27] Although the ministers were able to press their interests directly to the transition team, there was no assurance that the conversation would receive general media coverage and thus effectively compete for a position on the Fox agenda.

Taking advantage of this well-publicized opportunity, the Supreme Court's media-savvy president, Genaro Góngora Pimentel, held a press conference immediately after the transition team breakfast. He announced that he had presented the team with a thirteen-page comparative analysis of budgetary rules concerning Latin American judiciaries.[28] In it, Góngora vigorously argued for a fixed judicial budget. Important for the coverage the Court would receive on the following day, the DCS had previously prepped beat reporters covering the meeting on the interests of the Court, paving the way for coverage that focused not just on what Fox cared to promote, but on the ministers' interests as well. In somewhat of a public relations coup for the Court, the following day's newspaper coverage highlighted the Court's budgetary proposal alongside Fox's justice system reform (see, for example, Torres 2000).

The budget continued to be a hot reform issue for the Court over the next two years. President Góngora pushed this issue as a regionwide concern for judicial independence, promoting the reform at both national con-

---

[27] In particular, Fox proposed to move the federal agrarian, labor, and administrative courts from the executive to the judicial branch. He also proposed to transform the Office of the Attorney General (PGR) into something like the United States' Justice Department and to create a new cabinet position on security and justice services (Lizárraga 2000).

[28] This brief study is entitled *Debilidad constitucional en el Presupuesto de Egresos del Poder Judicial de la Federación*. It may be obtained from the Judiciary's Office of Social Communication upon request (www.cjf.gob.mx/comsocial/default.asp).

ferences and a series of international meetings of high court judges.[29] In August 2002 the Congress formally began to consider the proposal; however, the initiative seems to have died during the early months of 2003. The results of the Court's efforts on the budgetary reform suggest that the ministers were successful in generating media coverage and eventually inducing Congress to formally consider the measure, but they have been incapable of generating institutional change.

Judicial Authority

The Supreme Court has promoted three significant reform initiatives since 1994 concerning its jurisdiction, constitutional review powers, and administrative authority. Its most successful proposal involved a plan to redefine the authority of the CJF. The initiative arose out of a conflict between the CJF and the Court over whether the CJF's administrative decisions could be challenged through *amparo* (Aranda 1998). The fundamental political issue involved whether the Supreme Court sat at the top of the judicial hierarchy.

In January 1999 the Court, hoping to clarify its position, sent a formal proposal to President Zedillo, who submitted the proposal to Congress with limited modifications. The changes adopted by Congress reduced the tenure of CJF counselors from six to three years and required that the current members of the CJF resign. More important, the reform changed CJF selection procedures. Originally the Court selected three of the seven counselors randomly from a list of qualified applicants. The reform granted the Court the power to select members of its choosing, giving it direct control over a majority of the judicial council's membership. This reform, which was driven largely by the Court's direct lobbying efforts, undoubtedly increased its administrative authority, allowing the ministers to create a fully coherent strategy for developing the federal judiciary.

The Court has also promoted a constitutional amendment granting it the power to initiate bills on subjects concerning the judiciary. The Court's preferred reform would grant it the ability to initiate laws related to federal jurisdiction and, predictably, the judicial budget. For two years beginning in 2000, President Góngora repeatedly called on President Fox and Congress to proceed with this change. On June 26, 2001, Góngora testified before the Chamber of Deputies' Special Committee on State Reform. He

---

[29] See the findings from the 7th Cumbre Iberoamericana de Cortes y Tribunales Supremos de Justicia, at www.cjf.gob.mx.

argued that because the Supreme Court best understands which of its institutions require reform, it ought to be granted the power to initiate its own laws. Such a power would not interfere with the authority of the other two branches of government, because Congress could always reject its proposals and the president could always veto them. Such a power, on Góngora's account, would simply allow the Court to ensure the consolidation of democracy.[30] PAN deputy Margarita Zavala introduced a constitutional reform in December 2003 that would grant the Court the power to initiate laws concerning the Organic Law on the Federal Judiciary; however, the proposal denies the ministers formal influence over the judicial budget. As of March 2004 the bill still sat in committee.

Clearly, the most well-developed reform measure on the Court's authority involves a drastic change in the Amparo Law. On November 17, 1999, President Góngora formally installed a seven-member commission charged with investigating how best to reform *amparo*.[31] The commission sought proposals from members of the legal community and the general public. The elaborate process of submission and review generated 1,430 distinct reform recommendations. Of the 247 articles in the Amparo Law, only 18 did not receive any attention by those making proposals. With the written proposals and the commission's own summaries in hand, the commission hosted eleven public conferences on the subject of the reform in cities around Mexico between March 3 and April 7, 2000.[32] These meetings were attended by 955 lawyers and included 89 presentations on the

---

[30] See Comunicado 421, Dirección General de Comunicación Social, Suprema Corte de Justicia de la Nación.

[31] The commission, designed to be as inclusive as possible, comprised judges, legal scholars, and attorneys. Minister Román Palacios chaired the panel. The members included Minister Silva Meza, José Ramón Cossío Díaz, César Esquinca Muñoz, Héctor Fix Zamudio, Javier Auijano Baz, Manuel Ernesto Saloma Vera, and Arturo Zaldívar Lelo de Larrea. At the time of their appointments, Cossío Díaz was chair of the Department of Law at the Instituto Tecnológico Autónomo de México; Esquinca Muñoz was general director of the Instituto Federal de la Defensoría Pública; Fix Zamudio was Emeritus Researcher at the Universidad Nacional Autónoma de México's Instituto de Investigaciones Jurídicas; Saloma Vera was a professor at the Instituto de la Judicatura Federal; and Zaldívar Lelo and Saloma Vera were in successful private practices. See review in Suprema Corte 2001.

[32] Conferences were held in Baja California, Guanajuato, Tlaxcala, Querétaro, Durango, Oaxaca, Chiapas, San Luis Potosí, Cuernavaca, Zacatecas, and Ciudad Victoria.

Amparo Law. By making this process so public, the Court attempted to build wide support for the initiative it would send to Congress.

On August 29, 2000, the commission submitted its formal reform to the ministers. In light of the monumental number of individual recommendations that the commission deemed reasonable, its members opted to draft an entirely new law. This draft was accepted by a majority of the Court and was subsequently sent to the president and both chambers of Congress for consideration.[33] The proposal's most controversial article involves a reconsideration of the famous Otero Formula, which limits the effects in *amparo* to the parties immediately involved in the suit. Although the proposal allows the Court to continue making decisions that establish only specific effects, it also provides a mechanism wherein the ministers may speak generally on the constitutionality of laws.[34] If the Supreme Court establishes a formal jurisprudential thesis on the unconstitutionality of a law or regulation, within thirty days it may set general effects by declaring this law or regulation unconstitutional, thereby abrogating the norm.

If adopted, this reform would clearly change the Court's ability to control constitutional meaning. Of course, it would also fundamentally alter the original formulation of *amparo*, rendering it much more similar to the individual constitutional complaint evident in many European systems of constitutional review (Stone Sweet 2001: 43–45). Despite some important criticisms from traditional Mexican legal scholars, the Court has been resolute in its search for this new power.[35] That said, Congress has never formally undertaken consideration of the Court's proposal, even after the grand effort to mobilize public support.

Efficiency

Many of the Court's reform measures affecting judicial efficiency have not required the assistance of the elected branches of government. Efforts such

---

[33] Minister Juventino V. Castro y Castro, himself a former public prosecutor, filed an important dissent on the proposal concerning the removal of the Ministerio Público. The Court has published this dissent in a book entitled *Réquiem para el Ministerio Público en el Amparo.*

[34] Proyecto, Arts. 232–235.

[35] In particular, Doctor Ignacio Burgoa, author of the definitive work on *amparo* and law professor to many of the ministers, filed his disagreement with the Supreme Court in November 1999. In response, Góngora made a point of publicly thanking Burgoa and welcoming further criticism. See Comunicado 303, Dirección General de Comunicación Social, SCJN.

as creating an internal network for employees of the federal judiciary, creating a school for the continuing education of members of the judicial career, and automating the storage of jurisprudential theses were all carried out within the judiciary itself. Other reform measures have required the participation of the elected branches.

In 1999 the ministers proposed a constitutional amendment to grant the Supreme Court the authority to distribute cases among its benches and the collegial circuit courts. The problem, as the Court saw it, was that it was being weighed down by *amparo* appeals upon which it had already defined jurisprudential theses. Without the authority to decide for itself on the kinds of appeals it could remit to the circuits, the Court would have had to appeal directly to Congress each time it believed there could be gains from a more efficient distribution of jurisdiction. The Court's efforts in this regard were successful.[36]

The Court and the CJF's efforts to create a greater number of judgeships and courts have necessitated a significant increase in the judicial budget. Such increases required congressional acquiescence and, accordingly, some reasonable justification from the judiciary. The number of federal courts has increased tremendously since the 1994 reform. Fix-Fierro reports that the federal judiciary added seventy-six district courts between 1995 and 2001 and eighty-three collegial circuit courts over the same period. Unfortunately for the Court's interests, the number of cases per judge has increased along with the increase in the number of courts, and thus there has not been an appreciable decrease in the average workload of federal judges (Fix-Fierro 2001: 41). That said, data compiled by the World Bank suggest that the Mexican federal judiciary may be making some progress, at least in civil *amparo* cases. Among the sixteen countries for which it collected sufficient data in 2000, Mexico ranked highest on its clearance measure, the ratio of cases disposed to cases filed in a particular year.[37] The sample included regional neighbors Costa Rica, Nicaragua, Ecuador, Peru, Argentina, and Colombia. While this result is encouraging, Schatz, Concha, and Magaloni Kerpel's contribution to this volume reminds us that the Mexican judicial system is multi-tiered and incredibly complex. Accordingly, we ought not to infer that all Mexican courts are becoming increasingly efficient. Moreover, insofar as these data are limited to civil *amparo* cases in

---

[36] See Ley Orgánica de la Federación, Art. 11, V.

[37] The data are stored at http://www4.worldbank.org/legal/database/. I can produce a table for July if requested.

2000, they do not even allow the inference that all federal courts are becoming more efficient.

Summary

Since 1994 the Mexican state has been building a healthier judiciary, and the ministers of the Supreme Court have played an important role in molding the substance of the process. Still, the ministers have had to address a number of obstacles that limit their ability to promote reform. First, they could not implement many changes without the support of the elected branches of government. Second, as judges they lacked a natural constituency from which they might have leveraged support for their proposals. Third, they lacked a mechanism through which they might directly communicate their proposals to the Mexican public.

I suggested above that the Court attempted to address these problems by directly lobbying members of the executive and legislative branches. They implemented a coordinated public relations effort designed to create accurate media coverage and promote reform messages to the public. Substantively, the Court has been relatively successful in its attempts to frame the reform debate. Although the ministers have been successful in some cases, two of their most important reform proposals—the Amparo Law reform and the budgetary reform—have not been enacted. Moreover, since the beginning of 2003, the Court has greatly reduced its public relations work. These patterns suggest a number of limitations on the ability of judges to affect the policy choices of elected officials on judicial institutions. I end with a discussion of these limitations.

CONCLUSIONS

The notion that judges might be able to shape the legislative or executive reform agenda adds a degree of substance to the theoretical literature analyzing why politicians might choose to build healthy judiciaries. The models I review above suggest two ways of understanding the incentive to reform. Still, they do not offer much more than general predictions about delegation. That is, it is not clear what either the insurance or credible commitment accounts have to say about the particular institutional choices that elected officials make. For many political scientists, perhaps this is not important. To understand the plausible incentive structures that induce delegation might be enough. Still, if we want to either accurately describe the world or understand how actual judicial institutions are created, we might do well to consider the role of judges in helping to shape the reform agenda. Of course, there are important limitations on the effects we might suspect judges to have.

Going Public

Clearly, part of the Supreme Court's program to influence judicial reform has involved an effort to explain its positions to the Mexican public. This part of the Court's public relations strategy is crucial insofar as the ministers do not represent a relevant set of constituents outside the members of the judiciary itself. If the Court wants leverage, it has to create it through developing wide public support for its interests. Yet this effort to generate support for particular reform measures may be limited by the Court's concomitant desire to present itself as fundamentally apolitical (see Silva Mena 2000). Making sales pitches directly to voters risks developing a politicized image, precisely what most judges, and certainly the ministers of the Mexican Supreme Court, would like to avoid. Moreover, strong appeals for coverage may invite negative as well as positive analysis. In fact, recent articles on the Mexican judiciary in the newspaper *Reforma* have focused on the rise of already high judicial salaries and questions regarding the judiciary's decisions to increase the number of judges and courts (see Fuentes 2003a, 2003b; Fuentes and Jiménez 2002).

Appeals to the public for support concerning judicial reform thus present judges with a compelling trade-off. Remaining inactive and largely detached from the political arena limits the ability of judges to create support for their reform efforts. However, running an aggressive public relations campaign risks developing an image of a politicized judiciary. The clearly noticeable reduction in the Supreme Court's public communication with the press since January 2003 suggests that the ministers may perceive that the marginal benefits obtained by continuing the Court's previously aggressive public relations work may now be outpaced by the marginal costs of appearing to be just another political branch of government.

A future model of this process might more systematically evaluate the conditions under which judges will be more likely to risk developing an overly politicized image. At first blush, one might hypothesize that such a choice will be nonlinear in the degree of public trust enjoyed by the judiciary. That is, we might expect judges who enjoy little trust and judges who are greatly trusted to engage in fairly aggressive public relations, while judges that fall somewhere in the middle might be expected to be more careful. The idea here, though underdeveloped, is that while judges who enjoy little trust likely will have less impact on public opinion, they will also have little to lose by generating a negative image. Judges who enjoy much trust might expect their appeals to be particularly persuasive. In contrast, judges who are neither significantly trusted nor distrusted might not expect to greatly affect public opinion and perceive the costs of appearing politicized to be significant. Clearly, both theoretical and empirical work on this issue is in order.

Political Responses

Successfully convincing executives or congressional delegates to consider reform proposals does not mean that those proposals will be enacted. Given their role as high-ranking officials of the state, we might expect high court judges to obtain relatively easy access to policymakers. Indeed, the Mexican Supreme Court seems to have been quite capable of directly lobbying the most important elected officials of the state. That said, the Court has failed to successfully promote both its *amparo* and budget reforms, issues on which it has expended considerable resources. In the end, it would appear that the ministers have been largely successful in obtaining desired results in areas that did not directly affect significant sources of legislative or executive power, especially power over the judiciary itself. The conflict with the CJF was largely an intra-judicial battle, not one whose result would affect important legislative interests. The same can be said for the reform to the Court's power to remit certain cases to the circuits.

In contrast, the Court has been fairly unsuccessful in its attempts to gain budgetary independence and expanded powers of constitutional review in *amparo*. Although reformers might expect gains from judicial independence on both the insurance and commitment accounts, they must trade independence off against judicial accountability (see Burbank and Friedman 2001: 14–17). Similarly, reformers must trade legislative authority off against judicial power. Granting the judiciary further budgetary independence would have surely created a more independent set of courts; however, it would have rendered those courts less accountable as well. Budgetary authority is an important check on the power of the judiciary, one that might be carefully guarded by institutional equals. Also, the Supreme Court has been increasingly willing to challenge the authority of both Congress and the president, especially since the 2000 transition (Finkel 2003). Enhancing the Court's powers in *amparo* might allow the Court to more efficiently control constitutionality. However, it would also mean that the Court could better control public policy. Without a pressing legislative reason for change, it is not surprising that the *amparo* reform has stalled.[38]

For future research, the point here is a simple one. All things equal, we might expect judges to be at least as successful as other powerful interest groups in shaping reform debates. However, we should expect judges to have less success influencing the outcomes of debates in areas that directly enhance their powers over public policy or affect the ability of the elected branches to hold judges accountable for their actions than in areas that do not.

References

Aguinaco Alemán, José Vicente. 1998. *El nuevo poder judicial de la Federación*. Mexico City: Suprema Corte de la Nación.

Aguirre Anguiano, Sergio. 2001. Comments by Minister Aguirre Anguiano at the 7th Iberoamerican Summit of Supreme Tribunals and Courts, November 28. Summarized in Comunicado 581, Dirección General de Comunicación Social, SCJN.

Aranda, Jesús. 1998. "Resurge la pugna entre la Corte y el Consejo de la Judiciatura," *La Jornada*, August 24.

Baker, Richard D. 1971. *Judicial Review in Mexico: A Study of the Amparo Suit*. Austin: University of Texas Press.

Burbank, Stephen B., and Barry Friedman. 2001. "Reconsidering Judicial Independence." In *Judicial Independence at the Crossroads: An Interdisciplinary Approach*, ed. Stephen B. Burbank and Barry Friedman. Thousand Oaks, Calif.: Sage.

Burgoa O, Ignacio. 1998. *El juicio de amparo*. 24th ed. Mexico City: Porrúa.

---

[38] An alternative explanation for the death of the *amparo* reform is that Mexicans have become accustomed to the current *amparo* legislation, and as such the Court's failure was a result of some sort of policy inertia. It was simply too costly to try to get the gigantic Amparo Law to move in a drastically different direction. If this argument is correct, then the entire 1994 judicial reform, which radically changed the structure of the federal judiciary and created a new constitutional action, would seem all the more puzzling. It would appear that inertia undermines all significant policy reforms, not just the Mexican *amparo* reform. We might ask how an inertia story would explain why the Court has been unable to win its fixed budgetary amendment. Has the Mexican public become too accustomed to the president submitting the budget? While the political account I suggest certainly may be falsified, its chief advantage is that it suggests a consistent explanation for a variety of the Court's policy successes and failures.

Buscaglia, Edgardo, and Maria Dakolias. 1996. "Judicial Reform in Latin America." Washington, D.C.: World Bank.

Camacho Guzmán, Óscar. 1999. "El presidente de México no tiene privilegios en la Suprema Corte," *Milenio Diario*, October 11.

Carranco Zúñiga, Joel. 2000. *Poder Judicial*. Mexico City: Porrúa.

Concha Cantú, Hugo Alejandro, and José Antonio Caballero Juárez. 2001. "Diagnóstico sobre la administración de justicia en las entidades federativas: un estudio institucional sobre la justicia local en México." Mexico City: Universidad Nacional Autónoma de México.

Domingo, Pilar. 2000. "Judicial Independence: The Politics of the Supreme Court of Mexico," *Journal of Latin American Studies* 32: 705–35.

Finkel, Jodi. 1997. "An Analysis of Mexico's 1994 Judicial Reform." Paper presented at the international congress of the Latin American Studies Association, Guadalajara, April.

———. 2003. "Supreme Court Decisions on Electoral Rules after Mexico's 1994 Judicial Reform: An Empowered Court," *Journal of Latin American Studies* 35 (November).

Fix-Fierro, Héctor. 2001. "Judicial Reform in Mexico: What Next?" Paper presented at the "Rule of Law Workshop: Legal and Judicial Reform in Developing Countries," Stanford Law School, February 26.

Fix Zamudio, Héctor, and José Ramón Cossío Díaz. 1995. *El poder judicial en el ordenamiento mexicano*. Mexico City: Fondo de Cultura Económica.

Fix Zamudio, Héctor, and Héctor Fix-Fierro. 1996. *El Consejo de la Judicatura*. Mexico City: Instituto de Investigaciones Jurídicas, Universidad Nacional Autónoma de México.

Fuentes, Víctor. 2003a. "Duplican salaries al Poder Judicial," *Reforma*, February 25.

———. 2003b. "Disfruta élite judicial de privilegios," *Reforma*, February 26.

Fuentes, Víctor, and Benito Jiménez. 2002. "Cuestionan crecimiento de poder judicial," *Reforma*, December 12.

Ginsberg, Thomas. 2002. "Economic Analysis of Constitutional Law: Economic Analysis and the Design of Constitutional Courts," *Theoretical Inquiries in Law* 3 (January): 49–85.

Hansen, John M. 1991. *Gaining Access: Congress and the Farm Lobby, 1919–1981*. Chicago: University of Chicago Press.

Kernell, Samuel. 1993. *Going Public: New Strategies of Presidential Leadership*. 2d ed. Washington, D.C.: CQ Press.

Landes, William M., and Richard A. Posner. 1975. "The Independent Judiciary in an Interest-Group Perspective," *Journal of Law and Economics* 18: 875–901.

Lizárraga, Daniel. 2000. "Negocian hoy reformas ministros y foxistas," *Reforma*, August 17.

Magaloni, Beatriz. 2003. "Authoritarianism, Democracy and the Supreme Court: Horizontal Exchange and the Rule of Law in Mexico." In *Democratic*

Accountability in Latin America, ed. Scott Mainwaring and Christopher Welna. New York: Oxford University Press.

North, Douglass, and Robert Paul Thomas. 1973. *The Rise of the Western World*. London: Cambridge University Press.

North, Douglass C., and Barry R. Weingast. 1989. "Constitutions and Commitment: The Evolution of Institutions Governing Public Choice in Seventeenth-Century England," *Journal of Economic History* 49 (December): 803–32.

O'Donnell, Guillermo. 1999. "Horizontal Accountability in New Democracies." In *The Self-Restraining State: Power and Accountability in New Democracies*, ed. Andreas Schedler, Larry Diamond, and Marc F. Plattner. Boulder, Colo.: Lynne Rienner.

Prillaman, William C. 2001. *The Judiciary and Democratic Decay in Latin America: Declining Confidence in the Rule of Law*. London: Praeger.

Schatz, Sara. 1998. "A Neo-Weberian Approach to Constitutional Courts in the Transition from Authoritarian Rule: The Mexican Case (1994–1997)," *International Journal of the Sociology of Law* 26: 217–44.

Silva Meza, Juan. 2000. "La Corte y la defensa de la constitución." In *Once voces*, ed. Alberto Aragón Bolado. Mexico City: Suprema Corte de Justicia de la Nación.

Solomon, Peter H., Jr. 2002. "Putin's Judicial Reform: Making Judges Accountable as Well as Independent," *East European Constitutional Review* 11: 117–24.

Staton, Jeffrey K. 2002. "Judicial Activism and Public Authority Compliance: The Role of Public Support in the Mexican Separation of Powers System." PhD dissertation, Washington University.

———. 2004. "Public Support and Spin: Judicial Policy Implementation in Mexico City and Mérida," *Journal of Comparative Politics* 37, no. 1 (October).

Stone Sweet, Alec. 2000. *Governing with Judges: Constitutional Politics in Europe*. Oxford: Oxford University Press.

———. 2001. *Governing UIT Judges: Constitutional Politics in Europe*. Oxford: Oxford University Press.

Suprema Corte de Justicia de la Nación. 2001. *Proyecto de la Ley de Amparo Reglamentaria de los Artículos 103 y 107 de la Constitución Política de los Estados Unidos Mexicanos*. Mexico City: Suprema Corte de Justicia de la Nación.

Torres, Mario. 2000. "Demanda SCJN 6% del presupuesto federal," *El Universal*, August 18.

Widner, Jennifer A. 2001. *Building the Rule of Law*. New York: W.W. Norton & Company.

Winkle, John W., III. 1990. "Judges before Congress: Reform Politics and Individual Freedom," *Polity* 22: 443–60.

PART IV

Crime and Society

CHAPTER 13

Citizen Access and Professional Responsibility in the Mexican Justice System

ROBERT M. KOSSICK, JR. AND RUBÉN MINUTTI Z.

Two of the most historically neglected dimensions of the Mexican legal system involve citizen access to justice and professional responsibility. Notwithstanding the emphasis that academic scholars and professional practitioners alike place on the importance of giving effect to the constitutional guarantee of the right to defend life, liberty, and property in an established tribunal, the practical reality is that access to justice has been circumscribed along economic, social, educational, linguistic, and urban-rural lines. Lacking the time, money, educational foundation, communications capabilities, alternative dispute resolution mechanisms, and/or pro bono services required to bring and see through claims or, more fundamentally, uphold the promise of due process, citizens have, in the past, been left with little choice but to contract the services of unlicensed intermediaries, forgo the pursuit of formal justice, suffer the consequences of a miscarriage of justice, or take the law into their own hands.

The concept of professional responsibility in Mexico has been similarly deficient. Here, the absence of transparency with respect to legal professionals and proceedings has combined with the existence of an impractical and ineffective framework of disciplinary rules and procedures to create a culture of nonaccountability and impunity. This outcome, to the extent it (1) obstructs the efficient administration of justice, (2) undermines confidence in legal institutions and actors, and (3) limits the ability of citizens to follow and understand the leading legal controversies of the day, has worked against the attainment of Mexico's growth and development objectives by facilitating a spirit of lawlessness and impeding citizen participation.

Mexico has undergone a substantial process of judicial modernization and reform over the course of the past ten years, as documented throughout this volume. This chapter identifies the scope and analyzes, from a comparative perspective, the effectiveness of the strategies and actions that have been spawned by this transformative dynamic with respect to the issues of citizen access to justice and professional responsibility. Basic descriptive statistics are provided where available, with an eye to bringing a degree of objective measurability to bear on issues and concepts that have traditionally been the object of more subjective analyses. These qualitative and quantitative observations are supplemented by the presentation of ad hoc policy recommendations geared toward strengthening citizen access and professional responsibility in the Mexican justice system. Pointing to the relatively incipient and still evolving nature of Mexico's overall program of judicial reform, this chapter concludes by arguing that access to justice and professional responsibility will be enhanced, respectively, by the passage of time and the continued toughening of transparency and accountability–oriented rules and procedures.

CITIZEN ACCESS TO JUSTICE

> *La garantía de acceso a la justicia es indispensable para alcanzar el fin de derecho. El Estado debe asegurar a todos los ciudadanos las mayores garantías, para que accedan a los servicios de justicia* [Guaranteed access to justice is essential to achieving the aims of the law. The State must guarantee its citizens' access to justice—SCJN (2001: 15).

> *Ultimately, institutions are not truly reformed unless they are accessible to citizens*—Ungar (2002: 187).

The Ideal and the Reality of Citizen Access to Justice

Article 14 of the Mexican Constitution guarantees individual citizens the right to defend their life, liberty, property, and possessions by means of trial in an established tribunal. In the event that a citizen facing criminal charges declines or is otherwise unable to secure counsel after having been instructed to do so, the courts of the Federal Judicial Power (Poder Judicial Federal, PJF) will, in the interest of assuring the defendant's adequate defense, designate a public defender (*Diario Oficial* 1917). In the Mexican context, where an estimated 40 percent of the population lives below the poverty line (CEPAL 2003), there is no constitutional-level presumption of innocence (CMDPDH 2002), and the guarantee of due process is loosely correlated with skin tone and/or social class (Reding 1995), these basic protections are crucial components of the overall formula for assuring access to justice.

Despite the apparent solidity of this framework, it is generally considered that Mexico's federal legal system has failed to protect the rights of the accused in an expeditious and gratuitous way. PJF defenders have traditionally been perceived as being overloaded, underpaid, incompetent, and corrupt (Yamin and Noriega García 1999). At times, court-appointed defenders have even been unlicensed (UNSR 2002). The U.S. Department of State's 2002 "Country Report on Human Rights Practices" for Mexico fleshes out some of the shortcomings associated with the work of Mexico's federal public defenders when it notes:

> While there is a constitutional right to an attorney at all stages of criminal proceedings, in practice, the authorities often do not assure adequate representation for poor defendants. Attorneys are not always available during the questioning of defendants; in some instances a defense attorney will attempt to represent several clients simultaneously by entering different rooms to certify that he was present although he did not actually attend the full proceedings. In the case of indigenous defendants, many of which do not speak Spanish, the situation is often worse. The courts do not routinely furnish translators for them at all stages of criminal proceedings, and thus defendants may be unaware of the status of their case (U.S. Department of State 2002: 25).

Andrew Reding (1995: 41) provides further insight into the deficient nature of the services provided by Mexico's public defenders when, referring to the findings of a National Indigenous Institute (INI) study, he notes that "courts had not sentenced 70% of indigenous prisoners, half of whom the authorities held in pretrial detention for longer than allowed by law." A 2000 study by Mexico's National Institute for Statistics, Geography, and Informatics (INEGI) involving the administrative capacity of Mexico's system of criminal justice reached the even more alarming conclusion that only one in ten of the country's criminal defendants is processed in accordance with the requirements of the law (*Reforma* 2002a).

The low quality of representation provided by federal public defenders has been perpetuated by the fact that Mexican law prohibits the filing of an *amparo* suit on the basis of deficient counsel. The federal government's failure to establish an effective mechanism for the purpose of assuring a minimum level of professional competence on the part of defenders has, in turn, been compounded by the frequency with which the intended beneficiaries of this supposedly gratuitous public service—the great majority of whom hail from the poorest segments of society—have been required to make irregular payments in connection with the receipt of legal assistance. Faced, accordingly, with the prospect of a prohibitively expensive private-sector lawyer or a government-furnished representative of doubtful effectiveness, many citizens have, in the past, elected to retain the services of unlicensed intermediaries popularly known as *coyotes*, *tinterillos*, or *gestores* (Monge 2002). This outcome increased the number of actors in the Mexican legal system who were both untrained and wholly outside of any type of professional oversight, thereby complicating Mexico's already challenged system of judicial administration and devaluing the constitutional ideal of universal access to justice.

In other cases, citizens have responded to the difficulty of obtaining access to justice and due process under law by simply taking matters into their own hands.[1] Some of the most galling incidents involved several high-profile mob lynchings in 2004. One involved three undercover federal investigators accused by an angry local mob of allegedly planning a child-napping; all three men were badly beaten for a lengthy period, and then two were killed by being burned alive.[2] The phenomenon of vigilantism—be it in the form of hostage taking, a lynching, or a politically motivated assassination[3]—underscores the nonresponsiveness of formal law and procedure to the real and increasingly complex needs of society at the same

---

[1] The increased willingness of citizens to take the law into their own hands is reflected in the fact that almost 60 percent of respondents in the *Encuesta Nacional sobre Cultura Política y Prácticas Ciudadanas* thought that unjust laws can be disobeyed (Secretaría de Gobernación 2001).

[2] A noncomprehensive electronic search of the Mexican newspapers *Reforma* and *El Norte* indicates that there were at least thirty-eight attempted lynchings between July 2002 and July 2003 in the Mexican states of Nuevo León, Hidalgo, Tlaxcala, Puebla, Estado de México, and Chiapas. Several of these resulted in death.

[3] As of March 2002, twenty-one high-level functionaries—on average, one every three weeks—had been killed in acts of politically motivated violence (*El Norte* 2002).

time that it communicates a socially dangerous message regarding the erosion of the rule of law in Mexico (*Reforma* 2002b; Peters 2002; *El Norte* 2002).

The Scope and Impact of Measures to Strengthen Citizen Access to Justice

Recognizing the failure of the system to guarantee, in practice, the public's access to justice, Mexico has undertaken a number of important remedial actions over the last ten years. Between 1994 and 2001, for example, Mexico overhauled the legal framework and institutional foundation associated with government-supplied counsel by introducing updated laws; establishing the Federal Institute of the Public Defender (IFDP) as an organ of the PJF vested with technical and operational autonomy (*Diario Oficial* 1998a); making the process of selecting public defenders and counselors more competitive (*Diario Oficial* 1998b); expanding the mandate of the public defender's office so as to encompass both penal and civil matters (*Diario Oficial* 1998a); loosening service eligibility requirements in the interest of enabling more citizens to qualify for legal assistance (*Diario Oficial* 1998c); improving public defender pay (*Diario Oficial* 2003);[4] and establishing an intragovernmental program geared toward securing the early release of indigenous prisoners from federal detention facilities.[5]

These actions have been accompanied by a concerted effort to augment both the human resources and physical infrastructure of the IFDP. The combined number of defenders (penal) and counselors (civil) increased in per capita terms (from one IFDP lawyer for every 178,715 citizens to one IFDP lawyer for every 155,255 citizens) between 1999 and 2002 (SCJN 2002).[6] This rise in the number of criminal and civil representatives has permitted the IFDP to take on a growing number of new matters. In this latter connection, the combined number of penal and civil matters accepted by the IFDP increased by 27 percent between 2000 and 2003 (table 13.1).

---

[4] The monthly salary for which a federal public defender is eligible ranges from a low of 25,787.06 pesos to a high of 85,858.60 pesos.

[5] The early release program was established in 1999 pursuant to an agreement made between the National Human Rights Commission (CNDH), INI, the Office of the Attorney General (PGR), the Interior Ministry (Gobernación), and the IFDP. Its operation has resulted in the expedited processing of over three thousand prisoners between 1999 and 2003 (U.S. Department of State 2002).

[6] These criminal and civil representatives serve 164 cities and towns distributed across a nationwide network of twenty-four delegations (IFDP 2003).

Table 13.1. Human Resources and Intake at the Federal Institute of the Public
Defender (IFDP)[a]

Year	Number of Staff Lawyers		New Matters Accepted	
	Public Defenders	*Counselors*	*Public Defenders*	*Counselors*
2003[b]	545	121	138,150	22,206
2002	509	114	133,143	17,739
2001	488	105	122,372	10,610
2000	447	88	118,020	8,432
1999	472	73	108,909	991
1997	n.a.	n.a.	46,369	n.a.
1996	n.a.	n.a.	57,083	n.a.
1995	n.a.	n.a.	49,274	n.a.

Sources: SCJN Informes, CJF Information Requests.
[a] And its antecedent, the Unidad de Defensoría del Fuero Federal.
[b] Through May 2003.
n.a. = not available.

The final and perhaps most important remedial measure that has been
taken with an eye to improving the service delivered by Mexico's federal
public defenders focuses on the nature and quality of the training received
by IFDP representatives. The centerpiece of this initiative is the Plan Anual
de Capacitación y Estímulos (Annual Training and Incentive Plan) (*Diario
Oficial* 1998a; SCJN 2002). Under this program, IFDP lawyers are able to
receive ongoing training with respect to subject matter that is closely related to the needs and reality of the citizens they serve, including, for example, federal criminal law, indigenous law, administrative law, and *amparo*. While voluntary, program participation is an important factor in the
overall process of determining which defenders and counselors advance
(*Diario Oficial* 1998a).

Pending Developments and Recommended Reforms

The foregoing measures have done much to strengthen the quality and
availability of government-supplied legal services in Mexico. This outcome
is positive in that it is helping to transform the concept of universal access
to justice from fiction into reality. Without meaning to minimize the significance of these developments, however, it is important to note that there
are two additional measures that could be taken for the purpose of extend-

ing the benefits of professional legal representation to an even larger number of citizens. The first of these involves the prohibition of unlicensed—and hence unaccountable—legal representatives (the so-called *coyotes*). To this end, an initiative requiring that representation in federal criminal matters be provided exclusively by licensed attorneys is currently pending before the Congress (*Gaceta Parlamentaria* 2001). The second measure entails the opening up of alternative sources of subsidized and/or free legal counsel. Actions that Mexico could take in this regard include the introduction of a U.S.-style *pro bono publico* requirement for licensed attorneys, the modification of the social service regime so as to allow for the meaningful involvement of law students in IFDP cases (under the responsible supervision of licensed public defenders) (*Diario Oficial* 1998a),[7] and the creation of "social justice" clinics within the country's law schools.[8] The latter two measures would present Mexico with pure upside insofar as they provided law students with valuable practical experience, benefited the indigent segment of society, and facilitated the development of a culture of "*civismo.*"

PROFESSIONAL RESPONSIBILITY IN THE MEXICAN JUSTICE SYSTEM

> *The legal profession in Mexico might be one of the worst in the world insofar as disciplinary procedures are concerned*—UNSR (2002: 25).

Mexico's System of Regulatory and Disciplinary Oversight with Respect to the Legal Profession

Scant attention has been paid historically to the professional conduct of Mexican judges and lawyers. The reasons for this situation are several and include the absence of a competition-based culture of accountability engendered by the executive branch's long period of domination over the judiciary and the legislature, the persistence of an inadequate regulatory framework, and the nonexistence of effective oversight mechanisms. The

---

[7] Students who elect to conduct their mandatory period of social service with the office of the federal public defender are accorded an auxiliary status and prohibited from intervening in substantive functions.

[8] Mexico could, to this end, formally create a status similar to that of the U.S. "student attorney." These individuals would work under the direct supervision and professional responsibility of attorney-clinical professors.

legacy of this hands-off approach to the regulation and oversight of judges and lawyers is manifest in (1) the fact that no federal judge or magistrate has ever been sanctioned for corruption,[9] despite the United Nations Special Rapporteur's recent finding that an estimated 50 to 70 percent of the federal judiciary is corrupt (UNSR 2002; Hughes 1995);[10] (2) the near absolute lack of demand on the part of Mexican attorneys for legal malpractice insurance coverage; and (3) the paucity of publicly disseminated information regarding clients' rights (in their capacity as consumers of legal services) and the disciplinary histories of lawyers and judges (notwithstanding the Ministry of Education's (SEP) obligation to publish information pertaining to developments that bear on the status of an attorney's license) (*Diario Oficial* 1945).

Realigning the Regulatory/Disciplinary Framework to Better Respond to Mexico's Evolving Political, Economic, and Social Reality

There has been growing recognition over the past ten years of the symbiotic relationship between the inculcation of a strong sense of professional responsibility and ethics within the legal community and the attainment of efficiency and certainty in the administration of justice. The measures that Mexico has introduced, consistent with this recognition, to better align the regulation and oversight of judges and lawyers with the needs of its rapidly evolving social, economic, and political reality are set out in the following sections.

Background Screening

One step taken in furtherance of this realignment involves screening the backgrounds of federal judicial candidates with an eye to identifying (and eliminating from further consideration) those individuals with criminal

---

[9] Interview with Lic. Luz del Carmen Herrera Calderón, executive secretary for discipline of the Federal Council of the Judiciary (CJF), Mexico City, June 2003; telephone interview with Lic. Adrián de la Rosa Cuevas, director of the Complaints and Denouncements Unit, Office of the Contraloría Interna of the Tribunal Federal de Justicia Fiscal y Administrativa, Mexico City, June 2003 (stating that no TFJFA magistrate had been disciplined for corruption between 1970 and 2002).

[10] Included within this estimate is the case of Ernesto Díaz Infante, the SCJN minister who in 1988 fled the country after being charged with accepting a half-million-dollar bribe to pressure a lower court magistrate to release a rich Mexico City businessman convicted of raping and murdering a child.

records (*Diario Oficial* 1995). This development is significant given the ease with which individuals had previously been nominated for and appointed to judicial posts with little if any meaningful review of their personal and professional records. This type of screening does not, however, extend to prospective lawyers. That is, unlike the moral character and fitness evaluation and criminal background check that their counterparts in the United States must pass prior to obtaining a law license, there are no official inquiries into the backgrounds of Mexican law students prior to their entry into the profession.

Asset Monitoring and the Management of Client Funds

In a related vein, the patrimonial declaration process applicable to all public servants—including judges and magistrates—has been strengthened. Prior to 2000, the patrimonial declarations required of judicial officials in Mexico were manually prepared, filed, and archived. This system did not rise to the level of its potential given the way it (1) conduced to data modification, error, and/or loss, and (2) complicated the efficient realization of asset monitoring and corruption-detection activities. The 2001 launch of the now obligatory "Declaranet" (http://www.declaranet.gob.mx) eliminates many of these problems by centralizing within the Ministry of Public Service (SFP), automating, and disintermediating the patrimonial declaration process. More importantly, in creating an accurate and searchable database, the Declaranet system provides government auditors and the public at large with an effective oversight resource. Mexican attorneys in private practice are not, alternatively, required to maintain a separate account (similar to the Interest On Lawyers Trust Account, or IOLTA, program of a U.S. attorney) for the purpose of preventing the comingling of client and counselor funds. The lack of clear and mandatory requirements in this regard works against the best interests of clients by making it difficult—if not impossible—to detect and/or remedy the misappropriation of funds entrusted to lawyers.

Transparency

The final measure that bears on the regulation and oversight of judges and lawyers involves the issue of transparency. The rigidly closed information policy maintained by Mexico throughout the better part of its modern history, together with the absence of basic verification and accountability mechanisms, produced a condition of information asymmetry characterized by the distortion of political and economic decision-making processes, de minimis levels of citizen participation, and widespread corruption. Alejandro Junco de la Vega, president and general director of one of the largest media groups in Mexico, captured the essence of the traditional state of transparency when he noted that Mexican citizens know more about the intimate details of Bill Clinton's sex life than the assassination of Donaldo Colosio (*Infosel Financiero* 2002).

This situation began to change in 2001 when Mexico, as part of its on-going drive to strengthen public institutions, embraced a principal-agent paradigm for conceptualizing the government-constituent relationship (Stiglitz 1987). A key outgrowth of this reorientation consisted of the promulgation of landmark legislation (the Law on Transparency and Access to Public Government Information, or LFTAIPG) establishing the federal government's obligation to disclose and the citizenry's right to request public-sector information of a nonreserved character (*Diario Oficial* 2002).[11] Viewed from the perspective of the PJF, an increased quantity of better-quality information can strengthen oversight capabilities, serve as a check against the high index of judicial corruption occasioned by the absolute secrecy shrouding the resolution of cases, and breed an understanding of the rule of law that is based, as former U.S. Supreme Court Justice William O. Douglas would say, less on "awe" and more on "confidence" (Douglas 1949). The Mexican Supreme Court (SCJN) directly acknowledges the importance of transparency in strengthening the administration of justice and the protection of individual rights when it states, "the duty of providing timely, truthful, and objective information constitutes the most adequate means of ratifying the PJF's commitment to society" (SCJN 2001: 13).

Notwithstanding the positive objectives and aspirations of the LFTAIPG, the combination of a deeply entrenched culture of nontransparency, weak administrative will, deficient request and delivery mechanisms, and opaque physical infrastructure[12] makes its implementation within the PJF problematic.

---

[11] This law builds on and gives meaning to the amendment that was made to Article 6 of the Mexican Constitution on December 6, 1977. The right of citizens to ask for and obtain information that is not manipulated, incomplete, or false was, furthermore, elevated to the level of an individual guarantee by two legislative acts of the Supreme Court (SJF 1996, 2000).

[12] Judicial transparency is physically compromised by the way in which the public is commonly separated from the space designated for the conduction of proceedings by a plastic or glass partition.

PJF information disclosed pursuant to the requirements of Article 7 of the LFTAIPG has, for the most part, been of low quality. Typical information shortcomings include the lack of temporal depth (thus precluding any understanding of how the PJF's performance is changing through time), the over-aggregation of categories or classification concepts (thus impeding a detailed understanding of the PJF's performance with respect to a particular issue), and/or the presentation of information in an unclear format (see table 13.2 for a summary of obstacles encountered). Consider, in this last connection, the salary and compensation information published on the SCJN's Web page in supposed satisfaction of its obligations under Article 7 of the LFTAIPG. The coded information contained in this example—considered in conjunction with the way in which the PJF's failure to provide an interpretive key prevents citizens from understanding which figure corresponds to the salary and compensation of a SCJN minister, tribunal magistrate, or district judge—fails to satisfy the LFTAIPG standard that disclosed information facilitate public "use and comprehension" (*Diario Oficial* 2002).

Table 13.2. Summary of Access to Information Obstacles

Obstacle
• Information disclosed lacks temporal depth.
• Information disclosed pursuant to over-aggregated categories and concepts.
• Information disclosed in coded form.
• Unidad de Enlace staff unprepared and/or uninformed.
• Unidad de Enlace staff willing to disregard established procedures in favor of informal solutions.
• Manual, nonautomated request and delivery mechanisms.
• Absence of obligation to dedicate human resources to task of extracting and furnishing an answer can be used as pretext for effectively withholding information, even if same exists, where (1) form of data sought does not conform to official registration and archiving practices and (2) requesting party resides far from Unidad de Enlace.
• Nature and scope of successor agency obligations unclear.
• Answers delivered in untimely manner.
• Answers incomplete or otherwise nonresponsive.
• Answers inconsistent with information available through other federal sources.

Table 13.3. Summary of Information Request Outcomes

Entity	Folio Number	On-line Request Mechanisms	Date of Request (dd/mm/yr)	On-line Delivery Mechanism	Timely Answer	Informal Discussion Suggested	Responsive Answer
SCJN	14	No	01/07/03	Yes	No	No	Partially
SCJN	25	No	03/07/03	Yes	Yes	No	Yes
SCJN	49	No	11/07/03	Yes	Yes	No	Yes
CJF	6	No	07/01/03	No	No	Yes	Partially
CJF	14	No	08/01/03	No	No	Yes	Partially
SEP	65803	Yes	11/08/03	Yes	Yes	No	No[a]
SEP	65903	Yes	11/08/03	Yes	Yes	No	No[a]
SEP	66003	Yes	11/08/03	Yes	No	No	No
TFJFA	None	Yes	24/07/03	Yes	No	No	Yes

[a] These decisions were overturned on administrative appeal.

Table 13.6. Disciplinary Actions Involving Federal Judges and Magistrates for Violations of Article 131 (XI), LOPJF or Article 47, LFRSP, 1995–2002

Suspensions		Dismissals		Disqualifications	
Judges	_Magistrates_	_Judges_	_Magistrates_	_Judges_	_Magistrates_
18	9	2	5	5	6

Source: CJF Information Requests.

Initial experience with regard to the filing of citizen information requests has not been much more promising. In contrast to the online information request and delivery mechanism used by the dependencies and entities of the Federal Public Administration (APF) and in violation of the LFTAIPG requirement that information be put at the "public's disposition pursuant to either local or remote means of electronic communication" (*Diario Oficial* 2002), information requests pertaining to the PJF must be made and retrieved in person at the Unidad de Enlace of the appropriate organ or entity. This type of manual approach can be highly disorganized, despite the fact that the LFTAIPG has been in effect for months. Officials at the Federal Tribunal for Fiscal and Administrative Justice (TFJFA) did not, for example, even realize that the entity had a Unidad de Enlace the first time this author attempted to make an information request. More disturbingly, the use of manual, in-person information request and delivery mechanisms elevates the probability that public servants will attempt to dispose of information requests via "informal" or "extra-official" methods—an outcome that is fundamentally inconsistent with both the spirit and terms of the LFTAIPG—or otherwise erect bureaucratic obstacles to the surrender of requested information. As table 13.3 indicates with respect to this latter issue, the only proposals received by this author to participate in an "informal" discussion regarding the contents of an information request correspond to those requests submitted via nonautomated methods.

The final problem encountered in connection with the request and/or delivery of information involves the fact that the LFTAIPG and its accompanying Reglamento do not obligate the Unidades de Enlace of governmental organs or entities to assign human resources to the task of sifting through and extracting information that is technically available but not exactly in the form requested by an investigator. This shortcoming in the law is problematic insofar as it can, in certain cases (for example, where distance makes it impossible for a requesting party to go, physically, to the administrative headquarters of the government organ or entity in question for the purpose of reviewing files), be used as a pretext to effectively withhold information that could and should otherwise be disclosed.

Setting aside the request and delivery mechanism issues, other information request–related problems that have been experienced to date involve the timeliness, accuracy, consistency, and utility of the government's substantive responses. In five out of nine cases, initial responses were delivered after the prescribed period (see table 13.3). Upon being in receipt of final answers, it subsequently became clear that information provided was, with inappropriate frequency, inconsistent with data published in SCJN annual reports or PJF databases, incomplete, and/or unclear. Although the fact that most initial responses were not challenged precludes a more definitive statement, it is worth noting that incomplete disclosure motivated by the desire to prevent the PJF from being cast in a less than positive light would have violated the interpretive presumption of openness established by Article 6 of the LFTAIPG.

Transparency is a relatively novel concept in Mexico and, as the preceding observations suggest, the country generally, and the government specifically, are going through an adjustment process characterized by resistance and uncertainty (*Reforma* 2003a, 2003b, 2002c). Former SCJN Minister Juventino V. Castro y Castro put this point into historical perspective by noting that the novelty of the guarantee of information is so new that "it is not possible to find clear and precise antecedents in our history" by which to better understand the issue (SCJN 2002: 859).

Going forward, there are several steps the federal government can take to overcome its reluctance to disclose information. The first focuses on transparency at the level of the legal system and involves the PJF's development and implementation of automated information-requesting mechanisms, as required by the LFTAIPG.[13] The second step centers on transparency at the level of the legal controversy and entails the amplification of the public's right of access to information regarding *pending* legal matters (save those that have been placed under a gag order or are otherwise reserved).[14] This latter action—in breaking with Mexico's contradictory policy of making legal proceedings open to the public (in theory) (*Diario Ofi-*

---

[13] Despite the statements made by representatives of PJF Unidades de Enlace to this author regarding their plans to move information request and delivery mechanisms online by the end of 2003, such mechanisms, based on information and communications technology (ICT), were, at the time of this chapter's preparation, still unavailable.

[14] Article 8 of the LFTAIPG requires that only final PJF decisions be made available to the public. Contrary to the fact that this provision extends to all PJF courts, the only final PJF sentences that are presently available to the public pertain to those of the SCJN. In the United States, by way of contrast, any person is able to request and review the file on any matter (assuming that it has not been sealed, expunged, or otherwise placed under a gag order)—pending or resolved—either in person, at the court clerk's office, or, in some cases, via the Internet. Chile offers its citizens a degree of access to information regarding pending and/or resolved legal matters similar to that found in the United States.

cial 1932), on the one hand, and restricting courtroom and case file access to parties with an accredited interest, on the other—would bring PJF transparency practices into line with those followed by the world's most efficient and rule of law–oriented legal systems. Mexican transparency expert Jorge Islas reinforces this idea when he remarks, "If there is a true volition on the part of the PJF, then they will open not only the final sentences but also all the writs and other resolutions generated by judges in the course of their work" (*Reforma* 2002d). Such an outcome would strengthen oversight capabilities with respect to the PJF (as well as those lawyers who practice in federal courts) and deepen public understanding of the procedural and substantive dynamics associated with the most controversial issues of the day (Lederer 1999). Armed with this information, Mexico's citizens and merchants would finally be in a better position to (1) assure accountability within the legal sector, and (2) participate in the administrative and legislative debates that bear on their interests as stakeholders in the nation's future.

Accountability

While on balance the foregoing measures have positively impacted the regulation and oversight of judges and lawyers, they do not go as far as they could and should in terms of driving meaningful change with respect to the values and practices of the Mexican legal system. Nowhere is this more evident than in the disciplinary framework applicable to members of the legal profession in Mexico.

The current patchwork of laws and regulations that collectively govern the conduct and performance of Mexican judges and lawyers is overly general, impractical, and lacunae-ridden. Mexico's approximately 40,000 attorneys and 801 federal judges and magistrates are, under the present system, criminally or administratively liable for the acts and omissions set forth in table 13.4.

Consistent with the long-standing tradition of focusing disciplinary efforts on less serious and more easily resolved violations (in lieu of investigating and prosecuting larger-scale and more serious conduct)—and despite the substantial rhetoric currently heard in Mexico about "reforming the state," establishing "good government," reducing corruption, and introducing accountability—little tangible progress has been made over the course of the past eight years in terms of suspending or removing the 50 to 70 percent of the federal judicial population that the United Nations special rapporteur identified, on the basis of information supplied by the Mexican legal community, as being corrupt. The number of judges, magistrates, and

Table 13.4. Principal Disciplinary Regulations Applicable to the Federal Judiciary and Lawyers

Subject	Conduct	Law
Judge	Compromising independence or impartiality of judiciary	Art. 131, LOPJF
Judge	Providing counsel to parties with pending matters	Art. 225, CPF
Judge	Abuse of authority	Art. 8 (I), LFRASP
Judge	Overt acts of corruption	Art. 8 (XII), LFRASP
Judge	Conflict of interest	Arts. 39–42, CFPC; Art. 47 (XIII), LFRSP
Judge	Failure to recuse	Arts. 47–53, CFPC
Judge	Admission of malicious or improper filings	Art. 57, CFPC
Public defender	Negligent representation	Art. 233, CPF
Law student/ lawyer	Untitled practice of law	Arts. 29, 30, 62, Ley Reglamentaria 5; Art. 250, CPF
Lawyer	Failure to apply all professional knowledge for benefit of client	Arts. 33, 64, Ley Reglamentaria 5
Lawyer	Failure to guard secret or privileged communications	Art. 36, Ley Reglamentaria 5, Art. 210, CPF
Lawyer	Professional negligence, incompetence	Art. 2615, Código Civil
Lawyer	Conflict of interest	Art. 232, CPF
Lawyer	Making false statement, engaging in dilatory tactics	Art 231, CPF

Note: CPF, Código Penal Federal; CFPC, Código Federal de Procedimientos Civiles; LOPJF, Ley Orgánica del Poder Judicial Federal; LFRASP, Ley Federal de Responsabilidades Administrativas de los Servidores Públicos.

other judicial servants who have been suspended or removed for having incurred some type of administrative responsibility has remained relatively static (see tables 13.5 and 13.6 [the latter is presented with table 13.3]).

Table 13.5. Disciplinary Actions Involving Federal "Judicial Servants," 1995–2002

	Suspensions	Dismissals	Disqualifications	Average Combined Number of Suspensions, Dismissals, and Disqualifications
2003	5	5	1	3.6
2002	5	5	2	4.0
2001	11	2	2	5.0
2000	5	4	1	3.3
1999	4	2	2	2.6
1998	4	1	2	2.3
1997	6	5	n.a.	n.a.
1996	8	6	5	6.3
1995	n.a.	1	n.a.	n.a.
Total	48	31	15	n.a.

Source: SCJN Informes.
n.a. = not available.

In a similar vein, Mexican attorneys rarely, if ever, become the object of administrative complaints or legal malpractice actions (Mears 2003). While the Ministry of Education's effective refusal to deliver information regarding the number of Mexican attorneys who have had their *cédulas profesionales* either suspended or terminated for disciplinary reasons in the years 1970, 1980, 1990, and 2000 precludes the making of a statement of absolute certainty, anecdotal evidence suggesting the accuracy of the preceding assertion abounds. Considering the United Nations special rapporteur's observation that the discipline-driven revocation of attorney licenses involves a "complicated procedure" that is "never implemented" (UNSR 2002: 26), the Ministry of Education's unwillingness to deliver *cédula* revocation information likely reflects the simple fact that no attorney licenses were revoked during the targeted years. This inference is borne out by practical experience. One of the authors of this chapter has for several years practiced as a foreign legal consultant in Mexico, yet he has yet to meet or learn of any Mexican attorney who has had his/her license suspended or terminated for disciplinary reasons. By way of sharp contrast—and using information that could be freely obtained within a matter of minutes over the Internet—4,269 (out of an active total of 1,231,888) U.S. lawyers were reprimanded, suspended, or disbarred in 2002 (ABA 2003).

The reasons underlying this situation of weak lawyer accountability are threefold. First, the absence of an obligatory, specific, and publicly disseminated set of professional standards and responsibilities makes clients less likely to seek redress for the delivery of poor-quality legal services. Second, this fact is compounded by the criminal nature of the regulations most relevant to matters of attorney discipline. Faced with the prospect of having to meet the higher burden of persuasion associated with a criminal—as opposed to a civil—action, many clients determine that the benefits to be derived from a malpractice suit are outweighed by considerations of time, cost, and inconvenience. The third reason stems from the nonexistence of mandatory bar associations with disciplinary committees empowered to hear and rule on matters of professional misconduct. Unlike the situation in the United States, where disciplinary complaints can be quickly and cheaply brought at the administrative level, the only grievance action available in Mexico entails the initiation of a resource-consuming legal proceeding. The latter two factors—really two sides of the same coin—are, to the extent they leave Mexican citizens inclined to forgo valid malpractice claims, contrary to the objectives of strengthening the administration of justice and improving public confidence in the legal system. The unjust nature of this situation is captured by Héctor Fix-Fierro when he states:

> The most significant problem in the relationship between lawyers and their clients is that the latter are almost completely at the mercy of the former.... [Lawyers] are largely not accountable, and there is little recourse against a disloyal, negligent, or dishonest lawyer (Fix-Fierro, this volume).

Recommended Reforms

Several measures can be taken, prospectively, to strengthen Mexico's system of judicial and attorney oversight. The first entails decentralizing the regulation of lawyers by transferring the responsibility of administrative and disciplinary oversight from the Education Ministry to an interrelated network of national and state-level bar associations (similar in concept to the way that bar associations function as administrative agencies for the judicial branch at the state level in the United States).[15] This proposed measure—consistent as it is with both the spirit of *"federalismo"* that currently prevails in Mexico and pan-Latin trends—would transform Mexico's extant bar associations from voluntary and essentially ceremonious organizations into entities with mandatory memberships and real disciplinary authority (Mantellini González 1995). Furthermore, the implementation of this measure could give local consumers of legal services a greater stake in assuring the effective administration of justice at the same time that it reduced the spatial scope of the nationwide license to practice that is presently conferred on Mexican lawyers. The latter potential outcome— inasmuch as it prevented a Chiapas attorney, for instance, from practicing in Nuevo León without having been first admitted to the state bar or otherwise authorized to appear in a *pro hac vice*–type capacity—would mitigate against the risk of malpractice or negligence occasioned by attorney ignorance of the way in which the process of political and legislative decentralization is making federal and state laws increasingly dissimilar.

The second measure that can be taken to strengthen the regulatory framework applicable to the conduct and performance of lawyers involves the introduction of a comprehensive and mandatory code of professional responsibility.[16] Such a code could provide clear and pragmatic guidance with respect to conduct that is inadequately addressed at present, including, for example, *ex parte* communications, advertising, specialization, client fund management, referrals, fee splitting, and so on. Such a measure should, importantly, be accompanied by the introduction of a mandatory and detailed code of ethics for the federal judiciary.[17] The speedy imple-

---

[15] This is not a new concept in Mexico, the same basic idea having been presented at the First Annual Congress of Federal District Judges held in Mexico City in 1999. Though no progress has been made in this regard, the federal judges attending the conference proposed the creation of a decentralized organ with the authority to uphold attorney ethics and to intervene in the face of abusive litigation tactics (*Reforma* 2002e).

[16] The Mexican Bar Association does have a comprehensive "Código de Ética Profesional." The value of this code of ethics is diminished, however, by the voluntary nature of membership in the association (BMA 2003).

[17] The National Center for State Courts has been working actively with the Instituto de Estudios Judiciales del Tribunal Superior de Justicia del Distrito Federal to introduce a code of ethics for federal district judges and magistrates (NCSC 2003). Mexico's states have, pursuant to the objectives set at the

mentation of the latter part of this measure, considered in light of the way in which public perceptions regarding the role and relevance of Mexico's judges and magistrates continue to change, is more important than ever.

The final corrective measure that can be taken consists of improving the quantity and quality of information disseminated regarding (1) the professional disciplinary record of judges and lawyers, and (2) the rights of and grievance procedures available to citizen consumers of legal services. Taking U.S. experience again as an example, this measure could be realized by distributing information concerning professional license suspensions and terminations (together with a brief yet illustrative account of the facts that gave rise to the disciplinary action), the duties and obligations of attorneys and judges, and grievance filing procedures via a combination of traditional and virtual public-sector and private-sector channels.

The implementation of the foregoing measures could, to the extent they resulted in increased levels of accountability, lead judges and attorneys to conduct their professional affairs with an enhanced degree of caution and care. This outcome, in turn, could improve the administration of justice and strengthen citizen confidence in Mexico's legal system.

CONCLUSION

It is evident from the preceding discussion that the program of judicial reform launched almost ten years ago in Mexico is beginning to have a positive impact on citizen access to justice and on professional responsibility. Evidence of this progress is easy to come by. There are today a greater number of better-paid and better-trained federal public defenders and counselors than at any other time in Mexico's history. Shifting, alternatively, to the subject of professional responsibility, recent reforms have had the effect of increasing the quantity and quality of information available with respect to both the personal histories of judges and magistrates and the progression of legal controversies.

Notwithstanding the positive initial results that have been achieved within the relatively short time span of just a few years, it is also clear from the preceding discussion that Mexico's program of judicial reform is a work in progress. That is, a fundamental determinant of the success that Mexico encounters in maximizing the benefits of its judicial reform program involves the government's capacity for further strengthening citizen

---

Segunda Reunión Nacional de Tribunales de Justicia de los Estados, also determined to develop and implement a code of ethics (*Reforma* 2002f).

access to justice and professional responsibility. Key issues that remain to be taken up and/or acted upon in this regard include (1) the introduction of access-enhancing pro bono requirements for registered attorneys; (2) the development of social justice clinics within the nation's law schools; (3) the innovation of additional means of protecting citizens—particularly the poor and the indigenous—from wrongful detentions, forced confessions, and ineffective representation; (4) the conduction of investigations into the prior civil, criminal, and administrative records of prospective attorneys; (5) the disintermediation of LFTAIPG-based information request and delivery mechanisms; (6) the amplification of the scope of judicial branch transparency so as to encompass both prejudgment filings and rulings and the actual monitoring of legal proceedings; (7) the promulgation of a more consumer-friendly and practical framework for regulating the attorney-client relationship; (8) the creation and implementation of a mandatory code of ethics for the judiciary; and (9) the improvement of Mexico's record with respect to the disciplining of judges and attorneys.

The realization of this agenda for additional reform is no small task. While it is easy to change rights and duties by legislative fiat, the reprogramming of culturally determined and temporally reinforced institutional and personal values and practices in furtherance of the ideal of enhancing access to and accountability in the justice system is a much more difficult challenge. The patient maintenance of the positive aspects of the current program of judicial reform (that is, funding, training, and so on), together with the satisfactory rectification of the justice system's extant deficiencies, will, it is finally submitted, facilitate the elimination of the perceptions of ineffectiveness and impunity that erode citizen and investor confidence in Mexico's legal institutions and actors and will contribute to the establishment of a culture of justice that is organically responsive to the country's past experience, present needs, and future aspirations.

References

ABA (American Bar Association). 2003. "Survey on Lawyer Discipline Systems." At http://www.abanet.org/cpr/discipline/sold/sold-home.html.

BMA (Barra Mexicana, Colegio de Abogados). 2003. "Código de Ética Profesional." At http://www.bma.org.mx/.

CEPAL (Comisión Económica para América Latina y el Caribe). 2003. "Panorama social de América Latina 2002–2003." At http://www.eclac.cl/prensa/noticias/comunicados/4/12984/presentacionPS2002-2003jao.pdf.

CMDPDH (Comisión Mexicana de Defensa y Promoción de los Derechos Humanos). 2002. *Análisis y propuestas de reformas mínimas para el fortalecimiento del sistema de procuración y administración de justicia en México*. Mexico: Impresos Escorpión.

Diario Oficial de la Federación. 1917. "Constitución Política de los Estados Unidos Mexicanos," February 5.

————. 1932. "Código de Procedimientos Civiles para el Distrito Federal," September 1.

————. 1945. "Ley Reglamentaria del Artículo 5 Constitucional, Relativo al Ejercicio de las Profesiones en el Distrito Federal," May 26.

————. 1995. "Ley Orgánica del Poder Judicial de la Federación," May 26.

————. 1998a. "Ley Federal de Defensoría Pública," May 28.

————. 1998b. "Bases Generales de Organización y Funcionamiento del Instituto Federal de Defensoría Pública," November 26.

————. 2002. "Ley Federal de Transparencia y Acceso a la Información Pública Gubernamental," June 11.

————. 2003. "Acuerdo por el que se Autoriza la Publicación de los Sueldos, Prestaciones y Demás Beneficios de los Servidores Públicos del Poder Judicial de la Federación," February 26.

Douglas, William O. 1949. "Stare Decisis," *Columbia Law Review* 49: 735–54.

El Norte. 2002. "Servidores públicos: bajo la sombra de la muerte," March 17.

Gaceta Parlamentaria. 2001. "Iniciativa de Reforma al Código de Procedimientos Penales y a la Ley Orgánica del Poder Judicial de la Federación." Cámara de Diputados del H. Congreso de la Unión, November 21. At http://gaceta.diputados.gob.mx/Gaceta/58/2001/nov/20011122.html.

Hughes, Sallie. 1995. "Law and Disorder," *Mexico Business*, April, pp. 8–12.

IFDP (Instituto Federal de Defensoría Pública). 2003. "Delegaciones." At http://www.ifdp.cjf.gob.mx/Delegaciones/default.asp.

Infosel Financiero. 2002. "Es estado de derecho base para pacto nacional," July 4.

Lederer, Fredric. 1999. "The Foundation for the Virtual Courtroom: Today's Developing Technologies." National Center for State Courts. At http://www.ncsc.dni.us/NCSC/TIS/TIS99.

Mantellini González, Pedro. 1995. "The Role of Bar Associations in Judicial Reform." In *Judicial Reform in Latin America and the Caribbean*, ed. Waleed Malik et al. Washington, D.C.: World Bank.

Mears, Rona. 2003. "The International Lawyer's Creed: A Code of Ethics for International Lawyers." Haynes and Boone, LLP. At http://www.haynesandboone.com/briefings/mears7.tm.

Monge, Raúl. 2002. "La justicia mexicana: corrupción," *Proceso*, July, pp. 35–38.

NCSC (National Center for State Courts). 2003. "Ética Judicial." National Center for State Courts. At http://www.ncsc.com.mx/etica_judicial.htm.

Peters, Gretchen. 2002. "In Mexico Hostage Crisis, Seeds of Unrest," *Christian Science Monitor.* At http://www.csmonitor.com/2002/0715/p01s04-woam.html.

Reding, Andrew. 1995. *Democracy and Human Rights in Mexico.* New York: World Policy Institute.

Reforma. 2002a. "Rebasan denuncias al sistema judicial," June 24.

———. 2002b. "Alertan sobre riesgo de ingobernabilidad," October 4.

———. 2002c. "Rechazan magistrados abrir el poder judicial," August 28.

———. 2002d. "Piden apertura judicial total," June 23.

———. 2002e. "Inicia segundo congreso de jueces," June 3.

———. 2002f. "Planean tribunales un código de ética," April 13.

———. 2003a. "Reconoce IFAI incertidumbre en dependencias," August 13.

———. 2003b. "Detectan temor en apertura," July 4.

SCJN (Suprema Corte de Justicia de la Nación). 2001. *Informe de Labores.* Mexico: Poder Judicial Federal.

———. 2002. *Informe de Labores.* Mexico: Poder Judicial Federal.

Secretaría de Gobernación. 2001. *Encuesta Nacional sobre Cultura Política y Prácticas Ciudadanas.* Mexico: Secretaría de Gobernación.

SJF (Seminario de Justicia de la Federación). 1996. "Garantías individuales (derecho a la información). Violación grave prevista en el segundo párrafo del artículo 97 constitucional. La configura el intento de lograr la impunidad de las autoridades que actúan dentro de una cultura del engaño, de la maquinación y del ocultamiento, por infringir el artículo 60 también constitucional," 513.

———. 2000. "Derecho a la información. La Suprema Corte interpretó originalmente el artículo 60 constitucional como garantía de partidos políticos, ampliando posteriormente ese concepto a garantía individual y a obligación del Estado a informar verazmente," 72.

Stiglitz, Joseph. 1987. "Principal and Agent." In *The New Palgrave: A Dictionary of Economics,* ed. John Eatwell et al. New York: Macmillan.

Ungar, Mark. 2002. *Elusive Reform, Democracy and the Rule of Law in Latin America.* Boulder, Colo.: Lynne Rienner.

UNSR (United Nations Special Representative). 2002. U.N. Document E/CN.4/2002/72/Add.1 (58th Sess., Provisional Agenda Item 11(d), at 25). New York: United Nations.

U.S. Department of State. 2002. *2002 Human Rights Report.* Washington, D.C.: The Department.

Yamin, Alicia Ely, and María Pilar Noriega García. 1999. "The Absence of the Rule of Law in Mexico: Diagnosis and Implications for a Transition to Democracy," *Loyola Los Angeles International and Comparative Law Journal* 21: 467–95.

CHAPTER **14**

Unweaving the Social Fabric: The Impact of Crime on Social Capital

PABLO PARÁS

Today we understand only a portion of the impact that crime exerts on a society. Most research focuses exclusively on crime's economic or psychological consequences.[1] The economic costs are the sum of resources that a society loses to crime or invests to protect against it, and these are often taken as the social cost of crime.[2] No matter how immediate or obvious, this perspective is limited. The other common cost perspective is the psychological, in which the focus falls on the individual rather than on the society. But again, this perspective is limited, as it only looks into the wounds and scars suffered by the victims, and often only focuses on the most violent or traumatic types of crime, which affect only a very small percentage of victims.[3]

Much less attention has been devoted to assessing the other consequences of crime. In Mexico, these other consequences appear to reach well beyond crime's economic impacts or physical and psychological impacts

---

[1] In this essay I use the terms "costs" and "consequences" interchangeably.

[2] The most commonly researched are direct economic costs, such as the loss of property, and indirect costs, as for individual protection. Projections from ICESI's 2001 victimization survey estimated that the direct economic cost of crime in Mexico that year was nearly 1 percent of the nation's total gross domestic product (http://www.warebox.net/icesi-org-mx/images/pdf/Inseguridad_01.pdf). Another set of costs, often referred to as the "social costs of crime," are the resources that a society invests in combating, preventing, or managing crime.

[3] I am speaking here in a quantitative, not a qualitative, sense. The latter is more properly the focus of a psychological perspective. It is not my intent to treat different types of crime or victims as comparable cases.

on victims. Since the mid-1990s, Mexican society has been in the grip of a collective sense of insecurity. As noted elsewhere in this volume, this sense of public insecurity has led to decreased reporting of crimes, individual and mob vigilantism, and mass protests demanding action by public authorities. In this chapter, I explore the impact that crime has on how individuals form their opinions, define their preferences, and shape their attitudes and behavior. In so doing, I seek to enhance our understanding of the erosion of social capital that accompanies crime and the ways in which this social degradation and undermining of community represents a substantial cost in Mexico.

Using public opinion surveys, this chapter focuses specifically on the social consequences of crime in Mexico City. Mexico's capital city offers a useful case study for two reasons. On one hand, its incidence of crime is alarmingly high: surveys report that in any given twelve months, one of every four adults in Mexico City is the victim of an assault. Nearly half of the city's population (45 percent) report that a close relative has been the victim of a crime (survey results from Data OPM, TC time series).[4] Further, the threat or use of violence represents 55 percent of all crimes, and half of these involve the use of a firearm (http://www.warebox.net/icesi-org-mx/images/pdf/Inseguridad_01.pdf). Presently there are few surveys that allow comparison between victims and nonvictims, and that allow for measurement of key social constructs such as interpersonal trust, networking, membership, fear, well-being, and institutional trust.[5] The survey instrument used in this research was specifically designed to measure each of these constructs and was tested using confirmatory factor analysis. Relations between constructs are shown using causal analysis, assigning temporal precedence to the condition of being a victim (victimization experience).

CRIME AND SOCIAL CAPITAL

Much research has been directed at identifying the causes of crime. Theories of crime causation include choice theory, trait theories, social structures theories, social process theories, conflict theory, and integrated theories (Siegel 2000). However, apart from assessing the economic or

---

[4] Data OPM is a private polling firm in Mexico City. It conducted a longitudinal survey, the "Termómetro Capitalino" (the capital's thermometer, or TC), referred to in this chapter as the TC times series.

[5] The focus of these studies has been, rather, to compare respondents' positions on issues such as the death penalty and use of weapons, for example.

psychological impacts of crime, relatively little has been done to determine other types of consequences. The relationship between social capital and crime has been addressed in recent work, but the focus of most of the literature gives causal priority to the former. That is, crime itself has not been researched in depth as an important determinant of social capital. My research examines this line of causation. "Social capital" is useful to my work for three reasons: there is comprehensive research on how to measure it; it can be an effective indicator (proxy) of the well-being of a society; and there is extensive work on its consequences, including its impacts on democracy, development, and economic growth.

There is ample debate about the scope and measurement of social capital (see Grootaert 1997). For the purposes of my research, I use a combined definition of social capital in order to incorporate both the cognitive and structural aspects of the concept. Social capital is defined as "the capability that arises from the prevalence of trust in a society" (Fukuyama 1997: 26) and "any aspect of informal [or formal] social organization that constitutes a productive resource for one or more actors" (Coleman 1994: 170). The first part of the definition includes the cognitive dimension of the term; the second incorporates the structural aspect of social capital while emphasizing its productive quality, a key component because it gives the term greater social relevance.

Although there is consensus about the need to identify the origins of social capital, there is substantial debate about how social capital is formed within a society.[6] According to Krishna (2002: 19) there are three competing hypotheses on the causal placement and theoretical importance of the concept of social capital. The first is the "social capital thesis," presented in the work of those who explain most other social phenomena as being causally related to social capital. The "structuralists" or "institutionalists" present the opposite argument, treating social capital as a residual of structures. "The structuralist rejoinder against social capital picks up on what is perhaps the weakest point of the social capital thesis: the issue of origins. How is social capital brought into being, and why do levels of social capital vary from one society to another?" (Krishna 2002: 14–19). The intermediate position asserts only marginal causality. The model I test identifies crime as one of the possible factors that explain the levels of social capital, and it

---

[6] Early theorists such as de Tocqueville, Durkheim, and Weber are relevant sources for the idea of social capital (see Healy and Côte 2001: 40). However, Bourdieu, Coleman, and Putnam "have generally been credited with introducing it to the theoretical debate" (Baron , Field, and Schuller 2000: 1).

assumes that social capital will have important effects on individual opinions, perceptions, preferences, and behavior.[7] Of greater importance for my research design are the dimensions and key forms of social capital that explain its importance and operationalization.

Groeter and Bastelaer effectively illustrate the dimensions of social capital on two continuums: micro to macro, and structural to cognitive. The first is self-explanatory; for the second they offer the following definition:

> *Structural* manifestation refers to the more visible and perhaps more tangible aspects of the concept, such as local institutions, organizations and networks among people, which can be set up for cultural, social, economic, political, or other objectives. *Cognitive* social capital refers to more abstract manifestations, such as trust, norms, and values, which govern interactions among people (Grootaert and Bastelaer 2002: 342).

According to Woolcock (2001: 13), the most common sources of capital are bonding, bridges, and linkages. Healy and Côte offer concise definitions of these terms:

> Bonding refers typically to relations among members of families and ethnic groups. Bridging social capital refers to relations with distant friends, associates and colleagues. Linking refers to relations between different social strata in a hierarchy where power, social status and wealth are accessed by different groups (Healy and Côte 2001: 42).

It seams plausible to assume that crime can undermine these three sources by affecting a victim's future trust of others. Trust thus plays an important role in my research because it may be the strongest theoretical

---

[7] Further discussions of the concept of social capital and its origin are beyond the scope of this work. Most recent works on the topic include a review of its evolution, shapes, forms, and applications. The use of the concept has been the focus of recent research over a range of topics: from the nature of capital and education to development and democracy; from community to nation; from quantitative to qualitative. Perhaps the most salient is the work of Putnam (1993, 2000). Important treatments of the concept and how it is measured can be found in Grootaert 1997; Grootaert and van Bastelaer 2002; Portes 1998; Woolcock and Narayan 2000; Krishna 2002.

link between crime and social capital and because it is a crucial component of it. Fukuyama (1997: 26) offers a definition of trust that has clear social implications for the three basic forms presented above. He defines trust as the "expectation that arises within a community of regular, honest and co-operative behavior, based on commonly shared norms, on the part of other members of the community." Putnam notes that trust carries many desirable spillover effects:

> Other things being equal, people who trust their fellow citizens volunteer more often, contribute more to charity, participate more often in politics and community organizations, serve more readily on juries, give blood more frequently, comply more fully with their tax obligations, are more tolerant of minority views, and display many other forms of civic virtues (Putnam 2000: 136).

Although my work tests a complex causal model, one of my key objectives is to see if trust is indeed being affected by personal victimization experiences.

Smith uses a different but related dependent variable: misanthropy. He finds that "recent negative life events (including criminal victimization and violence, health problems, unemployment, and traumas in general) increase misanthropy" (Smith 1997: 184). He also finds that misanthropy is higher in persons living in large cities. Although misanthropy is not part of my work, I suspect it correlates with trust, with causal precedence on the latter. Putnam reaches a similar conclusion: "victims of crime and violence—wherever they live—express reduced social trust" (Putnam 2000: 138). Further, at the aggregate level there is evidence suggesting a correlation between crime rates and measures of social capital. "Higher levels of social capital, all else being equal, translate into lower levels of crime" (Putnam 2000: 308). But again, further research is needed on the issue of causality and effect size.

Looking at homicide rates and controlling by "fear of crime," Putnam concludes that "the causal arrows runs, at least in part, from social capital to crime" (2000: 309). While this finding is important, it is limited for two reasons: homicides account for only a very small fraction of criminal activity, and Putnam's social capital index is structural rather than cognitive. My research includes both the (direct and indirect) experience of crime and the fear of crime. It is also more comprehensive in terms of the crimes it covers, and it includes structural and cognitive constructs of social capital. An additional difference is that Putnam reaches his conclusion using aggregate-level data, while I work with individual-level differences. One of the most relevant research approaches for work on this topic, which also draws its conclusions from individuals rather than aggregates, is that of Brehm and Rahn. These authors note that one characteristic of social capital is that it is "an aggregate concept that has its basis in individual behavior, attitudes, and predispositions." Further, "it is not a 'community' that participates or builds trust, but the people who comprise that community who belong to civic organizations and acquire positive feelings towards others" (Brehm and Rahn 1997: 1000–1003). We should expect that our personal experiences with crime would affect what we think, what we do, and how we do it. It is very plausible to expect that a community, depending on its levels of trust or networks, would prevent or allow crime (a buffering effect). However, that does not necessarily mean that crime is caused by the lack of social capital. Social structure theories of crime give emphasis to the economic indicators of a community as they "view disadvantaged economic class position as a primary cause for crime" (Siegel 2000: 190). It is very likely that economic strata will correlate with social capital stocks, but crime is more likely to be caused by a depressed economic position than by a failure to attend PTA meetings. It may be that correlations between crime and social capital are spurious as they share a common causal antecedent. Brehm and Rahn make a similar point, referring to the correlation between trust and democracy and noting how both could share a causal antecedent: economic development (1997: 1008). They find that victimization undermines interpersonal trust, although the effect size is minimal compared to other substantive or demographic predictors (1997: 1012). I expect a larger effect size for Mexico, where the incidence of personal victimization is high.

Mexico City provides an ideal setting for this research for three reasons. First, as noted above, the incidence of direct personal victimization experiences—one in four adults—is high, and indirect experiences with crime are at least double that figure (survey results from Data OPM, TC time series). Second, there is evidence that the levels of social capital, at least in their principal structural components, have not changed significantly over time.[8]

---

[8] Based on a comparison of the 1990 and 2000 data for Mexico in the World Values Survey conducted by the University of Michigan. There are mixed results on the Social Capital indicators. While structural aspects (formal participation) have remained the same and perceptions of live satisfaction and happiness have increased, indicators of interpersonal trust have decreased significantly.

And third, most of the seminal and most salient work on social capital has been based on research from the developed world; systematic analysis using data from Mexico will help to confirm or challenge these established theories.

Much scholarly research has demonstrated the positive link between social capital and democracy (see Baron, Field, and Schuller 2000: 39). Although this link will be used in the construction of my causal model, it is largely beyond the scope of my research except to note that social capital has external and internal effects on democracy. The external effects can be summarized as a mean of social action in which "individual and otherwise quiet voices multiply and are amplified" (Putnam 2000: 338). The internal effect is concisely defined as a "school for democracy" (Putnam 2000: 339). Both kinds of effect are particularly important in Mexico's transition to and/or consolidation of democracy. Krishna, whose work is focused on the developing world, finds that there is a need to activate social capital in order to make it more productive; stocks are not enough. In her words, "some form of agency is usually necessary for converting social capital into flows of benefits" (2002: 12). Although social capital stocks, measured by group membership, appear to be low in Mexico (survey results from Data OPM, TC time series), it maybe crucial to find ways to "detonate" them in favor of development. If crime rates harm or disable a community's available social capital stocks, then the cost of crime can include significant harm to the successful development of a society.

Figure 14.1 presents my model, which gives causal priority to crime as it impacts the cognitive aspects of social capital, directly and indirectly (using "feeling unsafe" as a proxy for fear). The figure also shows that the system of social capital (comprising cognitive and structural variables) has a direct impact on perceptions, opinions, preferences, and behavior, which can be important to democracy and development.

My general hypothesis is that individuals who have personally experienced victimization are less likely than nonvictims to possess or generate social capital. Stated more specifically, my research tests the following hypothesis:

- Individuals with personal victimization experiences are less likely than nonvictims to (a) trust other individuals, (b) trust institutions, (c) be members of formal organizations, (d) report good personal health, and (e) prefer democracy.

Figure 14.1. Causal Model of the Impact of Crime on Social Capital

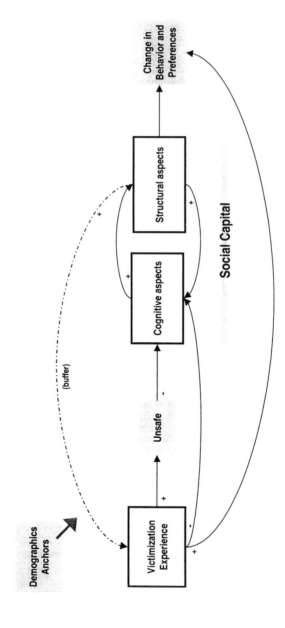

Source: Data OPM: Termómetro Capitalino Time Series.

METHODOLOGY

My unit of analysis is the individual. I examine 1,006 respondents to a survey conducted on April 12–13, 2003. These respondents constitute a representative sample of residents of Mexico's Federal District who are eighteen years of age or older. The survey is wave 17 of a longitudinal survey called the "Termómetro Capitalino" (the capital's thermometer, or TC). The TC is one of a few surveys—perhaps the only one—in Mexico that do not use any kind of quota control for sample selection.[9] The results have a margin of error of +/–3 percent at a 95 percent confidence level.

A personal victimization experience is defined as being the victim of a crime within the preceding twelve months. It has been argued that questions about crime experiences may be unreliable because the respondent must rely on memory, more so when the questions refer to a relatively long timeframe. I concur. From 1997 to 2001, I myself was a victim of crime on three different occasions. I can recall each with precision, but I cannot provide an accurate date or other crucial details for these events. It can be argued that the more traumatic the event, the more likely a person will remember it (incorrectly) as a more proximate incident. Yet it can also be argued that the event will be more likely to be remembered more clearly over time.

My research does not intend to provide a precise figure for the frequency with which crimes occur, the "cifra roja" as it is referred to in victimization surveys. Rather, my interest is in comparing victims to nonvictims. Even though operationalizing this variable can overestimate the incidence of crime, I am confident that it will identify those who at some point (usually within the timeframe of my questions) were victims of crime. A comparison of my the time series for the relevant questions reveals that the survey results are internally consistent (within-series consistency). Figure 14.2, which reports the personal victimization experiences of

---

[9] The Termómetro Capitalino, conducted by Data OPM, uses the list of electoral sections in the Federal District as its sample framework. Sample selection is a multi-stage process. The first stage is systematic random selection of electoral sections, with probability of selection proportional to the number of registered voters for each section. A total of 101 sections were chosen using this procedure. Ten interviews are conducted in each selected section. Two residential blocks are randomly selected in each section, and five households are selected within each of these, using a systematic random procedure. Finally, one person within the household is selected using the last-birthday method.

Figure 14.2. Direct Victimization Experience in the Federal District, 1999–2003

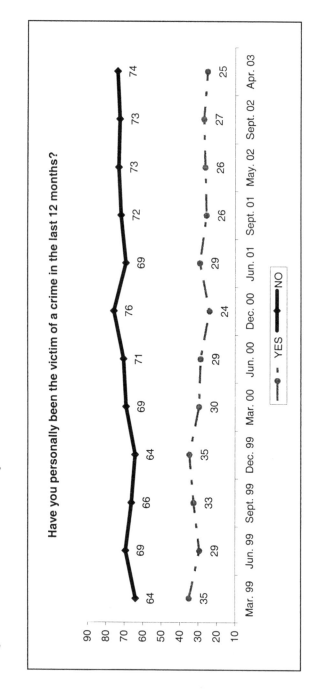

Have you personally been the victim of a crime in the last 12 months?

Mexico City residents over a four-year period, suggests that crime is slowly decreasing. The figure also confirms that the question asked has been consistent over time. A twelve-month period was chosen as optimal because that timeframe provides a sizable sample of "victims" (25 percent of the total sample). In addition to the internal consistency of the TC survey results, the survey was compared with research conducted by other polling firms in order to obtain an external evaluation of the survey's reliability.[10]

I anticipated that some individuals would report more than one victimization experience for the timeframe; the variable reflects this by assigning a higher value to such individuals. I expected to find similar behavior among individuals who had experienced either indirect or direct victimization. Indirect victimization experience is defined as having at least one household member and/or close family member who was a victim of a crime within the preceding twelve months. It is very possible that indirect victimization experience is overreported, given that it relies on indirect, and thus less precise, information. A variable labeled UNSAFE was constructed as a proxy for "fear." This variable was measured by asking respondents how safe/unsafe they feel in different places. These three variables—direct victimization, indirect victimization, and feelings of being unsafe—were combined to reflect the Victimization Experience System (VES). For this research, the "social capital" measure was based on a combination of the following variables: interpersonal trust (thick, thin, and trustworthiness), formal networks (membership), and institutional trust.[11]

Reliability Tests for Constructs

The measurement model that was tested includes fourteen variables. Five are single-item variables; the rest are latent variables (multi-item constructs).

---

[10] For example: ratings of the performance of Mexico City Mayor Andrés Manuel López Obrador, as reported in the newspaper *Reforma*, were 77 percent approve, 17 percent disapprove (Grupo Reforma, January 18–21, 2003). Wave 17 of DATA OPM-TC found similar numbers in April 2003: 77 percent approve and 12 percent disapprove.

[11] The survey, which was conducted in a single weekend, had a refusal rate of 24 percent. It is important to mention that no recalls were conducted. This may impact the measurement of social capital stock because individuals with greater trust (a key component of social capital) may be more likely to respond to a survey (thus the results may overestimate social capital). But again, my purpose is not to measure the amount of social capital but to assess individual differences.

The multi-item constructs are the following: Bridging (thin trust), Change in Behavior, Unsafe, Formal Networks (membership), Health, Indirect Victimization Experience, Institutional Trust, Preference for Democracy, and Trustworthiness. A confirmatory factor analysis was conducted to test the internal and external consistency of the construct. Table 14.1 shows that these constructs are reliable and internally consistent. The right-most column shows the number of items from the original survey that were excluded because of an unsatisfactory factor loading or lack of external consistency. Items included in the constructs display the following three characteristics: a loading of at least 0.3, internal and theoretical consistency, and external reliability. The description of items, transformation of variables, and factor loadings are presented in the addendum to this chapter.

Table 14.1. Results of Confirmatory Factor Analysis for Constructs

Construct (alphabetically)	No. of Items	Alpha	No. of Items Not Included
Bridging (active thin trust)	7	.73	0
Change in Behavior (stop doing activities)	7	.80	0
Unsafe (proxy for fear)	6	.74	3
Formal Network (membership)	10	.68	1
Health (well-being)	6	.76	0
Indirect Victim Experience	2	.55	0
Institutional Trust	10	.84	2
Preference for Democracy	2	.41	1
Trustworthiness	2	.41	0

Path Analysis

To test for the expected relationships between variables, a causal analysis model was constructed using the PMOD 5.0 computer program. The model includes fourteen variables—the nine constructs presented in table 14.1 plus the following single-item variables: Gender, Age, Socioeconomic Level (SEL), Bonding (thick trust), and Direct Victimization Experience. The results of the path analysis are represented in figure 14.3. The model has a root mean-squared error (RMSE) of 0.059. The RMSE, the most commonly used measure for assessing the overall "fit" of a model, is used to accept or reject a model based on how well it fits the collected data. The lower the RMSE, the better the fit. Values lower than 0.10 are considered to represent a good fit; at 0.059, our model has a very good fit.[12]

The numbers in figure 14.3 show the size of the effect of one variable on another. The arrows show the direction of the effect. The model is constructed from a correlation matrix in which all correlations are statistically significant. A positive number (effect size) shows a direct relationship between variables, and a negative number reflects an inverse relationship. The effect size represents how much the dependent variable will change for each one-unit increase in the predicting variable, with everything else held constant. In this case, for each one-unit increase in INDIRECT Victim, UNSAFE will increase 0.13.

The model shows multiple relationships. In the previous example, UNSAFE is caused by the INDIRECT Victim. However, UNSAFE also affects several other variables. For example, individuals with higher values for fear (UNSAFE) display lower values for BRIDGING (thin trust). For this example, the model shows an arrow from UNSAFE to BRIDGING, with a value of −.13 (an inverse relationship).

The model shows both direct and indirect effects. Directs effects are represented in figure 14.3 by arrows leading from one variable to another, as discussed above. An indirect effect is the impact that one variable has on another through one or more other variables. Indirect effects are multiplicative. Table 14.2 shows the total effect that Fear (UNSAFE) has on Institutional Trust. This total effect is −.198, a sum of an indirect effect of −.13 and an indirect effect of −.068. For the purpose of this essay, I only discuss direct effects. However, the reader should keep in mind that any effect size discussed could be larger if the indirect effects were taken into account.

FINDINGS

In order to facilitate the following discussion, I will refer to the causes or impacts of two systems within the model: the Victimization Experience System (VES) and the Social Capital System (SCS). The Victimization Experience System (VES) is composed of Direct Victimization Experience, Indirect Victimization Experience, and the UNSAFE construct. Direct Victimization Experience (DV) and Indirect Victimization (IV) Experience both have a small positive impact on UNSAFE. However, the path coefficients

---

[12] The chi square (198.52 with 59 degrees of freedom) significance test is not included in the text because it is not relevant for large samples like the one used in this study.

Figure 14.3. Path Diagram

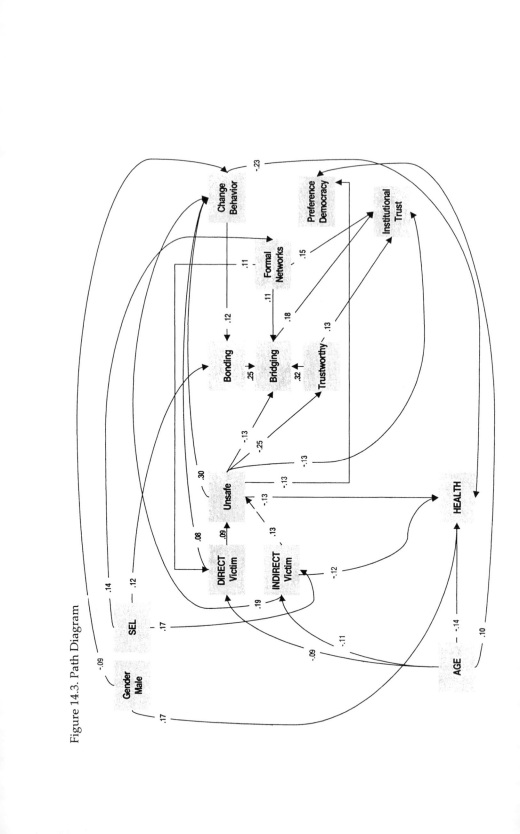

Table 14.2. Total Effect of UNSAFE on Institutional Trust

Type of Effect	Path	Multiplicative	Effect Size
Direct	UNSAFE → Institutional Trust	-.13	-.130
Indirect	UNSAFE →Trustworthy → Institutional Trust	-.25 x .13	-.033
Indirect	UNSAFE →Bridging → Institutional Trust	-.13 x .18	-.023
Indirect	UNSAFE →Trustworthy → Bridging → Institutional Trust	-.25 x .32 x .18	-.014
Indirect	UNSAFE→ Change in Behavior → Bonding → Bridging → Institutional Trust	.30 x .12 x .25 x .18	.002
	Total Effect		-0.198

are lower than expected ($\rho = 0.09$ and $\rho = 0.13$, respectively). There are two possible explanations for this. One involves the construction of the DV and IV predictors and the fact that their distribution is not normal.[13] The other is that, in Mexico City, the condition of being a victim, regardless of how we measure it, is no longer functioning as a variable but rather as a constant. This would imply that *being a victim* is embedded in the condition of living in the Federal District.

Indeed, we may find a very high incidence of persons reporting being a crime victim once in their lifetime, or even once in the last three, five, or ten years. If this worst-case scenario is even partly true, it means that the social consequences of being a victim are present to some degree in all residents of Mexico's capital city. An additional finding is that higher-income individuals report greater exposure to crime (a path coefficient of $\rho = 0.17$ from SEL to Indirect Victim). Younger individuals also run a higher risk of exposure to crime ($\rho = -0.09$ and $\rho = -0.11$ going from Age to DV and IV, respectively).

The Social Capital System (SCS) includes the three cognitive variables/constructs (Bonding, Bridging, and Trustworthiness) and the structural one (Formal Networks/Membership). Figure 14.3 shows that all of the variables within the system have an impact on Bridging. Those who have greater trust in family members (Bonding) have more trust in others, such as co-workers and neighbors ($\rho = 0.25$). The same is found for Trustworthiness ($\rho = 0.32$). It is interesting to note that people who are more active, as measured by membership in formal networks, are also more likely to trust others ($\rho = 0.11$). This finding, which has been reported in much of the literature, is an important component of a reinforcing process that supports the reproduction of social capital stocks. The following discussion addresses the way in which these two systems interrelate and what impacts they exert on other key social constructs.

Although DV and IV do not have a direct significant effect on SCS, the condition of feeling unsafe appears to exert a significant impact on the *thinner* levels of trust. Feeling unsafe has a negative effect on both Trust-

---

[13] For Direct Victimization Experience, 75 percent of the sample report no crime experience; 16 percent report one crime incident, 6 percent report two such incidents, and 3 percent report three or more. This presents the problem of an irregular (non-normal) distribution; range restrictions also reduce the construct's power. The same issue may be occurring with Indirect Victimization Experience.

worthiness ($\rho = -0.25$) and Bridging ($\rho = -0.13$). This means that feeling unsafe undermines the trust we have in others.

Bonding is not at all affected by the Victimization Experience System. This is something I expected given the Mexican context, a cultural environment with relatively strong nuclear family relations. This may well be the greatest asset of Mexican society, at least in terms of social capital theory.

We find no impacts of the VES on the structural component of the SCS in the direction hypothesized. Interestingly, the model reports a small causal relationship between Formal Networks and Direct Victimization Experience. This derives from the composition of the Formal Networks construct, which reflects active membership in ten different types of organizations (see the addendum for details). This causal link means that individuals who are more active—with "activity" measured in terms of organizational memberships—are victims in proportionately greater numbers than those who are less active. This result can be viewed as an "exposure dilemma," which can also take a toll on social capital. A more active a person is, the more likely he or she will be exposed to crime when going out in public to fulfill membership obligations. If this pattern holds over time, it can have important social consequences; it could increase the likelihood that the "most active" individuals will become inactive in order to reduce their exposure to personal risk.

More research is needed to assess this and other findings presented here. A good approach for future research would be to conduct panel studies that track how individuals change over time.

One of the most strongly affected constructs is Institutional Trust, in large part because of the close conceptual relationship between interpersonal trust and institutional trust. Institutional Trust experiences significant positive impacts from Bridging, Trustworthiness, and Formal Networks ($\rho = 0.18, 0.13$, and 0.15, respectively). Thus the more an individual trusts others and the more he or she is an active member of formal organizations, the higher the institutional trust that person will have. An important and direct negative effect is the impact that Unsafe has on Institutional Trust ($\rho = -13$). The VES also impacts Institutional Trust indirectly (an indirect negative effect through the SCS).

If the citizenry's trust in institutions is a desired component in a democracy, then one important consequence of crime is that it adversely impacts democracy (mainly through the Fear proxy, the condition of feeling unsafe). Another direct negative outcome of feeling unsafe is its impact on one's preference for democracy (ρ = −0.13). The more a person feels unsafe, the more likely it is that he or she will favor an authoritarian regime. Another interesting finding is that older individuals appear to prefer democracy in higher proportions than do younger people (ρ = 0.10). As discussed above, younger individuals are victims in higher proportions than are older persons. Thus we could witness an undesirable generational impact of crime on democracy, in which younger Mexicans' preference for democracy is negatively affected by their feelings of insecurity.

As a system, the VES exerts its strongest impact on Change in Behavior, the construct that encompasses behaviors that people avoid or cease doing, such as going out at night, visiting relatives, or riding in taxis. There are direct positive impacts on Change in Behavior from the three variables of the VES: Direct Victimization (ρ = 0.08), Indirect Victimization (ρ = 0.19), and Feeling Unsafe (ρ = 0.30). This "chilling effect" that these three variables have on behavior is also an undesirable social impact in the long term: people who stop engaging in activities such as those measured by this latent variable are more likely to reduce their trust in others and be less active in formal and informal networks.

Interestingly, Change in Behavior has a significant positive effect on Bonding (ρ = 0.12). This could mean that individuals distancing themselves from the world are turning inward to "thicker" levels of trust, such as trust in close family members. However, this does not necessarily mean that their bonding will result in "thinner" trust (Bridging or Trustworthiness), precisely because their behavior is indicating otherwise. Finally, the model also shows that the VES has a direct negative impact on reported individual Health (IV ρ = −0.12, and Unsafe ρ = −.13). However, the biggest effect on Health is exerted by Change in Behavior (ρ = −.23). Thus the condition of being a victim and Change in Behavior cause poorer reported health, at least as measured by this survey instrument. Health is a central component of Human Capital Theory (see Healy and Côte 2001) and together with social capital represents the fundamental assets of any society.

CONCLUSIONS AND POLICY IMPLICATIONS

This study is not intended to merely reaffirm that crime is "socially regrettable."[14] Rather, my findings provide valuable clues about the additional social costs of crime. The numbers show that the Victimization Experience

---

[14] This term is borrowed from Healy and Côte 2001: 12.

System—operating mainly through fear—affects social capital stocks and human capital. That is, victims feel less safe, become less trusting of others, and avoid certain important social activities. The data also show that these effects could weaken democracy by undermining institutional trust and augmenting a preference for an authoritarian system.

This result has clear policy implications. In a more general sense, investing in the containment, prevention, and eradication of crime may yield higher return rates than expected or than would result from other types of public expenditure. Specifically, increasing the levels of "perceived individual safety" appears to be of crucial importance.

I began my research using social capital as a convenient and powerful way to illustrate these undesirable consequences of crime. I was drawn to this construct not so much for its links to almost every social phenomenon, but rather for its potential to generate egalitarian growth. It has great potential to reintroduce a social dimension into capitalism, as Baron, Field, and Schuller advocate (2000: 13), and Mexico would do well to take full advantage of its potential.[15] Mexico is experiencing a historical public security crisis amidst political change, power struggles, and major reforms to the legal system. As Paterson (2000: 54) suggests, a nation in the middle of such changes has an important opportunity to promote positive social change, since the creation of social capital may be fundamentally determined by "moments of sharp social conflict, where power relations are shifting, and where the outcome is not determined in advance because there is a myriad of possible new networks to be formed." Thus it is up to us, in the present, to ensure that the appropriate actions are taken to reduce crime's impact on social capital in Mexico.

References

Baron, Stephen, John Field, and Tom Schuller. 2000. *Social Capital: Critical Perspectives*. New York: Oxford University Press.

Brehm, John, and Wendy Rahn. 1997. "Individual-Level Evidence for the Causes and Consequences of Social Capital," *American Journal of Political Science* 41, no. 3 (July): 999–1023.

Coleman, James S. 1994. "A Rational Choice Perspective on Economic Sociology." In *The Handbook of Economic Sociology*, ed. Neil Smelser and Richard Swedberg. New York: Russell Sage.

---

[15] I borrow here from the work of Krishna (2002) on the need to provide "agencies" for increasing social capital.

Fukuyama, Francis. 1997. *Trust: The Social Virtues and the Creation of Prosperity*. New York: Free Press.

Grootaert, Christian. 1997. "Social Capital: The Missing Link?" In *Expanding the Measure of Wealth: Indicators of Environmentally Sustainable Development*. Washington D.C.: World Bank.

Grootaert, Christian, and Thierry van Bastelaer, eds. 2002. *The Role of Social Capital in Development: An Empirical Assessment*. Cambridge: Cambridge University Press.

Healy, Tom, and Sylvain Côte. 2001. *The Well-being of Nations: The Role of Human and Social Capital*. Paris: Organisation for Economic Co-operation and Development.

Krishna, Anirudh. 2002. *Active Social Capital: Tracing the Roots of Development and Democracy*. New York: Columbia University Press.

Paterson, Lindsay. 2000. "Civil Society and Democratic Renewal." In *Social Capital: Critical Perspectives*, ed. Stephen Baron, John Field, and Tom Schuller. New York: Oxford University Press.

Portes, Alejandro. 1998. "Social Capital: Its Origins and Applications in Contemporary Sociology," *Annual Review of Sociology* 24: 1–24.

Putnam, Robert D. 1993. *Making Democracy Work: Civic Traditions in Modern Italy*. Princeton, N.J.: Princeton University Press.

———. 2000. *Bowling Alone: The Collapse and Revival of American Community*. New York: Touchstone.

Siegel, Larry. 2000. *Criminology*. 7th ed. Belmont, Calif.: Wadsworth/Thomson Learning.

Smith, Tom W. 1997. "Factors Relating to Misanthropy in Contemporary American Society," *Social Science Research* 26, issue 2 (June): 170–96.

Woolcock, Michael. 2001. "The Place of Social Capital in Understanding Social and Economic Outcomes," *ISUMA* 2, no. 1 (Spring). At http://www.isuma.net/v02n01/woolcock/woolcock_e.pdf.

Woolcock, Michael, and D. Narayan. 2000. "Social Capital: Implications for Development Theory, Research and Policy," *World Bank Research Observer* 15, no. 2: 225–49.

Addendum: Variables in the Causal Model, Index Construction, and Factor Loadings

Anchors and Single Variables

Name	Variable	Recoded Values (original code on questionnaire)
GENDER (male)	Q1 Gender	1 = male
		0 (2) = female
AGE	Q2 Age	18–97 years
SE	Income (number of possessions)	1 to 5
		3 (6) = intermediate
BONDING		(1) = a lot
		(2) = some
	BD1 Trust Family	(3) = a little
		(4) none
		(9) intermediate
DIRVICT		(4) = three or more times
(direct victim)		= twice
	DV1 Victim within the last 12 months	(2) = once
		(1) = none
		(9) = intermediate

Index Construction

Name	Item	Factor Loading	Recoded Values (original code questionnaire) = Category
INSTRUST (Institutional Trust)	IT3 Press	54	
	IT4 Television	51	
	IT5 Unions	50	
Alpha = .842	IT6 Political parties	63	4 (1) = a lot
	IT7 Big corporations	58	3 (2) = some
	IT8 Federal government	58	1 (3) = a little
	IT9 Congress	66	0 (4) none
	IT10 Public officials	65	2 (9) = intermediate
	IT11 Judges	62	
	IT12 Policy	61	
BRIDGING (Thin Trust)	BR1 Trust neighbors	57	4 (1) = a lot
	BR2 Trust co-workers	43	3 (2) = some
Alpha = .728	BR3 Trust clerks where you shop	44	1 (3) = a little
			0 (4) = none
			2 (9) = intermediate
	BR5 Trust the majority of one's neighbors	60	3 (1) = agree
			2 = neither agree nor disagree
			1 (3) disagree
			2 (9) = intermediate
	BD2 Leave keys with neighbor	46	3 (1) = agree
			2 = neither agree nor disagree
			1 (3) disagree
			2 (9) = intermediate
	N12 The neighborhood is united	57	3 (1) = agree
	N13 Neighbors have helped me	61	2 = neither agree nor disagree
			1 (3) disagree
			2 (9) = intermediate

Name	Item	Factor Loading	Recoded Values (original code questionnaire) = Category
TRUSTW (Trustworthiness)	BD3 Most people can be trusted	53	3 (1) = most people can be trusted 1 (2) = you cannot be too careful 2 (9) = intermediate
Alpha = .413	BR4 Trust people in the street	53	4 (1) = a lot 3 (2) = some 1 (3) = a little 0 (4) none 2 (9) intermediate
NETWORK (Membership)	N2 Member, work-related group	30	
	N3 Member, neighborhood group	51	
	N4 Member, education-related group	47	
Alpha = .678	N5 Member, credit union	49	4 (1) = active member 3 (2) = just member 1 (3) = was a member 0 (4) never has been member 2 (9) intermediate
	N6 Member, political party	39	
	N7 Member, sports organization	47	
	N8 Member, cultural organization	45	
	N9 Member, religious organization	31	
	N10 Member, informal financial group	32	
	N11 Member, NGO/charity	48	

Name	Item	Factor Loading	Recoded Values (original code questionnaire) = Category
HEALTH	HE1 Headaches	54	
	HE2 Get scared easily	60	0 (1) = yes
Alpha = .755	HE3 Frequently feel nervous	71	3 (2) = no
	HE4 Difficulty doing routine activities	51	3 (9) intermediate
	HE5 Feel tired most of the time	69	
	HE6 Personal health	46	5 (1) = very good
			4 (2) = good
			3 = regular
			2 (4) = bad
			3 (9) regular
INDVICT	IV2 Household member victim	63	1 to 7
(Indirect Victim)	within last 12 months		0 (99) = no, intermediate
	IV5 Family member victim within	63	1 to 7
Alpha = .551	last 12 months		0 (99) = no, intermediate
UNSAFE	F1 Feel safe at home	35	1 = completely safe
(Fear of Crime)	F2 Feel safe at work	37	2 = somewhat safe
	F4 Feel safe in street	74	4 (3) = somewhat unsafe
Alpha = .738	F5 Feel safe in supermarket	74	5 (4) = completely unsafe
	F6 Feel safe in public transportation	71	3 (9) = intermediate
	F7 Feel safe in private transportation	52	
BEHAVE	BE1 Stop visiting relatives	57	
(Change in	BE2 Stop going out at night	62	
Behavior)	BE3 Stop going out very early	59	1 = yes
	BE4 Stop taking a taxi	66	0 (2, 9) = no
Alpha = .799	BE5 Stop using public transportation	61	
	BE6 Stop carrying cash	59	
	BE7 Stop dressing a certain way	57	

Name	Item	Factor Loading	Recoded Values (original code questionnaire) = Category
PREFDEMO (Preference for Democracy)	K1 Authoritarianism	53	5 (1) = democracy is preferable
			1 (2) under some circumstances, authoritarianism is desirable
			3 (9) Intermediate
Alpha = .413		53	5 (1) = strongly agree
			4 (2) = somewhat agree
	K3 Democracy is preferable		2 (3) = somewhat disagree
			1 (4) = strongly disagree
			3 (9) = intermediate

Binational Civic Action for Accountability: Antiviolence Organizing in Cd. Juárez–El Paso

KATHLEEN STAUDT AND IRASEMA CORONADO

For all the praise of Mexico's "transition to democracy," civic activists still have great difficulty obtaining political accountability, professional responses from the criminal justice system, or even respectful acknowledgment of public problems, particularly those affecting women and families in poverty. In fact, some activists face threats, harassment, and intimidation for their efforts to make public problems visible and for their criticism of government nonresponsiveness. This chapter focuses on antiviolence organizing in the binational Ciudad Juárez–El Paso region, particularly organizing efforts by nongovernmental organizations (NGOs) around the murders of over three hundred girls and women over the last decade (Washington Valdez 2002; Gonzales 2002; Benítez et al. 1999; Staudt and Coronado 2002: chap. 6; Ortiz 2002).

The first section briefly outlines the facts and chronology of the Juárez murders as well as the official responses. The second section examines the accountability challenges that complicate public action in borderlands. The third section analyzes cross-border civic action and includes consideration of successful strategies. The chapter draws on multiple sources: interviews, observation, and participant observation in antiviolence organizations, including the cross-border Coalition Against Violence toward Women and Families at the U.S.-Mexico Border (hereinafter the Coalition Against Violence), which involves activists and organizations from both Ciudad Juárez and El Paso. The underlying thread in this chapter is the need for institutional mechanisms that can provide leverage and resources for successful binational action coupled with oversight from civil society. Although Mexico and the United States have signed numerous agreements on topics ranging from free trade and the environment to air traffic control and plant viruses, no human rights agreement exists to address public safety, sexual serial killers, or the overall lawless climate in cities like Ciudad Juárez.

THE JUÁREZ MURDERS AND THE OFFICIAL RESPONSE

Borderlands are often characterized as wild frontiers. Ciudad Juárez, Mexico's fifth-largest city, is no exception. Juárez has long been considered a "boom town" (Martínez 1978). The Border Industrialization Program of the 1960s and the growth of assembly-line production in the *maquiladora* industry attracted migrants from the interior of Mexico and drove dramatic population increases in the region. After the U.S. War on Drugs made drug trafficking from Colombia through Florida more difficult, El Paso–Ciudad Juárez became a major trafficking corridor (Bowden 2002; U.S. Department of Justice 2003), and illegal drug trafficking is perhaps the city's major business.[1] Yet despite the characterization of the U.S.-Mexico border as wild and lawless, it is also subject to heavy law enforcement and what has been called the "militarization of the border" (Dunn 1996; selections in Spener and Staudt 1998; Williams and Coronado 1994). Border law enforcement aims to regulate and control immigration, commerce and trade, firearms (the special concern of Mexico), and drug traffic (the special concern of the United States). At the federal level, the Federal Bureau of Investigation (FBI) and Drug Enforcement Administration (DEA), among others, work in Mexico (Paterson 2001). Likewise, the Office of the Mexican Attorney General (PGR) has branch offices in the United States. Binational cooperation in law enforcement exists at the higher echelons of government, setting a precedent for cooperation at all government levels, including at the state and municipal/local levels.

In the early to mid-1990s, Juarenses began noticing a pattern in media reports about female homicides. The bodies of women were being found in the desert or in fields within the city limits; many had been raped before death. They fit a certain profile: slender, poor, young, dark-haired. Most were between eleven and twenty-one years of age and died after being subjected to particular practices, such as being set on fire or having their breasts cut off. When questioned, public officials discounted the victims' value and appeared to blame them for "leading a double life," "dressing provocatively," or "being out at night." In fact, the victims' style of dress

---

[1] Ciudad Juárez is the home base of the Carrillo-Fuentes cartel.

was varied, and some were killed during daytime hours. Police files contain some information about the victims, but all too many of these records were shoddily assembled and are incomplete.

The first person to be charged for the murders was Abdel Latif Sharif Sharif. The fact that Sharif is a foreigner fit with the city's sentiment that "Mexicans don't do such things."[2] When the killings continued despite Sharif's detention, the authorities charged members of the Los Rebeldes gang, claiming that they took orders from Sharif. The next group to be charged included bus drivers contracted to transport second- and third-shift *maquiladora* workers to the plants.[3]

Still the killings continued, giving rise to a surge of public consciousness. People began painting pink and red crosses on black backgrounds in public spaces to call attention to the murders. A large wooden cross with nails to represent the murder victims was installed across from the international border bridge in downtown Ciudad Juárez. And media coverage has escalated on both sides of the border each time a new body has been found.

The precise number of victims has been in dispute, even between Chihuahua State's successive governments of the Institutional Revolutionary Party (PRI) and National Action Party (PAN). By 2002, the various figures were as follows: 254 (86 identified as serial killings) according to Casa Amiga, the antiviolence counseling center in Ciudad Juárez; 258, according to the Chihuahua State Attorney General's Office; and 320 (90 of them sex-related serial killings), according to the *El Paso Times* (Gaspar de Alba 2003; see also www.casa-amiga.org/Statistics.htm and www.elpasotimes.com/borderdeath). By this time, media coverage had extended beyond the border, to Mexico City newspapers, the *New York Times, Washington Post, Los Angeles Times,* and the Los Angeles-based *La Opinión,* the predominant Spanish-language newspaper in the United States. International coverage was extensive as well, and several European newspapers and magazines sent reporters and photographers to the border to cover the story.

---

[2] See Piccato 2001 on home-grown versions of serial killing in early-twentieth-century Mexico City.

[3] Many of the arrestees were mistreated (one died), in line with the Mexican tradition of forcing confessions (Human Rights Watch 1999). Others were released in the absence of real evidence. The early history is covered well in Lourdes Portillo's film *Señorita Extraviada* (2001). Portillo focused on the victims' families, the indifference of police and judicial authorities, and those who denounced the police as active participants in the rape and torture killings.

The police have generally treated the victims' families, most of whom live in poverty, with disdain (Staudt and Coronado 2002: chap. 6), to the point of being careless about retaining the victims' clothing and remains.[4] Activists allege that police misconduct has gone far beyond indifference and disdain, however, to include intimidation, fabricated evidence, incomplete and lost investigation files, and misidentification of remains, often causing the victims' families to relive the murders again and again. Police do not give consistent accounts to the victims' families, undermining any trust that this already skeptical population may have in their police.[5] In one case, a threatening message was left on the phone of a victim's family, instructing the family not to pursue the issue; Caller ID showed the source of the message to be the state judicial police number (authors' field notes, 2003).

During our research, family members reported that in some instances they did not even know where to report a missing daughter. Wracked with anguish over their missing children and hindered by their limited knowledge about government institutions, these poor and disenfranchised people report having endured frustrating experiences with law enforcement agencies at all levels. As one mother recalls:

> Our family went to one office, where we told them that our daughter had not come home. They made us wait, then sent us to an office where a man asked us all kinds of questions: name, age, address, where we worked, on and on. Then we finally got to our daughter, her name, her age, what she was wearing, and so on. The man said we should not worry because many young women like our daughter go and spend the night in a hotel with their boyfriend and oversleep, and they usually return the next day. I was shocked, like a pail of cold water had been thrown at me (authors' field notes, 2002).

The official went on to tell these parents that if their daughter did not return later in the day, they should go to another office, whose address he provided. "This is not where we deal with missing persons," he told them.

---

[4] When members of two cross-border coalitions searched the desert for evidence, they found underwear and other objects the police had left behind.

[5] See the chapter in this volume by Pablo Parás, on crime, public trust, and social capital stocks in Mexico City.

Family members have also reported that they have had to take days off from work to go to the police station to follow up on their cases. Families who do not have telephones have a difficult time getting through to the person in charge of their case, so they often come in person in the hope that they will get some information.

The situation has not changed much over the years despite the public's attention to these cases, and corruption is routine. As one mother reported:

> We were told by one police officer that they would look into my daughter's case a little more closely if we could provide an "incentive." Our family and friends gathered all the money we could and gave it to him, hoping that he would be able to tell us where our daughter was. At the time, you're in so much pain and anguish that you're not thinking clearly, and I felt that it was the right thing to do because I really wanted them to find my daughter (authors' field notes).

Following the supplication style of Mexico's clientelist politics, victims' families have gone to public officials and pleaded with them to "do something," to little avail. By the late 1990s, nongovernmental groups were emerging to fill the vacuum surrounding this issue, and established NGOs were beginning to act in solidarity with the families. One of the first groups (later disbanded) was Voces Sin Eco, composed of victims' family members. The first cross-border group to emerge was Amigos de las Mujeres de Juárez, based in Las Cruces, New Mexico. Other new NGOs included Mujeres por Juárez, Nuestras Hijas de Regreso a Casa, and Mujeres de Negro. This latter group, whose members dress in mourning at public events, has held solidarity actions in the United States and around the world, often at Mexican consulates and embassy offices. The binational Coalition Against Violence, discussed in greater detail below, was born at a labor solidarity event in Ciudad Juárez in November 2001. These groups were joined in 2003 by Amnesty International, which released a report on the murders, which it counted at 370, including 137 "sexual homicides" (Amnesty International 2003).

By this time, government officials no longer blamed the victims, at least not in public. Similar serial killings had spread to other border locations and to Chihuahua City, the state capital (Guillermoprieto 2003). Yet the municipal and state police continued to display indifference, incompetence, or, as suspected by the public, complicity with the killers, who were imagined to be members of rich families and/or drug cartels, all with sufficient money to buy protection. As the Mexican celebration of the Day of the Dead approached in 2003, *La Jornada* published a lengthy front-page article implicating prominent Juárez families in the case (Washington Valdez 2003; Burnett 2004).

Residents of Mexico generally distrust the police and believe they are corrupt.[6] These perceptions are exacerbated in Ciudad Juárez and the state of Chihuahua more generally, which is among the states with the highest rates of crime and organized crime (including drug trafficking) (as summarized in Moloeznik 2003). In fact, there is substantial evidence in support of the public's perception. Mexican police at the municipal, state, and federal levels are regularly fired or suspended for corruption and drug charges.[7] Although dated, a study conducted by the National Autonomous University of Mexico (UNAM) concluded that "cocaine traffickers spent as much as $460 million [dollars] on bribery in 1993—far more than the annual budget of the Mexican Attorney General's Office in 1993" (Andreas 2000: 62). After a decade more, the amounts have likely skyrocketed. Transparency International, an NGO that reports an annual Corruption Perception Index for most countries, scored Mexico at 3.3 in 2003, higher than the two lowest (Nigeria at 1.4 and Bangladesh at 1.3) but far from the top five (mostly Scandinavian) countries, which fell between 9 and 10 (Transparency International 2003).

Mexican citizens who criticize government corruption or inaction are subject to threats, intimidation, even death. For example, in February 2002, state police officers shot and killed attorney Mario Escobedo Anaya in Ciudad Juárez. Escobedo was defending one of the two bus drivers accused of raping and murdering eight women whose bodies were found in an empty lot in November 2001; Escobedo's father was defending the second bus driver. There are various accounts regarding what happened the night that the police chased Escobedo through the streets of Ciudad Juárez: the attorney crashed and died; the police shot him in self-defense; the police shot him after Escobedo crashed his car. When Escobedo's father arrived at the scene, state police were everywhere and his son was dead (http://www.nodo50.org/pchiapas/documentos/Juárez2.htm).

---

[6] In the multi-country World Values Survey (Inglehart, Basáñez, and Moreno 1998), approximately three of ten Mexicans trust the police, and five of ten trust the army. See Giugale, Lafourcade, and Nguyen 2001 for reviews of other research in Mexico.

[7] Andreas (2000: 64) reports that 10 percent of the federal judicial police were relieved of duty for corruption from 1992 to 1995.

The focus on the cases of the murdered women intensified with the election of President Vicente Fox in 2000.[8] In the summer of 2003, responding to national and international pressure to act on the murders and on official impunity, Fox authorized the stationing of hundreds of federal preventive police in Ciudad Juárez, and in 2004 he appointed a special commission to investigate the crimes. Guadalupe Morfín was appointed as the commission head, and María López Urbina as special prosecutor.[9] Yet despite this renewed attention, more than ten years have passed since the murders began and only Sharif Sharif has been convicted; his case remains under appeal.

BORDERLINE ACCOUNTABILITY

The fact that the international borderline runs through the Ciudad Juárez– El Paso metropolitan area complicates accountability relationships between the murder victims, their families, and government. The regional context involves two sets of political institutions that appear similar on the surface (federalism; presidential forms of government with separate executive, legislative, and judicial branches) but that operate quite differently. Periodically, binational cooperation on the issue has transcended borderlines,[10] as in the late 1990s, when data were run through the FBI database at Quantico, Virginia, with inconclusive results.

Article 33 of the Mexican Constitution prohibits foreigners' involvement in the nation's political affairs, and cross-border activists face the risk of being declared persona non grata or even jailed for their activities, with the concomitant risk of torture. During V-Day activities[11] on February 14, 2004

---

8 His election also further undermined cooperation between the levels of government in Mexico, exacerbating an already stressed situation in Chihuahua. Fox is a member of the PAN, as is Jesús Delgado, municipal president of Ciudad Juárez; Chihuahua's governor, Patricio Martínez, is from the PRI.

9 Their official titles are, respectively, Human Rights Commissioner to Prevent and Eradicate Violence against Women, and Special Prosecutor for the Attention of Crimes Related to the Homicides of Women.

10 There are many precedents for cross-border, binational cooperation between the United States and Mexico, including official organizations like the International Boundary and Water Commission (IBWC/CILA), nongovernmental organizations, registered nonprofit organizations, and informal networks and coalitions (Staudt and Coronado 2002). The two governments have cooperated on questions of water, toxic waste, air quality, trade, and commerce.

11 V-day is an annual event aimed at ending violence against women and girls.

(discussed below), a flier reminded non-Mexican participants of the potential legal consequences of their political activism in Ciudad Juárez.

Why are the Juárez murders a binational—even an international—issue? Cross-border activists point to several reasons. First, at least four of the victims were from the United States (El Paso), and others were from the Netherlands, Honduras, and Guatemala (Washington Valdez 2002). Furthermore, there is a larger population of *desaparecidos* (disappeared persons) that includes people from both sides of the border, which is of special concern to the cross-border Asociación de Familiares y Amigos de Personas "Desaparecidas" (Staudt and Coronado 2002: 150–51). It is impossible to know how many of these "disappeared" have been murdered, their bodies yet to be found in the vast stretches of the Chihuahuan desert on the periphery of Ciudad Juárez.

Second, the serial killers' nationality is not known. They could be border crossers from either country in these porous borderlands.[12]

Third, the two economies are linked, especially via the mostly U.S.-owned assembly plants where some of the victims worked. Ciudad Juárez's *maquiladoras* have become a magnet for migrants since 1965, and there were approximately 200,000 such firms in the area in 2003. Some border theorists believe that the related notion of a cheap, "disposable" labor force contributes to the lawless climate in the city (Biemann 2002).

And fourth, domestic efforts in Mexico have been insufficient to resolve the problem. Chihuahua's legislature has passed a variety of laws on domestic assault, rape,[13] and murder, but the language is often vague and the (underreported) crime data are not disaggregated by gender. The lack of disaggregated data allowed Chihuahua's Governor Patricio Martínez García to cavalierly state that murder rates in Ciudad Juárez are not as bad as in places like New York. Nevertheless, the female homicide rate per 100,000 population is glaringly high compared to other large cities in Mexico and elsewhere (Monárrez Fragoso 2002). Three of the thirty deputies in the current legislature are women and, despite their different party affiliations, they are cooperating to prioritize solutions for violence against women.

---

[12] In this regard, as the murders spread to Chihuahua City, authorities there forced a confession from a U.S. citizen, a woman whose husband is Mexican. Her confession contained references to blows inflicted to a part of the victim's body that was in fact untouched (Guillermoprieto 2003).

[13] Two years ago, activists had to fight an effort in the Chihuahua state legislature to reduce the penalty for rape below the penalty for injuring a cow (Martínez-Márquez 2002).

At the national level, numerous reports of violence against women have been made through Mexico's National Human Rights Commission (CNDH), but this entity lacks enforcement powers. Within the judicial branch, which since 1994 has enjoyed greater autonomy from the executive branch, national-level reforms have not spilled over to the state level. According to José Luis Soberanes, the "delivery of justice in Mexico depends on a structure that is complicated, slippery, and often corrupt" (Human Rights Watch 1999: 46). In a damning indictment, judicial experts conclude that Mexico does not extend rights and protections based on the "rule of law" (Domingo 1999).

In the absence of effective domestic strategies and mechanisms to resolve this problem, residents of Ciudad Juárez and El Paso have employed existing cross-border ties to promote binational civic action in search of accountability. The following section analyzes cross-border civic actions and the gains they have made. Although the public's awareness of the Juárez murders has increased, responses thus far have been modest. The Coalition Against Violence has united disparate groups that share the common goal of ending the violence and identifying the killers. However, other organized interests, such as the chambers of commerce, downtown merchants, and *maquiladoras*, have not pressed for government action even though it might help improve the image of Ciudad Juárez and promote economic investment in the region. Instead, the region's businesspeople have been quoted in the media as stating that the protestors put the city in a bad light.

CROSS-BORDER CIVIC ACTIONS

The Coalition Against Violence toward Women and Families at the U.S.-Mexico Border is a loose binational alliance of organizations and individuals concerned with issues of human and women's rights, labor, health care, counseling, and shelter in the border zone. The chronology below outlines the Coalition's evolution from regional network of activists to an organization that, with "the strength of weak ties" (Granovetter 1974), has gained leverage with networks at the national and the international level.

Cross-Border Organizational Birth and Growth

The Coalition Against Violence emerged to bring attention to the Juárez murders and also to pursue reformist strategies within the local binational economy. The El Paso and Ciudad Juárez governments have long cooperated on shared problems of interest to the business establishment, such as auto theft, water and air quality, and cross-border commerce. Yet such cooperation was lacking in the Juárez murder investigations. Despite the reluctance of the Coalition Against Violence's more "radical" members to look to the police for solutions, the group called for a binational task force to foster cooperation in investigating the crimes,[14] issuing the following challenge: "you can cooperate over auto theft; why not over these murders of girls and women?" (authors' field notes, 2002, 2003).

Activists also sought to link the Juárez murders to other policy areas, such as the framework for future health interventions. This linking effort was in response to the "Healthy Borders 2010" report, compiled by the U.S.-Mexico Border Health Commission, which failed to address violence against women as a health issue. Members of the Transborder Consortium on Gender and Health at the U.S.-Mexico Border drew on their expertise to draft a critique that proposed new language and got it on the Health Commission's agenda.

It is important to note that these activists sought to involve U.S. policymakers in what would otherwise be viewed as a "Mexican problem." Members of the Coalition Against Violence got strong support from Texas State Senator Eliot Shapleigh, who lent his name and official stationery for letters urging binational cooperation; the letters went to President Bush and to officials at the Departments of Justice and State. The replies, which arrived months later, tended to treat the issue as a narrow judicial matter to be resolved by Mexico alone, unless Mexico requested U.S. assistance. Yet through Senator Shapleigh's continued efforts, Coalition members were able to meet with FBI officials, who expressed their willingness to cooperate in training efforts—though not in the investigations directly.[15]

Another stage in the Coalition's evolution was its participation in luncheons hosted by the Twin Plant Wives Association and the Republican Women's Club, for which Coalition members dressed in mourning. At one such luncheon, First Lady of Texas Anita Perry was "pinned" with the black and pink cross that symbolizes the murder victims. She shared staff

---

[14] This included greater FBI involvement, especially in setting up a tip line. The Coalition also approached Crimestoppers, a nonprofit organization that offers financial rewards for tips that help solve crimes. However, this group decided not to collaborate because its directors felt that their involvement would imply criticism of the Mexican police.

[15] This occurred in 2002. The FBI had also collaborated earlier, in 1998.

lists and brainstormed over strategies with Coalition members, though little came of these and similar activities.

Only when the Coalition staged dramatic public events, with full media coverage, did regional, national, and international networks mobilize and draw a response from broader segments of the public. Media coverage tended to be most extensive in Mexico, especially by newspapers that were critical of the government and the dominant PRI party, which controlled the Chihuahua state government. The state government responded with the traditional Mexican strategy of misinformation campaigns and a lack of transparency. Chihuahua's Governor Martínez appointed longtime activist Vicky Caraveo to head the state's Instituto de la Mujer, which paid out stipends to some of the victims' mothers, but little is known about the institute's overall budget or priorities. The effect was to polarize human rights groups. "Who is profiting from our pain?" some of the mothers asked (authors' field notes).

In public educational events, the Coalition Against Violence has made dramatic use of symbols, colors, and icons to recall the murder victims. In April 2002, students in the Feminist Majority Leadership Alliance at the University of Texas at El Paso sponsored a silent vigil in a well-traversed section of the campus. Many news teams took photographs of the 150 "mourners," who held up placards of black and pink crosses. Shocking guerrilla theatre performances in Ciudad Juárez sparked further public awareness. Day of the Dead celebrations in Ciudad Juárez and El Paso have included displays with mementos of the deceased, and university students from both sides of the border have constructed elaborate altars to pay tribute to the murdered girls and women.

Political films and theatre performances have extended public education opportunities with memorable visuals. Lourdes Portillo's award-winning film, *Señorita Extraviada*, has been enormously important in increasing the visibility of the murders and the indifference of the police.[16] Eve Ensler's play *Vagina Monologues* has been performed several times in El Paso and Las Cruces. V-Day has linked the border region to the nation and the world. In the run-up to V-Day 2003, Esther Chávez Cano, who runs Casa Amiga for victims of violence in Ciudad Juárez, was named one of "21 Leaders for the 21st Century."

---

16 The film focuses on the murders and the victims' families. It has been shown many times in the border region, both for public education and for fundraising for antiviolence causes. The English version aired in the United States on national public television.

From Local/Regional to Transnational/Global Networks

Four more murder victims—three teens and a six-year-old—were found in a single week in February 2003. All had been raped and mutilated. Coalition Against Violence members reacted to the discovery with a press conference, and the Mexican and U.S. media gave the story broad coverage throughout the hemisphere. The Coalition then spoke with city and county representatives to press for passage of an antiviolence resolution and issuance of a proclamation for International Women's Day. The resolution was narrowly focused, calling for a binational task force and cross-border use of police resources. The proclamation's thrust was much broader: to educate people about systemic gender inequalities. The resolution and proclamation were approved by both the El Paso City Council and the El Paso County Commissioners Court, whose members were motivated by fears that the border region's declining image would deter investments. Such a strategy was not available to NGOs operating in Ciudad Juárez, where municipal council meetings are not open for public comment.

At a March 2003 press conference, El Paso's Mayor Ray Caballero and chief of police announced that there would be cooperation between judicial authorities on both sides of the border. The press conference format, in which journalists and NGO representatives were able to ask challenging questions, proved somewhat discomforting to the Mexican officials who were in attendance.

On March 8, 2003, mirroring the turnout of the previous year, hundreds of marchers attended the International Women's Day rallies at the border, along with numerous reporters and television crews. An AP wire reporter and photographer were present as well, and their story was picked up by outlets across the United States.

In March 2003, Coalition members were invited to New York City to participate in the 47th session of the United Nations Commission on the Status of Women. This presented another opportunity to press Mexican authorities and to develop network ties in distant locales.[17]

In April 2003, Senator Shapleigh and Representative Norma Chávez introduced a joint resolution in the Texas legislature on binational cooperation in criminal investigations. Members of the Coalition Against Violence and Austin-based activists were invited to testify at the legislative hearings (Staudt 2003), at which the legislators wore Coalition-supplied lapel pins of

---

[17] Human rights commissions generally report abuses rather than exercise authority to enforce solutions.

black and pink crosses. The resolution, HCR 59, passed in the 78th Legislative Session, amid endorsements of solidarity from around the world: antiviolence protests at Mexican consulates and a flurry of emails and photographs from Tokyo, Belgrade, Madrid, and elsewhere.

NGOs in Ciudad Juárez have worked extensively to network with international NGOs like Amnesty International and international organizations such as the Organization of American States and its InterAmerican Commission on Human Rights, in the interest of placing the Juárez murders on international agendas (Ortiz 2002). Amnesty International joined the group of organizations focused on this issue when, in the summer of 2003, it released a monograph on the Mexican criminal justice system, the history of the murders, and the government's failure to respond (Amnesty International 2003).

The Coalition's network also included the Mexico Solidarity Network and antiviolence coalitions in cities in both the United States and Mexico. Responding to the many Juarenses in her Los Angeles constituency, U.S. Congressional Representative Hilda Solís took the lead in organizing the Hispanic Caucus to encourage Mexican President Vicente Fox to push for Mexican federal involvement in the murders, with legal tools and precedents outlined in a letter to Fox.[18] The Coalition met with the staff of Congressman Silvestre Reyes (Texas, 16th District) to win his signature on the letter and his support for hearings at the border. In October 2003 Representative Solís led a congressional delegation to the border to talk to victims' families, NGO activists, and public officials, and to visit the sites where the bodies had been found. That visit spurred a great deal of media coverage. Solís has since introduced a bipartisan resolution in Congress (House Resolution 466, with three Republican and five Democratic co-sponsors) that encourages U.S. involvement in seeking binational solutions (Solís 2004).

Universities also organized events that made the murders more visible and increased the pressure on governments to act. In April 2003, Arizona State University-West sponsored a conference on "Gender, Justice, and the Border." Students and faculty decorated dresses for the 320 victims and hung the dresses on three-feet-high crosses in the campus courtyard.[19] From late October through November 2, 2003, the University of California–Los

---

[18] Mexico's 1996 Federal Law Against Organized Crime (LFCDO) provides authority to transfer jurisdiction from the State of Chihuahua to the federal Office of the Attorney General (PGR).

[19] Several of the dresses were included in the October 2003 exhibit in the UTEP Library commemorating the Day of the Dead.

Angeles hosted a conference entitled "Maquiladora Murders," which drew over a thousand participants. Conference speakers ranged from experts to victims' family members and activists from both sides of the border (see http://chavez.ucla.edu/maqui_murders). Under the banner of Operación Digna (named for assassinated human rights lawyer Digna Ochoa), cyber activists organized a "floodnet" of Mexican government agencies. Their effort was so effective that it prompted the mailing of a lengthy fax to organizers of the "Maquiladora Murders" conference, promising new coordinative bodies (authors' field notes, 2003).

New attention focused on Ciudad Juárez in early 2004 when bodies were found buried in city backyards. This prompted the removal of complicit state police and led to new binational initiatives—including an order by Governor Rick Perry of Texas to make the canine patrol available for investigations into murders of girls and women. Investigative reports in the *Dallas Morning News* included articles about victims being "abducted, raped, and killed to 'celebrate' successful drug runs," and these reports also implicated the police (Corchado and Sandoval 2004).

But the most visible attention to the murders came around V-Day 2004 (February 14). During the week prior to V-Day, students at the University of Texas at El Paso organized a day-long conference, men's workshops, art exhibits, and film series. On V-Day itself, an estimated 5,000 to 8,000 marchers crossed the border from El Paso to Ciudad Juárez in solidarity with victims of violence. This was the largest cross-border solidarity march in the region's history. Celebrities from Mexico and the United States performed from the *Vagina Monologues*,[20] and Eve Ensler wrote an additional monologue about the murders, which was performed at the border and in over a thousand cities around the world.

This loose chronology of the maturation of cross-border organizing illustrates how cross-border activists helped transform local/regional border organizing into national and international organizing around the murders of girls and young women in Ciudad Juárez. By 2003, although cross-border groups continued to demonstrate grounded expertise, national and international networks had taken the lead in making the murders visible and in pressing governments for binational solutions. Even so, each ad-

---

[20] Ensler visited Ciudad Juárez during the V-Day celebrations for cultural events but also for meetings with state judicial officials. She spoke at the final event of the day in front of the attorney general's office for the state of Chihuahua. Her new monologue about the murders will feature in future dramatic productions (see www.vday.org).

vance has triggered backlashes and resistance. The local business community has yet to respond, save to blame activists for the drop in tourism in downtown Ciudad Juárez and for the outflow of *maquiladora* jobs to China (in fact caused by a multitude of factors, the most prominent being China's lower labor costs). Meanwhile, the murders continue.

CONCLUSIONS AND STRATEGIES FOR CHANGE

The problem of violence against women is ancient and deep-seated, and has been tolerated as a private matter for centuries (Weldon 2002). Since the 1970s, activists in Mexico and the United States (and around the world), from the grassroots to national and international levels, have called attention to violence against women—domestic assault/abuse, rape, murder—as a public problem.[21] The Ciudad Juárez murders illustrate how the U.S.-Mexico border complicates such organizing, since the lines of accountability are rendered complex by the existence of distinct national sovereignties and multiple institutions. Cross-border organization around the murders in Ciudad Juárez therefore emerged as a unique strategy in the struggle to address violence against women.

Additional complications related to the lack of rule of law in Mexico include threats and intimidation of activists, lack of police professionalism, and low priorities for problems that women and poor people face. Although the North American Free Trade Agreement (NAFTA) and numerous bilateral agreements offer institutional mechanisms that provide policy leverage and resources for policymakers and stakeholders to address common North American problems at borders, such mechanisms do not exist for human rights and public safety. Binational cooperation among activists has begun with several tentative steps outlined in this chapter, but there are numerous regional, national, and international issues that must be addressed. Specifically, we recommend several short- and long-term actions for activists and authorities working to promote reform in Mexico:

- Mexico's federal government has refrained from involvement in the Ciudad Juárez murders out of alleged respect for the jurisdiction of local authorities. Yet given significant evidence of the ineptitude and possible corruption of local authorities, activists should demand federal involvement as authorized under the 1996 Federal Law Against Organized Crime (LFCDO).

---

[21] See Rodríguez 2003: 170 on national-level activism and response in Mexico.

- Activists should also press the federal government to use revenue-sharing incentives (an important tool of the Mexican federal government, documented by Rodríguez [1997]) to encourage reform at state and local levels, such as the freedom of information laws of 2003.

- Citizens should demand greater oversight by state legislators to whom state agencies should be accountable. Likewise, NGOs should press for a voice not only in selecting the director of the Instituto de la Mujer, but also in deciding the institute's priorities and budgetary spending.

- Lawmakers should make it possible for citizens to file civil lawsuits against intransigent police departments for monetary damage, or reparations and damage payments should be provided to all victims' families (not just those the government favors) in the form of the "stipends" that have long been a feature of Mexico's co-optation–based system.

- Public authorities and NGOs should collaborate to develop legal literacy campaigns that clearly explain the legal processes for reporting crimes, filing charges, and monitoring investigations and court procedures, so that all citizens can understand and access the system. Beyond that, streamlining complex steps may be in order, just as they emerged for businesses seeking "one-stop shops" for licenses and regulations.

- A variety of reforms are needed to promote professionalism in state and local police organizations, including domestic-violence training for police, proper evidence gathering and interrogation techniques (barring the use of torture), and better reporting and analysis of gender-disaggregated data on all sexual assaults and domestic violence.

- In Ciudad Juárez and elsewhere along the border, the government and private funding organizations should provide financial support and training to develop a network of shelters for battered women.

- *Maquiladora* managers should expand workplace safety initiatives to include surrounding areas and background checks, as well as routine drug tests for security guards, drivers of company buses on which potential female victims ride, and individuals subcontracted by the company. Managers could also fund workshops and self-defense classes for employees.

- Public school curricula should integrate anti–domestic violence and anti–sexual violence themes for male and female students. Criminal hyper-masculinity should be publicly criticized and no longer tolerated or celebrated as "cultural."

Above all, our research suggests that binational strategies are also necessary to ensure accountability in the border region. Mexico's domestic laws and organizations are insufficient to address the murders of girls and women in Ciudad Juárez, making this a major law enforcement and human rights concern of binational scope. Therefore, activists should maintain civic pressure in both Mexico and the United States through high-visibility events, media attention, and the use of symbols. Both activists and policymakers should also strive to connect the violence against women in Ciudad Juárez to related matters of binational concern. In other words, binational civic coalitions can be made more effective by including not only human rights activists but also those interested in public health, economic development, tourism, and foreign investment.

Yet resources are needed to provide support for such binational solutions. Binational initiatives frequently fall through the cracks along the border, since domestic government agencies and private funding sources often do not support such activities. For example, funds should be available to police departments and federal investigation agencies to support binational collaboration in training, use of laboratory and DNA testing facilities, and tip lines. Therefore, longer-term binational solutions will only be possible through the development of institutions to foster further civic activism and provide greater accountability, such as a strong Human Rights Treaty for the North American region.

References

Amnesty International. 2003. "Intolerable Killings: Ten Years of Abductions and Murders of Women in Ciudad Juárez and Chihuahua." At www.amnesty.org.

Andreas, Peter. 2000. *Border Games: Policing the U.S.-Mexico Divide*. Ithaca, N.Y.: Cornell University Press.

Benítez, Rohry, et al. 1999. *El silencio que la voz de todas quiebra: mujeres y víctimas de Ciudad Juárez*. Chihuahua, Chih.: Azar.

Biemann, Ursula. 2002. "Performing the Border: On Gender, Transnational Bodies, and Technology." In *Globalization on the Line: Culture, Capital, and Citizenship at U.S. Borders*, ed. Claudia Sadowski-Smith. New York: Palgrave.

Bowden, Charles. 2002. *Down by the River: Drugs, Money, Murder and Family*. New York: Simon and Schuster.

Burnett, John. 2004. "On the Job: Chasing the Ghouls: The Juárez Serial Murders, and a Reporter Who Won't Let Go," *Columbia Journalism Review* 2 (March/April). At http://www.cjr.org/issues/2004/2/burnett-mexico.asp.

Corchado, Alfredo, and Ricardo Sandoval. 2004. "Juárez Slayings: Inquiry Indicates Police, Drug Ties. Disturbing Reports Say Women Were Tortured and Slain as Celebration," *Dallas Morning News*. Reprinted in *STARS Voice* II, no. 1 (March): 2–3.

Domingo, Pilar. 1999. "Rule of Law, Citizenship and Access to Justice in Mexico," *Mexican Studies/Estudios Mexicanos* 15, no. 1: 151–91.

Dunn, Timothy. 1996. *The Militarization of the U.S.-Mexico Border, 1978–1992: Low-Intensity Conflict Doctrine Comes Home*. Austin: Center for Mexican American Studies, University of Texas at Austin.

Gaspar de Alba, Alicia. 2003. "The Maquiladora Murders, 1993–2003," *Aztlan: A Journal of Chicano Studies* 28, no. 2 (Fall): 1–17.

Giugale, Marcelo, Oliver Lafourcade, and Vinh Nguyen. 2001. *Mexico: A Comprehensive Agenda for the New Era*. Washington, D.C.: World Bank.

Gonzales, Sergio. 2002. *Huesos en el desierto*. Barcelona: Anagrama.

Granovetter, Mark. 1974. "The Strength of Weak Ties," *American Journal of Sociology* 78, no. 6: 1360–80.

Guillermoprieto, Alma. 2003. "Letter from Mexico. A Hundred Women: Why Has a Decade-long String of Murders Gone Unsolved?" *The New Yorker*, September 29.

Human Rights Watch. 1999. *Systemic Injustice: Torture, "Disappearance," and Extrajudicial Execution in Mexico*. New York: Human Rights Watch.

Inglehart, Ronald, Miguel Basáñez, and Alejandro Moreno. 1998. *Human Values and Beliefs. A Cross-Cultural Sourcebook: Political, Religious, Sexual, and Economic Norms in 43 Countries*. Ann Arbor: University of Michigan Press.

Martínez, Oscar. 1978. *Border Boom Town: Ciudad Juárez since 1848*. Austin: University of Texas Press.

Martínez-Márquez, Alejandra. 2002. "A Feminist Response to Changes in the Sexual Violence Law in the State of Chihuahua." Manuscript.

Moloeznik, Marcos Pablo. 2003. "The Challenges to Mexico in Times of Political Change," *Crime, Law and Social Change* 40: 7–20.

Monárrez Fragoso, Julia. 2002. "Feminicidio sexual serial en Ciudad Juárez: 1993–2001," *Debate Feminista*, April 13.

Ortiz, Marisela. 2002. "Crímenes contra mujeres: un desesperado grito de auxilio," *Chamizal* 2, no. 1 (July–December): 23–30.

Paterson, Kent. 2001. "Deepening U.S.-Mexico Security Cooperation: As NAFTA's Anti-narcotics Apparatus Focuses on Public Security, Human Rights Activists Grow Worried," *Borderlines* 84 (December). At http://americaspolicy.org/borderlines/2001/b184/b184security_body.html.

Piccato, Pablo. 2001. "'El Chalequero' or the Mexican Jack the Ripper: The Meanings of Sexual Violence in Turn-of-the-Century Mexico City," *Hispanic American Historical Review* 82, nos. 3–4: 623–51.

Rodríguez, Victoria. 1997. *Decentralization in Mexico: From Reforma Municipal to Solidaridad to Nuevo Federalismo*. Boulder, Colo.: Westview.

———. 2003. *Women in Contemporary Mexican Politics*. Austin: University of Texas Press.

Solís, Hilda. 2004. "In Search of Justice," *Center for Latin American Studies Newsletter*, Winter, pp. 3, 18–20.

Spener, David, and Kathleen Staudt, eds. 1998. *The U.S.-Mexico Border: Transcending Divisions, Contesting Identities*. Boulder, Colo.: Lynne Rienner.

Staudt, Kathleen. 2003. Testimony before the Texas Legislature Border Committees, April.

Staudt, Kathleen, and Irasema Coronado. 2002. *Fronteras No Mas: Toward Social Justice at the U.S.-Mexico Border*. New York: Palgrave.

Transparency International. 2003. Corruption Perception Index. At www. transparency.org. Accessed March 2004.

U.S. Department of Justice. 2003. "DEA Congressional Testimony," by Sandalio González, Special Agent in Charge, April 15. At www.usdoj.gov/dea. Accessed March 22, 2004.

Washington Valdez, Diana. 2002. "Death Stalks the Border," *El Paso Times*. At www.elpasotimes.com/borderdeath.

———. 2003. "Ciudad Juárez: así empezó todo," *La Jornada*, October 31.

Weldon, Laurel S. 2002. *Protest, Policy and the Problem of Violence against Women*. Pittsburgh, Penn.: University of Pittsburgh Press.

Williams, Edward, and Irasema Coronado. 1994. "The Hardening of the United States–Mexico Borderlands: Causes and Consequences," *Boundary and Security Bulletin* 1, no. 4.

CHAPTER 16

Different but Equal: Access to Justice for Mexico's Indigenous Peoples

ROSALVA AÍDA HERNÁNDEZ AND HÉCTOR ORTIZ ELIZONDO

The development in Mexico of an efficient, modern judicial system that can meet the needs of a plural, democratic nation requires the genuine incorporation of Mexico's cultural diversity. This objective requires a "reform of the state" that can offer the country's millions of indigenous citizens meaningful access to justice. Currently, the nation-state is structured as if it comprised a single culture, imposing a homogenizing judicial order with institutions based primarily on values held by a segment of the dominant mestizo population. In contrast, international legal trends have tended to promote the development of multicultural states, in which the reform of institutions and the basic concepts of law and justice themselves are grounded in pluralistic judicial models. The Mexican state barely started walking down this long and winding road in 1989, when it signed the International Labour Organization's Convention 169. Although this agreement represented a milestone in the recognition of the collective rights of indigenous peoples in modern Mexico, there is still a long way to go.

In this chapter we examine certain problems relating to the rule of law as it affects indigenous peoples, and the prospects for the construction of a multicultural state in Mexico under current conditions. We also discuss some of the advances achieved thus far in terms of reforming the legal system in matters concerning the rights of indigenous peoples. We start with a general overview of Mexican pluralism as it has existed since colonial times and as it was finally recognized in 1992 in the Mexican Constitu-

Translation by Patricia Rosas.

tion.[1] We then analyze the refusal of the legislature and judiciary to recognize cultural diversity and to incorporate it into legal concepts and practices. Next we present a case study to show how indigenous people in the state of Guerrero, through local practices for delivering justice, have developed their own strategies for resisting and negotiating federal law. Finally, we conclude with some reflections about the connection between justice and cultural citizenship, analyzing how indigenous women have responded to the critiques of the politics of cultural recognition and how they participate in the construction of a cultural citizenship that is nonessentialist and open to change and renewal.

EXCLUSION FROM UNIVERSAL CITIZENSHIP AND THE REALITY OF LEGAL PLURALISM

Since its very beginnings, the Mexican state—heir to the liberal doctrine of the Enlightenment and French liberalism—has taken as its premise the discourse of the equality of universal citizenship, which demands the unity of the law and emphasizes the individual legal personality (Marshall 1950). The triad formed by one people/one territory/one culture was a condition for state formation and a politics of acculturation and integration of indigenous peoples into a homogeneous and blended national culture. In the name of equality and the need to build a modern nation, indigenous peoples were denied the right to speak their own languages, and Spanish was enforced as the sole idiom. Laws were imposed on indigenous groups that they could not understand and that failed to take their cultural context into consideration. The authority of indigenous politico-religious institutions was illegitimated, and mestizo municipal officials, who often concentrated the political and economic power of entire regions, were forced upon the indigenous peoples (see Hernández Castillo 2001 for a detailed analysis). All of this was done in the name of the "right to equality," which hid the fact that these legal rights of citizenship were also imposed without consideration of cultural, economic, and social differences.

Paradoxically, while the state denied indigenous peoples access to their own institutions, at the same time it permitted the coexistence of parallel spaces for the delivery of justice that made possible the continuation of traditional forms of social organization. Judicial pluralism has therefore been a consistent reality in Mexico since its independence, partly the result

---

[1] Article 4, para. 1 of (now in Article 2, following a constitutional amendment).

of indigenous tradition, and partly the legacy of colonial law that created a parallel legal system for this native population through the Indigenous Republics.

What we now call indigenous law is made up of a plurality of normative practices that indigenous peoples have produced and re-created to resolve difficulties in their identities and communities. During the nineteenth and twentieth centuries, the isolation and marginalization of indigenous peoples, combined with their own resistance, were factors that made it unfeasible for the judicial system to have effective jurisdiction throughout the nation. This allowed these indigenous peoples to create their own spaces for conflict resolution.[2] Currently, those spaces are being continuously transformed and reinvented in an ongoing relationship with the nation's regular legal system and the specific conditions of each region.

While liberal jurists continued demanding the unity and universality of the law, disregarding the conditions of its actual practice, some lawyers and anthropologists who share a common interest in legal anthropology have been engaged in an analysis of the conflict-resolution mechanisms that coexist with national law and in the different notions of subject and of justice included in this parallel legal system. Through what are, today, classic ethnographies on litigation proceedings—from authors such as Laura Nader (1969) and Jane Collier (1995)—we know, for example, that Tzotzils and Zapotecs consider crime, the conflicts that arise from it, and their resolution to be a collective problem. Thus it is up to the community to seek solutions. We also know that the judicial authorities generally hold civic-religious positions and act as mediators, roles for which experience and age are important elements.

The work of these authors allows us to contrast the Mexican legal system with the indigenous one. The former is heir to the Spanish and Roman legal traditions, in which charges are filed with a public prosecutor, who is responsible for conducting the investigation based on criminal codes and procedures. That legal process is sorted out by means of written documents and without a public trial. In contrast, in the indigenous tradition, hearings occur in community meetings that are open to the public, and each party presents its own witnesses. Moreover, whereas the national legal arena is essentially punitive (despite the supposed goal of criminal

---

[2] The creation of local arenas for conflict resolution is not only occurring in indigenous communities. With a historian's perspective, Pablo Piccato (this volume) shows us similar efforts in Mexico City, which respond to the ineffectiveness of the state's justice system.

rehabilitation), carefully deliberated conciliation procedures predominate in indigenous communities.

Nevertheless, although such procedures have operated against the grain of state power, these arenas have never been, strictly speaking, "liberated spaces," since the state has sometimes made use of them to maintain control and hegemony over those territories through local caciques (Rus 1995; Garza Caligaris 2002). Later works show us that even if we acknowledge the existence of distinct cultural frameworks in mestizo and indigenous society (which must be analyzed in each regional context and be a starting point and not the final goal), we cannot continue to think about indigenous legal systems and the national legal system as two entirely separate spheres. Instead, both spheres continuously interrelate due to the legal strategies of social agents who resort to both arenas of justice (Sierra Camacho 1993, 1995). Thus we ought to think in terms of one single *legal map*, on which the two normative systems are overlapping, interrelated, and, in certain contexts, in opposition, in a productive dialogue that necessarily affects the very content of the distinct legal spaces.[3] However, until now, this ongoing relationship of mutual shaping between the two spaces for delivering justice has essentially been one of subordination, which allows neither a legal recognition of local forms of authority nor a true possibility for genuine political autonomy.

RELUCTANCE IN THE LEGISLATIVE BRANCH

The complex reality described above should have been addressed in the legislative proposition prepared by congressional representatives and senators from all political parties during the negotiation of a major indigenous reform in Mexico in 2001. This initiative resulted from the Agreements on Indigenous Rights and Culture (Acuerdos sobre Derechos y Cultura Indígena), better known as the San Andrés Accords, signed in 1997 by representatives of the Mexican government and the Zapatista Army of National Liberation (EZLN). Based on this agreement, the Peace and Harmony Commission (CO-COPA) would later prepare the initiative known as the COCOPA law. The importance of these negotiations, the broad nationwide consultations, and the

---

[3] We refer to de Sousa Santos's concept of legal maps. He describes legal pluralism as "various superimposed legal spaces, interpenetrated and mixed both in our minds and in our actions, on occasion, with qualitative leaps or devastating crises in our life trajectories as well as in the routine rhythms of our daily lives. We live in an era of legal porosity and porous legality" (1987: 289).

strong support expressed by various indigenous peoples around the country led Francisco López Bárcenas to remark, "of all propositions for transformation that have taken place in our country, the Agreements on Indigenous Rights and Culture have generated the greatest consensus" (López Bárcenas n.d.).

This legal initiative proposed the foundation for a new relationship between indigenous peoples and the Mexican state by amending the legal framework to collectively incorporate indigenous peoples as subjects of the law and recognize their right to self-determination and autonomy. Such a framework would enable Mexico's indigenous peoples to decide upon and exercise their own forms of social, political, economic, and cultural organization and to apply their own norms for conflict resolution. The initiative also aimed at guaranteeing indigenous peoples effective access to the state's jurisdiction and their collective rights over their territories (including the use of natural resources existing there), without denying the distinct cultural features of the indigenous peoples (López Bárcenas n.d.).

However, in April 2001, majorities in both houses of Congress altered the key propositions for self-determination that were originally included in the initiative and presented as a bill by the executive. Ultimately, a constitutional amendment was published on August 14, 2001, by virtue of which several articles were reformed.[4] The initiative endorsed by the Zapatistas, intellectuals, and representatives of the Mexican government was discarded, primarily because of a fear of the notion of indigenous autonomy. For most conservative sectors of the Mexican state, indigenous autonomy implied the disintegration or fragmentation of the nation. Thus the amended legislation begins with a clarification that "the Mexican nation is singular and indivisible," a statement that does not appear in other parts of the Constitution. The specter of national fragmentation, the fear of the collectivization of natural resources, and disapproval of the use of indigenous norms led the Mexican Congress to pass a law that did not respond to the central demands of the national indigenous movement.[5]

Certainly, the new legal framework achieves some greater specificity with regard to cultural diversity, and in this sense it represents an important advance from the monocultural and homogenizing discourses of the

---

[4] Currently, constitutional articles referring to indigenous rights are Article 2 (which replaces Article 4, to which we referred earlier); Article 18, para. 6; Article 27, sec. VII, para. 2; and Article 115, sec. III.

[5] For a legal analysis of the limitations of the new law, see Gómez 2000; López Bárcenas 2000a.

past. Yet ultimately it does not create the conditions for a new political pact between indigenous peoples and the Mexican state. Rather, it seems to mark the formation of an official approach to multiculturalism that disengages political and territorial issues from the concept of culture, and establishes a relationship based on the suspicion that indigenous peoples seek to undermine national unity. Furthermore, there remains a need to establish practical mechanisms to set the law in motion. As a result, the 2001 legislative reforms failed to achieve real structural transformations that would redefine power relations and facilitate access to justice for indigenous peoples.

This explains why the initiative was ultimately rejected by the same groups that worked so hard to achieve a broad mobilization of society in support of indigenous reform.[6] As approved, the law was rejected by the eighteen Mexican states with indigenous majorities. The EZLN and the national indigenous movement also rejected the new law, arguing that it betrayed the spirit of the San Andrés Accords. Although the reform that was finally approved recognized the right to self-determination, it did so with enough provisos and stipulations to postpone indefinitely its effective implementation. Consequently, the indigenous rights originally promised in constitutional Article 4 remain without any regulatory law specifying the meaning and scope originally stipulated.[7]

For example, the new framework empowers state-level constitutions and laws to determine how the autonomy of indigenous peoples will be recognized; it limits indigenous communities' collective usufruct rights to national resources to include only "preferential" access; and it negates the legal status of indigenous norms. Considering that most state assemblies are disinclined to promote further reform, the "right to free determination" —and, consequently, autonomy as guaranteed by constitutional Article 2— will be nothing more than paper tigers (*Diario Oficial*, August 14, 2001).

Moreover, the new framework does not recognize indigenous peoples (that is, ethnic or cultural groups) as legal entities, but instead consigns rights to indigenous *communities* (that is, geographically defined political entities). This implicitly recognizes the rights of the indigenous population

---

[6] The culmination of that support was a tour through 12 Mexican states by members of the EZLN leadership in early 2001, a meeting in Nurío, Michoacán, of 3,383 indigenous delegates from 41 ethnic groups, and the historic appearance of the Zapatista leadership before Mexico's Congress.

[7] Instead, Article 2 now combines substantive law with regulatory law, thus dodging future controversies.

as a whole, but it grants rights only to its territorial manifestations. In turn, this construes those communities as objects of the state's attention by changing their status from entities of public law to entities of public interest (Gómez 2000; López Bárcenas 2000a). The full incorporation of the indigenous peoples into the national structure implies redefining their place not only within the state but also within Mexican society itself. Thus this debate serves as the seed for a new conceptualization of citizenship.

For example, granting legal recognition to indigenous languages and cultural forms presents the need to restructure the country's educational, health care, and judicial systems so that they can function in contexts of diversity. Self-determination also implies the creation of sustainable development models that would reinstate traditional agricultural techniques and combine them with organic agriculture. Economic self-determination would provide indigenous peoples with the means to sell their own products without the need for intermediaries. Finally, the restoration of their normative systems and forms of government would call into question the use of electoral democracy as the sole route to broad political participation.[8]

In sum, despite its breadth, the reform of constitutional Article 2 does not grant legal personhood to indigenous peoples, nor does it guarantee that they will benefit from the natural resources in their territories. The new framework also does not specify the nature of self-determination, which is now decentralized to the discretion of state authorities, and it certainly does not include indigenous normative systems. Ultimately, indigenous peoples' struggle for autonomy is in conflict with the Mexican state and society, transnational corporations, local intermediaries, and political parties for whom their normative structures hold little value. In other words, it is a struggle on many fronts and is, therefore, full of complexities and obstacles.

RELUCTANCE IN THE JUDICIAL BRANCH

Needless to say, legislative reforms, while necessary, are insufficient to transform the indigenous peoples' relationship with the state or, even less, with the overall social structures. The very concept of "the constitution" refers to the project of a nation, not to its actual image. This is particularly

---

[8] For a review of various proposals for indigenous autonomy and specific experiences, see Díaz Polanco 1998; Mattiace 1996.

true regarding aspects relating to the acceptance of diversity, in all its aspects. Discrimination is a social practice that will not disappear in the absence of policies aimed at transforming the letter of the law into new forms of social coexistence. Ultimately, the debate does not end with the writing of a law. Instead, it gathers new dimensions through the reading and interpretation of that law.

Unfortunately, a sector that is particularly reluctant to modify its practices in accordance with the multicultural nature of the Mexican nation is the one comprising the legal practitioners themselves.[9] The lack of jurisprudence on indigenous matters and the Supreme Court's declaration of its lack of jurisdiction in constitutional controversies brought before it by a number of indigenous municipalities in response to the 2001 amendments show that the judicial branch has decided to sideline itself from the debate about indigenous rights (Escalante Betancourt 2002: 27). There are various areas of the judicial branch that merit a review, but in the following pages we will discuss only the need to modify procedures applied to the indigenous individuals subjected to trial or involved in lawsuits.

To begin, we must point out that, in both Mexico and the United States, apparent neutrality of the law obscures the fundamental predominance of an ethnocentric perspective and cultural and linguistic hegemony, which affect practices in law enforcement, the courts, and the prisons. This occurs even to the extent of permitting indigenous individuals to be jailed and tried without due legal assistance or without a legal defense. In extreme cases, this may result in the accused not knowing the charges against him or her or being subjected to psychiatric treatment because the indigenous person does not fit the concept of "normalcy" held by representatives of the justice system (see Ortiz Elizondo 1999; de León Pasquel 2001).

The legal practitioners' conduct does not necessarily fit what the regulations stipulate because it must pass through the interpretive sieve of their own socially and historically determined culture; through the judicial culture itself, which reduces cases to typologies; and through the material conditions in which legal practitioners perform their activities. These three elements, coupled with the persistence of de facto normative systems in indigenous communities, create dissonance between the state's regulations and empirical reality, and that shapes a web of legal fictions. Take, for

---

9 Fix-Fierro (this volume) critiques the teaching of law in Mexico by showing how the "traditional" perspectives of the 1950s (which, of course, do not contain any consideration of diversity) continue to be hegemonic in law school curricula today.

example, the handling of linguistic difference.[10] According to the regulations on interpreters in the Federal Criminal Code (CPF) and the Federal Criminal Procedures Code (CFPP), the determination of Spanish fluency falls on the agent of the Office of the Public Prosecutor. Thus the right to have an interpreter depends on what, in the judgment of the public prosecutor, is "sufficient" language ability.[11]

Even something as simple as entering into the record the defendant's status as a member of an indigenous community, which is the foundation for any and all rights relating to that condition, is frequently omitted. Take, for example, a sampling of court files held by the National Indigenous Institute (INI), now called the National Commission for the Development of Indigenous Peoples (CONADEPI). Some of the files do not even mention whether the accused is an indigenous person. Others acknowledge that the accused speaks an indigenous language or is an indigenous person but do not mention the rights relating to that condition. Only in a minority of cases is the person's membership in an ethnic group entered into the record and the rights relating to that condition indicated (Ortiz Elizondo 2003).

In December 2002, the CFPP was amended again so that Articles 15, 18, 124b, 128(4), 154, and 159 now require that interpreters and defense attorneys have knowledge of indigenous languages, culture, customs, and practices. This is an advance in the letter of the law. However, in legal practice, changes come slowly because the courtrooms do not have court-appointed public defenders who are indigenous or, at minimum, "have knowledge of the culture of the accused." Moreover, in places like Mexico City, the number of cases is proportionally so low and the number of languages and variants so high that it is not viable, even in the long term, for agencies to be staffed by people who meet those criteria. In consequence, the INI's Legal Enforcement Department (now disappeared) became a nonjudicial branch of the public defender's office. In its absence, universities or professional schools will have to replace it, but this is not yet taking place.

Something similar occurs with the mandate that judges and courts must consider the indigenous customs and practices of the defendant's people

---

[10] For a binational analysis of linguistic issues in trials of indigenous peoples, see Escalante Betancourt 2002.

[11] The 2002 reform of the CFPP tries to remedy this problem by including in Article 154 the prescription to inform the accused of the "right to be assisted by an interpreter and a defense attorney who knows the language and culture." The mechanisms for informing the accused of this right, without already having an interpreter present, remain to be resolved.

(*Diario Oficial*, December 11, 2002). A specialist, whether a professional or a practitioner, must be involved in collecting that information. However, the conditions that would call for that type of expert opinion have not been established, so that experts are sometimes called in for no reason; and at other times, when they could be of use, they are not present. Moreover, the judge is free to determine the requisites for someone to be considered an expert in indigenous matters. Thus anthropologists or lawyers, speakers of a variant of the language, or even indigenous leaders with conflicts of interest are all, at times, considered "experts."

In any case, considering the customs and practices of indigenous peoples or communities during trials only makes sense to the degree that the final result—the sentence—is altered by the existence of those elements. Indeed, even in cases where expert opinion has been offered to argue that cultural factors contributed to the commission of the crime, the result has not been the acceptance of customary practices or the legitimization of indigenous institutions or even a validation of those actions (Ortiz Elizondo 2003). The reasons bandied about by the judges for discarding expert testimony generally refer to equality before the law. So, in the end, what is the purpose of the expert?

In order for the notion of plurality to take root among legal practitioners, judicial practices and discourse must be modernized through innovative responses to changing social conditions. The lawyer's saying about the perfectibility of the law—"laws are not improved, they are only updated"—is only one form of hiding the historicity of norms and practices.

Two lone exceptions stand vis-à-vis the real integration of plurality through changes in government structures. One is the legislation on indigenous matters added to Oaxaca's constitution that, among other things, recognizes the character of indigenous peoples as public-law entities. This enables the application of the customary voting system as a mechanism for municipal elections, replacing the intermediation of political parties.[12]

The second exception is the legislation contained in Quintana Roo's 1997 Law on Indigenous Justice (Ley de Justicia Indígena), which creates an indigenous justice system with representation in Mayan ceremonial centers. This system is headed by a judiciary council for indigenous justice, which monitors the performance of traditional judges, whose decisions are admitted as *res judicata*. In this last case, the number of provisos incorpo-

---

[12] For a detailed critique of this legal framework, see López Bárcenas 2000b.

rated into the law is, unfortunately, very high. Among them we can mention the limitations on the traditional judges' jurisdiction over crimes involving livestock rustling (Art. 17, sec. II). In economic felonies, their jurisdiction is limited to damages involving up to one hundred minimum wages (Art. 15, sec. I; Art. 17, sec. II, III, IV, and VI). Notably, Quintana Roo's Judicial Branch Framework Law (Ley Orgánica del Poder Judicial) does not specify where the judiciary council or traditional judges fit into the structure.

In summary, a judicial apparatus that could incorporate plurality cannot depend solely on legislative amendments. It also requires a conceptual framework in which the actors recognize the importance of diversity and act accordingly. It also requires human capital that would establish non-discriminatory relationships with indigenous peoples and other forms of diversity. Finally, it requires being open to debate with social scientists and abandoning the prejudice that there is no other truth than one's own.

AN INDIGENOUS CONTRIBUTION TO PUBLIC SECURITY

Beyond the strictly legislative arena and most relevant for this chapter's purposes, a key problem regarding legal fictions is the persistence of indigenous legal systems despite their persecution and/or denial by the judicial system, government officials, and legal practitioners. Thus, for example, in the Costa Chica region of the state of Guerrero, a large group of Tlapanec, Mixtec, and, to a lesser degree, Nahua and mestizo communities, located primarily in the municipalities of San Luis Acatlán, Azoyú, and Malinaltepec, successfully developed a public security project known as "community police" (*policía comunitaria*) (Flores Félix 2001).[13] According to members and supporters, this project arose during a crime wave in the region during the first half of the 1990s. Heavily armed masked gangs operated freely because of the ineffectiveness—even the collaboration—of existing law enforcement agencies.[14] The day after the assembly of communities created the system, a document was sent to Guerrero's attorney general, with copies to the governor and Mexico's president, requesting

---

13 The official inaugural date was October 15, 1995, during an assembly in which thirty-eight communities participated. Participation is by community, but today even the municipality of San Luis Acatlán participates and supports the system.

14 Rowland (2003) discusses conflicts that the region's inhabitants had with Guerrero's state security apparatus.

that the state motorized police be replaced by the community police, the latter to be funded by the former's budget.

Originally, this Community Public Security System (Sistema de Seguridad Pública Comunitaria) was directed exclusively at policing. Presumed offenders were arrested and turned over to the public prosecutor's office. In contrast to the traditional structures that had been in force until then, the so-called *topiles*, or police, broadened their scope of action, surpassing the boundaries of the indigenous community to include neighboring roads and coordinating with other communities. However, two years later they decided that this system was not effective since offenders who were turned over to the public prosecutor's office often were not prosecuted (Martínez Sifuentes 2001: 47). So the original police structure was complemented with a new one, the Officers' Coordinating Body (Coordinadora de Autoridades), charged with "delivering justice according to the customs and practices of the peoples." This set of agencies is now called the Community System for Security, Justice Delivery, and Reeducation (Sistema Comunitario de Seguridad, Impartición de Justicia y Reeducación; hereinafter the community system), and over two hundred people are involved in it.

The community system's effectiveness is difficult to determine. Certainly highway robberies have declined and the population feels protected, but it is not possible to establish a cause-and-effect relationship without further research. The director of the penitentiary in San Luis Acatlán credits the community system with reducing the number of inmates since 1997, which may make that prison the only one in the country that is not overpopulated (*El Sol de Acapulco*, January 26, 2001).[15]

If we consider the self-image of the members of the community system, they speak proudly of the people's voluntary participation in the feeding of detainees, intercultural communication, and the validation of customs and practices that were being lost. Moreover, members believe that the "community has gained personhood" by assuming "the responsibility of working for its own welfare." They also count among their achievements the opening of a highway, increased production, coordination with the "government police" and the army, and the absence of bribery in freeing prisoners. Up to the year 2003, the community system had "rehabilitated" 150 people (disclosure statement "Promoting Hope, 8th Anniversary," n.d.).

---

15 Rowland (2003) mentions the importance of the perception of effectiveness vis-à-vis the measures taken, a requirement that is met in the region. Regarding prison conditions in Mexico, see Azaola and Bergman, this volume.

In its current structure, the community system is led by a general assembly of officers, composed of representatives from all the participating communities. This body determines an offender's guilt and the need to apply rehabilitation. Subordinate to the general assembly are a committee and a coordinating council. Each has six members of equal status who serve for one year. The committee members are called *comandantes* and are responsible for coordinating police activities involving arrests and patrolling in the communities and on neighboring roads. The coordinating council members are referred to as *comisarios* who, in their words, "deliver justice," which in fact means that they perform activities pertaining to investigative and judiciary agencies. A third body, comprising two delegates from each community, serves as a regulatory organ for the system. It works on internal regulations, the contents of which specify the obligations and powers of each body. The phrase "respect for human rights" is repeated in each chapter of the regulations. The regulations justify the existence of the community system based on the Mexican Constitution and ILO Convention 169. From the perspective of the community system's members, they are following the rules; the government of Guerrero is not.

The community system's central offices and the jail are located in an unfurnished residence with four rooms and a large patio, located four blocks from the municipal offices of San Luis Acatlán. This residence also houses the radio communications system that connects the communities in the system. In this office, local conflicts are heard, as are other cases the *comisarios* hand over—supposedly only those considered too serious to be settled by a *comisario*. All the cases that are presented and the conciliation agreements that are reached are recorded in writing, as are the names of those arrested, released, and imprisoned. It is a traditional system but one in which the collective memory does not depend on the elders but instead on the labors of a secretary.

The police officers serve rotating fifteen-day shifts by community. Their principal duties are to patrol the roads and communities, guard offices, and accompany cargo trucks and people who request an escort. They also guard prisoners while they perform maintenance work on roads, churches, schools, and so forth, a central aspect of the prisoners' reeducation. Each police officer is responsible for a rifle (these are usually low-caliber weapons, but supposedly there are some M1 rifles). While on duty, they must wear a uniform—a cap and T-shirt stamped in green or black with the emblem of the association. They carry identification cards (with a photograph and birthdate) issued by the municipal headquarters. Two nearly new pickup trucks, donated by the municipal government, carry the police between the communities.

If all this deployment were aimed at pursuing chicken thieves or those accused of putting a hex on their neighbors, or if it just involved dealing with drunks and abusive husbands, probably no one would care. However, the security system has taken on robberies, assaults, rapes, murders, and the planting of illegal drug crops, as well as all of the misdemeanors mentioned above. The more serious crimes demand sentences involving imprisonment, which has led to incarcerations for up to one year. The scope of this form of social organization has left the police open to accusations of subversion.

Such an extensive system cannot operate without funding. However, this support does not come from clandestine foreign interests but from public donations and subventions made openly. Some of the community system's firearms are hunting rifles, which for years had been in the possession of the people who carry them. The governor of Guerrero himself donated twenty rifles. The municipal government of San Luis Acatlán has been providing a subvention that in 2003 amounted to 50,000 pesos per month. As in the past, through a grant competition for justice projects, the Commission for Indigenous Development (CDI) provided the community police with more than 100,000 pesos to continue developing its activities that year. At one time there had also been cooperation with the National System for Family Development (DIF), which provided supplies for agents, and with Liconsa (a state-run milk distribution agency) in exchange for guarding their delivery trucks.

The activities of this security corps are clearly performed in good faith, publicly, and under the scrutiny of society. The relationship with various government agencies is ongoing and diverse, and it has included a training course on the handling of firearms run by the 48th Infantry Battalion (Martínez Sifuentes 2001: 70), with which there has also been coordination of police work during traditional festivals. The community system's weapons are duly registered, and one of the strongest aspirations of the system's members is to obtain a collective license to carry firearms. Their efforts to become a part of state legitimacy included steps in March 2000 to form a civic association.

The most relevant feature regarding cooperation with the state is that the community system respects a verbal agreement with the public prosecutor's office through which each side resolves the problems brought before it, and once one initiates a process, the other does not intervene. However, the system is illegal, not because the Constitution does not permit it but because the regulatory laws do not recognize it and government authorities persecute it and deny its existence.

Thus, for example, Julio Lorenzo Jáuregui, a judge in Guerrero's Superior Court, declared in February that the agreement made by the communities' general assemblies that created the indigenous security system "is entirely baseless, lacking legal foundation, and, consequently, contrary to the rule of law that must prevail in our state." No less significant was the statement by Guerrero's assistant public prosecutor: "I cannot say whether the community police is legal or not, because for us this body does not exist." Persecution and denial, it seems, reflect official responses to this indigenous legal system. Indeed, at the time of this study, there were nineteen arrest warrants against members of the community system, another five members were free on bond, and the CNDH (14/2003) had issued a recommendation to Guerrero's governor to free twenty-one prisoners undergoing reeducation (one of whom had been turned over to the community system by his own mother).[16]

Nevertheless, the Mexican Constitution, in paragraph 2 of amended Article 2, recognizes and guarantees the right of indigenous peoples to self-determination:

> To apply their own normative systems to regulate and resolve internal conflicts, subject to the general principles of this Constitution, with respect for civil liberties, human rights, and in a manner respecting the dignity and integrity of women. The law will establish the cases and procedures for verification by judges and the corresponding courts.

Undoubtedly this paragraph is open to various interpretations. For example, to the degree that the subject of the law is the community and not the ethnic group, one might argue that internal conflicts are only those that occur within the boundaries of the community, which would exclude assaults on nearby roads. Moreover, by saying that the "law will establish the cases and procedures for validation," it fails to specify to which law it is referring and whether that law already exists or is yet to be written. It also gives the state the right to establish the conditions for ratifying

---

16 That recommendation was not implemented because the prisoner was released at the request of his mother on May 4, an act with which his reeducation was considered complete.

indigenous regulations, which amounts to state interference in the shaping of those laws.

In any case, the judges and courts in Guerrero have not yet decided to ratify, either in part or in total, the indigenous security system that operates in the state. Ultimately, not all activities of legal practitioners are aimed against crime. At least some of them aim at preserving the system itself. The existence of the community system and other indigenous legal systems does indeed threaten the identity of the national, monocultural, and monolithic legal system.

ADMINISTRATIVE DECENTRALIZATION OR STATE REFORM: RETHINKING CITIZENSHIP

Some scholars have noted that granting indigenous peoples rights to autonomous justice systems, as has been achieved in several Latin American countries in recent years (Colombia, 1991; Paraguay, 1992; Peru, 1993; Bolivia, 1994; Venezuela, 1999), is still a limited response to indigenous peoples' demands for autonomy. Besides, it also responds to pressures from international financial organizations that call for the decentralization of state power (Sieder 2002). So-called indigenous law can play a role similar to mechanisms for alternative dispute resolution or restorative justice that presently exist in countries like the United States. These offer civic spaces for conflict resolution, and the legal apparatus supports them because they help to simplify the delivery of justice and the functioning of the state apparatus (see www.aic.gov.au/rjustice/index.html).

In Mexico, however, the coupling of the state-level judicial system with the indigenous spaces for the delivery of justice mainly reflects the state's inability to impose its law throughout the nation—and, therefore, a self-interested tolerance that may continue only until the state perceives that its power is being affected. As such, even in the light of democratic federalism, this type of decentralization has little to do with indigenous peoples' demands for autonomy or the recognition of their collective rights, which the Mexican government initially sanctioned in 1989 when it signed ILO Convention 169.

The demands for autonomy reflected in the COCOPA law initiative were not directed toward seeking administrative decentralization; instead, they sought a comprehensive state reform that would necessarily be accompanied by the construction of a new collective conceptualization of the nation. Although the indigenous movement has not laid claim to the concept, its demands point to the construction of a new type of ethnic or cultural citizenship. Under this vision, being ethnically or linguistically different from the dominant society would not deny the right to belong to or participate in the democratic processes of the state (Rosaldo 2000; de la Peña 1999, 2002).[17]

One problem with the construction of this new type of citizenship pact is the idealization of the indigenous past, which in part is a reaction against the racism with which some sectors of Mexican society treat indigenous cultures. The sharp dismissal of their cultural forms has led indigenous leaders, their advisers, and many sympathizers to portray an idealized version of the communities, one that emphasizes the harmonious nature of their regulatory systems, the focus on ecology in their cosmological vision, and the sense of democracy within their government forms. However, both the racist and the idealized visions are ahistorical and deny the complexity of cultural identities. This would suggest that there are only two possible representations: either the nineteenth-century one, which views indigenous culture as primitive, residual, backward, and thus discardable; or the essentialist one, which presents it as millenarian, ecological, and democratic, and then bases its legitimacy as a viable identity on those characteristics.

Indigenous women confront both representations by calling on the state to recognize their right to cultural difference and by calling on the indigenous movement to recognize their right to change cultural forms that affect women's freedom and dignity. In the Mexican Congress, in the National Indigenous Congress (CNI), and in the many arenas of debate that have appeared following the Zapatista uprising, the voices of these organized indigenous women show how to imagine indigenous autonomy from a dynamic conceptualization of the culture and with a historical perspective on ethnic and gender identities (Hernández Castillo 2002; Mattiace, Hernández, and Rus 2002).

Confronting the liberal critiques that accuse indigenous law of being backward and antidemocratic, indigenous women have pointed out the dynamic character of their normative systems, which are continuously being reconfigured and which, in recent years, reflect the transformations and struggles these women have promoted. Two indigenous women, Comandante Esther, the Zapatista leader, and María de Jesús Patricio, a CNI

---

17 Iris Marion Young (2000) develops the concept of differentiated citizenship in reference to the construction of a heterogeneous public space that considers differences of cultural, gender, and sexual preferences, in which interest groups would work together while maintaining their collective identities.

representative, defended the COCOPA law in speeches before the Mexican Congress. They challenged the static representations of tradition that have been used to dismiss indigenous practices and customs, saying instead that the indigenous communities' normative systems are being reworked and that indigenous women are playing a fundamental role in that process.

In this regard, María de Jesús Patricio pointed out:

> We indigenous peoples now recognize that there are practices we should combat and others we should encourage, and this is seen in the more active participation of women in the decisions of our community. Today, we women participate more in the decisions of the assemblies; today we are chosen to hold positions; and in general we participate more in community life (*La Jornada*, April 3, 2001: 9).

Comandante Esther focused on enumerating the inequalities and exclusions that the current legislation permits. She argued that the COCOPA initiative would serve to "allow us to be recognized and respected, as woman and as indigenous persons.... Our rights as women are included in that law, since now no one can impede our participation or our dignity and integrity in any endeavor, the same as men."[18]

CONCLUSION

In the hope of expediting trials and reducing paperwork, the possibility of incorporating a system of oral judgment and mediation for resolution of certain conflicts is under discussion in the state of Nuevo León. In Mexico's Federal District, a conciliation system has already been launched, and there is interest in adopting a "neighborhood policing" model to bring the activities of officers into closer connection with the people they serve. In indigenous communities, these features have already existed for a long time. However, legal practitioners do not generally refer to them as a model for such "innovation" or otherwise incorporate these practices into the existing legal system. From our viewpoint, this simply confirms the ignorance and

---

[18] Opponents to the COCOPA law frequently used women's issues as a reason to oppose indigenous peoples' struggle for self-determination. Yet the active participation of women in the San Andrés Larrainzar roundtable discussions ensured that the initiative indeed helped to protect women's rights and interests within indigenous justice-delivering systems.

disdain that exists in Mexico with regard to the cultural practices of indigenous peoples.

In the case of the community police in Guerrero, an important issue to confront in the future is the community system's capacity for expansion, especially because of its centralized character. To the degree that new communities are incorporated, the community dynamic may begin to lose the capacity to control the overall system. This potential shortcoming could also be remedied through formal recognition by and coordination with state structures. As noted throughout this essay, recent political and legislative endeavors in Mexico are not aimed merely at the constitutional recognition of indigenous peoples and their corresponding rights. What is mainly at stake is the need to rethink the national project and to establish a new social pact among Mexicans that would include indigenous peoples as an integral part of the Mexican state.

The challenge of access to justice for Mexico's indigenous peoples goes beyond administrative reforms to the judicial system. Pending is a true reform of the state that would incorporate diversity. Instances of autonomy that occur de facto in several indigenous regions, of which Guerrero's community police is only one example, and the active participation of women in the incipient national indigenous movement give us some clues about how to rethink cultural diversity from a nonessentialist perspective. Studying the experiences of indigenous men and women can give us some idea of how to imagine a multicultural state through a dynamic definition of culture. Diversity should not lead to disintegration or exclusion, but rather to specificity and heterogeneity. Multiculturalism requires that differences be considered as relational rather than as a product of categories or essential attributes, so that the right to citizenship does not imply renunciation or denial of cultural identity.

References

Collier, Jane. 1995. *El derecho zinacanteco: procesos de disputar en un pueblo indígena de Chiapas*. Mexico City: CIESAS/UNICACH.

de la Peña, Guillermo. 1999. "Reflexiones preliminares sobre la ciudadanía étnica." In *La sociedad civil, de la teoría a la realidad*, ed. Alberto Olvera. Mexico City: El Colegio de México.

———. 2002. "Social Citizenship, Ethnic Minority Demands, Human Rights and Neoliberal Paradoxes: A Case Study in Western Mexico." In *Multiculturalism in Latin America: Indigenous Rights, Diversity, and Democracy*, ed. Rachel Sieder. London: Institute of Latin American Studies, University of London.

de León Pasquel, Lourdes. 2001. "Lenguas minorizadas, justicia y legislación en México y Estados Unidos." In *Costumbres, leyes y movimiento indio en Oaxaca y Chiapas*, ed. Lourdes de León Pasquel. Mexico City: CIESAS/Miguel Ángel Porrúa.

de Santos Souza, Boaventura. 1987. "Law: A Map of Misreading. Toward a Postmodern Conception of Law," *Journal of Law and Society* 4, no. 3: 279–302.

Díaz Polanco, Héctor. 1998. *La rebelión zapatista y la autonomía.* Mexico City: Siglo Veintiuno.

Escalante Betancourt, Yuri. 2002. "La eliminación de la alteridad lingüística en los procesos judiciales." In *La experiencia del peritaje antropológico*, by Yuri Escalante Betancourt et al. Mexico City: Instituto Nacional Indigenista.

Flores Félix, José Joaquín. 2001. "Democracia, ciudadanía y autonomía de los indígenas en la región Costa Montaña del estado de Guerrero." In *Migración, poder y procesos rurales*, ed. Arturo López León, Beatriz Canabal Cristiani, and Rodrigo Pimienta Lastra. Mexico City: Universidad Autónoma Metropolitana/Plaza y Valdés.

Garza Caligaris, Anna María. 2002. *Género, interlegalidad y conflicto en San Pedro Chenalhó.* Mexico: Universidad Nacional Autónoma de México/UNACH-IEI.

Gómez, Magdalena. 2000. "Iniciativa presidencial en materia indígena: los desacuerdos con los Acuerdos de San Andrés." In *Autonomía y derechos de los pueblos indígenas*, ed. Gabriel García Colorado and Irma Eréndira Sandoval. Mexico City: Cámara de Diputados–Instituto de Investigaciones Legislativas.

Hernández Castillo, Rosalva Aída. 2001. *Histories and Stories from Chiapas: Border Identities in Southern Mexico.* Austin: University of Texas Press.

———. 2002. "National Law and Indigenous Customary Law: The Struggle for Justice of the Indigenous Women from Chiapas, Mexico." In *Gender, Justice, Development, and Rights*, ed. Maxine Molyneux and Shahra Razavi. London: Oxford University Press.

López Bárcenas, Francisco. 2000a. "La diversidad negada: los derechos indígenas en la propuesta gubernamental de reforma constitucional." In *Autonomía y derechos de los pueblos indígenas*, ed. Gabriel García Colorado and Irma Eréndira Sandoval. Mexico City: Cámara de Diputados–Instituto de Investigaciones Legislativas.

———. 2000b. "La diversidad mutilada: los derechos indígenas en la Constitución de Oaxaca." In *Autonomía y derechos de los pueblos indígenas*, ed. Gabriel García Colorado and Irma Eréndira Sandoval. Mexico City: Cámara de Diputados–Instituto de Investigaciones Legislativas.

———. n.d. "La lucha por la autonomía indígena en México: un reto al pluralismo." In *El Estado y los indígenas en tiempos del PAN*, ed. Rosalva Aída Hernández Castillo, Teresa Sierra, and Sarela Paz. Mexico City: CIESAS. In press.

Marshall, T.H. 1950. *Citizenship and Social Class and Other Essays*. Cambridge, Mass.: Cambridge University Press.

Martínez Sifuentes, Esteban. 2001. *La policía comunitaria: un sistema de seguridad pública comunitaria indígena en el estado de Guerrero*. Colección Derecho Indígena del INI. Mexico City: Instituto Nacional Indigenista.

Mattiace, Shannan. 1996. "Zapata Vive! The EZLN, Indian Politics and the Autonomy Movement in Mexico," *Journal of Latin American Anthropology* 3, nos. 1–2: 32–71.

Mattiace, Shannan, Rosalva Aída Hernández, and Jan Rus. 2002. *Tierra, libertad y autonomía: impactos regionales del zapatismo*. Mexico City: IWGIA/CIESAS.

Nader, Laura, 1969. "Styles of Court Procedures: To Make the Balance." In *Law in Culture and Society*, ed. Laura Nader. Chicago, Ill.: Adline.

Ortiz Elizondo, Héctor. 1999. "Impartición de justicia, ciencia y diferencia cultural: instantáneas de un viajero perdido," *Dimensión Antropológica* 15, no. 6. Special issue on racism and law.

———. 2003. "El reconocimiento de la diferencia cultural en los juzgados mexicanos," *Revista del Instituto de la Judicatura Federal* 15: 87–98.

Rosaldo, Renato. 2000. "La pertenencia no es un lujo: procesos de ciudadanía cultural dentro de una sociedad multicultural," *Desacatos* 3: 39–51.

Rowland, Allison M. 2003. "Local Responses to Public Insecurity in Mexico: A Consideration of the Policía Comunitaria of the Costa Chica and the Montaña de Guerrero." Paper presented at the international congress of the Latin American Studies Association, Dallas, March 27.

Rus, Jan. 1995. "La Comunidad Revolucionaria Institucional: la subversión del gobierno indígena en Los Altos de Chiapas (1936–1968)." In *Chiapas: los rumbos de otra historia*, ed. Juan Pedro Viqueira and Mario Ruz. Mexico City: CIESAS/CEMCA/Universidad Nacional Autónoma de México/UF.

Sieder, Rachel. 2002. "Introduction." In *Multiculturalism in Latin America: Indigenous Rights, Diversity, and Democracy*, ed. Rachel Sieder. London: Institute of Latin American Studies, University of London.

Sierra Camacho, María Teresa. 1993. "Usos y desusos del derecho consuetudinario," *Nueva Antropología* 13, no. 44 (August).

———. 1995. "Articulación jurídica y usos legales entre los nahuas de la Sierra Norte de Puebla." In *Pueblos indígenas ante el derecho*, ed. María Teresa Sierra and Victoria Chenaut. Mexico City: CIESAS.

Young, Iris Marion. 2000. *La justicia y la política de la diferencia*. Translated by Silviana Álvarez. Valencia, Spain: Ediciones Cátedra.

PART V

Best Practices and Policy Recommendations

CHAPTER 17

Exploring Roads to Police Reform:
Six Recommendations

ROBERT O. VARENIK

In the area of public security and policing, Mexico faces a painful dilemma, one that appears not to admit of a solution. Its police forces utterly lack public trust. Citizens betray a palpable fear that contact with the police will more likely cost them some of their rights (or goods) than preserve and protect them. In short, reform of the police is needed, urgently.

At the same time, the nation finds itself in the midst of the most troubling period of criminality in its modern history. The perception that crime is more common, better organized, more dangerous, and generally more out of control than before only exacerbates the enormity of the multiple challenges involved in vetting, retraining, managing, and radically upgrading police forces at every level and across the nation. For Mexicans, this is attempting to repair or replace a faulty parachute while free falling. Faced with dual emergencies, politicians run a great risk of seizing upon an approach that is too fast and not carefully considered, as a means of placating a public clamoring for action. The fact that police reform is a new endeavor and local police experts are scarce only enhances the potential for hazard.

This essay attempts to offer a lens through which to view this challenge and a few recommendations for public officials to consider. The focus is as much on initiating the processes for change as on the specific reforms themselves. The recommendations draw on the lessons of experiences elsewhere, because they are relevant and because Mexico's own lack of experience with democratic, responsive policing obligates its leaders to create a new tradition, supported by ideas adapted to local realities.

POLICE REFORM: A PROPOSED VIEW OF THE UNDERLYING CHALLENGE

As various observers have noted, two central characteristics set policing apart from many other aspects of the criminal justice process (and, indeed, many other occupations).[1] Analysis of the potential for police abuse (or inefficiency or corruption) often begins with the wide discretion that officers continually exercise and the low visibility of their daily decisions (Walker 1993: 21–25; see also Brown 1981). These are distinct from the often-mentioned police monopoly on the application of force, but concern over the combination of great discretion and little visibility is obviously amplified by the high stakes that are present when state agents wield the right to detain, subdue, even kill.

For comparison's sake, consider the work of a criminal court judge. Working within a normative framework that governs substantive matters—and, indeed, constitutes a formal process for assimilating facts and applying the law—judges are informed as well by the input and scrutiny that various collateral actors (prosecutors, defense counsel, appellate courts, to name a few) are obligated to provide as part of their own functions. A judge's decision is the culmination of formal proceedings, arguments, and (one hopes) deliberate reflection upon the proof and the law, with a careful eye toward what a superior tribunal might decide upon review of a potential appeal or writ.

Police work contrasts radically with this model. Much of an officer's work is "pre-process"—before the formalities of criminal justice begin to structure the actors' behavior—and comprises actions that require, above all, subtle and sometimes rapid reactions that are virtually impossible to define or prescribe a priori. Taking one of the more dramatic and difficult examples (but one that is fundamental to policing and the question of controlling police), how much force, for example, is justified in effecting the arrest of a suspect? In practice, an officer must calculate, in real time, factors such as the other's physical stature, whether and how he is armed, the consequences of his evading capture, and a host of other considerations that can only be determined (if at all) in the midst of the encounter. The law offers guides—principles of proportionality and necessity—but ultimately leaves the officer, in the heat of the moment, with little more than his reservoir of experience and good judgment. In other words, discretion.

---

[1] Two works that offer an idea of the breadth of discretionary decisions made by police officers are Davis 1975 and Walker 1992.

Second, neither the police hierarchy nor the judicial apparatus, which have defined responsibilities for supervising the actions of police personnel, are present at the moment of decision and action. (Few things highlight the different roles and modalities of judges and police more than the formers' oversight of the latter. Society mandates judges to second-guess the police and grants them the luxury of time and distance so that they might carefully contemplate what the officer had seconds to decide, perhaps with his own or others' safety at risk.) Officers are supposed to record some of their actions (how and how often varies from place to place), but there is nothing to compare with the reasoned memorials of judicial decisions. This is particularly true when officers decline to act. For instance, normally nothing is written up when the cop decides *not* to stop a car or write a ticket. In other cases, officers can make certain actions, even encounters with civilians, virtually invisible by simply failing to note or report them, even when required to do so.[2] In fact, for better or worse, officers pass the majority of their professional lives acting with little visibility and little scrutiny but with very high stakes. For these reasons the principal challenges in police reform are to examine, oversee, and occasionally bureaucratize discretion in order to ensure that, day in and day out, officers are doing what we hope they will and not what we fear.

Accountability is the operative principle behind a series of mechanisms for regulating the exercise of broad discretion and limiting bad, illegal, or nonperformance. In other words, the challenge is to bring the exercise of discretion within a system of institutional and societal controls. Achieving this is the nucleus of sustainable reform because it tends to ensure the return on other investments, such as better salaries, training, and equipment. Accountability is also particularly important for Mexico, which has lacked systemic approaches to public administration of police forces, precisely because it incorporates a focus on the institutional response as well as the individual conduct.

The focus on institutional conduct and development—making agencies act like real institutions—may be as alien to many Mexican reformers as it is urgently needed. In the area of criminal justice and policing, local debate

---

[2] Officers in the New York City Police Department have apparently used this tactic frequently. Although they are required to record "stop and frisk" encounters, there is reason to believe that often no form is completed or kept. Indeed, NYPD policy does not require officers to report all "stops," making the tracking of officer interventions difficult. See, for example, Office of the Attorney General 1999: 71–72.

is inordinately concentrated on reforming the criminal law (primarily the Penal Code, and secondarily the procedure) and renaming or rearranging which agencies have which responsibilities. Thus the plan advanced by the Fox administration talks primarily about unifying Mexico's two main federal police forces under a new roof, but it neglects entirely the issue of strengthening what goes inside the box on the organizational chart (Presidencia de la República. n.d.). Where to place authority over Mexico's police forces and how many to have are not, to be sure, trivial issues. But they pale in comparison to the questions of *how* the police are run: what they are paid, who evaluates them, what incentives govern behavior, what information they compile, how they utilize it for internal and external purposes, and so on. Mexico's public institutions—and police are among the most dramatic examples—too often resemble organizational shells for personnel and budget rather than dynamic institutions capable of demonstrating learning from experience, continuity of purpose, or even clear internal norms or standardized operating procedures. Ignoring this set of foundational issues is something Mexican decision makers have done, and continue to do, at their peril.

Accountability is a term not easily translated into Spanish. *Rendición de cuentas*, perhaps the term most often used, approximates but does not completely capture the dimensions of the concept as it is intended here. In Mexico in particular, *rendición de cuentas* conjures up the notion of making a report, often, if not always, about the use of public resources. It therefore carries a connotation of fiscal responsibility and oversight and does not, in common usage, necessarily include the idea of a response—a process or processes that determine and impose consequences if the action is found to be inappropriate or illegal. As used here, accountability connotes review of a broader range of conduct, investigation if necessary, a determination of appropriateness, and the application of sanction or reward as indicated by the circumstances. It also implies an atmosphere of transparency and the provision of information needed to allow the appropriate actors to make informed decisions.

Police should not interpret the focus on their discretion or the call for greater accountability solely as a "stick" or a crippling restriction on their judgment and action. Demonstrated accountability is also a key to credibility, closely related to what Lawrence Sherman calls "evidenced-based policing" (Sherman 1998: 4). As Sherman uses it, the term implies the presence of evaluation and accountability mechanisms as elements of modern management systems that permit the police hierarchy to know what officers are doing, with what results, and where to make changes—without which it would be hard to demonstrate impact, and thereby make a convincing case for public support, true civil service status, enhanced budgets, and so on.[3] Irrespective of the particular policing strategies employed—be they the so-called zero tolerance, community policing, or problem-solving policing—effective accountability mechanisms are needed to assure both the police and the public that, among other things, the inevitable officer discretion is not abused.

With accountability as the rubric for looking at the challenge of reform, the question shifts to where to begin and which other experiences might offer clues.

WHAT LESSONS DO OTHER EXPERIENCES OFFER?

The most dramatic reforms tend to arise in post-conflict situations (such as in Central America), upon independence (as in East Timor), after the disintegration of security structures from an old regime (for example, Haiti), or with the change of governmental paradigm (Russia after the breakup of the Soviet Union). In such cases, there is the political momentum to make fundamental, as opposed to incremental, changes. Often the government can rely upon external actors such as the United Nations, NATO, or the Organization of American States to deploy forces to shore up security during the transition to a new police. At times, donors are prepared to finance much of the process as well as underwrite significant portions of the new entity's budget. Where a thoroughly discredited old force is to be radically transformed or replaced, the focus tends to be on creating a new police with some measure of professional selection and training, formal independence from the military, and reasonable working conditions—pillars, if you will, of democratic policing. These efforts usually include some initiative around accountability in order to offer some response to a prevailing pattern of rights abuses committed by police officers.

Although the "rupture" or post-trauma situations just described are similar in some ways to the broad outlines of the Mexican scenario (to the extent that the situation in Mexico, a federal republic of some thirty-two

---

[3] One recent survey of New York City residents explored the things that motivate people to support the police, obey them, and help them. Fairness by the police in dealing with civilians was the most important factor in getting people to support police discretion, obey police orders, generally cooperate with them, or support budget increases for the police (Tyler n.d.).

state-level entities, can be generalized), they are quite different in others. Mexico cannot contemplate decommissioning entire police forces at once, lacking "blue helmets" (United Nations Civilian Police, or CIVPOL) to maintain security while it reinvents the police. And although foreign experts may be welcomed to offer their perspectives, Mexico's reform process will have to be its own, not directed by other nations or donor institutions, as in the other cases.

In stable countries, including those that enjoy a tradition of "democratic" policing, reform tends to be more evolutionary, even if episodic. Important changes have often tended to deal with more detailed issues, the creation or strengthening of internal control or oversight mechanisms, and the integration of different mechanisms into systems. In the most successful cases, these changes reflect the acceptance of accountability as a central thread in management and public administration, and not just a necessary evil in order to placate public pressure over human rights or corruption scandals. These may prove to be more apt examples, particularly at the federal and Federal District levels.

There are diverse lessons to be drawn from the wide range of experiences. They speak to the steps needed to create the impetus for reform and the steps needed to diagnose and address the challenge. Two initial recommendations are directed at the process for facilitating learning and agreement.

1. Acknowledge the technical aspects of this field of inquiry and practice, and seek formulas for avoiding political gridlock.

In Northern Ireland, after thirty years of conflict, the parties found themselves in extremely difficult negotiations that had as one of their central issues the reform of a police force that was, according to Catholics who had borne the brunt of their tactics, tainted by violence and impunity, but which for loyalist Protestants and the British government offered the main line of defense against IRA terrorism. It became clear that the parties alone would not likely resolve the question of what to do with the police, and that some alternative process would be required if progress were to be achieved. Faced with a strong possibility of paralysis and failure, bitterly opposed factions found a mechanism that promised a sound technical basis for a reform plan and offered a way around political impasse.

They agreed upon terms of reference for a commission charged with developing recommendations for reform. The terms of reference articulated not only the inclusive and democratic values that the Patten Commission (which came to be known by the name of its chief, Christopher Patten) was to emphasize but also various enhancements of a professional nature that appealed directly to the police themselves. The terms included an instruction to the commission to consult widely, and specifically mentioned nongovernmental organizations (NGOs), in order to ensure that interested sectors would have the opportunity to present their concerns and suggestions (Independent Commission 1999: annex 1).

Among the distinguished members of the commission, almost all of whom were well versed in the field, were foreign individuals. They were included partly to ensure that international experiences would enrich the commission's considerations, but also to establish presences within the panel that were not a partisan of any local cause or group and who could help ensure the technical focus. Those commissioners drawn from Northern Ireland, including some from the private sector, assured that political realities were not entirely ignored.

Northern Ireland's own experience taught that however good a commission or its recommendations, it would achieve little if there were no political will to implement its vision. The parties took various measures to prevent repetition of past failures. First, the Good Friday Agreement, which set forth the overall political settlement and created the Patten Commission, was submitted to a public referendum, where it obtained 71 percent of the vote. In one of its provisions, the agreement underscored the parties' determination that implementation not be frustrated, stipulating that the signatories would "introduce *and support* legislation" to give effect to specific portions of the agreement.[4] Although the portions dealing with police matters did not include the same language, a combination of factors—the referendum, the prestige of the commission and its members, the transparency of its work (it conducted more than forty public meetings),[5] and the detailed terms of reference—created an environment in which it

---

[4] Agreement between the Government of the United Kingdom of Great Britain and Northern Ireland and the Government of Ireland, 10 April 1998, Art. 1, para. iv ("Constitutional Issues").

[5] Among the participants in the public meetings, fourteen political parties, businesses, and unions made oral presentations. Besides the formal meetings convened by the commission itself, the commissioners participated in various meetings organized by different entities. The commission also consulted with twenty-nine different police forces and had private meetings with forty-four other organizations, including both rights NGOs and entities connected to the Royal Ulster Constabulary or its members.

was virtually impossible to renounce the commission's report and difficult to frustrate it by indirect means. The commission itself added another device: it suggested an oversight commissioner to review implementation of the reform plan, which was created after the commission delivered its final report.[6]

Mexico might benefit from adapting certain elements of the Northern Ireland approach. The administration of President Vicente Fox has found itself stymied on most legislative fronts, and the president has not yet demonstrated a convincing habit of consultation or the capacity to push reforms past the objections of opposition parties determined to deny his government easy victories. Despite a well-publicized announcement of a legislative reform package, the Fox government's approach holds out little promise so far of broader participation, and it may well run aground when three parties begin to debate its contents in legislative session. If President Fox were to use his political capital to promote an agreed process—one that involves an appropriate commission and in which all political parties share responsibility for implementing the commission's recommendations—Mexico might find itself with a recipe for moving forward in a difficult area. A serious group—one that combined the right mix of insider and outsider perspectives and took up the challenge of studying, broadly listening, and proposing—would provide Mexicans with nothing worse than a proposal that would enrich the debate, and if the parties honored their commitments, it could offer a great deal more. Bequeathing the future of reform to the traditional system of overly personalized politics, quasi-clandestine negotiation, and the exclusion of affected sectors of society cannot possibly be the best alternative.

2 Do not limit the learning to the government.

Local officials must take seriously the need to immerse themselves in the mechanics of modern police management and accountability. The challenge of making the police work is real and complex, as is the question of ensuring public security. Mexico does not enjoy the luxury of great local expertise on the subject, so it falls to the authorities to catalyze a learning process within and outside of the institutions themselves.

Reforming the police is a struggle that will consume years. Every relevant actor in this area is fully aware of this. However, there is reason to

---

[6] For information on the oversight commissioner's role and copies of reports, visit http://www.oversight.commissioner.org/background/default.asp?page=back.

doubt that official diagnoses will be sufficiently self-critical or that reform plans will be adequate. Without outside ideas, critiques, and support, Mexico would also lack a valuable resource for generating the political agreement to take needed action, and it would be far less likely to have needed scrutiny of the implementation.

Mexican human rights nongovernmental organizations have remained on the margin of the debate about police reform, leaving a noticeable void in public discourse. Reform-minded officials from various agencies have noted this absence, lamenting what they perceive as a lack of support in legislative and policy battles. Mexico's transition toward pluralistic politics carries with it a certain irony: now, with more official recognition of the institutional problems and need for profound changes, the NGOs that for years clamored for such changes have encountered difficulties in taking advantage of relative openness. They suffer from a lack of human and financial resources, as well as the same lack of familiarity with an increasingly technical subject matter—problems they share with many local officials and institutions.

South Africa offers an illustrative, if unfortunate, example in this regard. During the apartheid era, there evolved an impressive network of local NGO "advice offices" whose presence in urban centers and in the so-called homelands was a veritable lifeline for people taken away unjustly or otherwise victimized by the security forces. With the transition to multiracial democracy under the presidency of Nelson Mandela, the manifestation of police abuse changed somewhat, but the problem did not vanish.[7] However, five years after the initial transition, the number of advice offices had fallen from over 400 to about 250, casualties of the flow of attention and funds away from the NGO sector once the formal specter of apartheid had ended.[8]

Government wastes the potential of civil society at the risk of bad policies and poor governance. Certainly this is one of the lessons to be drawn from Mexico's last century. In fact, a book on comparative democratic policing, still one of the most recommended texts of its kind, is the result of an NGO effort to bolster Northern Ireland's official reform effort. *Human Rights on Duty*, published in 1997 by the Belfast-based Committee on the

---

[7] Civilian deaths at the hands of South African police are as much, if not more, of a problem today as they were under apartheid. See Inter-African Network 2001: 101–110.

[8] Personal interview with Black Sash organization member, Johannesburg, July 1996.

Administration of Justice (CAJ), compiles information on policing transitions in seven nations, thanks to the collaboration of more than a hundred officials, academics, and advocates who completed questionnaires and provided analysis and materials. The aim of this effort was to enrich the Patten Commission process and to educate officials and journalists, as well as a public whose only experience with the police had been with a force created and operated pursuant to a national security doctrine.

By taking an active role in the process, the CAJ and other NGOs gained influence. The participation of credible NGOs also helped sustain a certain level of social support for the reform plan, including some of its inevitable compromises. Some who had traditionally denounced the police as irretrievably evil invested time and resources in the effort to find lasting means of making them better. In a context so polarized, with such visceral rejection of most official initiatives, this sort of participation was significant.

To those Mexican officials who ask what they can do to achieve some of the same results, one answer is straightforward: initiate a joint learning effort, bringing together officials from different agencies and civil society, including NGO representatives. Mexican officials are already developing a taste for comparative study: a team of officials from Los Pinos (the president's residence) traveled to the United States and South America recently to look at other judicial systems, in search of ideas for reform proposals. There are other examples of the authorities' study abroad. But to date, few if any initiatives include those outside of government circles, and there appears to be little sharing of the lessons that were brought back. Indeed, President Fox's recent announcement of a proposal for reforming criminal procedure, making the Attorney General's Office independent, and combining different federal police forces may ultimately meet with support, but its content comes as a surprise to academics and civil society groups who were largely ignored throughout a very secretive incubation process. It remains to be seen whether the proposal (whose details are still closely held) lacks important elements that would have emerged through broader discussion.

A joint initiative might follow the Los Pinos example of traveling to different places where the experiences are illustrative. This might be complemented by comparative seminars, convened to bring experts from abroad to different forums in Mexico. Working groups might review and debate important texts in order to air different ideas and identify a few areas for more focused inquiry. NGOs that took part might obtain the building blocks of a new and appropriate role for themselves, an important advance in an area that has noticeably lacked their analysis and proposals. For the government's part, it would be a worthwhile and serious investment of time and money to catalyze a tangible collaboration between officials and the nongovernmental community, something that they have sought, at least at a rhetorical level. No party would have to give up its rights to dissent, loudly if necessary. Only the right of abstention from matters of public concern would be compromised.

3. Adopt the language of rights *and* security.

The very shape of public discourse about citizen security is one of the most crippling obstacles to joining forces in this area. Naturally enough, two principal values dominate discussion: the protection of the populace from crime and criminals (which implies, in turn, the prevention, prosecution, and punishment of crime), and clear respect for the rights of every person, whether victim, witness, or the accused. When, as inevitably happens, the two notions are posited as incompatible and in competition, opposing camps arise, each one emphasizing a different value. This essay does not address the many arguments against such a dichotomy, but instead suggests that all actors should acknowledge the importance of both values, in public and at each opportunity.

Mexican human rights groups have achieved something very important in this regard: public comment from police officials rarely omits some mention of the relevance of protecting human rights or fails to assert that it is official policy and practice to do so. Although one could argue about the consistency with which such a policy is actually applied, it is important to recognize that official language has evolved and to congratulate those authorities who have taken the first step of adopting the rhetoric of rights protection.

At the same time, NGOs rarely reciprocate by underscoring the legitimate and necessary battle against crime. By assimilating the idea that the police must be effective as well as fair, rights advocates could help change the way they see, and are seen by, the police. Without abstaining from criticism, they could contribute to a basis for more productive interchanges about how to satisfy both values to a greater degree, something that should interest both the activist and the officer.

4. Develop information mechanisms and practices.

One of the most often-stated concerns of Mexican police officials is how to change negative public perceptions of the police. It is readily apparent to them that this will demand more than changing the police themselves; some frustrated officials complain that little notice is taken of the changes they have wrought. Information policies (relatively underemphasized by reforms to date) can help achieve both aims—positive change and having the public begin to perceive it. Internally, there is room for great improvement in the management of data about, for example, officer conduct, supervision, and resource use. More important, this information could be tied to consequences (positive and negative) that would represent the incentive for improvement. And ultimately, processed data could highlight trends and impacts, strengths and weaknesses, that point to the need to sustain or change certain polices and operational methods—in other words, give police officials a continual sense of institutional health.

Addressing accountability issues is not the only option officials have open to them as they seek to win public confidence. There are numerous policing strategies available, each with its adherents. Before banking on beating back crime, consider that the crime indices are historically not terribly elastic in the short term nor subject to steep declines solely as a result of police actions. Police undoubtedly can affect crime, but their impact on a decidedly social phenomenon is necessarily partial and still not entirely understood or necessarily replicable, even in light of numerous dramatic declines like those experienced in cities across the United States. It is even less likely that the results will materialize in time for demandingly short political cycles, and it is virtually impossible that this would occur with a vastly flawed police that have not come close to overcoming their multiple defects. If officials can hardly rely on vastly improved crime statistics that will speak for themselves, it is worth considering a different way of demonstrating the will to change: a transparent process of cleansing and strengthening the institution, punishing bad conduct and rewarding good.

Police departments should create tracking and reporting mechanisms that would actively inform, via the Internet and other media, about various issues, including the manner in which the police have resolved citizen complaints or other administrative processes covering misconduct. This can be done without providing the public with any identifying data about the victim or alleged offender that might compromise confidentiality policies. (This is, in fact, the practice of many police forces, although it is generally considered good practice to provide, privately, the complainant with more detailed information.) Officials can create virtuous competitions by ordering the data according to police precincts or administrative units, so that the public becomes aware of which units stand out with fewer complaints or with the most appropriate handling of those that do arise. Simple questionnaires given to complainants can also yield valuable information about the public's experiences with the police and the accountability process, which can be tracked across both time and geography.

In general, more agile and transparent information systems and practices will help police forces to achieve several objectives central to the main goal of improving public perceptions of the police. For example:

- Evaluate the effort and results achieved by officers and their supervisors.

- Follow and interpret patterns of conduct at the individual, unit, and institutional levels, which will provide the feedback needed to modify recruitment and training practices or operational rules. In short, such an approach provides an informational foundation for deciding how to make the institution better.

- Sensitize and educate the public about police efforts to acknowledge and address the institutional problems, thereby helping to adjust expectations to accord with the profound difficulties of this transition. It is worth noting that a public that is well informed on such points can be an important source of support for a reform process that will inevitably encounter some resistance from within.

- Aid the police in obtaining a reliable understanding of what actions and services the public expects from the police. Here, too, more information may yield different demands on the police. If the police offer a compelling menu of services (prevention, assistance, and so on), conceivably the demand might evolve toward a force that defines its mandate less exclusively in terms of arrests, instead including a range of other functions.

5. Create police-specific external audit and advisory mechanisms.

Mexican officials should consider the creation, as an early priority, of an autonomous public entity to audit the performance of accountability and control mechanisms that apply to police forces. The official human rights commissions cannot play this role, given their government-wide mandates and orientation toward individual cases. A police-specific organ is needed, with personnel whose training and experience afford an appreciation of the difficulties of police work, as well as the capacity to evaluate institutional performance.

Having such expertise and oversight can bring powerful benefits to police managers and, in turn, to the rank and file. One dramatic example concerns the Special Counsel's Office for the Los Angeles County Sheriff's Department (LASD) in California. Los Angeles County contains eighty-eight municipalities, including the city of the same name. The LASD has responsibility for policing almost fifty of these municipalities, while the separate Los Angeles Police Department (LAPD) covers the city of Los Angeles.

The two forces display significant similarities. Police personnel levels are comparable (8,900 at LASD, 10,000 at LAPD), as are the respective populations they patrol (LASD, 2.7 million; LAPD, 3.5 million). In 1991, at the time of the Rodney King incident (involving an African American man who was brutally beaten by four LAPD officers, in the presence of at least ten of their colleagues), both departments had serious brutality problems. However, motivated by the high costs of police brutality litigation, which were running into the tens of millions of dollars and threatening to bankrupt Los Angeles County, officials decided to name a special counsel to examine institutional issues within the LASD. The Special Counsel's Office, which functions as an outside auditor, was given broad access to LASD data, processes, and personnel, and publishes serious semi-annual reports whose critical findings are always accompanied by detailed suggestions for improving department management and avoiding the problems that have plagued the force.

The results for the LASD—and the marked difference from post–Rodney King events around the LAPD, which stumbled from scandal to scandal—are impressive. Between 1991 and 1998, LASD halved the number of civilians killed by its officers. For years after, the LAPD did not even maintain complete data on its officer-involved shootings. However, six years after the LASD created its Special Counsel's Office, LAPD's total number of officer-involved shootings was 30 percent higher than LASD's.[9] From annual highs of 381 excessive force lawsuits and $17 million in damages and settlements paid, the LASD reached recent lows of 93 lawsuits and, in 2001, $2.1 million paid to complainants (Bobb 2002: 8–9). Indeed, LASD's relatively open approach to its officers' misconduct (the LAPD tended to whitewash bad incidents) and its decreasing numbers of officer-involved shootings (LAPD's rose between 1991 and 1998) prompted the *LA*

---

[9] The number of persons shot by LASD officers dropped from sixty-three in 1999 to eighteen in 2000, while the number of officers killed by gunfire dropped from ten to three between 1991 and 2001 (*LA Weekly* 1999).

Weekly to ask in 1999, "Why can't LAPD be more like the Sheriff's Department?"

There is an interesting footnote to this comparison, which sheds some light on the relationship between greater accountability and police aggressiveness against crime. Data covering 1997 to 2001 show that the LASD had a higher index of arrests (expressed as a percentage of crime) than did the LAPD (Prendergast n.d.). (Since 1998, when the worst scandal in its history forced the LAPD to implement more serious investigations of civilian complaints as part of a stricter accountability regime, the LAPD has suffered fewer cases of excessive force and lower litigation costs, and it is gradually coming to project a more positive image before the community.)

Mexico's Ministry of Public Service (SFP, primarily an anticorruption agency and formerly known as SECODAM) and the counterpart comptroller's offices in individual agencies are not a substitute for an effective accountability auditor. Their emphases have largely reflected the fiscal connotation of *rendición de cuentas* and, insofar as the police, have done little to evaluate or spur progress on other key police-specific fronts, such as the development of systems to review use of force, officer safety practices, and so on. Moreover, Mexico's experiments in accountability and anticorruption have largely reproduced the broader Latin American experience: the creation of innumerable additional requirements and rigid bureaucratic layers that have diminished both efficiency and fairness without producing a corresponding increase in service. As Esteban Moctezuma Barragán and Andrés Roemer, authors of a recent work on public service in Mexico, put it, the government ends up paying more to do the same (Moctezuma Barragán and Roemer 2000: 23). There is a continuing and urgent need for mechanisms that can offer the public a clear and coherent vision of the specific problems and a meaningful description of actions taken or actions needed.

Although it is beyond the scope of this chapter to revisit the literature on police accountability, it is probably safe to say that there have been a few key axes of debate, empirical research, and lesson taking. A fundamental dilemma surrounds the common inability and unwillingness of the police to police themselves adequately, along with one of the central empirical lessons of the movement toward accountability—that the results rarely live up to expectations if the police are not to some degree voluntarily brought into the process. Closely related is the question of how much can or should external mechanisms displace the police's own procedures for investigating, judging, and sanctioning those within their ranks. Finally, police reform history is littered with examples of scandal-provoked blue ribbon panels, ballyhooed conclusions and recommendations, and vanishing public attention to difficult processes of implementing changes in the institutional environment that often engender the attention-getting egregious behavior—and the entire cycle repeating itself over time in the same places. Continuity, often missing, has come to be seen as one of the important qualities of any oversight mechanism.

Drawing from this admittedly abbreviated rendering of a long and complex history, the currently favored recipe seems to call for an entity that enjoys a mix of independence and cooperation from the police in an ongoing oversight relationship focused not only on the symptoms of organizational problems but on the problems themselves. Happily there is an emerging model that in some instances promises to combine these virtues in practice: the independent police auditor.

Properly designed and executed, an audit mechanism promises to address the institution itself, and not just its miscreants, which from the perspective of sustained reform makes it a priority. By its nature, the auditor reviews the performance of the mechanisms that should condition and control conduct, bringing within its focus elements of internal management, supervision, training, promotion, and discipline. Academic studies, officer surveys, and the observations of experience all underline the important role of supervisors and commanders in defining what will be internally understood as good or bad police performance (see, for example, Christopher et al. 1991). An innovation designed to evaluate management's success in creating a culture of respect and accountability is, from this perspective, an even more urgent priority than the creation of an external entity devoted to receiving civilian complaints against the police. A complaints bureau will almost certainly be necessary (notwithstanding the current human rights commissions),[10] but its recommendations would have

---

[10] Mexico's current system of human rights commissions is extraordinarily expensive. The National Human Rights Commission (CNDH), which is responsible only for the acts of federal agents (a relatively tiny percentage of the whole), particularly as regards policing, has an annual budget in excess of US$50 million, to which are added the costs of maintaining thirty-two state-level commissions. However, the substantive breadth of the commissions' mandates and the lack of authority to compel official action have limited their impact on police misconduct. Over the years, the commissions have steadily decreased their issuance of case-based recommendations, their most powerful weapon. For example, Mexico City's commission, considered one

much greater impact if the internal systems were in place to deal with them—something that a well-designed audit mechanism can help to bring about.

Even so, Mexican authorities at every level should seriously study the possibility of a police ombudsman. Other nations have experimented with diverse forms of this model: Northern Ireland named a police ombudsman as a result of its Good Friday Accord,[11] while South Africa created an independent complaints directorate to complement several internal mechanisms designed to regulate and monitor use of force.[12] Queensland, Australia, created a criminal justice commission to review police conduct in the wake of egregious abuse and corruption scandals.[13] Following inquiries by an ad hoc public committee and various government reports throughout the 1980s, Israel created an external complaints board in 1992, while Colombia, with one of the highest rates of state violence in the world, named a complaints commissioner which, though initially short-lived (it was abolished after a brief period and recently reinstated), by its mere presence forced internal reforms in the police, who wised to avoid losing control over accountability to an external body (Goldsmith 2000). Even New York City's police, who had long fought an independent civilian complaint review board, finally accepted an external board in 1993. In 2001, then Mayor Rudolph Giuliani responded to widespread concern over the police commissioner's frequent decisions to ignore the board's findings that punishment was warranted, proposing to augment the board's authority to prosecute the cases administratively, in lieu of the police officials who previously had this responsibility.[14] Canada has had a complaints board solely for the fabled Royal Canadian Mounted Police (RCMP) since 1988, which conducts investigations that are separate from but complementary to the RCMP's own internal disciplinary procedures.[15] Peru has created a police ombudsman of a different sort. In addition to inculcating respect for

---

of the nation's most active, has issued 100 recommendations in a decade of operations, having received more than 45,000 complaints.

[11] See http://www.policeombudsman.org/index.cfm for the ombudsman's Web site.

[12] See http://www.icd.gov.za/ for the directorate's Web site.

[13] See http://www.cjc.qld.gov.au/ for the commission's Web site.

[14] See http://www.ci.nyc.ny.us/html/ccrb/html/news.html for a summary of the proposal and subsequent developments.

[15] Background on the Complaints Commission can be located at http://www.cpc-cpp.gc.ca/DefaultSite/Home/index_e.aspx?ArticleID=1.

human rights among officers, the office is dedicated to defending the rights of officers. It handles cases ranging from challenging abuses of administrative disciplinary processes to assisting surviving spouses to secure death benefits.[16]

The truth of citizen oversight mechanisms is that they have not proven to be sufficient by themselves to bring about needed institutional changes. For one thing, it is difficult to obtain political agreement over their powers, particularly the tools needed to remain effective in the face of resistance. The essential lesson from experience seems to be that such mechanisms are part of the solution, and should necessarily share authority with the police. They represent a potentially powerful source of oversight, but they are not a substitute for the proper internal application of the rules.

The most prudent approach might include opting for creation of an audit mechanism while examining different options for a police ombudsman. The experiences of Mexico's human rights commissions should be evaluated, with attention given to the relationship between them, the audit mechanism, and an eventual ombudsman.

Different models can be used to fulfill the function of receiving and investigating civilian complaints. As other experiences suggest, perhaps more important than the specific design is achieving a balance of different internal and external forces. Police officers and government officials acknowledge privately that many police reject the human rights commissions and NGOs, considering them implacable. Although understandable, this attitude appears to be premised on a flawed perception. The tendency of police to view the monitors as too critical, too closely scrutinizing their acts, probably reflects the rule that public politics abhors a vacuum. Police forces in Mexico do not offer the public sufficient tangible evidence that they are engaged in self-correction, and therefore other actors feel compelled (often by public pressure) to demonstrate that they are filling the gap. Consider an alternate, vastly preferable scenario: internal accountability systems begin to demonstrate that they are exercising effective control over police actions, and external actors begin to feel freer to change the emphases in their work, devoting resources to a different type of focus on the police or turning to another set of issues altogether. For example, outside groups or a potential police complaints bureau would be unlikely to feel as much pressure to confront the police if an audit mechanism had

---

[16] Interview with former *defensora de la policía* Susana Villarán; see also http://www.mininter.gob.pe/article/articleview/849/1/12/.

begun reporting credible evidence of better discipline and improved police performance.

6. Design a federal entity to support experimentation and study.

Federated republics face challenges relatively unknown to unitary systems. On one hand, responsibilities and resources divided among so many diverse jurisdictions, and the variety of legal frameworks and institutional designs, can make coordination extremely difficult. On the other hand, federations offer the extraordinary opportunity to take advantage of different experiences at the state and municipal levels. This harvesting of knowledge will not happen by accident, and efforts should be made to ensure that it is neither haphazard nor unevenly distributed. Mexico's federal officials, acting in their unique national capacity, should create an entity that will exploit this potential by promoting study, experimentation, and dissemination of the results of local efforts.

Washington, D.C., offers a useful example. As happens in Mexico, the U.S. federal government and its different police forces (FBI, INS, Border Patrol, and so on) have limited jurisdiction, touching only federally defined crimes, while the vast majority of street crime is in the hands of local forces. However, since 1968 Washington has carved out an important supporting role that has been essential to the development of state and local policing techniques.

In the 1960s, after decades without figuring significantly on the political radar, crime (and the accompanying multiple social tensions) prompted President Lyndon Johnson to name a technical commission (see recommendation 1, above) on law enforcement and the administration of justice, which in a sentence captured a good deal of the problem of then-prevalent antiquated law enforcement practices: "the revolution of scientific discovery has largely bypassed the problems of crime and crime control."[17] Congress responded by creating the National Institute of Justice (NIJ). In its thirty-five years of operation, the NIJ has financed innumerable studies and pilot projects, which are carefully documented and accessible to scholars, police officials, and other interested readers. It is worth noting that the NIJ typically does not vouch for or control the findings, opinions, or policies advanced by the projects, which often touch on issues that are sensitive for police officials at all levels of government. The net effect is to pro-

---

[17] For background on the creation of the NIJ, see the timeline "Tracking an Era," at http://nij.ncjrs.org/timeline/time_60.html.

vide a rich assortment of academic study and concrete experience distilled from federalism's great asset: an array of state and local laboratories for testing new ideas and—with the support of the NIJ—an ongoing virtual conversation among them. Although recent shifts in Washington's priorities threaten NIJ's ability to sustain what it has created, it has built a record that makes it a model worth exploring.

* * *

These six recommendations do not pretend to be solutions, only ideas. Even if implemented, they will not begin to exhaust the decisions that police officials face as they confront existing policing challenges. Even within the area of accountability, there are difficult choices: what sort of mechanisms (needed and wanted), what level of public transparency, what mix of internal and external controls? This chapter aims to help define some of the questions and to offer a basis for tackling them. It is virtually impossible to predict where the process of reform will lead, but perhaps not impossible to determine where to begin. Mexico's challenges are its own, but they are not entirely unique, and there is much for Mexico to draw on from the world around it.

References

Bobb, Merrick J. 2002. "Civilian Oversight of the Police in the United States." Paper delivered at the Global Meeting on Civilian Oversight of Police, Rio de Janeiro, September.

Brown, Michael K. 1981. *Working the Street: Police Discretion and the Dilemmas of Reform*. New York: Russell Sage Foundation.

Christopher, Warren, et al. 1991. "Report of the Independent Commission on the Los Angeles Police Department." July.

Committee on the Administration of Justice. 1997. *Human Rights on Duty: Principles for Better Policing–International Lessons for Northern Ireland*. Belfast: The Committee.

Davis, Kenneth Culp. 1975. *Police Discretion*. St. Paul, Minn.: West.

Goldsmith, Andrew J. 2000. "Police Accountability Reform in Colombia." In *Civilian Oversight of Policing: Governance, Democracy, and Human Rights*, ed. Andrew J. Goldsmith and Colleen Lewis. Oxford: Hart Publishing.

Independent Commission on Policing for Northern Ireland. 1999. *A New Beginning for Policing in Northern Ireland*. Norwich, Eng.: H.M.S.O.

Inter-African Network for Human Rights and Development. 2001. *Police Brutality in Southern Africa: A Human Rights Perspective*. Lusaka: Afronet.

LA Weekly. 1999. "Departmentally Disturbed," November 12–18. At http://www.laweekly.com/ink/99/51/city-haefele.php.

Moctezuma Barragán, Esteban, and Andrés Roemer. 2000. *Por un gobierno con resultados.* 2d ed. Mexico City: Fondo de Cultura Económica.

Office of the Attorney General of the State of New York. 1999. "The New York City Police Department's 'Stop & Frisk' Practices." December.

Prendergast, Canice. n.d. "Selection and Oversight in the Public Sector, with the Los Angeles Police Department as an Example." At http://www.worldbank.org/research/projects/service_delivery/paper_prendergast.pdf.

Presidencia de la República. n.d. "La reforma al Sistema de Justicia Penal mexicano: combatir la delincuencia y proteger los derechos humanos." Powerpoint presentation.

Sherman, Lawrence. 1998. "Evidence-Based Policing," *Ideas in American Policing* (newsletter), July.

Tyler, Tom. n.d. "What Works in Police Policy." Presentation of study results. At http://www.gmu.edu/depts/pia/adj/center/1.

Walker, Samuel. 1992. *The Police in America: An Introduction.* Boston, Mass.: McGraw-Hill.

———. 1993. *Taming the System: The Control of Discretion in Criminal Justice, 1950–1990.* New York: Oxford University Press.

CHAPTER **18**

Evaluating the Zero Tolerance Strategy and Its Application in Mexico City

MARIO ARROYO JUÁREZ

Authorities and criminologists in Mexico have historically attempted to improve law enforcement by drawing on contemporary criminological theories and approaches, though with mixed success (see the chapters by Buffington and Speckman Guerra in this volume). In 2002, Mexico City Mayor Andrés Manuel López Obrador made international headlines when he hired the consulting firm of former New York City Mayor Rudolf Giuliani to offer recommendations on fighting crime in Mexico's capital. Giuliani's apparent success in reducing crime in New York was accomplished through the application of what is commonly called a "zero tolerance" approach born from modern criminological theories in the United States. Is it feasible for Mexico City to apply the "zero tolerance" strategy as it was developed in New York City under Mayor Rudolph Giuliani? This chapter considers that question, paying special attention to the factors that might impede the strategy's implementation in Mexico City.

The first section discusses some of the basic differences between New York and Mexico City in terms of population, the justice administration system, crime rates, and cultural context. The second section examines the factors that are obstacles to implementing zero tolerance. Two basic hypotheses are examined. First, whereas in New York zero tolerance was a political slogan based on criminology and law enforcement tactics, in Mexico City the strategy might end up being merely a political slogan. The second hypothesis suggests that the implementation of zero tolerance in Mexico City is flawed at its source because, basically, the city leaders chose

---

Translation by Patricia Rosas.

the strategy without first understanding the problem they face. As a consequence, the chapter opens with a brief discussion of the need to use an integral approach to crime control in Mexico City, instead of using a solution like the one employed in New York, which was developed in a very distinct legal and cultural environment.

WHAT IS "ZERO TOLERANCE"?

A few points need clarification before we analyze the feasibility of implementing the zero tolerance law enforcement strategy in Mexico City. First, we must define what is meant by zero tolerance, and second, we need to understand the origin of the term. Although the origin is uncertain, many have noted its ongoing presence as a theme in political and official discourse since the 1970s. The term has referred to the objective of restraining deviant behavior by imposing controls on juvenile delinquents, on decaying schools, and even in the labor arena (Morgan and Newburn 1997: 14). Today it is most commonly used as a synonym for a crime policy based on the administrative transformation of the police, the change from a reactive to a proactive orientation, community involvement, the efficient use of technology, and accountability. As such, it seeks to meet the basic objectives of the police: to reestablish public order, raise the quality of life for citizens, and punish all crimes or misdemeanors, large or small, thereby giving back to the people clean and safe urban areas.

As frequently occurs with public initiatives, it is hard to determine who coined the term "zero tolerance." Rudolph Giuliani—whom the media, first in the United States and eventually internationally, identified as its author—has publicly pointed out that the name does not reflect what was, in reality, done in New York City. Instead, he prefers to use the label "fixing broken windows" in reference to the famous article by George Kelling and James Q. Wilson: "Broken Windows: The Police and Neighborhood Safety" (Kelling and Wilson 1982). In later publications, Kelling has left no doubt that "zero tolerance" distorts the meaning of their original arguments, and he goes even further, calling it "the bastard child of the broken windows theory" (Kelling 1999: 1). William Bratton, the first police commissioner under Giuliani, has also distanced himself from the name. Whenever Bratton talks about New York's experience and the police reforms in which he participated, he avoids the term: "In New York City, we restructured the Police Department, we reinvented the strategy of policing, and we rediscovered that the police could control crime in any neighbor-hood, in any city" (Bratton and Andrews 1999: 1).

It is curious that an apparently successful law enforcement strategy can be both so widely known and so thoroughly disavowed. This estrangement from the term "zero tolerance" has to do with the criticisms of the strategy, which aimed to highlight the police brutality that accompanied it. The ongoing complaints about human rights violations, particularly from mi-nority ethnic groups and marginalized social groups, earned the strategy the epithets of "racist" and "police-against-the-poor."

The disavowal of zero tolerance by its own originators is relevant to the Mexican case. Even Mexico City's Ministry of Public Security (SSP) dis-credited the term. At the end of 2002, the SSP hired the services of the Giuliani Group, LLC, to consult on reducing the crime rate, for a fee of US$4.3 million. The SSP justified the contract by saying that "one of the key strategies for combating crime in New York City was the 'Mayor's Quality of Life Initiative,' incorrectly identified by the media as zero tolerance." And it distanced itself by saying, "That term can generate negative reac-tions in those who do not understand what it means, due to the assump-tion that it implies an absence of compassion and the presence of police brutality and the suppression of civil liberties. However, the essence of the concept is not intolerance but trust" (http://www.ssp.df.gob.mx). This denial of zero tolerance only serves to support Kelling by pointing to it as a bastard child, a grand idea without a creator, and thus a great myth which, like all myths, exists not because we see it but because we believe in it.

UNRAVELING THE ZERO TOLERANCE MYTH

If the principal actors involved in crime reduction in New York City deny paternity when it comes to zero tolerance, can we then conclude that it does not exist? Certainly not, when we recognize that someone coined the term and the media, through repetition, transformed it into something concrete. This forces us to trace its origin and, above all, to describe its implementation. Some of its history goes back to the "law and order" de-bate that was prevalent in the 1970s. The zero tolerance strategy came to represent a break with the fatalism that was embodied in the idea that "nothing is working." In other words, the police are incapable of reducing crime, the prisons do not rehabilitate their inmates, crime is increasingly violent, and, in short, nothing that we do works. With zero tolerance, a decision was made to put an end to every symptom of impunity and make it utterly clear that the law exists to be obeyed. The question as to why it is disobeyed is irrelevant. What matters is enforcing it, and whoever transgresses the law will have to face the consequences. In other words, the old and well-known formula of the "all-out war against crime" transfigured itself linguistically into a subtler phrase: zero tolerance. With that, the attempt was made to convince the public that the strategy is a positive measure, one that will help win back streets now overtaken by crime.

In sum, zero tolerance is an ideology about crime that is nourished by moral principles and that arises from administrative criminology. Its objective is to prove that crime statistics can be reduced, thus demonstrating that the arguments of conventional criminology theories—which attribute the causes of crime to socio-structural factors such as poverty, unemployment, or the demographic structure of the population—are ideological in nature and incorrect.[1] Those assertions may have been on Giuliani's mind when he was being questioned about the difficulties that Mexico City confronts. He pointed out that "There are certainly differences between New York City and Mexico City, but I am not convinced that those differences are relevant to reducing crime" (Giuliani 2003). Next we will explore a few of those differences.

MEXICO CITY AND NEW YORK CITY: A COMPARISON

Mexico's Federal District contains sixteen political divisions, called *delegaciones*, with a combined population of 8,489,000 (INEGI 2001).[2] New York City has a population of 7,746,000 (NYPD 2003). According to the data on reported crimes, New York has the higher crime rate of the two. In 1999, 2,592 crimes per 100,000 inhabitants were reported in Mexico City (Go-

---

[1] In the *Programa General de Desarrollo del Distrito Federal 2000–2006* (Gobierno del Distrito Federal 2001), the leftist-oriented government of Mexico City declares that crime is caused by exactly the factors that zero tolerance theory posits as insuperable. It says, "To attack the multifactor causes of crime, a set of social development policies and plans for sustainable economic development will be promoted that will contribute to creating sources of employment as well as recreational and sports activities." This contradiction serves to demonstrate the lack of planning in matters of crime policy, and it even demonstrates how public security policy responds more to a political agenda of circumstantial nature than to a long-term strategy for public well-being.

[2] However, it is surrounded by the thirty-four municipalities of México State, in which another 8,295,000 people live. Together, this forms the Mexico City Metropolitan Area, with a population of 16,784,000 people (INEGI 2001).

bierno del Distrito Federal 2000), compared to 4,037 per 100,000 for New York City. This type of comparison must be viewed cautiously, however, given the possible difference in how crime is recorded and because of the Mexican *cifra negra* (unreported crime). Eager to avoid possible omissions, I compared the crime rates for those offenses that, consensus holds, are reported most frequently (homicide, burglary, and vehicle theft). Although rape often goes unreported, rape rates were also compared (see tables 18.1 and 18.2). New York City reflected higher rates than Mexico City for the compared crimes, with the exception of homicide.

Table 18.1. Murder and Rape Rates for New York City and Mexico City, 1999

	Murders per 100,000 Inhabitants	Rapes per 100,000 Inhabitants
New York City	9.0	22.9
Mexico City	10.0	15.5

Sources: Prepared by the author from data from NYPD 2003; INEGI 2001 (Mexico City population data), and Gobierno del Distrito Federal 2000 (reported crime data).

Table 18.2. Burglary and Vehicle Theft Rates for New York City and Mexico City, 1999

	Burglaries per 100,000 Inhabitants	Vehicle Thefts per 100,000 Inhabitants
New York City	544.7	534.3
Mexico City	93.8	510.8

Sources: Prepared by the author from data from NYPD 2003; INEGI 2001 (Mexico City population data), and Gobierno del Distrito Federal 2000 (reported crime data).

Any careful observer would immediately notice that the data do not align with Mexico City's image as one of the world's most violent cities, with high incidences of kidnapping, robbery, and homicide, or as the hemisphere's largest city, whose millions of residents are—in the words of Bensinger (2002)—waiting for "Rudolph Giuliani to make crime and police corruption vanish." To get beyond the folklore created by the media and the oft-repeated numerical inaccuracies, I next analyze certain obstacles to implementing zero tolerance in Mexico City.

OBSTACLES TO IMPLEMENTING ZERO TOLERANCE

Shortcomings in Data Sources

The first obstacle for the zero tolerance strategy is a lack of data. The Mexico City police are divided based on two primary functions. The Ministry of Public Security is assigned to preventing crimes and misdemeanors, whereas the Office of the Attorney General of the Federal District (PGJDF) and its auxiliary, the judicial police, investigate crimes once they have occurred. Each compiles and records statistical information on crime, but for legal purposes the PGJDF data are accepted as the crime rate.

The statistical data from the SSP are not made available to the public, and the PGJDF information is, in general, incomplete.[3] Rather than providing historical data series, it reports only on recent crimes, and it fails to disaggregate crime categories (see figure 18.1). And rather than providing data on the frequency of crimes, the PGJDF reports on the percentage reduction in crime rates, thus making an eminently propagandistic use of that information. The authorities do not have an open information policy for crime statistics, and there is no official publication of any type in this respect. Thus analyses by academics and government offices often have to rely on partial, outdated, or fragmented data.

Mexico has no official victimization survey, despite the wide international use of that research tool for designing crime policies. Nor is there an official survey taken in Mexico City itself. Yet several related studies, including Guillermo Zepeda Lecuona's work in this volume and elsewhere, indicate that 80 percent of the crimes committed in Mexico City go unreported.[4] This means that of every 100 crimes that occur in Mexico City, only 20 are recorded. If we apply this ratio to the 1999 figures for reported crimes, we would find that, instead of 227,212 crimes, there were in fact 1,136,060, a rate of 12,960 crimes committed per 100,000 inhabitants rather than the 2,592 figure that was based on reported crimes (see figure 18.2).

---

[3] SSP Internet pages contain information relative to the institution's operation, such as numbers of prisoners, how many appear before a judge, misdemeanors, towing of automobiles, and so forth. However, this information is incomplete because, rather than presenting historical series, the data show administrative periods, which are ultimately of little use for public policy analysis.

[4] Several victimization surveys—one conducted periodically by *Reforma*, one by the Comité Nacional de Consulta y Participación de la Comunidad en Seguridad Pública in 2000, and, more recently, two by the Instituto Ciudadano de Estudios sobre la Inseguridad—support this, despite using different methodologies (telephone polls or door-to-door surveys). See also Zepeda 2004.

Figure 18.1. Sample of Information Available from the Office of the Attorney
General of the Federal District (Total Crimes, 1993–2003)

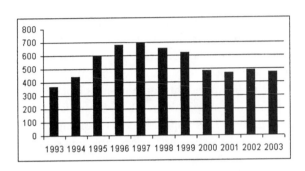

1993   1994   1995   1996   1997   1998   1999   2000   2001   2002   **Febrero 2003**

Source: Procuraduría General de Justicia del Distrito Federal Web site (www.pgjdf.gob.mx) as of
April 4, 2003.

Figure 18.2. Crimes Reported versus Crimes Committed, Based on
Victimization Surveys, Mexico City, 1999

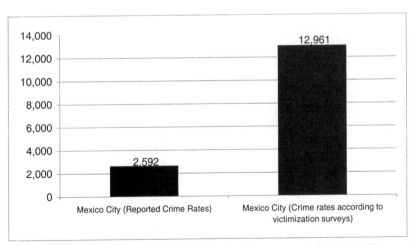

Sources: Prepared by the author. Various victimization surveys indicate that 80 percent
of all crimes go unreported. For data on reported crimes and the reference population, see Gobierno del Distrito Federal 2000; INEGI 2001.

Inflexible Politico-Administrative Divisions

A second obstacle to implementing the zero tolerance strategy is geographic and administrative in nature. The geographic issue, arising from the failure to take a metropolitan view of the problem, lies in the decision to implement the strategy in Mexico City but not in the surrounding municipalities. This makes the collection of statistical data difficult, but to solve that problem would imply coordinating at least thirty-four separate local police forces (from the thirty-three municipalities and Mexico City), whose distinguishing trait is that each is controlled by one of the three main political parties. This impedes cooperation among the police forces, the governments of the sixteen *delegaciones*, the government of Mexico City, and the federal government.

Although the obstacles are technically surmountable, under such circumstances it is difficult to use a system like CompStat.[5] As noted, the first problem is the lack of statistics. The SSP collects and uses information based primarily on administrative rather than criminological criteria. Its information reflects event frequency only, omitting data on variables that would be useful in policy development, such as the sociodemographic characteristics of victims, the crime site with its geographical referents, and the circumstances and characteristics surrounding the event (such as the date and hour of the crime and the presence of aggravating factors, including alcohol, drugs, or firearms). A second, technical problem is that the SSP currently does not have digitized maps of the seventy police precincts into which the city is divided, nor does it provide estimates of the number of crimes that occur in each.

Another problem associated with the decentralization of police power is that the sixteen *delegaciones* have democratically elected representatives from the three political parties, and so they do not have unified crime policies or budgets. Moreover, no *delegación* has authority over its police, so the various police forces rely on the norms set by police headquarters and are thus subject to arbitrariness. If we add the fact that the preventive police forces in Mexico City do not have the legal authority to investigate crimes (as will be seen below), it is understandable that their performance is limited.

---

[5] The CompStat Unit was created to provide the New York Police Department with preliminary statistics in advance that would aid in the planning and use of resources in combating crime. This unit creates digital maps that show where crimes have occurred throughout the city.

A Deficient Law Enforcement Structure

The factors that contribute to police deviance pose a third insurmountable obstacle to applying zero tolerance in Mexico City. In theory, the mission of the police is to prevent crime; in practice, most police officers protect criminals, and the police even commit crimes. According to an SSP report, the main problems seen in the police are: underqualified personnel, desertion, corruption, lack of employee benefits, low salaries, absenteeism, and a high job-vacancy rate (SSP 1998: 8). Reconciling this diagnosis with some empirical findings and examples of police performance reveals three factors that explain the dysfunctional nature of the police in Mexico City: poor selection, training, and salaries; impunity; and corruption.

Poor selection, training, and salaries affect police deviance because they contribute to low self-esteem and lack of interest in the work, and they promote corruption among police officers. The problem of training begins with the substandard selection process. To become a preventive police officer, a person must be Mexican by birth; be between eighteen and twenty-eight years of age; measure at least 1.65 meters (men) or 1.55 meters (women); have no criminal record; present copies of birth certificate, secondary school diploma, proof of military service, voter card, and identification card (*clave única de registro de población*); and submit a letter giving the reasons for wanting to join the force. Once admitted, recruits take a basic, six-month course where they train in self-defense, marksmanship, surveillance techniques, and first aid, among other things. Having graduated, the individual receives a uniform, and he or she is ready to perform duties as a police officer. Given that the period of training is extremely short and, for the most part, primarily theoretical, these rookie officers feel very unsure of themselves when they first go out on the street.

Being a police officer in Mexico City today is risky, never more so than when the poor organization and deficient equipment of the police department results in an officer's death. Although no current statistics are available, estimates indicate that about 80 police officers die annually in Mexico City, or one every five days. Nationwide, between 200 and 500 officers die yearly (González et al. 1994: 26). It is not uncommon to hear an officer say, "I'm not going to risk my life for a handful of pesos and leave my family destitute." We can take that to mean that the police prefer not to enforce the law and, in the prevailing context of corruption, would rather take a bribe than a bullet (Arroyo 1998). A police officer in Mexico City earns only US$6,000 annually. The low salary explains the lack of interest in the career, the high level of vacancies and desertion rates, and often the corruption. In addition to the poor training and low salaries, the precarious work environment negatively affects officers' attitudes toward their work. There are only limited employee benefits, such as lowered insurance premiums, limited access to housing, and inadequate health services (table 18.3).

Table 18.3. Police Force Employee Benefits, New York City and Mexico City

New York City Police Benefits	Mexico City Police Benefits
• Choice of various paid medical and dental programs	• Medical services for the officer and his or her family
• 20 paid vacations days to start	• Two vacations per year
• 27 paid vacations days after 5 years	• Pension plan
• Unlimited sick leave with full pay	• Savings fund
• Optional retirement at one-half salary after 20 years of service	• After 5 years, the right to participate in home loan raffle
• Annuity fund	• Can continue to pursue the undergraduate degree in Police Administration or specialized courses in different areas
• Home ownership assistance programs	
• Over 70 college and graduate school scholarships	• Uniform
• Excellent promotional opportunities	
• Various work assignments	

Source: Prepared by the author with data from the New York City Police Department (www.nypd2.org) and the Secretaría de Seguridad Pública (www.ssp.df.gob.mx).
Note: The NYDP annual starting salary is US$34,514; the SSP's, US$6,000.

Impunity is a second factor in police deviance. The failure to punish someone for a crime is very common in Mexico City. Comparing filed crime reports with the number of presumed criminals brought before the lower court in 1999, we generally find that in only 7 percent of the crimes reported in Mexico City is a presumed offender detained. Thus 93 percent evade any punishment. In homicide cases, more than 50 percent go unpunished; in rape, 76 percent; and in bodily harm, 87 percent (table 18.4).[6]

---

[6] Table 18.4 could be criticized for comparing two different years and distinct data sources. However, I believe it is useful to consider the number of crimes

Table 18.4. Comparison of Crime Statistics from the Office of the Attorney General and the Courts, Federal District, 1999–2000

	All Crimes	Homicide	Bodily Harm	Rape
Number of reported crimes	227,212	880	23,926	1,355
Number of presumed offenders	17,591	468	3,122	325
Percentage of crimes for which an offender is identified	7.7%	53.2%	13.0%	24.0%
Number of offenders who are sentenced	14,862	583	1350	274
Percentage of crimes for which an offender is sentenced	6.5%	66.3%	5.6%	20.2%

Sources: Frequency data prepared by Rosario Robles, from Gobierno del Distrito Federal 2001: 23; data on presumed offenders and number sentenced from INEGI 2001. Data are for 2000 and reflect the number of presumed offenders brought before courts of the first instance for the local jurisdiction and/or those sentenced.

Impunity is also visible in the daily behavior of the preventive police. For example, around midnight on November 30, 1997, a couple of police officers stopped two men because they seemed suspicious, exactly as directed by the operational handbook for New York's Quality of Life Initiative. But this was happening in Mexico City. The officers demanded personal identification and then asked for a bribe to set the suspects free. One of the men had only 12 pesos, the equivalent of about a dollar. That annoyed one of the officers, who ordered the man to run, threatening that if the incident were ever reported, the officer would take his revenge. The man began to walk away when the officer fired his weapon in the air to reinforce the threat. When the other suspect protested, the police officer shot him and fled. The officer is still a fugitive (*La Crónica*, November 30, 1997).

The third factor, corruption, is key to explaining police deviance in Mexico City. Based on fieldwork, José Luis Ortiz discovered how the police authorities work under a "secret code," with the goal of rising through the ranks, maintaining their positions, or working in specific locations (for

reported in one year along with the number of offenders sentenced the following year (whether for a particular crime or overall).

example, being assigned a beat outside a financial institution rather than at a busy intersection). Ortiz discovered how all police officers, whether on foot or in a patrol car, must pay between US$5 and $22 per day, plus an extra $12 every two weeks, in order to keep their jobs (Ortiz 1997: 37). If we consider that the preventive police have between 25,000 and 30,000 officers in their ranks, we can assume that about US$5 million per month is generated from corruption. One can see how this money flows from the base of the pyramid to the top, and that it is the product of extortion that the police inflict on citizens as well as presumed criminals. These estimates do not take into account the money that officers carry off in their pockets, and it supposes that everyone participates (one must remember that, in total, the police forces comprise some 90,000 officers). Nevertheless, other findings and testimonies confirm that corruption is very common. As one man declared when he and his fellow officers were accused of homicide, "We are corrupt, but we aren't murderers" (*Reforma*, June 5, 1997).

Legal Limitations for Crime Investigations

The fourth obstacle is perhaps the primary limitation that will be encountered in implementing the zero tolerance strategy in Mexico City: preventive police can neither investigate nor pursue crimes. Thus a controversial but apparently effective corps, such as New York's Street Crime Unit, which is legal there, would be illegal in Mexico City. Practices as common as stop-and-frisk, legal in New York, would violate Mexican constitutional rights.

Article 21 of the Mexican Constitution states that public security is a duty of the federal government, the Federal District, the states, and the municipalities. Article 22 stipulates that the president of Mexico is in charge of the police force in the Federal District and is responsible for appointing the public servant who will run it. For its part, Mexico City's Public Security Law (Ley de Seguridad Pública) not only endorses what the Constitution mandates, but it also establishes that "public security is a service that, in the framework of respect for civil liberties, belongs exclusively to the state, and has as its objectives: the maintenance of public order; protecting the physical integrity of individuals and their possessions; preventing the commission of crimes and violations of government and police regulations; collaborating in the investigation and prosecution of crimes; and aiding the population in the event of natural disasters or calamities" (Estados Unidos Mexicanos 2002: 21–22).

The law dictates that the SSP can only *collaborate* in the investigation and prosecution of crimes and infractions. The obligation to investigate and prosecute crime is exclusively the jurisdiction of the Office of the Attorney General of the Federal District through the work of its auxiliary forces, as well as the judicial police and experts, the preventive police, and any other police forces contemplated in the legal framework.

Beyond strategies, the crux of the matter for Mexico City is that the system for crime investigation is completely overwhelmed. Consider, for example, that in 1999 alone, 227,212 crime reports were filed (and do not forget that this is scarcely 20 percent of actual crimes committed). To handle that caseload, the Attorney General's Office has 73 *agencias* (branch offices), 1,085 agents from the public prosecutor's office, and 3,400 officers on the judicial police force. In light of these figures, it is structurally unlikely that the police, even if they were honest and dedicated to fulfilling their legal functions, would have sufficient capacity to satisfy the demand for investigative services.

Citizen Mistrust and Police Deviance

One of the principal characteristics of the Mexican police forces, including that of Mexico City, is their ongoing abuse of power. This characteristic, on top of what has already been mentioned (impunity, corruption, and so forth), has generated a general lack of public trust toward the police. The democratic dilemma for the police—apparent in U.S. law enforcement in the 1960s (see Skolnick 1966)—was not a problem for Mexico until democracy began to be realized. In some ways, this is a sign of the importance of the police as a topic for study in analyzing the Mexican political regime. During more than seven decades of authoritarianism, the police were on the margins of public and academic debate. The fundamental objective of police work was to provide security not to the citizens of Mexico but to the regime. This meant there was little planning concerning law enforcement functions and no interest whatsoever in regard to its professionalization, accountability, and so forth.

The media have periodically echoed the demands of certain sectors to replace the police with military personnel because of police inefficiency and corruption, which they believe exist because the police are civilians. Finally, Mexico is, after all, part of Latin America, and military solutions always resurface in that region, driven by citizen desperation and, above all, by the authorities themselves. In 1997 the government of Mexico City decided to replace three thousand civilian police with military personnel.

A retired army officer explained why: "Corruption has been part of the daily life of Mexico City. If they are poorly paid, they will be inclined to take bribes, whether from citizens or from criminals" (*La Jornada*, November 16, 1997). This officer argued that only the military can establish discipline and order in the police force. The change was not easy. An initial episode of conflict between police with military backgrounds and police with civil backgrounds occurred in May 1997, when nearly five hundred officers blocked some streets to protest the military-type training that was being required of them. Following this physical confrontation of police against police, fifty-five of those with a civilian background were dismissed and charged with inflicting bodily harm. The then-secretary of the SSP, a military general, declared that the military training would continue despite the protests (*La Jornada*, November 21, 1997).

Whether under civilian or military command, the tactical operational mode for the Mexico City police has been based traditionally on "surprise operations," involving a large number of officers who are sent to "high-crime areas." Such operations generally occur in response to pressure from public opinion through the media because of some coexisting event. The only difference in the operations is the "civilian" or "military" background of the officers. "Civilian" has come to represent corruption and lack of capacity; "military" has come to represent honesty and capacity. With time, reality has demonstrated that police deviance in Mexico City is not a problem of "background," whether military or civil, but a structural problem.

If the cases of Amadou Diallo, Abner Louima, and Anthony Baez constitute an unforgettable precedent of police brutality for New Yorkers and American citizens,[7] for the Mexican people, their own history is full of police abuse and massacres, committed with the complicity of—or, in the worst cases, perpetrated directly by—the police. Just one brief example: At the beginning of September 1997, a nationwide, nighttime newscast aired a videotape of a criminal gang committing the armed robbery of a driver in his car in the Buenos Aires neighborhood of Mexico City. The novelty of the case was that, immediately after the robbery, the criminals walked over to a patrol car that was driving past the scene of the crime and gave the police officer a bribe. After the patrol car left the area, the criminals contin-

---

[7] The three men were killed as a result of police brutality. These were high-profile cases because of the social mobilization generated and the vehement defense that Mayor Giuliani made of the abusive police officers. An excellent account of these and other cases can be found in McArdle and Erzen 2000.

ued robbing other drivers. The day after the images were broadcast, the media, echoing the public's indignation, demanded government action to stop crime and end police corruption. The pressure of public opinion obliged the police to act, especially in the Buenos Aires neighborhood.

Days later, on September 8, after another armed robbery in the same area, a police officer and a citizen were murdered. To find the responsible parties, the preventive police initiated a rapid-response operation in charge of the elite corps called the "Zorros" (the Foxes). The operation ended with the capture of six suspects who, in a highly irregular manner, were not sent to the public prosecutor's office, as the law requires. Facing pressure from relatives of the detained men and from human rights organizations that demanded to know their whereabouts, the judicial police began an investigation that ended with the discovery of the bodies of three of the suspects. It was clear they had been tortured. Two weeks later the other suspects were found in similar conditions except that these bodies were dismembered and the body parts scattered in a radius of over 100 yards.

Public outrage over these events was such that the federal government ordered the army to initiate an investigation, even though, legally, criminal investigation is the jurisdiction of local authorities through the public prosecutor's office. Leaving aside the issue of legality, the army's investigation determined that twenty-four officers from the preventive police, members of two elite corps (the Zorros and the Jaguars), had been responsible for the homicide and torture of the six presumed offenders.

These events further eroded public confidence in the police and in the criminal justice system in general. Most people reacted against the police brutality and demanded that the laws be enforced. After these events, the SSP secretary and his highest-ranking officers went to the Buenos Aires neighborhood to convince the residents that the responsible parties had been punished. The police officials left the area after an angry crowd threatened to lynch them. However, they did not escape the political lynching. The president of Mexico's National Human Rights Commission (CNDH) declared that the military should not exercise police functions given that they were prone to human rights violations. She based her arguments on the fact that the commission had received 350 complaints against army officers during 1997, the majority concerning illegal detentions and torture. She declared that the absence of professional training had led the police to substitute torture for modern investigative methods. "Torture," she said, "continues to be a police practice that recalls the behavior not of the Middle Ages but of the Stone Age" (*La Jornada*, November 23, 1997).

Little Respect for the Sciences

Another obstacle to implementing zero tolerance in Mexico's Federal District is that little value is accorded in Mexico to new scientific perspectives on crime prevention and policing. Knowledge plays a crucial role in all disciplines, and the area of crime policy is no exception. International advances in crime policy rarely arrive in Mexico in a timely manner. An obvious example is the debate over community policing. Whereas in the United States, and later in other countries, the usefulness of the police and its institutional practices had been debated since the 1960s, in Mexico this discussion began toward the end of the 1990s, and it came not from academia but from the "public policy" arena. It was the first democratically elected government in Mexico City (1997–2000) that decided to initiate an exercise in community policing. To accomplish this, the SSP secretary selected the "highest-crime areas" and gave officers a three-month training course to teach them to coexist with the members of the community. Selected patrol cars and police guard stations were painted with the words "Community Police," and that was all that was done.

A few years later and without having conducted any evaluation, the Mexico City government, through a speech delivered by the then-SSP secretary, announced that a neighborhood policing program (Policía de Barrio) would be initiated. It had taken "several months to prepare and plan, and it had as its objective … to establish a bridge of trust, reconciliation, and joint action between the citizenry and community and the officers of the preventive police." In contrast to the studies that officials and academics had carried out for several decades in Newark, Nashville, and Kansas City (see Kelling and Coles 1996), the chief of police of Mexico's capital city did not need to conduct studies to select community policing. For him, it was enough just to have heard about the international experiences of Japan, Chile, and Spain and, above all, to recall oral tradition, "because," as the official noted, "no study has been made of the subject in Mexico City, but we all remember that during the 1950s and for most of the 1960s the police had very strong support from the community" (Ebrard 2003a).

Unfortunately, recollections should not be substituted for the appropriate inputs for a crime policy, which are data, planning, organization, and budget. In comparison and to show the premature nature and lack of a solid technical foundation for this "new community-policing initiative," we should recall the ten principles that Robert B. Trojanowicz, one of the leading theoreticians of community policing, has cited: change, leadership, vision, fraternity, problem solving, fair-mindedness, trust, empowerment, service, and accountability (Trojanowicz and Bucqueroux 1998: 8). These are principles that cannot be put in place in a matter of months.

Lack of Social Responsibility and Forward-Looking Vision

A principal problem for Mexico City is the lack of professionalization in the police leadership and the fact that the post of chief of police is political, rather than technical, in nature. The head of government in the Federal District nominates a candidate to lead the SSP, and the president of Mexico makes the appointment. By definition, this situation causes the position of chief of police to be an eminently political post since, rather than choosing the best candidate based on technical considerations, it involves the selection of someone based on consensus arising from the political moment. The fact that the post is held by a professional politician rather than a civil servant is in detriment to the continuity and quality of security policy. In a strict sense, no impediment would emerge if high-ranking police officials were supported by well-defined public policies based on information and technical knowledge. However, having been trained to obtain power by means of political struggle, they ignore the fact that, once they hold a public post, they must exercise their power, and that requires administrative techniques. This apparently straightforward solution is difficult to apply while governing, and for that reason their "acts of government" appear to be more the stuff of "electoral campaigns."

In Mexico City's current administration (2000–2006), examples of this abounded well before the extraordinary removal of SSP Secretary Marcelo Ebrard by President Fox in 2004, after the failure of Mexico City police to respond to a brutal mob lynching of three federal undercover police. One earlier example clearly illustrated the political nature of the SSP secretary's position. Midway through his term, Ebrard launched a vehement campaign against the sale of replicas of guns. At one point he even declared that 40 percent of the assaults in the Federal District in January 2003 that involved public transportation had been carried out with toy guns. For that reason, he promoted an initiative to reform the District's criminal code "to establish clearly that for a criminal such instruments have the same effect as any weapon" (Ebrard 2003b). That initiative won him a lot of media airtime as well as opportunities to make important connections with federal officials.[8] Although the initiative may have been praiseworthy, real fire-

---

[8] He called together officials from, among other places, the Federal Attorney General's Office for Consumer Affairs and the Economic Ministry. The latter

arms unfortunately continue to be one of the principal risk factors associated with crime and, above all, one of the principal means for committing murder. During 1998, of the 1,216 registered homicides in Mexico City, 66 percent were perpetrated with a firearm (figure 18.3). Thus, although toy guns may be eliminated, real firearms continue causing injury and death.

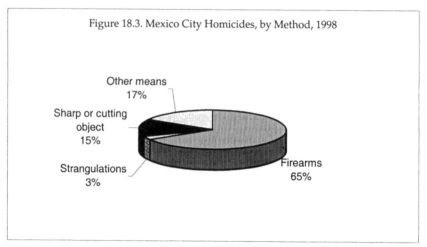

Figure 18.3. Mexico City Homicides, by Method, 1998

Source: Secretaría de Salud 1998.

Theoretical and Methodological Errors in Choosing Zero Tolerance

For many, the basic arguments sustained by the broken windows theory are only too familiar. However, the SSP's answer to the question "Why Giuliani?" serves to summarize it. Besides noting that the Giuliani administration's achievements constitute one of the most successful cases of reducing crime anywhere in the world, the SSP explains that "the Quality of Life Initiative has its roots in the broken windows theory developed by the criminologists James Q. Wilson and George Kelling, which maintains that tolerating misdemeanors and minor crimes generates an environment that propitiates the commission of more serious crimes. From that comes the

---

issued an emergency regulation requiring that toy guns be made of plastic, preferably transparent or in fluorescent colors (not silver, grey, or black) and that they not have the same dimensions as real firearms.

importance of duly punishing crimes, however minor they may seem to be. This theory is based on the premise that social disorder and crime are intrinsically linked" (http://www.ssp.df.gob.mx).

There are those who have questioned the theoretical validity of these arguments. Nevertheless, the important thing here would be to demonstrate that the hypothesis of social disorder, at least in the case of Mexico, may be biased above all because the evidence shows that corruption and impunity have greater causal weight. And this is without even considering the importance of other factors, both those that are outside the security arena and those related to organized crime that are outside the jurisdiction of the Mexico City police (arms trafficking, drug trafficking, and trafficking in human beings, among other things).

Figure 18.4. Diagram of the Integral Approach

The methodological "error," like the theoretical error, is certainly subjective. There are various ways to confront a problem or design a public policy. However, the established consensus, including among international organizations, is that any crime policy must be integral in nature (see figure 18.4). Attempting to tackle crime exclusively with strategies of a law enforcement, judicial, or public-security nature will produce limited results. A more useful proposal would be the following: if the objective is crime reduction, then a series of policies must be deployed in a variety of arenas—health, education, development, security and justice, legislation, information and technology, the media, and citizen participation. The requirements for implementation are leadership, coordination, consensus, confidence, and the political will to construct an alternative for the future.

CONCLUSIONS

The first conclusion is that, whereas in New York City zero tolerance was a political slogan based on criminology and law enforcement tactics, in Mexico City it could end up being no more than a political slogan. The second conclusion is that the application of zero tolerance—or whatever one chooses to call it—would have very limited effects in Mexico City given the obstacles analyzed here:

- shortcomings in data sources;
- inflexible politico-administrative divisions;
- a deficient law enforcement structure—including poor selection, training, and pay, along with impunity and corruption;
- legal limitations for crime investigations;
- citizen mistrust and police deviance;
- little respect for relevant scientific findings;
- lack of social responsibility and a forward-looking vision; and
- theoretical/methodological errors in selecting the zero tolerance strategy.

The third conclusion indicates that, given the current characteristics of the police, not only will abuse continue but corruption will increase.

The fourth conclusion shows that the selection of the zero tolerance strategy may not be adequate because, in choosing it, the most rudimentary principles for public policy design were ignored. A correct public policy design requires the deployment of at least seven basic steps: data collection, data analysis and interpretation, strategy selection, design of programs, training, implementation, and monitoring and evaluation. These processes must be situated geographically at various levels: the national, regional, state, and local (see figure 18.5).

The fifth conclusion would be to recommend the application of an integral approach, fundamentally because it synthesizes knowledge arising from different disciplines and techniques: criminology, anthropology, psychology, sociology, geography, public health, system engineering, law, marketing, statistics, and administration, among others. That approach is based on four widely agreed-upon and basic suppositions. First, criminality is multi-causal because we encounter risk factors on at least four levels: the individual, the family, the community, and society. Second, the study of criminality requires a multidisciplinary approach; unitary approaches are incomplete and, in general, biased. Third, crime intervention requires the participation of multiple actors. And fourth, it is necessary to switch from the reactive approaches of the past to ones that are proactive.

Figure 18.5. Diagram of the Methodology for the Integral Approach

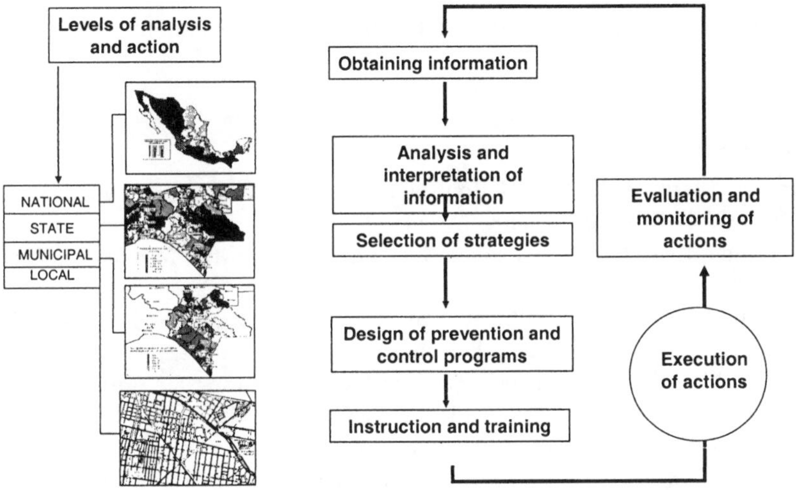

Sources: Geographic disaggregation prepared by Arturo Cervantes Trejo and Marco Antonio Rosas Pulido. Schematic diagram of public policy adapted and translated by the author from Ekbolm 1988.

Obviously, this chapter's results are a forward-looking exercise, an evaluation of the feasibility and potential impact of zero tolerance. Given the abrupt termination of SSP Secretary Ebrard, it is unclear whether the Giuliani strategy will be fully implemented in the last years of Mayor

López Obrador's administration. Considering the political context leading toward Mexico's next presidential election, the Giuliani strategy may have been a political gambit intended to raise the public visibility of both the SSP Ministry and the mayor. However, sooner or later, the need will arise to evaluate the feasibility of implementing policies similar to zero tolerance in the Federal District or elsewhere in Mexico. By examining the cultural, political, and technical obstacles to importing such strategies in Mexico, this chapter illustrates the need to construct new paradigms that adapt to the characteristics of Mexican society. I believe that the integral approach discussed here could assist in this effort because it brings together scientific knowledge, the political moment, and citizen demands. Most importantly, such an approach allows us to design a future agenda that would make it possible to assign resources and responsibilities to everyone involved in the task of building a more secure society. Above all, it would move the issue of crime prevention out of the political arena and into the policy realm.

References

Arroyo, Mario. 1998. "Social Control in Modern México." Presented at the World Congress of Sociology, Montreal, July 30.

Bensinger, Ken. 2002. "Can Giuliani Clean Up Mexico City?" *Washington Times,* December 23.

Bratton, William J., and William Andrews. 1999. "Crime and Punishment: What We've Learned about Policing," *City Journal* 9, no. 2: 1–6.

Ebrard, Marcelo. 2003a. Speech made on March 20 during the presentation of the Community Police in the Plaza de la Constitución.

———. 2003b. Speech made on February 28 to CANACINTRA.

Ekbolm, P. 1988. "Getting the Best Out of Crime Analysis." Home Office Crime Prevention Unit Paper No. 10. London: Home Office.

Estados Unidos Mexicanos. 2002. "Constitución Política de los Estados Unidos Mexicanos," *Prontuario Jurídico de la Procuraduría General de la República.* Mexico City: INACIPE.

Giuliani, Rudolph. 2003. Statement broadcast on the BBC News World Edition, May 11.

Gobierno del Distrito Federal. 2000. "III Informe de Gobierno." Statistical Appendix. Mexico City.

———. 2001. *Programa General de Desarrollo del Distrito Federal 2000–2006.*

González, Samuel, et al. 1994. *Seguridad pública en México.* Mexico City: Universidad Nacional Autónoma de México.

INEGI (Instituto Nacional de Estadística, Geografía e Informática). 2001. "Cuaderno de Estadísticas de la Zona Metropolitana." Mexico City: INEGI.

Kelling, George. 1999. Interview published in *Law Enforcement News* 25, nos. 511–512 (May 15 and 31): 1–8.

Kelling, George, and Catherine Coles. 1996. *Fixing Broken Windows*. New York: Simon and Schuster.

Kelling, George, and James Q. Wilson. 1982. "Broken Windows: The Police and Neighborhood Safety," *Atlantic Monthly* 249, no. 3: 29–38.

McArdle, Andrea, and Tanya Erzen. 2000. *Zero Tolerance: Quality of Life and the New Police Brutality in New York City*. New York: New York University Press.

Morgan, Rod, and Tim Newburn. 1997. "Tough on Zero Tolerance," *New Statesman*, May 30, pp. 14–15.

NYPD (New York Police Department). 2003. Division of Criminal Justice Services, Criminal Justice Indicators. New York City, 1997–2001.

Ortiz, José Luis. 1997. "La seguridad pública en el DF: contra el crimen organizado y la delincuencia," *El Cotidiano* 82: 32–43.

Secretaría de Salud. 1998. *La violencia un problema de salud pública*. Mexico City.

Skolnick, Jerome H. 1966. *Justice without Trial: Law Enforcement in Democratic Society*. New York: Wiley and Sons.

SSP (Secretaría de Seguridad Pública). 1998. "Programa Integral de Seguridad Pública 1998–2000." Mexico City.

Trojanowicz, Robert, and Bonnie Bucqueroux. 1998. *Community Policing: How to Get Started*. Cincinnati, Oh.: Anderson.

Zepeda, Guillermo. 2004. *Crimen sin castigo: procuración de justicia penal y ministerio público en México*. Mexico City: Centro de Investigación para el Desarrollo, A.C./Fondo de Cultura Económica.

CHAPTER 19

Assessing Decentralization: What Role for Municipal Government in the Administration of Justice?

ALLISON ROWLAND

In Mexico, decentralization of government functions to the municipal level has been linked since the early 1980s—both in rhetoric and in practice—to the broader processes of democratization, reform of the state, and the construction of "true" federalism (Cabrero Mendoza 1998; Guillén 1996; Merino 1992; Rodríguez 1997; Rowland and Graham 2002). As both cause and effect of this process, municipal governments as a group have become more important actors in many spheres of public life, including local public-service provision, land use regulation and planning, and revenue generation. This growth in activity and capacity has not gone unnoticed by citizens, who increasingly turn to the municipal level for the resolution of many daily problems of community life. In essence, the local arena has begun to take on political and governmental significance in ways that substantially differ from that of much of the twentieth century.

It is not surprising, then, that in recent years issues of crime and public safety also have become more pressing concerns for municipal governments. On one hand, citizens are increasingly likely to identify local government as a sphere of authority that can be useful for addressing issues that affect their lives. On the other, with increased levels of electoral competition among parties for local posts, municipal authorities have more reasons than ever to pay attention to, and try to resolve, the problems that residents present to them. Furthermore, to the degree that efficacy in pleasing local voters has become a test of electoral viability for politicians with ambitions to higher electoral office,[1] the issue of the formal assignment of

---

[1] Municipalities were proving grounds for up-and-coming politicians under the previous, one-party system as well, but in a different way: they sought to

powers among distinct levels of government (municipal, state, and central) has become a theme of substantial interest in public debate.

For these reasons, despite the inattention that most central and state authorities have given to these matters, the constitutional assignment of the functions of public order and preventive policing to the municipal level is anything but a minor detail in the lives of local authorities and most residents of Mexico. Article 21 of the Constitution defines local responsibility for public safety as a shared attribution of the three levels of government. Reforms in 1999 to Article 115 included preventive policing in the list of tasks in which municipal authority within local jurisdictions is preeminent over that of other levels.[2]

Still, despite shifts in politics and in formal rules, Mexican local governments appear to have progressed little in terms of policy approaches to crime control and prevention. A recent study of forty municipal programs concludes that, while local administrations are clearly feeling pressure from their residents to take action on these issues, virtually none has developed comprehensive approaches, nor are their policies likely to have any palpable impact on either crime rates or the public's fear of victimization (Rowland 2003a).

This chapter focuses on the possible reasons behind municipalities' failure to develop credible anticrime policies. It attempts to identify the limitations of municipal governments in addressing problems of crime and public safety by identifying the key issues that constrain local effectiveness in this area. The empirical evidence for this study is drawn from research carried out during 2001 in six municipalities located in three different states. This research included document collection and in-depth interviews with the major actors in municipal and state governments on their perceptions of insecurity, the role of local government, and the policymaking process.

The chapter begins with a brief discussion of the potential of local government in public safety and crime control, and explains why the lack of reliable crime statistics should not be of particular concern as we consider these issues. The next section sets forth the framework and methods used to answer the main research question: why do Mexican municipal governments fail in fighting crime and perceptions of danger? Evidence drawn

---

demonstrate their loyalty to superiors in the party hierarchy and to prove they could keep the peace and deliver the vote in their jurisdiction.

[2] This reform was designed to overcome the practices of many states, which routinely "kept" the most profitable and politically sensitive activities—and policing in Mexico is both—under their own control.

both from the broader literature on municipal government in Mexico and from the field research carried out for this study is then presented to help formulate answers to this question.

CAN LOCAL GOVERNMENT FIGHT CRIME?

This study takes as a point of departure that it is important to understand why municipalities in Mexico have not succeeded in developing policies that are likely to prevent crime and improve the public's sense of personal security. The assumption is that such an understanding can be used to help design ways to improve the effectiveness of local policies, and thus lower crime rates as well as fear of crime. However, before delving into the question of municipal policy failures, it is important to address two related issues. First, how do we know that they have not succeeded? And second, is it possible that this level of government *can* succeed in doing something about crime?

Measuring Local Policy Effectiveness in Crime Fighting

Studies of public policy are rightly concerned with detecting, measuring, and evaluating the intended and unintended outcomes of government action (or inaction). Thus, if we want to show that the policies of Mexican local governments are ineffective in preventing or combating crime, one way to do so would be to measure the changes in crime rates across a variety of local jurisdictions and try to trace these impacts back to differences in the kinds of policies implemented.

This approach would certainly be adequate for the study of many of the public services with which local governments are charged, such as water provision or zoning. However, in contrast to these relatively straightforward tasks, the complex—and eminently human—character of criminal behavior makes it much more difficult to link patterns observed in the real world to policies implemented by a local unit of government. Indeed, we can imagine the case of a local government that implements some optimal package of anticrime policies (whatever this may be) and nonetheless experiences a rise in crime rates. This situation could come about because of such diverse factors as a dramatic change in national macroeconomic conditions, the coming of age of an exceptionally large number of adolescents, or the sparking of a turf war among rival drug-trafficking factions active in the region. And the reverse is also possible: a local government that does nothing, or that implements patently stupid anticrime policies, could see a reduction of crime in its jurisdiction because of changes in other variables that affect the crime rate.

In addition, we can expect that many of the potential benefits of local policies—particularly the reform of police forces, training of new officers, and efforts to improve public order—will be felt only in the longer term. Given that the brief terms of Mexican local administrations are often accompanied by drastic zigzags in policy, any results of a single administration's efforts are difficult to detect.

These theoretical difficulties are daunting enough. But an additional reason for setting aside the search for "objective" measures of the effectiveness of local public policies is that the data upon which these would be based are highly problematic in Mexico.[3] Even where data are available and relatively reliable, the unit of measurement is generally the entire local jurisdiction (municipality or *delegación*). These local jurisdictions range in population from just over one hundred residents to nearly two million, and the wide disparity among neighborhoods in urban areas—arguably wider than in developed countries because of greater income disparities and mixed land uses—makes data that encompass these units difficult to interpret.

Do these problems imply that it is impossible, or simply useless, to study local government policies for crime control and prevention in Mexico? Not at all, but they do suggest that simple statistical measures of crime are inappropriate for this study. Still, other methodologies may bear fruit. Specifically, the research team for this project[4] used interviews with key informants to help evaluate the difficulties and the effectiveness of the policies in question. The information that such actors can offer is not, by its nature, of the clean and clear variety we expect from quantitative data, and it is sharply limited by the number of in-depth case studies that can be carried out within a comparable time period. However, these sources have a richness in terms of detail and causal explanation that raw numbers lack. Thus I argue that it is possible to offer some comment on the effectiveness of local crime control and prevention policies currently in place in Mexico and, beyond that, on the difficulties in formulating these policies and putting them to work. In addition, although municipal actions to improve

---

[3] Other studies in this volume explain the problems in more detail.

[4] The field research referred to here was carried out by Cristián Flores, Luis Gómez, and Beatriz Sánchez, as part of their master's theses in administration and public policy at the Centro de Investigación y Docencia Económicas in Mexico City. The work was funded in part by a grant from CONACYT.

public perceptions of personal risk or safety may have little impact on "real" crime rates, they are worthwhile because it is public perceptions, rather than data, that determine votes. This observation is of no small importance in newly competitive Mexican local governments.

Evidence of Local Effectiveness in Preventing and Controlling Crime and in Reducing Fear

Given that Mexican municipalities appear to have been unsuccessful so far in implementing local crime prevention and control policies, it is reasonable to ask whether, in fact, these governments are the appropriate level to take charge of such actions. Indeed, in countries with unitary structures of government, the very idea of municipal police and local anticrime programs is usually considered rather odd. Even in Mexico, in spite of its federal structure, recent crime-fighting policies have been concentrated at the federal (and to some extent the state) level as a political response to public concerns about the current crime wave. In many senses, municipal policing and crime control have been ignored or dismissed, either tacitly or openly.

In contrast, however, much of the vast research on crime and policing that has been carried out in federal countries (particularly the United States) takes as a given that local governments can have important impacts on levels of crime and fear. The recommended policy approaches cannot be imported directly, of course, since the list of formal responsibilities for municipal policing and justice administration in Mexico is not as comprehensive as those in other federal countries, and there are important differences in context and practice as well. Perhaps most importantly, there are no local detectives or local courts, and municipal police duties are restricted to prevention, order maintenance, and the apprehension of criminals caught in the act. In addition, some Mexican scholars point to vagueness and self-contradiction in the various legal structures that pretend to give form to local duties of policing and public security (Yáñez Romero n.d.).

Still, many of the tasks that Mexican local governments and their police forces have begun to assume have much in common with key areas of research in other federal countries. The difficulties in coordination among the police forces and public policies of multiple levels of government have not gone unnoticed in the United States (see, for example, Geller and Morris 1992), but the benefits of local control and local knowledge are usually judged to outweigh these complications. Three aspects in particular stand out as areas in which local policies to combat crime and fear may be effective. First, for historical and cultural reasons, the extensive literature on policing from the United States presumes that policies related to police organization and behavior are best formulated and implemented by local government (Lyons 1999; Walker 1999). Second, according to the related literature, municipal governments and police forces have better access to detailed knowledge about neighborhood and urban dynamics, which makes the findings about crime control through the imposition of public order and combat of "hot spots" clearly relevant (Murray 1995; Sherman, Gartin, and Buerger 1989; Skogan 1990; Taylor and Gottfredson 1986). Finally, questions of social capital and its role in crime prevention are focused precisely on interactions at the community and neighborhood levels, rather than on grand national strategies. The role of local government in fomenting higher levels of interpersonal trust and watchfulness is taken for granted in much of this literature (Bursik 1988; Merry 1981; Wilson 1995; Wilson and Kelling 1982).

Thus the lack of reliable statistics on crime rates in Mexican municipalities should not be considered a barrier to studying local policy approaches and suggesting ways to improve them. As noted above, "real" statistics are neither available nor particularly relevant, since it is likely that even theoretically perfect policies would have mixed impacts on crime rates, at least in the short run. Instead, this chapter takes evidence of the potential importance of local government actions in controlling and preventing crime from contexts outside of Mexico, under the assumption that similar principles of social interaction among residents, potential criminals, and police officers are valid in this country as well.

THE RESEARCH QUESTION AND METHODS

A superficial familiarity with Mexican municipalities is sufficient to suggest a variety of potential, overlapping factors to explain their failure to design and implement successful anticrime policies. This section begins with an outline of the most common and credible arguments and a brief evaluation of each. This sets the bases for the main hypothesis of this research: that it is institutional limitations, more than other factors, that explain municipal failure to develop credible anticrime policies.

For those who believe that organized crime, especially drug trafficking, is the primary source of crime and insecurity in Mexico, the local level is all but irrelevant. In essence, the argument is that, given the dimensions of the problem, crime fighting is simply "too big" a problem for local governments. That is, local governments' closer relationship with citizens, as well as specialized knowledge of local issues and characteristics, is not relevant to issues of public security. This position contrasts sharply with the literature discussed in the previous section, which suggests that Mexican local governments could be successful within a limited sphere of action, centered on tasks of improved policing, prevention, and maintenance of public order.

Another potential explanation for municipal failure to formulate credible anticrime policies, which is frequently alluded to in national discourse on crime, is that local officials are simply too corrupt, or easily corruptible, to undertake such delicate matters. In other words, they benefit (financially) from the status quo, whether or not their inaction suits local residents. According to this line of argument, municipal administrations inevitably undermine national and state attempts to fight crime. However, it seems farfetched to suggest that local authorities are somehow intrinsically more corrupt than their counterparts at other levels of government, especially now that electoral competition acts as an incentive to better local government performance nearly everywhere in the country.

A related explanation suggests that it is not moral lapses that explain municipal failures, but plain incompetence. As discussed below in more detail, in Mexico, local governments typically are not characterized by high levels of professionalism and expertise. Still, the implication of this argument is that there is just not enough intelligence to go around in Mexican government, and this gives little credence to the idea that local officials might learn and improve their capacities. While the traditional difficulties in attracting and maintaining high-caliber staff to posts in smaller municipalities cannot be overlooked, competition for elected office has not only increased the diversity and responsiveness of local governments, but it has also led to rapid improvements in municipal capacity in recent years (Cabrero Mendoza 2003, 1996; Guillén 1996; Ramírez Saiz 1998; Ziccardi 1995). Nevertheless, for this research project, I do ask whether there are reasons related to the design of municipalities that continue to hold back progress in many local areas, and I incorporate this question into the research framework.

A more credible suggestion is that—given numerous other public service responsibilities, combined with serious and long-standing service backlogs—crime fighting may simply not be a priority of local governments. The urgency of demands for other local services may combine with elected officials' frank assessment of the scant possibility of making palpable progress in reducing crime and fear during their three-year terms of office.

Figure 19.1. A Model of Constraints to Effective Local Crime Prevention and Control

Constraints	Indicators	Result
Administrative and technical deficiencies	• Lack of administrative and technical capacity • Financial limitations	Problems in the design and implementation of local government policies for crime prevention and control
Difficulties in incorporating citizen participation and preferences	• Inadequate formal mechanisms • Uncooperative citizens • Inadequate informal mechanisms	
Lack of state and federal support for local efforts	• Lack of formal mechanisms • Inadequate informal mechanisms	
Problems intrinsic to local policing	• Conflicts with residents • Inadequate organization • Lack of equipment • Limited faculties	

Thus, insufficient attention may be paid to the issue of crime prevention and control. Whether this truly occurs is another question incorporated into the research framework for explicit consideration in each case municipality.

The hypothesis that guides the research presented in this chapter considers the arguments presented above but focuses explicitly on the institutional limitations of municipal government in Mexico as an explanation of failures in local anticrime policies. This hypothesis is based primarily on a review of the problems that researchers have identified in municipal governments in general, rather than in crime fighting in particular, given that very little specific information exists about the latter. These broader studies also help establish a systematic framework for understanding governance in Mexican municipalities, as well as the common problems encountered. The framework (summarized in figure 19.1) posits that for any given sector of local public policy, local governments confront three major types of constraints: administrative and technical limitations, difficulties in the relationship with local residents, and the inattention of state and federal levels of government to their efforts and problems. In addition, local governments must deal with a set of issues unique to tasks of crime prevention and control. The presence of such constraints, according to this research framework, can be detected through informed actors' opinions about certain indicators in each municipal case—in other words, a self-diagnosis.

The division of local government functions presented here is somewhat arbitrary; in practice there is substantial overlap among the processes of local government, but it is useful to bring clarity and thoroughness to the discussion. It also allows for more detailed hypotheses about the specific ways in which institutional limitations present problems for Mexican local governments in their attempts to design and implement policies to prevent and control crime.

As alluded to earlier, despite rapid gains in recent years in the number and quality of studies about Mexican municipal government, the kind of information needed to understand the choices made by public officials is most readily and accurately available only through case studies of particular places. This research adopted the method of multiple, explanatory case studies to allow both a review of actions of specific local governments (for example, policies designed and implemented/not implemented) and interviews with local actors about successes and failures and the reasons for making certain decisions. Six municipalities were chosen to maximize the variety of possible combinations of the factors that the literature on crime

Table 19.1. Key Characteristics of the Municipal Cases (2001)

Municipality	State	Population	Municipal Party Affiliation	State Party Affiliation	Economic Base
Atlacomulco	México	76,750	PRI	PRI	Agriculture, trade
Chilpancingo	Guerrero	192,947	PRI	PRI	State capital, trade, services
Guadalajara	Jalisco	1,646,319	PAN	PAN	State capital, industry, trade, services
Naucalpan	México	858,711	PAN	PRI	Industry, trade, services
San Luis Acatlán	Guerrero	36,813	PRD	PRI	Agriculture, ranching
Tomatlán	Jalisco	34,329	PRI	PAN	Agriculture

Source: INEGI 2000.

Note: PRI = Institutional Revolutionary Party; PAN = National Action Party; PRD = Party of the Democratic Revolution.

and Mexican local government suggests are important, including region of the country, urban-versus-rural social structures, political party affiliation of municipal and state authorities, and the economic profile of the place (table 19.1). This study could not pretend to exhaust the list of possible factors and combinations, but it did attempt to focus on the issues judged most important for local policymaking. In recognition of the large role of states in determining the scope of municipal action, the municipalities were chosen in pairs for each of three states: Guerrero, Jalisco, and México State. As in all case studies of current government functioning, it was necessary to limit the study to cases in which the cooperation of local officials could be secured.

WHY DO MUNICIPALITIES FAIL TO DEVELOP EFFECTIVE ANTICRIME POLICIES?

The basic argument in this research is that local governments in Mexico differ in significant ways from those envisioned in the literature on federalism and decentralization, as well as from those presented in studies of crime prevention and control. These differences—including administrative deficiencies, difficulties in relationships with residents, and lack of intergovernmental support—in turn help explain the ineffectiveness of Mexican municipalities in preventing and controlling crime. The empirical evidence encountered in this study suggests that, in general terms, this argument holds in all six cases, albeit in slightly different ways. This section reviews the findings according to the categories described in the research framework, putting them in the context of municipal government generally.

Administrative and Technical Deficiencies in Local Government

Since the early 1980s, local government functions in Mexico have expanded from simple order maintenance and minor public works (Fagen and Tuohy 1972; Graham 1968), which required little in the way of administrative expertise, to a much broader list of tasks, including personnel management, budgeting and planning, organizing property tax registers, and providing basic public services, including local public security. The degree to which individual municipalities have developed the capacity to manage such tasks varies considerably, but urban municipalities have tended to be more successful than rural ones for several reasons, including their greater revenue bases and the larger and more educated population from which they can draw potential employees (Cabrero Mendoza 1996; Rowland 2001).

Still, few observers of this process would suggest that even the most advanced Mexican local governments can successfully carry out all aspects of their jobs. The very design of local government, including a brief three-year term of office with no possibility of immediate reelection, contributes to discontinuities between the programs of one municipal administration and the next. Not only is learning by elected officials lost with every change in administration, but also, because of rapid turnover and the lack of a professional civil service, training invested in personnel is usually lost as well.

Financial limitations contribute to these problems. Recent evidence suggests that almost two decades after national decentralization legislation was implemented, decentralization of public expenditures in Mexico is finally under way, with urban municipalities in particular beginning to generate revenue from local sources, principally the property tax and service charges (Cabrero Mendoza 1996, 1998). Still, the high dependence of nearly all municipalities on transfers from the federal level (*participaciones*) remains problematic; these transfers are processed and distributed by state governments, which often attach political strings to their use and amounts (Rowland 2001). The size of these transfers varies greatly and unpredictably from year to year as well, making municipal planning and budgeting much more difficult. To make matters worse, long-standing backlogs in public services imply that pent-up demand exists for spending in many other areas of local responsibility.

Deficiencies in administrative and technical capacity in local governments presumably act in direct and indirect ways on the potential of local governments to design and implement anticrime policies.[5] This research sought to determine whether these deficiencies lead to local strategies that are inadequate in the face of real conditions and that reflect an insufficient understanding of the scope and characteristics of the local crime problem. In addition, even where policies seemed reasonable, I tried to find out whether they were implemented fully and in the way their designers intended.

---

[5] Limits in administrative and technical capacity also probably exert an effect on the other factors considered here: the ability to organize participation of local residents in policy design and implementation, the management of intergovernmental affairs under adverse circumstances, and the ability to organize and reform local police, as well as to conceive of other options to improve crime prevention and control.

The evidence collected in all six municipal cases made clear that crime control and prevention is an issue of high priority for local governments. None of the administrations was insensitive to the political imperative to take action in this sector. However, the policy development process, even in the most sophisticated municipalities, remains primitive. The research team found evidence of little planning, few attempts to explicitly link policy inputs and outputs, and no efforts at evaluation of public security policies currently in place. Paradoxically, the incapacity to carry out basic tasks of policy design and implementation appears even more marked in the largest urban cases. Presumably this is because their local contexts, in both bureaucratic and social terms, are more complex than those of rural areas.

Two other findings in regard to administrative and technical capacity bear note. On one hand, while finances are certainly limited, few officials or other actors considered this the primary constraint to more effective anticrime policies. On the other hand, although the level of trust for police officers that is attributed to residents was very low, local actors' opinion of municipal governments more broadly is considered to be much more positive, regardless of the corruption that may exist in specific municipal offices. This suggests that residents are likely to cooperate, at least initially, with local government efforts to fight crime and to reduce the fear of becoming a victim.

Difficulties Incorporating Citizens into Policymaking

One presumed advantage of local government is that its proximity and smaller scale allow more frequent contact with local residents, allowing them to express their preferences more easily and offering greater and more specialized information to public officials (Dahl and Tufte 1973; Putnam 1993; Smith 1985; World Bank 1997, 2000). However, in Mexico the relationship between local residents and local authorities remains confused and often distant.[6] Thus, as municipal governments began taking on greater importance in local affairs over the past few decades, the ambiguity in the established forms of interaction between municipal governments and their residents has become more obvious.

---

[6] This problem has complex historical roots. Suffice it to say that under the traditional PRI organization of government, the interaction of citizens with local government on substantial policy issues was almost nil (Fagen and Tuohy 1972; Ramírez Saiz 1998; Ziccardi 1995).

In part, the problem is related to representation and the structure of local government, including the election by party slate of the mayor (*presidente municipal*) and the local council (*cabildo*). The post-electoral relationship of residents to their local representatives is not entirely clear, either in formal terms or by virtue of accepted practice. Under the one-party system, the mayor dominated local policymaking and politics, and the majority in the council simply rubber-stamped the initiatives forwarded to them for official approval. This pattern has changed (in most parts of the country) as a result of the increasing competitiveness of local and state elections since the late 1980s. Local councilors are now less likely to cooperate unconditionally with mayors, even of their own party. At the same time, candidates must appeal to voters to prevail over opposition slates, and one way to do so is to pledge to be more responsive to local problems.

While this seems like a reasonable, even laudable, development, it is complicated by the fact that there is no formal list of tasks for council members, nor oversight of their work on sectoral commissions. Indeed, in many cases their activities overlap and even conflict with those of the directors of municipal administrative departments, who are named by the mayors. Little has been published about the effectiveness of council members in affecting local policy (Guillén 1996 is one exception), but it is not easy to be optimistic given the formal structure and anecdotal information.

Given that the institutional design of interactions between local government and residents is ambiguous in formal terms, in practice there is substantial variation among municipalities and among different administrations of the same municipality. The evidence collected in the six cases suggests that municipalities indeed experience difficulties in finding a place for citizens in their processes of policy development in general, and especially in anticrime strategies.[7] There is no consensus on what role residents should play in preventing and controlling crime, and the predominant attitude appears to be that the issue is too pressing and too dangerous to permit extensive public input. Nor are citizens typically deemed trustworthy allies in fighting crime.

Meanwhile, low public confidence in police officers, fueled by perceptions (and the reality) of brutality and corruption, keeps the relationship

---

[7] The only exception is the municipality of San Luis Acatlán, where the current municipal administration works closely with an innovative, nongovernmental *policía comunitaria* that enjoys local public support and apparent success at lowering crime rates (Rowland 2003b; Hernández and Ortiz Elizondo, this volume).

between citizens and police officers from improving. Indeed, in issues of crime control and public security, the specific personnel responsible for this local service, as well as their training and ethics, take on far greater importance than in other areas of local government activity. In particular, the complexity of police duties, the intensity of the relationship between the police and the public, and the potential recourse by the police to physical force contribute to a dramatic difference in the types of interactions that these employees routinely have with citizens, as compared to, for example, municipal water engineers or garbage collectors.

Finally, the party affiliation of local government appears to have little predictable relationship with local policymaking in terms of its implications for either policy choices or intergovernmental relations. Indeed, the most profound effect of partisan issues was reported to be the distraction that these create for municipal governments in their search for systematic approaches to crime and security problems. In many municipalities, electoral jockeying makes consensus on policy goals nearly impossible, and it thus impedes progress not only in public security but also in other local issues.

Lack of Support for Municipal Efforts by State and Federal Governments

Intergovernmental relations are of relatively recent concern in Mexico, given that disputes traditionally were mediated behind closed doors within the hierarchy of the Institutional Revolutionary Party (PRI). The rise of electoral competition since the late 1980s, however, has led to a growing diversity of parties in power at the local and state levels. This diversity implies not only a greater degree of conflict among all three levels as they battle for public resources and voters' favor, but also the need for new mechanisms of dispute resolution (Rowland 2000). Unfortunately, in spite of decentralization efforts, the vulnerability of most Mexican local governments to impositions by state and national levels continues.[8]

Formal mechanisms of coordination between municipalities and states—beyond the general principles of liberty, autonomy, and cooperation set forth in the Constitution—are integrated into many national programs, in-

---

[8] Although the 1999 reforms did set more solid bases for municipal claims to jurisdiction over certain tasks, including public security, many states have been slow to adjust their local constitutions to reflect these changes. For example, the municipality of Mérida, capital of the state of Yucatán, only gained control of local policing duties in June 2003.

cluding the National Public Security System (SNSP) and the National System of Democratic Planning (Sistema Nacional de Planeación Democrática). However, the actual extent to which both the letter and the spirit of these laws—which presume ongoing communication, common goals, and mutual respect among equals—are complied with varies from state to state. In fact, it is generally the states that dictate the terms of these relationships since, as noted previously, the balance of power between the two levels of government is tilted in favor of this level.

The same logic holds for federal-municipal relations, with the added complication that many states consider themselves legitimate and indispensable intermediaries in this relationship. However, even in states that are willing to cooperate with federal initiatives to establish and maintain formal mechanisms of coordination with municipalities, central government appears to have difficulty formulating a useful role for municipalities in the control and prevention of crime. At the same time, it is not unusual for intergovernmental conflicts to play out on the streets between local police and their federal or state counterparts, either while members of different groups pursue the same suspects or—in situations more numerous than one might expect—when members of one police group are apprehended by another as suspects in a crime.[9]

The evidence from the case studies points up differences in practice between activities of state and federal police and military, on one hand, and the broader issues of administrative and financial support for local initiatives from state and federal governments, on the other. A certain limited tradition of interagency cooperation and assistance to municipal police forces appears to prevail, at least formally.[10] In fact, municipal respondents appeared grateful for this support in training and technical activities, and they were somewhat hesitant to openly criticize those who offer it. Informal

---

[9] A sampling of recently reported cases includes: "Con hombres armados el director de la policía municipal defendió a su chofer de los ministeriales," *Ecos de Morelos-La Unión de Morelos*, February 9, 2004; "Bronca de policías por un testigo," *Diario de Toluca*, December 19, 2003; "Denuncia edil hostigamiento de las BOM en Benemérito de las Américas," *Notimex*, November 5, 2003; "Lamenta gobernador de BC balacera entre policías," *CNI en Línea*, November 2, 2003.

[10] San Luis Acatlán again diverges from the pattern in the sense that state police and military troops are a recurrent source of problems for local residents (see Rowland 2003b).

mechanisms of communication among police and security forces of different levels of government were also reported. These consist of officials at differing levels who meet in an ad hoc manner when the need arises or simply pick up the telephone and discuss matters of importance with their counterparts. In spite of this collaboration, many municipal actors complained about interference in local affairs by state and federal police, as well as their alleged inattention to or collusion with organized crime. Indeed, both formal and informal intergovernmental relationships appear to be stymied in matters of crime control by mutual and widespread suspicions of corruption, including links to organized crime.

In broader terms, local officials and other local actors report disappointment with the level of support from state and federal government for their crime-fighting efforts. The influx of revenue earmarked for municipal public security from the federal Fund for Municipal Strengthening (FAFM, which is part of budget line item [*ramo*] XXXIII) was welcomed by all, but the belief was widespread that federal and state governments should do much more to help municipalities fight crime. For their part, the actions and attitudes of actors at higher levels suggest an underlying skepticism that municipalities can do much about crime, an opinion not shared by their local counterparts. This may, however, partly reflect differences in the kinds of crime—particularly drug trafficking and other forms of organized crime—that states and federal government view as most important.

Special Difficulties for Municipalities in Crime Control and Prevention

Aside from the aforementioned issues of administrative capacity, relationships with citizens, and intergovernmental relations, the specific local institutions dedicated to crime prevention and control appear incapable of responding adequately to the current crime wave. Indeed, despite being charged with "public security" under national and state constitutions, local governments have little power to do more than basic patrol and order maintenance. Municipal police are defined as merely "preventive," and they are empowered to make arrests only for crimes discovered in flagrante or of individuals for whom an arrest warrant has been issued by a state prosecutor. The prosecutor's office in many regions has become a source of complaints by local authorities as well as in the media, because of slowness in investigations and the numerous cases in which a suspected criminal is released from custody because of errors in the documentation submitted to the presiding judge. Its lack of coordination with local police in questions of information and intelligence is also the target of frequent criticism.[11]

There are also administrative difficulties in local policing, some of which echo the broader problems in local administration noted above. Shortfalls in technical personnel and administrative equipment (such as computers and radios) are common. In addition, the municipal police chief is a political appointee, and lack of job protection often results in high turnover rates and dramatic changes in department policies from one year to the next (Ramírez Saiz 1998).

These are not the only limits on local police. In addition, officer salaries are low, even by Mexican standards, ranging from around 1,500 pesos to 5,000 pesos per month.[12] Other types of benefits, including life insurance and basic equipment (bulletproof vests, uniforms) are often not included in the officers' salary package and must be purchased separately. Armament is outdated and in short supply, and the contrast between the weapons carried by local police and by the criminals they often face on the streets is alarming; the latter commonly are equipped with the latest in semiautomatic and fully automatic technology.

A chilling study co-written by an undercover participant observer who joined a municipal police force near Mexico City reports a number of additional problems, all of which are probably generalizable to other localities (see Arteaga Botello and López Rivera 1998). Recruits to local police forces tend to have little more than primary education, and many have been previously fired from other police forces or have their own criminal records. Once enrolled in the police academy (where these exist), cadets are not trained in law enforcement, police tactics, or the management of interpersonal conflicts. Instead, they are explicitly instructed in techniques of extortion of residents and businesses, as well as in the need to regularly bribe their superior officers. Indeed, according to this study, corruption is the basis upon which the daily activities of local police officers are organized, since they must pay off everyone from the medical examiner who declares them fit for service, to the instructors charged with giving them exams, to the commander who assigns them to profitable or unprofitable beats.

---

[11] See other chapters in this volume for more information on the specific problems of the criminal justice system in Mexico.

[12] The official minimum wage at the time of this writing was around 700 pesos for a 160-hour work month. The rate of exchange was approximately ten Mexican pesos to one U.S. dollar.

Perhaps not surprisingly, many local police chiefs report that available positions on their forces remain unfilled because candidates cannot be found. A vicious circle, beginning with low public esteem and miserable working conditions, leads to difficulties in recruiting competent and professional-minded cadets as police officers. Since those who are recruited tend to have little formal education and are inducted into patterns of corruption as part of their working environment, public officials are reluctant to defend proposals to increase officer salaries and improve their benefit packages. Thus the distance between the organizational culture of police officers and the preferences of local residents for their behavior can become a problematic issue in itself.

The municipal cases suggest that mistrust between police officers and local residents may be the most important stumbling block to improved municipal public security. As in large cities in most of the world, conflict was particularly serious in certain urban neighborhoods controlled by local gangs, often in collusion with residents, where local police forces are reluctant to enter at all. In contrast, citizen-police relationships were characterized as far less conflictive in small towns. This makes sense given that, in the latter context, the everyday social separation of officers from residents or particular neighborhoods is less feasible than it is in large cities.

Local actors in all six of the case municipalities considered the organization and training of municipal police to be deficient. In addition, while many of those interviewed reported efforts to restructure and reform the institutions of local policing, they rarely reported satisfaction with the outcomes, even of their own policies. There was also much complaint over perceived shortages of modern and functioning equipment for municipal police forces. These shortages may be real, but it is not clear that they pose more serious problems to policing and local policymaking than do the other problematic aspects of local government discussed here. The insistence on the gravity of this problem may simply indicate a bias among many actors in favor of a "technical" solution to crime and violence.

Surprisingly, apart from equipment shortages, many officials denied that revenue constraints were an important limitation to their anticrime strategies. Again, the locality's population size appears to play a key role in these differences, with both large and midsize cities reporting a distinct advantage in this sense. In addition, all the cases received additional funds from the FAFM, which appears to have alleviated revenue scarcity in the short term.

Finally, opinions were mixed among the actors interviewed about whether the legal constraints on local police activities play a part not only in difficulties in attacking crime at the local level, but also in motivating officers to do their jobs. While some respondents strongly support proposals to expand municipal attributions, a substantial proportion suggested that they have enough difficulty fulfilling their current functions and do not wish to complicate matters further.

CONCLUSIONS

The evidence from the six case studies selected for this project suggests that Mexican local governments suffer from built-in weaknesses that impede effective policymaking and implementation in issues of crime prevention and control. These problems, like many others encountered in local government, arise from local inexperience, which leads to ineffective policy design and implementation. This, in turn, provokes the mistrust of federal and state officials, and leads to continued exclusion from higher-level efforts and the subsequent failure to improve local capacity in this sector. To the extent that municipalities are considered at all, state and federal government policies to combat crime have emphasized municipal incompetence or, at most, the remediation of material shortages via targeted revenue transfers. The present research disputes the usefulness of these approaches with the argument that neither the centralization of crime-fighting functions nor throwing money at the problem is likely to improve the situation.

Indeed, locating the source of local government failures to develop effective anticrime policies at the systemic rather than individual level—if accurate—points us in a fruitful direction for helping local governments improve their responses to crime and fear of crime. Clearly the municipal level is not adequate for fighting some of the crime problems, particularly drug trafficking, that most preoccupy the federal and state levels. However, findings drawn from other federal countries about policing, public order, and crime prevention, as well as issues related to perceptions of personal safety, suggest that there is indeed a role for local governments in this sector of activity. Unfortunately, the key ingredient for the success of these programs—the actions of relatively autonomous and competent local governments—appears to be overlooked in Mexico. Involving, rather than excluding, municipalities and concentrating on ways to help them overcome their limitations would be promising first steps.

The present research also suggests that the nature of public security itself differentiates the personnel involved from that of other sectors of municipal activity and makes lack of local experience especially problematic. "Learning by doing" and other informal or incremental ways of gaining expertise in local tasks are risky in issues of crime control and prevention. Here, additional information on what works and what does not work in the Mexican context is of crucial importance to helping local governments do a better job of formulating successful local policy.

The improvement of municipal police forces can be a vicious circle in which low pay and low public esteem limit the quality of candidates for these jobs and, in turn, reinforce the idea that local police do not deserve better. Indeed, the experience with the nongovernmental police officers in one of the cases—San Luis Acatlán, Guerrero—suggests that concerted attention to the human element inherent in this public service may be fundamental to improving both the perceptions and the reality of citizen safety. In this case, resident involvement in crime fighting has accompanied improved police responsiveness, and each continues to reinforce the other (see Rowland 2003b).

While the precise model of San Luis Acatlán is unlikely to be replicable in culturally heterogeneous areas, including cities, it emphasizes the importance of integrating local populations and municipal governments in efforts to prevent and control crime. Even in the best cases, federal and state police generally have little direct, day-to-day contact with law-abiding citizens, and they rarely appear to consider the effects of their actions on the perceptions of residents of a particular locality. Nor do state and federal police forces, prosecutors, or courts have any pressing need to answer to local authorities about their actions. In other words, the incentives that face local governments to formulate effective policies for crime prevention and control, as well as to improve public perceptions of security, do not appear to affect higher levels to the same extent.

Thus the potential role for municipalities in crime prevention and control is closely related to other arguments in favor of decentralization. In fact, greater effectiveness in crime control and prevention may be one of the most compelling reasons to continue decentralization and the strengthening of municipalities in Mexico. Currently, their potential to contribute to this task is ignored or denied by other levels of government. However, comparative advantage among levels of government on an issue of such pressing public concern should not continue to be squandered.

References

Arteaga Botello, Nelson, and Adrián López Rivera. 1998. *Policía y corrupción.* Mexico City: Plaza y Valdés.

Bursik, Robert. 1988. "Social Disorganization and Theories of Crime and Delinquency: Problems and Prospects," *Criminology* 26: 519–52.

Cabrero Mendoza, Enrique, ed. 1996. *Los dilemas de la modernización municipal: estudios sobre la gestión hacendaria en municipios urbanos de México.* Mexico City: Miguel Ángel Porrúa.

———. 1998. *Las políticas descentralizadoras en México (1983–1993): logros y desencantos.* Mexico City: Miguel Ángel Porrúa.

———. 2003. *Políticas públicas municipales: una agenda en construcción.* Mexico City: Miguel Ángel Porrúa.

Dahl, Robert A., and E.R. Tufte. 1973. *Size and Democracy.* Stanford, Calif.: Stanford University Press.

Fagen, Richard R., and William S. Tuohy. 1972. *Politics and Privilege in a Mexican City.* Stanford, Calif.: Stanford University Press.

Geller, William A., and Norval Morris. 1992. "Relations between Federal and Local Police." In *Modern Policing,* ed. Michael Tonry and Norval Morris. Chicago: University of Chicago Press.

Graham, Lawrence S. 1968. *Politics in a Mexican Community.* Gainesville: University of Florida Press.

Guillén, Tonatiuh. 1996. *Gobiernos municipales en México: entre la modernización y tradición política.* Mexico City: Miguel Ángel Porrúa.

INEGI (Instituto Nacional de Estadística, Geografía e Informática). 2000. *XII Censo General de Población y Vivienda.* At www.inegi.gob.mx. Retrieved March 10, 2004.

Lyons, William. 1999. *The Politics of Community Policing: Rearranging the Power to Punish.* Ann Arbor: University of Michigan Press.

Merino, Mauricio. 1992. *Fuera del centro.* Xalapa: Universidad Veracruzana.

Merry, Sally E. 1981. *Urban Danger: Life in a Neighborhood of Strangers.* Philadelphia, Penn.: Temple University Press.

Murray, Charles. 1995. "The Physical Environment," *Crime* [Institute for Contemporary Studies, San Francisco]: 349–61.

Putnam, Robert D. 1993. *Making Democracy Work: Civic Traditions in Modern Italy.* Princeton, N.J.: Princeton University Press.

Ramírez Saiz, Juan Manuel, ed. 1998. *¿Cómo gobiernan Guadalajara? Demandas ciudadanas y respuestas de los ayuntamientos.* Mexico City: Miguel Ángel Porrúa/Universidad Nacional Autónoma de México.

Rodríguez, Victoria E. 1997. *Decentralization in Mexico: From Reforma Municipal to Solidaridad to Nuevo Federalismo.* Boulder, Colo.: Westview.

Rowland, Allison M. 2000. *Los municipios y la coordinación intergubernamental.* Series: Agenda de la Reforma Municipal en México. Mexico City: CE-SEM/IIS-UNAM/CIDE.

———. 2001. "Population as a Determinant of Variation in Local Outcomes under Decentralization: Illustrations from Small Municipalities in Bolivia and Mexico," *World Development* 29, no. 8: 1373–89.

———. 2003a. "La seguridad pública local en México: una agenda sin rumbo." In *Políticas públicas municipales: una agenda en construcción,* ed. Enrique Cabrero Mendoza. Mexico City: Miguel Ángel Porrúa.

———. 2003b. "Local Responses to Public Insecurity in Mexico: A Consideration of the *Policía Comunitaria* of the Costa Chica and the Montaña de Guerrero." Paper presented at the international congress of the Latin American Studies Association, March 27, Dallas.

Rowland, Allison M., and Lawrence S. Graham. 2002. "An Historical Perspective on Federalism and Decentralization in Mexico, Brazil, and the United States." Working Paper DT-DAP 112. Mexico City: Centro de Investigación y Docencia Económicas.

Sherman, L., P. Gartin, and M. Buerger. 1989. "Hot Spots of Predatory Crime: Routine Activities and the Criminology of Place," *Criminology* 27: 27–56.

Skogan, Wesley G. 1990. *Disorder and Decline: Crime and the Spiral of Decay in American Neighborhoods.* Berkeley: University of California Press.

Smith, Brian C. 1985. *Decentralization: The Territorial Dimension of the State.* London: Allen and Unwin.

Taylor, Ralph B., and Stephen Gottfredson. 1986. "Environmental Design, Crime, and Prevention: An Examination of Community Dynamics." In *Communities and Crime,* ed. Albert J. Reiss, Jr. and Michael Tonry. Chicago: University of Chicago Press.

Walker, Samuel. 1999. *The Police in America: An Introduction.* Boston, Mass.: McGraw Hill College.

Wilson, James Q. 1995. "Crime and Public Policy," *Crime* [Institute for Contemporary Studies, San Francisco]: 327–48.

Wilson, James Q., and George L. Kelling. 1982. "The Police and Neighborhood Safety: Broken Windows," *Atlantic Monthly,* March.

World Bank. 1997. *World Development Report.* Washington, D.C.: World Bank.

———. 2000. *World Development Report.* Washington, D.C.: World Bank.

Yáñez Romero, José Arturo. n.d. "Police and Policing in Mexico." Manuscript.

Ziccardi, Alicia, ed. 1995. *La tarea de gobernar: gobiernos locales y demandas ciudadanas.* Mexico City: Miguel Ángel Porrúa.

CHAPTER 20

Public Security, Criminal Justice, and Human Rights: A Critique of PAN Governance in Jalisco, 1995–2006

MARCOS PABLO MOLOEZNIK

In 1995 the state of Jalisco experienced political alternation for the first time, when the National Action Party (PAN) replaced the long-ruling Institutional Revolutionary Party (PRI) in the governor's office. As at the national level since the PAN's victory in the presidential election of 2000, Jalisco's transition ostensibly represented a change in public policy. Jalisco therefore provides a useful case to examine the effects of political alternation on security, criminal justice, and human rights in the context of Mexico's democratization. In this chapter I critique the performance of two consecutive PAN administrations that have governed in Jalisco since 1995 with regard to the basic duties of the state in providing security for and protecting the rights of its citizens. The chapter concludes with ten recommendations for the future design and implementation of public security policy to address the particular needs of the state of Jalisco.

PUBLIC SECURITY AND CRIMINAL JUSTICE IN JALISCO, 1995–2003

Located in the heart of western Mexico, Jalisco has almost 6.5 million residents (INEGI 2001). In 1995 it began a process of democratic transition with the arrival in power of PAN Governor Alberto Cárdenas Jiménez (1995–2000), the first "opposition" administration in the state's history to replace the PRI. Continued PAN rule was achieved in 2000 with the electoral victory of Governor Francisco Javier Ramírez Acuña (2000–2006), also from the ranks of the PAN. The PAN's victories in Jalisco were accompanied by high expectations for positive change. The PRI had controlled the state for

Translation by Patricia Rosas.

Table 20.1. Selected Crimes, Jalisco, 1993–2002

Type of Crime	1993	1994	1995	1996	1997	1998	1999	2000	2001	2002
Vehicle theft	9,659	10,307	15,876	18,661	19,904	16,264	14,705	15,455	10,721	13,402
Residential burglary	4,319	4,131	5,358	6,518	6,120	n.a.	5,400	5,533	6,345	6,013
Burglary of a business	5,632	5,257	6,649	7,748	6,585	5,405	5,637	5,708	6,931	7,332
Freight theft	7	34	224	317	747	860	761	n.a.	719	893
Bank robbery	15	26	69	81	55	39	50	12	6	18
Kidnapping	42	39	61	66	112	49	31	27	14	16
Intentional homicide	n.a.	n.a.	704	764	600	612	545	486	488	431
All reported crimes	70,677	73,722	85,701	96,791	91,312	84,328	82,468	85,984	n.a.	n.a.

Source: Gobierno del Estado de Jalisco, Poder Ejecutivo 1994–2003.
n.a.= not available.

Table 20.2. Possible Criminal Acts Reported to Federal and Local Authorities in Jalisco, 1997–2001

	Crime Reports		Federal Jurisdiction Crimes		Local Jurisdiction Crimes	
	Total	Per 1,000 Inhabitants	Total	Per 1,000 Inhabitants	Total	Per 1,000 Inhabitants
1997	104,853	16.82	4,421	0.71	100,432	16.11
1999	87,292	13.58	4,824	0.75	82,468	12.83
2000	90,301	13.85	4,317	0.66	85,984	13.19
2001	99,957	15.13	5,052	0.76	94,905	14.36

Source: Presidencia de la República 2002: 419.

several decades as a highly effective political machine government that relied on clientelistic networks of patronage, graft, and electoral chicanery. Consistent with the concept of "machine politics," this enabled the PRI to generate consistent political outcomes—that is, to maintain itself in power—until the massive electoral revolt that initially brought the PAN into office in the municipality of Guadalajara in 1997 and later at the state level.

Many of the challenges that faced the PAN in its first years in office resembled those that political reformers have faced in other contexts. After over a decade of PAN rule in Jalisco, however, there is little evidence of positive change in the areas of public security, criminal justice, and human rights. Below I examine the serious criminal justice challenges these governments have faced since 1995 and consider why political change has failed to resolve Jalisco's public security crisis. I, like other scholars, argue that the failure to effectively address these challenges in Jalisco is largely due to these governments' "failure to adjust to changing conditions" with effective strategies for reforming public administration (Dror 1996: 39).

Crime Patterns in Jalisco

The growth in crime in Jalisco, especially after 1997, calls for an assessment of the nature and the dynamics of illegal activity (see tables 20.1 and 20.2). Nationally, Jalisco has the fourth-highest crime rate based on the absolute number of reported crimes, and the thirteenth based on rate per 1,000 inhabitants (table 20.3). For Jalisco in 2001, the rate per 1,000 inhabitants was 14.36 crimes of local jurisdiction (*fuero común*) and 0.76 crimes of federal jurisdiction (*fuero federal*), slightly above the respective national averages of 14.24 (local) and 0.73 (federal). Of Mexico's thirty-two federal entities (the states plus the Federal District), thirteen—Baja California, Baja California Sur, Chihuahua, Federal District, Jalisco, México State, Morelos, Nuevo León, Querétaro, Quintana Roo, San Luis Potosí, Tamaulipas, and Yucatán—had high crime rates in 2000 (Poder Ejecutivo 2003: 15). This coincides, at least partially, with a nationwide crime map prepared by the Federal Preventive Police (PFP) that identifies fifteen high-crime priority zones in Mexico. One of these is metropolitan Guadalajara, encompassing four municipalities in central Jalisco: Guadalajara, Zapopan, Tlaquepaque, and Tonalá (Presidencia de la República 2001).

The most prevalent local jurisdiction crime reported to authorities in Jalisco tends to be theft in its various forms, followed by bodily harm and property damage (table 20.1). Of federal jurisdiction crimes, drug-related

Table 20.3. Possible Criminal Acts Reported to Federal and Local Authorities in Selected States, 2001

State	Crime Reports		Federal Jurisdiction Crimes		Local Jurisdiction Crimes	
	Total	Per 1,000 Inhabitants	Total	Per 1,000 Inhabitants	Total	Per 1,000 Inhabitants
México State	214,379	16.03	4,899	0.37	209,480	15.66
Federal District	187,157	21.20	15,688	1.78	171,469	19.42
Baja California	114,761	46.89	8,997	3.68	105,764	43.22
Jalisco	**99,957**	**15.13**	**5,052**	**0.76**	**94,905**	**14.36**
Chihuahua	64,284	20.62	2,674	0.86	61,610	19.76
Nuevo León	63,512	16.17	1,625	0.41	61,887	15.76
Puebla	61,560	11.78	1,796	0.34	59,764	11.44
Veracruz	60,996	8.52	2,158	0.30	58,838	8.22
Tamaulipas	48,509	17.45	2,557	0.92	45,952	16.53
Yucatán	43,703	25.69	651	0.38	43,052	25.31

Source: Presidencia de la República 2002: 418–21; author's emphasis.

offenses are the most common, followed by violations of the Federal Firearms and Explosives Law (Gobierno del Estado de Jalisco 1994–2003; Poder
Ejecutivo 2003: 31–32). Thus most crimes reported in Jalisco are property
crimes or are related to the production, trafficking, distribution, sale, or
consumption of stimulants or narcotics. However, as I will discuss below,
most of the crimes committed in Jalisco are actually never reported.

Marked differences and inconsistencies exist in the reports from the
various sources responsible for crime rate databases, so the above-
mentioned crime statistics cannot be considered entirely reliable. In particular, one should note that the rates reported by the Office of Criminal
Policy within the Secretariat of Public Security, Prevention, and Social
Rehabilitation (Secretaría de Seguridad Pública, Prevención, y Readaptación Social), established in Jalisco in 1999, are noticeably lower than those
published by federal agencies and nongovernmental organizations. This
chapter relies on the version issued by the head of the federal executive
branch, which appears to be more reliable than the state government's own
figures.

Major Problems in Law Enforcement

A variety of surveys and opinion polls indicate that the level of citizen
insecurity—or, better said, the public's sense of vulnerability—has resulted
in public security becoming a major concern for Jalisco's residents.[1] These
concerns are not the result solely of the crime increases noted above, but
also of persistent patterns of corruption, ineffective enforcement, lack of
judicial professionalism, frequent human rights violations, and a general
lack of leadership to promote justice reform. One exceptional study identified these concerns as "major problems," noting that "Jalisco's position as a
competitive, quality state depends on solving them" (CEED 1999: 115). I
examine these problems in turn below.

Official Corruption

A poll taken in Mexico's states and the Federal District by Transparency
International, an advocacy nongovernmental organization, places Jalisco
fifth on its global corruption index (table 20.4). This high level of corruption is also reflected in the large proportion of police officers in metropoli-

---

[1] Notably, the results of all surveys and opinion polls in the past five years list
citizen insecurity as the top priority for the public, even above the issues of
employment and education.

tan Guadalajara who are systematically dismissed from the ranks, primarily for committing or participating in corrupt acts (table 20.5). When Jalisco inhabitants were asked "What should Jalisco's state government do to lower crime levels significantly?" nearly one in three (31 percent) answered, "Combat corruption in the police forces" (Berumen y Asociados 2001).

Table 20.4. Corruption and Good Governance Rates (ICBG), by State

Rank	State	ICBG
32	Federal District	22.6
31	México State	17.0
30	Guerrero	13.4
29	Puebla	12.1
28	**Jalisco**	**11.6**
27	Michoacán	10.3
26	Durango	8.9
25	Tabasco	8.5
24	Querétaro	8.1
23	Veracruz	7.9
	National average	10.6

Source: Transparency International 2001; author's emphasis.

Table 20.5. Dismissals from Police Forces, 2001–2002

Force	Positions	Dismissals	Percentage
Guadalajara police	3,033	505	16.65
Zapopan police	1,875	402	21.44
Tlaquepaque police	650	155	23.85
Tonalá police	530	311	58.68
Total	6,088	1,373	22.55

Source: Direcciones Generales de Seguridad Pública, metropolitan Guadalajara, 2002.

A survey from a recent anticorruption program, initiated by the state's executive branch, cited agents of the Transit Department, police investigators, and officers from the state preventive police as the public servants against whom the most complaints were filed for corrupt acts (table 20.6). Paradoxically, those who are primarily being implicated in corruption are the very actors who are responsible for public security and crime investigation. One university study gave police and judicial institutions high corruption ratings of 7.16 and 8.29 out of 10, respectively (Jiménez Díaz 2003a).[2] A separate study found that investigative police, public prosecutors, and municipal police are the state and municipal government institutions that the business sector of Jalisco perceives as being the most dishonest (ITESM 2002).

Table 20.6. Complaints against Presumed Acts of Corruption (agencies receiving the most complaints)

Agency	Number of Complaints
Transit Department	221
Office of the State Attorney General (police investigators)	108
State Education Secretariat	95
Public Security Secretariat (preventive police)	70

Source: Contraloría del Estado de Jalisco 2003.

The failure of two consecutive PAN governments to eliminate police corruption illustrates its insidious and intractable nature. Police corruption results from multiple factors, including limited training in proper and professional officer conduct; insufficient compensation (which leads to corruption as a means of supplementing poor salaries); the particular internal cultures that develop within police organizations (including clientelistic bribery networks); inadequate internal review; limited protection for whistle-blowers (both inside and outside the force); and public patterns of behavior (including citizens who opt to pay bribes rather than follow proper procedures). Experience in other countries where police corruption has resulted from long periods of machine politics, including the United States, shows that these problems may take decades to resolve. Addressing them effectively requires an approach that is both long term and comprehensive.

Criminal Impunity and Ineffective Enforcement

Added to the scourge of corruption is the failure to effectively enforce the law and, therefore, the high level of impunity for those who commit crimes in Jalisco. As an illustration of this, official records report 9,125 vehicles

---

[2] The instructions were: "Where zero (0) is not at all corrupt and ten (10) is highly corrupt, please rate how corrupt you believe the judiciary and police to be."

stolen in Jalisco during 2002, of which only 4,067, or about 45 percent, were recovered (Gobierno del Estado de Jalisco 2003). Similarly, in this highly industrialized region, only 23.08 percent of freight stolen from trucks was recovered (PGJE 2003). A 2002 study corroborated these patterns when it reported that the impunity rate for crimes in Jalisco is, on average, 93 percent (table 20.7). The State Attorney General's Office (PGJE) does not even have the ability to enforce all arrest warrants, since almost 45 percent of warrants issued are never served.[3]

Table 20.7. Measures of Impunity, 1999 (selected states)

State	Institutional Performance	Arrest Warrants Fulfilled	Average Impunity
National average	48.89	25.00	89.20
Aguascalientes	53.70	34.67	83.16
Coahuila	70.35	42.61	75.69
Colima	57.75	29.16	71.81
Federal District	31.39	n.a.	81.58
Guanajuato	60.06	37.62	86.15
Jalisco	**57.77**	**55.14**	**93.00**
Michoacán	41.69	15.05	80.83
Nayarit		N.D.	64.64
Nuevo León	41.25	26.15	85.44
Querétaro	51.97	18.76	73.53
Sinaloa	36.74	14.48	84.12

Source: Zepeda Lecuona 2002: 66–67; author's emphasis.
n.a. = not available.

Moreover, considering that most crimes are never reported to the authorities, the magnitude of criminal impunity is even greater. One nationwide survey suggested that during the first half of 2002, only seventeen of every one hundred crimes were reported in Mexico (ICESI 2003); subsequent studies have corroborated that only roughly one in five crimes is reported to Mexican authorities (Zepeda Lecuona 2004). Reporting patterns in Jalisco are consistent with these larger national trends; it is estimated that no report is ever filed on approximately 80 percent of the crimes committed in the state (Moloeznik 1999).

---

[3] When a criminal court judge issues an arrest warrant in Mexico, it is because the suspect is considered guilty of the crime of which he or she is accused.

All this leads to the conclusion that in Jalisco crime *does* pay. In other words, *impunity can be considered a principal crime-generating factor* since criminals know that it is unlikely that they will face punishment. Although the responsibility for this falls fundamentally on the public prosecutor's office, we must not overlook the performance of judges for criminal matters, as well as the efforts of the preventive police.

Lack of Judicial Professionalism

Most crime victims in Jalisco fail to file a report primarily because of the patterns discussed above—the corruption and perceived ineffectiveness of judicial authorities. This is apparent in the results of a study that measured the state's judicial branch performance in terms of professionalism, the quality of decisions, and judicial impartiality. Under all three indicators and in comparison to other states in Mexico, Jalisco's performance was less than stellar (table 20.8).

Table 20.8. Judicial Branch Performance (selected states)

State	Professionalism	Quality of Decisions	Judicial Impartiality
Aguascalientes	6.46	8.00	8.10
Guanajuato	5.58	6.36	6.00
Nuevo León	5.52	6.46	6.60
Querétaro	5.52	6.58	6.36
Coahuila	5.50	7.02	6.78
Jalisco	**4.46**	**5.32**	**6.22**

Source: World Bank 2003; author's emphasis.

According to Jiménez Díaz, a researcher at the University of Guadalajara, case backlogs are also an issue, having reached levels of 60 percent during the period from August 1, 2001, to July 31, 2003 (Jiménez Díaz 2003b: 2). Jiménez Díaz concludes, "The judicial backlog is the most serious and alarming problem confronting society in Jalisco" since only the elite are able to pay when they appeal to the courts (p. 7). As suggested by Azaola and Bergman (this volume), this backlog directly affects the conditions in the state's prisons: the overwhelming majority of prisoners find themselves caught between the trial phase (during which guilt is established) and the sentencing phase of the criminal proceedings (DIGPRES 2003).

Table 20.9. Government Agencies Most Frequently Cited for Presumed Violations of Human Rights and Number of Citations, 2001–2003

Agency	2001	2002	2003
Office of the Attorney General of Jalisco	813	839	725
Guadalajara Public Security Department	343	370	351
Ministry of Public Security	208	265	263
Ministry of Education	141	167	204
Mexican Social Security Institute (IMSS)	131	145	105
Zapopan Public Security Department	129	156	151
Judicial Branch, State of Jalisco	117	89	81
Tlaquepaque Public Security Department	115	137	85
Municipal Government of Guadalajara	108	136	85
Puerto Vallarta Public Security Department	98	70	48
Transit Department	80	88	75
Tonalá Public Security Department	68	78	61

Source: CEDHJ 2002–2004.

In part, this backlog is related to the dramatic rise in crime in Jalisco. However, there are also indications of serious irregularities within the judicial branch that ostensibly is responsible for administering justice in Jalisco. In November 2001, an independent investigation showed that the judges of Jalisco's State Supreme Court paid fives times less in taxes than they should have. In March 2002, in a totally discretionary fashion, the twenty-eight judges at the top of the court hierarchy divided up and pocketed almost 6 million pesos that resulted from an apparent "budgetary surplus." That amount could have fully equipped thirty-seven courtrooms or paid the salaries of twelve court employees for four years and four months.[4]

This unethical behavior by court officials is likely the result of the fact that individuals who hold high-level posts in Jalisco's judiciary did not obtain office through any form of public competition or by virtue of merit-based civil service examinations. To the contrary. And negotiations of a political and partisan nature do nothing to guarantee the selection of those who would be ideal leaders of the institutions responsible for justice oversight in the state. Thus it is necessary to question the quality of the judicial branch personnel who have responsibility for justice.

Human Rights Violations

The Jalisco State Commission on Human Rights (CEDHJ) was founded a decade ago as an autonomous organization to protect basic rights. Despite that, the rights and guarantees that are conferred by the Constitution and by international legal instruments recognized by Mexico continue to be routinely broken (table 20.9). The most frequent violations reported during 2003 were, in order of seriousness, arbitrary detention, improper rendering of public service, inflicting bodily harm, and noncompliance with law enforcement duties (table 20.10). Particularly frequent were violations of the right of personal liberty, which can involve depriving a person of his or her freedom without a due hearing before a court of law, failing to respect the procedures contained in the laws applying to such a case, arbitrary detention, or exile.

---

[4] At the end of January 2003, those same top-level officials passed a salary increase of 60 percent for themselves while approving an increase of only 4 percent for the rest of the court personnel, replicating in the judicial branch the same abysmal income discrepancies that are visible throughout Mexican society.

Table 20.10. Most Frequent Presumed Human Rights Violations Committed by Government Agencies, 2003

Type of Violation	Number
Arbitrary detention	951
Improper rendering of public service	819
Inflicting bodily harm	608
Noncompliance with law enforcement duties	255
Illegal searches and home intrusions	218
Improper exercise of public duty	216
Threats	201
Violation of the rights of children	166
Torture	162
Robbery	152
Violation of the rights of prisoners or inmates	120
Obstructing justice	119

Source: CEDHJ 2003, especially chap. 3.

It is appropriate here to note the practice of arbitrary detention, which is an act by an official or public servant that results in depriving a person of liberty without a warrant from a judge having jurisdiction in the matter or, for urgent or flagrante delicto cases, a detention order from the public prosecutor. Arbitrary detention also includes failure to meet the obligation to stop or denounce an official or public servant who is illegally depriving someone of their liberty (CNDH 1998). Arbitrary detentions totally contradict the principle of innocence because the detention occurs in order to confirm a suspicion rather than to determine the likely party responsible for a crime. Illegal detentions, which are practiced systematically in Jalisco (United Nations 2002), turn this individual guarantee on its head. The primary transgressors of human rights are the Office of the Attorney General of Jalisco and Guadalajara's Public Security Department (Dirección General de Seguridad Pública). Once again, in terms of absolute numbers, both institutions were at the top of the list of agencies against which victims had filed complaints for presumed human rights violations (CEDHJ 2001, 2002, 2003).

In recent years, the number of citizen complaints filed with the CEDHJ for presumed violations of basic rights had been trending upward. However, that came to an end in 2003, when there was a noticeable decline in the absolute number of complaints. In the opinion of the CEDHJ, whatever cause(s) may explain the increase in the numbers of complaints, this can be interpreted as reflecting *a level of discord between civil society and the government*, since, as part of its routine work, the CEDHJ takes the pulse of the health of public administration in Jalisco.

Inadequate Leadership

Many of the above problems relate to the leadership crisis in the institutions charged with public security and law enforcement in Jalisco, primarily due to a lack of professionalism and consistency among officials appointed by PAN administrations. The officials appointed at the top of the public security hierarchy typically do not have the characteristics needed to fulfill these important responsibilities. On top of that, there has been high turnover in public prosecutors in Jalisco—including five during the Cárdenas Jiménez administration. Likewise, in the area of public security, there has been a veritable parade of four undersecretaries in the department of Public Security, Prevention, and Social Rehabilitation during the time it was under the State Secretariat General (Secretaría General de Gobierno), and three while it was under the State Security Secretariat (Secretaría de Seguridad). For example, of the ten directors general that have served since the creation of the department in 1999, including the coordinator of advisers, only four had the requisites needed for effective administration (Moloeznik 2002a). Similar patterns are repeated in the headquarters of the various public security and law enforcement agencies throughout metropolitan Guadalajara. As a result, civil society is notoriously distrustful of public authorities, whose image is heavily tarnished (table 20.11).

Table 20.11. Responses to Survey Question: "How much confidence do you have in each of these institutions?"

Institution	Great or Some	Little or None
Armed forces	66.4%	33.5%
Judicial system	45.4%	54.7%
Mexican political system	40.4%	59.5%
Police	36.8%	63.2%
Unions	30.9%	69.1%
Congressional representatives	24.6%	75.3%

Source: CEED 2002.

In short, the frequent turnover and often inadequate credentials of public officials in PAN administrations in Jalisco do not appear to reflect a genuine commitment to resolving the state's serious rule-of-law challenges. Moreover, this leadership crisis erodes support for—and generates animosities toward—PAN administrations among police and prosecutorial officers, marshals, and the investigative police. A lack of motivation, excessive cynicism, and a "laissez faire, laissez passé" attitude have dangerously taken over the personnel charged with the prevention, deterrence, and prosecution of crime in Jalisco (Moloeznik 2002b).

TRENDS IN THE ADMINISTRATION OF JUSTICE IN JALISCO

The magnitude of crime, citizens' perceptions of social vulnerability, and the critical issues analyzed, including government incompetence, highlight the fact that, during both PAN administrations, the state of public security, criminal justice, and human rights in Jalisco has not changed compared to the situation under prior PRI administrations. This overview of the status of security policy and human rights in Jalisco can and should be amplified with an analysis of the trends that are shaping the design and implementation of public policy in these areas, examined below.

Significant Interference from the Center

The tension between Mexico's constitutionally designed, decentralized federal system and the actual tendency toward excessive centralism is very apparent in the overlapping jurisdictions that exist in the public security arena and that correspond to a decentralized model of policing, in which federal, state, and municipal law enforcement agencies must coexist. Jalisco has not escaped this ongoing tension. The creation in 1995 of the National Public Security System (SNSP) was intended to help coordinate law enforcement agencies at all levels. However, this system also significantly centralizes the distribution of resources and the locus of decisions made in public security policy.

The imposition of greater federal intervention is also visible in new standards for the hiring of personnel for the judicial system and law enforcement agencies. That obliges states and municipalities to adapt to indicators constructed in the country's center of power. This trend is expected to continue in the future, particularly in light of the consolidation of the SNSP and its instruments. Despite this trend toward centralism, since the creation of the SNSP Jalisco has been among the most favored states in terms of the federal allocations it receives (table 20.12).

Militarization of Public Security

Jalisco experienced a significant degree of the militarization that is occurring nationwide (consistent with the findings of Arzt, this volume). This trend has been justified as part of the open-ended mission of domestic security that is attributed to the Mexican military apparatus. Indeed, under the PAN government, military personnel made up part of the *volantes*, or mobile contingents, that were formed in metropolitan Guadalajara at the beginning of the administration. It was only through the timely intervention of the president of the CEDHJ that these units were disbanded. Even so, members of the PAN party in Jalisco have even encouraged personnel from the Defense Department to undertake missions and assume roles that correspond to public security or are of a police nature.

Notably, in Jalisco's municipalities, increasing numbers of military personnel are assuming positions of leadership in the public security arena, and more mayors (*presidentes municipales*) rely on the armed forces to preserve law and order and social peace in their jurisdictions. On the other hand, it is worth noting that in 1997 the level of public insecurity in Jalisco led to the creation of the 41st Military Zone, headquartered in Puerto Vallarta. Its objective was to "implement maximum security measures to avoid illegal activities ... given that its sole goal is securing the safety of the public against arms trafficking, disturbances, and drug-related crimes" (Moloeznik and Andrade 2002: 43).

Privatization of Public Security

The increase in the number of private security companies during both PAN administrations has been widely discussed. For the local economy, this trend toward the "privatization of public security" is a double-edged sword. On the one hand, it presents a highly lucrative business opportunity for local security firms and has actually seemed to reduce insecurity in some respects. More specifically, the contracting out of private security services has apparently diminished local rates of freight theft. On the other hand, it also increases what foreign investors refer to as the "country cost," that is, the cost that private parties and businesses themselves must assume when the central state fails in its basic duty of guaranteeing public security (Moloeznik 2002b).

Table 20.12. Distribution of the Contribution Fund for Public Security in the States and Federal District,[a] by Recipient (based on the application of the distribution formula by state, in Mexican pesos)

State	2000		2003	
	Total	*Percentage*	*Total*	*Percentage*
México State	398,841,524	7.71	202,376,212	8.10
Federal District	371,565,433	7.19	154,274,578	6.17
Veracruz	247,840,849	4.79	124,479,842	4.98
Jalisco	**230,008,577**	**4.45**	**116,716,269**	**4.67**
Chiapas	220,846,429	4.27	109,512,890	4.38
Baja California	227,036,131	4.39	105,511,521	4.22
Sonora	223,495,279	4.32	104,527,429	4.18
Nuevo León	215,537,878	4.17	98,569,979	3.94
Tamaulipas	210,328,039	4.07	96,500,362	3.86
Michoacán	191,173,239	3.70	94,182,122	3.77
Total	5,170,000,000	100.00	2,500,000,000	100.00

Sources: Diario Oficial 2000, 2003; author's emphasis.

Note: One year earlier, under the Coordination Agreement for the Implementation of Public Security Actions in 2002, signed by the Ministry of Public Security and the State of Jalisco, the state received 144,882.759 pesos in funding from the Contribution Fund for Public Security. See *Diario Oficial* 2002.

[a] Fondo de Aportaciones para la Seguridad Pública de los Estados y del Distrito Federal.

Moreover, this trend toward privatization had an impact on Jalisco's urban and land-use development; in recent years, metropolitan Guadalajara's wealthiest residents have sought safe haven in private gated communities where they pay for their own guards and security systems. This trend toward "fortress communities" in urban spaces has been likewise criticized in other major modern metropolises, since it shifts the focus away from the government's obligation to ensure the security of its citizens and ultimately leaves the poor and underprivileged to fend for themselves (Davis 1998).

Increase in Organized Crime

In recent years, the growth in crime involving syndicates and mafias has reached critical levels: freight theft, car theft, drug trafficking, and black marketeering of firearms are only a few of the examples in Jalisco. Again, given that crime *does* pay due to the very low probability that a crime will be investigated and solved (or that the criminal will be punished), it is not surprising that Jalisco—in particular, metropolitan Guadalajara—has become a marketplace for organized crime. The state's geographic location in west-central Mexico allows it to function as a doorway to both the United States and the Pacific Rim, making it an ideal location for international crime syndicates. Indeed, Guadalajara has accordingly been a central base of operations for Mexico's most powerful narcotics operation, the Juárez cartel, for many years. In addition, the incompetence of the local officials in preventing and combating organized crime favors the establishment of mini-mafias and minor criminal gangs that mimic the modus operandi of more powerful organizations.

Internationalization of Police Work

As a counterpoint to the growth of organized crime, there has been an intensification of worldwide cooperation to combat the scourge of transnational organized crime, especially trafficking in arms, drugs, human beings, and vehicles. In the past few years, personnel from the U.S. Federal Bureau of Investigation (FBI) and the Drug Enforcement Administration (DEA) have made their presence felt, with representatives from both agencies being posted in the U.S. Consulate in Guadalajara. In addition to their investigative work, these agents teach specialized courses, primarily to the investigative police within the offices of the states' attorneys general in western Mexico. To the degree that the presence or involvement of other mafias becomes apparent, we can anticipate that we will see the participation of other police forces, such as the Colombian National Police, the Spanish National Police, and the French National Police, which already have permanent representatives in Mexico City.

Tension between Results and Respect for Human Rights

While political alternation and democracy would seem to contribute to reduced human rights violations, this is not necessarily the case in Jalisco, as has been shown in the previous section. One fundamental problem is the tension between the respect for basic human rights and the PAN administrations' focus on "results" in the provision of public security. Moreover, where results have been less than stellar, Jalisco's successive PAN administrations have tried to place the blame for indications of the underperformance of law enforcement and public security agencies on poor reporting or exaggerations by the CEDHJ. This type of denial tends to deliberately misinform civil society about the true extent of government incompetence or ineffectiveness both in preventing and prosecuting crimes and in protecting basic human rights.

Also troubling is the tendency toward new legislation to support more draconian measures in response to the state's public insecurity challenges. On June 4, 2003, the incumbent PAN gubernatorial administration and the outgoing 56th state legislature passed a major justice reform package consistent with the administration's long-stated goal of promoting the democratic rule of law in Jalisco (Gobierno del Estado de Jalisco 2001). Unfortunately, this reform represented a step backward, in the sense that it significantly hardened the criminal justice system in a manner that is of doubtful constitutionality.[5] Indeed, the resulting impact on the state's criminal code and procedures will most certainly negatively affect human rights in Jalisco in the coming years.

Emphasis on Quantitative over Qualitative Factors

Currently, local governments emphasize the quantitative aspects of police force structure, to the detriment of those elements that are more intangible or difficult to measure, such as effective leadership; correct police doctrine;

---

[5] This utilitarian criterion responds to the well-known authoritarian discourse of "emergency," which is based on the rights of the state and is inspired by current tendencies that call for "law and order."

professional recruitment processes; selection, training, and promotion qualifications; information systems; and codes of conduct. Quantification is given priority, whereas qualitative, nonmaterial elements in particular are ignored.

RECOMMENDATIONS FOR THE DESIGN AND IMPLEMENTATION OF SECURITY POLICY

In order to contribute to changing civil society's perception about public security and the principal actors involved in it, and to get the results that the public is demanding, there are a number of issues that must be examined and addressed in the local arena. In light of the trends in public security indicated above, there are ten key areas where intervention is needed.

- *Clearly define "domestic security."* As promulgated in Article 89, Sec. 6, of the Mexican Constitution, the notion of "domestic security" is not defined. This leads to confusion since the term appears in the Criminal Code of Jalisco (Código Penal para el Estado Libre 2004: 48–50), which specifies under that label crimes such as conspiracy (Art. 104), rebellion (Arts. 105–109), sedition (Art. 110), and mutiny (Art. 111). This coincides with what the federal-level criminal code contemplates under the rubric of "crimes against the nation" (Código Penal para toda la República 2003: 43–52) and what the Code of Military Justice labels as "rebellion" and "sedition" (Código de Justicia Militar 1991, vol. 1: 72–82). Thus, to overcome the present ambiguity that dominates the situation and is facilitating the potential for human rights violations, we need to develop a distinct definition of domestic security.

- *Revitalize the systemic conceptualization of public security.* Local PAN administrations have conceived of public security as a restricted issue, one that is exclusively the purview of the police. Given this reductionist interpretation of public security, we must revitalize the spirit of the National Public Security System. This could be done through a policy design that would recognize the complexity of the criminal phenomenon and antisocial behavior, and that would employ a systemic approach by incorporating all the subsystems involving crime prevention and dissuasion, prosecution, the courts, corrections, and services for crime victims.

- *Critically evaluate the judicial reform process in Jalisco and its effects on the position of the attorney general.* Given the uncertain prospects for a larger national justice reform, it is important to promote state-level initiatives that will contribute to the decentralization of the justice reform process. There are a number of key areas to target in Jalisco. The prosecutorial system, in both its law enforcement and judicial arms, has not experienced transformations leading to a fulfillment of justice, as demanded by the public. To ensure impartiality and speed in the judiciary would require a purge of those personnel who were supposed to be overseeing justice in the state. It would also require a reconsideration of the direction and goals of the judicial branch's General Counsel. With regard to the Office of the Attorney General for Jalisco, the struggle must be waged to separate it from the executive branch and make it an autonomous institution that truly guarantees the representation of societal interests.

- *Monitor and purge the public security agencies and auxiliary law enforcement organizations.* The greatest challenge for law enforcement reform is to guarantee that Jalisco's finest officers embrace their profession as their life project and see themselves as professionally and morally bound handmaidens of Justice. A necessary prerequisite is that police forces be purged of corrupt elements and that all incompetent or otherwise unqualified personnel are dismissed. To retain the most suitable and worthy people, the central state must guarantee appropriate levels of compensation that recognize both their professional value and the risks of the profession. In addition to increased salaries, possible incentives might include the development of a social security system that offers a range of benefits, from mortgage assistance programs to meaningful retirement packages.

- *Connect with institutions of higher education.* Until now, the PAN's self-described "governments of change" in Jalisco have been completely divorced from the universities, and in particular from the Universidad de Guadalajara, which has special research expertise in the field of criminal justice and public security. The government should take advantage of the critical mass of human resources that exists in the institutions of higher education, both to replenish personnel and to design and implement studies on the causes of crime, high-crime areas, and strategy and action plans. Because it is within universities that knowledge and analysis are generated and transmitted, those who deal with the crucial issues of security and criminal justice should drink from this fountain of higher learning.

- *Effectively supervise private security forces.* Greater oversight is needed to ensure that private security enterprises are regulated by an official framework and do not themselves engage in criminal behavior in conducting their functions, either deliberately or inadvertently. The emergence and development of private security companies, and private actors in general, is in response to the central state's failure to fulfill one of its basic functions. Thus the least we ought to be able to expect is that the government effectively regulate the private entities that provide security and guard services. The state government should therefore maintain a database of individuals employed in this field, possibly through the establishment of formal licensing and background checks for such individuals. This information should be made readily available to both companies and consumers to ensure transparent oversight of the industry.

- *Encourage the participation of civil society.* Social energies must be channeled and mechanisms for community participation must be encouraged, both in the prevention of crime and in its solution. It is very difficult to solve a crime without the cooperation of the public. In other words, law enforcement authorities should see the public as an ally and involve it in the fight against crime.

- *Establish intelligence systems to combat and defeat impunity.* Jalisco lacks a true system for gathering crime intelligence that would enable rational decision making. Moreover, misunderstandings and an absence of collaborative frameworks have traditionally marred the relationships among the subsystems in the security apparatus. Consequently, in order to have the public prosecutors' offices and state and municipal public security headquarters interact synergistically, we must establish a strategic alliance between each of the substantive functions in the security apparatus while simultaneously designing and integrating a system of police intelligence.

- *Construct evaluation tools and measurement indicators.* We must opt for the certification of each function in the public security system as well as the evaluation of the results of each strategy and line of action. However, this will require the construction of evaluation tools and measurement indicators. Moreover, public security is not free. It takes funding, and so it must be subject to accountability and a process of ongoing evaluation.

- *Public security must be state policy.* Some things should not be politicized. In Jalisco, the institutions responsible for justice and public security oversight have served private interests and have been the booty of the political parties. The two PAN administrations are no exception. Thus the political forces in Jalisco must make an agreement or pact to keep the judiciary, public prosecutor, and law enforcement agencies on the sidelines during partisan disputes. Whatever else, this would require a conceptualization of public security as *state policy*, one that would be permanent in nature, with high professional standards, and removed from the vicissitudes of politics.

FINAL THOUGHTS

Jalisco's government apparatus is characterized by limited managerial and mediation competency and by overwhelming bureaucratic meddling, which does nothing to resolve the issues at hand. The state government cannot even guarantee public security. Impunity in Jalisco is pervasive, with 93 percent of reported crimes never reaching the courts. However, we must also opt for a preventive model, because currently the punitive paradigm is marked by failure, and it punishes the most vulnerable segments of society. That is, we must design and build mechanisms for the prevention of crime and antisocial behavior, including a genuine intelligence community whose goal is to confront organized crime and encourage citizen involvement relating to situational or occasional crimes.

This does not mean that we should ignore the state coercive apparatus—in particular, the part responsible for dissuasive functions—even though the most important actor in the criminal drama in Jalisco is the judge. The quality of the judiciary requires us to question those who hold in their hands the outcome of justice in Jalisco. A judicial reform that would attract the brightest jurists, those who desire a career in the judiciary, must replace agreements that do not respect the popular will.

In summary, regarding the state of Jalisco, the PAN administrations in power since 1995 have not brought about a transformation in regard to public security, criminal justice, and human rights. The outlook is therefore not as promising as many citizens might have hoped at the outset of Jalisco's transition. We must hope that the security-intelligence apparatus and the judicial system will benefit from more effective future leadership in order to fulfill the mandate of Jalisco's constitution: justice, respect for basic rights, and public security as a duty of the state.

References

Berumen y Asociados. 2001. "Encuesta de opinión para la integración del Plan Estatal de Desarrollo 2001–2007." Unpublished study commissioned by the government of the State of Jalisco.

CEDHJ (Comisión Estatal de Derechos Humanos de Jalisco). 2001–2004. *Informe Anual de Actividades*. Guadalajara.

CEED (Centro de Estudios Estratégicos para el Desarrollo). 1999. *Jalisco a futuro (construyendo el porvenir 1999–2025)*. Guadalajara: CEED, Universidad de Guadalajara.

———. 2002. *Percepciones de la población de la zona metropolitana de Guadalajara sobre la corrupción*. At http://www.claves.udg.mx/pdf1/EncuestaCEED.pdf. Accessed April 7, 2004.

CNDH (Comisión Nacional de Derechos Humanos/Federación Mexicana de Organismos Públicos de Protección y Defensa de los Derechos Humanos). 1998. *Manual para la calificación de hechos violatorios de derechos humanos*. Mexico City: CNDH.

Código de Justicia Militar. 1991. Mexico City: Secretaría de la Defensa Nacional.

Código Penal para el Estado Libre y Soberano de Jalisco. 2004. Mexico City: Anaya Editores.

Código Penal para toda la República en Materia de Fuero Federal. 2003. Mexico City: Miguel Ángel Porrúa.

Contraloría del Estado de Jalisco. 2003. *Tercer informe de avances del programa "Jalisco Unido contra la Corrupción."* Guadalajara. At http://www.jalisco.gob.mx (link to "Contraloría").

Davis, Mike. 1998. *City of Quartz: Excavating the Future in Los Angeles*. London: Pimlico.

Diario Oficial de la Federación. 2000. "Criterios de asignación para la distribución del Fondo de Aportaciones para la Seguridad Pública de los Estados y del Distrito Federal," January 17.

———. 2002. "Poder Ejecutivo, Secretaría de Seguridad Pública," July 24.

———. 2003. "Criterios de asignación para la distribución del Fondo de Aportaciones para la Seguridad Pública de los Estados y del Distrito Federal," January 31.

DIGPRES (Dirección General de Prevención y Readaptación Social). 2003. *Sistema penitenciario de Jalisco*. CD-ROM.

Dror, Yehezkel. 1996. *La capacidad de gobernar (Informe al Club de Roma)*. Mexico City: Fondo de Cultura Económica.

Gobierno del Estado de Jalisco, Poder Ejecutivo. 1994–2003. *Informe Anual de Gobierno*. Guadalajara: Secretaría General del Gobierno del Estado de Jalisco.

———. 2001. *Plan Estatal de Desarrollo, Jalisco 2001–2007*. Guadalajara: Secretaría General del Gobierno del Estado de Jalisco.

ICESI (Instituto Ciudadano de Estudios sobre la Inseguridad). 2003. *Segunda encuesta nacional sobre inseguridad pública en las entidades federativas*. Mexico City: ICESI.

INEGI (Instituto Nacional de Estadística, Geografía e Informática). 2001. *Anuario estadístico de los Estados Unidos Mexicanos*. Aguascalientes: INEGI.

ITESM (Instituto Tecnológico y de Estudios Superiores de Monterrey). 2002. *Encuesta de gobierno y desarrollo empresarial*. Guadalajara: Centro de Estudios Estratégicos, ITESM.

Jiménez Díaz, José Gustavo. 2003a. "El acceso a la justicia," *Gaceta Universitaria*. Nueva Época II, 2 (319): 7.

———. 2003b. "El rezago judicial," *El Nuevo Siglo de Guadalajara*, October 10.

Moloeznik, Marcos Pablo. 1999. "Estudio básico sobre seguridad pública." In *Jalisco a futuro (construyendo el porvenir 1999–2025)*. Guadalajara: Centro de Estudios Estratégicos para el Desarrollo, Universidad de Guadalajara.

———. 2002a. "Mitos y realidades de la participación ciudadana: breves reflexiones sobre seguridad pública y ciudadanía bajo la gestión del PAN en Jalisco." In *Jalisco a siete años de la alternancia (ensayos sobre administración, gobierno y política)*, ed. Andrés Valdez Zepeda and Berta Ermila Madrigal Torres. Guadalajara: Universidad de Guadalajara.

———. 2002b. "La seguridad pública en transición: Jalisco antes y después del proceso de alternancia política." In *Jalisco antes y después de 1995*, ed. Jorge Regalado Santillán and Juan Manuel Ramírez Sáinz. Guadalajara: Universidad de Guadalajara.

Moloeznik, Marcos Pablo, and Edmundo Andrade. 2002. *Seguridad pública y criminalidad "Bahía de Banderas a Futuro."* Guadalajara: Universidad de Guadalajara.

PGJE (Procuraduría General de Justicia del Estado de Jalisco). 2003. "Informe robo de vehículos de carga pesada." Guadalajara: PGJE. Mimeo.

Poder Ejecutivo de la Federación. 2003. "Programa Nacional de Seguridad Pública 2001–2006," *Diario Oficial de la Federación*, January 14.

Presidencia de la República. 2001. *Primer Informe de Gobierno, Área de Orden y Respeto*. Mexico City: Government of Mexico.

———. 2002. *Anexo Segundo Informe de Gobierno*. Mexico City: Government of Mexico.

Transparency International 2001. *Encuesta nacional de corrupción y buen gobierno.* At http://www.transparenciamexicana.org.mx/encuesta_nacional.html.

United Nations. 2002. *Los derechos civiles y políticos, en particular las cuestiones de la tortura y la detención.* (Informe del Grupo de Trabajo sobre la Detención Arbitraria acerca de su visita a México.) At http://www.unhchr.ch/Huridocda/Huridoca.nsf/TestFrame/e0d30fad39c92e5fc1256ccc0035bb0a? Opendocument. Accessed April 7, 2004.

World Bank (with the Agrupación Civil UNETE, Consejo Coordinador Empresarial, Universidad Nacional Autónoma de México, and Instituto Tecnológico Autónomo de México). 2003. "Estudio sobre el desempeño del Poder Judicial." Mexico City: Universidad Nacional Autónoma de México. Mimeo.

Zepeda Lecuona, Guillermo. 2002. "'Las cifras de la impunidad': la procuración de justicia penal en México," *Revista Renglones* 51 (May–August): 63–71.

———. 2004. *Crimen sin castigo.* Mexico City: Fondo de Cultura Económica.

CHAPTER 21

Reforming the Administration of Justice in Mexico: Strategies and Requisites

JOHN J. BAILEY AND WAYNE A. CORNELIUS

A central goal of our project has been to provide guidance for public policy reform. Specific policy recommendations are offered in several of the preceding chapters, especially Robert Varenik's on police reform and Héctor Fix-Fierro's on legal education, as well as the introduction by David Shirk and Alejandra Ríos Cázares. In this concluding chapter we sketch some broader strategies for justice system reform and discuss their political and institutional requisites. Policy prescription is an important enterprise and requires a specific perspective. Description tells us *what* or *how* something is, and analysis guides us in breaking phenomena into their relevant pieces and studying the relationships among the pieces. Explanation attempts to account for *why* something is, that is, to give adequate reasons for it. Policy prescription takes another, even more difficult step, by asking: What are appropriate goals and what, concretely, should be done to reach them?

Policies related to public security and reform of justice form part of the larger agenda of reform of the State. These "second-generation" reforms are especially challenging in the context of democratic consolidation and the transformation of the economy. As Shirk and Ríos rightly note, useful data on insecurity and administration of justice remain scarce. There is no generally accepted policy wisdom to follow; rather, there are multiple competing diagnoses and recipes for action. Some of the recipes are fads, and many are more symbolic than substantive. Public officials are coping with strident public outcries that the security situation is unacceptably bad and demands that something be done about it now. The prescriptive questions then become: In what ways does democratic consolidation affect reform of justice administration? What is the nature of the problem in terms of agencies and arenas? What are broad options for reform? And under what circumstances might reform initiatives prosper?

We continue the consideration of reform where Shirk and Ríos left off in their introduction. We divide the discussion into four sections: (1) general relationships between consolidation and reform of criminal justice, summarized in terms of what might be characterized as "optimistic" and "pessimistic" models; (2) policy arenas and institutions, and logics of reform; (3) a brief cross-national, comparative perspective; and (4) prospects for justice system reform in Mexico.

Most of the preceding chapters described the problems of agencies, processes, actors, and resources. Our conclusions emphasize two key deficits of a different type. We argue that the lack of a stable governing or policy coalition points to a "political deficit" whose correction is a prerequisite to successful reform. Moreover, the lack of a coherent reform strategy points to an "ideas deficit" that hampers effective action.

DEMOCRATIZATION AND REFORM OF JUSTICE: CONTRASTING MODELS

Although this book comprehensively addresses the administration of justice in Mexico, the bulk of the analysis concentrates on criminal justice. Further, within criminal justice, the main focus is on crimes against persons and property, as opposed to tax or regulatory evasion, fraud, or diverse forms of white-collar crime. This more limited focus is appropriate given the project's interest in the connections between administration of criminal justice and issues of democratic governability. We have seen that the upsurge in violent crime and perceptions of insecurity coincided with the transition to democracy in Mexico in the mid-1980s through the late 1990s. Data reported in the preceding chapters (by Parás, for example) show that the average Mexican attaches high priority to public security problems.[1] Thus, in terms of the regime's legitimacy stemming from government effectiveness (as opposed to legitimacy derived from democratic procedure), reform of criminal justice is an urgent necessity.

---

[1] A national public opinion survey conducted in December 2005 found that crime and kidnappings are the most important source of fear among Mexicans. Nearly 20 percent feared crime and kidnappings more than anything else, followed by death (7.9 percent), economic insecurity (7 percent), and health problems (3.5 percent). See Consulta Mitofsky 2006.

We need to be clear, however, that reform of the criminal justice system is but one of many elements that make up rule of law. To the Madisonian world of checks and balances and the Hobbesian world of order, we need to add the Hamiltonian world of commerce and contracts. We should be cautious about generalizing from one arena of justice to another. Very likely, the Hamiltonian world is the most advanced in terms of quality and efficiency and the Hobbesian is the least, but we should not expect much spillover between them. In sum, we do not use the term "rule of law" in this conclusion, and when we refer to reforming the administration of justice we have criminal justice in mind.

This noted, how might we characterize the overall relationships between democratic transition and consolidation and the reform of the administration of justice? Does democratization create dynamics that enhance or that undermine justice reform? Or does it have little or no effect? Is the relationship linear, that is, does each incremental advance in democratic consolidation imply an equivalent improvement in administration of justice? Or is the relationship nonlinear? For example, the early stages of consolidation might produce a deterioration of administration of justice, but later stages might yield significant improvements.[2]

We can clarify these relationships with two highly stylized models that offer basic contrasts. An "optimistic" model suggests that democratic consolidation produces positive reforms in the administration of justice. This is because democracy implies periodic elections that are reasonably free and fair, competition among elites to win office, more or less free flows of information, and effective interest group pressures. These developments create conditions in which electorates and interest groups reward those elites that can deliver better-quality administration of justice. Thus democratic transition will create pressures for reforms in the sequence of arenas and institutions related to justice administration. In its simplest form, the optimistic logic posits: Citizenry demands public security → Conversion of demands into votes → Elite competition for votes → Effective interest group activity → Governing coalition formulates and implements justice reform initiative → Electorate and interest groups reward governing coalition → Repeated iterations of positive policy reform cycle → Deepening of democratic consolidation.

---

[2] Thomas Carothers argues for a "loose fit" between democracy and rule of law. "It would be much more accurate to say that the rule of law and democracy are closely intertwined but that major shortcomings in the rule of law often exist within reasonably democratic political systems" (Carothers 2006: 19).

The simple version of the optimistic cycle assumes a law-abiding, engaged civic culture, elite commitment and capacity in problem solving, and competent, responsive public agencies and associated professions. It also assumes that the volumes of crime confronting the society and state apparatus are manageable, that the problem indeed has a solution. Pushed a bit further, the optimistic logic suggests that initial successes in justice reform will lead to a positive trajectory in path dependence.

In its bare bones, a pessimistic model suggests very different sequences: Citizenry demands public security → Conversion of demands into votes → Elite competition for votes → Ineffective, sporadic interest group activity → Inability to construct a stable governing coalition (or even policy coalition) → Inability to formulate or implement a justice reform initiative → Voter and interest group alienation and apathy → Repeated iterations of the negative policy reform cycle → Stagnation of democratic consolidation.

The pessimistic model suggests that democratic consolidation proceeds at uneven rhythms, that advances in some arenas (such as electoral competition, free and fair elections, transparency, free flows of information) proceed much more rapidly than in other arenas (for example, problem-oriented politicians, effective governing coalitions, competent, professional public services, democratic civic culture). Further, the pessimistic approach recognizes the embeddedness of criminality in structural features of the economy (including extensive unemployment, large informal sector, extreme income inequality) and the society (large numbers of young, under-employed males; and the enormity and complexity of the Mexico City metropolitan area, for example). The embedded character plus the sheer volume of criminality exceeds the capacity of the state to respond. Finally, failures of policy reform in the early stages of consolidation increase the likelihood of further failures, undermine support for democratic governance, and thus point toward a path dependence of frustration and stagnation of consolidation.[3]

These are highly stylized simplifications of polar extremes, but they point to potential weak links in the democratic policy logic, the scope and embeddedness of the problems of criminality, and the path dependence of success or failure. For our purposes, the key weak link is the inability to construct a stable governing coalition (or even a policy coalition) and, con-

---

[3] Pablo Parás's chapter analyzes the negative effects of perceptions of criminality on support for democracy. Davis (2006) provides an interesting "pessimistic" analysis with respect to democratization and police reform in Mexico City.

sequently, the failure to formulate an effective justice reform initiative during the Vicente Fox administration (2000–2006). The failure to form a stable governing coalition after the democratic breakthrough of Fox's election owes much to features of Mexico's particular democratic regime. Obstacles to implementation are found in the character of the public bureaucracies and services that make up the core of the state.

REGIME AND STATE AS OBSTACLES TO REFORM

The concept of "regime" refers to rules governing access to political power, the processes of policymaking, and relationships of participation and accountability between government and the citizenry. "State" refers to nationalism and territoriality, collections of public agencies and services, the constitutional-legal framework, and systems of justice administration. The transition from an authoritarian to a democratic regime implies new relationships between civil society, policymakers, and state agencies, as emphasized in the introduction to this volume. But state agencies and the justice system, conditioned by decades of operation under authoritarianism, can effectively resist the optimistic democratic logic.[4]

Hence a stable governing coalition is needed in order to formulate and implement justice reform. Optimally this would take the form of a governing coalition (an ongoing alliance among parties in the congress that can negotiate a range of policies with the presidency), but at minimum an issue coalition for justice reform is required to provide continuous backing over the period of time needed to formulate and implement significant programs. Precisely how much time is required is unclear. We know from cross-national experience that significant, integral reform of justice administration requires decades. In optimal terms, reforms implemented in one *sexenio* should be ratified and extended into the succeeding presidential term in order to lay the foundation for a positive reform dynamic.[5] The institutional arrangements of Mexico's democratic regime, however, im-

---

[4] The point is fundamental. See Garretón et al. 2003: 1–6 for a useful discussion of the differentiation among regime, state, society, and economic development models in Latin America.

[5] A good example is Mexico's welfare assistance policy, which traces its origins to the Luis Echeverría presidency (1970–1976) and has been ratified and improved in succeeding administrations. See Ward 1986; Skoufias and Parker 2001; de Janvry, Finan, and Sadoulet n.d.

pede this sort of coalition formation and policy continuity. Without going into detail, we can summarize some of the more important obstacles.

In formal-legal terms, the Mexican presidency is weak compared with other Latin American cases (Shugart and Mainwaring 1997: 48–52). The Mexican case is one of several in the region that combine presidentialism with a multi-party system. Mexico's mixed system of single-member districts and proportional representation has produced a three-party system at the national level, made up of fairly coherent, disciplined parties. The three-party system reduces the president's chances of coming to power with majority control in either house of Congress. The single most important feature of the party-electoral system is the no-reelection rule. Elected officials may serve a single term in a particular office, although they may be elected successively to different offices. For example, a deputy in the national Chamber of Deputies may not be reelected (immediately) to that body, but she might seek immediate election to a different national office, such as the Senate, or to a state or local office.

As one might expect, the incentive for career politicians is to curry favor with actors that control access to nominations to office. Two such sets of actors are the thirty-two state governors (including the mayor of the Federal District) and the state and national party leadership. Governors, by and large, focus on particular state-level issues or on their own agendas of advancing to national-level office. Party leaders, particularly at the national level, exercise significant influence over their legislative delegations and tend to place tactical-strategic calculations of winning elections ahead of legislative tasks of coalition building and problem solving. Over the course of the six-year presidential term, the dense calendar of dozens of state-level and thousands of local-level elections effectively precludes the formation of a governing coalition and allows precious few spaces to permit formation of a policy coalition to support justice reform. Despite the general public's preoccupation with insecurity, piecemeal and symbolic responses to such perceptions are sufficient for the parties to compete in electoral contests. Such responses can be merged with varieties of other issues and appeals. In sum, the institutional arrangements conspire against a governing coalition and complicate the negotiation of policy coalitions.

But let us assume a counterfactual: that a policy coalition in support of justice reform could be created and maintained over a significant period. The two additional requirements are (1) a coherent strategy of reform, and (2) the resources, organizational capacity, and skills to implement the strategy. Assuming that the strategy focuses on the public sector, it needs to confront an interconnected chain of policy arenas, agencies, and associated professions and public employee unions. The arenas include crime prevention, crime repression and investigation, criminal prosecution, justice administration, administration of sanctions (such as imprisonment, parole, probation), and rehabilitation. A major component, justice administration itself, is situated in a constitutionally separate branch, the judiciary. Each of these arenas involves clusters of bureaucracies and interconnections with civil society from the neighborhood to transnational levels. A crime prevention policy, for example, might include agencies and programs ranging from urban planning to public education, parks and recreation, youth employment, community policing, and foreign relations (such as agreements with the United States about mechanisms for the deportation and repatriation of Mexican criminal offenders).

One way to think about reform strategy is as a choice between "big push" versus "targeted leverage." "Big push" means a simultaneous, coordinated intervention into all of the relevant policy arenas and institutions. The "targeted leverage" approach means focusing on one or two arenas with the goal of multiplying positive effects on other arenas. The "big push" approach has strong appeal because change in any one arena can have multiplier effects in the others. For example, hiring more police—a very popular policy response—means more arrests, which quickly increases pressure on the courts, prison system, and rehabilitation programs to perform more efficiently and effectively. But the big-push approach hugely increases the resource requirements and implies, in practical terms, that justice reform would crowd out other essential priorities, such as education, health care, and poverty alleviation. While the Fox administration's reform proposals sought comprehensive changes within the criminal justice system, it arguably lacked the more holistic vision and concerted effort of a "big push."

Targeted leverage becomes the typical default strategy. But the policy blueprint for this option is uncertain.[6] That is, reformers do not know precisely where intervention might produce multiple positive spillovers. Too often, targeted leverage becomes "target of opportunity": reformers steer resources to the arena that appears most responsive. Or the option may become "target of expediency": politicians steer the resources in ways that

---

6 Carothers (2006) provides a useful discussion of the recent history of efforts to reform justice systems. He emphasizes the knowledge gaps that reformers typically bring to their task.

reduce public pressure or bring political gains. For example, the public demands more police on the streets, and politicians comply.

Having assumed a stable policy coalition, let us further assume that a coherent strategy presents itself. The focus then turns to the availability of resources and the quality of the public agencies and services at hand to implement the strategy. As the preceding chapters suggest, Mexico's federal government has thrown a good many pesos at the insecurity problem. The stronger constraints involve the poor quality of agencies and personnel, complicated by the effects of corruption. Thus, given the combination of regime features that prevent a stable policy coalition, the difficulties of formulating a coherent strategy, and the multiple weaknesses of agencies and personnel, policy failure in criminal justice reform at Mexico's central government level would seem to be "overdetermined."

However, Mexico's 2006 federal elections and key state races brought some movement toward a consensus on directions for justice system reform. To be sure, there was a notable difference between the positions of the National Action Party (PAN) and Institutional Revolutionary Party (PRI)—which emphasized a "get tough" approach to public security—and that of candidate Andrés Manuel López Obrador of the Party of the Democratic Revolution (PRD), who argued that crime must be addressed by targeting poverty.[7] Nevertheless, it was notable that all three major presidential candidates endorsed key tenets of the Fox justice system reform package (see the appendix to this volume). For example, all three agreed on the need for oral argument to bring greater transparency and efficiency to criminal proceedings. They also agreed that the public prosecutor's office, or *ministerio público*—responsible for investigating, prosecuting, and trying cases—should have greater autonomy, to ensure more vigorous prosecution of corrupt public officials and prevent undue influence from politicians. All three major candidates concurred on the need for changing the criminal code to standardize crime categories and sentencing guidelines nationwide, to ensure a more uniform application of the law. Finally, the candidates agreed that greater efforts are needed to dismantle bureaucratic barriers to interagency cooperation across the federal, state, and municipal levels. What remains to be seen is whether consensus in campaign rhetoric will translate into a stable policy coalition across the three

---

[7] All three presidential candidates were roundly criticized by Mexican academics for a lack of in-depth understanding of the insecurity problem and a lack of originality in their policy prescriptions. See, for example, Peñalosa 2006; Rubio 2006.

major parties, particularly in the wake of the highly contentious 2006 electoral process.

JUSTICE REFORM IN COMPARATIVE PERSPECTIVE

What does the experience of other Latin American countries teach us about success in carrying out significant reform of the criminal justice system? Given space constraints, we limit our discussion to three cases: one arguable success and two apparent failures. Unsurprisingly, the keys to success involve a stable governing coalition and effective institutions operating in a context of low levels of violent crime.

Chile teaches us something about success in justice reform. This relatively small, centralized system put priority on judicial reform following the democratic transition of 1989, which suggests a "targeted leverage" approach in our terms. Within the judicial arena, however, the reform was a balanced, incremental advance on several fronts (Prillaman 2000). Further, Chile produced a stable governing coalition that also received support from the opposition with respect to policy. "(T)he legal reform movement arose as a response to the need to establish controls over the use of power and to prevent corruption as the country moved away from authoritarian rule" (Bhansali and Biebesheimer 2006: 304). The left-of-center governing coalition put priority on dismantling the institutional legacies of authoritarianism, but the powerful right-of-center forces also favored justice system reforms. *Fortuna* intervened as well: a scandal involving the Supreme Court and a highly publicized kidnapping mobilized strong public support for justice reform.

Another lesson from Chile is that police involvement and cooperation is central to police reform. Chile is unique in the Latin American region as a country where the national police have substantial public approval. This, along with the institutional coherence and professionalism of the *carabineros*, a historical off-shoot of the army, has meant that the police have played the lead role in organizing the public debate about police reform (Candina 2005). Finally, as noted in the introduction to this volume, Chile suffers much less corruption than other systems in the region and confronts much lower levels of violent crime.

Mexico's recent experience with justice reform more nearly resembles the failed cases of Brazil and Argentina. All three are large-scale, federal systems, and all three have experienced the deleterious effects of authoritarian rule (although of markedly different kinds) on police and justice systems. Much of criminal justice administration in these countries is carried out at the state level, with the federal level focused on selected crimes (smuggling, for example) and on coordination among the states.

Again, the key is a stable governing coalition. Mercedes Hinton paints a gloomy picture of regime failure with respect to police reform in the cases of the cities of Buenos Aires, Argentina, and Rio de Janeiro, Brazil. The failures there echo the Mexican experience:

> Shaped by cultural toleration for corruption in public office, low accountability, impunity, and destructive corruption, the political game in Argentina and Brazil is consumed by an overriding interest in self-preservation and predicated on an insular form of governance that primarily benefits particularistic interests. In countries where mechanisms of vertical and horizontal accountability function only haltingly, there is an enormous window of opportunity for all players to exploit an already weakened concept of public good.... Faithful to the praxis of expediency, Argentine and Brazilian governments set up alternative mechanisms or created new institutions rather than fix existing ones. With each pledge to increase resources to the police, to purchase more vehicles and equipment, to put more officers on the street, or to purge police ranks, they provided an illusion of reform that helped to temporarily assuage a frightened population (Hinton 2006: 192, 194).

In Hinton's view, vacillation and expediency in police reform continued into the governments of Néstor Kirchner in Argentina and Luis Inácio "Lula" de Silva in Brazil.[8] The parallels to Mexico's experience from 2000 to 2006 are discomfortingly clear.

PROSPECTS FOR REFORM IN MEXICO: ACTORS AND VENUES

Successful national-level justice reforms in Latin America are, indeed, exceptional. The positive formula seems distant from the Mexican case. Reform works best in settings of stable governing coalitions, strong institutions, and low levels of violent crime. Mexico may be more "normal" in its *inability* to date to achieve significant national-level improvements in the administration of justice. If this is the case, we need to consider alternative

---

[8] Hinton's analysis coincides with that of González (2005).

routes to improvement. In this vein, we make two arguments: (1) prospects for reform are more likely at the subnational (state) level; and (2) justice reform is more likely a product of policy entrepreneurship by political and civil society leadership than a by-product of democratic consolidation per se.

The greater Mexico City metropolitan area, a mega-region of over twenty million inhabitants, is a unique challenge. Further, Allison Rowland's chapter finds multiple constraints on justice reform at the municipal level generally, including constitutional-legal restrictions and a lack of resources. The record at the state level reflects important challenges and limitations as well, which we saw in Marcos Pablo Moloeznik's discussion of Jalisco. Nevertheless, as Robert Varenik has observed, an important advantage of pursuing justice system reform at the state level is the presence of "fewer moving parts" than in the national case. Relatively strong governors have the same six-year term as the president but deal with a unicameral *congreso local*. By and large, the state governors also exercise considerable control over their own parties and thus confront simpler challenges in forming a governing coalition. Although bound by the no-reelection rule, governors typically think in terms of moving on to the national political stage, and thus institutional incentives provide motivation for policy success.

Unlike municipalities, state governments also have sufficient constitutional authority to deal with important aspects of criminal justice (*fuero común*). Further, fiscal decentralization is proceeding rapidly, and—while still underfinanced—the states receive substantially more resources each year. And because they operate outside of the media "fishbowl" which is Mexico City, one might argue that the states have more latitude to cooperate with external actors, such as foreign governments, foundations, and professional associations.

What are political arguments against innovation at the state level? States are often the unfortunate "meat" in a partisan "sandwich." Anti-reform partisanship can be applied from above and below. Presidents may provide less help (perhaps even create obstacles) to governors from opposition parties. Governors need to be able to work effectively with *presidentes municipales* of the principal cities in their states.

In terms of legal framework, we must recognize that the states lack jurisdiction over important types of organized crime, such as drug and weapons trafficking. These types of crime are principal engines of corruption and violence, carried on by gangs with organization, technology, and firepower superior in many cases to those of the state police. The lack of legal jurisdiction and the presence of powerful and violent criminal gangs often tempts governors to "pass the peso" to the national government. Corruption and violence become federal problems, and the hapless citizenry is left unprotected by either level.

On balance, however, the possibilities for significant reform seem better at the state than at the national level. Part of the argument is simple statistical probability. Thirty-one governors, along with the mayor of Mexico City, seek to ascend to the national level. If in a single case the various political planets and forces come into alignment and a governor "gets it right," the dynamics of success and diffusion can come into play.

There has, in fact, been an explosion of activity at the state and local levels in recent years to promote justice system reform. Many states have begun to adopt key elements of the Fox reform package (introduced to the federal Congress in April 2004), such as new transparency measures for the justice sector, oral trial proceedings, and alternative dispute resolution mechanisms. In 2000, Coahuila's state government introduced new alternative dispute resolution (ADR) mechanisms that have helped to reduce caseloads and delays in the regular court system. In 2005 the state of Nuevo León enacted legislation that helped bring unprecedented transparency to judicial proceedings. Similarly, in Oaxaca, state judges have begun to employ innovative legal practices, including oral trials, that will promote greater efficiency and accountability. In June 2006, the state of Chihuahua approved a package of comprehensive reforms that promise to fundamentally overhaul the state's judicial system by introducing oral arguments, ADR mechanisms, and other changes that expedite the prosecution process. As this volume went to press, similar reforms were under consideration in the state of Jalisco, which if enacted would go far to address the concerns discussed in Moloeznik's chapter in this volume. These innovations reflect the newfound subnational political pluralism and invigorated spirit of federalism that have accompanied Mexico's democratic transition. However, such initiatives are still largely untested and require further study to determine whether they might offer a blueprint for success at the national level.

If the state level is the most likely venue for justice reform in the short term, what processes are likely to foster it? If our analysis is accurate, the key requisites are political. Structures and institutions clearly matter, as do the dimensions and tenacity of the problems of violent crime; but the key is a stable coalition, which requires leadership. Further, the leadership needs to combine consensus building with policy entrepreneurship. This perspective takes us toward a state-centered, policy-elite approach, which is well summarized by Grindle and Thomas:

> In our view, specific policy choices are the result of activities that take place largely within the state and that are significantly shaped by policy elites who bring a variety of perceptions, commitments, and resources to bear on the content of reform initiatives, but who are also clearly influenced by the actual or perceived power of societal groups and interests that have a stake in reform outcomes. Our model of the policy process begins with two sets of factors. One set focuses on background characteristics of policy elites; the other emphasizes the constraints and opportunities created by the broader contexts within which they seek to accomplish their goals (Grindle and Thomas 1991: 33).

Grindle and Thomas go on to make a persuasive case for their argument with respect to economic, social, and administrative reforms in a number of developing countries. They do not, however, take on the hard case of justice reform in settings of democratic consolidation with high levels of violent crime and corruption. Even so, the near-legendary case of Bogotá, Colombia, under the leadership of Antanas Mockus supports their view. Colombia suffers from homicide rates among the highest in the Americas, and Bogotá's rate in the 1980s was high even by regional standards. Though the details take us beyond the scope of this chapter, Mockus's leadership was central to building a consensus, formulating a policy strategy, and then demonstrating the entrepreneurship needed to implement it.[9]

Our argument leads us to focus on quality of leadership more than on socioeconomic development or technical-legal factors. Other than the potential of large numbers, is there any reason to expect better leadership at the state than at the national level? Unfortunately, the political game at the state level in Mexico appears to date to echo Hinton's points about Argentina and Brazil as "consumed by an overriding interest in self-preservation and predicated on an insular form of governance that primarily benefits particularistic interests" (Hinton 2006: 192).

---

[9] For an overview of the thinking behind the policy reform, see Mockus and Corzo 2003; for a detailed record of the policy reform, see Martin and Ceballos 2004.

The case of Baja California is a cautionary tale. Baja California is among Mexico's more developed states in socioeconomic terms, and it experienced the nation's first officially recognized election of a governor from an opposition party (the National Action Party, in 1988). Since then the PAN has held the governorship continuously, with control of the state legislature during most of this period. The political leadership of the state, however, has not evolved toward consensus building and effective problem solving. Rather, in the view of an astute local observer, the leadership is

> a political elite in decline, not only in terms of its democratic content and its ability to represent citizen interests, but also in terms of technical capacity. Because of complicity, disinterest, or simple apathy, it is virtually impossible to initiate deep institutional reforms from within this elite that encompass all public entities (especially the police and security forces more generally). Rather, it is civil society that has conceived and proposed preventive solutions, ranging from the use of new technologies, to institutional reform of the security and justice apparatus, to social development initiatives. But these overtures rarely receive a response from municipal and state authorities. These conditions of institutional precariousness basically constitute an open invitation to complicity and corruption, in all of their guises. As long as the responsible parties—the entire political elite, not only the officials who are most immediately involved—lack an effective representational linkage to social interests and the capacity to respond to them, there can be no solution to insecurity (Tonatiuh Guillén, personal communication, May 22, 2006).

This observation suggests that the political deficit runs deeper than an inability to form policy coalitions; it points to a crucial prerequisite: the absence of problem-oriented politicians, even in one of Mexico's most developed and politically modern states.

We conclude that justice administration is likely to remain a "lagging" sector in the reform of the Mexican state. And criminal justice reform will probably trail behind improvements in other areas, such as constitutional or commercial law. If our analysis is correct, however, the dynamics of democratization will continue to create pressures and opportunities for improvement. Over time, some states will begin to show results in their efforts to improve justice administration, to make their police more professional and law-abiding, their courts more efficient and transparent, and the overall corrections system more humane and effective. These leading states can provide cues and resources for other states to deal more effectively with violent crime. But the same federalism that facilitates decentralized innovation also provides multiple openings for the more adept and dynamic criminal organizations, especially those engaged in transnational smuggling. Probably the best that the leading states can achieve is to cope better with the corrupting effects of such organizations, while the lagging states can expect an even greater presence of criminal violence.

References

Bhansali, Lisa, and Christina Biebesheimer. 2006. "Measuring the Impact of Criminal Justice Reform in Latin America." In *Promoting the Rule of Law Abroad: In Search of Knowledge*, ed. Thomas Carothers. Washington, D.C.: The Carnegie Endowment.

Candina, Azún. 2005. "Carabineros de Chile: una mirada histórica a la identidad institucional." In *Seguridad y reforma policial en las Américas: experiencias y desafíos*, ed. Lucía Dammert and John Bailey. Mexico: Siglo Veintiuno.

Carothers, Thomas. 2006. "The Problem of Knowledge." In *Promoting the Rule of Law Abroad: In Search of Knowledge*, ed. Thomas Carothers. Washington, D.C.: The Carnegie Endowment.

Consulta Mitofsky. 2006. "Los miedos y fobias del mexicano: encuesta en viviendas." México, D.F.: Consulta Mitofsky, www.consulta.com.mx.

Davis, Diane E. 2006. "Undermining the Rule of Law: Democratization and the Dark Side of Police Reform in Mexico," *Latin American Politics and Society*.

de Janvry, Alain, Frederico Finan, and Elizabeth Sadoulet. n.d.. "Can Conditional Cash Transfer Programs Serve as Safety Nets to Keep Children in School and Out of the Labor Market?" *Journal of Development Economics*, forthcoming.

Garretón, Manuel Antonio, et al. 2003. *Latin America in the 21st Century: Toward a New Sociopolitical Matrix*. Miami, Fl.: North-South Center Press.

González, Gustavo. 2005. "Intentos de reformas policiales en Argentina: los casos de las provincias de Santa Fé y Buenos Aires." In *Seguridad y reforma policial en las Américas: experiencias y desafíos*, ed. Lucía Dammert and John Bailey. Mexico: Siglo Veintiuno.

Grindle, Merilee S., and John W. Thomas. 1991. *Public Choices and Policy Change: The Political Economy of Reform in Developing Countries*. Baltimore, Md.: Johns Hopkins University Press.

Hinton, Mercedes S. 2006. *The State on the Streets: Police and Politics in Argentina and Brazil*. Boulder, Colo.: Lynne Rienner.

Martin, Gerard, and Miguel Ceballos, eds. 2004. *Bogotá: anatomía de una transformación: políticas de seguridad ciudadana, 1995–2003*. Bogotá, Colombia: Editorial Pontificia Universidad Javeriana.

Mockus, Antanas, and Jimmy Corzo. 2003. *Cumplir para convivir: factores de convivencia y su relación con normas y acuerdos*. Bogotá, Colombia: Universidad Nacional.

Peñalosa, Pedro José. 2006. "Candidatos, partidos, y seguridad pública," *Este País* 182 (May): 4–9.

Prillaman, William C. 2000. *The Judiciary and Democratic Decay in Latin America: Declining Confidence in the Rule of Law*. Westport, Conn.: Praeger.

Rubio, Luis. 2006. "La inseguridad," *El Seminario*, June 29.

Shugart, Matthew Soberg, and Scott Mainwaring. 1997. "Presidentialism and Democracy in Latin America: Rethinking the Terms of the Debate." In *Presidentialism and Democracy in Latin America*, ed. Scott Mainwaring and Matthew Soberg Shugart. Cambridge: Cambridge University Press.

Skoufias, Emmanuel, and Susan K. Parker. 2001. "Conditional Cash Transfers and Their Impact on Child Work and Schooling: Evidence from the PROGRESA Program in Mexico," *Economía: Journal of the Latin American and Caribbean Economic Association* 2, no. 1: 45–96.

Ward, Peter. 1986. *Welfare Politics in Mexico: Papering Over the Cracks*. London: Allen & Unwin.

Appendix: Candidates' Justice-Related Platforms

compiled by Robert Donnelly, with assistance from Verónica López Arellano

FELIPE CALDERÓN HINOJOSA

"I don't plan to offer the aggressor a seat at the negotiation table; I'm going to put him in jail" (*Mural* 2006).

On police operations, tactics, and techniques, supports:
- Metropolitan police force for Mexico City/México State exurban zones.
- Centralized federal police corps; Agencia Federal de Investigación, Policía Federal Preventiva under single command.
- Streamlined coordination among federal, state, municipal police corps.
- National Police Academy to standardize police techniques, methods.
- Centralized criminal database, Sistema Único de Información Criminal (SUIC) to warehouse information on firearms, automobile registrations; profiles of criminals, and so on.
- Creation of National Public Security/Safety and Criminal Justice Institute to produce data-driven analyses on crime in Mexico.
- Boosted police compensation through alternative means, performance bonuses, "standardized [and] dignified" salaries.
- Transformation of promotions structure to reward merit, public service.

On organized crime, supports:
- Specialized judges, prosecutors to handle federal organized crime cases from investigation, through prosecution, through sentencing.
- Constitutional reforms so local jurisdictions can pursue drug traffickers.

On victims' rights, supports:
- Restitution fund for crime victims, financed from seized drug-trade assets.
- Reorientation of criminal justice system to favor victims.

On international law, supports:
- Prioritizing international efforts against human smuggling, drug trafficking, the illicit arms trade, money laundering, terrorism.

- Facilitating overseas extradition of Mexican criminals and/or international fugitives.

On sentencing procedures and alternative dispute resolution mechanisms, favors:

- No-parole life sentence for certain heinous acts, including mutilation of kidnap victims.
- Critical review of existing laws that allow violent offenders to receive lenient "*pena privativa de libertad*" form of sentencing, as opposed to the harsher "*pena de reclusión.*"
- Alternative dispute resolution mechanisms for "swifter and more effective justice."
- Creation of a Federal Institute of Alternative Justice, to more economically and efficiently administer justice without compounding prison overpopulation.

On national security, endorses:

- Making National Security Council's governing body a coordinating agency for domestic intelligence gathering, to streamline national security policy and operations.

On reforms to justice system, proposes:

- That federal attorney general hold post for eight years, overlapping presidential administrations, thus increasing autonomy to encourage more vigorous prosecution.

On human rights, suggests:

- Reparations fund for damages caused from human rights violations by authorities when allegations have been vouched for by National Human Rights Commission.

On government transparency, proposes:

- Publicizing bureaucrat salaries to detect corruption (if individual living beyond means).

ANDRÉS MANUEL LÓPEZ OBRADOR

"Fighting crime is much more than a cops-and-robbers affair. The integral solution—the most efficient and probably the least expensive—includes fighting unemployment, poverty, domestic abuse, (immorality), and (hopelessness)" (López Obrador 2005).

On police procedures, tactics, and techniques, advocates:

- "Integral," multi-faceted crime-fighting, crime-prevention strategy.
- Amendments to existing laws that circumscribe activities of Federal Preventive Police (PFP), Attorney General's Office (PGR), and federal laws against organized crime.

On reforms to justice system, supports:

- Standardization of local statutes, laws to make more uniform sentencing guidelines and justice procedures, to eliminate inconsistencies in administration of justice.
- That National Criminal Sciences Institute has authority to train, evaluate prosecutors.
- Increased oversight of "all judicial authorities."
- Review of nation's Judiciary Council (Consejo de la Judicatura), which oversees federal-level appointments, because of track record of "inefficiencies" regarding corruption, "impartial evaluation and administration" of judicial appointments.
- Further reforms to existing criminal justice system, such as changes to laws circumscribing judicial branch, amendments to laws governing court-issued injunctions (*amparos*), and changes to Federal Code of Criminal Proceedings.

On organized crime and anti–drug trafficking operations, favors:

- Giving army freer hand to fight drug traffickers.

On victims' rights, endorses:

- Creation of a victims' restitution fund.

On discrimination, espouses:

- Commitment to address injustices, discrimination against indigenous communities.
- Eradication of discriminatory and racist practices.

- Erasure of educational, social, economic inequalities suffered by indigenous groups.

On civil liberties and human rights, says:
- "We will respect freedom of expression and religious creed. We are in favor of dialogue, tolerance, plurality, equality, diversity, transparency, and human rights" (López Obrador 2005).
- Wants alignment between Mexico's domestic human rights policy and contents of 2002 accord signed by federal officials, United Nations High Commissioner for Human Rights.

On the "'Dirty War," says:
- "Never more will the armed forces be used to repress the people of Mexico" (*Mural* 2006).
- Supports creation of "truth commission" to investigate causes, history of Mexico's "Dirty War" and establish appropriate punishment for guilty parties.

On government transparency, promises:
- To review federal law on transparency and access to public information, as well as to review corresponding state laws.

On judicial independence and separation of powers, says:
- "We will obey the resolutions of the judicial branch. And we will continue to respectfully insist on the need for it to be reformed from within, a true system of controls and safeguards that averts corruption and guarantees the proper action of judges, magistrates and ministers" (López Obrador 2005).

On official corruption, says:
- "We will fight corruption, impunity, and influence peddling to the core. To combat corruption is a moral imperative" (López Obrador 2005).

ROBERTO MADRAZO PINTADO

"Keep laughing; keep laughing [because] you have very little time left" (in a promise to crack down on white-collar criminals, in *Mural* 2006).

On police operations, tactics, and techniques, supports:
- Giving preventive police authority to investigate crime.

On organized crime, endorses:
- Using the army's *"facultades fuertes,"* or "strong faculties," to fight drug trafficking using modern technology (from transcript of second presidential debate).

On sentencing procedures, supports:
- Short on specifics but avows commitment to make sentencing more rigorous.

On trial procedures, endorses:
- Implementation of "accusatory, oral, and public" criminal process for certain cases, crimes, and situations.

On reforms to justice system, recommends:
- That judges—not Public Prosecutor's Office—determine when cases should go to trial. Also, that judges be devolved power to determine whether crime is "grave" or "minor."

On victims' rights, suggests:
- Making it easier for crime victims to denounce aggressors directly to judges in court, instead of through mediating public prosecutor's office, by amending criminal code.

SIMILARITIES AND DIFFERENCES BETWEEN PLATFORMS

While their platforms differ on several points, the presidential candidates shared similar stances on a few justice- and law-and-order-related issues.

SIMILARITIES:
Broad consensus on need for oral argument, "autonomous" public prosecutor's office, and reforms to criminal code.

- Oral argument: The three major candidates all voice support for the introduction of an oral argument phase to trial proceedings in Mexico. However, differences exist regarding the details of its implementation, specifically whether oral argument should be applicable in all court cases for all crimes.

- "Autonomous" Public Prosecutor's Office: Broad consensus exists among the candidates that the public prosecutor's office, or Ministerio Público, which is responsible for investigating, prosecuting, and trying cases, become more independent, presumably making it less vulnerable to undue influence from politicians and more vigorous in prosecution of corrupt public officials. However, candidates are not in complete agreement on how best to go about enhancing the "autonomy" of the public prosecutor's office.

- Penal code reforms: To a man, the candidates support an overhaul of the criminal code so that crime categories and sentencing guidelines may be standardized nationwide, ensuring a more uniform application of the law.

- Interagency cooperation: To fight organized crime, the candidates agree that greater strides in interagency cooperation must be achieved among the federal, state, and municipal police corps and efforts be made to dismantle the barriers that bureaucratically wall off the agencies.

DIFFERENCES:
Madrazo and Calderón stress a "get-tough" message, while López Obrador more prominently mentions discrimination, human rights, and the "Dirty War."

Note: *The vague, consensual language of campaign pledges may make it difficult to discern stark differences between candidates, especially considering that Calderón, López Obrador, and Madrazo seem to share many similar policy objectives. However, though they may not serve as meaty policy statements, such campaign pledges may in effect provide hints as to the inclination and orientation of prospective incoming administrations. The following bullet points attempt to demonstrate the ways in which each individual candidate, through his own campaign statements, contrasts with his competitors on key law and justice themes:*

- López Obrador: More prominently mentions poverty as root cause behind crime; eschews Madrazo's and Calderón's "get-tough" approaches; furthers an "integrated" strategy to fight crime; promises to battle discrimination, racism against indigenous people; supports truth commission, sanctions against those found guilty of repressing dissidents during "Dirty War."

- Madrazo: Fewer published policy goals on law and justice issues than either López Obrador or Calderón. Cultivates a "tough-on-crime" image. Promises to wield *"mano dura,"* or *"heavy hand,"* to fight crime.

- Calderón: Also pushes a "get-tough-on-crime" message. Proposes centralization of national police corps under single command; advocates standardization of police techniques and procedures. Suggests overhaul of criminal code. Pushes alternative sentencing mechanisms but lobbies for longer prison sentences for abductors.

References

López Obrador, Andrés Manuel. 2005. "50 compromisos para recuperar el orgullo nacional," July 17.

Mural. 2006. "Marcan candidatos sus cartas," June 5.

Acronyms

AFI	Agencia Federal de Investigaciones / Federal Investigative Police
APF	Administración Pública Federal / Federal Public Administration
BMA	Barra Mexicana, Colegio de Abogados / Mexican Bar Association
CDHDF	Comisión de Derechos Humanos del Distrito Federal / Human Rights Commission of the Federal District
CDI	Comisión para el Desarrollo Indígena / Commission for Indigenous Development
CEDHJ	Comisión Estatal de Derechos Humanos de Jalisco / Jalisco State Commission on Human Rights
CENDRO	Centro de Planeación para el Control de Drogas / National Drug Control Center
CENEVAL	Centro Nacional de Evaluación para la Educación Superior / National Center for the Evaluation of Higher Education
CFPP	Código Federal de Procedimientos Penales / Federal Criminal Procedures Code
CIDAC	Centro de Investigación para el Desarrollo, A.C. / Research Center for Development
CIDE	Centro de Investigación y Docencia Económicas / Center for Teaching and Research in Economics
CISEN	Centro de Información y Seguridad Nacional / National Information and Security Center
CJF	Consejo de la Judicatura Federal / Federal Council of the Judiciary
CNDH	Comisión Nacional de Derechos Humanos / National Human Rights Commission
CNI	Congreso Nacional Indígena / National Indigenous Congress
CNSP	Consejo Nacional de Seguridad Pública / National Public Security Council
COCOPA	Comisión de Concordia y Pacificación / Peace and Harmony Commission

CONADEPI	Comisión Nacional para el Desarrollo de los Pueblos Indígenas / National Commission for the Development of Indigenous Peoples
CPC	Consejo de Participación Ciudadana / Council of Citizen Participation
CPF	Código Penal Federal / Federal Criminal Code
DCS	Dirección General de Comunicación Social / Office of Public Relations
DEA	U.S. Drug Enforcement Administration
DIF	Sistema Nacional para el Desarrollo Integral de la Familia / National System for Family Development
ERUM	Escuadrón de Rescates y Urgencias Médicas / Emergency Rescue Squad
EZLN	Ejército Zapatista de Liberación Nacional / Zapatista Army of National Liberation
FAFM	Fondo de Aportaciones para el Fortalecimiento de los Municipios / Fund for Municipal Strengthening
FBI	U.S. Federal Bureau of Investigation
FEADS	Fiscalía Especializada para la Atención de los Delitos contra la Salud / Office of the Special Prosecutor for Crimes against Health
GAFES	Grupos Aeromóviles de Fuerzas Especiales / Mobil Air Special Forces Groups
ICBG	Índice de Corrupción y Buen Gobierno / Corruption and Good Governance Rates
ICESI	Instituto Ciudadano de Estudios sobre la Inseguridad, A. C. / Citizens' Institute for Security Studies
IEE	Instituto Estatal Electoral / State Electoral Institute
IFDP	Instituto Federal de Defensoría Pública / Federal Institute of the Public Defender
IFE	Instituto Federal Electoral / Federal Electoral Institute
IIJ-UNAM	Instituto de Investigaciones Jurídicas de la Universidad Nacional Autónoma de México / Institute for Juridical Studies, National Autonomous University of Mexico
IMSS	Instituto Mexicano del Seguro Social / Mexican Social Security Institute
INACIPE	Instituto Nacional de Ciencias Penales / National Penal Sciences Institute

INCD	Instituto Nacional de Combate a las Drogas / National Institute to Combat Drugs
INEGI	Instituto Nacional de Estadística, Geografía, e Informática / National Institute for Statistics, Geography, and Informatics
INI	Instituto Nacional Indigenista / National Indigenous Institute
LFCDO	Ley Federal Contra la Delincuencia Organizada / Federal Law against Organized Crime
LFTAIPG	Ley Federal de Transparencia y Acceso a la Información Pública Gubernamental / Law on Transparency and Access to Public Government Information
NAFTA	North American Free Trade Agreement
NGO	nongovernmental organization
NIJ	National Institute of Justice
PAN	Partido Acción Nacional / National Action Party
PEMEX	Petróleos Mexicanos / Mexican Petroleum Company
PFP	Policía Federal Preventiva / Federal Preventive Police
PGJDF	Procuraduría General de Justicia del Distrito Federal / Office of the Attorney General of the Federal District
PGJE	Procuraduría General de Justicia del Estado / State Attorney General's Office
PGR	Procuraduría General de la República / Office of the Attorney General
PJDF	Policía Judicial del Distrito Federal / Judicial Police of the Federal District
PJE	Policía Judicial de los Estados / State Judicial Police
PJF	Policía Judicial Federal / Federal Judicial Police
PNSP	Programa Nacional de Seguridad Pública / National Public Security Program
PRD	Partido de la Revolución Democrática / Party of the Democratic Revolution
PRI	Partido Revolucionario Institucional / Institutional Revolutionary Party
PVEM	Partido Verde Ecologista de México / Mexican Green Party
SCJN	Suprema Corte de Justicia de la Nación / Mexican Supreme Court
SECODAM	Secretaría de Contraloría y Desarrollo Administrativo / Ministry of Comptrollership and Administrative Development
SEDENA	Secretaría de la Defensa Nacional / National Defense Ministry

SEP	Secretaría de Educación Pública / Education Ministry
SE-SNSP	Secretariado Ejecutivo del Sistema Nacional de Seguridad Pública / Executive Secretariat of the National Public Security System
SFP	Secretaría de la Función Pública / Ministry of Public Service
SHCP	Secretaría de Hacienda y Crédito Público / Ministry of the Treasury
SIEDF	Subprocuraduría de Investigación Especializada en Delitos Federales / Office of the Deputy Attorney for Special Investigation of Federal Crimes
SIEDO	Subprocuraduría de Investigación Especializada en Delicuencia Organizada / Office of the Deputy Attorney for Special Investigation of Organized Crime
SM	Secretaría de Marina / Mexican Navy
SNSP	Sistema Nacional de Seguridad Pública / National Public Security System
SRE	Secretaría de Relaciones Exteriores / Ministry of Foreign Affairs
SSP	Secretaría de Seguridad Pública / Ministry of Public Security
SSP-DF	Secretaría de Seguridad Pública del Distrito Federal / Public Security Secretariat of the Federal District
TEPJF	Tribunal Electoral del Poder Judicial de la Federación / Electoral Tribunal of the Federal Judiciary
TFJFA	Tribunal Federal de Justicia Fiscal y Administrativa / Federal Tribunal for Fiscal and Administrative Justice
UECLD	Unidad Especializada Contra el Lavado de Dinero / Special Anti–Money Laundering Unit
UEDO	Unidad Especializada contra la Delicuencia Organizada / Special Anti–Organized Crime Unit
UNAM	Universidad Nacional Autónoma de México / National Autonomous University of Mexico

About the Authors

Mario Arroyo Juárez is Director General of Sistemas de Información para la Seguridad Humana and a doctoral candidate in Criminology at the Instituto Nacional de Ciencias Penales and in Sociology at the Universidad Nacional Autónoma de México. An expert in security and crime control, he has conducted research on criminality, public security, and victimization and also served as adviser on these issues to government agencies and private and nongovernmental organizations in Mexico.

Sigrid Arzt is founder and current Director of Democracia, Derechos Humanos y Seguridad and a doctoral candidate in Comparative Politics and International Relations at the University of Miami. Ms. Arzt has taught at several Mexican universities and has developed workshops on crime and violence prevention jointly with SEDESOL-SSPF and the World Bank to build local institutional capacity on security matters. Among her publications are: "Un sistema de justicia para combatir el narcotráfico y la delincuencia en México" (*Diálogo Político* 2005) and *El desafío democrático de México: seguridad y estado de derecho* (co-editor, 2001).

Elena Azaola is a Senior Researcher at the Centro de Investigaciones y Estudios Superiores en Antropología Social. She has been an adviser to the National Human Rights Commission and is currently a member of the Federal District Human Rights Commission. Dr. Azaola has conducted research on juvenile and women's justice institutions and on violent crime, topics on which she has published widely. She recently conducted research on the Mexico City police and is co-coordinating the National Report on Violence in Mexico for the World Health Organization.

John J. Bailey is Professor of Government and Foreign Service at Georgetown University, where he also directs the Mexico Project in the Center for Latin American Studies. His most recent book, *Public Security and Police Reform in the Americas* (co-editor, 2006), compares the experiences of six countries. A Spanish language edition was published by Siglo XXI. Dr. Bailey's current research project concerns the problem of "security traps" and their effects on democratic governability in Latin America.

Marcelo Bergman, a sociologist, is a Senior Investigator and Professor at the Centro de Investigación y Docencia Económicas (CIDE) in Mexico City. He has published in the areas of tax evasion in Latin America, rule of law, and criminology. He recently directed the first inmate survey in Mexico and a panel design victimization survey in that country. He teaches at the Law School at CIDE and directs several research projects in legal and crime data collection.

Robert Buffington is Associate Professor of History at Bowling Green State University. He is the author of *Criminal and Citizen in Modern Mexico* (2000), published in Mexixco as *Criminales y ciudadanos en el México moderno* (2001) and co-editor of *Reconstructing Criminality in Latin America* (2000).

Hugo Concha is a Researcher at the Instituto de Investigaciones Jurídicas of the Universidad Nacional Autónoma de México. His research focuses on the administration of justice and comparative law. Among his recent publications are: *Transparentar al Estado: la experiencia mexicana de acceso a la información* (co-editor, 2005) and *Cultura de la Constitución en México: una encuesta nacional de actitudes, percepciones y valores* (co-author, 2004).

Wayne A. Cornelius is Distinguished Professor of Political Science and founding Director of the Center for Comparative Immigration Studies at the University of California, San Diego, where he holds the Gildred Chair in U.S.-Mexican Relations. He was also the founding Director of UCSD's Center for U.S.-Mexican Studies. His current research includes a comparative study of the impacts of immigration control policies on Mexico-to-U.S. migration and Ecuadorean/Moroccan migration to Spain, and a study of binational political incorporation among U.S.-based Mexican immigrants. Recent books include *Controlling Immigration: A Global Perspective* (co-author/co-editor; 2nd ed., 2004); *Impacts of Border Enforcement on Mexican Migration: The View from Sending Communities* (co-editor, forthcoming); and *Mayan Journeys: The New Migration from Yucatán to the United States* (co-editor, forthcoming).

Irasema Coronado is Associate Professor and Chair of Political Science at the University of Texas at El Paso. She has worked extensively on women and gender issues on the U.S.-Mexico border and is co-chair of the Coalition Against Violence Towards Women and Families on the Border. She is the author of "Resistance on the Global Frontlines: Gender Wars at the

U.S.-Mexico Border" (in *Critical Theories, World Politics and the Anti-Globalisation Movement*, 2005) and "Women Leaders at the Border: Styles, Strategies and Issues"(forthcoming in *Border Women in Movement*).

Héctor Fix-Fierro is a Researcher at the Instituto de Investigaciones Jurídicas at the Universidad Nacional Autónoma de México and since July 2003 has been a visiting researcher at the University of Bremen, Germany. His main areas of research are judicial reform and legal change. His recent publications include: "Judicial Reform in Mexico: What Next?" (in *Beyond Common Knowledge. Empirical Approaches to the Rule of Law*, 2003) and *Courts, Justice and Efficiency. A Socio-Legal Study of Economic Rationality in Adjudication* (2003).

Rosalva Aída Hernández is a Research Professor at the Centro de Investigaciones y Estudios Superiores en Antropología Social. For the past fifteen years she has been conducting research in Chiapas with Guatemalan refugees and Mayan peasants. Her work with indigenous women in the Chiapas Highlands has been focused particularly on legal and educational issues. Among Dr. Hernández's publications are: *Histories and Stories from Chiapas: Border Identities from Southern Mexico* (2001) and *Mayan Lives, Mayan Utopias* (co-editor, 2003).

Robert M. Kossick, Jr., an attorney, has been a visiting researcher specializing in public administration at the Centro de Investigación y Docencia Económicas and is currently a doctoral candidate in International Development and Technology Transfer at Tulane University. His publications include "The Rule of Law and Development in Mexico" (forthcoming) and "The Role of Information and Communications Technology in Strengthening Citizen Participation and Shaping Democracy: An Analysis of Mexico's Initial Experience and Pending Challenges."

Ana Laura Magaloni Kerpel is a Law Professor at the Centro de Investigación y Docencia Económicas. She has been a visiting researcher at Harvard University's European Law Research Center, visiting professor at the International and Comparative Law Research Center at the University of California, Berkeley, and Director of Mexico's National Human Rights Commission. Ms. Magaloni was a member of the team of consultants working with the Office of the President on the 1994 constitutional amendments that modified the composition and powers of Mexico's Su-

preme Court and the structure of its judicial branch. Among her most recent publications is *The Constitutional Precedent in the U.S. Judicial System.*

Rubén Minutti Z.'s academic interests are focused on issues involving
constitutional law and alternative dispute resolution systems. Mr. Minutti
has held a variety of positions as a private consultant and in academia.
Since 2003 he has sat as magistrate on the Tribunal de lo Contencioso Administrativo del Distrito Federal. Previously, as a partner in Minutti-
Trapala Abogados, he specialized in constitutional, administrative, and
civil law. He has also been a member of the law faculties at the Universidad Iberoamericana and the Universidad La Salle. His work on constitutional law, regulatory systems, political reform, mediation, the public's
right to know, and corporate law has appeared in a variety of legal journals.

Marcos Pablo Moloeznik, who holds a doctorate in Law, is a Research
Professor in the Political Science Department of the Universidad de Guadalajara. He has taught at universities in Germany, Argentina, and Poland,
and also served as a disseminator of international humanitarian law
through the International Committee of the Red Cross. His recent publications include "El debate sobre la participación de las Fuerzas Armadas
Mexicanas en misiones de paz bajo el mandato de la Organización de Na-
ciones Unidas" (*Praesidium, Intrerdisciplinary Journal of Latin American and
Cross Cultural Studies*, 2004–2005) and "La naturaleza de un instrumento
militar atípico: las fuerzas armadas mexicanas" (*Revista Fuerzas Armadas y
Sociedad*, 2005).

Héctor Ortiz Elizondo, a researcher, writer, and consultant, is currently
pursuing a graduate degree in History and the Philosophy of Science at the
Universidad Autónoma Metropolitana–Iztapalapa. Mr. Ortiz has served as
chief investigator in the legal advocacy arm of the Instituto Nacional Indigenista and within the mental health department of the DIF, a prominent
government social welfare agency in Mexico. He participated in the Mexican ethnography project sponsored by the Instituto Nacional de Antropología e Historia and has taught courses on anthropology and law at the
Escuela Nacional de Antropología e Historia.

Pablo Parás has researched public opinion in Mexico for over fifteen years.
Before establishing the DATA Opinión Pública y Mercados consulting

firm, Parás was Director of the Centro de Estudios de Opinión Pública and of MORI de México. Dr. Parás founded the Banco de Encuestas de Latinoamérica, is a consultant for the magazine *Este País*, and is a founding member of Biomaya, a company dedicated to ecotourism in southeastern Mexico.

Pablo Piccato is Associate Professor of History at Columbia University. His published work includes *City of Suspects: Crime in Mexico City, 1900–1931* (2001), *Congreso y Revolución: El parlamentarismo en la XXVI Legislatura* (1991), *El Poder Legislativo en las décadas revolucionarias* (editor 1997), and *Actores, espacios y debates en la historia de la esfera pública en la ciudad de México* (co-author, 2005). In addition to crime and penal issues in Mexico, his research deals with notions of honor and the development of the public sphere in modern Mexico.

Benjamin Nelson Reames is a doctoral candidate in Political Science at Columbia University, dissertating on police reform in Brazil and the United States. During 2005, he researched transparency projects throughout Latin America as an accountability specialist at Partners of the Americas. He previously worked for the Lawyers Committee for Human Rights (now Human Rights First) on their Mexico Policing Project. He has contributed chapters to edited volumes on policing and has articles forthcoming in the *Journal of Urban History* and *Latin American Politics and Society*.

Alejandra Ríos Cázares is a doctoral candidate in Political Science at the University of California, San Diego. Her research focuses on comparative democratization, more specifically, bureaucratic accountability in developing presidential regimes. Before entering UCSD, she worked as head of a research project at the Mexican Senate's Institute of Legislative Research and as an analyst at the Office of Advisers to Mexico's Secretary of the Interior. In September 2003, she joined the Project on Reforming the Administration of Justice in Mexico and has coordinated this project's activities since September 2005.

Allison Rowland is Professor in the Department of Public Administration at the Centro de Investigación y Docencia Económicas. Her research in recent years has focused on issues of local public security in Mexico. Recent publications include: "The Interaction of Municipal and Federal Governments in Mexico: Trends, Issues and Problems" (in *Multilevel Govern-*

ance in Comparative Perspective, 2006) and "Local Responses to Public Insecurity in Mexico: The Policía Comunitaria of the Costa Chica and the Montaña de Guerrero" (in *Public Security and Police Reform in Latin America*, 2005).

Sara Schatz is a visiting scholar at the Center for Latin American Studies, Ohio State University. Her principal research interests are law and society, social movements, and the state. Two recent publications are *Conceptual Structure and Social Change: The Ideological Architecture of Democratization* (co-author, 2002) and "The Mexican Legal System" (in *Legal Systems of the World: A Political, Social and Cultural Encyclopedia*, 2002).

David A. Shirk is Director of the Trans-Border Institute and Assistant Professor of Political Science at the University of San Diego. He received his Ph.D. in Political Science at the University of California, San Diego and was a predoctoral fellow at the Center for U.S.-Mexican Studies in 1998–99 and 2001–2003. Dr. Shirk is the author of *Mexico's New Politics: The PAN and Democratic Change* (2005). He coordinated the Project on Reforming the Administration of Justice in Mexico and presently directs the Justice in Mexico Project, an outgrowth of the former project.

Carlos Silva, a sociologist from Uruguay, teaches at the Mexico City campus of the Facultad Latinoamericana de Ciencias Sociales (FLACSO). He is currently completing his doctoral dissertation at El Colegio de México on police behavior and the use of force in Mexico City. He also works in the Office of Applied Research at the Universidad Nacional Autónoma de México and at GIES A.C., where he has been involved in research on political culture and human rights.

Elisa Speckman Guerra is a Researcher in the Instituto de Investigaciones Históricas of the Universidad Nacional Autónoma de México, and a member of the Mexican Academy of Criminal Justice Sciences and the Mexican Academy of Sciences. She is the author of *Crimen y castigo: legislación penal, interpretaciones de la criminalidad y administración de justicia*, and editor of *De normas y transgresiones: enfermedad y crimen en América Latina*. Dr. Speckman has taught at the Universidad Nacional Autónoma de México, El Colegio de México, El Colegio de Michoacán, el Instituto Tecnológico Autónomo de México, and the Escuela Nacional de Antropología e Historia.

Jeffrey K. Staton is Assistant Professor of Political Science at Florida State University. His research considers how judicial institutions affect domestic and international politics. His most recent publications have appeared in the *American Journal of Political Science* and the *Journal of Politics* and *Comparative Politics*. He is currently working on projects concerning how institutions affect Latino immigration, a state's human rights practices, and the success of judicial reform efforts.

Kathleen Staudt is Professor of Political Science and Director of the Center for Civic Engagement at the University of Texas at El Paso. She has published many books, including: *The U.S.-Mexico Border: Transcending Divisions, Contesting Identities* (co-editor, 1998) and *Fronteras No Mas* (co-author, 2002). Dr. Staudt is active in community/binational organizations and co-chairs Border Interfaith. Her forthcoming book, *Violence and Activism at the Border: Gender, Fear and Everyday Life*, is based on research and action relating to domestic violence and female homicide in Ciudad Juárez–El Paso.

Robert O. Varenik serves as the Director of Programs for the Open Society Justice Initiative. He was previously based in Mexico City with the Law Faculty of the Centro de Investigación y Docencia Económicas, where he coordinated work on criminal justice and public security reform. In Mexico, he also designed and directed projects for the Instituto para la Seguridad y la Democracia, which he helped found in 2003.

Guillermo Zepeda Lecuona, an attorney also trained in political science and the sociology of law, coordinates the project on "Justice, Crime, and Human Rights in Mexico" at the Centro de Investigación para el Desarrollo. His research interests include institutional development, judicial reform, public security, and penal justice. His most recent publications are *Crimen sin castigo: procuración de justicia penal y ministerio público en México* and "Inefficiency at the Service of Inpunity: Criminal Justice Organizations in Mexico" (in *Transnational Crime and Public Security: Challenges to Mexico and the United States*, 2002).